Money, Payments, and Liquidity

Money, Payments, and Liquidity

Second edition

Guillaume Rocheteau and Ed Nosal

The MIT Press
Cambridge, Massachusetts
London, England

This book was set in Palatino Roman by diacriTech, Chennai.

Library of Congress Cataloging-in-Publication Data

Names: Rocheteau, Guillaume, author. | Nosal, Ed, author.
Title: Money, payments, and liquidity / Guillaume Rocheteau and Ed Nosal.
Description: Second edition. | Cambridge, MA : MIT Press, [2017] | Ed Nosal appeared as the first named author on the earlier edition. | Includes bibliographical references and index.
Identifiers: LCCN 2016034551| ISBN 9780262035804 (hardcover : alk. paper) | ISBN 9780262533270 (pbk. : alk. paper)
Subjects: LCSH: Liquidity (Economics) | Monetary policy. | Money.
Classification: LCC HG178 .N68 2017 | DDC 339.5/3–dc23 LC record available at https://lccn.loc.gov/2016034551

Contents

To our parents.

Acknowledgments

The starting point of this book is a Federal Reserve Bank of Cleveland policy discussion paper. We began work on the policy discussion paper in 2004, and our objective was to provide a concise overview of the literature on the economics of payments using a unified framework. During this phase of the project we benefitted from the great working environment and resources provided by the Research Department at the Federal Reserve Bank of Cleveland. We want to acknowledge the unwavering support provided by the research director, Mark Sniderman, and by our colleagues Dave Altig, Mike Bryan, Bruce Champ, John Carlson, Joe Haubrich, and Peter Rupert.

The content of the book has been shaped by our collaborations with many researchers in the field of monetary theory and payments: David Andolfatto, Boragan Aruoba, Aleksander Berentsen, Ricardo Cavalcanti, Ben Craig, Ricardo Lagos, Yiting Li, Sebastien Lotz, Peter Rupert, Shouyong Shi, Christopher Waller, Neil Wallace, Pierre-Olivier Weill, and Randall Wright. Several sections or chapters in the book come directly from our own work with these coauthors. For instance, the chapter on money under alternative trading mechanisms comes from some work with Boragan Aruoba, Christopher Waller, and Randall Wright. The sections on the divisibility and recognizability of money are derived from some work with Aleksander Berentsen and Yiting Li. The section on money and capital comes from some work with Ricardo Lagos. The model on liquidity in over-the-counter markets is also a joint work with Ricardo Lagos based on a paper by Darell Duffie, Nicolae Garleanu, and Lasse Pedersen.

In writing this book, we stand on the shoulders of many scholars. In particular, the basic research agenda for the field of monetary theory has been largely shaped by Neil Wallace. The search-theoretic approach to monetary economics was pioneered by Nobu Kiyotaki and Randall

Wright, and the framework that we use throughout the book was developed by Ricardo Lagos and Randall Wright. This framework itself benefitted from the earlier work of Shouyong Shi, Alberto Trejos, and Randall Wright.

We would like to thank Steve Williamson for his comments on the 2005 policy discussion paper that led to this book; David Andolfatto, for his insightful comments on the first half of the book; Aleksander Berentsen, who used this book to teach monetary theory at the universities of Basel and Zurich; and Stan Rabinovich, who provided detailed comments for the entire book. We also thank graduate students at the Institute for Advanced Studies, Vienna; National University of Singapore; the Singapore Management University; and the University of California, Irvine, especially Giovanni Sibal and Cathy Zhang. Finally, we have benefitted from the support of MIT Press.

Preface to the Second Edition

The New-Monetarist approach to payments and liquidity is a fast growing field. A lot of progress has been made since our first edition was written to describe economies with competing means of payments, including money and credit, to explain liquidity differences across assets, the role of liquid assets for the macroeconomy in general and the labor market in particular, the dynamics of asset prices in decentralized (over-the-counter) asset markets, and monetary policy in its conventional and non-conventional forms. Changes in the second edition of our book reflect this progress.

We added three new chapters: Chapter 9 on unemployment and liquidity, Chapter 14 on asset price dynamics, and Chapter 16 on crashes and recoveries in over-the-counter markets. Our chapter on the coexistence of money and other assets has been divided into two revised chapters: Chapter 11 focuses on money and physical capital and Chapter 12 specializes on money and nominal assets (another currency and nominal bonds). Chapter 11 has a new section on mechanism design with multiple assets. This section provides a novel result according to which rate-of-return dominance is an essential property of monetary economies. Chapter 12 has a new section on open-market operations and liquidity traps. Chapter 4 on the role of money has been entirely rewritten. We adopt a mechanism design approach to characterize the set of all incentive-feasible allocations in monetary economies. Moreover, we extend the model to introduce two-sided ex-post heterogeneity in bilateral matches so that barter trades are feasible. We believe that this extension illustrates more clearly the role of money and makes it transparent that our economy is fundamentally different from a cash-in-advance economy.

Other chapters have been revised and extended. Chapter 2 has new sections on pure credit economies under limited commitment.

We decentralize allocations with endogenous debt limits, characterize dynamic equilibria, and introduce heterogeneity under private information to explain default in equilibrium. Chapter 8 has a new section investigating the coexistence of money and credit under limited commitment. Chapter 13 has a new section to endogenize the pledgeability of assets with informational frictions.

When preparing this second edition we have benefitted from the help and suggestions from many of our students and colleagues, including Ayushi Bajaj, Bill Branch, Francesca Carapella, Tai-Wei Hu, Yiting Li, Pedro Gomis Porqueras, Sebastien Lotz, Antonio Rodriguez, Mario Rafael Silva, Russell Wong, Sylvia Xiao, and Cathy Zhang.

General Introduction

Economics is all about gains from trade. But if gains from trade are to be realized, people must exchange one object for another. How does exchange happen?

Exchange can be easy. If John has apples but likes strawberries more, and Paul has strawberries but likes apples more, then John and Paul can directly exchange strawberries for apples when they meet. There is a double coincidence of wants: John has what Paul wants and Paul has what John wants. In Figure 1 we represent the endowments and preferences of John and Paul. The "×" beside the names are their endowments and the arrows indicate the goods they would like to consume.

Unfortunately, life is not that easy. So let's complicate things just a bit by adding another person, George, and a third commodity, tangerines, to the picture. George has tangerines and likes apples more but hates strawberries; Paul has strawberries and now likes tangerines more but hates apples; and John has apples and still likes strawberries more but hates tangerines. The preferences and endowments for John, Paul, and George are now depicted in Figure 2.

How do the lads—John, Paul, and George—trade? If they can all meet at the same time and place, then exchange is just as easy as above. John gives apples to George, George gives tangerines to Paul, and Paul

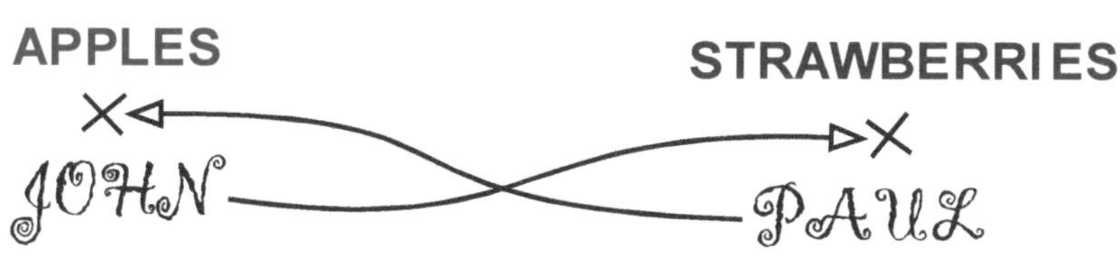

Figure 1
Double coincidence of wants

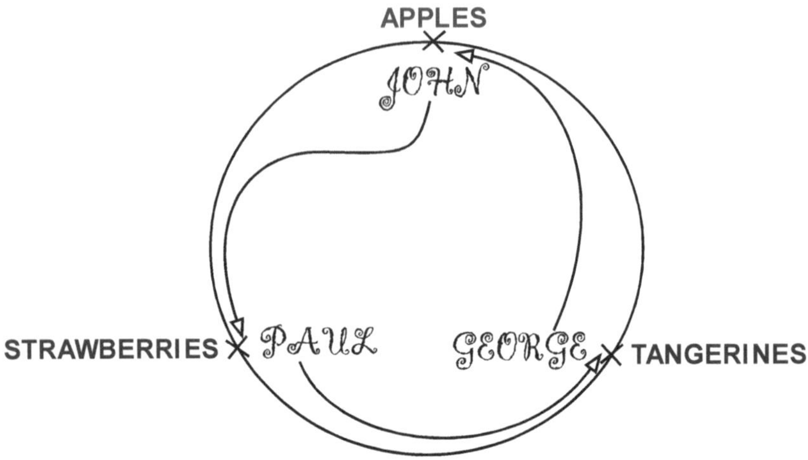

Figure 2
A lack-of-double-coincidence-of-wants problem

gives strawberries to John. But what if the lads can only meet in pairs? For concreteness, one can think that at different times, two of the lads are randomly chosen and are brought together in a meeting in Las Vegas. Why Vegas? Since what happens in Vegas, stays in Vegas; so what the lads do in their meetings remains private information.

If the lads can commit, then exchange is still easy. John can commit to give apples to George, George can commit to give tangerines to Paul, and Paul can commit to give strawberries to John. Sooner or later, all of the desirable exchanges will take place via pairwise meetings. But commitment seems rather strong; it is not a characteristic found in abundance in human interaction. So, suppose that the lads are unable to commit.

The above trading arrangement—give your partner in a meeting your good if he desires it more than you—will not work. For example, if John gets strawberries from Paul, then he has no incentive to give apples to George, provided that John likes apples a little, because he gets nothing in return from George. Hence, John might as well consume his own apples. So when the lads meet in pairs we have the famous double-coincidence problem. Two coincidences are required if trade is to take place, so there is a problem if lad A really likes what lad B is holding, but lad B does not like what lad A is holding.

If the lads are only willing to trade the good they have for the good they desire most, then the outcome is autarky. Autarky, however, need not be the outcome. For example, perhaps Paul will accept John's apples in exchange for strawberries, even though Paul doesn't like apples. After this transaction, when Paul meets George, Paul can trade his apples for George's tangerines. In this example, apples are used as medium of exchange, meaning that the apple is accepted in trade by Paul not to be consumed, but to be traded later on for some other good, tangerines. This medium of exchange is useful or *essential* in the following sense. If there is no medium of exchange, then the outcome, autarky, is worse than the allocation that can be obtained with a medium of exchange.

Typically, people have to pay for the goods they acquire. And depending on the situation, the payment instruments—or media of exchange—can be commodities, real assets, and/or fiat money. What ends up serving as the economy's payments instruments depends on many factors, such as the cost of storing apples compared to the cost of storing strawberries or tangerines, or how easy it is to recognize the quality of apples relative to that of strawberries or tangerines. What media of exchange will emerge in an economy? What are the factors that determine what will and will not be media of exchange? These are questions that this book addresses. But whatever the payment instruments are, the only kind that we study in this book are ones that are essential in the sense described above.

Models where money is useless

One of the most obvious and ubiquitous payment instruments is money. Although much ink has been spilled on the topic of money, some observers, e.g., Banerjee and Maskin (1996), believe that "money has always been something of an embarrassment to economic theory." One reason for this unsatisfactory situation is that the "wrong" model is used to study money. The benchmark model in economics is that of Arrow and Debreu (1954) and Debreu (1959). The environment is frictionless: markets are complete and people can commit to all future actions. At the beginning of time, a market opens up and individuals choose the goods they want to buy and sell over all future contingencies. The only constraint an individual faces is a budget constraint. As the future unfolds, people make or accept delivery of goods as promised at the beginning of time. In the standard Arrow-Debreu environment, a competitive equilibrium is Pareto optimal. This necessarily implies that money cannot play an essential role in the economy. This observation also applies to the workhorse model of modern macroeconomics, the neoclassical growth model developed by Cass (1965) and Koopmans (1965), and Kydland and Prescott (1982).

Fiat money has been forced into these models so that monetary policy can be studied. Since money is not essential, it has to enter the picture in some ad-hoc fashion. Real money balances can be assumed to be a productive good, and can enter either utility functions, e.g., Patinkin (1965), or production functions, e.g., Fisher (1974). This assumption seems odd. Fiat money is an intrinsically useless object but is being treated as a standard consumption or intermediate good. Equally puzzling is that the price level enters the utility or the production functions. Along similar lines, Niehans (1971, 1978) captures a transactions role for money by introducing exogenous transaction costs, and assuming that money has the lowest of these costs.

Another popular approach, initiated by Clower (1967), is based on the observation that in monetary economies, goods are not traded for other goods directly. Goods are traded for money. To capture this "stylized fact" of monetary economies, Clower (1967) and Lucas (1980) introduce a restriction that requires that consumption goods be purchased only with money, a so-called "cash-in-advance constraint." The problem with this description is that money enters the economy as a constraint that reduces the welfare of the economy, and not as a mechanism that overcomes exchange problems and enlarges the set of allocations that are feasible.

The most prominent framework for policy analysis nowadays, the New-Keynesian model of monetary policy proposed by Woodford (2003), takes money completely out of the picture by focusing on so-called "cashless economies." In such economies, money only matters as a unit of account given that prices are set in this unit of account and can only be readjusted infrequently.

Models where money is essential

Following Wallace (1998, 2001, 2010), we believe a reasonable modeling goal in the study of money, or any payment instrument, is that it be essential. None of the approaches described above satisfy the so-called Wallace (1998) Dictum:

> "[T]he proposed dictum is that money should not be a primitive in monetary theory. It is easy to describe in the abstract how to construct models that satisfy this dictum: specify both the physical environment and the equilibrium concept of the model in a way that does not rely on the concept called *money* or force the modeler at the outset to specify which objects will play a special role

> in trade. The physical environment and the equilibrium concept may include features that make trade difficult, more difficult than in the S[tochastic Competitive] G[eneral] E[quilibrium] model—features such as trading posts that are pairwise in objects, asymmetric information, or pairwise meetings. The model may also include assets that differ in their physical characteristics. For example, some assets may be indivisible and others not, some may be fiat objects while others throw off a real dividend at each date, some may physically depreciate more than others, some may be more recognizable than others, and some may yield disutility because they give off a noxious odor. Given such a specification, the model determines—but, in general, not uniquely because there may be multiple equilibria—the *values* of the different assets and their distinct roles, if any, in exchange. Money should not be a primitive in monetary theory.

There are a number of models of essential, or useful, money grounded in a competitive environment. The competitive equilibrium in an overlapping generations (OLG) model, developed by Samuelson (1958), need not be Pareto efficient because of the double infinity of goods and agents. In an OLG model, people are born at different dates, live finite lives, and the economy continues forever. The structure of the model implies that credit—i.e., borrowing and lending—is not incentive feasible. If the (non-monetary) competitive equilibrium is not Pareto efficient, then the introduction of fiat money results in a Pareto improvement. Money is essential because it allows agents to engage in Pareto-improving (intertemporal) trades. The OLG model was the standard model for monetary economics for well over a decade. It is the environment that Lucas (1972) used to revolutionize macroeconomics. The authoritative statement and accomplishments of this framework can be found in Wallace (1980).

As in the OLG model, money can play a useful role in Townsend's (1980) turnpike model. The model has infinitely-lived agents moving along an endless linear "highway," or turnpike, from one location to the next. Agents receive endowments in alternating periods, which creates a need for intertemporal trade. But agents with different endowment processes move in opposite directions along the turnpike. So agents of different types meet at most once, which makes credit arrangements infeasible. Just as in the OLG model, the introduction of fiat money leads to an allocation that is preferred by all agents in the economy.

Ostroy (1973), Starr (1972), and Ostroy and Starr (1974, 1990) focused on the transactional role of money in an otherwise standard general equilibrium model. The exchange process, by which agents move from their initial endowments to a final allocation, is modeled by (many) rounds of bilateral trade. In a round of bilateral trading, the value of goods that agent 1 wants from agent 2 may exceed the value of goods that agent 2 wants from agent 1. Because of this lack of double coincidence of wants, it can take many rounds of trade before all agents are able to move from the initial endowment to their final (equilibrium) allocation. If money is introduced, then additional quantities of goods can be bought and sold, implying there will be fewer rounds of bilateral trading. If trading is costly, money is useful.

A competitive environment, however, is not the most natural one to think about issues relating to money. For example, there is a strategic aspect to money: I accept an intrinsically useless object in trade because I rationally think others will accept it. As well, the mechanics of exchange—how people meet and exchange goods—is not formalized in a competitive environment. So it is difficult to think about double-coincidence problems in such an environment.

A natural way to capture strategic and double-coincidence issues is in a model of bilateral meetings. Jones (1976) was the first to model the double-coincidence problem in a bilateral random meeting context. Diamond (1982) constructed a fully coherent equilibrium search model, but without money. In Diamond's (1982) model, a person cannot consume the good he produces, but goods produced by anyone else are perfect substitutes in consumption. Since there is never a double-coincidence problem, there are no impediments to exchange, once people have met. Diamond (1984) introduced money into his search model but it was accomplished by imposing a cash-in-advance constraint. In a series of papers, Kiyotaki and Wright (1989, 1991, 1993) added the double-coincide problem identified by Jones (1976) into Diamond's (1982, 1984) equilibrium search model.

The big innovation in Kiyotaki and Wright (1989, 1991, 1993) was the introduction of heterogeneity over tastes and goods. The original Kiyotaki and Wright (1989) model focused almost exclusively on the emergence of commodity money as a medium of exchange. In a simple three-person environment, they designed the pattern of specialization, consumption, and production to create a lack of double coincidence of wants between agents. This heterogeneity is similar to that described in the John, Paul, and George example. They showed that certain goods will emerge as a medium of exchange depending on preferences, endowments, and beliefs. A somewhat stunning result was that in some equilibria, the good that serves as medium of exchange is the good with the highest storage cost, or the lowest rate of return. This finding was interpreted as a possible resolution for the long-standing rate-of-return dominance puzzle. The rate-of-return dominance puzzle, identified by Hicks (1935), is the lack of a compelling explanation for the observation that the rate of return on a medium of exchange is less than the ones of other assets in the economy. The puzzle is why people wouldn't hold and use higher rate of return instruments as media of exchange.

Kiyotaki and Wright (1991, 1993) extended the previous analysis to include an intrinsically useless object and demonstrated that this object can be valued in exchange and can raise society's welfare. The equilibrium, however, is not unique. If, for example, people believe that money will be accepted as a means of payment in the future, then a monetary equilibrium prevails with fiat money as a universally accepted means of payments. Alternatively, if people believe that money will not be accepted as a means of payment in the future, then the equilibrium is characterized by barter only.

The models described above are rather stark and simple. All objects are indivisible; agents can hold at most one unit of output or one unit of fiat money; and in all meetings, objects trade one-for-one. One may reasonably ask, other than demonstrating that a medium of exchange can emerge, what can one learn from such a stylized environment. The answer is: a lot. Here are two examples.

Kiyotaki, Matsui, and Matsuyama (1993) adopted a two-country, two-currency version of the Kiyotaki-Wright model where they investigated the conditions under which a currency would emerge as an international currency, meaning a currency that is accepted as a medium of exchange in both countries. This question was virtually impossible to address in reduced-form monetary models. Their answer was both intuitive and insightful. They found that the status of international currency depends on both fundamentals, such as the sizes of the countries and their degree of integration, as well as (self-fulfilling) beliefs and conventions.

Williamson and Wright (1994) formalized the old idea developed by Jevons (1875) that recognizability is a key property for a good or commodity to be used as money. They considered an environment where there is a double coincidence of wants in all meetings, as in Diamond (1982, 1984), but goods can be produced in different qualities, and agents have some private information about the quality of their goods. They showed that (fully recognizable) fiat money can play a useful role even if there is no double-coincidence problem. By introducing a good of recognizable quality, fiat money, consumption goods of unknown quality become less acceptable, and hence agents have less incentive to produce them.

Although the Kiyotaki-Wright model provides useful insights, it is unable to satisfactorily address some important and interesting questions in monetary theory. For example: how is the exchange value of money determined? The Kiyotaki-Wright model essentially evades this question since, by assumption, people can only hold at most one unit of indivisible money, and one unit of money trades for one unit of output. To answer this and other interesting policy questions, these extreme assumptions have to be relaxed in a number of directions.

The first step to generalize the model environment, undertaken by Shi (1995) and Trejos and Wright (1995), was to endogenize the value of money. This was accomplished, in spite of the restriction that people hold at most one unit of indivisible money, by making output divisible. With divisible output, the quantity of goods that is traded for one unit of money is determined by bargaining between the two parties; hence, one can speak sensibly about the value of money. Osborne and Rubinstein (1990) provide a systematic treatment of markets with bilateral trade and bargaining.

The models of Shi (1995) and Trejos and Wright (1995) impose a pricing (or trading) mechanism in bilateral meetings between agents. Although the mechanism typically has axiomatic or strategic foundations, it is chosen arbitrarily and might not lead to allocations with good properties from society's point of view. An alternative approach, proposed by Kocherlakota (1998) and strongly endorsed by Wallace (2010), is that of mechanism design. In a mechanism design approach, a planner chooses the trading mechanism among all incentive-feasible mechanisms. The mechanism that the planner chooses satisfies some desirable property; for example, it maximizes social welfare. A mechanism design approach can be helpful for establishing the essentiality of money. Recall that money is essential if, given the specification of the environment, there is no other way to achieve (desirable) allocations.

Regardless of how the value of money is determined—whether using strategic or axiomatic approach or a mechanism design approach—it is possible to examine how a change in the aggregate stock of money affects the value of money and output. However, because agents are restricted to hold at most one unit of money, then the more interesting policy question of how a continuous change in the money supply affects inflation and output cannot be addressed. Initial progress on the modeling of money growth was made by simply relaxing the unit upper bound constraint on money holdings, within the context of a Shi-Trejos-Wright-type environment. Zhu (2003, 2005) provided existence results when money holdings are richer than {0,1} for both indivisible and divisible money. Camera and Corbae (1999) and Molico (2006) provided numerical based solutions for these richer money holdings environments. Green and Zhou (1998) and Zhou (1999) assumed price posting by sellers and indivisible goods which made the model a bit more tractable. All these papers, however, demonstrate that departing from the unit money upper bound assumption significantly complicates the analysis. The complications arise from the fact that the equilibrium is, in part, characterized by a distribution of money holdings that is determined jointly with terms of trade in bilateral matches. And characterizing these equilibrium objects jointly is not easy (at least, analytically).

An alternative and clever approach to deal with unrestricted money holdings and divisible money is to change the economic environment in a way that implies that, in equilibrium, the money holdings of all agents of the same type are identical just before they are bilaterally matched. Since the distribution of money holdings is degenerate, the model becomes analytically tractable. Shi (1997), taking the lead from Lucas (1990), assumed that households are composed of a continuum of members—buyers and sellers—who pool their money holdings. This large-household structure implies that risks associated with the random matching process for individual buyers and sellers can be completely diversified away at the household level.

Lagos and Wright (2005), instead, introduced competitive markets that operate periodically and quasi-linear preferences. The competitive markets allow agents to adjust their money holdings following random-matching shocks. Since quasi-linear preferences eliminate wealth effects, all agents will make the same choices in the competitive market, except for the choice of the "quasi-linear good." The Lagos-Wright environment can accommodate different pricing mechanisms in the decentralized exchange market (Rocheteau and Wright 2005), such as bargaining, price posting, and Walrasian pricing. Moreover, the existence of periodic competitive markets allows for the reintroduction of Arrow-Debreu-type general equilibrium apparatus, such as state contingent commodities (Rocheteau, Rupert, Shell, and Wright 2008). Because of its flexibility, the Lagos-Wright model has already generated a large body of applications and extensions (see Williamson and Wright 2010a, 2010b). We use it throughout the book.

Beyond monetary exchange: Credit and liquidity

In this book we are interested in understanding how gains from trade can best be exploited in economic environments characterized by different sets of frictions. We do not require that trade be mediated by money since different frictions may dictate the use of different payment instruments.

One of the key challenges in monetary theory is to provide an explanation for the coexistence of money and credit. To address this issue we allow agents to use bilateral credit arrangements, or IOUs, to facilitate trade, as in Diamond (1987, 1990) and Shi (1996). One reason why coexistence is a challenge is that the frictions that are needed to make money essential typically make credit infeasible, and environments where credit is feasible are ones where money is typically not essential. By constructing environments where money and credit coexist, we are able to study interactions between monetary policy and the use of credit. We also study the notion of settlement, the process by which an obligation created by a credit relationship is ultimately extinguished. We examine how frictions in the settlement process affect the role of the monetary authority.

Over time, financial innovations such as securitization have made the distinction between monetary and nonmonetary assets somewhat fuzzy. Individuals and firms have access to checkable equity and bond mutual funds, they can get home and car equity loans that are effectively consumption loans collateralized by assets, and they can use government bonds as collateral in many instances. So at least indirectly, people use all sorts of assets to facilitate trade. In some extensions of our basic model we allow people to use assets other than fiat money or credit to facilitate exchange; assets such as capital, land, and government debt. Again, whether or not agents use these assets to conduct their transactions depends on the properties of assets, such as divisibility and recognizability, and on the frictions they face.

In practise, monetary policy is conducted through open-market operations, where the monetary authority trades fiat money for bonds. A fully coherent model of monetary policy should include these two assets, and must explain how they coexist even though bonds pay interest but money doesn't. Or, put another way, a coherent model of monetary policy should address the rate-of-return dominance puzzle. We provide explanations for this puzzle based on the physical properties of the interest bearing asset, such as recognizability, and on conventions or self-fulfilling beliefs. Our approach to address the rate-of-return dominance puzzle can also be applied to other types of asset pricing anomalies. For instance, Lagos (2010a,) showed that a monetary model with bonds and equity can address the risk-free rate and equity premium puzzles.

There is no universally accepted definition of liquidity. It is precisely because the concept of liquidity is somewhat vague that a model can be useful to clarify it. Clearly, when there are no frictions associated with trade, then all assets (and goods) are equally liquid, as in the Arrow-Debreu model. However, if there are frictions associated with exchange, then some assets may be able to command greater amounts of goods in trade than other assets. Generally speaking, the liquidity of an asset has to do with the ease at which it can be used to finance a random spending opportunity. If it can only be sold on short notice at a discounted price or not at all, then the asset is said to be illiquid. One of our objectives will be to explain why different assets have different liquidity properties. When assets do have different liquidity properties, we investigate the implications that liquidity has for the distribution of asset returns, and for the relationship between asset prices and monetary policy.

The notion of liquidity has a time, volume, and price dimension, and can be quantified by using measures related to the ease at which assets can be bought and sold. For example, liquidity can be measured by transaction costs, such as bid-ask spreads, trading delays, the time that it takes to buy or sell an asset, and by trading volume. We will use the structure of our basic model, with decentralized trades and bilateral matches, to describe an over-the-counter asset market that can be used to think about these measures of liquidity.

Tour of the book

The book is organized in 16 chapters. In the first chapter we present the basic environment we will use throughout the book. Even though we introduce different twists along the way, the models we use all have some common ingredients: an alternating market structure with competitive and bilateral trades, and quasi-linear preferences, as in Lagos and Wright (2005).

In Chapters 2 through 5, we present benchmark economies with a single method of payment. In Chapter 2, all trades are conducted with credit. We are interested in understanding whether an economy can achieve good allocations with credit for different sets of frictions. In Chapter 3, we examine an economy whose frictions rule out credit arrangements and show that there is a role for fiat money. We characterize allocations that emerge under different pricing mechanisms in the decentralized market. Chapter 4 adopts a mechanism design approach to determine the essentiality and role of fiat money. Chapter 5 studies how the properties of money, such as divisibility, portability, and recognizability affects allocations and impacts on its role as a medium of exchange.

Chapters 6 and 7 are devoted to monetary policy. In Chapter 6 we characterize the optimal rate of growth of money supply under various price mechanisms and frictions in the decentralized trade market. We explain when the Friedman rule is feasible, optimal, and achieves the first-best allocation. In Chapter 7, we examine the relationship between inflation and output under different information structures when the money growth rate is assumed to be random.

Chapters 8, 9, and 10 examine economies where monetary exchange coexists with credit transactions. In Chapter 8 we propose several environments where money and credit can coexist and study how monetary policy affects the use of credit. In Chapter 9 we introduce firm entry and a frictional labor market in order to study the interactions between liquidity and unemployment. In Chapter 10, we introduce settlement frictions and investigate how these frictions affect the allocations and if there is an optimal policy response.

Chapters 11 through 14 consider the coexistence of money and other assets, such as another money, capital, and bonds. Chapter 11 studies monetary equilibria with productive capital and focuses on the rate-of-return dominance puzzle. Chapter 12 studies money and nominal assets, a second currency or a nominal bond, and the implications for exchange rates and open-market operations. Chapter 13 investigates the implications for asset prices and monetary policy. Chapter 14 examines the dynamics of asset prices in economies where liquidity considerations matter.

Finally, in Chapters 15 and 16 we use a continuous-time version of our basic model with intermediaries to understand the functioning of over-the-counter markets and to study how trading frictions affect asset markets, asset prices, different measures of liquidity, and dealers' inventories in normal times and in times of crises.

1 The Basic Environment

This book studies issues directly related to society's need for media of exchange. Any such study requires a departure from the standard Arrow-Debreu model economy. In the Arrow-Debreu model, markets are frictionless and complete, all agents can get together at the beginning of time to buy and sell contracts, and they can commit to deliver or accept delivery of goods over all possible dates and contingencies. The basic structure of the Arrow-Debreu model implies that the economy can achieve a Pareto-efficient allocation without needing objects like money or other financial institutions.

A good model of media of exchange should incorporate a number of key ingredients. We view the following as being necessary ingredients:

1. *People cannot commit.* If people can commit, then they can promise to repay their debts or make gifts, and there is no need for a medium of exchange.
2. *The monitoring or record keeping of actions must be imperfect.* As we will see later, a well-functioning record-keeping device can replicate the role played by a medium of exchange.
3. *It must be costly for people to interact with one another.* If people could costlessly get together to trade, then many trades could be arranged among groups of people without having to resort to a medium of exchange. A natural way to think about costly connections between people is that they meet in pairs. Moreover, if people meet in pairs, then monitoring what happens in these meetings may be difficult.
4. *There must be a problem of lack of double coincidence of wants.* If there is not a double-coincide problem, i.e., in every pairwise meeting each person wants what the other person has, then there trades can be conducted through barter.

5. *The model must be dynamic.* It would be difficult to think about a number of (financial) assets if the model was not dynamic. For example, who would be willing to accept fiat money, an intrinsically worthless piece of paper, in a static environment?; or What is the meaning of debt, a promise to do something in the future, in a static model?

It is, of course, possible to add to this list. For example, one may want to include imperfect recognizability as a key ingredient since it is useful in explaining the emergence of a uniform currency or the acceptability of an asset as a medium of exchange. We use the assumption of imperfect recognizability in many parts of the book, e.g., to help explain the coexistence of money and higher rate of return assets.

If assets are held, then they must be priced. It would be desirable to have these assets priced in competitive markets if only for convenience. So, although we require that bilateral trading relationships exist, we do not insist that all trades be conducted on a bilateral basis; i.e., some trades can be conducted on a competitive market.

Finally, although it is not an absolute requirement, it would certainly be desirable if the model is analytically tractable. Tractability facilitates a better understanding of some issues or insights, and extending the model to address a large variety of topics related to money and payments.

1.1 Benchmark Model

The *benchmark* model we use throughout the book will have the following characteristics.

Time is discrete and continues forever. Each period is divided into two subperiods, called *day* and *night*, where different activities take place. During the day, trades occur in *decentralized* markets according to a time-consuming bilateral matching process. We will label the day market DM, which can also stand for decentralized market.

In the DM, some agents can produce but do not want to consume, while other agents want to consume but cannot produce. For convenience, we label the former agents *sellers* and the latter *buyers* which captures the agents' roles in the DM. Our assumption on preferences—sellers have no desire to consume in the DM—and technologies—buyers are not able to produce in the DM—generates a double-coincidence problem in matches between buyers and sellers. The measures of buyers and sellers are equal, and are normalized to one.

A buyer meets a seller, and a seller meets a buyer, with probability σ. The parameter σ captures the extent of the trading frictions in the market. If $\sigma = 1$, the trading frictions are shut down (except for the pairwise meeting friction) and each agent can find a trading partner with certainty. The parameter σ can be interpreted as capturing heterogeneity in terms of the goods that sellers produce and that the buyers consume. We call the good that is produced and traded in the DM either the DM good or the *search good*, since trade requires a search activity.

Exactly how production and trade are organized at night will depend on the issue that is under investigation. What can be said about the night market is that, in general, it will be characterized by fewer frictions than those that plague the DM. We will label the night market CM, since this market will typically be a competitive market. At night, all agents can produce and consume. The good that is produced and consumed in the CM will be called either the CM good or the *general good*. Typically, buyers will produce the general good in order to settle their debt or to readjust their asset holdings, and sellers will consume the general good in order to reduce their asset holdings.

All goods, whether produced in the DM or in the CM, are nonstorable, so a search good cannot be carried into the CM and a general good cannot be carried into the next DM. The perishability of consumption goods will prevent them from being used as means of payment.

The preferences of the buyer and seller are given by $\sum_t \beta^t U^b(q_t, x_t, y_t)$ and $\sum_t \beta^t U^s(q_t, x_t, y_t)$, respectively, where $U^b(q,x,y)$ and $U^s(q,x,y)$ are the buyer's and seller's period utility functions, $q \in \mathbb{R}_+$ is the quantity of the search good consumed and produced in the DM, $x \in \mathbb{R}_+$ is the quantity of the general good consumed in the CM, and $y \in \mathbb{R}_+$ is the amount of work undertaken in the CM. All agents discount between the night and the next day at rate $r = \beta^{-1} - 1$, where $\beta \in (0,1)$ is the discount factor. Although it is not crucial, we assume that the period utility functions are separable across subperiods; i.e.,

$$U^b(q,x,y) = u(q) + U(x,y)$$

and

$$U^s(q,x,y) = -c(q) + U(x,y).$$

More importantly, for tractability we will require that an agent's utility function in the CM is linear in their hours of work, i.e., $U(x,y) = v(x) - y$. As we argue later, linearity plays a role in eliminating wealth effects and facilitates the determination of the terms of trade in the DM.

The production technologies in the DM and CM are both linear in labor, where one unit of labor produces one unit of output. Therefore, $c(q)$ is the seller's disutility (or cost) of labor in the DM and y is the agent's disutility of labor in the CM.

If $v(x)$ is strictly concave, then we would typically get the choice of consumption in the CM satisfying $x = x^*$, where $v'(x^*) = 1$. For most of the book, and without loss of generality, we will simply assume that $v(x) = x$, so there is no gain from producing the general good for oneself. The timing of events and the preferences of agents are described in Figure 1.1.

In summary, the specification of the period utility functions for buyers and sellers are

$$U^b(q,x,y) = u(q) + x - y, \tag{1.1}$$

$$U^s(q,x,y) = -c(q) + x - y, \tag{1.2}$$

respectively. We assume $u'(q) > 0$, $u''(q) < 0$, $u(0) = c(0) = c'(0) = 0$, $u'(0) = +\infty$, $c'(q) > 0$, $c''(q) > 0$, and $c(\bar{q}) = u(\bar{q})$ for some $\bar{q} > 0$. We assume that the utility for the buyer in the DM is bounded below, which matters when there is negotiation between a buyer and a seller in the DM, so that utilities are not unbounded in the case of disagreements. Without loss of generality, we assume that $u(0) = 0$. An example of a DM utility function for buyer is $u(q) = (q+b)^{(1-a)} - b^{(1-a)}$, where $b > 0$ but small. If $a \in (0,1)$, then b can be set equal to zero. This utility function is reminiscent of a constant relative risk aversion utility function, and approaches such a function as b goes to zero.

Let q^* denote the level of production and consumption of the search good that maximizes the match surplus between a buyer and seller, $u(q) - c(q)$. It solves $u'(q^*) = c'(q^*)$. Preferences in the DM are represented in Figure 1.2. It can be seen graphically that q^* maximizes

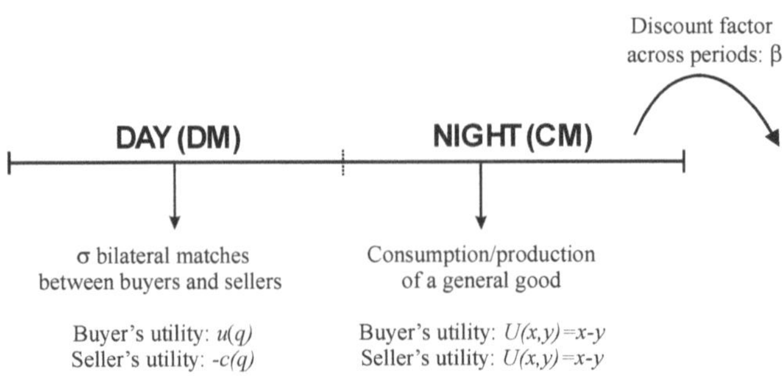

Figure 1.1
Timing

the size of the gains from trade in the DM, i.e., the difference between $u(q)$ and $c(q)$.

The assumption that the utility functions for both buyers and sellers are linear in the general good is made for tractability purposes. In versions of the model where agents can hold assets, such as money or capital, a more general specification for preferences would tend to generate a distribution of asset holdings when agents are subject to idiosyncratic shocks in the DM. The idiosyncratic shocks arise because of the randomness in the matching process in the DM. The heterogeneity in asset holdings is not eliminated by trading in the CM under a more general specification of preferences due to wealth effects. In contrast, with (quasi-) linear utility, there are no wealth effects and agents, conditional on their type, will choose the same asset positions in the CM. The linearity of the CM utility function, $U(x, y)$, greatly simplifies the determination of the terms of trade in the DM, which usually occurs through bargaining, and payment arrangements in bilateral matches. This linearity makes the continuation values in the bargaining problem linear. Note that the linear specification for the utility over goods produced and consumed in the CM implies that there is no benefit associated with producing the general good for one's own consumption.

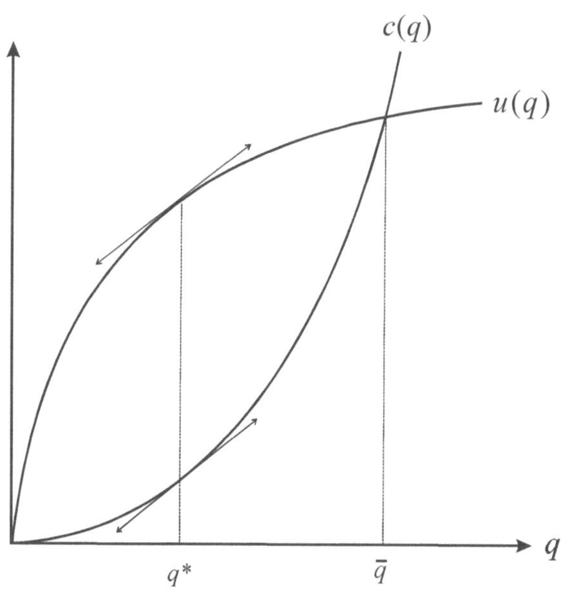

Figure 1.2
Preferences in a bilateral match

The benchmark model can be reinterpreted as a representative household model, where the buyers are the households and the sellers are neoclassical firms. Each firm has a technology that requires a discrete investment of k units of the general good in the CM to produce exactly one unit of a perfectly divisible intermediate good. The intermediate good is durable for one period, i.e., until the next CM. The firm can use the intermediate good in the subsequent period to produce the DM good and/or the CM good. The DM good is produced from the intermediate good according to a linear technology. The CM good is produced from the intermediate good according to the technology $f(x)$, where $f(0) = 0$, $f'(0) = +\infty$ and $f'(1) = 0$. The opportunity cost for the firm to produce the DM good is given by $c(q) = f(1) - f(1-q)$. Assume that $-k + \beta f(1) = 0$ so that a firm makes no profits from producing only the general good. The profits of the firms are transferred to households in a lump-sum fashion.

1.2 Variants of the Benchmark Model

Generally speaking, we adopt some version of this benchmark model specification throughout the chapters that follow. In all chapters, there will be a DM, with bilateral matching of agents, and there will be a CM, where trades are more centralized and agents have linear utility. However, we will depart from some aspects of our benchmark model in order to focus on the problem at hand. For example, when we want to talk about capital formation, we will allow some goods to be storable; when we want agents to be able to borrow or lend before entering the DM, and after exiting the CM, we will introduce additional subperiods and match-specific heterogeneity; if we think that policy may affect the nature of the matching process, we will endogenize the extent of the search frictions; and when it simplifies the analysis, we will consider the case of finitely-lived agents. When we do depart from the benchmark specification, we will be very clear in explaining both how and why we are modifying the model.

1.3 Further Readings

Jones (1976) examines a model with a double-coincidence problem, where agents meet in pairs and fiat money appears to be useful. The analysis, however, departs from rational expectations. Fully consistent models of bilateral exchange with trading frictions were introduced by Diamond (1982, 1984). Kiyotaki and Wright (1989, 1991, 1993) extend these models to incorporate a double-coincidence problem and a meaningful role for a medium of exchange. For related approaches, see also Oh (1989) and Iwai (1996).

The basic model we consider adopts the environment of Lagos and Wright (2005). The version with ex ante heterogeneous buyers and sellers comes from Rocheteau and Wright (2005). In most of the book we assume that the utility function in the centralized market is fully linear, as in Lagos and Rocheteau (2005). Rocheteau, Rupert, and Wright (2007) examine an environment where agents' CM utility functions are neither linear nor separable, but labor is indivisible and agents have access to lottery devices. Chiu and Molico (2010) do not use quasi-linear preferences, but resort to numerical methods to solve the model. Wong (2015) shows that a degenerate asset distribution is featured under a broad class of preferences including constant return to scale, constant elasticity of substitution, CARA, and others from a range of macroeconomic literatures. Rocheteau, Wong, and Weill (2015b) show that the exact same environment as the one described throughout the book with an upper bound on labor, $y \leq \bar{y}$, can lead to equilibria with nondegenerate distributions of money holdings that can be characterized in closed form. A continuous time version of this model is studied in Rocheteau, Wong, and Weill (2015a).

Even though most of the book focuses on household finance, it would be easy to reinterpret the environment as one where firms hold liquidity to finance investment opportunities. Such environments are provided by Silveira and Wright (2010, 2015), Chiu and Meh (2011), Chiu, Meh, and Wright (2015), and Rocheteau, Wright, and Zhang (2016).

Shi (2006) explains the rationale that underlies the microfoundations of money, and why they are necessary for monetary economics. Surveys and summaries of the literature are provided by Wallace (1998, 2000, 2010), Williamson and Wright (2010a, b), and Lagos, Rocheteau, and Wright (2016).

2 Pure Credit Economies

Consider an encounter between two individuals. One is hungry in the morning and wants to consume, but is only able to produce at night. Call him the *buyer*. The other can produce in the morning, but is only hungry at night. Call him the *seller*. If the buyer has nothing tangible to offer the seller in exchange for consumption goods, then the buyer and seller are unable to engage in a morning spot trade. In this event, a simple solution would be for the buyer to promise to deliver some consumption goods in the future in exchange for some consumption goods now. Such a credit arrangement, however, may fail to materialize if the seller believes that after he produces for the buyer, the buyer will not repay his debt.

In this chapter we are interested in characterizing the conditions under which bilateral credit is feasible, and the set of allocations that can be obtained in such *credit economies*. We are particularly interested in knowing if the best—socially desirable—allocations are feasible. We consider four related environments that can support credit arrangements but differ in terms of the amount of commitment, or trust, that agents possess, and on the punishments that can be imposed on a debtor who reneges on his obligation.

We will start by considering the best of all possible worlds—similar to the standard Arrow-Debreu framework—where agents are always trustworthy. That is, agents can commit to repay their debts. In such an environment, there is nothing that prevents intertemporal gains from trade from being fully exploited: socially desirable allocations can always be achieved. In such a perfect world, payment arrangements between agents are quite trivial.

In our second environment, we assume that, with positive probability, buyers are not able to produce when it is time to repay their debt.

Different buyers may have different probabilities of default. If the buyer does not know any more than the seller regarding his ability, or probability, of repaying his debt—i.e., information is symmetric—then socially desirable allocations are still feasible. In this case, the terms of trade reflect the possibility of default. If, however, the buyer knows his probability of debt repayment and sellers don't—i.e., information is asymmetric—then it becomes harder to achieve socially desirable allocations. In particular, if buyers are sufficiently different in terms of their probabilities to repay their debts, then the socially desirable allocations can no longer be obtained.

In the final two environments, we abandon the idea that agents can be trusted. If trade is to take place, trading arrangements must be self-enforcing. In the third environment, we assume there exists a technology—a public record-keeping device—that makes agents' production levels publicly observable. This technology opens up the possibility of punishing someone who does not produce when he is supposed to. Whether or not socially desirable allocations can be achieved depends on how agents value future consumption, the size of the gains from trade, and the structure of the market. When allocations are decentralized, we show that the incentive constraint that ensures debt repayment can be represented by a simple borrowing constraint with an endogenous debt limit. We characterize dynamic (nonsteady-state) equilibria and modify the environment to allow for the possibility of strategic default in equilibrium.

In the fourth environment, we assume that there does not exist a public record-keeping device, but, at times, agents are able to trade repeatedly among themselves. Repeated interactions allow for the possibility of trust building, where trust can be maintained by the punishment scheme of destroying a valuable partnership. We show that socially optimal allocations are feasible if it is hard to form a relationship—e.g., because the trading frictions are sufficiently severe—and if relationships are sufficiently stable.

2.1 Credit with Commitment

The environments we consider have the following characteristics: first, matches between buyers and sellers are formed during the day, DM, and are maintained at night, CM. The fact that agents are matched for the entire period allows them to make promises—or negotiate debt contracts—during the day that can be settled at night. Second, there are no frictions—e.g., no difficulties for debtors and creditors to find one another—or no costs—e.g., no administrative or enforcement costs—associated with settling debt at night: an agent can settle his debt by producing the general good at night, and transferring it to his creditor. Third, there are no tangible assets, such as money or capital, that agents can use for trade purposes. We first consider an economy where buyers can commit to repay their debts; then we consider environments where they cannot.

We describe the set of allocations that are feasible—e.g., the buyer's consumption in a match cannot be greater than the seller's production—and individually rational—meaning that trade is voluntary. We restrict the set of allocations to be symmetric across matches and constant over time. When a match is formed during the day in the decentralized market, DM, the buyer and seller must decide—either simultaneously or sequentially—whether to accept or reject the allocation (q,y), where q is the quantity of the DM good produced by the seller for the buyer in DM, and y is the amount of the CM good that the buyer promises to produce and deliver to the seller at night in the centralized market, CM. The buyer and seller will trade allocation (q,y) only if both of them accept it. We are agnostic in terms of how the allocation (q,y) is determined. For example, it might be the case that the allocation is an outcome from some bargaining protocol. For the time being our objective is to describe all feasible and individually rational allocations that can be obtained through any trading mechanism.

The sequence of events within a typical period is illustrated in Figure 2.1. At the very beginning of the period, all agents are unmatched. During the DM, each agent finds a trading partner with probability σ. A buyer and seller who are in a match decide to accept or reject a proposed allocation (q,y). If either player rejects the proposal, then the match is dissolved; otherwise, the seller produces q units of

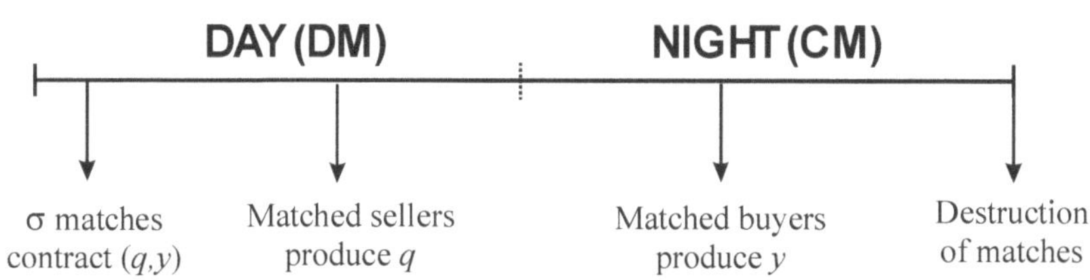

Figure 2.1
Timing of the representative period

the search or DM good for the buyer during the DM, and the buyer produces y units of the general or CM good for the seller at night in the CM. At the end of the period, all matches are destroyed.

The expected lifetime utility of a buyer, evaluated at the beginning of the DM, is

$$V^b = \sigma\left[u(q) - y\right] + \beta V^b, \tag{2.1}$$

assuming that both the buyer and seller accept allocation (q, y). According to (2.1), in the event that the buyer meets a seller, with probability σ, he consumes q units of the DM good and produces y units of the CM good. Since we focus on stationary allocations, time indexes are suppressed. The expected lifetime utility of a seller evaluated at the beginning of the DM is

$$V^s = \sigma\left[-c(q) + y\right] + \beta V^s. \tag{2.2}$$

Equation (2.2) has an interpretation similar to (2.1), except for the fact that during the DM sellers produce (and buyers consume) the DM good and in the CM sellers consume (and buyers produce) the CM good.

Since agents are able to commit, the only relevant constraints are buyers' and sellers' *participation constraints*, which are evaluated at the time that a match is formed. The participation constraints indicate whether agents are willing to participate in the trading arrangement (q, y), i.e., whether they agree to the proposed contract. These constraints are

$$u(q) - y + \beta V^b \geq \beta V^b, \tag{2.3}$$

$$-c(q) + y + \beta V^s \geq \beta V^s. \tag{2.4}$$

According to (2.3), a buyer will accept allocation (q, y) if the lifetime utility associated with acceptance—the left side of (2.3)—exceeds the lifetime utility associated with rejection—the right side of (2.3)—or if his surplus from the trade, $u(q) - y$, is nonnegative. Condition (2.4) has a similar interpretation for the seller. Note that (2.3) and (2.4) only consider single deviations to show the optimality of buyers' and sellers' strategies. After a deviation, we assume that agents return to their proposed equilibrium strategies with their associated payoffs, given by the right sides of (2.3) and (2.4). From (2.3) and (2.4), the set of *incentive feasible* allocations, $\mathcal{A}^C$, is

$$\mathcal{A}^C = \left\{(q, y) \in \mathbb{R}^2_+ : c(q) \leq y \leq u(q)\right\}. \tag{2.5}$$

This set is represented graphically by the shaded area in Figure 2.2. The gains from trade are maximized if agents produce and consume q^*

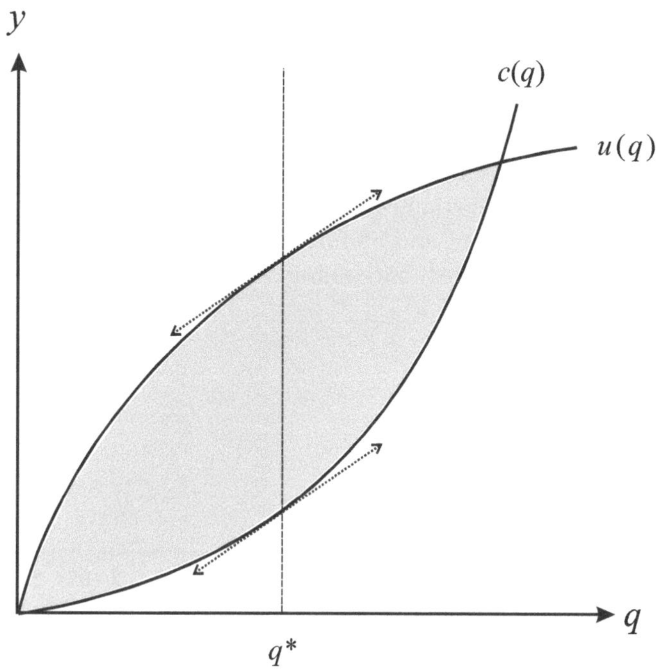

Figure 2.2
Incentive-feasible allocations under commitment

units of the search good in the DM, where $u'(q^*) = c'(q^*)$. From (2.5) it is easy to check that $\{q^*\} \times [c(q^*), u(q^*)] \subseteq \mathcal{A}^C$.

When agents are able to commit, the intertemporal nature of the trades or any issues associated with search frictions are irrelevant for incentive feasibility; i.e., the efficient level of production and consumption of the search good, q^*, is incentive-feasible for any values of β and σ. The level of output for the general good, y, will determine how the gains from trade are split between the buyer and seller.

Since any allocation in $\mathcal{A}^C$ is incentive-feasible, questions naturally arise regarding how the proposed allocation (q, y) will be chosen, and whether it will be efficient. One way to address these questions is to impose an equilibrium concept or, equivalently, a trading mechanism on bilateral matches, and to characterize the outcome of this procedure. For example, we can assume that the allocation (q, y) is determined by the generalized Nash bargaining solution, where the buyer's bargaining power is $\theta \in [0, 1]$. If an agreement is reached, then the buyer's lifetime utility is $u(q) - y + \beta V^b$; if they fail to agree, his lifetime utility is βV^b. Similarly, if they reach an agreement, the seller's lifetime utility is $y - c(q) + \beta V^s$; if they fail, then his lifetime utility is βV^s. The generalized Nash bargaining solution maximizes a weighted geometric mean of the buyer's and seller's surpluses from trade, $u(q) - y$ and $-c(q) + y$, respectively, where the weights are given by the agents' bargaining powers and a surplus is simply the difference between lifetime utility when there is agreement and lifetime utility when there is disagreement. The generalized Nash bargaining solution is given by the solution to

$$\max_{q,y} [u(q) - y]^{\theta} [y - c(q)]^{1-\theta} \tag{2.6}$$

subject to

$$u(q) - y \geq 0 \tag{2.7}$$

$$y - c(q) \geq 0. \tag{2.8}$$

The solution to (2.6)-(2.8) is $q = q^*$ and $y = (1-\theta)u(q^*) + \theta c(q^*)$. See the Appendix for details. The intuition that underlies the generalized Nash solution can be diagrammatically illustrated. The buyer's surplus from a trade is $S^b = u(q) - y$, while the seller's surplus is $S^s = -c(q) + y$. Hence, the total surplus from a match is $S^b + S^s = u(q) - c(q)$, and it is at its maximum when $q = q^*$. All the pairs of surpluses (S^b, S^s) that can be reached through bargaining, i.e., the pairs such that $S^b + S^s \leq$

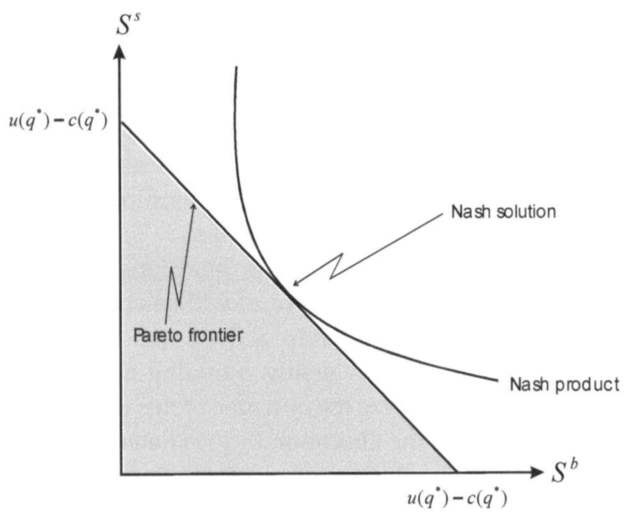

Figure 2.3
Nash bargaining

$u(q^*) - c(q^*)$, constitute the bargaining set, which is represented by the shaded area in Figure 2.3. The Pareto frontier of the bargaining set is the pairs such that $S^b + S^s = u(q^*) - c(q^*)$. The Nash solution is obtained graphically at the tangency point between a curve representing the Nash product, $[u(q) - y]^{\theta} [-c(q) + y]^{1-\theta}$, and the Pareto frontier of the bargaining set.

Note that the allocation is efficient for any value of the buyer's bargaining power $\theta \in [0,1]$. Furthermore, as one varies θ over $[0,1]$, the set of generalized Nash bargaining solutions varies over $\{q^*\} \times [c(q^*), u(q^*)]$. Diagrammatically speaking, as θ increases, the solution moves down the Pareto frontier in Figure 2.3.

2.2 Credit Default

In the previous section, credit arrangements work remarkably well. In reality, however, they may not function so smoothly. In particular, given the intertemporal nature of a debt contract, there is always a risk that something (bad) can happen between the time the contract is negotiated and the time it must be settled. For example, a buyer may be unable to, or does not want to, produce at the time of settlement; i.e., the buyer may default. For our first pass at capturing the notion of default, we assume that a buyer in a match can commit to produce in the CM if he is able to. But the buyer is subject to an exogenous, idiosyncratic productivity shock which implies he is able to produce in the CM with probability δ and is unable to produce with probability $1 - \delta$. Equivalently, $1 - \delta$ can be interpreted as the probability of an exogenous default.

If buyers are homogenous in terms of their default probabilities, then the expected lifetime utility of a buyer, evaluated at the beginning of the DM, is now given by

$$V^b = \sigma [u(q) - \delta y] + \beta V^b, \tag{2.9}$$

assuming that both the buyer and seller accept allocation (q, y). This value function is similar to (2.1), except that y is replaced with δy, since there is a $1 - \delta$ probability the buyer will not produce in the CM. Similarly, the expected lifetime utility of a seller evaluated at the beginning of the DM is now given by

$$V^s = \sigma [-c(q) + \delta y] + \beta V^s. \tag{2.10}$$

The set of incentive-feasible allocations is almost identical to (2.5), except that, like the above value functions, y is replaced by δy; i.e., the buyer's promised CM output production is simply adjusted to compensate for the risk of default. This observation is valid as long as the production of the general good is unrestricted. In this case, the risk of default has no effect on the set of incentive-feasible allocations. If, however, there is an upper bound on the quantity of goods buyers can produce in the CM, then for a sufficiently high probability of default, the set of feasible allocations will be reduced.

Next, we will see that default risk matters in the presence of heterogenous buyers and private information. Assume that buyers are heterogenous in terms of their probabilities of default. There is a measure π_H of buyers with a high probability of repayment, δ_H, and a measure $\pi_L = 1 - \pi_H$ with a low probability of repayment, where $\delta_L < \delta_H$. We assume that $\delta \in \{\delta_L, \delta_H\}$ is an idiosyncratic shock realized by the buyer at the beginning of the period, and these shocks are identically and independently distributed across periods, implying that buyers are ex ante identical. We denote the average probability of repayment by $\bar{\delta} = \pi_H \delta_H + \pi_L \delta_L$.

Assume that the probability of repayment is private information to the buyer. Upon being matched, the trading mechanism offers the buyer a menu of allocations $\{(q_L, y_L), (q_H, y_H)\}$. The buyer either chooses an allocation from the menu, or he declines the offer. If an allocation is chosen, then the seller can either accept or reject it. Trade occurs if both agents accept an allocation. We consider menus of allocations that are stationary, symmetric across agents of a given type, and incentive-compatible. By incentive compatibility, we mean that L-type buyers choose allocation (q_L, y_L) over (q_H, y_H) and H-type buyers choose allocation (q_H, y_H) over (q_L, y_L).

The value function for a buyer of type $\chi \in \{L, H\}$ evaluated at the beginning of the DM is

$$V_\chi^b = \sigma\left[u(q_\chi) - \delta_\chi y_\chi\right] + \beta \mathbb{E}[V_\chi^b], \qquad \chi \in \{L, H\}, \tag{2.11}$$

where $\mathbb{E}[V_\chi^b] = \pi_H V_H^b + \pi_L V_L^b$ is the ex ante expected value function of the buyer. The value function is analogous to (2.1), where the term $\delta_\chi y_\chi$ takes into account the probability that the buyer repays his debt. The value function of a seller evaluated at the beginning of the DM is

$$V^s = \sigma \mathbb{E}\left[-c(q_\chi) + \delta_\chi y_\chi\right] + \beta V^s. \tag{2.12}$$

The expectation is with respect to the type χ of buyer with whom the seller is randomly-matched, and (2.12) assumes that a χ-type buyers chooses allocation (q_χ, y_χ).

A menu of allocations is incentive-feasible if the following conditions are satisfied:

$$u(q_\chi) - \delta_\chi y_\chi \geq 0, \qquad \chi \in \{L, H\} \tag{2.13}$$

$$-c(q_\chi) + y_\chi \mathbb{E}\left[\delta | (q_\chi, y_\chi)\right] \geq 0, \qquad \chi \in \{L, H\} \tag{2.14}$$

$$u(q_L) - \delta_L y_L \geq u(q_H) - \delta_L y_H \tag{2.15}$$

$$u(q_H) - \delta_H y_H \geq u(q_L) - \delta_H y_L. \tag{2.16}$$

The conditions (2.13) and (2.14) are the participation constraints for buyers and sellers, respectively. In (2.14), $\mathbb{E}\left[\delta | (q_\chi, y_\chi)\right]$ represents the seller's expected value of δ, given that the buyer chose allocation (q_χ, y_χ). Both of these conditions indicate that each agent finds the proposed menu of allocations acceptable. Inequality (2.15) specifies that an L-type buyer has no incentive to choose the allocation intended for H-type buyers. Similarly, inequality (2.16) says that an H-type buyer (weakly) prefers allocation (q_H, y_H) to allocation (q_L, y_L).

Let's first consider a pooling menu of allocations: these are allocations where $(q_H, y_H) = (q_L, y_L) = (q, y)$. Note that for a pooling menu, the incentive-compatibility conditions (2.15) and (2.16) are automatically satisfied and, since the choice of the allocation in the first stage of the game conveys no information about the buyer's type, $\mathbb{E}\left[\delta | (q, y)\right] = \bar{\delta}$. As well, if condition (2.13) is satisfied for $\chi = H$, then it is automatically satisfied for $\chi = L$ since it is more costly for the H-type buyer to fulfill his obligation; i.e., $u(q) - \delta_L y \geq u(q) - \delta_H y$. Hence, conditions (2.13) for $\chi = H$ and (2.14) define the set of incentive-feasible pooling allocations, $\mathcal{A}^P$, which is given by

$$\mathcal{A}^P = \left\{ (q, y) \in \mathbb{R}_+^2 : \frac{c(q)}{\bar{\delta}} \leq y \leq \frac{u(q)}{\delta_H} \right\}.$$

The set of incentive-feasible pooling allocations, which is represented by the grey area in Figure 2.4, shrinks as the ratio δ_H/δ_L increases. This is because there is a wedge between the expected cost of promising to repay one unit of the general good by the H-type buyer, δ_H, and the expected benefit of such a promise for the seller, $\delta_H\pi_H + \delta_L\pi_L$. As δ_H/δ_L increases, the expected cost for the H-type buyer increases, relative to the seller's expected benefit, and, as a result, trade opportunities diminish. The efficient level of production and consumption of the search

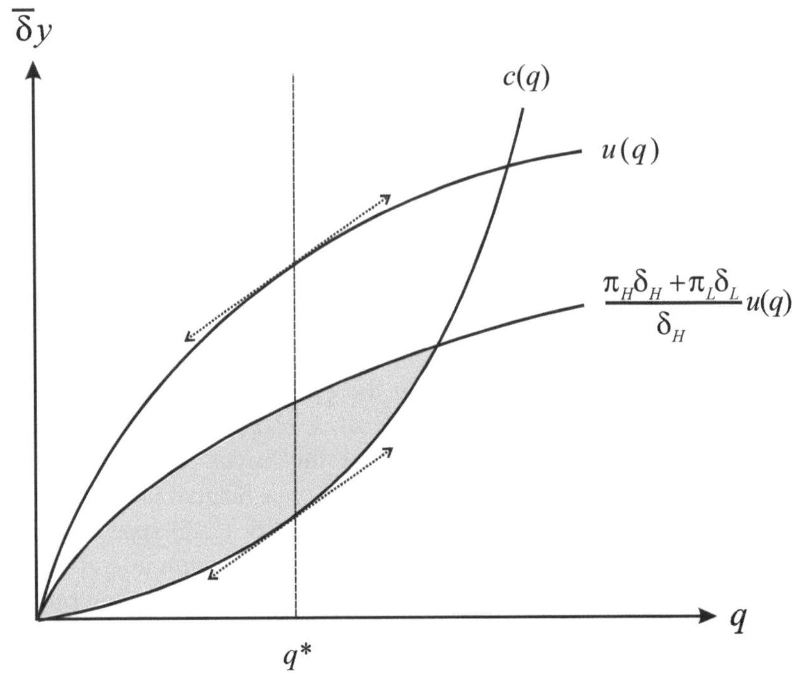

Figure 2.4
Incentive-feasible, pooling allocations under exogenous default

good, q^*, can be implemented if

$$c(q^*) \leq \left(1 - \pi_L \frac{\delta_H - \delta_L}{\delta_H}\right) u(q^*).$$

If $\delta_H = \delta_L$, then this condition is always satisfied. As δ_H/δ_L increases, the right side of the inequality decreases, which makes it less likely that the condition will hold.

Consider next a separating menu of allocations: these are menus that have allocations characterized by $(q_H, y_H) \neq (q_L, y_L)$. The buyers' incentive constraints, (2.15) and (2.16), can be rearranged to read

$$\delta_L(y_L - y_H) \leq u(q_L) - u(q_H) \leq \delta_H(y_L - y_H), \tag{2.17}$$

while their participation constraints, (2.13) and (2.14), can be written as

$$c(q_\chi) \leq \delta_\chi y_\chi \leq u(q_\chi), \qquad \chi \in \{L, H\}. \tag{2.18}$$

Since $\delta_H > \delta_L$, the incentive constraints (2.17) can only be valid if $y_L \geq y_H$ and $q_L \geq q_H$, and, because the allocation is a separating one, these inequalities are strict. As a result the low-probability repayment buyer consumes more, and produces more, than the high-probability repayment buyer in a separating menu. Hence, a separating contract cannot implement an efficient allocation since high- and low-type buyers trade different quantities in the DM.

If there is a limit to the amount of general goods that an agent can produce in the CM—and this limit can be arbitrarily large—then, from (2.18), as δ_L approaches zero, q_L tends to zero. From (2.17) $q_H \leq q_L$, which implies that q_H tends to zero as well. Hence, in a menu characterized by separating allocations, trade will completely shut down if one of the buyer types defaults with probability one.

2.3 Credit with Public Record-Keeping

In the previous section, a default by the buyer was an exogenous event. There was a risk that the buyer would be unable to produce and, hence, repay his debt. In this section, we allow for the possibility of strategic default by relaxing the commitment assumption. By strategic default we mean that the buyer chooses to default even though he has the ability to produce. In order to support trade in a credit economy when agents cannot commit, they must be punished if they do not deliver on their promises. The punishment that we impose is autarky: if an agent fails to deliver on a proposed allocation, then no one will trade with him in the future. Furthermore, we will assume that the punishment is global, in the sense that all agents in the economy revert to autarky if at least one agent deviates from proposed play.

The basic methodology that underlies the environment comes from the theory of repeated games. This literature teaches us that cooperative outcomes can be achieved by using threats of punishments that are credible. For such punishments to be feasible, players' actions must be observable. Hence, there is a need for a public record-keeping technology. We can formally define a record as a list $[q(i), y(i)]_{i\in[0,\sigma]}$, where i represents a match and $[0, \sigma]$ denotes the set of all matches. This record is made available to everyone at the end of each CM. Note that the public record lists only quantities and not the names of the agents associated with the produced quantities. It is for this reason that any deviation from proposed play will result in a global punishment. If names were associated with quantities, then non-global, personalized punishments would be possible. It turns out, however, that very little is changed if individual punishments are possible. We discuss these issues at the end of this section.

The chronology of events is as follows: at the beginning of the DM, a measure σ of buyers and sellers are randomly matched. In each match, the allocation (q,y) is proposed, which agents simultaneously accept or reject. If the allocation is accepted, then the seller produces q units of the search good for the buyer. In the CM, the buyer chooses to either produce y units of the general good for the seller or to renege on his promise and produce nothing. At the end of the CM, a record $[q(i),y(i)]_{i\in[0,\sigma]}$ of the DM and CM production levels for all matches is publicly observed. Based on this record, agents simultaneously decide whether to continue to trade in the subsequent period or to revert to autarky by playing the global punishment strategy. The global punishment strategy requires that all sellers refuse to extend credit to buyers in all future period matches. Given this punishment strategy, a particular seller in a match has no incentive to extend credit to a buyer since the buyer will not repay his debt. The buyer will renege because he cannot be (further) punished for this behavior; i.e., the buyer will not get credit in future matches.

We restrict our attention to symmetric, stationary allocations (q,y) that are incentive-feasible. Incentive-feasibility implies not only that the buyer and the seller agree to allocation (q,y), as before, but also that the buyer is willing to repay his debt when it is his turn to produce. We assume that all agents revert to autarky at the end of the CM whenever $[q(i),y(i)] \neq (q,y)$ for some $i \in [0,\sigma]$; i.e., there is at least one trade that is different from the proposed one. Indeed, having all agents revert to autarky is an equilibrium outcome in this situation.

During the DM, matched buyers and sellers agree to implement allocation (q,y) if

$$-c(q)+y+\beta V^s \geq 0, \tag{2.19}$$

$$u(q)-y+\beta V^b \geq 0. \tag{2.20}$$

Condition (2.19)—which is the seller's participation constraint—says that a seller prefers allocation (q,y) plus the continuation value of participating in future DMs and CMs, βV^s, to autarky. The seller compares the payoff associated with acceptance to that of autarky because if the seller rejects the proposal, a $(0,0)$ trade will be recorded and such a trade will trigger global autarky. Condition (2.20) has a similar interpretation but for the buyer; i.e., the buyer prefers suggested trade (q,y) plus the continuation value of participating in future trades to autarky. Note that the participation constraints (2.19) and (2.20) differ from the participation constraints when agents could commit—(2.3) and (2.4), respectively—since now agents go to autarky if they do not accept the proposed allocation (q, y), instead of just being unmatched for the current period.

We now need to check that the buyer has an incentive to produce the general good since this production occurs after he consumes the search good in the DM. The buyer will have an incentive to produce the general good if

$$-y + \beta V^b \geq 0. \tag{2.21}$$

The left side of inequality (2.21) is the sum of the buyer's current and continuation payoffs if he repays his debt by producing y units of output for the seller; the right side is his continuation (autarkic) payoff of zero if he defaults. Note that the buyer's participation constraint, (2.20), is automatically satisfied if his incentive constraint (2.21) is satisfied.

The value functions for the buyer and seller at the beginning of the period are still given by equations (2.1) and (2.2), respectively; i.e., $V^b = \sigma\left[u(q) - y\right]/(1-\beta)$ and $V^s = \sigma\left[-c(q) + y\right]/(1-\beta)$. These functions imply that the seller's participation constraint (2.19) and the buyer's incentive constraint (2.21) can be rewritten as,

$$-c(q) + y \geq 0, \tag{2.22}$$

$$\frac{\sigma\left[u(q) - y\right]}{r} \geq y, \tag{2.23}$$

respectively, where $r = \beta^{-1} - 1$. Condition (2.22) simply says that the seller is willing to participate if he gets some surplus from trade. It is interesting to note that this participation condition does not depend on discount factors or matching probabilities. Condition (2.23) represents the incentive constraint for the buyer to repay his debt. The left side of (2.23) is the buyer's expected payoff beginning next period, assuming that he does not renege on his debt obligation this period; it is the discounted sum of expected surpluses from future trade. This expression depends on both the frequency of trades, σ, and the discount rate, r. The right side of (2.23) represents the buyer's (lifetime) gain if he does not produce the general good for the seller this period. Not surprisingly, a necessary, but not sufficient, condition for inequality (2.23) to hold is that the buyer's surplus from the trade is positive; i.e., $u(q) - y \geq 0$. Note that (2.22) and (2.23), along with (2.1) and (2.2), imply that $V^s \geq 0$ and $V^b \geq 0$; i.e., agents are better off continuing to trade than being in autarky.

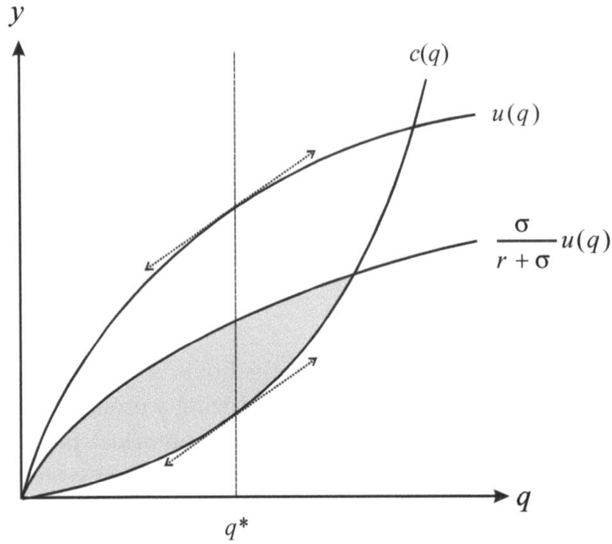

Figure 2.5
Incentive-feasible allocations under public record-keeping

The set of incentive-feasible allocations when agents cannot commit, but when public record-keeping is available, $\mathcal{A}^{PR}$, can be obtained directly from inequalities (2.22) and (2.23); i.e.,

$$\mathcal{A}^{PR} = \left\{ (q,y) \in \mathbb{R}^2_+ : c(q) \le y \le \frac{\sigma}{r+\sigma} u(q) \right\}. \tag{2.24}$$

This set, which is represented by the grey area in Figure 2.5, is smaller than the set of incentive-feasible allocations when agents can commit, $\mathcal{A}^C$; see Figure 2.2. This is a consequence of the additional incentive constraint, (2.21), that must be imposed when buyers are unable to commit to repay their debts. The set $\mathcal{A}^{PR}$ expands as the frequency of trades, σ, increases or as agents become more patient, i.e., when r decreases. Note also that $\mathcal{A}^{PR} \to \mathcal{A}^C$ when $r \to 0$, since the cost of defaulting, which is the expected discounted sum of future trade surpluses, becomes infinite. The efficient production and consumption level of the search good, q^*, will be incentive-feasible if

$$c(q^*) \le \frac{\sigma}{r+\sigma} u(q^*). \tag{2.25}$$

Suppose that inequality (2.25) holds for particular values of σ and r. If the probability of finding a future match, σ, is decreased, then the benefit of avoiding autarky is reduced. If σ decreases sufficiently, then there will be no value for y that gives the buyer an incentive to repay his debt, and makes the seller willing to produce q^*. In this situation, the efficient level of production and consumption of the search good, q^*, is not incentive feasible. One can see this graphically, if the $\sigma u(q)/(r+\sigma)$ curve in Figure 2.5 intersects the $c(q)$ curve at a value of q less than q^*.

Similarly, if buyers discount the future more heavily; i.e., if β decreases or if r increases, the buyer will have a greater incentive to renege on his debt since he cares more about his current payoff than future payoffs. For each level of search friction in the DM, $\sigma \in (0,1]$, there exists a threshold for the discount factor, $\bar{\beta}(\sigma)$, such that if $\beta \geq \bar{\beta}(\sigma)$, then an efficient allocation (q^*, y) is incentive-feasible. This threshold $\bar{\beta}(\sigma)$ is a decreasing function of σ, which means that the efficient level of production and consumption of the search good, q^*, is easier to sustain when there are lower frictions in the DM. If, however, $\beta < \bar{\beta}(\sigma)$, then the incentive-feasible allocations will be characterized by an inefficiently low level of the search good; i.e., $q < q^*$.

Two of the assumptions regarding punishments can be relaxed. First, we have assumed that if an agent in a match does not accept the proposed offer in the DM, then the economy will forever revert to autarky starting in the next period. This is reflected by the zero payoff on the right sides of (2.19) and (2.21). This assumption is harmless in the sense that if agents were not punished for rejecting the proposed offer, then they would still accept all of the equilibrium offers that are supported by the autarky punishment. Formally, we could replace the two participations constraints (2.19) and (2.20) with (2.3) and (2.4).

Second, we have assumed that if an agent defects from proposed play, then the economy will revert to global autarky forever. Such an assumption is necessary when an agent who defects from equilibrium play cannot be identified by other agents in the economy. If, however, a record is now the list $[q(i), y(i), b(i), s(i)]_{i \in [0,\sigma]}$, where $b(i) \in [0,1]$ is the identity of the buyer in match i and $s(i)$ is the identity of the seller in match i, then it is possible to support credit arrangements through *individual* punishments. That is, all of the above credit arrangements can be sustained without having to revert to global autarky in the event of a defection from a proposed allocation.

2.4 Credit Equilibria with Endogenous Debt Limits

We have characterized the set of all stationary, symmetric, incentive-feasible allocations when agents cannot commit—there is a limited commitment friction—and there exists a public record technology. In this section we characterize equilibrium allocations by assuming that the terms of the loan contract are determined in a DM match by a bargaining protocol. The buyer's incentive constraint that prevents default can be compactly represented by a borrowing constraint. This constraint simply says that a buyer cannot borrow more than some specified debt limit, $\bar{b}$; i.e., the borrowing constraint is

$$y \le \bar{b}. \tag{2.26}$$

For the time being we treat the debt limit $\bar{b}$ as being exogenous; below, we endogenize it by appealing to an incentive constraint similar to (2.21).

We start with a simple bargaining game where the buyer has all of the bargaining power and makes a take-it-or-leave-it offer to the seller. The buyer's problem is given by,

$$\max_{q,y} [u(q) - y] \quad \text{s.t.} \quad -c(q) + y \ge 0 \text{ and } (2.26). \tag{2.27}$$

According to (2.27) the buyer maximizes the utility of his DM consumption net of the repayment in the CM, $u(q) - y$, subject to the seller's participation constraint, $y \ge c(q)$, and the borrowing constraint, (2.26). The solution to this problem is $y = c(q)$ and $c(q) = \min\{c(q^*), \bar{b}\}$. If the buyer's borrowing capacity $\bar{b}$ is larger than $c(q^*)$, then the buyer asks for the efficient quantity, q^*, and promises to repay $y = c(q^*)$. Otherwise, the buyer borrows up to the debt limit $\bar{b}$ and consumes the maximum amount that the seller is willing to produce in exchange for $\bar{b}$, which is $q = c^{-1}(\bar{b})$. The left panel in Figure 2.6 plots the match surplus as a function of the debt limit, $\bar{b}$. The right panel plots the terms of trade, (q, y), as a function of the debt limit, $\bar{b}$. Notice that $q = \min\{c^{-1}(\bar{b}), q^*\}$ and $y = \min\{\bar{b}, c(q^*)\}$.

We have characterized the terms of trade, (q, y), as a function of an exogenous debt limit, $\bar{b}$. We now determine the maximum debt limit that can be sustained in an equilibrium. Any equilibrium debt limit $\bar{b}$ must satisfy an incentive constraint that is essentially identical to (2.21),

$$-\bar{b} + \beta V^b \ge 0. \tag{2.28}$$

If the buyer defaults on his debt, then he is sent to autarky forever and receives a lifetime expected utility of 0. According to (2.28), it is optimal for the buyer to repay his debt if the lifetime expected utility associated with debt repayment, βV^b, exceeds the debt limit, $\bar{b}$. When (2.28) holds

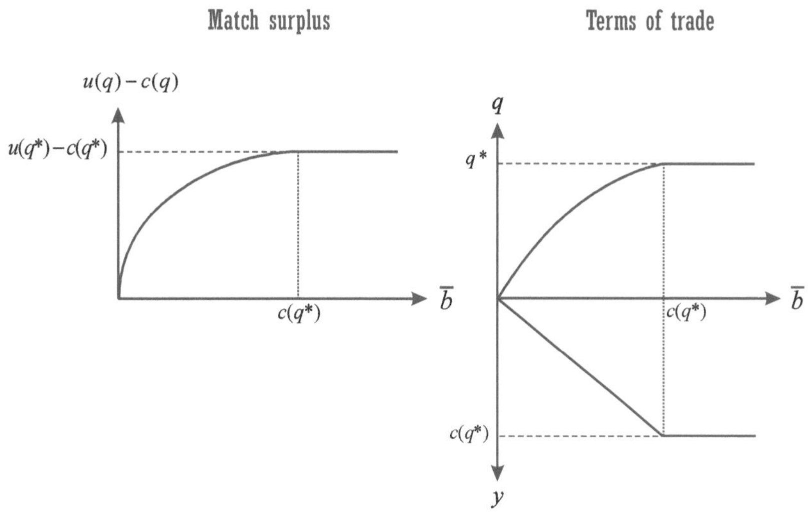

Figure 2.6
Match surplus and terms of trade under take-it-or-leave-it offers

at equality so that the debt limit is at its maximum, $b^{\max}$, the borrowing constraint is said to be "not-too-tight." The debt limit $b^{\max} = \beta V^b$ is sufficiently tight to prevent default but not too tight, i.e., too small, so as to leave unexploited gains from trade on the bargaining table.

If we substitute the buyer's value function $V^b = \sigma\left[u\left(q\right) - y\right] / \left(1 - \beta\right)$ from (2.1) into the buyer's incentive constraint, (2.28), we get

$$r\bar{b} \leq \sigma\left[u\left(q\right) - c(q)\right], \tag{2.29}$$

where $c(q) = \min\left\{c(q^*), \bar{b}\right\}$. The right side of (2.29) is a strictly concave function in $\bar{b}$ for all $\bar{b} < c(q^*)$ and is constant for all $\bar{b} \geq c(q^*)$, while the left side of (2.29) is linear in $\bar{b}$; see Figure 2.7. The grey area in Figure 2.7 indicates where the buyer's incentive constraint, (2.28) or (2.29), is satisfied. Any $\bar{b} \in \left[0, b^{\max}\right]$ implies that, in equilibrium, the buyer has no incentive to default; i.e., $\bar{b} \in \left[0, b^{\max}\right]$ is consistent with either (2.28) or (2.29).

It is interesting to note that there are a continuum of stationary credit equilibria indexed by the buyer's borrowing capacity, $\bar{b} \leq b^{\max}$. Intuitively, if sellers believe that buyers will be able to borrow up to $\bar{b}$ in the future, then they are willing to lend $\bar{b}$ in the current period. One might think, however, the buyer would be able borrow more if $\bar{b} < b^{\max}$ which implies that a debt limit of $\bar{b} < b^{\max}$ cannot be an equilibrium. For example, if the buyer offers $\bar{b} + \varepsilon$, it should be accepted by the seller

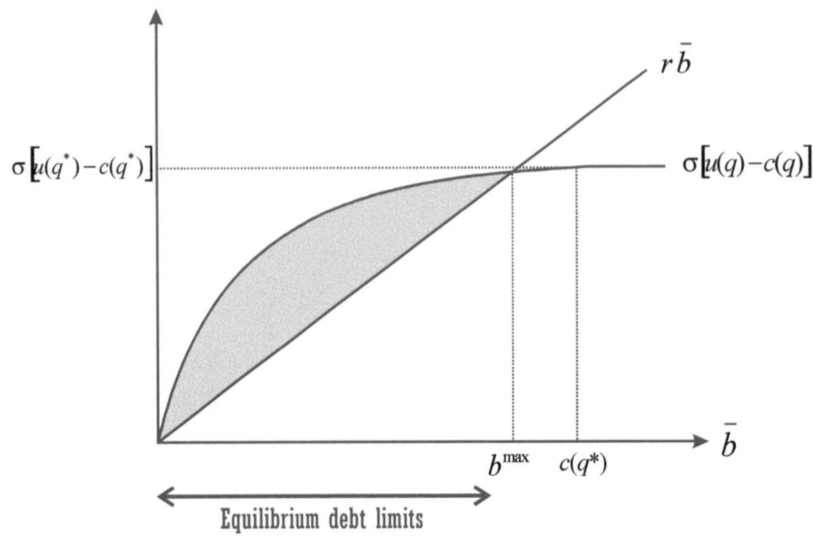

Figure 2.7
Endogenous debt limits under buyers' take-it-or-leave-it offers

since $\bar{b}+\varepsilon < b^{\max}$ implies that the buyer has an incentive to repay the slightly higher debt. But repeated games with perfect monitoring are typically characterized by a large multiplicity of equilibria and equilibria with $\bar{b} < b^{\max}$ can be supported in a number of ways. For example, suppose that sellers believe that a "trustworthy" buyer always repays up to the debt limit $\bar{b} < b^{\max}$ but never more than that limit. Therefore, in the out-of-equilibrium event where a buyer is extended a loan of size $y' > \bar{b}$, the buyer will partially default on his loan; he repays $\bar{b}$ and defaults on $y' - \bar{b}$. By doing so, the buyer remains trustworthy to future sellers—so he is able borrow $\bar{b}$ in the future—but does not incur any negative consequences from the partial default. Hence, a current seller has no incentive to extend a loan that exceeds $\bar{b}$ since he understands that the buyer will default on the amount that exceeds $\bar{b}$. Note that by the same logic, autarky, $(q,y)=(0,0)$, is always an equilibrium; i.e., autarky can be interpreted an equilibrium with loan size $\bar{b}=0$.

Now let's focus on equilibria where the borrowing constraints are "not-too-tight," i.e., $\bar{b}=b^{\max}$, so that the gains from trade are maximized. A credit equilibrium is characterized by the pair $(q,\bar{b})$ that solves,

$$r\bar{b} = \sigma\left[u(q)-c(q)\right]$$
$$c(q) = \min\left\{c(q^*),\bar{b}\right\}.$$

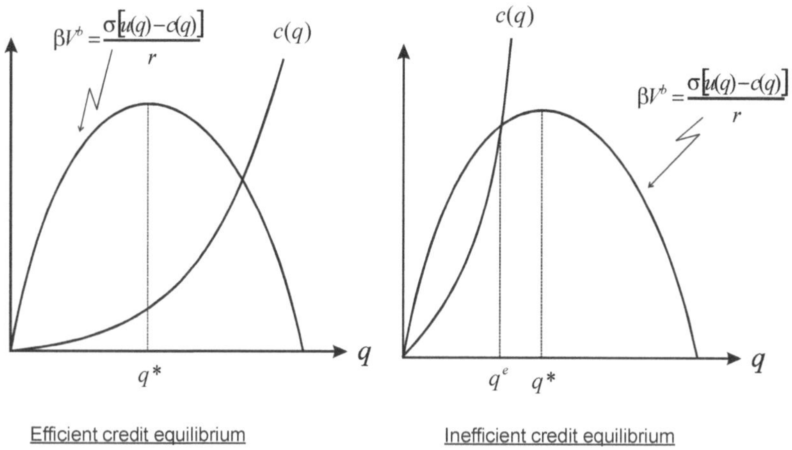

Figure 2.8
Credit equilibrium under take-it-or-leave-if offers by buyers

The credit equilibrium implements an efficient allocation if and only if $c(q^*) \leq \sigma [u(q^*) - c(q^*)] / r$. This condition is depicted in the left panel of Figure 2.8. Notice that this condition is equivalent to (2.25), which implies that whenever the first-best allocation is incentive-feasible, it can be implemented by a simple mechanism that has the buyer making a take-it-or-leave-it offer to the seller. If, however, $c(q^*) > \sigma [u(q^*) - c(q^*)] / r$, then the quantity traded in a credit equilibrium is given by the strictly positive solution to $c(q) = \sigma u(q) / (r + \sigma)$. The right panel of Figure 2.8 depicts this equilibrium, where the quantity traded is $q^e < q^*$. It is easy to see from the diagram that the quantity traded, q^e, increases with σ and decreases with r.

We have assumed that the buyer has all of the bargaining power. We can generalize the trading mechanism by assuming that the terms of the loan contract are determined by the generalized Nash solution. The generalized Nash solution to the bargaining problem is based on three axioms: Pareto efficiency, invariance to rescaling of agents' payoffs, and independence to irrelevant alternatives. It can be shown that these three axioms imply that the solution maximizes the weighted geometric average of the buyer's and seller's surpluses from trade, where the weights are given by the agents' bargaining powers. (We provide more details on bargaining solutions in the next chapter.) In this case, the terms of trade (q, y) are given by the solution to the following maximization problem,

$$\max_{q,y} [u(q) - y]^{\theta} [y - c(q)]^{1-\theta} \quad \text{s.t. } y \leq \bar{b}, \tag{2.30}$$

where $\theta \in [0,1]$ is the buyer's bargaining power. This problem is similar to the Nash bargaining problem under full commitment, (2.6), except that the current problem has a borrowing constraint, $y \leq \bar{b}$, which captures the limited commitment friction. If $\bar{b} \geq \theta c(q^*) + (1-\theta)u(q^*)$, then the solution to (2.30) is

$$q = q^* \tag{2.31}$$

$$y = \theta c(q^*) + (1-\theta)u(q^*). \tag{2.32}$$

If the debt limit is sufficiently large to guarantee the seller a share $1-\theta$ of the first-best surplus, $y - c(q) = (1-\theta)\left[u(q^*) - c(q^*)\right]$, (2.32), then agents trade quantity q^*, (2.31). If, however, $\bar{b} < \theta c(q^*) + (1-\theta)u(q^*)$, then $y = \bar{b}$ and the maximization problem (2.30) can be written as,

$$\max_q \left\{\theta \log\left[u(q) - \bar{b}\right] + (1-\theta)\log\left[\bar{b} - c(q)\right]\right\}. \tag{2.33}$$

The first-order condition to this problem is,

$$\frac{\theta u'(q)}{u(q) - \bar{b}} = \frac{(1-\theta)c'(q)}{\bar{b} - c(q)}. \tag{2.34}$$

The solution can be reexpressed as

$$\bar{b} = \frac{\theta u'(q)c(q) + (1-\theta)c'(q)u(q)}{\theta u'(q) + (1-\theta)c'(q)} \tag{2.35}$$

$$y = \bar{b}. \tag{2.36}$$

Buyers borrow up to their debt limit, (2.36), and consume less than the efficient quantity. The payment made to the seller is a weighted average of the utility of the buyer, $u(q)$, and the disutility of the seller, $c(q)$, (2.35). The weight assigned to the buyer's utility, $(1-\theta)c'(q)/\left[\theta u'(q) + (1-\theta)c'(q)\right]$, is increasing in q. Hence, since $u(q) > c(q)$, q is an increasing function of the debt limit, $\bar{b}$.

If we assume that the borrowing constraint is "not-too-tight," i.e., $\bar{b} = b^{\max}$, the debt limit solves (2.28) at equality, which for generalized Nash bargaining, is given by

$$r\bar{b} = \sigma \frac{\theta u'(q)}{\theta u'(q) + (1-\theta)c'(q)}\left[u(q) - c(q)\right]. \tag{2.37}$$

The right side of (2.37) corresponds to the buyer's expected utility in the DM: the buyer is in a match with probability σ, in which case he receives the share $\Theta(q) \equiv \theta u'(q)/\left[\theta u'(q) + (1-\theta)c'(q)\right]$ of the total match surplus, $u(q) - c(q)$. The share $\Theta(q)$ is decreasing in q and the total match surplus is increasing in q. For q close to q^*, the first effect dominates, so that the buyer's surplus is decreasing in q and, hence, decreasing in $\bar{b}$. It follows that the right side of (2.37) is hump-shaped: it equals 0 at $\bar{b} = 0$ and equals $\sigma\theta\left[u(q^*) - c(q^*)\right]$ for all $\bar{b} \geq \theta c(q^*) + (1 - \theta)u(q^*)$. Therefore, there are two solutions to (2.37): $\bar{b} = 0$ and $\bar{b} > 0$. A credit equilibrium is a triple, $(q, y, \bar{b})$, that solves (2.31)-(2.32) if $\bar{b} \geq \theta c(q^*) + (1 - \theta)u(q^*)$, (2.35)-(2.37) if $\bar{b} < \theta c(q^*) + (1 - \theta)u(q^*)$. An equilibrium achieves the first best if and only if

$$r \leq \frac{\sigma\theta\left[u(q^*) - c(q^*)\right]}{\theta c(q^*) + (1 - \theta)u(q^*)}. \tag{2.38}$$

Since the right side is increasing in θ, the first best is more likely to be achieved when buyers have more bargaining power.

2.5 Dynamic Credit Equilibria

Up to this point we have focused on steady-state credit equilibria. We now examine non-stationary credit equilibria where the debt limit varies over time. Owing to the multiplicity of stationary equilibria, it is possible to construct dynamic equilibria where the debt limit b_t varies over time; for example, the debt limit can increase, decrease, or cycle. Here, we restrict our attention to equilibria where the borrowing constraint is "not-too-tight" in all time periods, which implies that (2.28) holds at equality; i.e.,

$$\bar{b}_t = \beta V_{t+1}^b. \tag{2.39}$$

(We now make time indices explicit.) We assume for simplicity that the terms of the loan contract are determined by take-it-or-leave-it offers by buyers, which is described by (2.27). The solution to the bargaining problem (2.27) is given by $y_t = c(q_t)$ and $c(q_t) = \min\left\{c(q^*), \bar{b}_t\right\}$. The lifetime expected discounted utility of a buyer is

$$V_t^b = \sigma\left[u(q_t) - y_t\right] + \beta V_{t+1}^b. \tag{2.40}$$

Using (2.39), we obtain a first-order difference equation in the debt limit,

$$\bar{b}_t = \beta\left\{\sigma\left[u(q_{t+1}) - c(q_{t+1})\right] + \bar{b}_{t+1}\right\}. \tag{2.41}$$

Notice (2.41) has the interpretation of an asset pricing equation: the date t debt limit is the discounted value of the date $t + 1$ debt limit plus the

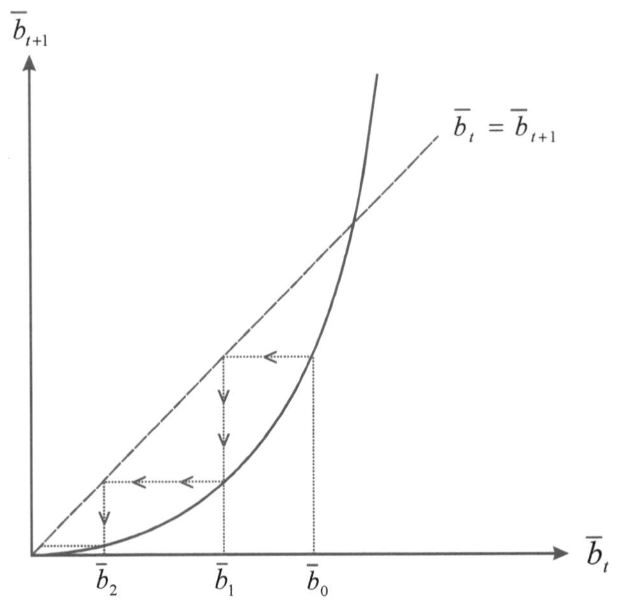

Figure 2.9
Phase diagram of a credit economy under limited commitment

expected surplus in the DM. A credit equilibrium is now a sequence, $\{\bar{b}_t\}_{t=0}^{+\infty}$, solution to (2.41). The right side of (2.41) is increasing and concave in $\bar{b}_{t+1}$ and is strictly concave for all $\bar{b}_{t+1} < c(q^*)$. We represent (2.41) in a phase diagram in $(\bar{b}_t, \bar{b}_{t+1})$ space; see Figure 2.9. There are a continuum of equilibria indexed by the initial debt limit, $b_0 \in [0, b^{\max}]$. For all $b_0 \in (0, b^{\max})$, the equilibrium is characterized by a debt limit that decreases over time. If sellers believe that a buyer's borrowing capacity decreases over time, i.e., the buyer becomes less trustworthy over time, then this belief is self-fulfilling. As a result, DM output also decreases over time.

2.6 Strategic Default in Equilibrium

We now revisit the possibility of default in credit economies. In Section 2.2 default occurs because exogenous shocks prevent buyers from producing and, hence, repaying their debt. We now suppose that buyers can always repay their debt in the CM, but they may choose not to. Moreover, only a fraction δ of the buyers are viewed as being trustworthy by sellers and have a positive debt limit, $\bar{b} > 0$. The remaining

$1-\delta$ buyers are viewed as being untrustworthy. Since these buyers do not have access to credit in the future, they never find it optimal to repay their debt today.

Suppose that the identity of the buyer—trustworthy or untrustworthy—is not perfectly observable in the DM when matches are formed. In particular, with probability Λ a seller can observe a buyer's identity and has access to his trading history through the record-keeping technology. In such matches only trustworthy buyers are able to borrow up to $\bar{b} > 0$. In the remaining $1-\Lambda$ matches, the identity of the buyer is not observed by the seller at the time of the loan contract. However, the identity is observed at the time of repayment and the actions of the buyer are publicly recorded. So, a trustworthy buyer who would not repay his debt becomes untrustworthy.

In uninformed matches, we focus on pooling equilibria of the bargaining game and select the equilibrium that maximizes the utility of trustworthy buyers. Specifically, the terms of trade in uninformed matches, (q^u, y^u), are given by the solution to,

$$\max_{q,y} [u(q) - y] \text{ s.t. } -c(q) + \delta y \geq 0 \text{ and } y \leq \bar{b},$$

where the first equality constraint is the participation constraint of a seller in a pooling equilibrium of an uninformed match. The solution to this bargaining problem is given by: $q^u = \hat{q}_\delta$, where $\delta u'(\hat{q}_\delta) = c'(\hat{q}_\delta)$ if $\bar{b} \geq c(\hat{q}_\delta)/\delta$; otherwise, $c(q^u) = \delta\bar{b}$ and $y^u = \bar{b}$. Because the outcome is pooling, the $1-\delta$ untrustworthy buyers are able to borrow y^u and consume q^u in the DM; but because they are untrustworthy, they default on their debt in the subsequent CM. The trustworthy buyer's debt limit satisfies

$$-\bar{b} + \beta V^b \geq \beta V^{ub}, \tag{2.42}$$

where V^{ub} is the value function for an untrustworthy buyer. From the right side of (2.42) if a trustworthy buyer defaults, then he is perceived as being untrustworthy by sellers.

Assuming that borrowing constraints are "not-too-tight," the debt limit of trustworthy buyers solves (2.42) at equality, where

$$V^{ub} = \sigma(1-\Lambda)\frac{u(q^u) - c(q^u)/\delta}{1-\beta}$$

$$V^b = \sigma\frac{\Lambda\left[u(q) - c(q)\right] + (1-\Lambda)\left[u(q^u) - c(q^u)/\delta\right]}{1-\beta},$$

and q represents the DM output in matches where the seller can observe the buyer's type. Substituting these expressions into (2.42), the debt limit solves

$$r\bar{b} = \sigma\Lambda\left[u\left(q\right) - c(q)\right]. \tag{2.43}$$

The right side of (2.43) represents the flow cost from defaulting: the buyer will not be able to trade in the fraction Λ of matches where his identity is observed. It increases with Λ, which implies that the debt limit increases with the level of information in the DM.

2.7 Credit with Reputation

The public nature of the record-keeping technology is a rather strong assumption. In this section, we illustrate that a much weaker record keeping technology, private memory, can still be quite powerful in terms of sustaining credit arrangements when buyers and sellers have repeated interactions. It is well known that cooperation can be sustained when agents repeatedly interact with one another. With repeated interactions, agents are able to develop reputations for behaving appropriately. We assume that agents who are in a trade match during the DM can form a long-term partnership that can be maintained beyond the current period. That is, agents can continue their trade match or partnership into the next period if they so desire.

We allow for both the creation and destruction of a partnership. At the end of each period, an existing partnership is exogenously destroyed with probability $\lambda \in (0,1)$. One can justify this exogenous destruction by supposing that the buyers and/or the sellers are hit by a relocation shock and, as a result, permanently lose contact with one another. Agents can also choose to terminate a partnership at-will. For example, the seller may choose to dissolve the partnership by looking for alternative trading partners if the buyer does not deliver on his promise to produce the general good. This sort of termination is important because it provides the seller with a punishment vehicle—namely, the destruction of the asset value of an enduring match or partnership—that is required to make a partnership viable in the first place. Notice that walking away from a partnership when the buyer does not deliver on his promise to produce the general good is a subgame perfect equilibrium since both players make their decisions

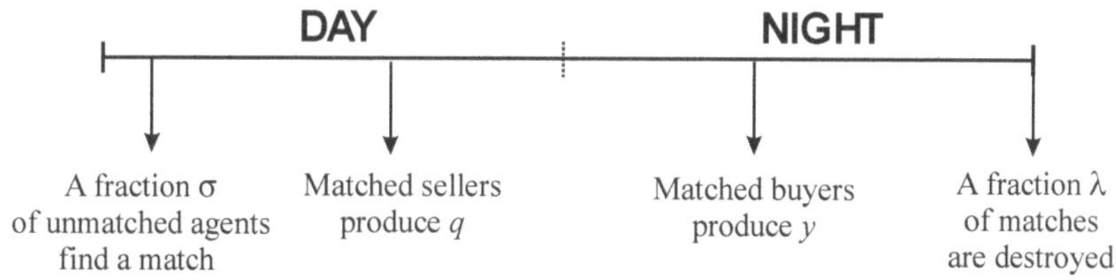

Figure 2.10
Timing of the representative period

simultaneously. That is, since agents make their decisions simultaneously, walking away from a partnership is a best-response for an agent to the same strategy by the other agent.

The chronology of events is illustrated in Figure 2.10. At the beginning of the DM, unmatched buyers and sellers participate in a random matching process. With probability σ, a buyer (seller) is matched with a seller (buyer). Buyers and sellers whose match was not destroyed at the end of the previous period simultaneously and independently decide whether to look for the previously matched partner or look for a new partner. If two old partners search for each other, then they find one another with probability one, and the partnership is maintained. If either one of them looks for a new partner, the match is terminated.

In each match, an allocation (q, y) is proposed, which agents can either accept or reject. If both agents accept the offer, the seller produces q units of the search good for the buyer in the DM. In the CM, the buyer chooses whether or not to honor his implicit obligation by producing y units of the general good for the seller. At the end of the CM, either the partnership is exogenously destroyed or it can continue into the next period. Partnerships can be formed and maintained only during the random matching process at the beginning of the DM.

We will characterize the set of symmetric stationary equilibrium allocations for this economy. Let e_t denote the total measure of partnerships during the DM in period t, after the matching phase is completed. Assuming that buyers do not renege on their promises, the law of motion for e_t is

$$e_{t+1} = (1 - \lambda)e_t + \sigma(1 - e_t + \lambda e_t). \tag{2.44}$$

According to (2.44), if there are e_t partnerships in period t, a fraction $(1 - \lambda)$ of them will be maintained into period $t + 1$. Among the $1 - e_t + \lambda e_t$ agents who are unmatched at the beginning of $t + 1$, a fraction σ find new partners. In the steady state, $e_{t+1} = e_t = \bar{e}$ which, from (2.44), implies that

$$\bar{e} = \frac{\sigma}{\sigma + \lambda(1-\sigma)}. \tag{2.45}$$

The number of matches increases with the matching probability σ and decreases with the destruction probability λ.

Let V_e^b be the value function for a buyer who is in a partnership at the beginning of a period and V_u^b the value function for a buyer who is not, where e stands for employed in a partnership and u for unmatched. Then, assuming that the buyer does not renege and neither party voluntarily terminates the partnership,

$$V_e^b = u(q) - y + \lambda\beta V_u^b + (1-\lambda)\beta V_e^b, \tag{2.46}$$
$$V_u^b = \sigma V_e^b + (1-\sigma)\beta V_u^b. \tag{2.47}$$

According to (2.46), the buyer receives q units of search goods in the DM and produces y units of general good in the CM. The partnership is exogenously destroyed with probability λ, in which case the buyer goes to the random matching process at the beginning of the next period to find a new partner. According to (2.47), an unmatched buyer finds a seller with probability σ. If the buyer does not get matched, then, with probability $1-\sigma$, he starts the next period unmatched. The closed form solutions for V_e^b and V_u^b, whose derivation can be found in the Appendix, are given by

$$V_e^b = \frac{[1-(1-\sigma)\beta]\,[u(q)-y]}{(1-\beta)\,[1-(1-\sigma)(1-\lambda)\beta]} \tag{2.48}$$
$$V_u^b = \frac{\sigma\,[u(q)-y]}{(1-\beta)\,[1-(1-\sigma)(1-\lambda)\beta]}. \tag{2.49}$$

Let V_e^s be the value function for a seller who is in a partnership at the beginning of the period and V_u^s the value function for a seller who is not. Then,

$$V_e^s = -c(q) + y + \lambda\beta V_u^s + (1-\lambda)\beta V_e^s, \tag{2.50}$$
$$V_u^s = \sigma V_e^s + (1-\sigma)\beta V_u^s. \tag{2.51}$$

According to (2.50), the seller produces q units of the search good during the DM and consumes y units of the general good in the CM. With probability λ the partnership is destroyed, in which case the seller enters the random matching process at the beginning the next period. According to (2.51), with probability σ, the seller is matched with a buyer who likes his search good. The closed form solutions for V_e^s and V_u^s are given by

$$V_e^s = \frac{[1-(1-\sigma)\beta]\,[-c(q)+y]}{(1-\beta)\,[1-(1-\sigma)(1-\lambda)\beta]} \tag{2.52}$$

$$V_u^s = \frac{\sigma\,[-c(q)+y]}{(1-\beta)\,[1-(1-\sigma)(1-\lambda)\beta]}. \tag{2.53}$$

Allocation (q, y) can be implemented as an equilibrium outcome if three sets of conditions are satisfied. First, agents who enter the DM unmatched, and subsequently become matched, will accept the proposed allocation (q, y) if the following participation constraints hold,

$$V_e^s \geq \beta V_u^s, \tag{2.54}$$

$$V_e^b \geq \beta V_u^b. \tag{2.55}$$

If the seller and buyer accept the allocation (q, y), then their expected payoffs are given by the left sides of (2.54) and (2.55), respectively; and if they reject, the continuation payoffs are given by the right sides.

Second, at the beginning of a period, matched sellers and buyers who do not receive a relocation shock will agree to continue their partnership if

$$V_e^s \geq V_u^s, \tag{2.56}$$

$$V_e^b \geq V_u^b. \tag{2.57}$$

If the seller and the buyer choose to continue the partnership, their payoffs are given by the left sides of (2.56) and (2.57), respectively; if either or both choose to dissolve the partnership, the expected payoffs are given by the right sides. Clearly, conditions (2.56) and (2.57) imply that (2.54) and (2.55) hold, respectively. Note that from (2.48) and (2.49), and (2.52) and (2.53), the surpluses that a buyer and a seller receive are given by, respectively,

$$V_e^b - V_u^b = \frac{(1-\sigma)\,[u(q)-y]}{1-(1-\sigma)(1-\lambda)\beta} \tag{2.58}$$

$$V_e^s - V_u^s = \frac{(1-\sigma)\,[-c(q)+y]}{1-(1-\sigma)(1-\lambda)\beta}. \tag{2.59}$$

From these surpluses, we can deduce that (2.56) and (2.57) are satisfied if $u(q) - y \geq 0$ and $-c(y) + y \geq 0$.

Third, a buyer in a partnership must be willing to produce the general good for the seller in the CM. This requires that

$$-y + \lambda\beta V_u^b + (1-\lambda)\beta V_e^b \geq \beta V_u^b. \tag{2.60}$$

If the buyer produces y units of the general good, then his expected payoff is given by the left side of (2.60). If, however, he deviates and does not produce, then the partnership will be dissolved at the beginning of the subsequent period and the buyer will start the next DM seeking a new match; the utility associated with this outcome is given by the right side of (2.60). This constraint can be reexpressed as $y \leq (1-\lambda)\beta\left(V_e^b - V_u^b\right)$ or, using (2.58), $y \leq \beta(1-\lambda)(1-\sigma)u(q)$.

The set of incentive-feasible allocations that can be supported by reputation is given by

$$\mathcal{A}^R = \{(q,y) : c(q) \leq y \leq \beta(1-\lambda)(1-\sigma)u(q)\}. \tag{2.61}$$

This set is represented by the grey area in Figure 2.11. The buyer's incentive-compatibility condition, (2.60), generates an endogenous borrowing constraint, $y \leq \beta(1-\lambda)(1-\sigma)u(q) \equiv b^{\max}$. This borrowing constraint indicates that the maximum amount the buyer can promise to

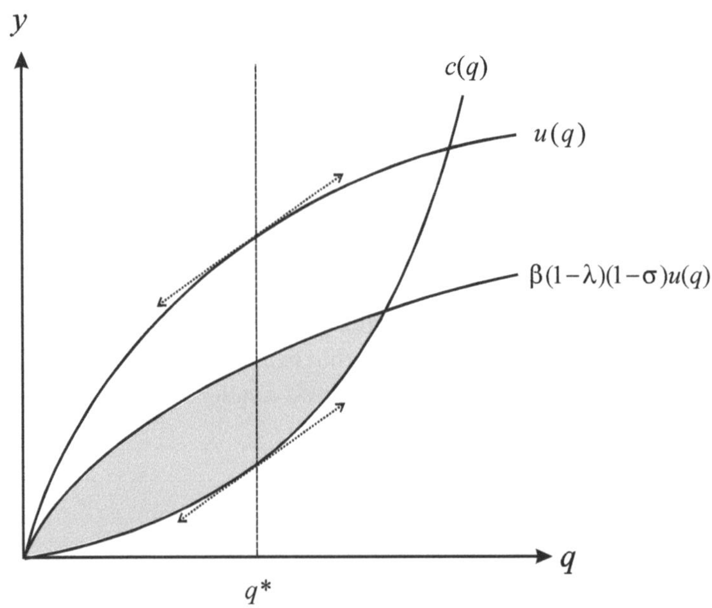

Figure 2.11
Incentive-feasible allocations with reputation

repay in the CM depends on his patience, β, the stability of the match, λ, and market frictions, σ. The buyer is able to credibly promise to repay more, the more patient he is, i.e., the higher is β; the more stable is the match, i.e., the lower is λ; the greater is the matching friction, i.e., the lower is σ; and the higher is his consumption the next DM, i.e., the higher is q.

Note that the set of incentive feasible allocations, $\mathcal{A}^R$, will be empty if either all matches are destroyed at the end of a period, if $\lambda = 1$, and/or if agents can find partners in the DM with certainty, if $\sigma = 1$. The existence of credit relationships relies on the threat of termination, but such a threat only has bite if matches are not easily destroyed *and* if it is difficult to create a new trade match.

The efficient production and consumption level of the search good, q^*, is implementable if and only if $(q^*, y) \in \mathcal{A}^R$,

$$c(q^*) \leq \beta(1-\lambda)(1-\sigma)u(q^*). \tag{2.62}$$

Agents are able to trade the quantity q^* through long-term partnerships if the average duration of a long-term partnership is high, i.e., if λ is low, if the matching frictions are severe, i.e., if σ is low, and if agents are patient, i.e., if β is close to one. Figure 2.11 characterizes a situation where the efficient production and consumption level of the search good is implementable. Diagrammatically speaking the $\beta(1-\lambda)(1-\sigma)u(q)$ curve must intersect the $c(q)$ curve at a $q > q^*$ in Figure 2.11.

The model environment in this section provides an example where social welfare is not monotonic in the underlying search friction σ. Social welfare at the steady state, W, is defined to be the measure of trade matches, $\bar{e}$ given by (2.45), times the surplus of each match; i.e.,

$$W = \frac{\sigma}{\sigma + \lambda(1-\sigma)} \left[u(q) - c(q) \right].$$

Let W^* denote the maximum social welfare over the set of incentive-feasible allocations,

$$W^*(\sigma) = \max \left\{ \frac{\sigma}{\sigma + \lambda(1-\sigma)} \left[u(q) - c(q) \right] : (q, y) \in \mathcal{A}^R \right\}.$$

To see that $W^*(\sigma)$ is not a monotonic function of σ, note that the measure of matches, $\bar{e}$, is increasing in σ while the set of incentive-feasible q's shrinks as σ increases. If $\sigma = 0$ or $\sigma = 1$, then $W^* = 0$ since at $\sigma = 0$ the number of matches is zero and at $\sigma = 1$ the set of implementable allocation is $\mathcal{A}^R = \{(0,0)\}$; if, however, $\sigma \in (0,1)$, then $W^*(\sigma) > 0$.

Finally, we show that if the planner were free to choose the extent of the search frictions, σ, in the DM, then the optimal σ would have the repayment constraint, $c(q) \leq \beta(1-\lambda)(1-\sigma)u(q)$, bind and $q < q^*$. To see this, define σ^* as the solution to $c(q^*) = \beta(1-\lambda)(1-\sigma^*)u(q^*)$. Clearly, for all $\sigma \in [0, \sigma^*]$, the repayment constraint is not violated at $q = q^*$; hence, a planner would never choose $\sigma < \sigma^*$. As σ increases above σ^*, the number of matches increases, but the repayment constraint starts to bind. A small increase of σ above σ^*, therefore, has a first-order effect on the number of matches, but only a second-order effect on match surplus, $u(q) - c(q)$. Hence, the optimal σ is greater than σ^*, which implies that the repayment constraint binds and $q < q^*$.

2.8 Further Readings

Pairwise credit in a search-theoretic model was first introduced by Diamond (1987a,b, 1990). The environment is similar to Diamond (1982), where agents are matched bilaterally and trade indivisible goods. As in our setup, credit is repaid with goods. The punishment for not repaying a loan is permanent autarky.

There are several models where agents have some private information about their ability to repay their debt. Aiyagari and Williamson (1999) consider a random-matching model where agents receive random endowments that are private information and exchange is motivated by risk-sharing. The optimal allocations have several features similar to those of real-world credit arrangements, such as credit balances and credit limits. Smith (1989) constructs an overlapping generations model where agents have stochastic endowments and can misrepresent the nature of the liabilities they issue. Jafarey and Rupert (2001) study an economy with alternating endowments, where the set of agents who issue debt is divided into two classes: safer and riskier borrowers. The former have a higher probability of redeeming their debt than the latter.

Kocherlakota (1998a,b) describes credit arrangements in different environments, including a search-matching model with a public record of individual transactions. He uses mechanism design to characterize the set of symmetric, stationary, incentive-feasible allocations. Kocherlakota and Wallace (1998) extend the model to consider the case where the public record of individual transactions is updated after a probabilistic lag. They establish that society's welfare increases as the frequency with which the public record is updated increases. As pointed out by Wallace (2000), this is the first model that formalizes the idea that technological advances in the payment system improve welfare. The model by Kocherlakota and Wallace has been extended by Shi (2001) to discuss how the degree of advancement of the credit system affects specialization.

Seminal contributions on limited-commitment economies include Kehoe and Levine (1993), Kocherlakota (1996), and Alvarez and Jermann (2000). Kocherlakota (1996) adopts a mechanism design approach in a two-agent economy with a single good. Gu, Mattesini, Monnet, and Wright (2013a) conduct a similar mechanism design exercise for a large economy with imperfect monitoring to explain the essentiality of banks. Kehoe and Levine (1993) establish conditions for first-best allocations to be implementable. Alvarez and Jermann (2000) introduce the notion of endogenous debt limits and "not-too-tight" borrowing constraints. They prove a First Welfare Theorem where constrained-efficient allocations can be implemented with competitive trades and not-too-tight borrowing constraints. Sanches and Williamson (2010) introduce the "not-too-tight" borrowing constraints in a model with pairwise meetings and bargaining and study steady-state equilibria. Gu, Mattesini, Monnet, and Wright (2013b) investigate dynamic equilibria and credit cycles in a related economy. Bethune, Hu, and Rocheteau (2014) show that the set of equilibria derived under "not-too-tight" borrowing constraints is of measure zero in the whole set of Perfect Bayesian Equilibria. Under some conditions constrained-efficient allocations cannot be implemented with "not-too-tight" borrowing constraints. They also establish the existence of a continuum of endogenous credit cycles of any periodicity and a continuum of sunspot equilibria, independent of the assumed trading mechanism. Carapella and Williamson (2015) study asymmetric equilibria with trustworthy and untrustworthy agents under asymmetric information in order to generate default in equilibrium. Monnet and Sanches (2015) study a competitive banking system composed of bankers who cannot commit to their promises and show it is inconsistent with an optimum quantity of private money.

Most search-theoretic models of the labor market, e.g., Pissarides (2000), assume long-term partnerships. However, in these economies trades do not involve credit and are free of moral hazard considerations. Corbae and Ritter (2004) consider an economy with pairwise meetings, where agents can form long-term partnerships to sustain credit arrangements. A related model of reciprocal exchange is also presented by Kranton (1996).

Appendix

The Generalized Nash Bargaining Solution

The Nash solution is an axiomatic bargaining solution proposed by Nash (1953). It is based on four axioms—Pareto efficiency, scale invariance, independence of irrelevant alternatives, symmetry—and it predicts a unique outcome to a bargaining problem. Moreover, it has solid strategic foundations, see, e.g., Osborne and Rubinstein (1990). In our context, the generalized Nash Bargaining solution, which generalizes the Nash solution by dropping the axiom of symmetry, is given by the solution to (2.6), i.e.,

$$(q,y) = \arg\max_{q,y} \{\theta \ln [u(q) - y] + (1-\theta) \ln [y - c(q)]\}$$

The first-order conditions are

$$\frac{\theta u'(q)}{u(q)-y} - \frac{(1-\theta)c'(q)}{y-c(q)} = 0 \tag{2.63}$$

$$-\frac{\theta}{u(q)-y} + \frac{(1-\theta)}{y-c(q)} = 0. \tag{2.64}$$

It is immediate that $u'(q) = c'(q)$, or $q = q^*$, and $y = (1-\theta)u(q^*) + \theta c(q^*)$.

Derivation of Equations (2.48) and (2.49)

The system (2.46)-(2.47) can be rewritten under the following matrix form:

$$\begin{pmatrix} 1-(1-\lambda)\beta & -\lambda\beta \\ -\sigma & 1-(1-\sigma)\beta \end{pmatrix} \begin{pmatrix} V_e^b \\ V_u^b \end{pmatrix} = \begin{pmatrix} u(q)-y \\ 0 \end{pmatrix}.$$

By inverting the first matrix we obtain

$$\begin{pmatrix} V_e^b \\ V_u^b \end{pmatrix} = \Delta^{-1} \begin{pmatrix} 1-(1-\sigma)\beta & \lambda\beta \\ \sigma & 1-(1-\lambda)\beta \end{pmatrix} \begin{pmatrix} u(q)-y \\ 0 \end{pmatrix},$$

where $\Delta = [1-(1-\lambda)\beta][1-(1-\sigma)\beta] - \sigma\lambda\beta$. The determinant of the matrix can be reexpressed as

$$\Delta = (1-\beta)[1-(1-\sigma)(1-\lambda)\beta] \in (0,1).$$

Consequently, the closed-form solutions for the value functions of a buyer are

$$V_e^b = \frac{[1-(1-\sigma)\beta]\,[u(q)-y]}{(1-\beta)\,[1-(1-\sigma)(1-\lambda)\beta]}$$

$$V_u^b = \frac{\sigma\,[u(q)-y]}{(1-\beta)\,[1-(1-\sigma)(1-\lambda)\beta]}.$$

By similar reasoning, we can solve for the closed-form solution of a seller:

$$V_e^s = \frac{[1-(1-\sigma)\beta]\,[-c(q)+y]}{(1-\beta)\,[1-(1-\sigma)(1-\lambda)\beta]}$$

$$V_u^s = \frac{\sigma\,[-c(q)+y]}{(1-\beta)\,[1-(1-\sigma)(1-\lambda)\beta]}.$$

3 Pure Currency Economies

In the previous chapter we showed that credit arrangements allow agents to take advantage of intertemporal gains from trade. If, however, creditors do not trust debtors to repay their debts, then trade by credit may not be incentive-feasible. If agents are to trade with one another, then some sort of tangible medium of exchange must emerge. According to Kiyotaki and Moore (2002), a lack of trust is of primary importance for a theory of money: as they say, "distrust is the root of all money."

In this chapter, we assume that buyers and sellers never trust one another because they cannot commit to repay their debts, and there is no record-keeping technology or reputational device that can make debt contracts self-enforcing. In the absence of some tangible means of payment, buyers and sellers live in autarky. In order to give trade a chance we introduce an intrinsically useless asset, fiat money. The objective is to investigate whether fiat money can be valued in equilibrium and can serve as a medium of exchange.

The model presented in this chapter is the core framework to study issues related to money, payments, and liquidity for the rest of the book. We will provide a detailed guideline on how to solve the model and analyze monetary equilibria. We will study stationary and non-stationary equilibria and characterize outcomes that can occur in pure currency economies. Moreover, we will consider different trading protocols in pairwise meetings that have either explicit axiomatic or strategic foundations, and we will explore the normative and positive implications of such protocols.

We show that pure currency economies have a rich set of non-stationary equilibria. Some of these equilibria are characterized by inflation, even though there is a constant money supply. Other equilibria are characterized by the value of money fluctuating over time, which generates output cycles even though fundamentals are not changing. This multiplicity of equilibria reenforces the notion that the value of fiat money is sustained by self-fulfilling beliefs.

For all of the trading protocols we study, the model has similar positive implications, e.g., the value of money at a steady-state equilibrium depends on the fundamentals of the economy, such as preferences, technologies and search frictions. In terms of normative implications, we isolate a key inefficiency of monetary exchange that is common to all trading protocols: quantities traded in the DM tend to be too low. In terms of policy, money is neutral, in the sense that a one-time change in the money supply does not affect the allocations or welfare, for all of the trading protocols we consider.

Even though we identify a number of features that are common to the various trading protocols, equilibrium allocations, welfare, and the value of fiat money are not invariant to the protocol. For example, quantities traded and social welfare tend to be higher under a competitive protocol in the DM compared to bargaining when the buyer does not have all of the bargaining power.

3.1 A Model of Divisible Money

The environment is similar to the previous chapter. A major departure, however, is that we now assume that there is no commitment or enforcement, no record-keeping, and no long-term relationship. Hence, agents are anonymous and cannot be trusted to honor their future obligations. There is an intrinsically useless object called fiat money. This object does not provide any utility to its owner and it is not an input in the production of goods. It is durable, perfectly divisible, and recognizable—it cannot be counterfeited. The aggregate stock of fiat money is constant over time, and equal to M.

The timing of events in a typical period is as follows. At the beginning of the DM, a measure σ of buyers and sellers are randomly matched, where the buyer has $m \in \mathbb{R}_+$ units of money and the seller has $m_s \in \mathbb{R}_+$. Unless otherwise specified, we assume that the measures of buyers and sellers in the economy are both equal to 1. In each match, the buyer makes a take-it-or-leave-it offer (q, d) to the seller, where q represents the amount of the search good to be produced by the seller and $d \in \mathbb{R}_+$ the amount of money that he receives. At the end of the day, all matches are broken up. At night, all buyers and sellers participate in a competitive market in the CM, where agents can exchange money for general goods at price ϕ_t, where one unit of fiat money buys ϕ_t units of the CM good.

The model is solved in four steps:

1. We characterize some key properties of the value functions in the CM;
2. We determine the terms of trade in a bilateral match in the DM;
3. We characterize the value functions in the DM; and
4. We determine the buyer's and seller's choice of money holdings in the CM.

The value function for a buyer holding $m \in \mathbb{R}_+$ units of money, evaluated at the beginning of the CM, satisfies

$$W_t^b(m) = \max_{m' \in \mathbb{R}_+, x, y} \left\{ x - y + \beta V_{t+1}^b(m') \right\} \tag{3.1}$$

$$\text{subject to} \quad x + \phi_t m' = y + \phi_t m. \tag{3.2}$$

From (3.2), the buyer finances his end-of-period money balances, m', and general good consumption, x, with production of the general good, y, and money balances brought into the CM, m. Notice that the value functions in (3.1) and prices in (3.2) are indexed by time since we allow the value of money and allocations to vary over time. Substituting $x - y$ from (3.2) into the maximand of (3.1), we get

$$W_t^b(m) = \phi_t m + \max_{m' \geq 0} \left\{ -\phi_t m' + \beta V_{t+1}^b(m') \right\}. \tag{3.3}$$

Equation (3.3) tells us that the buyer's CM value function is linear in the money balances, m, brought into the CM. This is an important result which comes about from the linearity of the CM utility function, $x - y$. An implication of such preferences is that the buyer's wealth, which is composed only of real balances, does not affect his choice of money holdings for the future. This result is crucial for the tractability of the model because otherwise the idiosyncratic trading shocks in the DM—a buyer is matched with probability σ—would create a non-degenerate distribution of money holdings when buyers exit the subsequent CM. The non-degeneracy would occur because buyers who are matched in the DM hold fewer money balances when they enter the subsequent CM than buyers who are unmatched. In the presence of wealth effects, the heterogeneity in money holdings that results from the trading shocks in the DM would persist into the subsequent CM, as well as in subsequent periods. Generally speaking, it is difficult to obtain analytical solutions when this sort of heterogeneity is present; one must, instead, rely on numerical methods. The value function of the buyer in the CM is illustrated in Figure 3.1.

By a similar line of reasoning, the seller's CM value function is

$$W_t^s(m) = \phi_t m + \max_{m' \geq 0} \left\{ -\phi_t m' + \beta V_{t+1}^s(m') \right\}. \tag{3.4}$$

The seller's value function, like the buyer's, is linear in real balances. The linearity of these value functions will also prove to be convenient when solving the bargaining problem.

The evolution of the distributions of money holdings for buyers and sellers over a period is represented in Figure 3.2. Buyers start the period with m_b units of money, where m_b is typically equal to the money supply, M. Sellers start with m_s, typically equal to zero. The fraction σ of buyers who are matched end the DM with $m_b - d$ units of money, where d is the amount spent in a match. Similarly, the fraction σ of sellers who are matched end the DM with $m_s + d$ units of money. In the CM, buyers and sellers readjust their money holdings so that all buyers end the period with m_b units of money and all sellers end the period with m_s units of money.

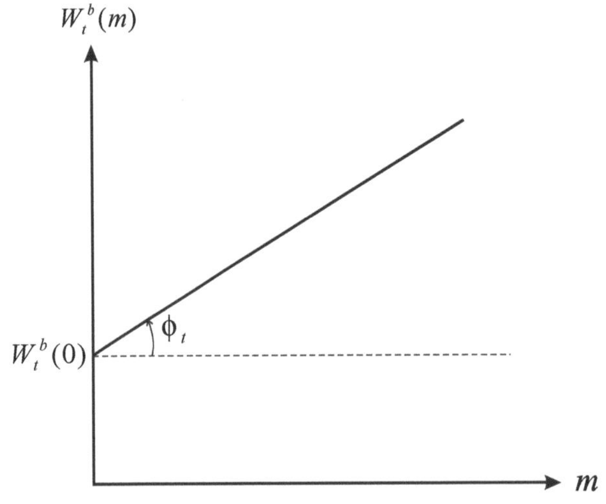

Figure 3.1
Buyer's value function

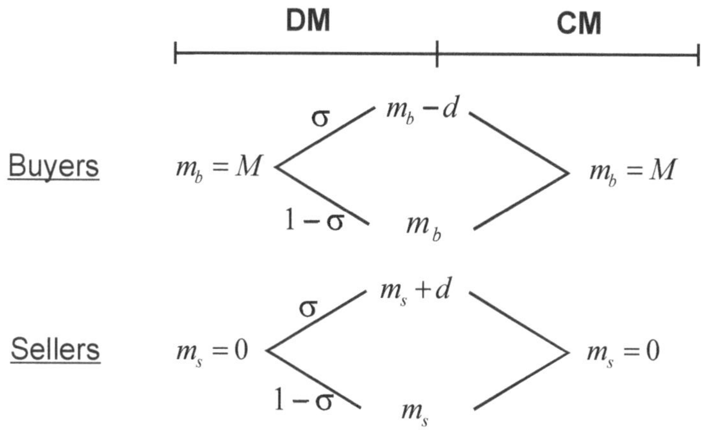

Figure 3.2
Evolution of the distributions of money holdings over a period

The terms of trade in the DM of period t are determined in a bilateral match between a buyer holding m units of money and a seller holding m_s units. The buyer chooses an offer, (q,d), that maximizes his expected utility subject to satisfying the seller's participation constraint. The buyer's offer solves

$$\max_{q,d} \left[u(q) + W_t^b(m-d)\right] \tag{3.5}$$

$$\text{s.t.} \quad -c(q) + W_t^s(m_s+d) \geq W_t^s(m_s) \tag{3.6}$$

$$-m_s \leq d \leq m. \tag{3.7}$$

The seller's participation constraint is (3.6), and (3.7) is a feasibility constraint that says the buyer cannot offer to transfer more units of money than he holds, or he cannot ask for more units of money than the seller holds. Since the value functions W_t^b and W_t^s are linear, (3.5)-(3.7) can be simplified to

$$\max_{q,d} \left[u(q) - \phi_t d\right] \quad \text{s.t.} \quad -c(q) + \phi_t d \geq 0, \quad -m_s \leq d \leq m. \tag{3.8}$$

The constraint, $-m_s \leq d$, is never binding since otherwise the seller's surplus would be negative. Hence, the terms of trade, (q,d), do not depend on the seller's money holdings. As well, the seller's participation constraint must hold at equality. If this was not the case, then the buyer could increase his surplus by slightly reducing the amount that he offers to pay the seller so that the seller would still find the offer acceptable. Therefore, the solution to (3.8) is

$$q = \begin{cases} q^* \\ c^{-1}(\phi_t m) \end{cases} \text{if } \phi_t m \begin{cases} \geq \\ < \end{cases} c(q^*), \tag{3.9}$$

$$d = \frac{c(q)}{\phi_t}. \tag{3.10}$$

The buyer can obtain the socially-efficient quantity, q^*, if his real balances, $\phi_t m$, are large enough to compensate the seller for the disutility to produce, (3.9). The solution to the buyer's bargaining problem is depicted in Figure 3.3. In this diagram, one can trace out the buyer's offer (q, d) by varying m.

The buyer's DM value function, $V_t^b(m)$, is given by

$$V_t^b(m) = \sigma\left[u(q) + W_t^b(m-d)\right] + (1-\sigma)W_t^b(m), \tag{3.11}$$

where q and d are determined by (3.9) and (3.10). According to (3.11), the buyer is matched in the DM with probability σ, in which case he consumes q units of the DM good and gives up d units of money. With complementary probability, the buyer is unmatched and enters the CM with his beginning-of-period money balances. Since $q = c^{-1}(\phi_t d)$ and

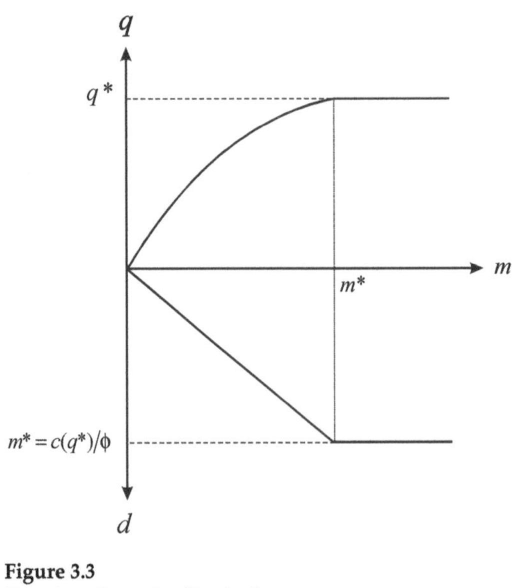

Figure 3.3
Take-it-or-leave-it offers by buyers

$W_t^b(m) = \phi_t m + W_t^b(0)$, the buyer's DM value function can be expressed as

$$V_t^b(m) = \sigma \max_{d \in [0,m]} \left[u \circ c^{-1}(\phi_t d) - \phi_t d \right] + \phi_t m + W_t^b(0). \tag{3.12}$$

Substituting the right side of (3.12), indexed by $t+1$ and m', for $V_{t+1}^b(m')$ in (3.3), we get

$$\begin{aligned} W_t^b(m) &= \phi_t m + \max_{m' \geq 0} \left\{ -\phi_t m' + \beta \left[\sigma \max_{d \in [0,m']} \left[u \circ c^{-1}(\phi_{t+1} d) - \phi_t d \right] \right. \right. \\ &\qquad \left. \left. + \phi_{t+1} m' + W_{t+1}^b(0) \right] \right\} \\ &= \phi_t m + \beta W_{t+1}^b(0) + \max_{m' \geq 0} \left\{ -(\phi_t - \beta \phi_{t+1}) m' \right. \\ &\qquad \left. + \beta \left[\sigma \max_{d \in [0,m']} \left[u \circ c^{-1}(\phi_t d) - \phi_t d \right] \right] \right\}, \end{aligned}$$

where the term $\beta W_{t+1}^b(0)$ has been taken outside of the maximization problem because it is independent of the buyer's choice of money holdings. Since the first two terms on the right side of the equation above are independent of m', the buyer's problem reduces to

$$\max_{m \in \mathbb{R}_+} \left[-\left(\frac{\phi_t}{\beta \phi_{t+1}} - 1 \right) \phi_{t+1} m + \sigma \max_{d \in [0,m]} \left[u \circ c^{-1}(\phi_{t+1} d) - \phi_{t+1} d \right] \right]. \tag{3.13}$$

According to (3.13), the buyer chooses his money balances to maximize his expected surplus in the DM net of the cost of holding real balances.

To characterize both the solution to the buyer's problem and the equilibrium, we distinguish different cases depending on whether the (gross) rate of return of currency, ϕ_{t+1}/ϕ_t, is equal to, smaller than, or greater than the (gross) discount rate, β^{-1}.

1. If $\phi_t/\phi_{t+1} < \beta$, then there is no solution to problem (3.13), as the buyer would demand infinite money balances. Consequently, there cannot be an equilibrium where the rate of return of currency is larger than the discount rate.
2. If $\phi_t/\phi_{t+1} = \beta$, then money is costless to hold. In this situation, the buyer carries sufficient balances in order to purchase q^* from the seller. Hence, $d = c(q^*)/\phi_{t+1}$ and any $m \geq c(q^*)/\phi_{t+1}$ is a solution.
3. If $\phi_t/\phi_{t+1} > \beta$, then money is costly to hold. Because of this, buyers do not accumulate more money balances than they expect to spend

in the DM; i.e., $d = m$. The first-order (necessary and sufficient) condition of the buyer's problem (3.13) is given by

$$\frac{u' \circ c^{-1}(\phi_{t+1}m)}{c' \circ c^{-1}(\phi_{t+1}m)} = 1 + \frac{1}{\sigma}\frac{\phi_t/\phi_{t+1} - \beta}{\beta}. \tag{3.14}$$

By a similar line of reasoning, the seller's DM value function, which is evaluated at the beginning of the period, is

$$V_t^s(m) = \sigma\left[-c(q) + \phi_t d\right] + W_t^s(m) = \phi_t m + W_t^s(0),$$

where we have used the fact that the seller does not receive any surplus in the DM, i.e., $c(q) = \phi_t d$. Hence, we can rewrite the seller's choice of money balances problem in the CM, described in (3.4), as

$$\max_{m \geq 0}\left\{-\left(\frac{\phi_t}{\beta\phi_{t+1}} - 1\right)\phi_{t+1}m\right\}. \tag{3.15}$$

From (3.15), if $\phi_t/\beta\phi_{t+1} = 1$, then the seller is indifferent between holding money or not, and $m \geq 0$. If, however, $\phi_t/\beta\phi_{t+1} > 1$, then $m = 0$ since the seller's money holdings are costly to carry from one period to the next but do not affect the terms of trade in the DM. As above, if $\phi_t/\beta\phi_{t+1} < 1$, then a solution does not exist.

The aggregate money demand correspondence, $M^d(\phi_t)$, is the sum of the individual money demands across buyers and sellers. From the above cases, the aggregate demand correspondence is

$$M^d(\phi_t) = \begin{cases} \left[\frac{c(q^*)}{\phi_{t+1}}, +\infty\right) & \text{if } \phi_t = \beta\phi_{t+1} \\ \{m\} \text{ where } m \text{ solves (3.14) if } \phi_t > \beta\phi_{t+1} \end{cases}.$$

The aggregate money demand correspondence is represented in Figure 3.4. It is equal to an interval when $\phi_t = \beta\phi_{t+1}$, and is single-valued otherwise. Moreover, it is decreasing in ϕ_t. Market clearing requires $M \in M^d(\phi_t)$. If $M \geq c(q^*)/\phi_{t+1}$, then $\phi_t = \beta\phi_{t+1}$. Otherwise, ϕ_t solves (3.14) with $m = M$. Consequently, $\{\phi_t\}_{t=0}^{\infty}$ is the solution to the difference equation

$$\phi_t = \beta\phi_{t+1}\left\{1 + \sigma\left[\frac{u' \circ c^{-1}(\phi_{t+1}M)}{c' \circ c^{-1}(\phi_{t+1}M)} - 1\right]^+\right\}, \tag{3.16}$$

where $[x]^+ \equiv \max(x, 0)$.

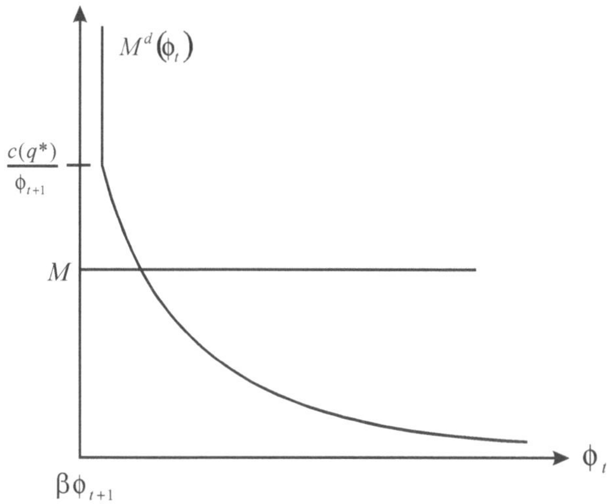

Figure 3.4
Aggregate money demand

According to (3.16) the price of money in period t is equal to its discounted price in period $t+1$ plus a liquidity factor,

$$\sigma\beta\phi_{t+1}\left[\frac{u'\circ c^{-1}(\phi_{t+1}M)}{c'\circ c^{-1}(\phi_{t+1}M)}-1\right]^{+},$$

that captures the marginal benefit of holding real balances in the DM. If money is costly to hold, then buyers don't bring enough real balances in the DM to purchase q^* if they are matched, $\phi_{t+1}M < c(q^*)$. As a consequence, the liquidity factor is positive since a buyer would value having an additional unit of money to spend in the DM. If money is costless to hold, then in the CM of period t buyers accumulate sufficient balances to purchase q^* in the DM of period $t+1$ if they are matched, which implies that $\phi_{t+1}M \geq c(q^*)$. Here, the liquidity factor is zero; i.e.,

$$\left[\frac{u'\circ c^{-1}(\phi_{t+1}M)}{c'\circ c^{-1}(\phi_{t+1}M)}-1\right]^{+}=0$$

since a buyer would not value having an additional unit of money to spend in the DM.

An equilibrium of an economy with divisible money is a bounded sequence $\{\phi_t\}_{t=0}^{\infty}$ solving the first-order difference equation (3.16). Note that we do not impose an initial condition because the dynamic equation for the value of money, (3.16), is forward looking. The value of money is not determined by what happened in the past; it depends entirely on expectations about its future value. In other words, ϕ_0 is an endogenous variable.

3.1.1 Steady-State Equilibria

We first examine stationary equilibria, where $\phi_t = \phi_{t+1} \equiv \phi^{ss}$. Since fiat money has no intrinsic value, there always exists an equilibrium where money has no exchange value, where $\phi_t = \phi_{t+1} = 0$. Now consider stationary equilibria where the production and consumption of the search good are strictly positive, $q_t = q_{t+1} = q^{ss} > 0$, and $q^{ss} = \min\{c^{-1}(\phi^{ss}M), q^*\}$. Equation (3.16) can be simplified to

$$\frac{u'(q^{ss})}{c'(q^{ss})} = 1 + \frac{r}{\sigma}, \tag{3.17}$$

where $r = (1-\beta)/\beta$. The left side of (3.17), which is decreasing in q^{ss}, goes to infinity as q^{ss} approaches zero; i.e., $u'(0)/c'(0) = \infty$, and is equal to one if $q^{ss} = q^*$. See Figure 3.5. Consequently, there is a unique q^{ss}

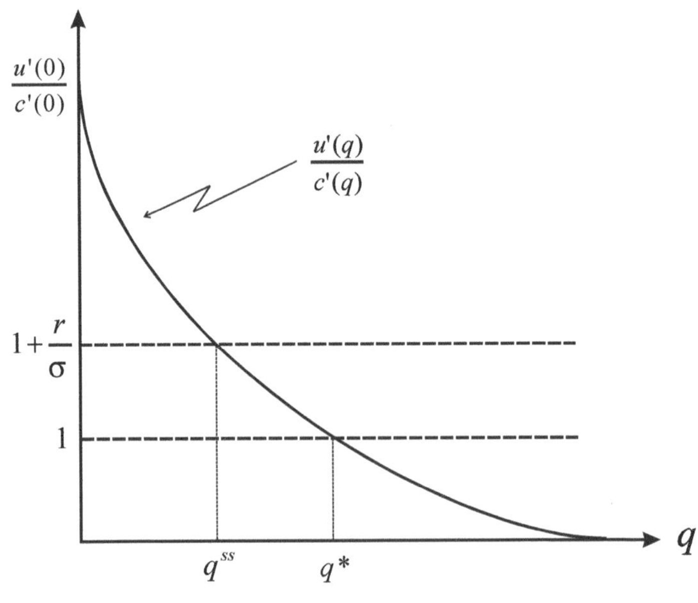

Figure 3.5
Determination of the steady-state equilibrium

satisfying (3.17). Since $r/\sigma > 0$, $q^{ss} < q^*$ and the unique ϕ^{ss} is pinned down by

$$\phi^{ss} = \frac{c\left(q^{ss}\right)}{M}. \tag{3.18}$$

Hence, output will be inefficiently low when $r > 0$. Moreover, output increases as trading frictions decrease, $\partial q^{ss}/\partial\sigma > 0$, and decreases as money becomes more costly to hold, $\partial q^{ss}/\partial r < 0$. One can interpret the term r/σ in (3.17) as a measure of the cost of holding real balances: it is the product of the rate at which agents depreciate future utility, r, and the average number of periods it takes to get matched, $1/\sigma$. As this cost increases, buyers reduce their real balances, and DM output falls. As the rate of time preference approaches zero, q^{ss} tends to q^*.

Finally, notice that a one-time change in the stock of money, M, does not affect the real allocation: money is neutral. From (3.17), output in the DM, q^{ss}, is unaffected by a change in the aggregate stock of money, since a change in the aggregate stock affects neither the frequency of trade, σ, nor the rate of time preference, r. Hence, aggregate real balances, ϕM, are constant—equal to $c\left(q^{ss}\right)$—and the change in the price level, $1/\phi$, is proportional to the change in M.

3.1.2 Nonstationary Equilibria

There exists other equilibria that are not stationary. The exact nature of these equilibria, however, depend upon functional forms and parameter values. The curve representing graphically the relationship between ϕ_{t+1} and ϕ_t as defined by (3.16) is called a phase line. It is continuous, it goes through the origin and the positive steady state, (ϕ^{ss}, ϕ^{ss}). For all $\phi_{t+1}M > c\left(q^*\right)$, the phase line is linear, $\phi_t = \beta\phi_{t+1}$. Consequently, in the (ϕ_t, ϕ_{t+1}) space, the phase line intersects the 45° line from below. See the Appendix for details.

Consider the following functional forms: $c(q) = q$ and $u(q) = q^{1-a}/(1-a)$ with $a < 1$. For this specification, $q^* = 1$ and (3.16) becomes

$$\phi_t = \begin{cases} \beta\left\{(1-\sigma)\,\phi_{t+1} + \sigma\left(\phi_{t+1}\right)^{1-a}(M)^{-a}\right\} \text{ if } \phi_{t+1}M < 1 \\ \beta\phi_{t+1} \text{ if } \phi_{t+1}M \geq 1 \end{cases}. \tag{3.19}$$

As shown in Figure 3.6, the phase line, given by (3.19), is monotonically increasing and convex in the (ϕ_t, ϕ_{t+1}) space when $\phi_{t+1}M < 1$ and linear with slope $\beta^{-1} = 1 + r$ otherwise.

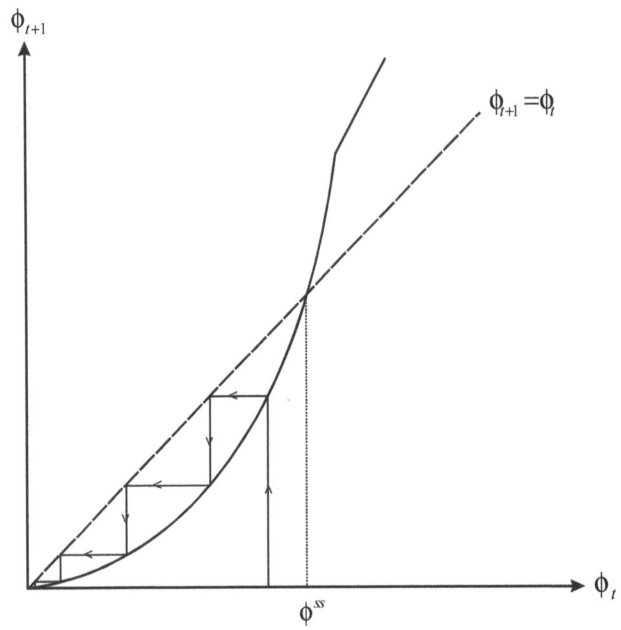

Figure 3.6
Phase diagram: $c(q) = q$ and $u(q) = \frac{q^{1-a}}{1-a}$ with $a \in (0,1)$

There are a continuum of equilibria converging to the nonmonetary equilibrium: if $\phi_0 < \phi^{ss}$, then ϕ_t approaches 0 as t goes to infinity. For all these equilibria, ϕ_t is decreasing and the price level, $1/\phi_t$, is increasing over time. Hence, it is possible to have a positive inflation, in equilibrium, even though the money supply is constant. In this situation, beliefs about a depreciating value of currency can be self-fulfilling. If $\phi_0 = \phi^{ss}$, then the equilibrium is stationary. If $\phi_0 > \phi^{ss}$, then there does not exist an equilibrium since $\{\phi_t\}_{t=0}^{\infty}$ is unbounded.

For the above example, there is a unique equilibrium where the value of money does not vanish asymptotically; it corresponds to the stationary equilibrium, where $\phi = \phi^{ss}$ in Figure 3.6. For alternative functional forms and model parameters, the solution to the difference equation (3.16) can involve time-varying values of money, where the value of money is bounded away from 0.

Suppose now that $\sigma = 1$, $c(q) = q$, and

$$u(q) = \frac{(q+b)^{1-a} - b^{1-a}}{1-a},$$

with $a > 1$ and $b \in (0,1)$. As b approaches zero, $u(q)$ tends to a constant relative risk aversion utility function, with relative risk aversion equal to a. For this particular specification, the difference equation (3.16) becomes $\phi_t = \Gamma(\phi_{t+1})$ where

$$\Gamma(\phi_{t+1}) = \begin{cases} \beta \frac{\phi_{t+1}}{(\phi_{t+1}M+b)^a} \text{ if } \phi_{t+1}M < 1-b \\ \beta\phi_{t+1} \text{ if } \phi_{t+1}M \geq 1-b \end{cases}. \tag{3.20}$$

The steady-state is given by $\phi^{ss} = (\beta^{1/a} - b)/M$, which is positive if $b < \beta^{1/a}$. In the neighborhood of the steady state, the difference equation, $\phi_t = \Gamma(\phi_{t+1})$, can be approximated by the following first-order Taylor series approximation,

$$\phi_t = \Gamma(\phi_{t+1}) \approx \Gamma(\phi^{ss}) + \Gamma'(\phi^{ss})(\phi_{t+1} - \phi^{ss}). \tag{3.21}$$

By definition, $\Gamma(\phi^{ss}) = \phi^{ss}$, so (3.21) becomes

$$\phi_{t+1} - \phi^{ss} = \frac{\phi_t - \phi^{ss}}{\Gamma'(\phi^{ss})}.$$

The solution to this linear difference equation is

$$\phi_{t+1} = \phi^{ss} + \left(\frac{1}{\Gamma'(\phi^{ss})}\right)^t (\phi_0 - \phi^{ss}).$$

It is then clear that the slope of the phase line, $\Gamma'(\phi^{ss})$, is crucial for the stability of the steady-state equilibrium. If $|\Gamma'(\phi^{ss})| < 1$, then ϕ_t tends to diverge from its steady-state value, while if $|\Gamma'(\phi^{ss})| > 1$, then ϕ_t approaches its steady-state value for any initial condition close to the steady state. Differentiating (3.20), we obtain

$$\Gamma'(\phi^{ss}) = 1 - \frac{a(\beta^{\frac{1}{a}} - b)}{\beta^{\frac{1}{a}}}. \tag{3.22}$$

If $ba/(a-1) < \beta^{1/a}$ (recall that $a > 1$), then the slope of the phase line at the steady state is negative. In this case, the phase line defined by (3.20) bends backwards. If b is close to zero, then $\partial\phi_t/\partial\phi_{t+1} \approx 1 - a$ at the steady state. In the neighborhood of $a = 2$, $\Gamma'(\phi^{ss}) \approx -1$, and the local stability of the steady state changes for small changes in a around $a = 2$: for values of a smaller than 2 the steady state is an "unstable" spiral while for values of a greater than 2 the steady state is a "stable" spiral. When the steady state becomes "stable," for an initial condition ϕ_0 close to ϕ^{ss} the system converges to the steady state. As illustrated in Figure 3.7, there are a continuum of equilibria leading to the steady

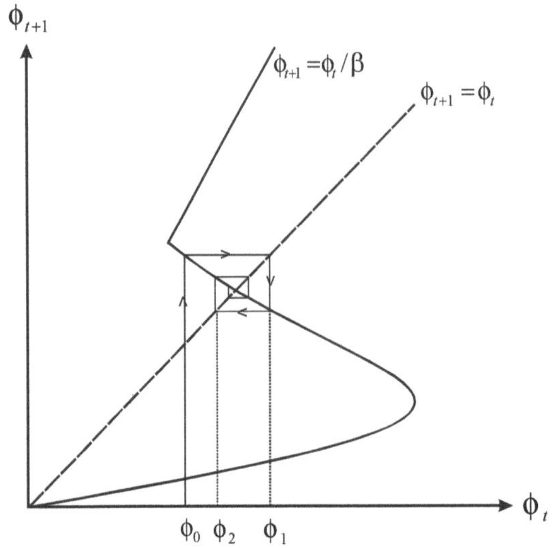

Figure 3.7
Phase line: $\sigma = 1$, $c(q) = q$, $u(q) = \frac{(q+b)^{1-a}-b^{1-a}}{1-a}$, $b > 0$ and $a(\beta^{\frac{1}{a}} - b) > 2\beta^{\frac{1}{a}}$

state. Along any one of these equilibrium paths the value of money, ϕ_t, fluctuates.

In Figure 3.8, we illustrate, by way of numerical examples, the above discussion. We plot the phase line, $\phi_{t+1} = \Gamma(\phi_t)$, for the following parameter values: $b = r = 0.1$ and $\sigma = M = 1$. The coefficient a is equal to 0.5 in the top left panel, 1.5 in the top right panel, 2.2 in the bottom left panel, and 4 in the bottom right. As a increases above one, the phase line bends backward, and it becomes flatter at the steady state as a increases.

In the bottom right panel, we plot both the phase line, $\phi_t = \Gamma(\phi_{t+1})$, and its mirror image with respect to the 45° line, $\phi_{t+1} = \Gamma(\phi_t)$. We enlarged the phase diagram in the neighborhood of the steady state. Two-period cycles are obtained at the intersection of the phase line and its mirror image. If the intersection is not on the 45° line, we obtain a proper cycle. In our example, there is a two-period cycle where the value of money alternates between a low value, $\phi_L \approx 0.85$, and a high value, $\phi_H \approx 0.95$. Hence, output in a bilateral match alternates between $q_L \approx 0.85$ and $q_H = q^* = 0.9$. Note that in the high state, buyers' holdings are larger than the level required to buy the efficient quantity. The buyer is willing to hold this additional currency because the rate of return on currency is exactly equal to r.

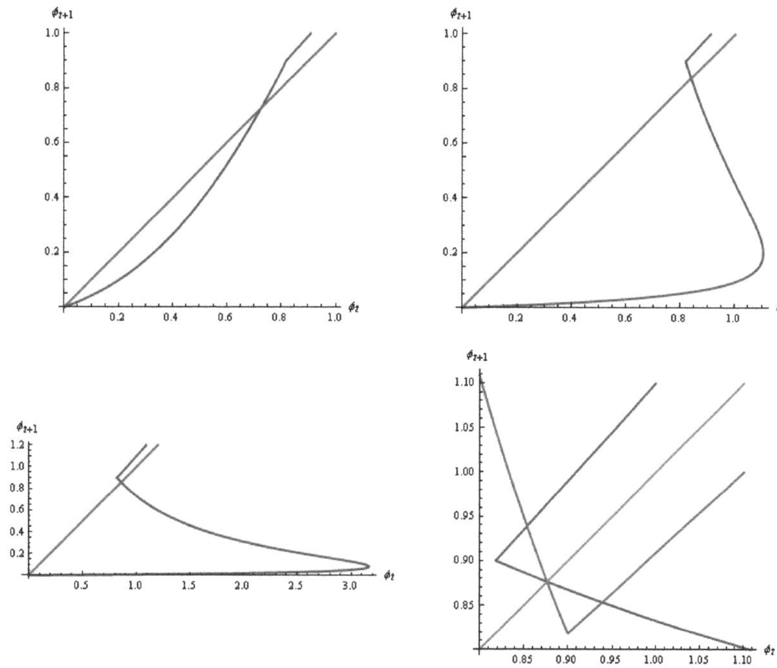

Figure 3.8
Phase diagrams. Top left: $a = 0.5$; Top right: $a = 1.5$; Bottom left: $a = 2.2$; Bottom right: $a = 4$

3.1.3 Sunspot Equilibria

To conclude this section, we introduce the notion of extrinsic uncertainty—uncertainty that does not affect fundamentals, such as technologies and preferences. The sample space of the extrinsic random variable, called a sunspot, is $E = \{\ell, h\}$. The sunspot $e \in E$ is observed by all agents at the beginning of the CM, and follows a two-state Markov chain, with $\lambda_{ee'} = \Pr[e_{t+1} = e' \,|e_t = e]$. That is, there is a (possibly new) sunspot realization at the beginning of each CM and the probability that the new realization is e', given that the previous realization was e, is $\lambda_{ee'}$. We now characterize stationary equilibria when there is extrinsic uncertainty, where by stationarity we mean that the value of money, ϕ_e, depends on the realization of the sunspot state, but does not depend on time.

Following the same reasoning as above, the buyer's choice of money holdings in state s is given by

$$\max_{m \geq 0} \left\{-\phi_e m + \beta\sigma \left\{u\left[q(\bar{\phi}_e m)\right] - c\left[q(\bar{\phi}_e m)\right]\right\} + \beta\bar{\phi}_e m\right\}, \tag{3.23}$$

where $\bar{\phi}_e = \sum_{e' \in E} \lambda_{ee'} \phi_{e'}$ is the expected price of money in the next CM conditional on the current state e. We have that $q(\bar{\phi}_e m) = q^*$ if $\bar{\phi}_e m \geq c(q^*)$ and $q(\bar{\phi}_e m) = c^{-1}(\bar{\phi}_e m)$ otherwise. According to (3.23), in the sunspot state e, the buyer purchases m units of money at the price ϕ_e. In the subsequent DM, buyers purchase $q(\bar{\phi}_e m)$ units of goods and transfer $c\left[q(\bar{\phi}_e m)\right]$ real balances to sellers. In the DM, agents value money according to its future expected price in the CM.

The first-order condition of the buyer's problem, (3.23), together with the market-clearing condition $m = M$, is

$$\phi_e = \beta \bar{\phi}_e \left\{ 1 + \sigma \left\{ \frac{u'\left[q(\bar{\phi}_e M)\right]}{c'\left[q(\bar{\phi}_e M)\right]} - 1 \right\} \right\}. \tag{3.24}$$

As above, the value of money is equal to its expected discounted value in the next CM plus a liquidity premium factor. The liquidity premium factor is strictly positive if an additional unit of money relaxes the budget constraint of the buyer in a bilateral match in the DM. A stationary sunspot equilibrium is a pair (ϕ_ℓ, ϕ_h) that satisfies (3.24) for $e = \ell, h$.

There is always an equilibrium where agents simply ignore sunspots, $\phi_\ell = \phi_h = \phi^{ss}$, since sunspot states do not affect fundamentals in any way. There can also be proper sunspot equilibria, where the economy jumps from one state to another state, where states are associated with different values for money and different quantities traded in the DM. In general, one can construct sunspot equilibria from the multiplicity of steady-state equilibria. However, this won't work in our case where one equilibrium is the nonmonetary one because the value of money in the low state is constrained to be non-negative. This would work in the case where there is a cost to carry money, as in Chapter 5.2, and if we use the two monetary equilibria to construct a sunspot equilibrium. One can construct a sunspot equilibrium from a two-period-cycle equilibrium when it exists, as mentioned above. Suppose $\lambda_{\ell h} = \lambda_{h\ell} = 1$. Then, the solutions ϕ_ℓ and ϕ_h to (3.24) corresponds to the values of money in the two-period cycle. By continuity, for $\lambda_{\ell h}$ and $\lambda_{h\ell}$ close to one, there exists other proper sunspot equilibria where the change in the state is not deterministic.

3.2 Alternative Bargaining Solutions

We have considered a trading protocol in the DM where a buyer makes a take-it-or-leave-it offer to the seller. This protocol is interesting because the agent who enters the DM with money is able to extract all the gains from trade. This arrangement, however, is quite special and one should examine the positive and normative implications associated with alternative trading protocols. We now propose a number of different trading protocols for the DM, which include alternative bargaining solutions, a Walrasian protocol where agents are price-takers, and a price-posting protocol, where sellers compete to attract buyers. We start by defining the bargaining set in a bilateral match, and then review the solutions to alternative bargaining protocols.

3.2.1 Bargaining Set

Consider a match between a buyer holding m units of money and a seller holding none. (It is straightforward to generalize the argument to the case where sellers hold positive money balances.) An agreement is a pair (q, d), where the buyer receives $q \geq 0$ units of the search good produced by the seller in exchange for $d \in [0, m]$ units of money. If an agreement is reached, then the buyer's utility is $u^b = u(q) + W^b(m - d)$, and the seller's is $u^s = -c(q) + W^s(d)$. If there is no agreement, then buyer's utility is $u_0^b = W^b(m)$, and the seller's is $u_0^s = W^s(0)$. Because W^b and W^s is linear in money, we have $u^b = u(q) - \phi d + u_0^b$ and $u^s = \phi d - c(q) + u_0^s$. Hence, the buyer's surplus from an agreement is $u^b - u_0^b = u(q) - \phi d$, the seller's surplus is $u^s - u_0^s = \phi d - c(q)$, and the total surplus, the sum of the buyer's and seller's surpluses, is $u\,(q) - c\,(q)$.

To illustrate the role that money plays in exchange, suppose that the buyer cannot spend more than $\tau \leq m$ units of money. Let $\mathcal{S}(\tau)$ represent the set of feasible utility levels for the buyer and seller, when the buyer can spend at most τ units of money; i.e.,

$$\mathcal{S}(\tau) = \left\{ \left(u(q) - \phi d + u_0^b, \phi d - c(q) + u_0^s\right) : d \in [0, \tau] \text{ and } q \geq 0 \right\}.$$

The equation for the Pareto frontier of $\mathcal{S}$ is derived from the program $u^b = \max_{q,d} [u(q) - \phi d] + u_0^b$ s.t. $-c(q) + \phi d \geq u^s - u_0^s$ and $d \leq \tau$, for $u^s \geq u_0^s$. If $\phi\tau \geq c(q^*) + u^s - u_0^s$, then the solution to the Pareto problem is

$$q = q^*,$$
$$\phi d = c(q^*) + u^s - u_0^s,$$

and if $\phi\tau < c(q^*) + u^s - u_0^s$, then the solution is

$$q = c^{-1}\left[\phi\tau - (u^s - u_0^s)\right],$$
$$d = \tau.$$

The equation for the Pareto frontier is

$$u^s - u_0^s = \begin{cases} u(q^*) - c(q^*) - (u^b - u_0^b) & \text{if } \phi\tau \geq c(q^*) + u^s - u_0^s \\ \phi\tau - c\left[u^{-1}(u^b - u_0^b + \phi\tau)\right] & \text{otherwise} \end{cases}. \tag{3.25}$$

If τ units of money are sufficient to purchase q^* and to provide the seller with a surplus of $u^s - u_0^s$, i.e., if $\phi\tau \geq c(q^*) + u^s - u_0^s$, then the buyer and seller will split the total surplus, $u(q^*) - c(q^*)$, according to $u^b - u_0^b$ and $u^s - u_0^s$, respectively. If, however, τ units of money are insufficient to purchase q^* and to provide a surplus of $u^s - u_0^s$ to the seller, then the buyer will spend all τ units of his money and $q < q^*$. It can be checked from (3.25) that $d^2u^s/(du^b)^2 = 0$ if $\phi\tau - c(q^*) - u^s + u_0^s \geq 0$ and $d^2u^s/(du^b)^2 < 0$ otherwise. That is, when $q = q^*$ the Pareto frontier is linear and when $q < q^*$ it is strictly concave.

In Figure 3.9, we illustrate the bargaining set $\mathcal{S}(\tau)$ for $\tau_3 > \tau_2 > \tau_1$. The maximum possible surplus of a match is denoted by Δ^*, where $\Delta^* = u(q^*) - c(q^*)$. Note that the match surplus is always less Δ^* for bargaining set $\mathcal{S}(\tau_1)$ in Figure 3.9, i.e., by construction all of the allocations in $\mathcal{S}(\tau_1)$ are characterized by $q < q^*$ since $\phi\tau < c(q^*)$. For the bargaining sets $\mathcal{S}(\tau_2)$ and $\mathcal{S}(\tau_3)$, the match surplus is equal to Δ^*

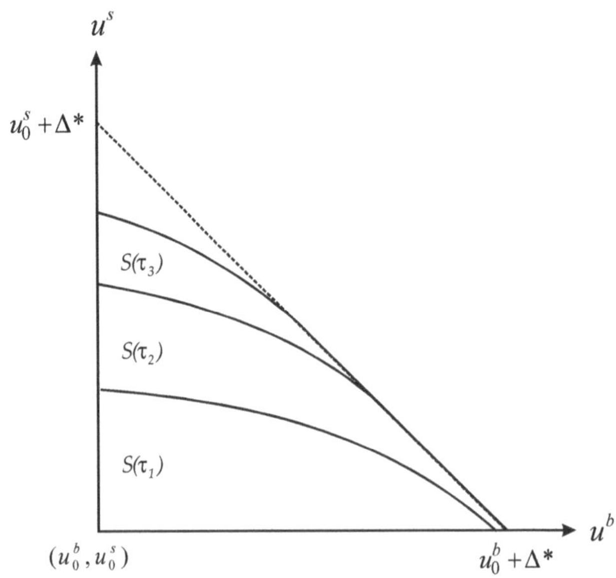

Figure 3.9
Bargaining set

along their linear portions of the respective sets. However, trades are characterized by $q < q^*$ where the frontiers are strictly concave. Note that the bargaining set is larger when the buyer is able to use more of his money balances, i.e., $\mathcal{S}(\tau_1) \subset \mathcal{S}(\tau_2) \subset \mathcal{S}(\tau_3)$. This expansion of the bargaining set illustrates the idea that fiat money allows traders to achieve utility and output levels that otherwise would not be attainable.

3.2.2 The Nash Solution

A solution to the bargaining problem can be interpreted as a function that assigns a pair of utility levels to every bargaining game. The generalized Nash solution maximizes the weighted geometric average of the buyer's and seller's surpluses from trade, where the weights are given by the agents' bargaining powers. Figure 3.10 provides a graphical illustration of the Nash solution. The grey shaded area, denoted by $\mathcal{S}$, represents the set of feasible utility levels for the buyer and seller—the bargaining set—and the bargaining solution chooses one point from this set. Since the Nash solution is Pareto efficient, the solution will lie on the Pareto frontier. The downward-sloping, convex curve represents the combinations of the weighted geometric average of the agents' surpluses that generates the same value. The Nash solution is given by the tangency of this curve with the bargaining set. Since, in Figure 3.10, the tangency occurs on the strictly concave part of the Pareto frontier, the Nash solution is characterized, in part, by $q < q^*$.

In the context of our monetary environment, the generalized Nash solution, $[q(m), d(m)]$, can be expressed as

$$[q(m),\ d(m)] = \arg\max_{q,d \le m} [u(q) - \phi d]^{\theta} [-c(q) + \phi d]^{1-\theta} \tag{3.26}$$

where $\theta \in [0,1]$ represents the buyer's bargaining power, $1-\theta$ represents the seller's, and m is the buyer's money holdings. If the constraint $d \le m$ does not bind, then the solution to (3.26) is

$$q = q^*,$$
$$d = m^* \equiv \frac{(1-\theta)u(q^*) + \theta c(q^*)}{\phi}.$$

If, however, $m < m^*$, then the constraint $d \le m$ binds, i.e., $d = m$. In this case, the generalized Nash solution for the level of DM output can be expressed as

$$\arg\max_{q} \left\{\theta \ln [u(q) - \phi m] + (1-\theta) \ln [-c(q) + \phi m]\right\}. \tag{3.27}$$

The solution to (3.27) is

$$\phi m \equiv z_\theta(q) = \frac{(1-\theta)c'(q)u(q) + \theta u'(q)c(q)}{\theta u'(q) + (1-\theta)c'(q)}. \tag{3.28}$$

According to (3.28), in order to buy $q < q^*$ the buyer spends all of his money, and DM output, $q < q^*$, is determined by a weighted mean of the buyer's utility of consuming q and seller's disutility of producing q. It should be clear from (3.26) or (3.27) that the outcome, $[q(m), d(m)]$, is independent of the seller's money balances due to the linearity of the seller's value function. Since money is costly to hold and the seller's money holdings do not influence the terms of trade, the seller will not accumulate money in the CM to bring into the DM.

For the remained of this chapter, we will focus only on steady-state equilibria. The buyer's DM value function is, therefore, given by

$$V^b(m) = \sigma\left\{u[q(m)] + W^b[m - d(m)]\right\} + (1-\sigma)W^b(m). \tag{3.29}$$

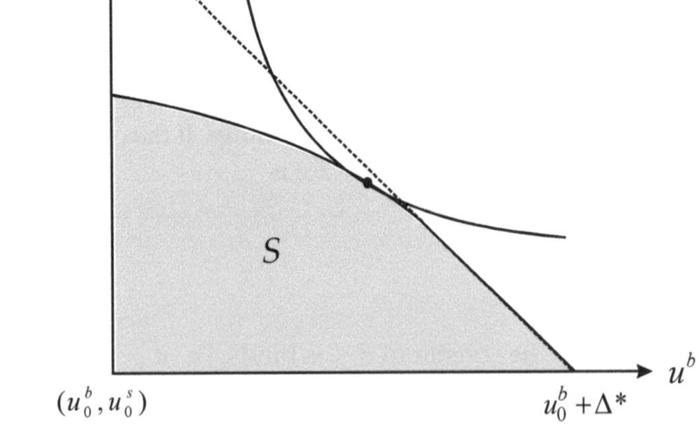

Figure 3.10
The Nash solution

Since the buyer's CM value function is linear in money, i.e., $W^b(m) = \phi m + W^b(0)$, the choice his money holdings is given by the solution to

$$\max_{m \in \mathbb{R}_+} \{-r\phi m + \sigma \{u[q(m)] - \phi d(m)\}\}. \tag{3.30}$$

Provided that $r > 0$, the buyer will never accumulate more balances in the CM than he would spend in the DM, which implies that $d = m \leq m^*$. Using (3.28) and (3.30), the buyer's choice of consumption in the DM at a steady-state equilibrium is

$$\max_{q \in [0,q^*]} \{-rz_\theta(q) + \sigma [u(q) - z_\theta(q)]\}. \tag{3.31}$$

Note that problem (3.31) is a generalization of problem (3.13) when $\phi_t = \phi_{t+1} = \phi$, where in the latter problem the buyer has all of the bargaining power. The buyer maximizes the expected surplus from a trade in the DM, $\sigma [u(q) - z_\theta(q)]$, minus the cost of holding real balances, $rz_\theta(q)$. While the objective function in (3.31) is not necessarily concave—because $z_\theta(q)$ is not convex—it is continuous and the choice of q is in the compact set $[0, q^*]$. Therefore, a solution exists.

Assuming an interior solution, the first-order condition to (3.31) is

$$\frac{u'(q)}{z'_\theta(q)} = 1 + \frac{r}{\sigma}. \tag{3.32}$$

Note that if $\theta = 1$, then $z_\theta(q) = c(q)$ and the solution to (3.32) coincides with (3.16). In particular, as r tends to zero, the quantities traded in the DM approach q^*. In contrast, however, if $\theta < 1$, then $q < q^*$ even in the limit when $r \to 0$. To see this, we can express the relationship between real balances and output in (3.28) as

$$z_\theta(q) = [1 - \Theta(q)]\, u(q) + \Theta(q)c(q) \tag{3.33}$$

where

$$\Theta(q) = \frac{\theta u'(q)}{\theta u'(q) + (1-\theta)c'(q)}.$$

It is easy to check that $\Theta(q^*) = \theta$, and $\Theta'(q) < 0$ for all q. Hence, $z'_\theta(q^*) = u'(q^*) - \Theta'(q^*)\,[u(q^*) - c(q^*)] > u'(q^*)$. Therefore, as q approaches q^*, the buyer's surplus, $u(q) - z_\theta(q)$, falls. There are two effects associated with an increase in $q < q^*$: first, total match surplus, $u(q) - c(q)$ increases, and second, the buyer's share of the surplus decreases. For q close to q^*, the second effect dominates the first. Consequently, even if it is not costly to hold real balances, $r \approx 0$, the buyer will not bring sufficient real balances into the DM to be able to purchase q^*. So, in addition to the monetary inefficiency created by discounting, there is an inefficiency associated with Nash bargaining. This result is a consequence of the fact that the buyer's surplus is not always increasing in his real balances: The generalized Nash bargaining solution is said to be non-monotonic.

Note that if the buyer has no bargaining power, $\theta = 0$, then $z_\theta(q) = u(q)$, and the solution to problem (3.31) is $q = 0$. Since the buyer receives no surplus from purchasing the DM good from the seller, and it is costly to accumulate real balances, the buyer optimally chooses not to trade in the DM. Hence, a necessary condition for trade to take place is $\theta > 0$; buyers must have some bargaining power.

3.2.3 The Proportional Solution

In contrast to the generalized Nash solution, the proportional bargaining solution requires that agents' surpluses increase as the bargaining set expands, which implies that the solution is monotonic. The proportional bargaining solution is also Pareto efficient, i.e., (u^b, u^s) lies in the Pareto-frontier of $\mathcal{S}$ and has each player receiving a constant share of the match surplus, i.e., $u(q) - \phi d = \theta[u(q) - c(q)]$ and $-c(q) + \phi d = (1-\theta)[u(q) - c(q)]$ or

$$u^b - u_0^b = \frac{\theta}{1-\theta}(u^s - u_0^s), \tag{3.34}$$

where, as above, $\theta \in (0,1]$ is the buyer's bargaining power. The outcome of the proportional solution is illustrated in Figure 3.11.

In the context of our monetary model, (q, d) solves

$$(q,d) = \arg\max_{d \le m}[u(q) - \phi d] \tag{3.35}$$

$$\text{subject to } u(q) - \phi d = \frac{\theta}{1-\theta}[\phi d - c(q)], \tag{3.36}$$

$$d \le m. \tag{3.37}$$

Substituting ϕd by its expression from (3.36), i.e., $\phi d = (1-\theta)u(q) + \theta c(q)$, into (3.35) and (3.37), this problem can be simplified to

$$q = \arg\max_{q} \theta[u(q) - c(q)] \tag{3.38}$$

$$\text{subject to } (1-\theta)u(q) + \theta c(q) \le \phi m. \tag{3.39}$$

If (3.39) binds, then q is simply the solution to

$$\phi m \equiv z_\theta(q) = \theta c(q) + (1-\theta)u(q). \tag{3.40}$$

This expression is similar to the Nash solution, (3.33), except that the buyer's share in the Nash solution, $\Theta(q)$, is a function of q, whereas for the proportional solution it is a constant.

The buyer's problem in the DM is given by (3.31), which, thanks to (3.40), can be rewritten as

$$\max_{q\in[0,q^*]} \{-rz_\theta(q) + \sigma\theta\,[u(q) - c(q)]\} \tag{3.41}$$

or

$$\max_{q\in[0,q^*]} \{[\sigma\theta - r(1-\theta)]\,u(q) - (r+\sigma)\,\theta c(q)\}. \tag{3.42}$$

The analysis assumes that (3.39) binds; it should be pointed out that as long as $r > 0$, (3.39) will always bind. A necessary condition for the buyer's CM problem to admit a positive solution is $\sigma\theta - r(1-\theta) > 0$ or $\theta/(1-\theta) > r/\sigma$. This condition implies that buyers must have enough bargaining power if money is to be valued. If $\theta/(1-\theta) > r/\sigma$, then the buyer's objective in (3.42) is strictly concave. The first-order condition

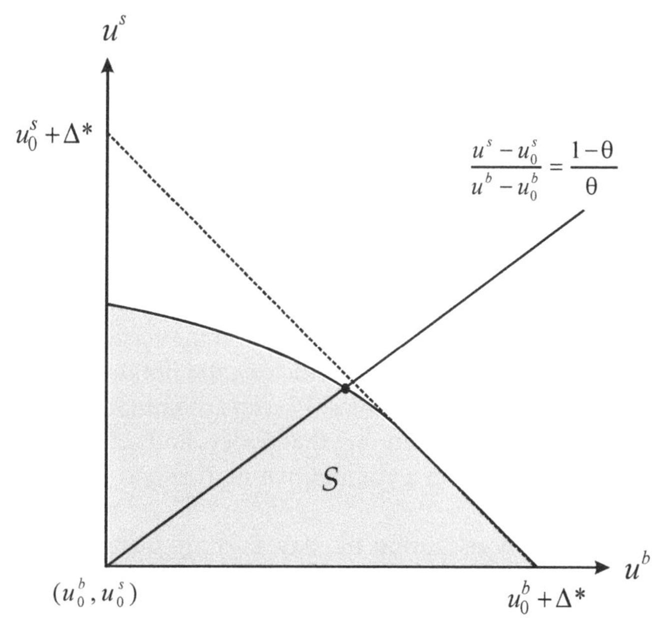

Figure 3.11
The proportional bargaining solution

to (3.42) is given by (3.32). This condition, with the help of (3.40), can be rewritten as

$$\frac{u'(q) - c'(q)}{z'_\theta(q)} = \frac{r}{\theta\sigma}. \tag{3.43}$$

The left side of (3.43) is the marginal increase of the match surplus generated by an increase of the buyer's real balances, while the right side of (3.43) is a monetary wedge introduced by discounting, r, search frictions, σ, and the buyer's bargaining power, θ. An increase in the seller's bargaining power—which reduces θ—raises the monetary wedge through a holdup problem. The buyer will tend to underinvest in real balances since he incurs the proportional cost r/σ from holding real balances, but only receives a fraction θ of the match surplus. It can be checked that q increases with θ.

As r tends to zero, the cost of holding real balances vanishes, as does the holdup problem. Consequently, match output approaches q^* as r approaches zero, which is in contrast to the generalized Nash solution. With proportional bargaining, the buyer's surplus is strictly increasing in his real balances, until the match output q^* is achieved. Hence, if the cost of holding money balances is zero, then the buyer will accumulate sufficient real balances to purchase the efficient level of the search good, q^*.

3.3 Walrasian Price Taking

We have assumed so far that buyers and sellers meet bilaterally in the DM. We favor this sort of arrangement since it provides an explicit description of how trades take place and prices are formed. We show in subsequent chapters that the assumption of bilateral meetings is crucial for generating certain optimal policy results, and the coexistence of assets with different rates of return. Nevertheless, the notion of competitive markets is pervasive in economics. We can accommodate such a trading protocol in the DM by assuming that buyers and sellers meet in large groups during the day in a competitive market and that they are anonymous.

Since agents are anonymous during the day, they are unable to use credit arrangements. We continue to label the day market as decentralized, DM, and reinterpret the idiosyncratic matching shocks, σ, as preference and productivity shocks. In particular, a fraction σ of buyers want to consume during the day, while a fraction $1-\sigma$ do not, and a fraction σ of sellers are able to produce, while a fraction $1-\sigma$ cannot.

We denote the price of the day good expressed in terms of the night good as p; i.e., if $\hat{p}$ is the dollar price for a unit of DM output and ϕ is amount of CM goods that can be purchased with a dollar, then $p \equiv \hat{p}\phi$.

The problem that an active seller faces in the DM, i.e., a seller who can produce, is to choose the quantity to supply, q^s. This problem is given by

$$q^s = \arg\max_q \left[-c(q) + pq\right]. \tag{3.44}$$

The first-order condition to this problem is

$$p = c'(q^s). \tag{3.45}$$

Sellers produce until their marginal disutility is equal to the real price of the DM good, measured in terms of CM good.

The problem that the buyer faces in the CM is how much money to bring into the DM or, equivalently, how much of the DM good to consume. The buyer makes this choice before he learns whether he is active in the DM. The buyer's problem is

$$q^b = \arg\max_q \left\{-rpq + \sigma\left[u(q) - pq\right]\right\}. \tag{3.46}$$

From (3.46), in order to consume q in the DM, the buyer must accumulate pq real balances—measured in terms of the next period's CM output—in the CM, where the cost of holding real balances is equal to the rate of time preference, r. The first-order condition to (3.46) is

$$u'(q^b) = \left(1 + \frac{r}{\sigma}\right)p. \tag{3.47}$$

From (3.47), there is a monetary wedge equal to r/σ between the buyer's marginal utility of consumption and the price of the good in the DM. This wedge arises because the buyer must accumulate real balances in the period before entering the DM. As well, there is a risk the buyer will not need the real balances if he receives a preference shock that implies he does not want to consume.

Since the measures of active buyers and sellers are both equal to σ, the clearing condition for the DM goods market requires that $q^b = q^s = q$. From (3.45) and (3.47), we have that

$$\frac{u'(q)}{c'(q)} = 1 + \frac{r}{\sigma}. \tag{3.48}$$

This equation is identical to the one obtained under the bargaining protocol, where the buyer has all of the bargaining power, (3.17). In both these cases, q approaches q^* as r tends to zero.

The value of money is given by the solution to $pq = \phi M$, which, by (3.45), implies that $c'(q)\,q = \phi M$ or

$$\phi = c'(q)\,q/M.$$

If $c(q)$ is strictly convex, $c'(q)q > c(q)$, then the value of money is larger than in a bargaining environment where the buyer makes a take-it-or-leave-it offer. Intuitively, when the buyer makes a take-it-or-leave-it offer, DM goods are priced according to average cost and when pricing is Walrasian, DM goods are priced according to marginal cost.

3.4 Competitive Price Posting

In many markets, sellers post prices for their goods. Buyers observe these prices—or contracts—and then decide where to buy. We formalize this notion of trade by appealing to the concept of competitive search. Competitive search has been developed to provide a foundation for competition in environments where agents meet in pairs, and their participation decisions are associated with thick-market and congestion externalities. By having sellers compete before matches are formed, competitive search allows one to price congestion or waiting times in the market, where the surplus that an agent receives reflects his social contribution to the matching process.

We assume that the economy is composed of different submarkets in the DM, where a submarket is identified by its terms of trade, (q,d). The terms of trade for the DM good in period t are posted by sellers at the beginning of the previous night, in period $t-1$. Sellers can commit to their posted prices. Buyers can observe all of the terms of trade in all of the submarkets. Based on the observed terms of trade, buyers decide which particular submarket they will visit in the subsequent DM, and the amount of real balances to accumulate in that CM. The timing of events is illustrated in Figure 3.12.

Submarkets are not frictionless. The search frictions that exist in competitive search environments attempt to capture heterogeneity of goods and capacity constraints. For example, in each submarket, buyers and sellers face the risk of being unmatched. So, even though a buyer can direct his search to a location where he knows the terms of trade, he still has to find a match with a seller who produces the type of good he wants. In addition, even if the buyer finds a desirable seller, sellers may face capacity constraints, such as only being able to produce for one buyer.

We can describe the matching process more formally. Suppose there is a measure B of buyers and a measure S of sellers in a submarket that has posted terms of trade (q,d). Denote the ratio of buyers per seller as $n = B/S$. A matching technology specifies the measure of matches in a submarket as a function of the matching friction, σ, and the measures of buyers and sellers. We assume that the matching technology is given by $\sigma \min(B,S)$; i.e., the measure of matches is a fraction, σ, of the measure of agents on the short side of the market. If $\sigma = 1$, then all agents on the short side of the market are matched. The actual buyers and sellers that are matched are chosen at random in their respective submarkets. Consequently, the matching rate of a buyer is $\sigma \min(B,S)/B = \sigma \min(1,1/n)$, and the matching rate of a seller is $\sigma \min(B,S)/S = \sigma \min(n,1)$.

When a seller posts his terms of trade at the beginning of the night subperiod, he takes as given the utility that buyers expect to receive when optimally choosing the submarket to search for sellers. If U^b represents the expected surplus of a buyer in the DM, net of the cost of holding real balances, then in any active submarket,

$$-r\phi d + \sigma \min\left(1, \frac{1}{n}\right)[u(q) - \phi d] = U^b. \tag{3.49}$$

A seller's choice of his terms of trade, (q,d), determines the length of the queue, n, in his submarket, where n is given by the solution to (3.49). The length of queue is such that a buyer is indifferent between going to a particular submarket associated with terms of trade (q,d) or going to his best alternative that guarantees him an expected utility equal to U^b.

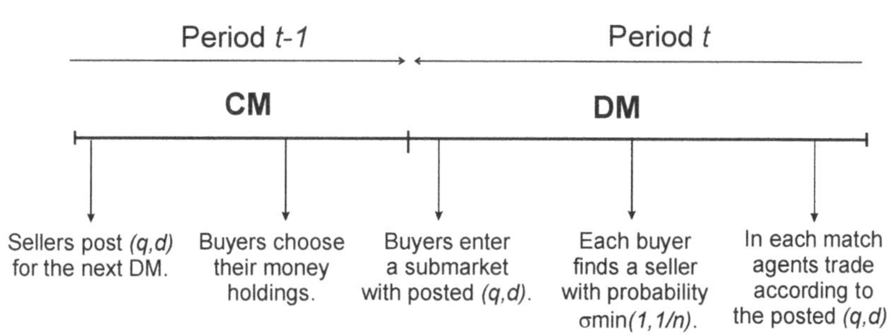

Figure 3.12
Competitive search: Timing of events

The seller's posting problem can be represented by

$$\max_{q,d,n} \sigma \min(1,n)\left[-c(q)+\phi d\right] \text{ subject to (3.49).} \tag{3.50}$$

The seller chooses the terms of trade to post, (q,d), and, via constraint (3.49), the implied queue length, n, so as to maximize his expected utility in the DM.

Let $\bar{U}^b$ represent the upper bound of the buyer's expected utility that can be achieved in any equilibrium. This upper bound will be attained if the buyer receives the entire match surplus, $u(q)-c(q)$, and if his matching probability is at its maximum value, σ. In this case, the buyer will only bring enough real balances to compensate the seller for his production cost, $c(q)$. More formally, the upper bound of the buyer's expected utility is given by

$$\bar{U}^b = \max_q \left\{-r\phi d + \sigma\left[u(q)-\phi d\right]\right\} \text{ s.t. } -c(q)+\phi d = 0,$$

or $\bar{U}^b = \max_q \left\{-rc(q)+\sigma\left[u(q)-c(q)\right]\right\}$.

Qualitatively speaking, the buyer's expected utility, U^b, can fall into one of four ranges.

1. If $U^b > \bar{U}^b$, then sellers have no incentives to make markets, or post prices, since they cannot offer buyers their market expected utility without generating a negative payoff for themselves. Clearly, $U^b > \bar{U}^b$ is inconsistent with an equilibrium.
2. If $U^b = \bar{U}^b$, then the buyer's surplus is at its maximum value. Any solution to (3.50) implies that buyers receive the entire surplus of a match, i.e., $\phi d = c(q)$, and that they are on the short side of the submarket, $n \leq 1$. Hence, the seller's payoff is zero.
3. If $U^b \in \left(0,\bar{U}^b\right)$, then $u(q)-\phi d > 0$. This implies, however, that $n > 1$ cannot be an equilibrium, i.e., a solution to (3.50). If $n > 1$ was a solution, then the seller could slightly increase d such that, via (3.49), n decreases but still remains greater than or equal to 1. Hence, the seller's expected utility increases, which is a contradiction. Intuitively, if $n > 1$, then there is congestion on the buyer's side. Sellers don't benefit from this congestion since their matching probability is σ, which is independent of n, whereas buyers must be compensated for the congestion by better terms of trade. Clearly, it is optimal for sellers to eliminate the congestion, since doing so results in better terms of trade for themselves without affecting their matching probability. Therefore, in any equilibrium it must be the case that

$n \leq 1$. Since $n \leq 1$, $\min(1,1/n) = 1$. If we substitute the expression for ϕd given by (3.49) with $\min(1,1/n) = 1$ into the objective function, (3.50), the seller's problem becomes

$$\max_{q,n\leq 1} \left\{ \sigma n \frac{-rc(q) + \sigma [u(q) - c(q)] - U^b}{r+\sigma} \right\}. \tag{3.51}$$

Assuming an interior solution, the first-order condition with respect to q is

$$\frac{u'(q)}{c'(q)} = 1 + \frac{r}{\sigma}. \tag{3.52}$$

Hence, the quantity traded when $U^b \in (0, \bar{U}^b)$ is the same as that for the Walrasian price taking protocol and the bargaining protocol where the buyer has all the bargaining power. Finally, if $U^b \in (0, \bar{U}^b)$, the ratio expression in the inner braces of (3.51) will be strictly positive, which implies that $n = 1$ is the solution.

4. If $U^b = 0$, then a buyer is indifferent between (actively) participating or not in the DM. If a buyer participates, then solution to (3.50) is such that $n = 1$ and q solves (3.52). The value of the money transfer, d, will adjust so that the left side of (3.49) is zero. There may also be some buyers who choose not to participate and enter an inactive submarket, i.e., a submarket that implicitly has $d = q = 0$ and $n = \infty$, i.e., $\sigma \min(1,1/n) = 0$, see constraint (3.49).

The equilibrium value of being a buyer, U^b, is determined such that the ratio of buyers per seller in the different submarkets is consistent with the measures of buyers and sellers in the economy. Suppose that the market is composed of a unit measure of sellers and a measure N of buyers, where $N > 0$. Then, we can define the aggregate demand for active buyers by sellers, N^d, and the aggregate supply of active buyers, N^s, by

$$N^d \equiv \int n(j)dj = N^s \equiv N - n_0, \tag{3.53}$$

where $n(j)$ is the measure of buyers per seller in the submarket of seller j and n_0 is the measure of buyers who do not participate; i.e., they enter the inactive submarket. From the above results, if $U^b < \bar{U}^b$, then from points 3 and 4, above, $\int n(j)dj = 1$. Moreover, if $U^b > 0$, then $n_0 = 0$ and $N^s = N$. If $U^b = \bar{U}^b$, then from point 2, above, $n(j) \in [0,1]$ and $\int n(j)dj \in [0,1]$. Finally, if $U^b = 0$, then from point 4, above, buyers are

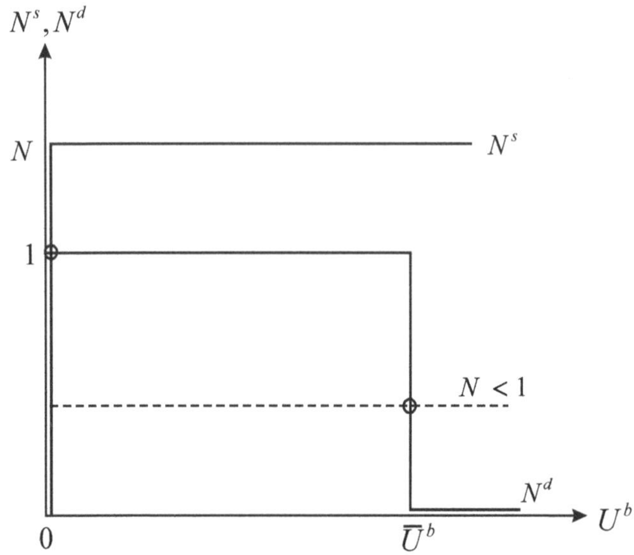

Figure 3.13
Equilibrium with posting

indifferent between participating and not participating, which means that $n_0 \in [0, N]$ and $N^s \in [0, N]$.

We illustrate the various equilibrium outcomes in Figure 3.13. The step function in Figure 3.13 labelled N^d represents the aggregate number of buyers desired by sellers across all submarkets for various levels of the buyer's surplus. The step function labelled N^s represents the aggregate number of buyers who are willing to participate, i.e., the active buyers. Note that the step function N^s corresponds to the case where $N > 1$. The "market-clearing price" that equalizes aggregate supply of buyers and aggregate demand of buyers is the buyer's expected utility, U^b.

If $N > 1$, then $U^b = 0$ since N^s intersects N^d at $U^b = 0$ in Figure 3.13. In any equilibrium, $n(j) = 1$ for all sellers; a measure $N - 1$ of buyers go to the inactive market, and a unit measure will allocate themselves one-for-one with sellers. The inactive buyers get zero utility and, since they are inactive in the DM, they do not accumulate real balances in the CM. The unit measure of buyers who are active also receive zero utility, and the seller's posted price is characterized by $\phi d = \sigma u(q)/(r + \sigma)$, which follows from constraint (3.49).

If $N < 1$, then $U^b = \bar{U}^b$, since the horizontal dashed line, which represents the supply of active buyers when $N < 1$, intersects N^d at $U^b = \bar{U}^b$ in Figure 3.13. In any equilibrium, $n(j) \leq 1$ for all sellers j. The seller's posted contract, (q, d), is the one that maximizes the expected surplus of the buyer, subject to the seller receiving zero surplus; i.e., it is characterized by $\phi d = c(q)$. This outcome is identical to the outcome under the bargaining protocol when the buyers have all of the bargaining power since the buyers are on the short side of the market and have all the market power.

Finally, if $N = 1$, then $U^b \in [0, \bar{U}^b]$, since the horizontal line emanating from 1 and its continuation in Figure 3.13 represents the supply of active buyers when $N = 1$. In any equilibrium, $n(j) = 1$ for all sellers j, q is determined by (3.52), and $\phi d \in [c(q), \sigma u(q)/(r + \sigma)]$. The steady-state value of money is indeterminate since the market value of the buyer, U^b, is indeterminate, where the indeterminacy results from the different possible divisions of the match surplus, i.e., $U^b \in [0, \bar{U}^b]$. This set of outcomes here is represented by the horizontal line with height equal to one between $U^b = 0$ and $U^b = \bar{U}^b$ in Figure 3.13.

3.5 Further Readings

Search models with divisible money include Shi (1997), Green and Zhou (1998, 2002), Zhou (1999), Lagos and Wright (2005), Laing, Li, and Wang (2007), and Faig (2008). The formalization adopted in this section follows the one in Lagos and Wright (2005). Aliprantis, Camera, and Puzzello (2006, 2007) provide a formal definition of anonymity for this model. Wright (2010) proposes a uniqueness proof for monetary steady state. Duffy and Puzzello (2014, 2015) study the Lagos-Wright model in the laboratory. The large household model of Shi (1997a) is presented in the Appendix. Alternative models of monetary exchange are surveyed in Wallace (1980) and Townsend (1980).

Kamiya and Sato (2004), Kamiya, Morishita, and Shimizu (2005), and Kamiya and Shimizu (2006, 2007a, 2007b) study the real indeterminacy of stationary equilibria in matching models with perfectly divisible fiat money and nondegenerate distribution of money holdings.

The dynamics of the Kiyotaki and Wright (1989, 1993) models and the existence of sunspot equilibria is studied by Wright (1994, 1995). See Ennis (2001) for sunspot equilibria in the Shi-Trejos-Wright model with barter. Coles and Wright (1998) investigate the nonstationary equilibria of the Shi-Trejos-Wright model with indivisible money but divisible goods. They provide an explicit characterization of the bargaining game out of steady state and show that the outcome differs from the axiomatic Nash solution. Ennis (2004) studies the Coles-Wright bargaining solution in the context of sunspot equilibria. Lagos and Wright (2003) study dynamic monetary equilibria in the context of a search model with divisible money. They show that the model can generate a wide variety of equilibria, including cycles, chaos, and sunspot equilibria. Baranowski (2015) and Branch and McGough (2016) characterize dynamics in the Lagos-Wright model under learning and heterogeneous beliefs. Related dynamics in the context of overlapping generations models can be found in Grandmont (1985) and Tirole (1985). Lomeli and Temzelides (2002) show that under take-it-or-leave-it offers, dynamic equilibria in a discrete time random matching model of money are a "translation" of dynamic equilibria in the standard overlapping generations model. Azariadis (1993) is a good reference book for dynamic systems, phase diagrams, cycles, and sunspot equilibria in the context of overlapping generation economies.

Dating back to Shi (1995) and Trejos and Wright (1993, 1995), search models of money use the generalized Nash bargaining solution or extensive bargaining games with alternating offers to determine the terms of trade in bilateral matches. The methodology to formalize markets with bargaining is developed in Osborne and Rubinstein (1990).

Rocheteau and Wright (2005) and Aruoba, Rocheteau, and Waller (2007) compare different bargaining solutions and alternative pricing mechanisms, including price-taking and competitive price posting (or competitive search). Jean, Rabinovich, and Wright (2010) study price posting with indivisible goods. Dong and Jiang (2014) study price posting with undirected search under private information. Silva (2015) incorporates monopolistic competition and endogenous variety.

Competitive search with a Leontief matching function—the formulation used in this chapter—was introduced by Faig and Jerez (2006). Moen (1997) developed the notion of competitive search equilibrium in the context of search models of the labor market. See also Mortensen and Wright (2002), and for a somewhat related concept, Howitt (2005). Galenianos and Kircher (2008) study auctions with indivisible goods and show that their model generates a distribution of money balances and prices. Julien, Kennes, and King (2008) examine price posting with divisible goods and indivisible money. Dutu, Julien, and King (2012) study price posting and auctions with free entry of sellers. Conditions are identified under which auctions (with price dispersion) dominate posted prices (without dispersion).

We have been arguing that money supports trade in a world without enforcement. In contrast, Camera and Gioffre (2014) describe a game in which monetary equilibrium can break down in the absence of adequate enforcement institutions.

Appendix

A1. Difference Equation (3.16)

We prove some properties of the difference equation (3.16) that defines an equilibrium of the economy with divisible money. First, we show that the right side of (3.16) approaches 0 as $\phi_{t+1} \to 0$. To see this, for all ϕ_{t+1} such that $\phi_{t+1} < \frac{c(q^*)}{M}$, the right side of (3.16) is

$$\begin{aligned} RHS &= \beta\phi_{t+1}[1-\sigma+\sigma\frac{u'\circ c^{-1}(\phi_{t+1}M)}{c'\circ c^{-1}(\phi_{t+1}M)}] \\ &= (1-\sigma)\beta\phi_{t+1}+\beta\phi_{t+1}\sigma\frac{u'\circ c^{-1}(\phi_{t+1}M)}{c'\circ c^{-1}(\phi_{t+1}M)} \\ &= M^{-1}[\beta c(q_{t+1})(1-\sigma)+\beta\sigma\frac{q_{t+1}u'(q_{t+1})/u(q_{t+1})}{q_{t+1}c'(q_{t+1})/c(q_{t+1})}u(q_{t+1})], \end{aligned}$$

where $c(q_{t+1}) = \phi_{t+1}M$. Since $q_{t+1}u'(q_{t+1})/u(q_{t+1}) \leq 1$ and $q_{t+1}c'(q_{t+1})/c(q_{t+1}) \geq 1$,

$$RHS \leq M^{-1}\{\beta(1-\sigma)c(q_{t+1})+\beta\sigma u(q_{t+1})\}.$$

But $\beta(1-\sigma)c(q_{t+1})+\beta\sigma u(q_{t+1})$ tends to 0 as q_{t+1} approaches 0. Hence, $\phi_t = \phi_{t+1} = 0$ is a solution to (3.16).

Second, we evaluate the slope of the phase line defined by (3.16) at the positive steady-state equilibrium, $\phi^{ss} > 0$. Differentiate (3.16) for ϕ_{t+1} such that $\phi_{t+1} < c(q^*)/M$ and use (3.17) to get

$$\frac{\partial\phi_t}{\partial\phi_{t+1}} = 1+\sigma\beta\phi^s M\left[\frac{u''(q^{ss})c'(q^{ss})-u'(q^{ss})c''(q^{ss})}{[c'(q^{ss})]^3}\right] < 1,$$

where $q^{ss} = c^{-1}(\phi^{ss}M)$. In the space (ϕ_t, ϕ_{t+1}) the phase line representing *RHS* intersects the 45° line from below.

A2. Shi's (1997) Large Household Model

In Section 4.1 we described a simple search-theoretic model with divisible money. Even though there are idiosyncratic trading shocks in the DM, the distribution of money holdings at the beginning of each periods is degenerate, which keeps the model tractable. This result arises thanks to a competitive market in the second subperiod and quasi-linear preferences. The former allows agents to readjust their money holdings and latter eliminates wealth effects, so that the choice of money holdings of an agent is independent of his trading history in the previous decentralized markets.

The first search model with divisible money and a degenerate distribution of money holdings was proposed by Shi (1997, 1999, 2001). This model does not assume competitive markets nor quasi-linear preferences. The trick to keep the model tractable, which is borrowed from Lucas (1990), is to assume that households are composed of a large number of members that can pool their money holdings, thereby providing insurance against the idiosyncratic trading shocks in the DMs. We will describe a slightly modified version of the large household model that is similar to the model used in this book.

Each household consists of a unit measure of buyers and a unit measure of sellers. Buyer and sellers carry out different tasks but regard the household's utility as the common objective. Buyers attempt to exchange money for consumption goods, and sellers attempt to produce goods for money. When carrying out these tasks, household members follow strategies that have been given to them by their households. In each period, the probability that a seller of a given household meets a buyer from another household is σ, and the probability that a buyer meets a seller from another household is σ. At the end of each period, buyers and sellers of the same household pool their money holdings, which eliminates aggregate uncertainty for households. Finally, the utility of the household is defined as the sum of the utilities of its members.

We refer to an arbitrary household as household h. Decision variables for this household are denoted by lowercase letters. Uppercase letters denote other households' variables, which are taken as given by the representative household h. Because we focus on steady state equilibria, we omit the time index t. Nevertheless, variables corresponding to the next period are indexed by $+1$, and those corresponding to the previous period are indexed by -1.

The chronology of events within a period is as follows. At the beginning of each period, household h has m units of money per buyer, which it divides evenly among its buyers. The household specifies the trading strategies for its members. Then, agents are matched and carry out their exchanges according to the prescribed strategies. Within a period, a buyer cannot transfer any of his money to another member of the same household. After trading concludes, buyers consume the goods they acquired, and sellers bring the money that they received for producing back to the household. At the end of a period, the household has money holdings m_{+1} that is carried into period $t+1$.

The quantity of money in the economy is assumed to be constant and equal to M units per buyer. The (indirect) marginal utility of money of household h is $\phi = \beta V'(m_{+1})$, where $V(m)$ is the lifetime discounted utility of a household holding m units of money.

We assume that the terms of trade in bilateral matches are determined by a take-it-or-leave-it offer by the buyer. When matched, household members cannot observe the marginal value of money of their trading partners, $\beta V'(m_{+1})$. As a consequence, households' strategies depend on the distribution of their potential bargaining partners' valuations for money. In a symmetric equilibrium, this distribution is degenerate: all households have the same marginal value of money, Φ.

A buyer's take-it-or-leave-it offer is a pair (q,d), where q is the quantity of goods produced by the seller for d units of money. If the seller accepts the offer, then the acquired money, d, is added to his household's money balances at the beginning of the next period. Because each seller is atomistic, the amount of money obtained by a seller is valued at the marginal utility of money, Φ. Since the seller's cost associated with producing q is $c(q)$, the seller accepts offer (q,d) if $\Phi d \geq c(q)$. Thus, any optimal offer—optimal from the buyer's household perspective—satisfies

$$\Phi d = c(q). \tag{3.54}$$

Because a buyer cannot offer to exchange more money than he has, offer (q,d) satisfies

$$d \leq m. \tag{3.55}$$

In each period, household h chooses m_{+1} and the terms of trade (q,d) to solve the following problem,

$$V(m) = \max_{q,d,m_{+1}} \{\sigma [u(q) - c(Q)] + \beta V(m_{+1})\} \tag{3.56}$$

subject to (3.54), (3.55), and

$$m_{+1} - m = \sigma (D - d) \tag{3.57}$$

The variables taken as given in the above problem are the state variable m and other households' choices, Q and D. The first term in the maximand of (3.56), $\sigma u(q)$, specifies the consumption utility of the household. This utility is defined as the sum of utilities of all its members, (recall there is no aggregate uncertainty at the household level). The measure of buyers is one, and the probability of meeting an appropriate seller is σ, so that the number of single-coincidence meetings involving a buyer in each period is σ. The second term in the maximand, $-\sigma c(q)$, specifies the household's disutility of production.

The law of motion of the household's money balances is given by (3.57). The first term on the right-hand side specifies sellers' money receipts from producing goods, and the second term specifies buyers' expenses when exchanging money for goods.

If we denote λ as the the multipliers associated with constraints (3.55), recognizing that these constraints are applicable only when buyers are involved in single-coincidence meetings that occur with probability σ, and take note that (3.54) can be written as $q = c^{-1}(\Phi d)$, then the household's problem (3.56)-(3.57) can be expressed as

$$V(m) = \max_d \sigma \left[u \circ c^{-1}(\Phi d) - c(Q)\right] + \beta V\left[m + \sigma(D - d)\right] + \sigma\lambda(m - d).$$

The first-order conditions and the envelope condition are,

$$\frac{u'(q)}{c'(q)} = \frac{\lambda + \phi}{\Phi} \tag{3.58}$$

$$\lambda(d - m) = 0 \tag{3.59}$$

$$\frac{\phi_{-1}}{\beta} = \sigma\lambda + \phi. \tag{3.60}$$

Equation (3.58) states that, for a buyer in a match, the marginal utility of consumption must equal the opportunity cost of the amount of money that must be paid to acquire additional goods. To buy another unit of a good, the buyer must give up $\frac{c'(q)}{\Phi}$ units of money (see equation (3.54)). Increasing the monetary payment has two costs to the buyer. He gives up the future value of money ϕ, and he faces a tighter constraint (3.55). Together, ϕ and λ measure the marginal cost of obtaining a larger quantity of goods in exchange for money. Equation (3.59) is the Kuhn-Tucker condition associated with the multiplier λ. Finally, equation (3.60) describes the evolution of the marginal value of money. It states that the marginal value of money today, $\frac{\phi_{-1}}{\beta} = V'(m)$, equals the discounted marginal value of money tomorrow, $\phi = \beta V'(m_+)$, plus the marginal benefit of relaxing future cash constraints, $\sigma\lambda$.

We focus on symmetric equilibria, where the value of money is the same across all households, $\phi = \Phi$ and across time. In addition, symmetry implies that the values for the different variables associated with household h equal the values of the same variables of all other households. Consequently, upper- and lowercase variables equal to one another, $m = M$ and $(d, q) = (D, Q)$, and $\phi_{-1} = \phi = \beta V'(M)$. A steady-state, symmetric, monetary equilibrium is a collection (q, λ, d, ϕ) satisfying equations (3.54) and (3.58)–(3.60), and $\phi > 0$.

From (3.58),

$$\frac{u'(q)}{c'(q)} = 1 + \frac{\lambda}{\phi},$$

and from (3.60), $r\phi = \sigma\lambda$. Consequently,

$$\frac{u'(q)}{c'(q)} = 1 + \frac{r}{\sigma}.$$

This equation is identical to the one found in our model of Section 3.1, see (3.17), where instead of a large household, there exists a competitive market that allows agents to rebalance their money holdings. For all $r > 0$, the quantities traded in bilateral matches are inefficiently low, $q < q^*$. Moreover, as r increases or σ decreases, the quantities traded fall. The transfer of money in a match is $d = M$ and the value of money is $\phi = c(q)/M$.

A key difference between the large household model and the model with alternating market structures and quasi-linear preferences is that in the former the value of money, ϕ, is household specific, whereas in the latter it is a market price taken as given by all households. This subtle difference can generate intricate technicalities, which are discussed in Rauch (2000), Berentsen and Rocheteau (2003), and Zhu (2008).

4 The Role of Money

In previous chapters we studied two extreme economies: a pure credit economy, where gains from trade are exploited through bilateral credit arrangements, and a pure currency economy, where fiat money is the only means of payment. We want to compare the set of stationary allocations in a credit economy with public record-keeping and limited commitment with that of a monetary economy with no record-keeping technology. In making this comparison we depart from the approach taken in the previous chapters where the terms of trade are determined by a particular bargaining solution, e.g., Nash or proportional bargaining. Indeed, we establish that these arbitrary trading mechanisms generate only a subset of all incentive-feasible allocations and are generally not socially optimal. Instead, we take a *mechanism design approach,* which characterizes the complete set of allocations that can be implemented by a trading protocol—or mechanism—satisfying some basic optimality properties such as individual rationality and pairwise Pareto efficiency. We pay special attention to the set of incentive-feasible allocations that maximize social welfare.

A key insight is that the set of stationary allocations in the pure currency economy coincides with the set of allocations of the same economy without money but with a public record-keeping technology. Hence, the role of money can be identified with record-keeping: *money is memory.* We also show that the trading mechanisms used in Chapter 3 are suboptimal because they do not provide the right incentives to accumulate liquidity. If money is indivisible and there is exactly one unit of money per buyer, then constrained-efficient allocations can be decentralized by a mechanism that simply gives all of the bargaining power to the buyer.

Finally, we elaborate on the role of money by slightly modifying our environment so that in pairwise meetings each agent is both a consumer and a producer, which means there is double coincidence of wants in (almost) all matches. In a typical match, agents value each other's goods asymmetrically: one agent might value his potential trading partner's good more highly than the trading partner values his. In the absence of fiat money, agents can engage in barter trades. These barter trades, however, are typically socially inefficient. The reason for the inefficiency is that commodities play a dual role in the match: they provide a direct flow of utility to those consuming them and they serve as a means of payment. As a result, if an agent likes the good produced by his partner a lot but the reverse is not true, then he is willing to produce a lot of his own good in order to acquire a small quantity of his trading partner's good. But social efficiency dictates the opposite. In order to achieve a better allocation one needs to disentangle the real consumption services provided by a commodity from its liquidity services. This decoupling can be accomplished by introducing fiat money which, by construction, provides only liquidity services.

4.1 A Mechanism Design Approach to Monetary Exchange

In the previous chapter the terms of trade in pairwise meetings are determined by a particular bargaining solution, e.g., Nash, proportional or take-it-or-leave-it bargaining. There is no guarantee that such trading mechanisms deliver socially desirable outcomes. In this section we propose a simple mechanism that describes the set of allocations that satisfy incentive constraints arising from the frictions in the environment, such as lack of commitment and the absence of a monitoring technology. From this set of allocations, we identify those that are socially optimal in the sense that they maximize social welfare. We then compare the allocations that can be implemented under the optimal mechanism to those of a pure credit economy.

We describe the mechanism in a very general way since we do not want to place arbitrary restrictions on it. To this end, we define the DM mechanism as a set of strategies and a function mapping strategies into outcomes. Assuming that both the buyer and seller agree to play the mechanism, the set of strategies that describe the mechanism is simply the buyer's choice of real money holdings, $z = \phi m \in \mathbb{R}_+$, and the outcome function maps the buyer's money holdings into the pair $(q,d) \in \mathbb{R}_+ \times [0,z]$, where q is the quantity produced by the seller and consumed by the buyer and d is a transfer of real balances from the buyer to the seller. Implicit in this formulation is that money holdings are common knowledge in a match. (We argue later on that agents have no incentive to hide their money under the optimal mechanism.) Note that the mechanism cannot be made contingent on individual trading histories since there is no monitoring. The mechanism first proposes the outcome function $[q(z), d(z)]$, where the outcome (q, d) is a function of the buyer's real balances z. Following the proposal, the buyer and the seller simultaneously announce either "yes" or "no." If they both announce "yes," then the trade takes place according to $[q(z), d(z)]$; otherwise, the outcome is no trade. Notice that by allowing agents to reject a proposal, the mechanism ensures that all trades are individually rational since there is no enforcement technology to force the trade. In addition, we require the proposal to be pairwise Pareto efficient in the sense that the buyer or seller cannot come up with a different offer that would make both of them better off.

We focus on mechanisms that implement stationary and symmetric allocations. Symmetry means that proposals do not depend on the identities of the agents in a match. Stationarity means that the proposals are constant across time. The outcome implemented by the mechanism is the triple (q^p, d^p, z^p), where (q^p, d^p) is the trade in the DM match and z^p is the buyer's real balances. (The superscript "p" stands for planner.) Notice that market clearing of the CM money market implies that $z^p = M\phi$. The challenge is to design a mechanism so that both buyers and sellers agree to (q^p, d^p) in the DM and buyers agree to accumulate z^p real balances in the CM.

Given a mechanism, which for convenience we denote as $[q(z), d(z)]$, the DM Bellman equation for a buyer holding $z = \phi m$ units of real balances is

$$V^b(z) = \sigma \{u [q(z)] + W [z - d(z)]\} + (1 - \sigma) W^b(z), \tag{4.1}$$

where $W^b(z)$ is the CM value function of the buyer. According to (4.1) the buyer meets a producer with probability σ. He consumes q units of goods and delivers d units of real balances (expressed in terms of CM output) to his trading partner.

The CM problem of the buyer is

$$W^b(z) = z + \max_{\hat{z} \geq 0} \left\{ -\hat{z} + \beta V^b(\hat{z}) \right\}. \tag{4.2}$$

Substituting $V^b(\hat{z})$, given by its expression (4.1), into (4.2), and using the linearity of $W^b(z)$ and ignoring the constant terms, one can rewrite the agent's problem in the CM as

$$\max_{z\geq 0}\{-rz+\sigma\{u[q(z)]-d(z)\}\}, \quad \text{where } r=(1-\beta)/\beta. \tag{4.3}$$

The optimal choice of real balances maximizes the expected DM surplus of the buyer net of the holding cost of real balances. From (4.3), a necessary condition for (q^p, d^p, z^p) to be the equilibrium outcome of the mechanism $[q(z), d(z)]$ is

$$-rz^p+\sigma[u(q^p)-d^p]\geq 0. \tag{4.4}$$

We interpret (4.4) as the buyer's CM participation constraint. The left side of (4.4) is the buyer's expected DM surplus of net of the cost of holding real balances for the proposed allocation. It is always feasible for the buyer to deviate from the proposed allocation by not accumulating money in the CM and not trading in the DM; i.e., the buyer is in autarky. The expected payoff associated with this defection, which is the right side of (4.4), is 0.

Similarly, the Bellman equation for a seller in the DM solves

$$V^s=\sigma\{-c[q(z^p)]+d(z^p)\}+\beta V^s, \tag{4.5}$$

where we have used the fact that sellers do not carry real balances from the CM to the DM—since having sellers holding money is not socially optimal—and buyers hold z^p on the proposed equilibrium path. The allocation must satisfy the seller's participation constraint,

$$-c(q^p)+d^p\geq 0. \tag{4.6}$$

There is a similar DM participation constraint for buyers, $u(q^p)-d^p\geq 0$, but it is implied by the buyer's CM participation constraint, (4.4).

Any allocation (q^p, d^p, z^p) that satisfies (4.4) and (4.6) can be implemented by the following simple mechanism. If the buyer in a pairwise meeting holds at least the amount of real balances he is supposed to have on the equilibrium path, $z\geq z^p$, then the mechanism chooses terms of trade that maximize the seller's payoff subject to the constraint that the buyer enjoys at least his equilibrium path surplus. More formally, the mechanism solves

$$[q(z),d(z)]=\arg\max_{q,d\leq z}[d-c(q)] \;\text{ s.t. }\; u(q)-d\geq u(q^p)-d^p \;\text{ if }\; z\geq z^p.$$

If, however, a buyer enters a DM meeting with fewer real balances than what he is supposed to have along the equilibrium path, $z < z^p$, the mechanism imposes the harshest credible punishment on the buyer: he obtains zero surplus from the DM trade. Formally, the mechanism chooses an offer that maximizes the seller's payoff subject to the buyer receiving no surplus,

$$[q(z), d(z)] = \arg\max_{q, d \leq z} [d - c(q)] \text{ s.t. } u(q) - d = 0 \text{ if } z < z^p.$$

Figure 4.1 illustrates this mechanism. The buyer's surplus from a trade is denoted by $U^b = u(q) - d$, while the seller's surplus is $U^s = -c(q) + d$. As shown in Chapter 3, the Pareto frontier that relates U^b and U^s is downward sloping and concave when $q < q^*$. (The frontier is linear when $q = q^*$.) The utility levels associated with the proposed trade, (q^p, d^p), where we assume $q^p < q^*$, are denoted by $\bar{U}^b$ and $\bar{U}^s$ for a buyer and seller, respectively. If the buyer holds $z > z^p$, then the Pareto frontier shifts outward. The mechanism selects the point on the Pareto frontier marked by a circle that assigns the same surplus level, $\bar{U}^b$, to the buyer. If the buyer holds less than z^p, the Pareto frontier shifts inward. The mechanism selects the point on the frontier marked by a circle that assigns zero surplus to the buyer, $U^b = 0$.

We now prove that an allocation (q^p, d^p, z^p) that satisfies (4.4) and (4.6) can be implemented by the mechanism. To see this, notice, as illustrated

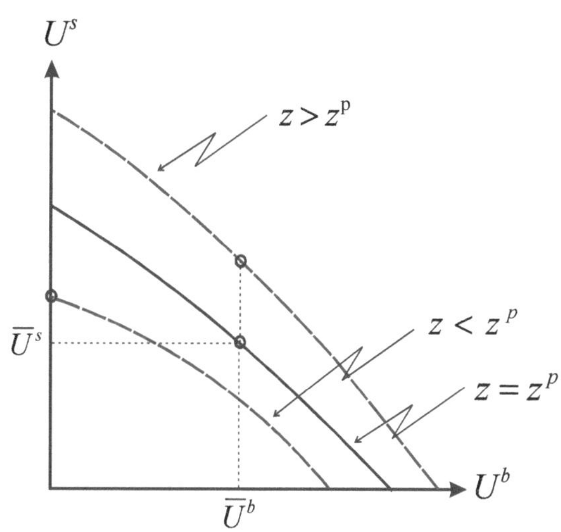

Figure 4.1
Implementation of incentive-feasible allocations

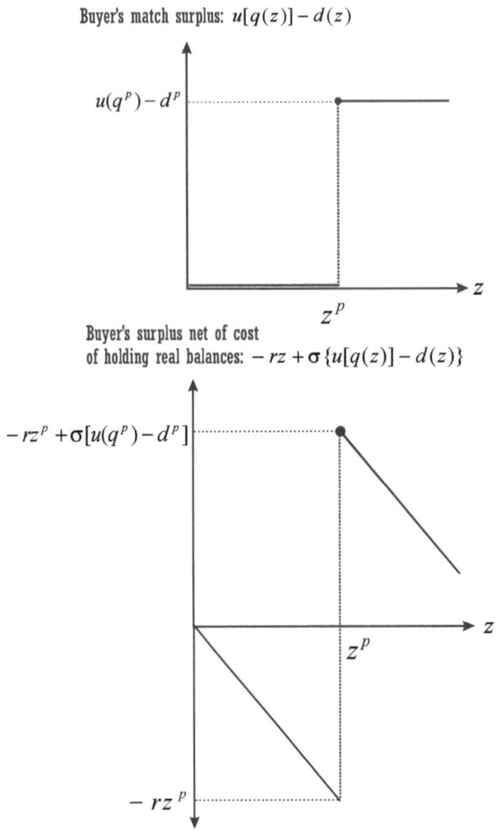

Figure 4.2
Optimal trading mechanism and buyer's payoff

in the top panel of Figure 4.2, the buyer's surplus is (weakly) monotonically increasing in his real balances. This implies that if the buyer's money holdings were private information, he would not have an incentive to hide them. The bottom panel represents the buyer's surplus net of the cost of holding real balances. From (4.3) and the bottom panel of Figure 4.2, it is easy to check that the buyer will choose $z=z^p$ if (4.4) holds. Since the buyer accumulates z^p real balances in the CM, the DM trade chosen by the mechanism is (q^p, d^p).

From the above discussion, the set of symmetric, stationary outcomes that can be implemented in a monetary economy is given by the set of triples (q^p, d^p, z^p) that satisfy

$$0 \leq rd^p \leq rz^p \leq \sigma\left[u\left(q^p\right)-d^p\right] \text{ and } c(q^p) \leq d^p.$$

Since d^p corresponds to the seller's consumption in the CM, $d^p = y$, (and following the same notation used in Chapter 2) the set of incentive-feasible allocations for a monetary economy, $\mathcal{A}^M$, is given by

$$\mathcal{A}^M = \left\{ (q,y) \in \mathbb{R}_+^2 : c(q) \leq y \leq \frac{\sigma}{r+\sigma} u(q) \right\}. \tag{4.7}$$

This set is larger than the set of incentive-feasible allocations that would prevail in an economy without money, which is $\{(0,0)\}$. In that economy, agents are forced into autarky because credit arrangements are not incentive feasible owing to a lack of commitment and a record-keeping technology. Note that the set $\mathcal{A}^M$ includes allocations that are preferred to the autarky allocation by both buyers and sellers. It is in this sense that money plays an essential role in this economy. Money can implement some allocations that are otherwise incentive-infeasible, and these new allocations increase the welfare of society.

We are now in a position to address the role that money performs in an economy. We do so by comparing the set of implementable allocations in the monetary economy with that of a credit economy with public record keeping. The set of incentive-feasible allocations for the latter, defined by $\mathcal{A}^{PR}$, is characterized by equation (2.24) in Chapter 2. Notice that the set of incentive-feasible allocations for a monetary economy, $\mathcal{A}^M$, is identical to the set of incentive-feasible allocations for a credit economy; i.e., $\mathcal{A}^M = \mathcal{A}^{PR}$. It is in this sense that money is equivalent to a public record-keeping technology: money has the technological role of memory because an agent's money holdings conveys information about his past trading behavior. By holding a unit of money at the beginning of a DM, a buyer signals that, in the past, he produced in the CM (for a seller) after a seller produced for him in the DM. If he does not have any money, it means that in the past he reneged on his "promise" to produce for a seller in the CM. In this situation, the buyer is "punished" since he is unable to enjoy gains from trade in the DM and the punishment will be lifted only when he fulfills his promise and produces in the CM.

We say that an implementable allocation is optimal if it maximizes society's welfare, where welfare is defined to be $\sigma\,[u(q) - c(q)]$. An optimal, incentive-feasible allocation is given by the solution to

$$\max_{q,d \leq z} \sigma\,[u(q) - c(q)] \tag{4.8}$$

$$\text{s.t.} \quad -c(q) + d \geq 0 \tag{4.9}$$

$$-rz + \sigma\,[u\,(q) - d] \geq 0. \tag{4.10}$$

The mechanism described above can implement the solution to this problem. We can, without loss of generality, set $d = z$ since it is suboptimal to require buyers to hold more real balances than they will transfer to sellers in their DM pairwise meetings. The first-best allocation, $q = q^*$, solves the above problem and, hence, is implementable if and only if constraints (4.9) and (4.10) are satisfied at $q = q^*$, or if

$$c(q^*) \leq \frac{\sigma}{r+\sigma} u(q^*). \tag{4.11}$$

Notice that the first-best allocation is implementable if agents are sufficiently patient, i.e., if r is lower than some threshold. If condition (4.11) holds, then there exists an optimal mechanism that prescribes a transfer of real balances that just compensates sellers for their disutility of production, $z^p = d^p = c(q^*)$. The cost associated with holding such real balances for buyers is $rc(q^*)$ and they will be willing to follow this recommendation as long as their DM expected surplus, $\sigma\left[u(q^*) - c(q^*)\right]$, is larger than the cost of holding real balances. This result—that the first-best allocation can be implemented if buyers are sufficiently patient—is in sharp contrast with those in Chapter 3, where under standard bargaining mechanisms we get $q < q^*$ whenever $r > 0$.

If the first-best allocation, q^*, is not implementable, then the optimal trading mechanism will require buyers to hold $z^p = c(q^p)$ real balances, where q^p is the largest solution to

$$-rc(q^p) + \sigma\left[u\left(q^p\right) - c(q^p)\right] = 0.$$

It is easy to check that q^p is decreasing in r, which implies that as agents become less patient the set of DM output levels that are implementable shrinks.

4.2 Efficient Allocations with Indivisible Money

In the previous section we characterized the optimal trading mechanism in pairwise meetings. This mechanism does not resemble any of the standard (bargaining) mechanisms described in Chapter 3. These standard mechanisms are socially inefficient because they fail to incentivize agents to hold sufficient liquidity. We now show that when money is indivisible, $m \in \mathbb{N}_0 \equiv \{0, 1, 2, \ldots\}$, and the money supply is exactly one unit per buyer, $M = 1$, the constrained-efficient allocation described in the previous section can be obtained under a simple trading mechanism where buyers make a take-it-or-leave-it offer. The idea behind this implementation result is that if money is indivisible, agents will be constrained to hold at least one unit if they want to trade. Provided that the endogenous value of money is large enough, agents can trade the first best DM allocation q^*.

The value function for a buyer at the beginning of the CM satisfies

$$W^b(m) = \phi m + \max_{m' \in \mathbb{N}_0} \left\{ -\phi m' + \beta V^b(m') \right\}. \tag{4.12}$$

The novel aspect of (4.12) is that money holdings are restricted to the set of integers, $m' \in \mathbb{N}_0$, instead of real numbers, $m' \in \mathbb{R}_+$. We omit the seller's value function since we know that sellers never find it optimal to accumulate real balances in the CM. We assume that a buyer who is holding m real balances makes a take-it-or-leave-it offer to the seller; hence, the buyer's offer is given by the solution to

$$\max_{q,d \in \{0,\ldots,m\}} [u(q) - \phi d] \text{ s.t. } -c(q) + \phi d = 0. \tag{4.13}$$

Note that d is a transfer of nominal money balances. The value function for a buyer holding m units of money at the beginning of the period satisfies

$$V^b(m) = \sigma \max_{d \in \{0,\ldots,m\}} \left[u \circ c^{-1}(\phi d) - \phi d \right] + \phi m + W^b(0). \tag{4.14}$$

According to (4.14), the buyer is matched with probability σ, in which case he chooses a transfer of money balances that maximizes his surplus, which equals the entire match surplus. His continuation value is linear in his real balances. Substituting the expression for $V^b(m)$ given by (4.14) into the buyer's CM value function, (4.12), his CM money holdings problem can be described more compactly as

$$\max_{m \in \mathbb{N}_0} \left\{ -r\phi m + \sigma \max_{d \in \{0,\ldots,m\}} \left[u \circ c^{-1}(\phi d) - \phi d \right] \right\}. \tag{4.15}$$

Equation (4.15) has the standard interpretation: there is a cost associated with holding real balances, which equals the rate of time preference, r, per unit of real balances. The benefit associated with holding real balances equals the expected surplus that can be obtained in the DM, $\sigma [u(q) - \phi d]$. Since $r > 0$, buyers holds only real balances that they intend to spend in the DM; i.e., $d = m$. As a result, $c(q) = \phi m$ and the buyer's portfolio problem, (4.15), can be further simplified to

$$\max_{m \in \mathbb{N}_0} \left\{ -r\phi m + \sigma \left[u \circ c^{-1}(\phi m) - \phi m \right] \right\}. \tag{4.16}$$

Since $u \circ c^{-1}(\cdot)$ is strictly concave in m, the buyer's maximization problem (4.16) has a unique solution *if money is perfectly divisible*. This solution is denoted as $m^* \in \mathbb{R}_+$ in Figure 4.3. However, this solution may not be feasible since money is indivisible. Let $[m^*]$ denote the integer part of m^*. Consequently, (4.16) has, at most, two solutions which are $[m^*]$ and $[m^*]+1$.

At the beginning of time all buyers receive exactly one unit of money, $M=1$. The market clearing condition in the CM requires that buyers prefer holding one unit of money instead of two or zero. These conditions can be written as

$$-r\phi + \sigma\left[u \circ c^{-1}(\phi) - \phi\right] \geq -r2\phi + \sigma\left[u \circ c^{-1}(2\phi) - 2\phi\right], \tag{4.17}$$

$$-r\phi + \sigma\left[u \circ c^{-1}(\phi) - \phi\right] \geq 0. \tag{4.18}$$

Condition (4.17) is the requirement that a buyer prefers holding one unit of money to two and (4.18) says that a buyer prefers holding one unit of money to none. A stationary equilibrium is any $\phi \geq 0$ that satisfies (4.17) and (4.18). We represent these equilibrium conditions in Figure 4.4. The grey area represents the gain from holding one unit of money instead of two. Values of ϕ that are consistent with market clearing are those ϕ where the gain is positive. Notice there is a range of such values.

We now determine the conditions under which $q=q^*$ is part of an equilibrium. Since buyers have all of the bargaining power and

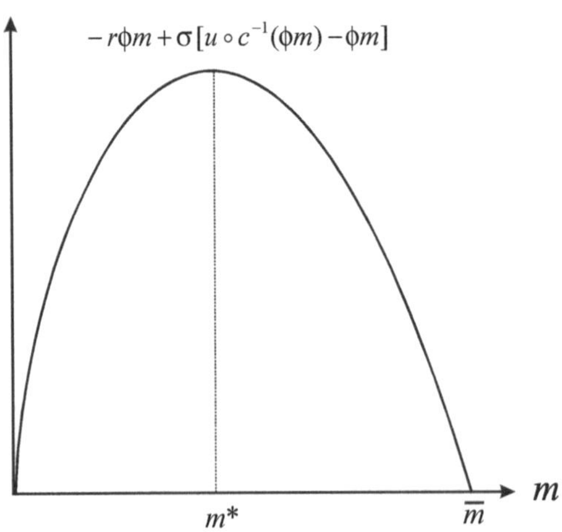

Figure 4.3
Buyer's net payoff from holding money

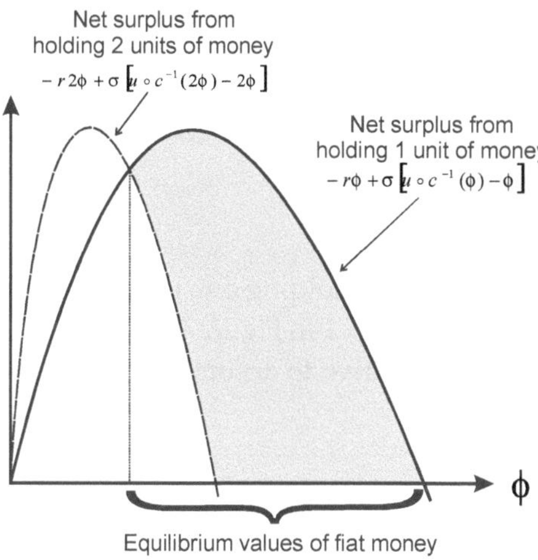

Figure 4.4
Market clearing conditions when money is indivisible

$d=m=1$, we have $\phi=c(q^*)$. Condition (4.17) can be rewritten as

$$-r2\phi+\sigma\left[u\circ c^{-1}(2\phi)-2\phi\right]\leq -r\phi+\sigma\left[u(q^*)-c(q^*)\right].$$

Since $u\circ c^{-1}(2\phi)-2\phi<u(q^*)-c(q^*)$, it is immediate that (4.17) is satisfied. Intuitively, by accumulating one unit of money, the buyer maximizes the match surplus. A second unit of money is not useful since it cannot increase the match surplus but it is costly to hold. Graphically, $\phi=c(q^*)$ is located in the downward-sloping part of the net surplus from holding one unit of money, $-r\phi+\sigma\left[u\circ c^{-1}(\phi)-\phi\right]$, and this part of the curve is located above the curve representing the net surplus from holding two units of money, see Figure 4.4. Condition (4.18) can be rewritten as

$$c(q^*)\leq\frac{\sigma}{r+\sigma}u(q^*). \tag{4.19}$$

Hence, if the efficient level of consumption and production in the DM is implementable with divisible fiat money, then it can also be implemented with indivisible money by giving all of the bargaining power to the buyer. Note that with indivisible money we do not have to worry about buyers not bringing enough liquidity in a match since they must carry at least one unit of money in order to trade and there is exactly one unit of money per buyer.

If the efficient DM allocation, q^*, is not incentive-feasible, i.e., if $c(q^*)>\sigma u(q^*)/(r+\sigma)$, then the best incentive-feasible allocation can still be implemented by the trading protocol that gives all of the bargaining power to the buyer. To see this, suppose that q^* is not incentive feasible; then the highest incentive feasible $q < q^*$ is given by (4.18) holding at equality, i.e.,

$$c(q) = \frac{\sigma}{r+\sigma}u(q).$$

In this case, the buyer is indifferent between holding one unit of money or zero and this outcome is illustrated by $\bar{m} = 1$ in Figure 4.3. This figure makes it clear that the buyer has no incentive to accumulate a second unit of money.

4.3 Two-Sided Match Heterogeneity

To deepen our understanding on the role that fiat money plays in mitigating inefficiencies in barter economies, we extend our model to include two-sided match heterogeneity in the DM. We assume there is a continuum of DM goods, where a good is represented by a point on a circle of circumference equal to $2\bar{\varepsilon}$. In a DM match, each agent is a consumer *and* a producer and agents derive utility from consuming goods except their own production good. We identify an agent type by his least preferred consumption good on the commodity circle. An agent's utility of consuming a good that is $\varepsilon \in [0, \bar{\varepsilon}]$ in arc length distance away from his least preferred good on the commodity circle is $\varepsilon u(q)$, see Figure 4.5. The good produced by an agent is chosen at random from the circle of commodities. An agent's (net) utility in a DM match is given by

$$\varepsilon u(q^b) - c(q^s),$$

where q^b is the quantity consumed of a good that is ε away from his least preferred good and q^s is the quantity produced. We will assume that producing q units of a good yields disutility $c(q) = q$.

In almost all matches there is a double coincidence of wants since each agent values the other agent's production good. But, in a typical match agents' preferences will not be symmetric. If agent i is matched with agent j, the match type is given by the pair $\boldsymbol{\varepsilon} = (\varepsilon_i, \varepsilon_j) \in E = [0, \bar{\varepsilon}]^2$. That is, the good that j produces is ε_i away from i's least preferred consumption good and the good that i produces is ε_j away from j's least preferred consumption good. Denote the distribution of types $(\varepsilon_i, \varepsilon_j)$ across matches by μ. If we assume that agents and goods are uniformly

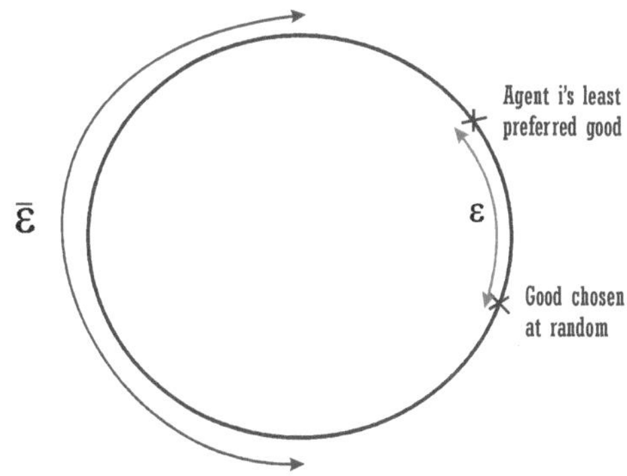

Figure 4.5
Commodity circle

distributed on the circle of circumference $2\bar{\varepsilon}$, and each agent produces a good chosen at random on that circle, the distribution of match types is given by $\mu(d\varepsilon_i, d\varepsilon_j) = d\varepsilon_i d\varepsilon_j / \bar{\varepsilon}^2$. The set of matches is represented in Figure 4.7. We identify three different match types that have figured prominently in the literature: $(\bar{\varepsilon}, \bar{\varepsilon})$ represents a symmetric double coincidence of wants match and $(\bar{\varepsilon}, 0)$ and $(0, \bar{\varepsilon})$ represents a single coincidence of wants matches.

4.3.1 The Barter Economy

Consider first a barter economy, where agents in a match trade goods for goods. A match type is denoted by $\boldsymbol{\varepsilon} = (\varepsilon_i, \varepsilon_j)$ and the levels of output produced in a match $\boldsymbol{\varepsilon}$ by $q^b_{\boldsymbol{\varepsilon}}$ and $q^s_{\boldsymbol{\varepsilon}}$, where $q^b_{\boldsymbol{\varepsilon}}$ is i's consumption—and j's production—and $q^s_{\boldsymbol{\varepsilon}}$ is j's consumption—and i's production. (We define the output levels from the perspective of the first agent type in the pair $\boldsymbol{\varepsilon} = (\varepsilon_i, \varepsilon_j)$.) By definition $q^b_{\boldsymbol{\varepsilon}} = q^s_{\boldsymbol{\varepsilon}'}$ for all $\boldsymbol{\varepsilon} = (\varepsilon_i, \varepsilon_j)$ and $\boldsymbol{\varepsilon}' = (\varepsilon_j, \varepsilon_i)$. Social welfare is at a maximum if, for each match type $\boldsymbol{\varepsilon} \in E$, the terms of trade, $(q^b_{\boldsymbol{\varepsilon}}, q^s_{\boldsymbol{\varepsilon}})$, maximize the total surplus of the match, S, where $S = \varepsilon_i u\left(q^b_{\boldsymbol{\varepsilon}}\right) - q^s_{\boldsymbol{\varepsilon}} + \varepsilon_j u\left(q^s_{\boldsymbol{\varepsilon}}\right) - q^b_{\boldsymbol{\varepsilon}}$. Match surplus is maximized at $q^b_{\boldsymbol{\varepsilon}} = q^*_{\varepsilon_i}$ and $q^s_{\boldsymbol{\varepsilon}} = q^*_{\varepsilon_j}$ where

$$\varepsilon u'\left(q^*_{\varepsilon}\right) = 1 \qquad \forall \varepsilon \in [0, \bar{\varepsilon}]; \tag{4.20}$$

i.e., the marginal utility of consumption for each agent must equal the marginal disutility of production for his partner in the match.

Assuming the realizations of the preference shocks, $(\varepsilon_i, \varepsilon_j)$, are common knowledge in a match, two reasonable properties for allocations in a decentralized economy are Pareto efficiency—there does not exist an alternative allocation that would raise the surplus of one agent without lowering the other agent's surplus—and individual rationality—the allocation is weakly preferred to no trade. We start by characterizing the Pareto frontier of a match. Let $S_i = \varepsilon_i u(q^b_\varepsilon) - q^s_\varepsilon$ denote i's surplus and let $S_j = \varepsilon_j u(q^s_\varepsilon) - q^b_\varepsilon$ denote j's surplus. The Pareto frontier is determined by

$$S_i = \max_{q^b_\varepsilon, q^s_\varepsilon} \left\{ \varepsilon_i u(q^b_\varepsilon) - q^s_\varepsilon \right\} \text{ s.t. } \varepsilon_j u(q^s_\varepsilon) - q^b_\varepsilon \geq S_j,$$

for $S_j, S_i \geq 0$. The allocation is chosen to maximize i's surplus subject to the constraint that j must get at least S_j. Pareto efficiency in a match requires that

$$\varepsilon_i u'(q^b_\varepsilon) = \frac{1}{\varepsilon_j u'(q^s_\varepsilon)}. \tag{4.21}$$

To understand (4.21), suppose that $\varepsilon_i u'(q^b_\varepsilon) > 1/\left[\varepsilon_j u'(q^s_\varepsilon)\right]$. In this case, if we ask j to produce an additional small quantity, $dq^b > 0$, and i to produce an additional $dq^s = \varepsilon_i u'(q^b_\varepsilon) dq^b > 0$, then the utility of i would be unchanged while the utility of j would increase by

$$\varepsilon_j u'(q^s_\varepsilon)(dq^s) - dq^b = \left[\varepsilon_j u'(q^s_\varepsilon)\varepsilon_i u'(q^b_\varepsilon) - 1\right] dq^b > 0.$$

Hence, an allocation in a match type $(\varepsilon_i, \varepsilon_j)$ is Pareto efficient if and only if (4.21) is satisfied. Along the Pareto frontier there is a negative relationship between the surplus of agent i and the surplus of agent j, i.e., since $S_i = \varepsilon_i u[S_j - \varepsilon_j u(q^s_\varepsilon)] - q^s_\varepsilon$ and

$$\frac{dS_j}{dS_i} = -\frac{1}{\varepsilon_i u'(q^b_\varepsilon)} < 0.$$

Moreover, the Pareto frontier is concave, i.e., $d^2 S_j / dS_i^2 < 0$. For example, if $u(q) = 2\sqrt{q}$, the Pareto frontier will correspond to the set of pairs, $S_i = 2\varepsilon_i \sqrt{q^b_\varepsilon} - \left(\varepsilon_i \varepsilon_j\right)^2 / q^b_\varepsilon$ and $S_j = 2\varepsilon_i \left(\varepsilon_j\right)^2 / \sqrt{q^b_\varepsilon} - q^b_\varepsilon$ for $q^b_\varepsilon \in [(\varepsilon_i \varepsilon_j^2/2)^{2/3}, (2\varepsilon_i \varepsilon_j^2)^{2/3}]$.

In Figure 4.6 we represent the Pareto frontier of the bargaining set when $\varepsilon_i > \varepsilon_j$. The line $S^* S^*$ represents every possible split (S_i, S_j) of the maximum total surplus of the match $S^* = S_i^* + S_j^*$, where $S_i^* = \varepsilon_i u(q^*_{\varepsilon_i}) - q^*_{\varepsilon_j}$ and $S_j^* = \varepsilon_j u(q^*_{\varepsilon_j}) - q^*_{\varepsilon_i}$. One can interpret $S^* S^*$ as a Pareto frontier in an environment with transferable utility. Note that (S_i^*, S_j^*) is at the tangency point between the Pareto frontier of the barter economy and the line $S^* S^*$.

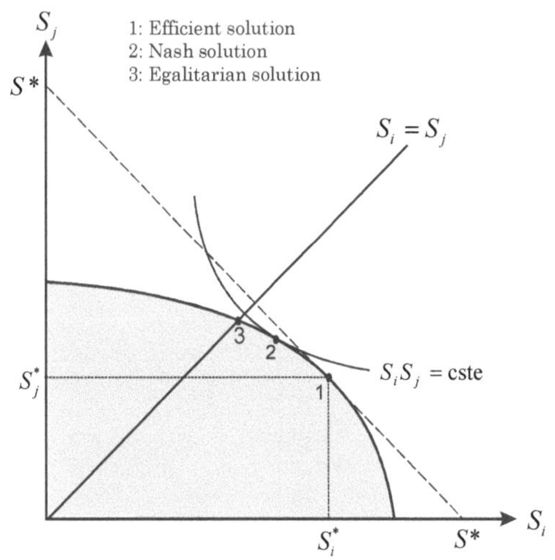

Figure 4.6
Pareto frontier in a match without money and $\varepsilon_i > \varepsilon_j$

An allocation, $(q^b_{\boldsymbol{\varepsilon}}, q^s_{\boldsymbol{\varepsilon}})$, is individually rational if $S_i \geq 0$ and $S_j \geq 0$. Therefore, the efficient allocation is individually rational if $\varepsilon_i u(q^*_{\varepsilon_i}) - q^*_{\varepsilon_j} \geq 0$ and $\varepsilon_j u(q^*_{\varepsilon_j}) - q^*_{\varepsilon_i} \geq 0$. If the match is symmetric, i.e., $\varepsilon_i = \varepsilon_j$, then $q^*_{\varepsilon_i} = q^*_{\varepsilon_j}$, $S^*_i = S^*_j = \max_q \{\varepsilon_i u(q) - q\} \geq 0$ and the efficient allocation is individually rational. If the match is asymmetric with $\varepsilon_i > \varepsilon_j$, then it is easy to see that $S^*_i = \max_q \{\varepsilon_i u(q) - q\} + q^*_{\varepsilon_i} - q^*_{\varepsilon_j} > 0$ since $q^*_{\varepsilon_i} > q^*_{\varepsilon_j}$. Hence, the agent with the highest valuation is always willing to go along with the efficient trade since he is a net buyer. If, however, the asymmetry in preferences is large, then S^*_j may be negative in which case the efficient allocation is not individually rational for agent j. This implies that for given ε_i, there is a threshold for ε_j, $\varepsilon_R > 0$, below which agent j is not willing to trade the efficient allocation since $S^*_j < 0$. This threshold solves the problem

$$\max_q \{\varepsilon_R u(q) - q\} = q^*_{\varepsilon_i} - q^*_{\varepsilon_R},$$

which is increasing in ε_i. For example, if $u(q) = 2\sqrt{q}$, then it is straightforward to show that $\varepsilon_R = \varepsilon_i/\sqrt{2}$. In Figure 4.7 we represent the set of match types for which the efficient trade is individually rational—$\varepsilon_j \geq \varepsilon_i/\sqrt{2}$ if $\varepsilon_i \geq \varepsilon_j$ and $\varepsilon_i \geq \varepsilon_j/\sqrt{2}$ otherwise—by a white area. The set of match types for which the efficient allocation is not individually rational is indicated by a grey area in Figure 4.7: when matches are sufficiently asymmetric, the efficient allocation cannot be implemented by any individually-rational mechanism.

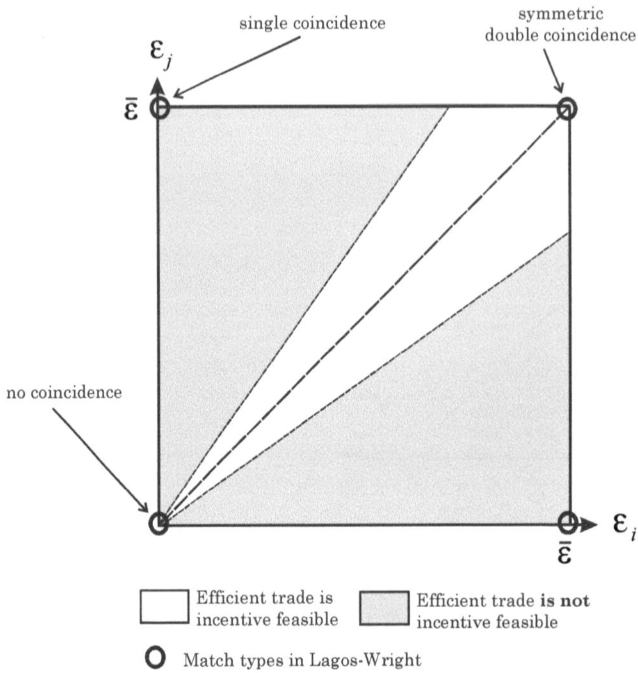

Figure 4.7
Match types and individually-rational, socially-efficient allocations

Now let's turn to allocations in bilateral matches that are determined by a bargaining solution. The symmetric Nash solution maximizes the product of the agents' surpluses, $S_i S_j$. The first-order conditions for this problem can be represented as

$$\frac{\varepsilon_j u\left(q^s_{\boldsymbol{\varepsilon}}\right) - q^b_{\boldsymbol{\varepsilon}}}{\varepsilon_i u\left(q^b_{\boldsymbol{\varepsilon}}\right) - q^s_{\boldsymbol{\varepsilon}}} = \frac{1}{\varepsilon_i u'\left(q^b_{\boldsymbol{\varepsilon}}\right)} = \varepsilon_j u'\left(q^s_{\boldsymbol{\varepsilon}}\right). \tag{4.22}$$

Notice that the Nash solution $(q^b_{\boldsymbol{\varepsilon}}, q^s_{\boldsymbol{\varepsilon}})$ is Pareto efficient since it is consistent with (4.21). One important property of this decentralized bargaining solution is that if $\varepsilon_i > \varepsilon_j$, then $q^b_{\boldsymbol{\varepsilon}} < q^*_{\varepsilon_i}$ and $q^s_{\boldsymbol{\varepsilon}} > q^*_{\varepsilon_j}$. To see this, note that if $q^b_{\boldsymbol{\varepsilon}} = q^*_{\varepsilon_i}$ and $q^s_{\boldsymbol{\varepsilon}} = q^*_{\varepsilon_j}$, then $\varepsilon_i u'\left(q^b_{\boldsymbol{\varepsilon}}\right) = \varepsilon_j u'\left(q^s_{\boldsymbol{\varepsilon}}\right) = 1$ but the left side of (4.22) implies that

$$\frac{\varepsilon_j u\left(q^*_{\varepsilon_j}\right) - q^*_{\varepsilon_i}}{\varepsilon_i u\left(q^*_{\varepsilon_i}\right) - q^*_{\varepsilon_j}} < 1$$

and, hence, (4.22) is violated. The Nash bargaining condition (4.22) can be restored only if agent i produces more than $q^*_{\varepsilon_j}$ and agent j

produces less $q^*_{\varepsilon_i}$. Although the Nash solution is pairwise Pareto efficient, it prescribes that traders exchange socially inefficient quantities when they have asymmetric tastes for each other's goods. The reason for the observed inefficiencies is that in barter economies the quantities produced and consumed simultaneously determine both the size and the split of the total surplus of the match.

A second important property of the Nash solution is in regard to the relative levels of production in an asymmetric match. When $\varepsilon_i > \varepsilon_j$, the Nash bargaining solution for match type $(\varepsilon_i, \varepsilon_j)$ has agent i producing more and consuming less than agent j, $q^b_{\boldsymbol{\varepsilon}} < q^s_{\boldsymbol{\varepsilon}}$, even though social efficiency dictates the opposite, $q^*_{\varepsilon_i} > q^*_{\varepsilon_j}$. To see this, suppose that $q^b_{\boldsymbol{\varepsilon}} = q^s_{\boldsymbol{\varepsilon}} = q$ and $u(q) = 2\sqrt{q}$. From (4.21), we have $u'(q) = 1/\sqrt{\varepsilon_i \varepsilon_j}$. If we multiply the left side of (4.22) by $\varepsilon_i u'(q) = \sqrt{\varepsilon_i}/\sqrt{\varepsilon_j}$, we get

$$\frac{\sqrt{\varepsilon_i}[\varepsilon_j u(q) - q]}{\sqrt{\varepsilon_j}[\varepsilon_i u(q) - q]} < 1 \text{ when } \varepsilon_i > \varepsilon_j,$$

but condition (4.22) requires that the right side of the above inequality equals 1. To restore the equality, $q^s_{\boldsymbol{\varepsilon}}$ must increase and $q^b_{\boldsymbol{\varepsilon}}$ decrease. Hence, the Nash solution will require i to produce more than j.

The same inefficiencies in production and consumption occur if the outcome is given by the egalitarian solution which equates the surpluses of agents in a match. More formally, the egalitarian solution must satisfy

$$\frac{\varepsilon_j u(q^s_{\boldsymbol{\varepsilon}}) - q^b_{\boldsymbol{\varepsilon}}}{\varepsilon_i u(q^b_{\boldsymbol{\varepsilon}}) - q^s_{\boldsymbol{\varepsilon}}} = 1, \tag{4.23}$$

which necessarily implies $q^s_{\boldsymbol{\varepsilon}} > q^b_{\boldsymbol{\varepsilon}}$ if $\varepsilon_i > \varepsilon_j$. In Figure 4.6, the Nash bargaining solution is determined by the tangency point between the Pareto frontier and a Nash product curve, $S_i S_j$ (the convex curve). The egalitarian solution is determined by the intersection of the 45° line and the Pareto frontier. Under both solutions bartering is socially inefficient because $(S_i, S_j) \notin S^* S^*$, which means that the terms of trade do not exploit all the gains from trade; i.e., they do not maximize the total surplus of the match.

4.3.2 The Monetary Economy

When a real commodity has the dual role as a means of payment and a consumption good, the production of this commodity might be socially inefficient. We now consider an economy that has an explicit payments instrument, fiat money. We assume that the supply of fiat money, M, is constant and that its price is strictly positive in the CM, $\phi > 0$. The lifetime expected utility of an agent holding m units of money at the beginning of the CM is

$$W(m) = \phi m + \max_{m' \geq 0} \{-\phi m' + \beta V(m')\}. \tag{4.24}$$

Note that the value functions do not have subscripts for buyers and sellers since agents are both consumers and producers in (almost) all matches. Consider now a DM meeting between agent i holding m_i units of money and agent j holding m_j units of money where $\varepsilon_i \geq \varepsilon_j$. An allocation in a match is described by a triple, $(q^b_{\boldsymbol{\varepsilon}}, q^s_{\boldsymbol{\varepsilon}}, d_{\boldsymbol{\varepsilon}})$, where $d_{\boldsymbol{\varepsilon}} \in [-m_j, m_i]$ indicates a transfer of money from i to j. Feasibility requires that i does not transfer more than he has or does not receive more than what j holds.

The surpluses of agents i and j are now characterized by

$$S_i \equiv \varepsilon_i u(q^b_{\boldsymbol{\varepsilon}}) - q^s_{\boldsymbol{\varepsilon}} + W(m_i - d_{\boldsymbol{\varepsilon}}) - W(m_i) = \varepsilon_i u(q^b_{\boldsymbol{\varepsilon}}) - q^s_{\boldsymbol{\varepsilon}} - d_{\boldsymbol{\varepsilon}}\phi$$
$$S_j \equiv \varepsilon_j u(q^s_{\boldsymbol{\varepsilon}}) - q^b_{\boldsymbol{\varepsilon}} + W(m_j + d_{\boldsymbol{\varepsilon}}) - W(m_j) = \varepsilon_j u(q^s_{\boldsymbol{\varepsilon}}) - q^b_{\boldsymbol{\varepsilon}} + d_{\boldsymbol{\varepsilon}}\phi.$$

If (S_i, S_j) is achievable without money, then any pair $(S_i - d_{\boldsymbol{\varepsilon}}\phi, S_j + d_{\boldsymbol{\varepsilon}}\phi)$ with $d_{\boldsymbol{\varepsilon}} \in [-m_j, m_i]$ is achievable with money. A Pareto-efficient match allocation must still satisfy (4.21). Moreover, any Pareto-efficient allocation with $d_{\boldsymbol{\varepsilon}} \in (-m_j, m_i)$ is characterized by $q^s_{\boldsymbol{\varepsilon}} = q^*_{\varepsilon_j}$ and $q^b_{\boldsymbol{\varepsilon}} = q^*_{\varepsilon_i}$, i.e., $S_i + S_j = S^*$. Indeed, if $q^s_{\boldsymbol{\varepsilon}} > q^*_{\varepsilon_j}$ and $q^b_{\boldsymbol{\varepsilon}} < q^*_{\varepsilon_i}$ and $d_{\boldsymbol{\varepsilon}} < m_i$, then it is feasible to reduce the inefficiently high $q^s_{\boldsymbol{\varepsilon}}$ and increase the inefficiently low $q^b_{\boldsymbol{\varepsilon}}$ by increasing the transfer of money from i to j while maintaining $S_i \geq 0$ and $S_j \geq 0$. If the feasibility constraint on $d_{\boldsymbol{\varepsilon}}$ binds, then the match allocation is socially inefficient and the Pareto frontier is strictly concave at those allocations.

In Figure 4.8 we illustrate how the Pareto frontier is transformed when money is introduced into the economy and all agents hold the same amount of money M. The Pareto frontier of a match without money is the envelope of the light grey area while the Pareto frontier of a match with valued fiat money is the envelope of the dark grey area. The set of individually-rational agreements in the monetary economy contains the set of individually-rational agreements in the barter economy. It is in this sense that fiat money plays an essential role in the economy. The socially-efficient pair of surpluses, (S^*_i, S^*_j), is the only point on the Pareto frontier of the barter economy that maximizes the total match surplus; i.e., the point is on the S^*S^* line. In an economy with valued fiat money, the pair of surpluses $\left(S^*_i - d\phi, S^*_j + d\phi\right)$,

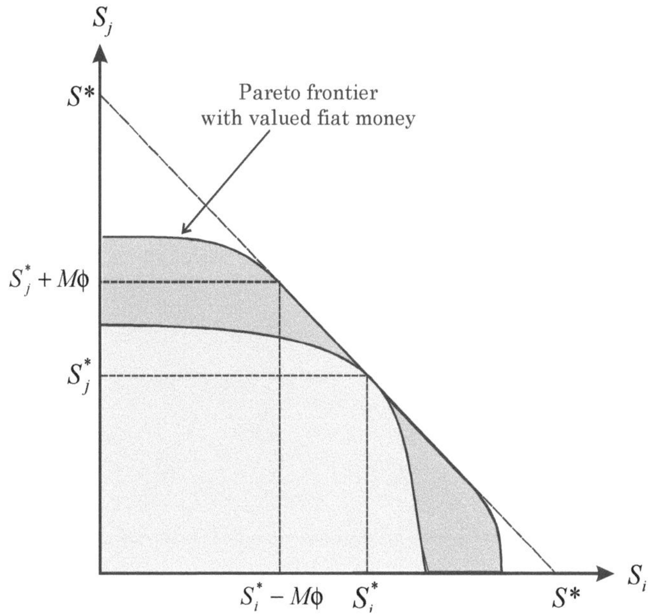

Figure 4.8
Pareto frontier with money

where $d \in (-M, M)$, is feasible and corresponds to an allocation where i and j produce $q^*_{\varepsilon_i}$ and $q^*_{\varepsilon_j}$, respectively, and i transfers d units of money to j. Hence the segment between points $(S^*_i + M\phi, S^*_j - M\phi)$ and $\left(S^*_i - M\phi, S^*_j + M\phi\right)$ on $S^*S^*$is part of the Pareto frontier, and any allocation on this segment is socially efficient.

The efficient allocation, $(q^*_{\varepsilon_i}, q^*_{\varepsilon_j})$, where $\varepsilon_i \geq \varepsilon_j$, is individually rational with fiat money if there is a transfer $d_{\boldsymbol{\varepsilon}} \in \left[-m_j, m_i\right]$ such that

$$q^*_{\varepsilon_i} - \varepsilon_j u(q^*_{\varepsilon_j}) \leq d_{\boldsymbol{\varepsilon}}\phi \leq \varepsilon_i u(q^*_{\varepsilon_i}) - q^*_{\varepsilon_j}. \tag{4.25}$$

The transfer of real balances must be sufficiently large to compensate j for his production cost net of his utility of consumption but should not be larger than i's utility of consumption net of his production cost. Condition (4.25) is satisfied for some $d_{\boldsymbol{\varepsilon}}$ if $m_i\phi \geq q^*_{\varepsilon_i} - \varepsilon_j u(q^*_{\varepsilon_j})$. It follows that if all agents hold the same amount of money, $m_i = m_j = M$, the efficient allocation is individually rational in all matches if $M\phi \geq q^*_{\bar{\varepsilon}}$, since the buyer has enough real balances to compensate the seller for his production cost in the single coincidence match where $\boldsymbol{\varepsilon} = (\bar{\varepsilon}, 0)$.

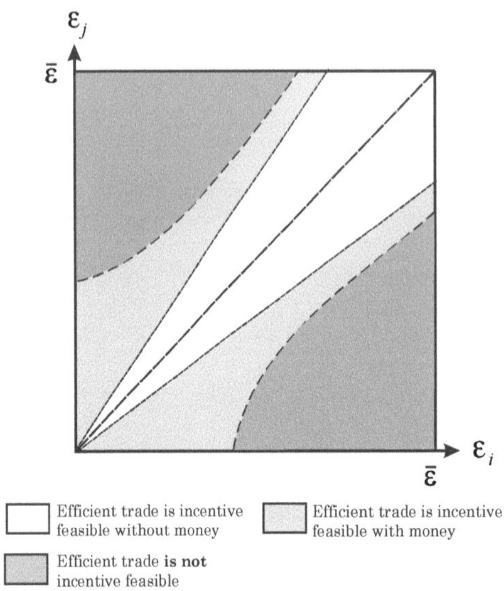

Figure 4.9
Incentive-feasible, socially-efficient allocations with and without money

Suppose for example that $u(q)=2\sqrt{q}$. Then the socially-efficient trades are individual rational when real balance holdings are $M\phi$ if $(\varepsilon_i)^2 \le M\phi + 2(\varepsilon_j)^2$ (assuming that $\varepsilon_i \ge \varepsilon_j$). In Figure 4.9 we represent the set of match types for which the efficient trade is not individually rational without money by the light-grey area but is individually rational with money. As $M\phi$ increases, the light grey area expands and the dark-grey area disappears as $M\phi \to (\bar{\varepsilon})^2$.

Up to this point we have simply assumed that agents hold M balances. We now examine the conditions under which agents are willing to accumulate sufficient real balances in the CM—before matches are formed—so that socially-efficient DM allocations can be implemented. A necessary condition for an agent to be willing to accumulate $\phi M = q^*_{\bar{\varepsilon}}$ real balances is

$$-\phi M + \beta V(M) \ge \beta W(0). \tag{4.26}$$

An agent can choose not to accumulate money in the CM and not to trade in the following DM (two consecutive deviations), which is the right side of the above inequality. (Note that in principle an agent who does not hold money can still engage in barter trades in the DM.

Inequality (4.26) is just a necessary condition for participation.) Assuming that agents have sufficient real balances to implement the socially efficient levels of DM production, the value function of an agent in the DM, $V(m)$, is given by

$$V(m) = \int_E \left[\varepsilon_i u(q^*_{\varepsilon_i}) - q^*_{\varepsilon_j} - \phi d_{(\varepsilon_i,\varepsilon_j)}\right] d\mu(\varepsilon_i, \varepsilon_j) + W(m). \tag{4.27}$$

The first term on the right side of (4.27) is the weighted sum of all DM surpluses while the second term is the continuation value in the next CM. Using the linearity of $W(m)$ and the fact that $d_{(\varepsilon_i,\varepsilon_j)} = -d_{(\varepsilon_j,\varepsilon_i)}$, the CM participation constraint (4.26), can be simplified to

$$r\phi M = rq^*_{\bar{\varepsilon}} \leq \int_E \left[\varepsilon_i u(q^*_{\varepsilon_i}) - q^*_{\varepsilon_j}\right] d\mu(\varepsilon_i, \varepsilon_j). \tag{4.28}$$

According to (4.28) the cost of holding real balances, as measured by the rate of time preference r, cannot be larger than the weighted sum of the surpluses in all matches. Using the same arguments as in Section 4.1 and assuming money holdings are observable, we can construct a trading mechanism that specifies if an agent fails to show that he has at least M units of money in a bilateral match, then he receives zero surplus from trade in the match. If the condition (4.28) holds, then such a mechanism can implement the socially efficient output levels. Hence, the efficient allocations can be implemented in all matches with a constant money supply provided that agents are sufficiently patient.

Let's now examine equilibrium outcomes when the terms of trade in a match are determined by a bargaining protocol. Consider a match where $\varepsilon_i \geq \varepsilon_j$ where agent i holds m units of money. We adopt the egalitarian bargaining solution, where $(q^b_{\boldsymbol{\varepsilon}}, q^s_{\boldsymbol{\varepsilon}}, d_{\boldsymbol{\varepsilon}})$ maximizes S_i subject to $S_i = S_j$ and $d_{\boldsymbol{\varepsilon}} \leq m$. (The logic and implications would be similar for the Nash bargaining solution, but the analysis would be a bit more tedious.) The constraint $S_i = S_j$ can be written as

$$d_{\boldsymbol{\varepsilon}}\phi = \frac{\left[\varepsilon_i u(q^b_{\boldsymbol{\varepsilon}}) - q^s_{\boldsymbol{\varepsilon}}\right] - \left[\varepsilon_j u(q^s_{\boldsymbol{\varepsilon}}) - q^b_{\boldsymbol{\varepsilon}}\right]}{2}. \tag{4.29}$$

The egalitarian bargaining solution implies that the transfer of real balances from agent i to j is half of the difference between the utilities of consumption of the two agents net of their disutility of production. Let $\lambda_{\boldsymbol{\varepsilon}} \geq 0$ denote the Lagrange multiplier associated with the feasibility constraint $\phi d_{\varepsilon} \leq \phi m$. Agent i's match surplus, $S_{(\varepsilon_i,\varepsilon_j)}(m)$, solves

$$\max_{q^b_{\varepsilon},q^s_{\varepsilon}} \left\{ \frac{\varepsilon_i u(q^b_{\varepsilon}) - q^s_{\varepsilon} + \varepsilon_j u(q^s_{\varepsilon}) - q^b_{\varepsilon}}{2} \right.$$
$$\left. + \lambda_{\varepsilon} \left[\phi m - \frac{\left[\varepsilon_i u(q^b_{\varepsilon}) - q^s_{\varepsilon}\right] - \left[\varepsilon_j u(q^s_{\varepsilon}) - q^b_{\varepsilon}\right]}{2} \right] \right\}, \tag{4.30}$$

for all ε such that $\varepsilon_i \geq \varepsilon_j$. The first-order condition of (4.30) with respect to q^b_{ε} is

$$\lambda_{\varepsilon} = \frac{\varepsilon_i u'(q^b_{\varepsilon}) - 1}{\varepsilon_i u'(q^b_{\varepsilon}) + 1}. \tag{4.31}$$

From (4.29) notice that by holding an additional Δz units of real balances, agent i can increase his consumption by Δq^b_{ε} that solves $\left[\varepsilon_i u'(q^b_{\varepsilon}) + 1\right] \Delta q^b_{\varepsilon}/2 = \Delta z$. Hence, agent i's surplus increases by $\varepsilon_i u'(q^b_{\varepsilon})\Delta q^b_{\varepsilon} - \Delta z = \lambda_{\varepsilon}\Delta z$. For all ε such that

$$\frac{\left[\varepsilon_i u(q^*_{\varepsilon_i}) - q^*_{\varepsilon_j}\right] - \left[\varepsilon_j u(q^*_{\varepsilon_j}) - q^*_{\varepsilon_i}\right]}{2} > \phi m,$$

the constraint $d_{\varepsilon} \leq m$ binds and, hence, $\lambda_{\varepsilon} > 0$. In this case, the terms of trade are socially inefficient, where $q^b_{\varepsilon} < q^*_{\varepsilon_i}$ and $q^s_{\varepsilon} > q^*_{\varepsilon_j}$. In contrast, if $d_{\varepsilon} \leq m$ does not bind, then $\lambda_{\varepsilon} = 0$ and, from (4.21) and (4.31), the allocation is socially efficient.

In summary, when $\varepsilon_i > \varepsilon_j$ efficiency requires that agent j produces a larger quantity of DM output than agent i. Agent j will agree to such an allocation if agent i is able to compensate him by transferring sufficient claims to future consumption, i.e., by transferring money. If i's constraint on money holdings does not bind, then i and j exchange the socially efficient quantities. If, however, i's constraint on money holdings binds, then i transfers all of his real balances to j and bargaining results in socially inefficient DM quantities.

The lifetime expected utility of agent i at the beginning of a period, (4.27), can be expressed as

$$V(m) = \int_{\varepsilon_i > \varepsilon_j} S_{(\varepsilon_i,\varepsilon_j)}(m) d\mu(\varepsilon_i,\varepsilon_j) + \int_{\varepsilon_i \leq \varepsilon_j} S_{(\varepsilon_j,\varepsilon_i)}(M) d\mu(\varepsilon_i,\varepsilon_j) + W(m). \tag{4.32}$$

If the DM match is such that $\varepsilon_i > \varepsilon_j$, then agent i is the buyer in the match and he transfers output and money to j to finance his consumption, (consumption that is produced by j). Agent i's match surplus,

$S_{(\varepsilon_i,\varepsilon_j)}(m)$, is given by (4.30). If the DM match is such that $\varepsilon_i \leq \varepsilon_j$, then the agent i's partner transfers money to him to finance his—agent j's—consumption. In this case, the surplus of agent i is $S_{(\varepsilon_j,\varepsilon_i)}(M)$, where M is j's money holdings. (In equilibrium, agent $j \neq i$ holds money balances equal to M.) Since we are assuming the egalitarian bargaining solution, we have that $S_{(\varepsilon_i,\varepsilon_j)}(m) = S_{(\varepsilon_j,\varepsilon_i)}(M)$ when $\varepsilon_i \leq \varepsilon_j$.

In the CM, each agent chooses his real balances in order to maximize his expected surplus net of the cost of holding money, (4.24). Substituting $V(m)$, given by (4.32), into (4.24) the agent's CM money demand problem becomes,

$$\max_{m \geq 0} \left\{ -r\phi m + \int_{\varepsilon_i > \varepsilon_j} S_{(\varepsilon_i,\varepsilon_j)}(m) d\mu(\varepsilon_i, \varepsilon_j) \right\}. \tag{4.33}$$

Notice that problem (4.33) only considers matches where agent i is the buyer, $\varepsilon_i > \varepsilon_j$, since these are the only matches where i requires money to trade with his partner. Using $S'_{(\varepsilon_i,\varepsilon_j)}(m) = \phi\lambda_{\boldsymbol{\varepsilon}}$, the solution to (4.33) is simply

$$-r + \int_{\varepsilon_i > \varepsilon_j} \lambda_{\boldsymbol{\varepsilon}} d\mu(\varepsilon_i, \varepsilon_j) \leq 0, \tag{4.34}$$

with an equality if $m\phi > 0$. Each agent chooses his money holdings so that the rate of time preference r, which is the cost of holding money, is equal to the expected shadow value of money across all matches. As long as $r > 0$, there is a positive measure of matches for which the constraint $d_{\boldsymbol{\varepsilon}} \leq M$ is binding. Provided that $\lambda_{\boldsymbol{\varepsilon}} > 0$, (4.31) implies that $\lambda_{\boldsymbol{\varepsilon}}$ is a decreasing function of $m\phi$. As $m\phi$ approaches 0 the marginal value of real balances, $\lambda_{\boldsymbol{\varepsilon}}$, tends to its value in the barter economy, which is bounded above by 1. So from (4.34) a necessary condition for money to be valued is $r < 1$. From (4.29) the transfer of real balances in the most asymmetric match, $\boldsymbol{\varepsilon} = (\bar{\varepsilon}, 0)$, if efficient quantities are traded is:

$$d_{(\bar{\varepsilon},0)}\phi = \frac{\bar{\varepsilon}u(q^*_{\bar{\varepsilon}}) + q^*_{\bar{\varepsilon}}}{2}.$$

Hence, if $\phi M \geq \left[\bar{\varepsilon}u(q^*_{\bar{\varepsilon}}) + q^*_{\bar{\varepsilon}}\right]/2$ then $\lambda_{\boldsymbol{\varepsilon}} = 0$ in all matches. By market clearing (4.34) determines a unique $M\phi \in \left(0, \left[\bar{\varepsilon}u(q^*_{\bar{\varepsilon}}) + q^*_{\bar{\varepsilon}}\right]/2\right]$ provided that r is sufficiently small. As agents become infinitely patient, r goes to 0, $M\phi$ approaches $\left[\bar{\varepsilon}u(q^*_{\bar{\varepsilon}}) + q^*_{\bar{\varepsilon}}\right]/2$ and the efficient allocation is traded in all matches.

In Figure 4.10 we represent the Pareto frontier of the most asymmetric match with $(\varepsilon_i, \varepsilon_j) = (\bar{\varepsilon}, 0)$. If fiat money is not valued, then agents'

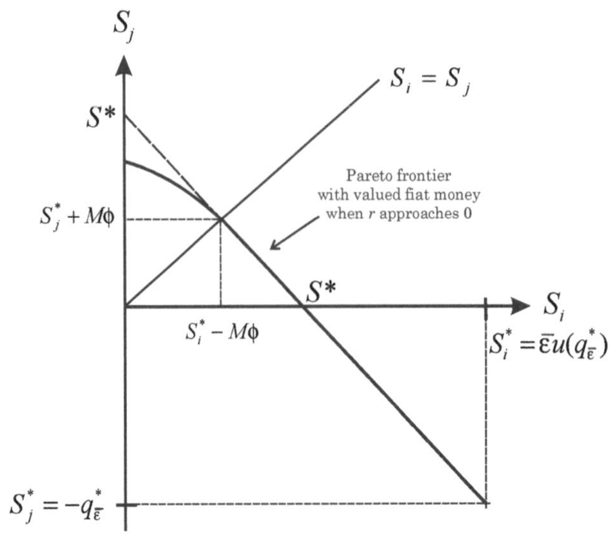

Figure 4.10
Pareto frontier of the single-coincidence match, $(\varepsilon_i, \varepsilon_j) = (\bar{\varepsilon}, 0)$, when r tends to 0

surpluses at the first best are $S_i^* = \bar{\varepsilon}u(q_{\bar{\varepsilon}}^*) > 0$ and $S_j^* = -q_{\bar{\varepsilon}}^* < 0$. Clearly, such a trade is not incentive feasible. If money is valued and r tends to 0, then ϕM tends to $\left[\bar{\varepsilon}u(q_{\bar{\varepsilon}}^*) + q_{\bar{\varepsilon}}^*\right]/2$ so that $S_i^* - \phi M = S_i^* + \phi M = \left[\bar{\varepsilon}u(q_{\bar{\varepsilon}}^*) - q_{\bar{\varepsilon}}^*\right]/2$. Now the first best levels of output are incentive feasible. Graphically, the Pareto frontier is linear and coincides with the S^*S^* lines until it intersects the 45°-line imposed by the proportional bargaining solution.

4.4 Further Readings

Mechanism design has been applied to the Lagos and Wright (2005) model by Hu, Kennan, and Wallace (2009). The presentation in this chapter is based on Rocheteau (2012). Kocherlakota (1998) and Kocherlakota and Wallace (1998) were the first to use implementation theory to prove the essentiality of money. Applications of mechanism design to monetary theory include Cavalcanti and Erosa (2008), Cavalcanti and Nosal (2009), Cavalcanti and Wallace (1999), Deviatov (2006), Deviatov and Wallace (2001), Koeppl, Monnet, and Temzelides (2008), and Mattesini, Monnet, and Wright (2010). Wallace (2010) provides a review of the literature.

The record-keeping role of money is emphasized by Ostroy (1973), Ostroy and Starr (1974, 1990) and Townsend (1987, 1989), among others. Kocherlakota (1998a,b) uses a mechanism design approach to establish that the technological role of money is to that of a societal memory device that provides agents with access to certain aspects of the histories of their trading partners. As a corollary, imperfect knowledge of individual histories is necessary for money to play an essential role in the economy (Wallace 2000). For further discussions on the essential role of money as memory, see Araujo (2004), Aliprantis, Camera, and Puzzello (2007), and Araujo and Camargo (2009). Araujo, Camargo, Minetti, and Puzzello (2012) study the essentiality of money in environments with centralized trade.

The section with two-sided heterogeneity in pairwise meetings is based on Berentsen and Rocheteau (2003) in the context of the large-household model of Shi (1997). Ex-post heterogeneity across matches has been studied in Kiyotaki and Wright (1991) to endogenize the set of barter and monetary trades; in Berentsen and Rocheteau (2002, 2003) to study the role of divisible money with and without double-coincidence-of-wants meetings; in Peterson and Shi (2004) to account for price dispersion and its relationship to inflation; in Jafarey and Masters (2003), Lagos and Rocheteau (2005), and Nosal (2011) to study the effects of inflation on output and the velocity of money; and in Curtis and Wright (2004), Faig and Jerez (2006), and Ennis (2008) to study price posting under private information. Asymmetric valuations for the goods arise endogenously in models with private information about the quality of goods, such as Williamson and Wright (1994), Trejos (1999), and Berentsen and Rocheteau (2004) among others.

Engineer and Shi (1998, 2001)—in an environment with indivisible money—and Berentsen and Rocheteau (2003)—in an environment with divisible money—emphasize the role of money to transfer utility perfectly across agents. In those models fiat money allows traders to separate the decisions of how much to produce and how to split the resulting total surplus. In contrast, real production is an imperfect device for transferring utility, because the marginal utility of the consumer and the marginal cost of the producer vary with the quantity produced and exchanged and, in general, they do not coincide. Jacquet and Tan (2012) use a related argument to explain why fiat money has a higher liquidity than Lucas trees. In their model, Lucas trees that yield state-dependent dividends are valued differently by agents with different hedging needs. It follows that agents have an endogenous preference for money as a means of payment because in contrast to Lucas trees they are valued equally by all agents. The result that fiat money is socially useful because it reduces over-production of some goods is closely related to the idea that money prevents the over-accumulation of capital, as in Wallace (1980)—in overlapping-generations economies—and Lagos and Rocheteau (2008)—in search economies.

Camera and Chien (2016) argue that the cash-in-advance and the Lagos-Wright models neither induce fundamental theoretical nor quantitative differences in results. Our model with two-sided heterogeneity makes it clear that this statement is not true in general. The outcome of our model could not be replicated by a cash-in-advance model since agents finance their purchases with both money and their own output. Moreover, cash-in-advance models are not amenable to the mechanism design approach described in this chapter. Finally, reduced-form models have nothing to say about the underlying frictions that generate a role for money and prevent other assets, such as credit, capital, and bonds, from being used as media of exchange.

This book emphasizes the role of money as a medium of exchange. Doepke and Schneider (2013) complement our approach by studying the role of money as a unit of account and how this role relates to the redistributional effects of inflation.

5 Properties of Money

"In a simple state of industry money is chiefly required to pass about between buyers and sellers. It should, then, be conveniently portable, divisible into pieces of various size, so that any sum may readily be made up, and easily distinguishable by its appearance, or by the design impressed upon it."

William Stanley Jevons, *Money and the Mechanism of Exchange* (1875, Chapter 5)

The role that an asset plays as a medium of exchange depends on the nature of the frictions in the economy and on its physical characteristics. In Chapters 3 and 4, the absence of record-keeping and commitment implied that a tangible medium of exchange is needed to facilitate trade, and fiat money fulfills that role. In those chapters, although some physical properties of fiat money were made explicit—such as its divisibility or lack thereof—other important, and desirable, properties were left implicit. For example, it was implicitly assumed that fiat money did not depreciate or wear out over time, that it could be carried costlessly from one market to another, and that it could not be counterfeited.

In this chapter we examine how the physical properties of money can affect its value and ability to perform the role of a medium of exchange. We reexamine the issue of divisibility, and investigate the implications for a medium of exchange that is costly to carry or that can be counterfeited. We are interested in how allocations and equilibria are affected when the physical properties of money depart for their ideal state.

Commodity money systems have, at times, been plagued with a scarcity of certain types of coins. Since money cannot be scarce if it is perfectly divisible, we examine an environment where money is indivisible and there are fewer units of money than there are buyers. Obviously, in this situation the total number of trades will be too low. In order to illustrate other important inefficiencies associated with indivisible and scarce money, we assume that buyers have heterogeneous valuations for the goods produced by sellers. Because of this, the economy will be characterized by a number of trade inefficiencies, where some of these inefficiencies would not arise if money was perfectly divisible.

The second property of money we investigate is its portability. According to Jevons (1875, Chapter 5),

> "Many of the substances used as currency in former times must have been sadly wanting in portability. Oxen and sheep, indeed, would transport themselves on their own legs; but corn, skins, oil, nuts, almonds, etc., though in several respects forming fair currency, would be intolerably bulky and troublesome to transfer."

If we assume that it is costly to carry units of money, then money will not be held nor valued when the cost of carrying money is higher than some threshold. If, however, the carrying cost of money is not too large, then there are multiple stationary equilibria where money has a positive value in exchange. This suggests that fundamentals, such as carrying costs, as well as conventions matter for the use of an object as a means of payment. In the equilibrium where money has its highest value, the value of money decreases as the carrying cost increases. Finally, money is not neutral since, in a monetary equilibrium, an increase in the money supply implies that agents will hold more nominal balances, which increases the total cost of holding money and, hence, reduces welfare.

The final property of money that we examine is its recognizability or, in Jevons' (1875, Chapter 5) words, its *cognizability*.

> "By this name we may denote the capability of a substance for being easily recognized and distinguished from all other substances. As a medium of exchange, money has to be continually handed about, and it will occasion great trouble if every person receiving currency has to scrutinize, weigh, and test it. If it requires any skill to discriminate good money from bad, poor ignorant people are sure to be imposed upon. Hence the medium of exchange should have certain distinct marks which nobody can mistake."

The art of counterfeiting has been around for as long as money. In medieval Europe, individuals clipped the edges of silver and gold coins and tried to pass off the depreciated coin as full bodied. During the nineteenth century in the US, vast quantities of counterfeit banknotes were produced and passed off as the real thing. To address the issue of counterfeiting, we examine an environment where fiat money can be counterfeited at a fixed cost, and sellers are unable to distinguish genuine from counterfeit notes. We show that the lack of recognizability results in an upper bound on the quantity of real balances that a buyer can transfer to the seller in a match. Even though counterfeiting does not occur in equilibrium, our model provides support for policies that make a currency harder to counterfeit: by raising the cost to produce counterfeits, policy makers can increase the velocity of money, output, and welfare.

5.1 Divisibility of Money

In this section we investigate the implications of money being indivisible. In Chapter 4.2, we considered a model with indivisible money and assumed that the supply of money was such that all buyers could exactly hold one unit of money, i.e., $M = 1$. We now assume that money is scarce or, equivalently, that there is a currency shortage, i.e., $M < 1$. In order to identify the inefficiencies associated with indivisible and scarce money we introduce buyer heterogeneity in the DM matches as in Chapter 4.3. In particular, the utility of a buyer in a bilateral match is $\varepsilon u(q)$, where ε is the realization of an idiosyncratic preference shock drawn from some cumulative distribution function $F(\varepsilon)$ with support in $\mathbb{R}_{+}$. A high ε means that the buyer's marginal utility for the seller's good is high, and a low ε means that it is low. The preference shocks are independent across time and across matches. They capture the idea that even though agents are ex ante identical, buyers have idiosyncratic preferences over the goods produced by sellers in the DM.

The timing of events in a representative period is illustrated in Figure 5.1. A fraction σ of buyers and sellers are matched in the DM. Upon being matched, a buyer draws a preference shock ε for the output produced by the seller. If the buyer has some money, then he can make a take-it-or-leave-it offer to the seller. At night, buyers and sellers trade money and the general good in a centralized competitive market, CM, where the price of a unit of money in terms of the general good is ϕ. We focus on stationary equilibria where this price is constant over time.

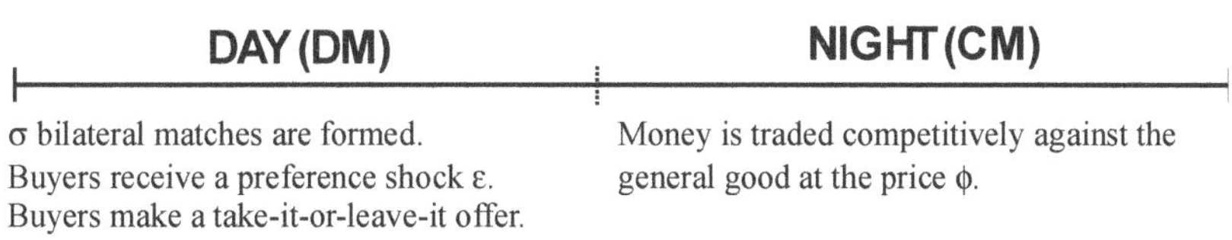

Figure 5.1
Timing of a representative period

5.1.1 Currency Shortage

Since there is less than one indivisible unit of money per buyer, clearing of the money market in the CM requires that a fraction M of buyers end up with one unit of money and the remaining $1-M$ end up with none. Moreover, buyers are indifferent between holding one unit of money and holding zero unit. The concavity of the buyer's value function implies that the buyer has no incentive to hold more than one unit of money. See the Appendix. Therefore,

$$-\phi+\beta V_1=\beta V_0, \tag{5.1}$$

where V_1 is the value of a buyer holding one unit of money in the DM and V_0 is the value of a buyer holding no money. The left side of (5.1) is the expected discounted utility of a buyer who obtains one unit of money in the CM: the unit of money costs him ϕ and his continuation value in the next DM is V_1. The right side of (5.1) is the expected discounted utility of a buyer who exits the CM without money.

In the DM, a matched buyer with one unit of money makes a take-it-or-leave-it offer, (q,d), to the seller where the only feasible transfer of money is $d=1$. The offer must satisfy the seller's participation constraint, $-c(q)+\phi\geq 0$. Hence, the buyer will choose the largest q he can afford with his unit of money, $q=c^{-1}(\phi)$, which is independent of the realization of his preference shock.

The value of a buyer without money in the DM solves

$$V_0=\max\left(-\phi+\beta V_1,\beta V_0\right)=\beta V_0=0. \tag{5.2}$$

The buyer cannot trade in the DM because he has no means of payment. In the CM, equilibrium requires that buyers are indifferent between holding or not holding one unit of money.

The value of a buyer with one unit of money at the beginning of the DM is

$$V_1=\sigma\int\max\left[\varepsilon u(q)-\phi+\beta V_1,\beta V_1\right]dF(\varepsilon)+(1-\sigma)\beta V_1. \tag{5.3}$$

With probability σ the buyer finds a seller. He draws a preference shock, ε, for the good produced by the seller. If the buyer chooses to make an offer, then his lifetime utility is $\varepsilon u(q)-\phi+\beta V_1$: he enjoys the utility of consumption and his continuation value in the CM is $-\phi+\beta V_1=\beta V_0$. If the buyer chooses not to make an offer, his continuation value is simply βV_1. The value function (5.3) can be simplified to

$$V_1=\sigma\int\max\left[\varepsilon u(q)-\phi,0\right]dF(\varepsilon)+\beta V_1. \tag{5.4}$$

If the surplus from trading is positive, $\varepsilon u(q) - \phi \geq 0$, then the buyer makes an offer. Otherwise, he chooses not to trade. Since $q = c^{-1}(\phi)$, the buyer chooses to trade if $\varepsilon u \circ c^{-1}(\phi) - \phi \geq 0$.

Let $\varepsilon_R(\phi) = \phi/[u \circ c^{-1}(\phi)]$ denote the threshold for ε, below which the buyer chooses not to trade. Since $u \circ c^{-1}(\phi)$ is strictly concave and $u \circ c^{-1}(0) = 0$, it can be shown that $\varepsilon_R(\phi)$ is an increasing function of ϕ. That is, as money becomes more valuable, buyers become more choosy, and are only willing to spend their indivisible unit of money on goods that they highly value. Using (5.1) and (5.2) i.e., $\beta V_1 = \phi$, (5.4) can be rewritten as

$$r\phi = \sigma \int_{\varepsilon_R(\phi)}^{\infty} \left[\varepsilon u \circ c^{-1}(\phi) - \phi\right] dF(\varepsilon). \tag{5.5}$$

According to (5.5), the value of money in equilibrium is such that the opportunity cost of holding one unit of money, the left side of (5.5), is equal to the expected surplus from a trade in the DM, the right side of (5.5). A steady-state equilibrium of the economy corresponds to a ϕ solution to (5.5).

We first examine the special case where $\varepsilon = 1$ in all matches. Then (5.5) becomes

$$r\phi = \sigma\{u \circ c^{-1}(\phi) - \phi\}, \tag{5.6}$$

or

$$\phi = \frac{\sigma}{r+\sigma} u \circ c^{-1}(\phi). \tag{5.7}$$

Given our assumptions about c and u, it is easy to check that there exists a unique $\phi > 0$ that satisfies (5.7). In terms of comparative statics associated with the purchasing power of money, note that ϕ is independent of the quantity of money, M. From (5.7), $\partial\phi/\partial\sigma > 0$ and $\partial\phi/\partial r < 0$. Intuitively, as the matching probability σ increases, a buyer has a higher chance of trading in the DM, which makes money more valuable. As a consequence, the quantities traded during the DM increase. And, as the rate of time preference, r, increases, agents become more impatient, and the cost of holding money increases. As a consequence, the value of money falls, and agents trade less in the DM.

We now generalize these results to the case where the distribution of preference shocks is nondegenerate. If we divide both sides of (5.5) by $u \circ c^{-1}(\phi)$ and use $\varepsilon_R = \phi/[u \circ c^{-1}(\phi)]$, then we get

$$r\varepsilon_R = \sigma \int_{\varepsilon_R}^{\infty} (\varepsilon - \varepsilon_R)\, dF(\varepsilon). \tag{5.8}$$

Equation (5.8) is a standard optimal stopping rule in sequential search models. It determines the reservation utility above which it is optimal to accept a trade. For the sake of interpretation it can be rewritten as

$$r\varepsilon_R = \sigma\left[1 - F(\varepsilon_R)\right]\mathbb{E}\left[\varepsilon - \varepsilon_R | \varepsilon \geq \varepsilon_R\right].$$

The left side is the flow value from agreeing to trade at the reservation utility, while the right side is the expected return from the search activity. The return from search for a buyer is the probability of meeting a seller, σ, times the probability that the match specific component is larger than the reservation value, $1 - F(\varepsilon_R)$, times the expected difference between ε and ε_R conditional on ε being larger than ε_R. Integrating the right side of (5.8) by parts, we get

$$r\varepsilon_R = \sigma \int_{\varepsilon_R}^{\infty} 1 - F(\varepsilon) d\varepsilon. \tag{5.9}$$

There is a unique $\varepsilon_R > 0$ that solves (5.9). To see this, notice that the left side is increasing in ε_R from 0 to ∞ as ε_R goes from 0 to ∞, while the right side is decreasing from $\sigma\varepsilon^e$, where ε^e denotes the mean of the distribution F, to 0 as ε_R goes from 0 to ∞. See Figure 5.2.

It is also immediate from (5.9) that $\partial\varepsilon_R/\partial\sigma > 0$ and $\partial\varepsilon_R/\partial r < 0$. If it is easier to find a seller in the DM, then buyers become more demanding and raise their reservation utility. In contrast, if buyers become

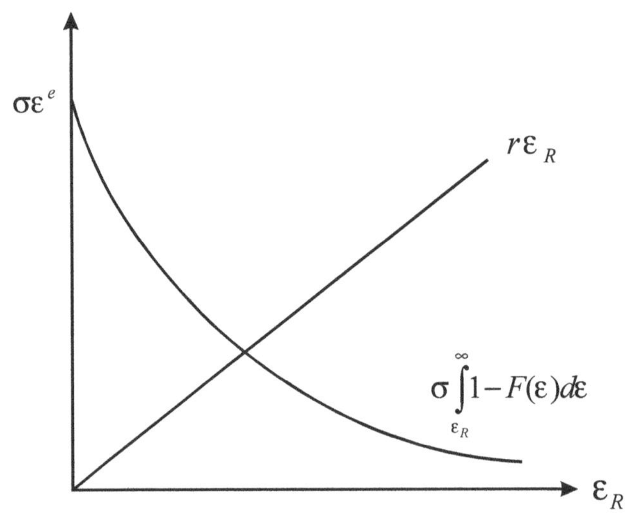

Figure 5.2
Reservation utility in the model with indivisible money

less patient, then they lower their reservation utility. Since $\varepsilon_R = \phi/[u \circ c^{-1}(\phi)]$, there is a positive relationship between the value of money and the buyer's reservation utility. Consequently, $\partial\phi/\partial\sigma > 0$ and $\partial\phi/\partial r < 0$.

We now turn to normative considerations. We measure social welfare by the discounted sum of utilities of buyers and sellers,

$$\mathcal{W} = \sigma(1-\beta)^{-1}M \int_{\varepsilon_R}^{\infty} [\varepsilon u(q_\varepsilon) - c(q_\varepsilon)]dF(\varepsilon),$$

where $M \in (0,1)$ and q_ε is the output traded in a match with idiosyncratic shock ε. (The net aggregate utility from consuming and producing the general good in the CM is zero.) In this situation, since a change in M affects the *extensive margin*—the number of trade matches—an increase in M raises welfare. This extensive margin result disappears when money is perfectly divisible. A change in M, however, has no effect on the *intensive margin*—the quantity produced in a particular trade match. In terms of efficient allocations, a social planner would choose ε_R^* and q_ε^* such that

$$\varepsilon_R^* = 0$$
$$\varepsilon u'(q_\varepsilon^*) = c'(q_\varepsilon^*).$$

The social planner would like agents to trade in all matches, and the quantities traded should equalize the marginal utility of consumption of the buyer with the marginal disutility of production of the seller.

In contrast, in equilibrium, $\varepsilon_R > \varepsilon_R^* = 0$. Buyers do not trade in matches when they have a low valuation for the seller's output. Hence, for low values of ε, there is a no-trade inefficiency. When $\varepsilon = \varepsilon_R$, by definition $\varepsilon_R u(q) - c(q) = 0$. However, when the socially efficient level of output is produced, we get $\varepsilon_R u(q_{\varepsilon_R}^*) - c(q_{\varepsilon_R}^*) > 0$. In this situation, agents trade too much from a social perspective, i.e., $q > q_{\varepsilon_R}^*$. Finally, for values of ε sufficiently large, agents trade too little from a social perspective, i.e., $q < q_\varepsilon^*$.

To explain the no-trade and too-much-trade inefficiencies, consider a buyer's consumption decision when his preference shock is in a neighborhood of ε_R, see Figure 5.3. If $\varepsilon = \varepsilon_R$, the buyer is just indifferent between consuming q units of the good in exchange for his unit of money and not trading. The seller is also indifferent between producing q units for one unit of money and not trading. If ε is slightly below ε_R, then no trade takes place, because the bid price of money—the quantity, $q_b = c^{-1}(\phi)$, the seller is willing to produce for one unit of

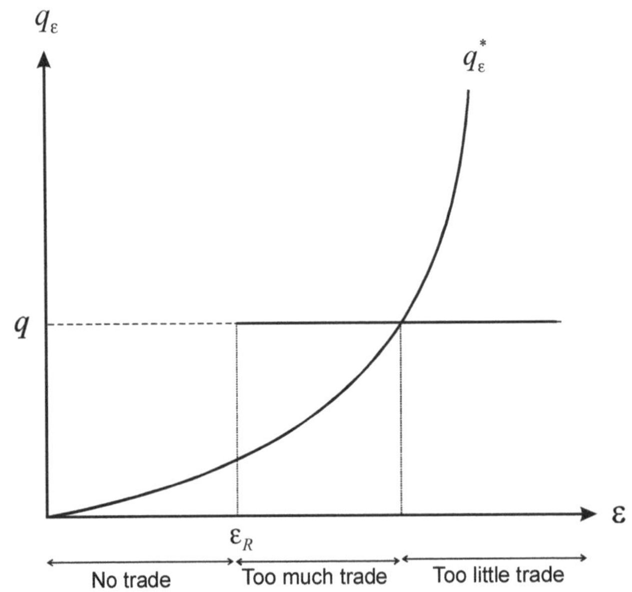

Figure 5.3
Trade inefficiencies with indivisible money

money—is smaller than the ask price of money—the quantity of output, $q_a = u^{-1}(\phi/\varepsilon)$, the buyer demands to give his unit of money up. In contrast, if ε is slightly above ε_R, then the bid price of money is larger than its ask price and, because of the buyer-takes-all bargaining protocol, a trade takes place at the bid price. The consumed quantity, however, is inefficiently large because of the buyer's low valuation for the seller's output.

In summary, the following inefficiencies arise when money is indivisible, see Figure 5.3:

1. The number of trade matches is too low if there is a shortage of currency, i.e., when $M < 1$.
2. For low values of ε, buyers do not trade even though it would be socially optimal to do so.
3. For intermediate values of ε, agents trade too much.
4. For high values of ε, agents trade too little.

5.1.2 Indivisible Money and Lotteries

When agents don't trade, $\varepsilon < \varepsilon_R$, or when they trade too much, $q > q^*_\varepsilon$, they could achieve a pairwise superior outcome in the DM if the buyer could somehow give up only a fraction of his unit of money to the seller. But this is not feasible since each unit of money is indivisible. The buyer could, however, overcome this indivisibility by offering to transfer his unit of money with some probability by using a lottery device.

Since output is perfectly divisible, a lottery is only needed for the money balances that are transferred from the buyer to seller in the DM. When lotteries are used, a take-it-or-leave-it offer by the buyer can be compactly described by $(q_\varepsilon, \varsigma_\varepsilon)$, where q_ε is the amount of the DM good produced by the seller, and $\varsigma_\varepsilon \in [0,1]$ is the probability that the buyer transfers his unit of money to the seller.

Consider a match between a buyer and a seller. The take-it-or-leave-it offer that a buyer with one indivisible unit of money makes to the seller, $(q_\varepsilon, \varsigma_\varepsilon)$, solves the problem,

$$\max_{q,\varsigma} [\varepsilon u(q) - \varsigma\phi] \quad \text{s.t.} \quad -c(q) + \varsigma\phi = 0, \quad \text{and} \quad 0 \leq \varsigma \leq 1. \tag{5.10}$$

The buyer maximizes his expected surplus, which is the difference between his utility of consumption in the DM minus the probability that he gives up his unit of money times the value of money in the CM. The offer is such that the seller is indifferent between accepting and rejecting. If $c(q_\varepsilon^*) \leq \phi$, then the solution to (5.10) is,

$$q_\varepsilon = q_\varepsilon^*,$$
$$\varsigma_\varepsilon = \frac{c(q_\varepsilon^*)}{\phi};$$

if $c(q_\varepsilon^*) > \phi$, then the solution is $q_\varepsilon = q = c^{-1}(\phi)$ and $\varsigma = 1$. In contrast to an environment without lotteries, buyers trade in all matches, which implies that $\varepsilon_R = 0$, and they never trade too much, i.e., $q_\varepsilon \leq q_\varepsilon^*$.

Following the same reasoning as above, see (5.5), the value of money is given by the solution to

$$r\phi = \sigma \int_0^\infty [\varepsilon u(q_\varepsilon) - \varsigma_\varepsilon\phi]\, dF(\varepsilon). \tag{5.11}$$

From the seller's participation constraint, $\varsigma_\varepsilon\phi = c(q_\varepsilon)$, (5.11) can be written as

$$r\phi = \sigma \int_0^\infty [\varepsilon u(q_\varepsilon) - c(q_\varepsilon)]\, dF(\varepsilon). \tag{5.12}$$

The opportunity cost of holding money, the left side of (5.12), is equal to the expected match surplus in the DM, the right side of (5.12).

Denote $\tilde{\varepsilon}$ as the threshold for the preference shock below which agents trade the socially efficient quantity, i.e., $\tilde{\varepsilon}$ is implicitly defined by $q^*_{\tilde{\varepsilon}} = c^{-1}(\phi)$. Then, (5.12) can be rewritten as

$$r\phi = \sigma \int_0^{\tilde{\varepsilon}} [\varepsilon u(q^*_\varepsilon) - c(q^*_\varepsilon)]\, dF(\varepsilon) + \sigma \int_{\tilde{\varepsilon}}^{\infty} \left[\varepsilon u \circ c^{-1}(\phi) - \phi\right] dF(\varepsilon). \quad (5.13)$$

It is easy to check that (5.13) determines a unique $\phi > 0$: the left side is linear in ϕ, while the right side is strictly increasing and concave in ϕ.

In the absence of lotteries, if a buyer's valuation for a good is very low, then the ask price of money, $q_a = u^{-1}(\phi/\varepsilon)$, is larger than the bid price of money, $q_b = c^{-1}(\phi)$, and consequently, no trade takes place. This no-trade inefficiency disappears with lotteries because when a buyer's valuation for a good is low, he simply delivers the indivisible money with a probability greater than zero, but less than one, in exchange for a small (and efficient) amount of the good. In the absence of lotteries, if the buyer's valuation for the good is low, but not too low, then the ask price of money is smaller than the bid price and, consequently, exchange takes place but at a level of DM output that is larger than the efficient level. Similar to the no-trade inefficiency, the too-much-trade inefficiency disappears with lotteries on indivisible money since the buyer can effectively deliver, in expected terms, less than a unit of money for the efficient level of DM output. Finally, note that lotteries do not eliminate the "too-little-trade" inefficiency, which occur when $\varepsilon > \tilde{\varepsilon}$.

If the support of the distribution of the preference shocks is not too large, it is quite possible to have agents trade the socially-efficient quantity in all matches. Consider the case where $\varepsilon = 1$ in all matches. We saw that with divisible money the output is too low provided that $r > 0$. With indivisible money and lotteries, the value of money is determined by (5.13),

$$\begin{aligned} r\phi &= \sigma\left[u(q^*) - c(q^*)\right] \text{ if } \phi > c(q^*), \\ &= \sigma\left[u \circ c^{-1}(\phi) - \phi\right] \text{ otherwise.} \end{aligned} \quad (5.14)$$

The determination of the equilibrium is illustrated in Figure 5.4.

It can easily be checked that $q = q^*$ if and only if the left side of (5.14) evaluated at $\phi = c(q^*)$ is less than the right side of (5.14) evaluated at $q = q^*$; i.e.,

$$c(q^*) \leq \frac{\sigma}{r+\sigma} u(q^*).$$

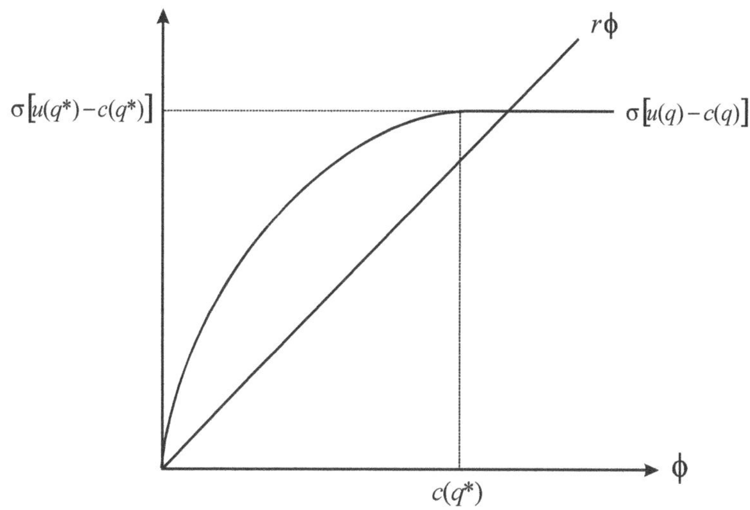

Figure 5.4
Equilibrium with indivisible money and lotteries

If the allocation $(q,y) = (q^*,c(q^*))$ is incentive-feasible in the environment with money—see Chapter 4.1 and the definition of $\mathcal{A}^M$ in (4.7)—or in a credit environment with public record keeping—see Chapter 2.3 and the definition of $\mathcal{A}^{PR}$ in (2.24)—then it can be implemented as an equilibrium in a monetary economy with indivisible money by a take-it-or-leave-it offer when buyers can use lotteries. Note, however, there is still an inefficiency due to the shortage of currency, $M < 1$, which reduces the number of matches.

5.1.3 Divisible Money

In this section we examine the case of a perfectly divisible money to see how these allocations compare to those with indivisible money. We will focus our attention on stationary equilibria.

When money is divisible and a buyer's preference shock is ε, a take-it-or-leave-it offer by the buyer in the DM is now a pair $(q_\varepsilon, d_\varepsilon)$, where q_ε is the amount of the search good produced by the seller, $d_\varepsilon \in [0,m]$ is the transfer of money from the buyer to the seller, and m is the buyer's money holdings. The buyer solves the problem

$$\max_{q,d} [\varepsilon u(q) - d\phi] \quad \text{s.t.} \quad -c(q) + d\phi = 0, \quad \text{and} \quad 0 \le d \le m. \tag{5.15}$$

This problem is analogous to (5.10). If $c(q^*_\varepsilon) \le m\phi$, then the solution is

$$q_\varepsilon = q^*_\varepsilon,$$
$$d_\varepsilon = \frac{c(q^*_\varepsilon)}{\phi};$$

if $c(q^*_\varepsilon) > m\phi$, then $q_\varepsilon = q = c^{-1}(m\phi)$ and $d = m$. The divisibility of money, just like the use of lotteries when money is indivisible, removes the no-trade and too-much-trade inefficiencies; i.e., $\varepsilon_R = 0$ and $q_\varepsilon \le q^*_\varepsilon$.

The expected lifetime utility of a buyer in the CM is

$$W^b(m) = \phi m + \max_{m'}\left\{-\phi m' + \beta\sigma\int_0^\infty \left[\varepsilon u(q_\varepsilon) + W^b(m' - d_\varepsilon)\right] dF(\varepsilon) \right. \tag{5.16}$$
$$\left. + \beta(1-\sigma)W^b(m')\right\},$$

where q_ε and d_ε are functions of the buyer's money holdings in the DM, m'. According to (5.16), the buyer readjusts his money holdings in the CM by acquiring $m' - m$ new units, which costs him $\phi(m' - m)$ in terms of the CM good. In the next DM, if the buyer is in a trade match, which occurs with probability σ, then he consumes q_ε units of the DM output and delivers d_ε units of money. Using the linearity of W^b, i.e., $W^b(m) = \phi m + W^b(0)$, and $\phi d_\varepsilon = c(q_\varepsilon)$, the buyer's choice of money holdings is given by the solution to

$$\max_{m\ge 0}\left\{-r\phi m + \sigma\int_0^\infty [\varepsilon u(q_\varepsilon) - c(q_\varepsilon)]\, dF(\varepsilon)\right\}$$
$$= \max_{m\ge 0}\left\{-r\phi m + \sigma\int_0^{\tilde\varepsilon(\phi m)} [\varepsilon u(q^*_\varepsilon) - c(q^*_\varepsilon)]\, dF(\varepsilon)\right. \tag{5.17}$$
$$\left. + \sigma\int_{\tilde\varepsilon(\phi m)}^\infty [\varepsilon u\circ c^{-1}(\phi m) - \phi m)]\, dF(\varepsilon)\right\},$$

where $\tilde\varepsilon$ solves $q^*_{\tilde\varepsilon} = c^{-1}(\phi m)$. The first-order condition with respect to m is

$$\frac{r}{\sigma} = \int_{\tilde\varepsilon(\phi m)}^\infty \left[\frac{\varepsilon u'\circ c^{-1}(m\phi)}{c'\circ c^{-1}(m\phi)} - 1\right] dF(\varepsilon). \tag{5.18}$$

For market clearing, $m = M$, which implies that (5.18) determines a unique $\phi > 0$.

For any $r > 0$, the right side of (5.18) must be positive, which implies that $q_\varepsilon < q^*_\varepsilon$ for some ε even if the support of $F(\varepsilon)$ is finite. The divisibility of money does not remove the too-little trade inefficiency. This inefficiency arises because there is a cost of holding real balances due to discounting. If this cost is driven to zero; i.e., $r \to 0$, then the right side of (5.18) is zero, meaning that real balances are sufficiently large to trade the socially-efficient quantities in all matches. Moreover, because money is divisible, it is feasible to endow all buyers with M units money at the beginning of a period, even when $M < 1$. Therefore, when money is perfectly divisible money, currency shortages cannot occur and the number of trade matches is at its maximum.

5.2 Portability of Money

We now consider another important physical attribute of a medium of exchange: portability. Portability describes the ease with which an object can be carried to where it is needed, i.e., into bilateral meetings. We equate portability with the cost of bringing money into the DM, and assume that at the beginning of each period, the buyer incurs a real cost $\kappa > 0$ for each unit of money he holds.

As in Chapter 3.1, the buyer's choice of money holdings in the CM of period t is given by

$$\max_{m \geq 0} \left\{ -\phi_t m + \beta V^b_{t+1}(m) \right\}. \tag{5.19}$$

However, the value of being a buyer in the DM is now given by

$$V^b_{t+1}(m) = -\kappa m + \sigma \max_{d \in [0,m]} \left[u \circ c^{-1}(\phi_{t+1} d) - \phi_{t+1} d \right] + \phi_{t+1} m + W^b_{t+1}(0), \tag{5.20}$$

where we have used $W^b_{t+1}(m) = \phi_{t+1} m + W^b_{t+1}(0)$ and, from the buyer-takes-all bargaining assumption, $q_{t+1} = c^{-1}(\phi_{t+1} d)$. The first term on the right side of (5.20) is new and represents the proportional cost from holding m units of money. Substituting this expression for $V^b_{t+1}(m)$ into (5.19), the choice of money holdings is now given by the solution to,

$$\max_{m \in \mathbb{R}_+} \left[-\left(\frac{\phi_t / \phi_{t+1}}{\beta} - 1 \right) \phi_{t+1} m - \kappa m + \sigma \max_{d \in [0,m]} \left[u \circ c^{-1}(\phi_{t+1} d) - \phi_{t+1} d \right] \right]. \tag{5.21}$$

The cost of accumulating $\phi_{t+1} m$ units of real balances has two components: the part due to inflation and discounting, $(\phi_t / \phi_{t+1} - \beta)/\beta$, and the part due to the imperfect portability of money, κ / ϕ_{t+1}. Provided that $(\phi_t/\phi_{t+1} - \beta)/\beta + \kappa/\phi_{t+1} > 0$, it is costly to hold money and, hence, $d = m$. Substituting $c(q_t) = \phi_t m$ into (5.21) and rearranging, we get

$$\max_{q_{t+1}\in\mathbb{R}_+} \left\{ -\left(\frac{\phi_t/\phi_{t+1}}{\beta} - 1 + \frac{\kappa}{\phi_{t+1}} \right) c(q_{t+1}) + \sigma \left[u(q_{t+1}) - c(q_{t+1}) \right] \right\}. \tag{5.22}$$

Assuming an interior solution, the first-order condition to this problem is given by

$$\frac{u'(q_{t+1})}{c'(q_{t+1})} = 1 + \frac{\phi_t/\phi_{t+1} - \beta}{\sigma\beta} + \frac{\kappa}{\sigma\phi_{t+1}}. \tag{5.23}$$

The money market clears if $m = M$, which implies from (5.23),

$$\phi_t = \beta\phi_{t+1} \left\{ \sigma \left[\frac{u'(q_{t+1})}{c'(q_{t+1})} - 1 \right] + 1 \right\} - \beta\kappa, \tag{5.24}$$

where $q_{t+1} = \min\left[q^*, c^{-1}(\phi_{t+1}M)\right]$. This equation generalizes (3.16) in an obvious way. Even though $\phi_t = \phi_{t+1} = 0$ does not solve (5.24), it should be noticed that for all $\kappa > 0$ there is a nonmonetary equilibrium, where the solution to (5.22) is a corner solution, and agents dispose of their money holdings since they have no value and they are costly to hold.

A monetary equilibrium is a sequence $\{\phi_t\}_{t=0}^{\infty}$ solving the first-order difference equation (5.24), where ϕ_t is bounded. Consider first stationary equilibria where money is valued, $q_t = q_{t+1} = q^{ss} > 0$. At a steady state, (5.24) can be rewritten as

$$\frac{u'(q^{ss})}{c'(q^{ss})} = 1 + \frac{r}{\sigma} + \frac{\kappa M}{\sigma c(q^{ss})}. \tag{5.25}$$

In contrast to the previous section, the steady-state monetary equilibrium with positive output, if it exists, is no longer unique. To see this, we assume the following functional forms and parameter values: $c(q) = q$, $u(q) = q^{1-a}/(1-a)$, $a < 1$, and $\sigma = 1$. Then, (5.25) can be rewritten as

$$(q^{ss})^{1-a} = (1+r)\, q^{ss} + \kappa M. \tag{5.26}$$

The left side is a strictly concave function of q^{ss} while the right side is linear with a positive intercept. Consequently, if κ is below a threshold, then there are two solutions $q^{ss} > 0$ to (5.26); otherwise, there is no monetary equilibrium. Suppose, for example, that $a = 1/2$. Then the two solutions to (5.26) are

$$q_H^{ss} = \left(\frac{1 + \sqrt{1 - 4(1+r)\kappa M}}{2(1+r)} \right)^2$$

$$q_L^{ss} = \left(\frac{1 - \sqrt{1 - 4(1+r)\kappa M}}{2(1+r)} \right)^2,$$

if $4(1+r)\kappa M < 1$.

The intuition behind the multiplicity of steady-state equilibria is that the cost of holding one unit of real balances is κ/ϕ, which depends on the value of money. If the value of money is low, then the cost of holding real balances is high. Buyers, then, do not want to accumulate large real balances, which makes the value of money low. A similar logic applies to the case where the value of money is high.

A monetary equilibrium is more likely to exist if the candidate object to be used as money is not too costly to hold. Hence, fundamentals matter for the use of an object as a means of payment. But good fundamentals are not sufficient for an object to be used as money since the liquidity property of the object—its acceptability—is endogenous. The following example illustrates this point.

Suppose there are two objects that can serve as a means of payments, called object 1 and object 2. There is a fixed supply of both objects, M_1 and M_2. The storage cost of object 1 is κ_1 and the storage cost of object 2 is κ_2. For simplicity, assume $u(q) = 2\sqrt{q}$, $c(q) = q$, and $\sigma = 1$. A steady-state monetary equilibrium where only object 1 is used as money exists if $4(1+r)\kappa_1 M_1 < 1$; a steady-state monetary equilibrium where only object 2 is used if $4(1+r)\kappa_2 M_2 < 1$. If $\kappa_2 M_2 > \kappa_1 M_1$, then whenever there exists an equilibrium where object 2 is used as money, there is also an equilibrium where object 1 is used as money, but the reverse is not true. In this sense, object 1 is more likely to be used as means of payment than object 2. An object is more likely to be used as means of payment if the aggregate cost from carrying this object is low; i.e., the storage cost per unit must not be too large and the object must not be too abundant. Still, the object with a large storage cost can emerge as the medium of exchange because of self-fulfilling beliefs.

Consider now the effects of an increase in κ on the high steady-state equilibrium. It can easily be checked that there is a negative relationship between q_H^{ss} and κ. When fiat money is more costly to carry, the DM output falls. Moreover, money is no longer neutral. As M increases, q_H^{ss}

decreases since carrying money involves additional real resources. The comparative statics at the low steady-state monetary equilibrium are opposite to those at the high steady-state monetary equilibrium.

Finally, let's consider nonstationary equilibria. If we adopt the same functional form and parameter values as above, then (5.24) becomes

$$q_t = \beta \left(q_{t+1}\right)^{1-a} - \beta \kappa M. \tag{5.27}$$

As illustrated in Figure 5.5, there are a continuum of trajectories leading to the low steady-state monetary equilibrium, while there is a unique trajectory—the stationary one—that leads to the high steady-state monetary equilibrium.

We have considered the case where $\kappa \geq 0$. If $\kappa < 0$, then the medium of exchange can be interpreted as a commodity money, or a real asset since it provides its holder with a real dividend. (We study this case in great details in Chapters 13 and 14.) When $\kappa < 0$, the phase line in Figure 5.5 would shift down and intersect the horizontal axis at a positive value of q_t. In contrast to the case where $\kappa > 0$, the phase line for

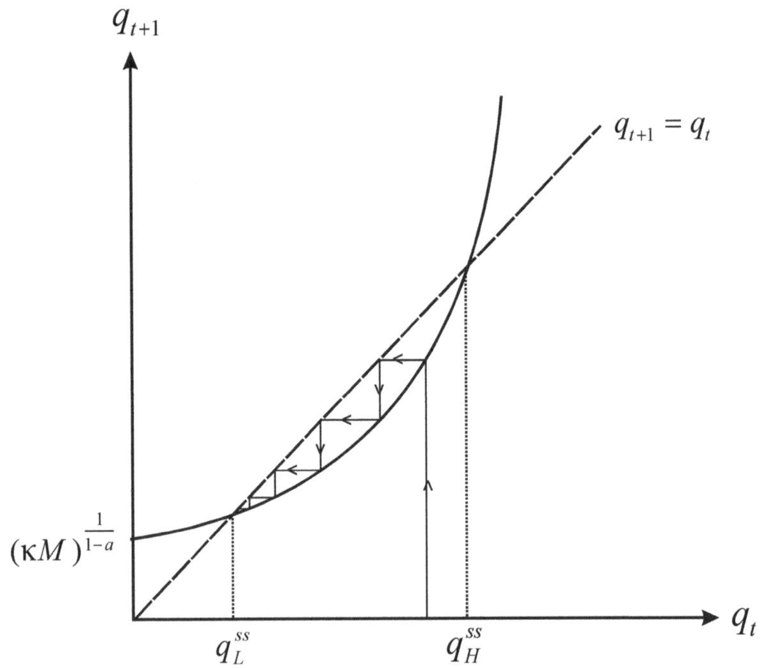

Figure 5.5
Dynamic equilibria under imperfect portability

$\kappa < 0$ would have a unique intersection with the 45°-line. As well, when $\kappa < 0$, a nonmonetary equilibrium no longer exists. This is because the price of money, ϕ, is bounded below by its fundamental value, which is given by $-\beta\kappa/(1-\beta) > 0$. If the price of money was below its fundamental value, say zero, then (5.22) would have no solution, as agents would demand an infinite amount of money in order to enjoy its real dividend.

Moreover, for the functional form used as above, there is a unique monetary equilibrium, and it is the stationary monetary equilibrium, $q_t = q_{t+1} = q^{ss}$. In a fiat monetary system, there is a continuum of equilibria that lead to the autarkic outcome, and in all these equilibria the value of money at any date is lower than what would prevail in a stationary (monetary) equilibrium. As a result, the stationary monetary equilibrium dominates, from a social welfare perspective, any of the inflationary equilibria. Since the presence of a commodity component eliminates any equilibria where money loses value overtime, there is a welfare gain associated with having a commodity money system.

5.3 Recognizability of Money

In this section, we analyze the implications of money being imperfectly recognizable. In particular, sellers are unable to distinguish genuine money from counterfeit money in the DM, and buyers can produce counterfeit bills at night, after the CM has closed. There is a fixed cost $k > 0$ associated with engaging in counterfeiting activities each night, but the marginal cost of producing a counterfeit note is zero. Moreover, the technology to produce counterfeits becomes obsolete after one period, so whenever an agent chooses to produce counterfeits at night he must incur the cost k. Counterfeits produced in period $t-1$ are all detected and confiscated as agents enter the CM of period t. Hence, the only venue to pass a counterfeit bill produced in period $t-1$ is the DM of period t. A seller in the DM of period t would never knowingly accept a counterfeit since it is worthless at night.

The terms of trade in the DM are determined by take-it-or-leave-it offers by buyers. Sellers do not observe the money holdings of the buyers or their decisions to produce counterfeits. To simplify the presentation, we assume that there are no search frictions in the DM, $\sigma = 1$.

The strategic interactions between a buyer—who decides the amount of genuine money to hold, whether to produce counterfeits and the terms of trade—and a seller—who must accept or reject the buyer's offer—can be represented by a simple game, where the buyer makes the first three moves. Things can be simplified a bit by noting that since the marginal cost of producing counterfeits is zero, a buyer will not need (or want) to accumulate genuine money if he produces counterfeits. Moreover, since money is costly to hold, i.e., $r > 0$, if a buyer decides to accumulate genuine money balances, then he will never hold more than what he intends to spend; i.e., $m = d$. Consequently, two of the buyer's moves can be collapsed into a one, in which he chooses either to produce d counterfeits or to accumulate d units of genuine money.

At the beginning of the CM of period $t-1$, the buyer anticipates that he will make the offer (q,d) in the subsequent DM. If the buyer chooses to accumulate d units of genuine money balances in the CM, given his anticipated offer (q,d), then, assuming this offer is accepted, his lifetime utility is

$$-\phi d + \beta \left[u(q) + W^b(0) \right]. \tag{5.28}$$

If, instead, he chooses to counterfeit d units of money, then his lifetime utility is

$$-k + \beta \left[u(q) + W^b(0) \right]. \tag{5.29}$$

The buyer is willing to accumulate genuine money if (5.28) exceeds (5.29), or if

$$\phi d \leq k. \tag{5.30}$$

Suppose that in the DM a seller is in a match with a buyer that offers terms of trade (q,d). Recall that the seller is unable to distinguish between genuine and counterfeit money. If (5.30) holds, then the seller concludes that the buyer is holding genuine money. The seller's reasoning is that (5.30) implies that a buyer's strategy of offering terms of trade (q,d) and producing d counterfeits is dominated by the strategy of offering (q,d) and accumulating genuine money; i.e., if (5.30) holds, then a buyer has no incentive to use counterfeit notes independent of the seller's decision to accept or reject. If, however, (5.30) does not hold, then we assume that the seller believes that the buyer in the match is holding counterfeit notes, and he rejects the offer. Therefore, a necessary, but not sufficient, condition for the seller to accept offer (q,d) is that (5.30) holds.

An equilibrium offer, (q,d), by the buyer must satisfy (5.30), as well as the seller's participation constraint. The buyer's equilibrium offer satisfies

$$(q,d) = \arg\max\{-(1-\beta)\phi d + \beta[u(q) - \phi d]\} \tag{5.31}$$

$$\text{subject to } -c(q) + \phi d \geq 0 \tag{5.32}$$

$$\text{and } \phi d \leq k, \tag{5.33}$$

where (5.31) is the buyer's expected utility, net of the continuation value $W^b(0)$, (5.32) is the seller's participation constraint, and (5.33) is the no-counterfeiting constraint.

The problem that determines the equilibrium terms of trade (q,d), (5.31)-(5.33), is similar to the one of the previous section, except that it incorporates an additional constraint, (5.33). Constraint (5.32) ensures that the seller will accept the offer with probability one, while constraint (5.33) ensures that the buyer has no incentive to produce counterfeit notes. The latter constraint places an upper bound on how many real balances the buyer can transfer. The amount of real balances that the buyer can transfer to the seller is equal to the cost of producing counterfeits.

A noteworthy property of this equilibrium is that no counterfeiting ever takes place. The buyer cannot benefit from counterfeiting since the seller understands the buyer's incentives, and accordingly adjusts his acceptance rule. We now examine this idea in greater detail. Suppose that constraint (5.33) does not bind, i.e., k is large; then the offer (q,d) is given by the solution to (5.31)-(5.32), i.e., (q,d) solves

$$\frac{u'(q)}{c'(q)} = 1 + r \tag{5.34}$$

$$\phi d = c(q). \tag{5.35}$$

Suppose, on the other hand, constraint (5.33) binds, i.e., k is small. Then the offer (q,d) is given by the solution to the constraints (5.32)-(5.33), i.e., (q,d) solves,

$$q = c^{-1}(k), \tag{5.36}$$

$$\phi d = k. \tag{5.37}$$

We can now define what we mean by k being large or small. There is a critical value for k, denoted $\bar{k}$, such that the solutions to (5.34) and (5.36) coincide; that is, the critical value $\bar{k}$ is given by the solution to

$$u'\left[c^{-1}(\bar{k})\right] = (1+r)c'\left[c^{-1}(\bar{k})\right]. \tag{5.38}$$

Therefore, if $k \geq \bar{k}$, then the constraint (5.33) does not bind and the buyer's offer (q,d) is given by the solution to (5.34) and (5.35); if, however, $k < \bar{k}$, then constraint (5.33) binds and the buyer's offer (q,d) is given by (5.36) and (5.37). In either case, the clearing of the money market implies $d = M$, which pins down the value of money ϕ.

The determination of the equilibrium level of the DM good production, q, is illustrated in Figure 5.6. When constraint (5.33) is not binding, or equivalently if $k > \bar{k}$, the equilibrium q is given by the intersection of the horizontal line representing the cost of holding money, $1+r$, and a downward sloping curve representing the function $u'(q)/c'(q)$. Provided that $u'(0)/c'(0) > 1+r$, which is true since we assume that $u'(0) = \infty$ and $c'(0) = 0$, there exists a monetary equilibrium. This condition is independent of k. The threat of counterfeiting does not make the monetary equilibrium less likely to prevail. In particular, if ϕM is sufficiently small it would be more costly for a buyer to incur the fixed cost to produce counterfeit money rather than going into the CM to produce ϕM units of the general good.

When constraint (5.33) binds, i.e., $k < \bar{k}$, the equilibrium level q is given by the intersection of the horizontal line representing the cost of holding money, $1+r$, and the vertical line emanating from (5.36),

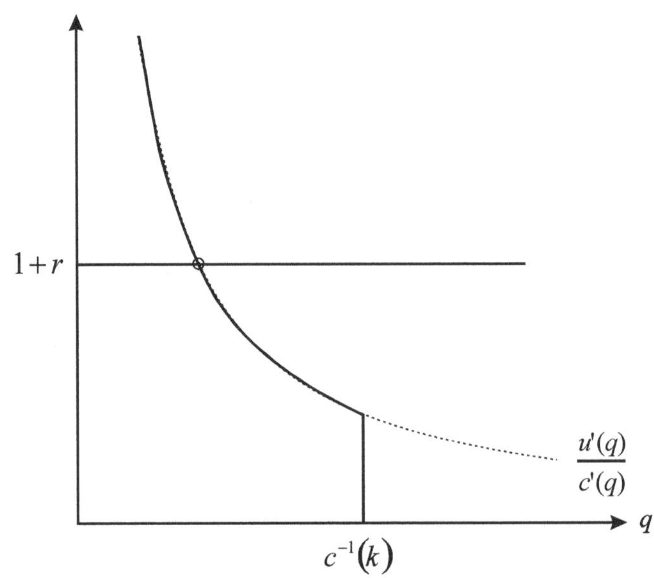

Figure 5.6
Determination of the equilibrium

$q = c^{-1}(k)$. In this case, note that $\partial q/\partial k > 0$ and $\partial \phi/\partial k > 0$. Diagrammatically speaking, an increase in k shifts the vertical line to the right, resulting in a higher production level of the DM good; as a result, money becomes more valuable. An implication of this result is that policies designed to make it harder to counterfeit fiat money, e.g., the use of special paper and ink, the frequent redesign of the currency and so on, can have real effects *even when counterfeiting does not take place.*

5.4 Further Readings

The first generations of search-theoretic models of monetary exchange assumed indivisible money and currency shortage. This includes Diamond (1984), Kiyotaki and Wright (1989, 1991, 1993), Shi (1995), Trejos and Wright (1995), and Wallace and Zhou (1997). Rupert, Schindler, and Wright (2000) extend the work of Trejos and Wright (1995) by generalizing agents' production choices and bargaining power. Berentsen, Molico, and Wright (2002) and Lotz, Schevchenko, and Waller (2007) introduced lotteries into the analysis. Shevshenko and Wright (2004) show that one can obtain partial acceptability of a means of payment by introducing heterogeneity across agents. Rupert, Schindler, and Wright (2000) provide a survey of search-theoretic models with indivisible money.

Camera and Corbae (1999) and Taber and Wallace (1999) relax the unit upper bound on money holdings and study price dispersion and divisibility of money. Molico (2006) has one of the first models with perfectly divisible goods and money. Redish and Weber (2011) build a random matching monetary model with two indivisible coins with different intrinsic values and study small change shortages.

The assumption of indivisible money in the presence of match specific preference shocks, and its implications for the efficiency of monetary exchange, are studied in Berentsen and Rocheteau (2002, 2003). Match specific shocks have also been used in Shi's (1997) large household model by Shi and Peterson (2004) and in the search labor literature by Marimon and Zilibotti (1997) and Pissarides (2000, Ch. 6).

Kiyotaki and Wright (1989) and Aiyagari and Wallace (1991) studied how storage costs affect the ability of a commodity to be used as means of payment. See also Kehoe, Kiyotaki, and Wright (1993) and Renero (1998, 1999).

The role of money as a recognizable asset has been emphasized in Brunner and Meltzer (1971) and Alchian (1977) and it has been formalized by King and Plosser (1986), Williamson and Wright (1994), and Banerjee and Maskin (1996). Williamson and Wright showed that money could be valued in a double-coincidence-of-wants environment if sellers have private information about the quality of the good they hold. Kim (1996) extended the model to endogenize the fraction of informed agents (who can recognize the quality of goods) in the economy. Trejos (1999) studied a version of the Williamson-Wright model with divisible goods, and Berentsen and Rocheteau (2004) considered the case with both divisible money and divisible goods. In order to establish the robustness of the monetary institution, Cuadras-Morato (1994) and Li (1995) showed that a good can be used as a medium of exchange even if its quality is uncertain.

Kultti (1996) and Green and Weber (1996) were the first papers to study counterfeiting of currency in a random-matching model with exogenous prices. Williamson (2002) investigated the counterfeiting of banknotes in a random-matching model with indivisible money but divisible output. Nosal and Wallace (2007) and Li and Rocheteau (2008) introduced lotteries as a proxy for divisible money and showed that it allows buyers to signal the quality of their money holdings. Cavalcanti and Nosal (2007) and Monnet (2005) adopted a mechanism design approach and focused on pooling allocations. A model of counterfeiting with perfectly divisible money, as examined in this chapter, was initially studied in Rocheteau (2008) and Li and Rocheteau (2009). These papers provide a more detailed analysis of the seller's beliefs. Quercioli and Smith (2015) introduced multiple denominations and a costly decision to verify currency in a non-monetary counterfeiting model.

Appendix

A1. Optimal Choice of Money Holdings in the Indivisible Money Model

We establish that the buyer has no incentive to accumulate more than one unit of money so that the support for the money distribution across buyers is $\{0,1\}$. Consider a buyer in a match holding m units of money with a preference shock ε. The buyer is willing to spend at least $d \in \{1,...,m\}$ units of money if

$$\varepsilon u \circ c^{-1}(\phi d) - \phi d \geq \varepsilon u \circ c^{-1}\left[\phi(d-1)\right] - \phi(d-1).$$

According to the inequality above, the buyer's surplus from spending d units of money is greater than the surplus from spending $d-1$ units of money. Define $\varepsilon_{R,d}$ the threshold for ε above which it is optimal to spend the dth units of money,

$$\varepsilon_{R,d} = \frac{\phi}{u \circ c^{-1}(\phi d) - u \circ c^{-1}\left[\phi(d-1)\right]}.$$

From the concavity of $u \circ c^{-1}(\phi d)$, it is easy to check that $\varepsilon_{R,d}$ is increasing in d.

Let $v(m)$ denote the expected surplus of the buyer in the DM from holding m units of money. It is given by

$$v(m) = \sigma \sum_{d=1}^{m-1} \int_{\varepsilon_{R,d}}^{\varepsilon_{R,d+1}} \left[\varepsilon u \circ c^{-1}(\phi d) - \phi d\right] dF(\varepsilon)$$
$$+ \sigma \int_{\varepsilon_{R,m}}^{\infty} \left[\varepsilon u \circ c^{-1}(\phi m) - \phi m\right] dF(\varepsilon).$$

Consequently, the utility gain associated with the mth units of money is

$$v(m) - v(m-1) = \sigma \int_{\varepsilon_{R,m}}^{\infty} \left\{\varepsilon\left[u \circ c^{-1}(\phi m) - u \circ c^{-1}(\phi(m-1))\right] - \phi\right\} dF(\varepsilon).$$

Using the definition of $\varepsilon_{R,m}$,

$$v(m) - v(m-1) = \sigma\left[u \circ c^{-1}(\phi m) - u \circ c^{-1}(\phi(m-1))\right]$$
$$\int_{\varepsilon_{R,m}}^{\infty} (\varepsilon - \varepsilon_{R,m})\, dF(\varepsilon).$$

Using integration by parts,

$$v(m) - v(m-1) = \sigma\left[u \circ c^{-1}(\phi m) - u \circ c^{-1}(\phi(m-1))\right] \int_{\varepsilon_{R,m}}^{\infty} 1 - F(\varepsilon) d\varepsilon.$$

Using the concavity of $u \circ c^{-1}(\phi m)$ and the fact that $\varepsilon_{R,m}$ is increasing in m, $v(m) - v(m-1)$ is decreasing with m.

Since the cost of holding an additional unit of money is $r\phi$, it is optimal to hold m units of money if

$$v(m) - v(m-1) \geq r\phi$$
$$v(m+1) - v(m) \leq r\phi$$

Using the definitions of $\varepsilon_{R,m}$ and $\varepsilon_{R,m+1}$, these inequalities can be rewritten as

$$\sigma \int_{\varepsilon_{R,m}}^{\infty} 1 - F(\varepsilon)d\varepsilon \geq r\varepsilon_{R,m}$$
$$\sigma \int_{\varepsilon_{R,m+1}}^{\infty} 1 - F(\varepsilon)d\varepsilon \leq r\varepsilon_{R,m+1}.$$

In the case of a currency shortage, $M < 1$, the first inequality holds at equality for $m = 1$, and the second inequality is satisfied from the fact that $\varepsilon_{R,m}$ is increasing in m, i.e., $\varepsilon_{R,2} > \varepsilon_{R,1}$.

A2. The Shi-Trejos-Wright Model of Indivisible Money

In Chapter 5.1.1 we presented a model with a currency shortage and indivisible money. A related model was first proposed by Shi (1995) and Trejos and Wright (1995). The environment in those models is similar to the one we consider, except that there is no centralized market where agents can readjust their money holdings. Moreover, individual money holdings are restricted to the set $\{0, 1\}$; i.e., an agent cannot accumulate more than one unit of money. An agent holding one unit of money is called a buyer, while the agent without money is called a seller.

The model is in continuous time. The Poisson arrival rate of a single-coincidence meeting—an encounter between an agent and a producer of a good he wishes to consume—is denoted by σ. This means that on a small interval of time of length dt, the probability of a single-coincidence meeting is σdt. For simplicity, we rule out double-coincidence-of-wants meetings, where two matched agents would like to consume their partner's output. For example, suppose there are $J \geq 3$ types of goods and J types of agents, where agents are evenly divided across types. An agent to type j produces good j but wishes to consume good $j+1$ (modulo J). Then, the probability of a single-coincidence meeting is $\sigma = \frac{1}{J}$ and the probability of a double-coincidence-of-wants meeting is zero. Finally, agents are matched at random. So conditional on a meeting, the probability that the partner holds one unit of money is M while the probability that he doesn't hold money is $1 - M$.

Given these assumptions, we can write the flow Bellman equations of a buyer and a seller as follows:

$$rV_1 = \sigma(1-M)\left[u(q) + V_0 - V_1\right] \tag{5.39}$$

$$rV_0 = \sigma M\left[-c(q) + V_1 - V_0\right]. \tag{5.40}$$

These flow Bellman equations (5.39) and (5.40) can be interpreted as asset pricing equations where V_1 and V_0 are the values of an asset in two different states. The left side of the flow Bellman equation represents the opportunity cost of holding the asset, while the right side is the expected return from holding the asset (dividend flows and capital gains or losses). According to (5.39), a buyer meets a seller who produces a good that he wishes to consumes with Poisson arrival rate $\sigma(1-M)$. In this event, the buyer enjoys the utility from consuming q units of the output produced by the seller, $u(q)$, and transfers his indivisible unit of money to the seller, which generates a capital loss $V_1 - V_0$. According to (5.40) a seller meets a buyer who wishes to consume the good he produces with probability σM. In this event, the seller suffers the disutility of producing q units of output, $c(q)$, but he receives one unit of money, which generates a capital gain of $V_1 - V_0$.

The quantity of output produced in a bilateral match, q, is determined by a take-it-or-leave-it offer by the buyer. The offer makes the seller indifferent between accepting and rejecting a trade,

$$c(q) = V_1 - V_0. \tag{5.41}$$

It follows from (5.40) that $V_0 = 0$, the seller gets no surplus from a trade. Substituting $V_1 = c(q)$ into (5.39), we obtain

$$c(q) = \frac{\sigma(1-M)}{r+\sigma(1-M)}u(q). \tag{5.42}$$

A steady-state equilibrium is a q that solves (5.42). First, $q = 0$ is a solution to (5.42). There always exists a nonmonetary equilibrium. Second, since the left side of (5.42) is convex and the right side of (5.42) is strictly concave, there is a unique $q > 0$ that solves (5.42). So there is a unique steady-state monetary equilibrium. It is easy to check that $\frac{\partial q}{\partial \sigma} > 0$, $\frac{\partial q}{\partial M} < 0$, and $\frac{\partial q}{\partial r} < 0$. So, in contrast to the model presented in Chapter 5.1.1, the quantity traded in bilateral matches is affected by the supply of money. This difference can be explained by the fact that in the Shi-Trejos-Wright model, a buyer is matched at random with any agent from the whole population, whereas in Chapter 5.1.1 buyers are only matched with sellers. Except for this difference, the two models have the same equilibrium condition.

We now describe the dynamics of the Shi-Trejos-Wright model. For simplicity, we adopt the normalization $c(q) = q$. The flow Bellman equations become

$$rV_1 = \sigma(1 - M)[u(q) + V_0 - V_1] + \dot{V}_1 \tag{5.43}$$

$$rV_0 = \sigma M[-q + V_1 - V_0] + \dot{V}_0 \tag{5.44}$$

where a dot over a value function indicates a time derivative. Equations (5.43)-(5.44) are generalizations of (5.39)-(5.40) where the expected return of the asset also includes the change of the value of the asset over time, the last terms on the right sides of (5.43) and (5.44). From the buyer-take-all assumption, (5.41), $q = V_1$ and $V_0 = 0$. Substituting $V_1 = q$ into (5.43), we obtain the following first-order differential equation:

$$\dot{q} = [r + \sigma(1 - M)]q - \sigma(1 - M)u(q). \tag{5.45}$$

The phase line associated with this differential equation, the right side of (5.45), goes through the origin and is strictly convex. It is represented in Figure 5.7. It has a unique intersection with the horizontal axis such that $q > 0$, which corresponds to the unique steady-state monetary equilibrium. The initial value of money cannot be greater than the positive steady-state value since otherwise the value of money would become unbounded and the match surplus would be negative. If the initial value of money is lower than the positive steady-state value, then the value of money decreases over time. Consequently, there are a continuum of nonstationary monetary equilibria converging to the nonmonetary equilibrium.

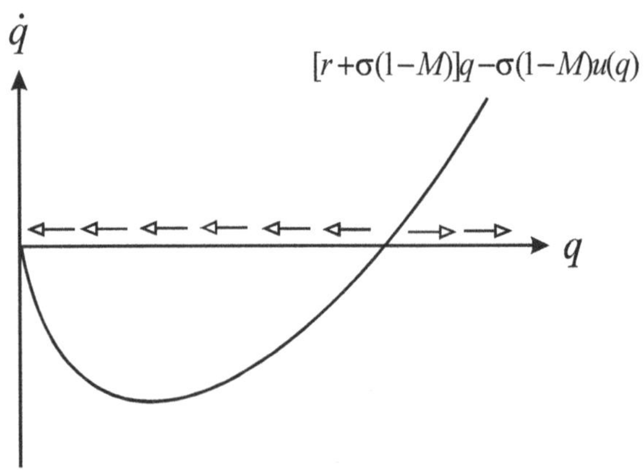

Figure 5.7
Dynamics of the Shi-Trejos-Wright model

6 The Optimum Quantity of Money

"Milton Friedman's (1969) doctrine regarding the 'optimum quantity of money'—according to which an optimal monetary policy would involve a steady contraction of the money supply at a rate sufficient to bring the nominal interest rate down to zero—is undoubtedly one of the most celebrated propositions in modern monetary theory, probably *the* most celebrated proposition in what one might call "pure" monetary theory (...) [T]he general equilibrium literature has shown that the question of optimal monetary policy cannot be settled—in the sense of producing explicit quantitative advice for policy makers—without needing to specify in relative detail a model of how money is used in the economy."

Michael Woodford, "The Optimum Quantity of Money," in *Handbook of Monetary Economics* (1990, Chapter 20)

By not specifying the frictions that make monetary exchange useful, reduced-form models do not fully articulate how monetary policy affects the economy. In contrast, we adopt the strategy of constructing economic environments where the presence of fiat money is essential, and the societal benefits of monetary exchange are explicitly spelled out. By following this strategy, we are able to show that the same frictions that support positively valued fiat money can also provide new insights for monetary policy.

So far, we have only considered a one-time change in the money supply. In this chapter, we go one step further and assume that monetary policy takes the form of a constant money growth rate. By changing the rate of growth of money supply, the monetary authority is able to affect the rate of return of currency and, hence, agents' incentives to hold real balances. This, in turn, has implications for equilibrium allocations, and society's welfare.

Under standard trading protocols, e.g., bargaining, price taking, price posting, optimal monetary policy is characterized by the so-called

Friedman (1969) rule. According to this policy prescription, the policy maker must engineer a rate of return for money that compensates agents for the cost of holding money balances. This can be accomplished by contracting the money supply at a rate approximately equal to the agent's rate of time preference. By doing this, the policy maker can drive the cost associated with holding real balances to zero, which in turn implies that agents will hold sufficient money balances to maximize their surpluses from trade.

While the Friedman rule is optimal under most trading protocols, it does not necessarily implement socially efficient allocations. For example, under the Nash bargaining solution, the quantities traded are inefficiently low even when the cost of holding real balances is driven to zero.

The optimality of the Friedman rule is a robust finding across various kinds of monetary models, but it is rarely observed in practice. In order to reconcile this observation with the predictions of our model, we first discuss the incentive-feasibility of the Friedman rule when the government's coercive power (to tax) is limited. Even though the policymaker would like to implement the Friedman rule through a contraction of the money supply, this policy may not be feasible. In particular, agents may choose not to participate in the market in order to avoid incurring the tax that is required to make the money supply contract at the optimal rate.

An alternative explanation for the non observance of the Friedman rule in practice is that it may not be the optimal monetary policy for some environments. We provide two extensions of the model where running the Friedman rule is feasible, but not optimal. In the first extension, we suppose that the number of trades in the decentralized market depends on the relative numbers of buyers and sellers in the market, and agents can choose whether to be buyers or sellers. It will turn out that the number of matches is inefficient because agents ignore the effect of their participation decisions on other agents' matching probabilities. Because inflation acts as a tax on participation, a deviation from the Friedman rule may be optimal.

In the second extension, we suppose that buyers receive uninsurable idiosyncratic productivity shocks. A growing money supply allows some redistribution of real balances among buyers, and provides some valuable insurance. Hence, in this situation, a strictly positive inflation rate is socially desirable.

We will conclude this chapter with a discussion of the welfare cost of inflation in this class of models. In the special case where buyers have all the bargaining power, the welfare cost of inflation coincides with the area underneath money demand. If sellers have some bargaining power, then the cost of inflation is larger. We will also see that the cost of inflation depends on trading frictions and externalities.

6.1 Optimality of the Friedman Rule

In this section, we determine the optimal growth rate of the money supply in the context of the divisible monetary economy studied in Chapter 3. Let M_t represent the aggregate stock of money at the beginning of period t, and $\gamma \equiv M_{t+1}/M_t$ the gross growth rate of the money supply. Money is injected, or withdrawn, in a lump-sum fashion in the competitive market, CM, at night. If $\gamma > 1$, then injections of money occur at the beginning of the CM; if $\gamma < 1$, then money is withdrawn at the end of the CM. If $\gamma < 1$, we assume that the government has sufficient coercive power to force agents to pay the lump-sum taxes.

The government is only able to tax in the CM because agents are anonymous in the decentralized market, DM, during the day, and, hence, cannot be monitored or coerced at that time. Since agents have quasi-linear preferences in the CM—preferences which eliminate wealth effects—we will assume without loss of generality that only buyers receive the monetary transfers. The timing of events is illustrated in Figure 6.1.

We focus on steady-state equilibria, where the real value of the money supply is constant over time, i.e., $\phi_t M_t = \phi_{t+1} M_{t+1}$. Note that the gross rate of return on money is $\phi_{t+1}/\phi_t = M_t/M_{t+1} = \gamma^{-1}$.

Since the price of money is not constant across time, we will write the value functions, V^b and W^b, as functions of the buyer's real balances, $z = \phi_t m_t$, expressed in terms of the general good traded in the current period. The transfer of real balances in a bilateral match from the buyer to the seller in the DM will be denoted d. (We keep the same notation as the one used for the transfer of nominal money balances in the previous chapter.) The value function of the buyer at the beginning of the CM, $W^b(z)$, satisfies

$$W^b(z) = \max_{x,y,z'} \left\{ x - y + \beta V^b(z') \right\} \tag{6.1}$$

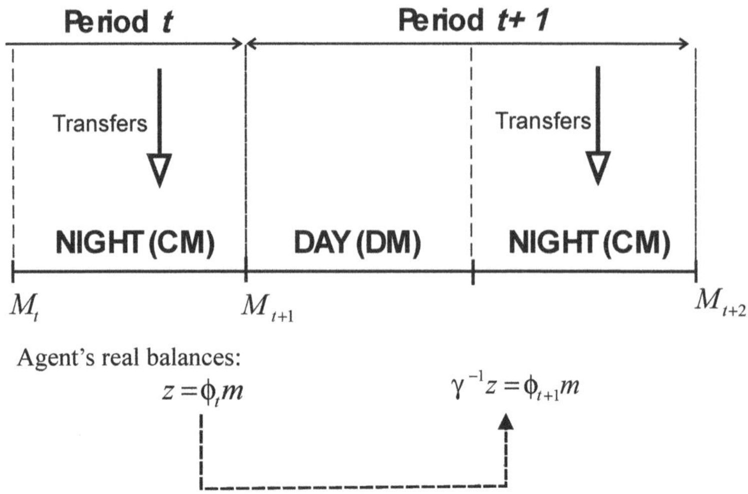

Figure 6.1
Timing of a representative period

subject to

$$x+\phi_t m' = y+z+T \tag{6.2}$$

$$z' = \phi_{t+1}m', \tag{6.3}$$

where T corresponds to the real value of the lump-sum transfer from the government; i.e., $T=\phi_t(M_{t+1}-M_t)=(\gamma-1)\phi_t M_t$. The first constraint, (6.2), represents the buyer's budget constraint in the CM and (6.3) describes the real value that m' units of money will have in the next period, $t+1$. Substituting $m'=z'/\phi_{t+1}$ from (6.3) into (6.2), and then into (6.1), and recalling that $\phi_t/\phi_{t+1}=\gamma$, the buyer's value function at the beginning of the CM can be expressed as

$$W^b(z) = z+T+\max_{z'\geq 0}\left\{-\gamma z' + \beta V^b(z')\right\}. \tag{6.4}$$

According to (6.4) the lifetime expected utility of a buyer in the CM is the sum of his real balances, the lump-sum transfer from the government, and his continuation value at the beginning of the next DM minus the investment in real balances. Recall that in order to hold z' real balances in the next DM, the buyer must obtain $\gamma z'$ real balances this CM.

The buyer's value function at the beginning of the DM, $V^b(z)$, is given by

$$V^b(z) = \sigma \left\{ u[q(z)] + W^b[z - d(z)] \right\} + (1-\sigma) W^b(z)$$
$$= \sigma \{ u[q(z)] - d(z) \} + W^b(z), \tag{6.5}$$

where we use the linearity of $W^b(z)$ in going from the first equality to the second. According to (6.5), the lifetime expected utility of a buyer at the beginning of the DM is the sum of his expected surplus in the DM plus his continuation value in the subsequent CM. The trade surplus in the DM is the difference between the utility of consumption and the transfer of real balances. We will consider trading protocols where the terms of trade (q, d) depend only on the real balances of the buyer.

The buyer's problem can be simplified by substituting $V^b(z)$ from (6.5) into (6.4), i.e.,

$$\max_{z \geq 0} \{ -iz + \sigma \{ u[q(z)] - d(z) \} \}, \tag{6.6}$$

where $1 + i = (1+r)\gamma$ and i can be interpreted as the nominal rate of interest on an illiquid bond; i.e., the bond cannot be used as a medium of exchange in the DM. If a one-period (illiquid) nominal bond issued in period $t-1$ pays one dollar in period t, then the dollar price of the newly-issued bonds in period $t-1$ is ω_{t-1}, where ω_{t-1} solves $\omega_{t-1}\phi_{t-1} = \beta\phi_t$; i.e., agents are indifferent between holding and not holding the bond. Hence, $\omega_{t-1} = \beta\phi_t/\phi_{t-1} = \beta/\gamma$. The nominal interest rate is then $i = (1/\omega_{t-1}) - 1 = (\gamma/\beta) - 1 = (1-r)\gamma - 1$, as stated above. The buyer chooses his real balances so as to maximize his expected surplus in the DM minus the cost of holding money balances, where the cost of holding money, i, is a function of the rate of time preference and the inflation rate.

Because it is costly to hold money, buyers will not hold more money than they intend to spend in a bilateral match in the DM; this implies that $d = z$. As a benchmark, we assume that the terms of trade are determined by a take-it-or-leave-it offer by the buyer. Since $i > 0$, buyers will not hold more real balances than what is necessary to compensate the seller for the efficient level of output, i.e., $z \leq c(q^*)$. The quantity traded in a match satisfies $c(q) = z$ whenever $z \leq c(q^*)$. Since there is a one-to-one relationship between q and z when $z \leq c(q^*)$, the buyer's problem (6.6) can be rewritten as a choice of q, i.e.,

$$\max_{q \in [0, q^*]} \{ -ic(q) + \sigma [u(q) - c(q)] \}. \tag{6.7}$$

The first-order (necessary and sufficient) condition to the buyer's problem (6.7) is

$$\frac{u'(q)}{c'(q)} = 1 + \frac{i}{\sigma}. \tag{6.8}$$

This equation is similar to (3.14) in Chapter 3, except the rate of time preference, r, has been replaced by the nominal interest rate, i. In Chapter 3, the money supply was assumed to be constant, which implies that $\gamma = 1$ and, hence, $i = r$. The cost of holding real balances, i, generates a wedge between the marginal utility of consuming and the marginal cost of producing q that is proportional to the average length of time to complete a trade in the DM, $1/\sigma$. The steady-state solution, q^{ss}, to (6.8) is depicted in Figure 6.2.

From (6.8), it is clear that the optimal monetary policy requires a zero nominal interest rate, $i = 0$, or, equivalently, $\gamma = 1/(1+r) < 1$. As a consequence, prices contract at a rate that is approximately equal to the rate of time preference. This is the so-called Friedman rule. By reducing the cost of holding real balances to zero, buyers will accumulate sufficient real balances in the previous CM so they can purchase the quantity, q^*, that maximizes the gains from trade in the DM. It is also clear from (6.8) and Figure 6.2, that an increase in inflation and hence, i, decreases

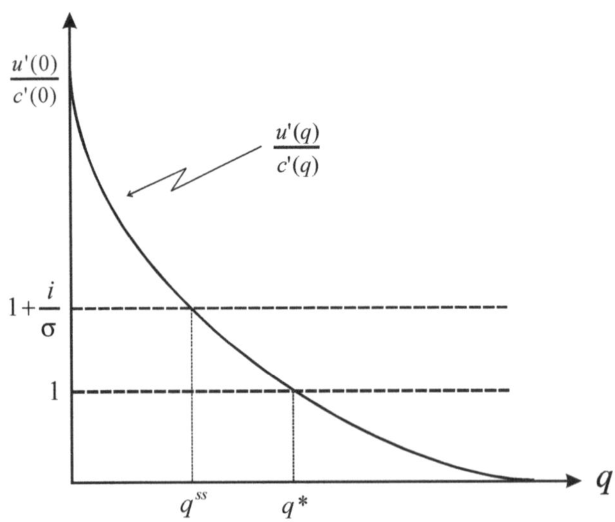

Figure 6.2
Stationary monetary equilibrium under a constant money growth rate

output produced in the DM. In summary, when buyers have all of the bargaining power, the allocation of the monetary equilibrium under the Friedman rule coincides with the socially-efficient allocation of the DM good, $q = q^*$.

6.2 Interest on Currency

We will now show that a policy that generates a rate of return for currency equal to the rate of time preference; i.e., the Friedman rule, does not need to be implemented by a contraction of the money supply. Instead, the policy maker can pay an interest on currency. This is effectively what happens when the central bank pays an interest on reserves.

Suppose that an agent holding m units of money at the beginning of the CM receives $i_m m$ units of money; i.e., the interest on currency is equal to $i_m \geq 0$. The budget constraint of the government is

$$T + i_m \phi_t M_t = \phi_t (M_{t+1} - M_t). \tag{6.9}$$

According to (6.9) the government finances its lump-sum transfer to buyers, T, and the interest payment on currency by the increase in the money supply.

The value of a buyer in the CM is

$$W^b(z) = \max_{x,y,z'} \left\{ x - y + \beta V^b(z') \right\} \tag{6.10}$$

subject to

$$x + \phi_t m' = y + z(1 + i_m) + T \tag{6.11}$$

$$z' = \phi_{t+1} m'. \tag{6.12}$$

From (6.11) the buyer receives a lump-sum transfer, T, and an interest payment on his money balances that he holds at the beginning of the CM, $i_m z$. The latter implies that the real value of one unit of money in the DM, measured in terms of the general good, is $(1 + i_m)\phi_t$. From (6.10)-(6.12), the buyer's value function at the beginning of the CM can be expressed as,

$$W^b(z) = T + (1 + i_m)z + \max_{z' \geq 0} \left\{ -\gamma z' + \beta V^b(z') \right\}, \tag{6.13}$$

where

$$V^b(z) = \sigma \left[u(q_t) - c(q_t) \right] + W^b(z), \tag{6.14}$$

and $c(q_t) = \min[(1+i_m)z, c(q^*)]$ from the buyer-takes-all assumption. From (6.14) the buyer enjoys the whole surplus from a match. The value of being seller in the CM is simply $W^s(z) = (1+i_m)z$.

From (6.13) and (6.14) the buyer's choice of money balances solves

$$\max_{z \geq 0} \{-\gamma z + \sigma\beta[u(q_t) - c(q_t)] + \beta(1+i_m)z\}. \tag{6.15}$$

We must assume that $\gamma \geq \beta(1+i_m)$, otherwise the buyer's problem has no solution. Note that the rate of return of currency is $\phi_{t+1}(1+i_m)/\phi_t = (1+i_m/\gamma)$. We focus our attention on stationary equilibria where $\phi_t M_t = \phi_{t+1}M_{t+1}$ or $\phi_t/\phi_{t+1} = M_{t+1}/M_t = \gamma$. The buyer's problem, (6.15), can be rearranged as

$$\max_{z \geq 0} \left\{ -\left(\frac{\gamma - \beta(1+i_m)}{\beta}\right) z + \sigma[u(q_t) - c(q_t)] \right\}. \tag{6.16}$$

Notice from (6.16) that the interest on currency reduces the cost of holding money, $[\gamma - \beta(1+i_m)]/\beta$. The first-order condition, assuming an interior solution, is

$$\frac{u'(q)}{c'(q)} = 1 + \sigma\frac{\gamma - \beta(1+i_m)}{\beta(1+i_m)}. \tag{6.17}$$

It is clear from (6.17) that in order to achieve the socially efficient allocation the policymaker must choose a combination for γ and i_m that satisfies

$$\gamma = \beta(1+i_m). \tag{6.18}$$

If $i_m = 0$, i.e., there is no interest on currency, then $\gamma = \beta$ and the money supply must contract at a rate that is approximately equal to the rate of time preference.

If for some reason the policy maker wants to avoid a deflation, it can set $\gamma = 1$. From (6.18) $\beta(1+i_m) = 1$ or, equivalently, $i_m = r$. Hence, the quantity traded will be at the efficient level if the policy maker sets the interest on currency equal to the rate of time preference, r, and maintains a constant money supply (through lump-sum taxes). This implies that the Friedman prescription for optimal monetary policy need not be associated with a contracting money supply.

Finally, if the policy maker does not make any lump-sum transfers (or doesn't levy any taxes); i.e., $T = 0$, then the interest on currency must be financed by an increase in the money supply. From (6.9), we have $i_m = \gamma - 1$ and from (6.17) we get,

$$\frac{u'(q)}{c'(q)} = 1 + r.$$

If the change in the money supply is engineered through proportional transfers to money holders, i.e., by interest on money holdings, then the quantity traded in a bilateral match is independent of the interest on currency and will be inefficiently low due to agents' impatience.

6.3 Friedman Rule and the First Best

When buyers receive the entire surplus from trade, the Friedman rule implements the efficient allocation, q^*. We want to check the robustness of this result by considering alternative trading protocols for the DM. We will see that the Friedman rule need not implement the efficient allocation for some trading protocols.

Let's first consider the generalized Nash bargaining solution. The Nash bargaining solution is appealing because it has strategic foundations; i.e., there are explicit alternating-offer bargaining games that generate the same outcome. The terms of trade, (q,d), are determined by the solution to

$$\max_{q,d}[u(q)-d]^{\theta}[-c(q)+d]^{1-\theta} \quad \text{s.t.} \quad d \leq z, \tag{6.19}$$

where $\theta \in [0,1]$ measures the buyer's bargaining power. Note that (6.19) is identical to (3.26) in Chapter 3.2.2. Since the constraint $d \leq z$ binds in any monetary equilibrium, because buyers do not hold more money than they intend to spend, the solution to (6.19) describes a relationship between q and z, and is given by

$$z = z_{\theta}(q) \equiv \frac{(1-\theta)c'(q)u(q)+\theta u'(q)c(q)}{(1-\theta)c'(q)+\theta u'(q)} = \Theta(q)c(q)+[1-\Theta(q)]\,u(q), \tag{6.20}$$

where

$$\Theta(q) = \frac{\theta u'(q)}{\theta u'(q)+(1-\theta)c'(q)}.$$

The definition of the transfer of real balances, (6.20), is identical to (3.28) in the Chapter 3.2.2, provided that $z \leq \theta c(q^*)+(1-\theta)u(q^*)$. Since there is a one-to-one relationship between q and z, the buyer's choice of real balances can be rewritten as a choice of q, i.e.,

$$\max_{q\in[0,q^*]} \{-iz_{\theta}(q)+\sigma[u(q)-z_{\theta}(q)]\}. \tag{6.21}$$

Note that (6.21) generalizes (3.31), which assumes a constant money supply. From the solution to the bargaining problem, q is no greater than q^*. At the Friedman rule, $i = 0$ and the buyer chooses q to maximize his surplus, $u(q) - z_\theta(q)$. We established in Chapter 3.2.2 that $u'(q^*) - z'_\theta(q^*) < 0$ whenever $\theta < 1$, which implies that the buyer's surplus is decreasing in q, when q is close to q^*. Therefore, to maximize his surplus, a buyer will choose, from a social perspective, an inefficiently low value for q when the cost of holding real balances is zero. This inefficiency is due to a non-monotonicity property of the Nash solution, according to which the buyer's surplus can fall even if the match surplus increases.

The buyer receives his maximum surplus at a value of $q < q^*$ when $\theta < 1$, as illustrated by the middle curve in Figure 6.3, and maximizes his surplus at $q = q^*$ when $\theta = 1$, as illustrated in the top curve. Despite the fact that real balances are too low when $\theta < 1$, the optimal monetary policy is still the Friedman rule. If, for example, $i > 0$, then buyers will choose an even lower amount of real balances, which implies an even lower social welfare.

The non monotonicity property of the Nash solution is crucial for the inability of the Friedman rule to generate the efficient allocation. But it

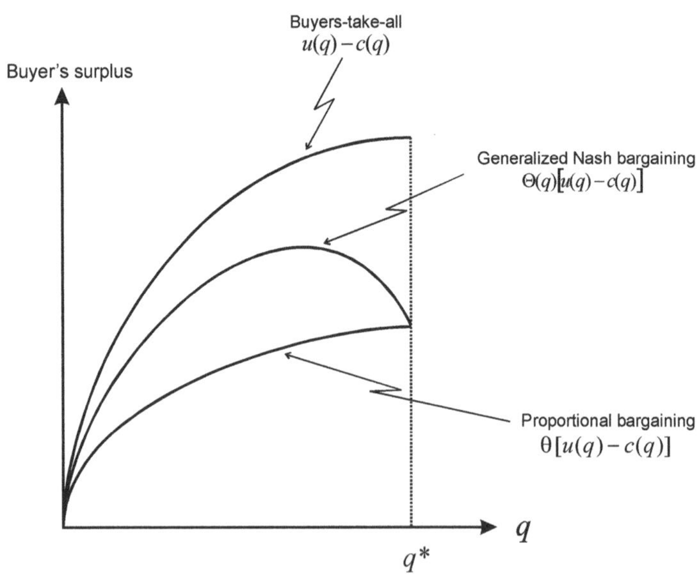

Figure 6.3
Buyer's surplus under alternative bargaining solutions

is not a generic property of all bargaining solutions. To see this, consider the proportional solution, where the buyer gets a constant share θ of the match surplus. With proportional bargaining we have

$$z_{\theta}(q) = \theta c(q) + (1-\theta)u(q).$$

The buyer's choice of real balances under proportional bargaining is given by the solution to

$$\max_{q \in [0,q^*]} \left\{-iz_{\theta}(q) + \sigma\theta\left[u(q) - c(q)\right]\right\}, \tag{6.22}$$

which generalizes (3.41) in Chapter 3.2.3. It is obvious that as i tends to 0, q approaches q^*. So, although buyers do not have all the bargaining power, the fact that the buyer's surplus is increasing in the total match surplus implies that both of these surpluses are maximized at $q = q^*$. See the bottom curve in Figure 6.3. Under proportional bargaining, the Friedman rule is optimal *and* guarantees that the efficient allocation, q^*, will prevail.

Finally, if the terms of trade are determined by either a Walrasian pricing protocol or a competitive posting protocol in the DM, then, as we demonstrated in Chapters 3.3 and 3.4, q is given by the solution to (6.8). Under both of these protocols, the buyer is able to extract the entire marginal contribution of his real balances to the match surplus. As a consequence, the Friedman rule implements the efficient allocation, q^*.

To summarize the results so far, while the Friedman rule is the optimal monetary policy under many trading protocols, it does not always achieve the efficient allocation. If the buyer obtains the marginal social return of his real balances, as is the case under buyers-take-all, competitive price posting or Walrasian price taking, then the Friedman rule implements the efficient allocation. And even if this condition does not hold, the Friedman rule can achieve the socially efficient allocation provided that the buyer's surplus from a trade increases with the total surplus of a match.

6.4 Feasibility of the Friedman Rule

We have assumed that the government has enough coercive power in the CM to force buyers to pay the lump-sum tax required to implement a deflation consistent with the Friedman rule. In this section we weaken the enforcement power of the government. We assume that the government has the ability to collect taxes from buyers in the form of money balances at the end of the CM, but cannot force buyers to produce or accumulate money balances. Consequently, a buyer can avoid paying the lump-sum tax by simply not producing in the CM and, hence, not accumulating money balances. If the buyer does not have enough money balances to pay all his taxes, but has some money balances, the government confiscates everything the buyer has. In this environment, taxes will only be collected from buyers. Since sellers have no incentive to accumulate money, they will never leave the CM with money balances and, hence, cannot be taxed.

If a buyer chooses to hold real balances at the end of the CM, then he will accumulate the optimal money balances defined by problem (6.6) in addition to the lump-sum tax. The reason is straightforward: if the buyer holds some money at the end of the CM but not enough to pay the tax, the government will confiscate all his money. So, if the buyer is going to pay the tax, he might as well accumulate the optimal amount of real balances for the subsequent DM.

A buyer will be willing to pay the lump-sum tax if

$$W^b(z) \geq z + \beta V^b(0), \tag{6.23}$$

where the right side says that the buyer consumes his real balances, z, in the CM and exits with no money balances. We assume that agents do not accumulate tax liabilities across periods, (e.g., the government has no memory). Nevertheless, if it is optimal for the buyer not to pay his taxes in, say, period t, then it is never optimal for him to pay any (current period) tax liabilities in future periods. From (6.4), (6.23) can be expressed as

$$T + \max_{z \geq 0} \left\{ -\gamma z + \beta V^b(z) \right\} \geq \beta V^b(0) = \beta W^b(0),$$

where $T < 0$ when there is a contraction of the money supply.

Using (6.5), this inequality can be rewritten as

$$T + \max_{z \geq 0} \{ -\gamma z + \beta\sigma \{ u[q(z)] - z \} + \beta z \} \geq 0; \tag{6.24}$$

i.e., the expected surplus from trade in the DM, net of the cost of holding money, must be greater than the lump-sum taxes collected by the government. The lump-sum transfer in the CM of period t is $T = (\gamma - 1)\phi_t M_t = (\gamma - 1)Z$, where Z represents aggregate real balances.

Let's assume that buyers make take-it-or-leave-it offers in bilateral matches in the DM. Then, $z = c(q)$ and, from (6.24), q solves $i \equiv (\gamma - \beta)/\beta = \sigma\left(u'(q)/c'(q) - 1\right)$. In equilibrium $z = Z = c(q)$, and (6.24) can be expressed as

$$-(1-\beta)c(q) + \beta\sigma\left[u(q) - c(q)\right] \geq 0.$$

Dividing by β, and rearranging terms, the above inequality holds if and only if

$$c(q) \leq \frac{\sigma}{r+\sigma}u(q), \tag{6.25}$$

The policy that consists in setting i equal to zero is incentive-feasible if

$$c(q^*) \leq \frac{\sigma}{r+\sigma}u(q^*). \tag{6.26}$$

Clearly, if r is sufficiently small, then the Friedman rule will be incentive-feasible; that is, buyers will be willing to pay the tax that is required to generate the optimal deflation.

It is important to point out that condition (6.26) coincides with the condition under which q^* can be implemented under a constant money supply if the trading protocol is chosen optimally, as in Chapter 4. This finding suggests that the Friedman rule is not an essential policy in environments with bilateral trades. Whenever the first-best can be achieved under the Friedman rule, it can also be achieved by a constant money supply, provided the trading protocol is designed appropriately. If (6.26) is violated, then the Friedman rule is not incentive-feasible and there is a lower bound $\underline{\gamma} \in (\beta, 1)$ for the incentive-feasible money growth rate. Notice that this lower bound is less than one, meaning that the optimal feasible policy is characterized by deflation.

6.5 Trading Frictions and the Friedman Rule

Although the Friedman rule is the optimal policy in many monetary environments, it is rarely implemented in practice. We have provided a couple of reasons for this. First, the government may lack the enforcement power required to implement the lump-sum tax needed to generate a deflation. Second, the Friedman rule may not be needed if the trading protocol that determines the terms of trade in the DM is appropriately designed as in Chapter 4. In this section, we describe an environment where the government has sufficient enforcement power to implement the Friedman rule, and the terms of trade are determined by a standard bargaining solution. However, the government may choose not to implement the Friedman rule—even though it is feasible—because it may be suboptimal. The novelty in this section is that DM search frictions are endogenously determined.

We slightly amend our benchmark model to endogenize the composition of buyers and sellers in the DM. We assume that there is a unit measure of ex ante identical agents that can *choose* to be either buyers or sellers in the DM. The decision to become a buyer or seller in period t is taken at the beginning of the previous CM, in period $t-1$. Suppose, for example, that at the beginning of the CM, individuals invest in a (costless) technology that allows them to either produce DM goods or consume them, and it is only possible to invest in one technology. One can think of the DM good as being an intermediate good, where sellers produce the intermediate good and buyers produce a final good that requires the intermediate good as an input. The final good is produced after the buyer and seller split apart. Therefore, the final good cannot be consumed by both the buyer and seller.

We assume that the government has coercive power in the CM to tax individuals. However, since it cannot observe agents' histories in the DM, the government cannot tax buyers and sellers at different rates. Figure 6.4 illustrates the timing of events for a typical period.

Let n denote the fraction of buyers in the DM and $1-n$ the fraction of sellers. The technology that matches buyers and sellers is the following: a buyer meets a seller with probability $1-n$, the fraction of sellers in the population, and a seller meets a buyer with probability n, the fraction of buyers in the population. Therefore, the number of matches in the DM is $n(1-n)$, and it is maximized when $n=1/2$.

As before, W^b (W^s) denotes the value function of an agent in the CM who chooses to be a buyer (seller) the next DM, and V^b (V^s) denotes the

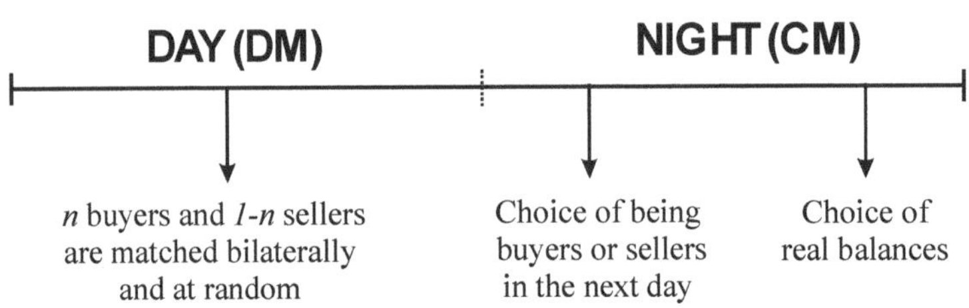

Figure 6.4
Timing of the representative period

value function for a buyer (seller) in the DM. The value function at the beginning of the CM is analogous to (6.4), and satisfies

$$W^j(z) = T + z + \max_{z' \geq 0} \left\{ -\gamma z' + \beta V^j(z') \right\}, \tag{6.27}$$

where $j \in \{b, s\}$. Since buyers spend all their money holdings in the DM if they are matched, the value of being a buyer in the DM satisfies

$$V^b(z) = (1-n)\{u[q(z)] - z\} + \max\left[W^b(z), W^s(z)\right]. \tag{6.28}$$

Substituting (6.28) into (6.27), and using the linearity of $W^b(z)$ and $W^s(z)$, the value of a buyer with z units of real balances at the beginning of the CM must satisfy

$$\begin{aligned} W^b(z) = T + z + &\max_{q \in [0, q^*]} \beta\{-iz(q) + (1-n)[u(q) - z(q)]\} \\ &+ \beta \max\left[W^b(0), W^s(0)\right]. \end{aligned} \tag{6.29}$$

From (6.29), the buyer chooses the quantity to trade in the next DM, taking as given his matching probability, $1-n$. By similar reasoning, the value of being a seller with z units of real balances satisfies

$$\begin{aligned} W^s(z) = T + z + &\beta n[z(q) - c(q)] \\ &+ \beta \max\left[W^b(0), W^s(0)\right]. \end{aligned} \tag{6.30}$$

Equation (6.30) embodies the result that sellers do not carry money balances into the DM—since they do not need them—and that the quantity traded q, or equivalently the buyers' real balances, is taken as given.

Since both $W^b(z)$ and $W^s(z)$ are linear in z, the choice of being a buyer or a seller does not depend on z. In a monetary equilibrium, agents must be indifferent between being a seller or a buyer, otherwise there will be no trade, and fiat money will not be valued. Consequently, we focus on monetary equilibria where $n \in (0,1)$ and $W^b(z) = W^s(z)$. From (6.29) and (6.30), n must satisfy

$$n[z(q) - c(q)] = (1-n)[u(q) - z(q)] - iz(q). \tag{6.31}$$

The left side of (6.31) is the seller's expected surplus in the DM, whereas the right side is the buyer's expected surplus, minus the cost of holding real balances. Hence, in any monetary equilibrium

$$n = \frac{u(q) - (1+i)z(q)}{u(q) - c(q)}. \tag{6.32}$$

Note that for given q, an increase in i reduces the measure of buyers. Intuitively, higher inflation increases the cost of holding real balances and, hence, reduces the incentives to be a buyer in the DM. From (6.29), q solves

$$\max_{q\in[0,q^*]} \{-iz(q) + (1-n)[u(q) - z(q)]\}. \tag{6.33}$$

A steady-state monetary equilibrium is a pair (q,n) such that $q > 0$ is a solution to (6.33) and $n \in (0,1)$ satisfies (6.32). Suppose that $z(q)$ is strictly increasing with q for $q \in (0,q^*)$, and the buyer's objective function in (6.33) is strictly concave and twice continuously differentiable. Then, the equilibrium is unique at the Friedman rule: q solves the first-order condition from (6.33), $u'(q) - z'(q) = 0$, and, given q, the measure of sellers is uniquely determined by (6.32).

Assuming the solution for n is interior, the effects of a change in i in the neighborhood of $i = 0$ are given by

$$\left.\frac{dq}{di}\right|_{i=0} = \frac{z'(q)}{(1-n)[u''(q) - z''(q)]}, \tag{6.34}$$

$$\left.\frac{dn}{di}\right|_{i=0} = -[u(q) - c(q)]^{-1}\left\{\left(\frac{n}{1-n}\right)\frac{z'(q)[u'(q) - c'(q)]}{u''(q) - z''(q)} + z(q)\right\}, \tag{6.35}$$

where n and q are evaluated at $i = 0$. Inflation has a direct effect on the equilibrium allocation by raising the cost of holding real balances and, therefore, by reducing q. The effect of inflation on the measure of buyers, n, is, in general, ambiguous. If, however, the pricing mechanism delivers $q = q^*$ under the Friedman rule, then n decreases with inflation since

$$\left.\frac{dn}{di}\right|_{i=0} = \frac{-z(q^*)}{u(q^*) - c(q^*)} < 0.$$

The intuition here is straightforward: since inflation is a direct tax on agents who hold money, as inflation increases fewer agents want to be buyers. As a result the matching probability of buyers, $1-n$, increases with inflation (close to the Friedman rule). Because there are fewer buyers, they spend their money balances in the DM faster. This is the so-called hot potato effect of inflation.

We measure social welfare by the sum of all trade surpluses in a period, i.e., $\mathcal{W} = n(1-n)[u(q) - c(q)]$. Equivalently, we could divide by $1-\beta$ to consider the discounted sum of those surpluses. Welfare is maximized when the surplus of each match is maximized—which requires $q=q^*$—and when the number of matches in the DM is maximized—which requires $n=1/2$.

Suppose that the trading protocol in the DM implements q^* at the Friedman rule. This would be the case, for example, under proportional bargaining. The first condition for efficiency, $q=q^*$, requires that the Friedman rule is implemented. The second condition for efficiency, $n=1/2$, requires, from (6.32), that

$$\frac{u(q^*)-z(q^*)}{u(q^*)-c(q^*)}=\frac{1}{2}. \tag{6.36}$$

Note that the left side of (6.36) represents the buyer's share of match surplus.

Equation (6.36) turns out to be a restatement of the so-called Hosios condition for efficiency in models with search externalities. Search externalities arise when agents' decisions to participate in a market affect the trading probabilities of other agents in the market. These search externalities are internalized when the elasticity of the matching function with respect to the measure of buyers is equal to the buyer's share in the match surplus. In other words, the buyer's contribution in the creation of matches in the DM must be rewarded by giving buyers a share in the match surplus that is equal to the fraction of matches that buyers are responsible for. The number of matches, i.e., the matching function, is $\Sigma=bs/(b+s)$, where b is the measure of buyers and s is the measure of sellers. Hence, the Hosios condition requires that

$$\frac{d\Sigma/\Sigma}{db/b}=\frac{s}{b+s}=1-n=\frac{u(q^*)-z(q^*)}{u(q^*)-c(q^*)}. \tag{6.37}$$

But, from (6.32), the right side of (6.37) is equal to n, and $n=1-n$ means that $n=1/2$.

The welfare effect of a change in i in the neighborhood of $i=0$ can be evaluated by totally differentiating the social welfare function and using (6.34) and (6.35), i.e.,

$$\left.\frac{d\mathcal{W}}{di}\right|_{i=0}=\frac{u'(q)\left[u'(q)-c'(q)\right]}{\left[u''(q)-z''(q)\right]}\frac{n^2}{1-n}+(2n-1)\,z(q). \tag{6.38}$$

Assuming that $q=q^*$ at the Friedman rule—which is valid under proportional bargaining—we can evaluate the welfare implications of a deviation from the Friedman rule by evaluating the second term in

(6.38), $(2n-1)z(q)$. A deviation will be optimal, i.e., $dW/di|_{i=0} > 0$, if and only if $n > 1/2$. From (6.32), this occurs when the buyer's share of the surplus is greater than one-half, in which case there are too many buyers from a social perspective. Under proportional bargaining, a deviation from the Friedman rule is optimal whenever $\theta \in (0.5, 1)$. In this case, the policy maker is willing to trade off efficiency on the *intensive margin*—the quantities traded in each match—in order to improve the *extensive margin*—the number of trade matches in the DM—by raising inflation. An increase in inflation will increase the number of sellers and decrease the number of buyers.

If, on the other hand, $\theta < 1/2$, then, at the Friedman rule, there are too many sellers. In this situation, a small deviation from the Friedman rule reduces welfare, since it further increases the number of sellers in the economy. Under proportional bargaining, using (6.32),

$$n = \theta - i\frac{[\theta c(q) + (1-\theta)u(q)]}{u(q) - c(q)}.$$

This means that for all $i > 0$, $n < \theta$. Recall that the total number of trades, $n(1-n)$, is increasing in n for all $n < 1/2$. Consequently, if $\theta < 1/2$, then $n < \theta < 1/2$, and the total number of trades is less than what it would be at the Friedman rule, $\theta(1-\theta)$. Consequently, a deviation from the Friedman rule reduces both the number of trades and the quantity traded in each match. So it is unambiguous that the Friedman rule is optimal, even though it fails to achieve a constrained-efficient allocation.

It should be pointed out that these sorts of welfare results depend critically on the DM trading protocol. For example, it can be shown that under a competitive search pricing protocol, the Hosios condition emerges endogenously and, as a consequence, the search externalities are internalized; i.e., the extensive margin is efficient. Therefore, since the competitive search pricing protocol results in an efficient intensive margin under the Friedman rule, a Friedman rule policy can implement an efficient allocation.

The envelope-type argument used above is only valid if the Friedman rule achieves an efficient intensive margin outcome, i.e., if $q = q^*$. The argument would not be valid for the generalized Nash bargaining protocol since $q < q^*$. When $q < q^*$ the first term on the right side of (6.38) is not equal to zero, and, as a result, one cannot evaluate the welfare implications of a departure from the Friedman rule by simply examining the value of n. One can, however, use numerical examples to establish that a deviation from the Friedman rule under the generalized Nash bargaining protocol can be optimal when the buyer's bargaining power is sufficiently high. Hence, the result that a deviation from the Friedman rule can be optimal is robust across different bargaining solutions.

At this point it would be natural to ask if there are other policy instruments that could be used to correct the extensive margin when $n \neq 1/2$ without distorting the intensive margin. If the policy maker could tax buyers and sellers differently, it would not need to resort to inflation to affect agents' incentives to participate in the market. However, because agents' trading roles in the DM are private information, the inflation tax seems to be a natural policy instrument to reduce agents' incentives to be buyers.

6.6 Distributional Effects of Monetary Policy

An inflationary monetary policy can be desirable when the distribution of money balances across agents is not degenerate. Indeed, a positive inflation, engineered by lump-sum money injections, redistributes wealth from the richest to the poorest agents in the economy. If some agents are poor because of uninsurable idiosyncratic shocks, then this redistribution can raise social welfare.

Money injections do not have a distributional effect in our benchmark model because, by construction, the distribution of money holdings across buyers at the end of the CM or beginning of the DM is degenerate. The assumption of quasi-linear preferences—which eliminates wealth effects—along with the fact that all buyers have access to the CM implies that all buyers will choose the same level of money holdings in the CM under the standard trading protocols we have examined.

One can obtain a nondegenerate distribution of money holdings by introducing some heterogeneity across buyers. For example, buyers could differ in terms of their marginal utility of consumption in the DM. Buyers with high marginal utilities of consumption would want to consume more than buyers with low marginal utilities of consumption, and, as a result, would hold larger real balances. In such an environment, however, the Friedman rule is still optimal since each type of buyer holds an amount of real balances that maximize his expected surplus in the DM.

To capture a distributional effect of monetary policy, we modify the benchmark model. We suppose that buyers and sellers live for only three subperiods. They are born at the beginning of the night subperiod and die at the end of the following period. Agents can potentially trade three times: in the CM when they are born, in the DM of the next period, and in the CM just before they die, see Figure 6.5. For simplicity, we assume that agents do not discount across periods, i.e., $r = 0$. This implies that the Friedman rule corresponds to a constant money supply or a zero inflation rate.

The utility function of a buyer is $x_y + u(q) + x_o$, where $x_y \in \mathbb{R}$ is the utility of consumption net of the disutility of production in the CM when young, x_o is the net utility of consumption in the CM when old, and $u(q)$ is the utility of consumption in the DM. Similarly, the utility function of a seller is $x_y - c(q) + x_o$. This overlapping generations structure does not, by itself, alter the allocation relative to the infinitely-lived agents model.

In order to obtain a nondegenerate distribution of money balances across agents, we assume that newly-born buyers differ in terms of their productivity in the first period of their lives. A fraction $\rho \in (0,1)$ of newly-born buyers are productive, while the remaining fraction is unproductive. As a result, newly-born productive buyers can participate in the CM to accumulate money balances, while unproductive ones cannot. Under a constant money supply policy, unproductive buyers do not consume in the DM because they have no money and cannot commit to repay their debt. Moreover, the productivity shocks to newly-born buyers are private information and, as a result, the government is unable to make differentiated transfers to productive and unproductive buyers.

The problem of a productive newly-born buyer, which is similar to (6.6), is

$$\max_{m \geq 0} \{-\phi_t m + \sigma \{u[q(\phi_{t+1} m)] - c[q(\phi_{t+1} m)]\} + \phi_{t+1} m\}. \tag{6.39}$$

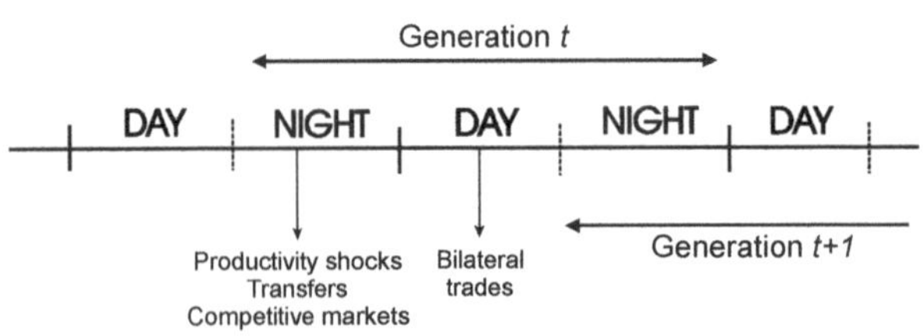

Figure 6.5
Overlapping generations

The productive buyer produces $\phi_t m$ units of the general good in exchange for m units of money in the CM when he is born. If he doesn't meet a seller in the subsequent DM, then he spends his money balances in the CM before he dies; if he does meet a seller, we assume that the buyer captures the entire surplus from the match. Denote $z = \phi_{t+1} m$ as the choice of real balances for a productive buyer born in period t for the subsequent DM. The productive buyer's problem (6.39) can be simplified to read

$$\max_{z \geq 0} \{-(\gamma - 1)z + \sigma \{u[q(z)] - c[q(z)]\}\}. \tag{6.40}$$

The first-order condition for this problem is

$$\frac{u'(q)}{c'(q)} = 1 + \frac{\gamma - 1}{\sigma}. \tag{6.41}$$

Therefore, if the money supply is constant, i.e., $\gamma = 1$, newly-born productive buyers consume q^* units of the DM good if they are matched. However, unproductive newly-born buyers do not consume in the DM since they cannot produce in the CM when they are born.

Assume now that there is a constant, positive inflation, $\gamma > 1$, and that money is injected into the economy through lump-sum transfers to all newly-born buyers in the CM. Let Δ_t denote a transfer at night in period $t - 1$ which can be used in the DM of period t. We have

$$\Delta_t = M_t - M_{t-1} = \frac{\gamma - 1}{\gamma} M_t. \tag{6.42}$$

Let m_t represent the money balances of a buyer in the DM of period t who had access to the CM when he was young. Equilibrium in the money market requires that

$$\rho m_t + (1 - \rho)\Delta_t = M_t. \tag{6.43}$$

The fraction ρ of productive buyers hold m_t units of money while the $1 - \rho$ unproductive buyers hold Δ_t. The sum of the individual money holdings must add up to the money supply, M_t. Substituting Δ_t from (6.42) into (6.43) and rearranging, we get

$$m_t = \frac{M_t}{\rho} \left(\frac{1 + \rho(\gamma - 1)}{\gamma} \right), \tag{6.44}$$

and, from (6.42) and (6.44), we get

$$\Delta_t = \frac{\rho(\gamma - 1)}{1 + \rho(\gamma - 1)} m_t. \tag{6.45}$$

Equation (6.45) implies that $\Delta_t < m_t$: unproductive buyers are poorer than productive ones.

Let $\tilde{q}$ denote the DM consumption of unproductive buyers. Unproductive buyers will spend all of their money balances in the DM because $\Delta_t < m_t$, and productive buyers spend all of their balances. From the buyer-takes-all bargaining assumption, $c(q_t) = \phi_t m_t$ and $c(\tilde{q}_t) = \phi_t \Delta_t$. Hence, (6.45) implies

$$c(\tilde{q}_t) = \frac{\rho(\gamma - 1)}{1 + \rho(\gamma - 1)} c(q_t). \tag{6.46}$$

From (6.46), $\tilde{q}_t < q_t$. As γ increases, q_t decreases through a standard inflation-tax effect, see (6.41). But inflation also affects the distribution of real balances across buyers. Indeed, the dispersion of real balances, as measured by $[c(q_t) - c(\tilde{q}_t)]/c(q_t) = 1/[1 + \rho(\gamma - 1)]$, decreases as γ increases. The policy maker, therefore, faces a trade-off between smoothing consumption across buyers and preserving the purchasing power of real balances.

We treat buyers and sellers from all the different generations symmetrically when we measure social welfare. In this case, the allocations of the general good are irrelevant and welfare can be measured by the sum of all surpluses across matches,

$$\mathcal{W} = \sigma\rho[u(q) - c(q)] + \sigma(1 - \rho)[u(\tilde{q}) - c(\tilde{q})]. \tag{6.47}$$

In the neighborhood of price stability, an increase in inflation only has a second-order effect on the match surpluses of productive buyers, $d[u(q) - c(q)]/d\gamma|_{\gamma=1^+} = 0$. However, it has a first-order effect on the match surpluses of unproductive buyers. Differentiating (6.46) with respect to γ, we get

$$\left.\frac{d\tilde{q}_t}{d\gamma}\right|_{\gamma=1^+} = \frac{\rho c(q^*)}{c'(0)}.$$

The welfare effect of an increase inflation from price stability is, from (6.47), given by

$$\left.\frac{d\mathcal{W}}{d\gamma}\right|_{\gamma=1^+} = \sigma(1 - \rho)\left[\frac{u'(0)}{c'(0)} - 1\right]\rho c(q^*) > 0,$$

since $u'(0)/c'(0) = \infty$. Hence, an increase in inflation from $\gamma = 1$ is welfare-improving because it allows unproductive buyers to consume, while the negative effect on productive buyers' welfare is only of second-order consequence.

6.7 The Welfare Cost of Inflation

Under most of the trading protocols examined thus far—bargaining, price taking, and price posting—inflation distorts allocations by inducing agents to reduce their real balances, and, hence, the quantities they trade in the DM. Qualitatively speaking, inflation typically reduces social welfare. The next step is to quantify this effect in order to determine whether the costs associated with inflation are large or small. If the costs associated with a moderate level of inflation are very small, then inflation will not be an important policy concern.

A typical calibration procedure adopts a representative-agent version of the model studied so far. The CM utility function takes the form $B \ln x - h$, where x is consumption, h is the hours of work, and h hours produces h units of the general good. With the linear specification used so far, CM output would be indeterminate. In contrast, with the quasi-linear preferences, production in the CM maximizes $B \ln x - h$, so $x = B$. One can interpret B as the quantity of goods that do not require money to be traded. The functional forms for utility in the DM are $u(q) = q^{1-\eta}/(1-\eta)$ and $c(q) = q$. The parameters (η, B) are chosen to fit money demand, as described in the model, to the data. The cost of holding real balances, i, is measured by the commercial paper rate and M is measured by $M1$, which is cash plus demand deposits. The model has been calibrated over long time periods, such as 1900-2000. The typical measure of the cost of inflation is the fraction of total consumption—in both the CM and DM—that agents would be willing to give up to have zero inflation instead of 10 percent inflation. The results of existing studies are summarized in Table 1.

Table 6.1
Summary of studies on the cost of inflation

Trading mechanism	Cost of inflation (% of GDP)
Buyers-take-all	1.2-1.4
Nash solution	3.2-3.3
Generalized Nash	up to 5.2
Egalitarian	3.2
Price posting (private info)	6.1-7.2
Price taking	1-1.5
Gen. Nash w/ ext. margin	3.2-5.4
Proportional w/ ext. margin	0.2-5.5
Comp. search w/ ext. margin	1.1

Under the buyer-take-all bargaining solution, the welfare cost of 10 percent inflation is typically between 1 percent and 1.5 per cent of GDP per year. One finds a similar magnitude for the welfare cost of inflation under Walrasian price taking or competitive posting, i.e., competitive search equilibrium. This is a sizeable number.

Graphically, this number is approximately equal to the area underneath the money demand curve. To see this, integrate the inverse (individual) money demand function, which is given by $i(z) = \sigma \{u'[q(z)]/c'[q(z)] - 1\}$, see (6.8), to obtain

$$\int_{z_{1.1}}^{z_1} i(z)dz = \sigma \{u[q(z_1)] - c[q(z_1)]\} - \sigma \{u[q(z_{1.1})] - c[q(z_{1.1})]\},$$

where z_1 represents real balances when $\gamma = 1$ and $z_{1.1}$ represents real balances when $\gamma = 1.1$. The left side of the above expression is the area underneath the individual money demand curve while the right side is the change in society's welfare.

In Figure 6.6 we represent the individual money demand function, $i(z)$. As the nominal interest rate approaches to 0, real balances approach their maximum level, z^*. Under the buyers-take-all bargaining protocol, $z^* = c(q^*)$. Consider two nominal interest rates, $i > 0$ and

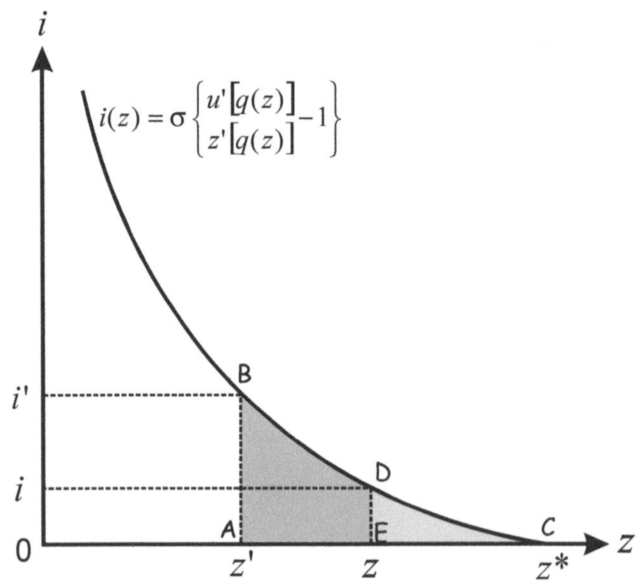

Figure 6.6
Welfare cost of inflation and the area underneath money demand

$i' > i$. The welfare cost from raising the nominal interest rate from i to i' corresponds to the area, $ABDE$, underneath money demand curve. The welfare cost from raising the interest rate from the rate associated with the Friedman rule, zero, to i' is given by the area ABC.

If sellers have some bargaining power, then the welfare cost of inflation is larger. Under the (symmetric) Nash solution or the egalitarian solution (i.e., proportional with $\theta = 0.5$), the welfare cost of 10 percent inflation is between 3 and 4 percent of GDP. The explanation for this large welfare cost of inflation is the following. Whenever $\theta < 1$ and $i > 0$, any bargaining solution generates a holdup problem for money holdings. Buyers incur a cost from investing in real balances in the CM that they cannot fully recover once they are matched in the DM. The severity of this holdup problem depends on the seller's bargaining power, $1 - \theta$, and the average cost of holding real balances, i/σ. As inflation increases, the holdup problem is more severe, which induces buyers to underinvest in real balances.

This argument can be illustrated using the area underneath the money demand function, see Figure 6.7. The inverse (individual)

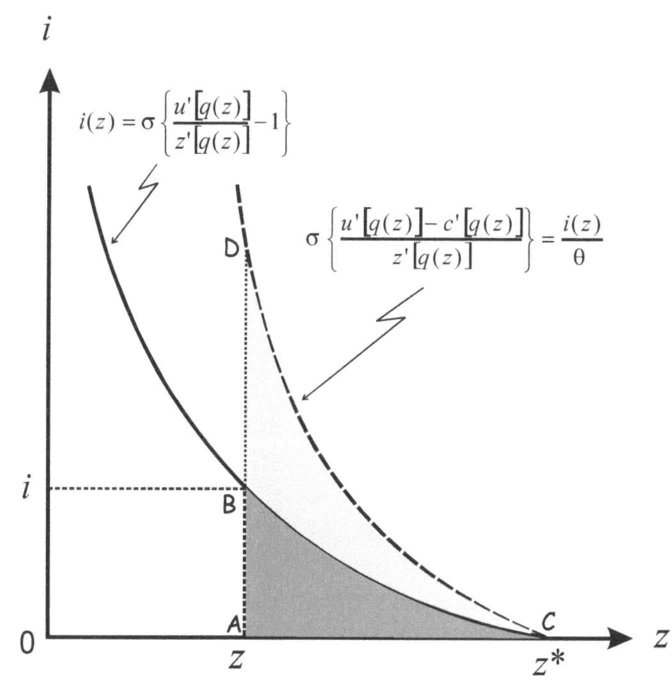

Figure 6.7
Holdup problem and the cost of inflation

money demand function is $i(z)=\sigma\{u'[q(z)]/z'[q(z)]-1\}$. The area underneath money demand is

$$\int_{z_0}^{z_1} i(z)dz=\sigma\{u[q(z_1)]-z_1\}-\sigma\{u[q(z_{1.1})]-z_{1.1}\}.$$

Under proportional bargaining, $u[q(z)]-z=\theta\{u[q(z)]-c[q(z)]\}$, the area underneath the money demand function is

$$\int_{z_0}^{z_1} i(z)dz=\theta\sigma\{u[q(z_1)]-c[q(z_1)]\}-\theta\sigma\{u[q(z_{1.1})]-c[q(z_{1.1})]\}.$$

The private loss due to an increase in the inflation rate corresponds to left side of the above expression. It is equal to a fraction θ of the welfare loss for society, the right side of the above expression.

In Figure 6.7 we represent the individual demand for real balances as well as the social return of those real balances (the dashed curve). The welfare cost from raising the nominal interest rate from 0 to i is given by the area ADC, while the welfare cost to the buyer is the area underneath money demand, ABC. To see this, notice that the marginal social return of fiat money is the increase in society's welfare arising from a marginal increase in real balances. Since social welfare is $\sigma\{u[q(z)]-c[q(z)]\}$, this is equal to

$$\sigma u'[q(z)]-c'[q(z)]\frac{dq}{dz}=\frac{\sigma[u'(q)-c'(q)]}{z'(q)}.$$

The private return to the buyer is

$$i(z)=\sigma\frac{u'(q)-z'(q)}{z'(q)}=\theta\sigma\frac{u'(q)-c'(q)}{z'(q)}.$$

So the individual money demand does not accurately capture the social value of holding money since it ignores the surplus that the seller enjoys when the buyer increases his real balances. If, for example, $\theta=1/2$, the egalitarian solution, then the social welfare cost of inflation is approximately twice the private cost for money holders. This private cost has been estimated to be about 1.5 percent of GDP, so the total welfare cost of inflation for society is then about 3 percent of GDP.

The introduction of an endogenous participation decision, as in Section 6.5, can either mitigate or exacerbate the cost of inflation, depending on agents' bargaining powers. As we saw earlier, in some instances, the cost of small inflation can be negative.

6.8 Further Readings

The result that the optimal monetary policy requires the nominal interest rate to be zero or, equivalently, deflation equal to the rate of time preference, comes from Friedman (1969). Different definitions and interpretations of the Friedman rule are discussed in Woodford (1990). The optimal monetary policy in a search model with divisible money was first studied by Shi (1997a), who showed that the Friedman rule is optimal when agents' participation decisions are exogenous. The ability of the Friedman rule to generate an efficient allocation when the terms of trade are determined according to the Nash solution is discussed in Rauch (2000) and Lagos and Wright (2005). Aruoba, Rocheteau, and Waller (2007) prove that an efficient allocation can be obtained even if sellers have some bargaining power, provided that the bargaining solution is monotonic. Lagos (2010) characterizes a large family of monetary policies that are necessary and sufficient to implement zero nominal interest rates. The optimality of the Friedman rule in different monetary models with heterogenous agents is discussed in Bhattacharya, Haslag, and Martin (2005, 2006) and Haslag and Martin (2007). Berentsen and Monnet (2008), Berentsen, Marchesiani, and Waller (2014), and Williamson (2015a) study the conduct of monetary policy through channel or floor systems. Araujo and Camargo (2008) discuss reputational concerns for the monetary authority.

The policy of paying interest on reserves has been advocated by Friedman (1960), and studied in overlapping generation economies by Sargent and Wallace (1985), Smith (1991) and Freeman and Haslag (1996). Andolfatto (2010) studies the payment of interest on money in a model similar to the one used in this book.

Using a mechanism design approach, Hu, Kennan, and Wallace (2009) show that the Friedman rule is not necessary to obtain good allocations. The incentive-feasibility of the Friedman rule when the government has limited coercive power is discussed in Andolfatto (2008, 2013), Hu, Kennan, and Wallace (2009), and Sanches and Williamson (2010).

The importance of trading frictions and search externalities for the design of monetary policy was first emphasized by Victor Li (1994, 1995, 1997), who established that an inflation tax could be welfare enhancing when agents' search intensities are endogenous. However, his results are subject to the caveat that prices are exogenous. Shi (1997b) found a related result in a divisible-money model where prices are endogenous. Faig (2008), Aruoba, Rocheteau, and Waller (2007), and Rocheteau and Wright (2009) revisit Shi's finding under alternative trading mechanisms. Berentsen, Rocheteau, and Shi (2007) establish that the efficient allocation is achieved when both the Hosios rule and the Friedman rule are satisfied. A necessary condition for a deviation from the Friedman rule to be optimal is that the Hosios condition is violated. Rocheteau and Wright (2005) study the optimal monetary policy in a model with free entry of sellers under alternative pricing mechanisms. Berentsen and Waller (2015) determine the optimal state-contingent monetary policy when there is a congestion externality. Camera, Reed, and Waller (2003) show that search externalities and holdup problems can arise when specialization is endogenous. Shi (1998) and Shi and Wang (2006) calibrate a model with an endogenous extensive margin to the U.S. time series data.

The first attempt to formalize the hot-potato effect of inflation in a search model of money is in Li (1994, 1995, 1997); in his model, prices are exogenous. Lagos and Rocheteau (2005) show that this effect vanishes in a model with divisible money and endogenous prices. Several attempts to resuscitate this hot-potato effect have been provided by Ennis (2009), Nosal (2011), and Liu, Wang, and Wright (2011). Hu and Zhang (2014) show that buyers' search intensity increases with inflation for low inflation rates under an optimal mechanism.

The welfare-improving role of a monetary expansion through distributional effects has been studied by Levine (1991), and in a search-theoretic environment by Deviatov and Wallace (2001), Berentsen, Camera, and Waller (2004, 2005), Molico (2006), Chiu and Molico (2010, 2011), and Rocheteau, Weill, and Wong (2015a,b). Zhu (2008) also shows a beneficial role for a positive inflation in the context of a search model with overlapping generations and strictly concave preferences. Wallace (2014) conjectures that for most pure currency economies there are transfer schemes (not necessarily lump sum) financed by money creation that improve ex ante representative-agent welfare relative to what can be achieved holding the stock of money fixed. Rocheteau, Weill, and Wong (2015a) check this conjecture in the context of a Bewley model in continuous time. Also in a Bewley-type model Lippi, Ragni, and Trachter (2015) determine the conditions under which an expansionary policy is desirable and study state-dependent optimal monetary policy. Boel and Camera (2009) calibrate a New-Monetarist model and show that inflation mostly hurts the wealthier and more productive agents, while those poorer and less productive may benefit from inflation. The converse holds if agents can insure against consumption risk with assets other than money. Berentsen and Strub (2009) study alternative institutional arrangements for the determination of monetary policy in a general equilibrium model with heterogeneous agents, where monetary policy has redistributive effects. Chiu and Molico (2011) show that in the presence of imperfect insurance the estimated long-run welfare costs of inflation are on average 40 to 55 percent smaller compared to complete markets, representative agent economy, and that inflation induces important redistributive effects across households.

The traditional approach to measuring the cost of inflation as the area underneath a money demand curve was developed by Bailey (1956). Lucas (2000) revisited this methodology and provided theoretical foundations using a general equilibrium model where money is an argument of the utility function. Lagos and Wright (2005) were the first to apply this methodology in the context of a model of monetary exchange. Rocheteau and Wright (2009) and Aruoba, Rocheteau, and Waller (2007) evaluate the cost of inflation under alternative trading mechanisms and in the presence of an extensive margin. Ennis (2008) considers a model with price posting under private information, Reed and Waller (2006) consider price-taking, and Faig and Jerez (2006) study competitive posting. Rocheteau (2012) shows that under an optimal mechanism the welfare cost of 10 percent inflation is 0% (of total consumption) whereas Wong (2016) shows that for a general class of preferences the first-best is not implementable in general. Aruoba, Waller, and Wright (2011) study quantitatively the effects of inflation in a search model with capital. Berentsen, Rojas Breu, and Shi (2012) investigate the welfare cost of inflation when liquidity promotes innovation and growth. Boel and Camera (2011) calibrate a model and estimate the welfare cost of anticipated inflation for 23 different OECD countries. Gomis-Porqueras and Peralta-Ava (2010) and Aruoba and Chugh (2008) study the optimality of the Friedman rule in the presence of distortionary taxes. Berentsen, Huber, and Marchesiani (2015) document and explain the breakdown of the empirical relation between money demand and interest rates. Wang (2014) studies the welfare cost of inflation in a monetary economy featuring endogenous consumer search and price dispersion. A review of this literature is provided in Craig and Rocheteau (2008).

7 Information, Monetary Policy, and the Inflation-output Trade-off

"The main finding that emerged from the research of the 1970s is that anticipated changes in money growth have very different effects from unanticipated changes. Anticipated monetary expansions have inflation tax effects and induce an inflation premium on nominal interest rates, but they are not associated with the kind of stimulus to employment and production that Hume described. Unanticipated monetary expansions, on the other hand, can stimulate production as, symmetrically, unanticipated contractions can induce depression."

Robert E. Lucas, "Monetary Neutrality," Nobel Prize Lecture, 1995.

How does money affect output? This is a classic and largely unresolved question in economics, dating back at least to David Hume. In the monetary economy described in Chapter 3, we show that money is *neutral*: a one-time, anticipated change in the money supply has no real effects, and nominal prices vary proportionally with the stock of money. Money is not, however, *superneutral* because a change in the rate of growth of money supply, even if anticipated, has real effects by reducing aggregate real balances, real output, and welfare.

In this chapter, we revisit the relationship between changes in money supply, output, and welfare. In contrast to Chapter 6, we assume that changes in the money supply are random and cannot be fully anticipated. Although the stochastic process driving the money supply is known to all, we make different assumptions regarding what agents know about the value of money at the time of trade. We consider the cases where information regarding the value of money is evenly distributed across agents, and cases where it is not.

We show that if all agents are uninformed about the realization of the money supply, then output is constant and uncorrelated with the changes in the money supply. In contrast, if all agents are fully informed, then output is negatively correlated with inflation: agents can trade larger quantities when the value of money is high.

We will spend most of this chapter analyzing the case where the buyers—the agents who hold and spend money in the decentralized market—have private information regarding the realization of the current money growth rate. In this case, inflation and output are positively correlated. A short-run Phillips (1958) curve emerges even though, in equilibrium, information is fully revealed, and prices are fully flexible. In this situation, buyers signal the high value of fiat money in the low-inflation state by hoarding a large fraction of their real balances, thereby reducing their consumption in bilateral trades. As a result, the model predicts a positive correlation between the velocity of money and inflation.

We demonstrate, by means of examples, that if agents assign a positive probability to a high-inflation state, then a policy maker can raise aggregate output and welfare by increasing the frequency of this high-inflation state. The optimal monetary policy requires the monetary authority to target the money growth rate—to make it deterministic—and to implement a rate of return for fiat money that is equal to the rate of time preference, i.e., the Friedman rule.

If the informational asymmetry between buyers and sellers is reversed; i.e., sellers have some private information regarding the future value of money, then the positive correlation between inflation and output disappears. In this case, buyers spend less money in the high-inflation state in order to reduce the informational rent captured by informed sellers. Hence, the informational structure regarding monetary policy is crucial in order to understand the output effects of unanticipated changes in the money supply.

7.1 Stochastic Money Growth

We extend the pure monetary economy described in Chapters 3 and 6. Let M_t represent the stock of money at the beginning of period t, and $\gamma_t \equiv M_{t+1}/M_t$ the gross growth rate of the money supply in period t. Money is injected or withdrawn in a lump-sum fashion in the centralized market, CM. This implies that in period t, the money supply in the decentralized market, DM, is M_t, and in the CM, after the monetary transfers have taken place, is M_{t+1}. We assume that agents always know the value of γ_t at the beginning of the CM and, without loss of generality, that only buyers receive the monetary transfers.

The value of fiat money in period t, ϕ_t, refers to the amount of CM goods that can be purchased by a unit of fiat money in period t. The novelty in this chapter is the assumption that the money growth rate, γ_t, is random. In each period, the money growth rate can take one of two values: high, $\bar{\gamma}$, or low, $\underline{\gamma} < \bar{\gamma}$, where the probability of a high money growth rate is α, i.e.,

$$\gamma_t = \begin{cases} \bar{\gamma} \text{ with probability } \alpha \in (0,1) \\ \underline{\gamma} \quad \text{with probability } 1-\alpha \end{cases}.$$

We focus on stationary equilibria where the real value of the money supply in the CM after the money transfer has taken place is constant over time, i.e., $\phi_t M_{t+1} = \phi_{t-1} M_t \equiv Z$. Note that if the growth rate of the money supply is constant, then this steady-state condition can be expressed as $\phi_t M_t = \phi_{t-1} M_{t-1}$, since $M_{t+1} = \gamma M_t$ for all t, which is the condition we specified for a constant real money supply in the previous chapter. Conditional on $\gamma_t = \underline{\gamma}$, the value of money in the CM is $\phi_t = \phi_{t-1}/\underline{\gamma}$, and conditional on $\gamma_t = \bar{\gamma}$, the value of money is $\phi_t = \phi_{t-1}/\bar{\gamma}$. Hence, the gross expected rate of return of money, conditional on the information available in the CM of $t-1$, $\mathbb{E}_{t-1}[\phi_t/\phi_{t-1}]$, is equal to $(1-\alpha)/\underline{\gamma} + \alpha/\bar{\gamma}$.

In the DM of period t, all agents know the current stock of money that is available for trade, M_t, and the value of money that prevailed in the previous period, ϕ_{t-1}. But in order to determine the terms of trade in the DM of period t, agents need to know the value of money that will prevail in the upcoming CM, ϕ_t. All agents will learn the money growth rate, γ_t, in the CM of period t, but some agents may learn it earlier.

In order to formulate the buyer's problem recursively, we will express the buyer's money holdings as a fraction of aggregate money balances. The value of a buyer in the CM of period $t-1$ after the transfer of money balances has been realized is

$$W^b\left(\frac{m}{M_t}\right) = \max_{x,y,m'}\left\{x - y + \beta V^b\left(\frac{m'}{M_t}\right)\right\}$$
$$\text{s.t. } x + Z\frac{m'}{M_t} = y + Z\frac{m}{M_t},$$

where $\phi_{t-1} = Z/M_t$. Note that the above budget constraint does not include the lump-sum transfer from the government because the utility of the buyer is measured after the transfer has been realized. Substituting the budget constraint into the objective function, we obtain

$$W^b\left(\frac{m}{M_t}\right) = Z\frac{m}{M_t} + \max_{m' \geq 0}\left\{-Z\frac{m'}{M_t} + \beta V^b\left(\frac{m'}{M_t}\right)\right\}. \tag{7.1}$$

As before, the buyer's value function is linear, $W^b(m/M_t) = Zm/M_t + W^b(0)$, and the buyer's choice of money balances, m', is independent of the balances he has when he enters the CM, m.

The value of the buyer at the beginning of the DM is

$$V^b\left(\frac{m}{M_t}\right) = \mathbb{E}_t\left[u(q_t) + W^b\left(\frac{m - d_t + (\gamma_t - 1)M_t}{\gamma_t M_t}\right)\right].$$

Buyers form expectations about the future growth rate—and, hence, value—of money, the terms of trade in the DM, and about the trading shock, σ, in the DM. Note that for the latter, the buyer must form expectations regarding what agents will know about the future value of money at the beginning of the DM. Note that in the expression for W^b, we take into account the lump-sum transfer from the government. Using the linearity of W^b, the above value function can be rewritten as

$$V^b\left(\frac{m}{M_t}\right) = \mathbb{E}_t\left[u(q_t) - d_t\frac{Z}{\gamma_t M_t} + m\frac{Z}{\gamma_t M_t}\right] + \mathbb{E}_t\left[\frac{(\gamma_t - 1)}{\gamma_t}Z\right] + W^b(0).$$

Hence, the buyer's choice of money holdings, given by the second term on the right side of (7.1), can be expressed as

$$\max_{m \geq 0}\left\{-Z\frac{m}{M_t} + \beta\mathbb{E}_t\left[u(q_t) + (m - d_t)\frac{Z}{\gamma_t M_t}\right]\right\},$$

or, since $\phi_{t-1} = Z/M_t$,

$$\max_{m \geq 0}\left\{-\phi_{t-1}m + \beta\mathbb{E}_t\left[u(q_t) + (m - d_t)\frac{\phi_{t-1}}{\gamma_t}\right]\right\}. \tag{7.2}$$

Before we examine the interesting case where different agents know different things about the money growth rate, we first consider the case where buyers and sellers are symmetrically informed regarding the money growth rate.

Symmetrically-uninformed agents Consider first the situation where both buyers and sellers learn the realization of the money growth rate, γ_t, at the beginning of the CM of period t. In this case, buyers and sellers will determine terms of trade in the DM based on the expected value of money, ϕ_t^e, where $\phi_t^e = \mathbb{E}_t(\phi_{t-1}/\gamma_t) = [(1-\alpha)/\underline{\gamma} + \alpha/\bar{\gamma}]\phi_{t-1}$. If we assume that buyers make take-it-or-leave-it offers to sellers in the DM, which implies that $c(q_t) = \phi_t^e d$, then, from (7.2), the buyer's choice of money holdings in the CM of period $t-1$ is the solution to,

$$\max_{m \geq 0} \{-\phi_{t-1} m + \beta \{\sigma [u(q_t) - c(q_t)] + \phi_t^e m\}\}, \tag{7.3}$$

where $c(q_t) = \min [c(q^*), \phi_t^e m]$. In period $t-1$, the buyer incurs the cost $\phi_{t-1} m$ to accumulate m units of money; in period t, the buyer enjoys the expected surplus from a trade, $\sigma [u(q_t) - c(q_t)]$, and can expect to resell his money holding for $\phi_t^e m$ units of output in the CM. Problem (7.3) can be rearranged to

$$\max_{q_t \in [0, q^*]} \{-ic(q_t) + \sigma [u(q_t) - c(q_t)]\},$$

where

$$i = \frac{1}{\beta \left(\frac{1-\alpha}{\underline{\gamma}} + \frac{\alpha}{\bar{\gamma}} \right)} - 1$$

is the nominal interest rate. The first-order condition for this problem is

$$\frac{u'(q_t)}{c'(q_t)} = 1 + \frac{i}{\sigma}. \tag{7.4}$$

There is a unique q_t that solves (7.4), and it is independent of time. Given q, the value of money is determined by $[(1-\alpha)/\underline{\gamma} + \alpha/\bar{\gamma}]\phi_{t-1} M_t = c(q)$ and, hence, real balances are constant across time. The level of output traded in the DM may differ from the efficient level because of a wedge between agents' rate of time reference and fiat money's expected rate of return. If, however, the expected rate of return on money is $(1-\alpha)/\underline{\gamma} + \alpha/\bar{\gamma} = \beta^{-1}$, then $q_t = q^*$. In words, if the rate of return on money is equal to the rate of time preference, then agents will trade the efficient level of output in the DM. This implies that there are many combinations of $\underline{\gamma}$ and $\bar{\gamma}$ that can implement the Friedman rule. While the DM output depends on the expected rate of return of money, it does not depend on the realization of the money growth rate in the current period. Consequently, the model predicts no correlation between inflation and output.

Symmetrically-informed agents Consider now the situation where buyers and sellers learn the period t money growth rate, γ_t, and hence the value of money, ϕ_t, before entering the DM of period t. One can imagine that the monetary authority makes a credible announcement at the beginning of each DM regarding the money growth rate that will prevail in the CM. If the monetary authority announces $\gamma_t = \underline{\gamma}$, then a buyer holding m_t units of money will ask for $q_t = q_H$, where

$$c(q_H) = \min\left[\frac{\phi_{t-1}}{\underline{\gamma}} m_t, c(q^*)\right].$$

If, alternatively, it announces $\gamma_t = \bar{\gamma}$, then the buyer asks for $q_t = q_L$, where

$$c(q_L) = \min\left[\frac{\phi_{t-1}}{\bar{\gamma}} m_t, c(q^*)\right].$$

Since $\bar{\gamma} > \underline{\gamma}$, it is obvious that $q_L(m_t) \leq q_H(m_t)$. Buyers consume more in periods where the money growth rate is low and the value of fiat money is high.

Since agents are symmetrically informed, the terms of trade in the DM of period t depend on the period t money growth rate. Assuming that buyers make take-it-or-leave-it offers to sellers in the DM, from (7.2), the buyer's choice of money holdings in the CM of period $t-1$ is given by the the solution to

$$\max_{m \geq 0} \{-\phi_{t-1} m + \beta\sigma(1-\alpha)\{u[q_H(m)] - c[q_H(m)]\} + \beta\sigma\alpha\{u[q_L(m)] - c[q_L(m)]\} + \beta\phi_t^e m\}, \tag{7.5}$$

where $\phi_t^e = [(1-\alpha)/\underline{\gamma} + \alpha/\bar{\gamma}]\phi_{t-1}$. This problem differs from (7.3) because now the quantity traded in the DM depends on the information regarding the money growth rate that agents receive before being matched. The first-order condition for this problem is

$$\frac{\hat{\imath}}{\sigma} = \left\{\left(\frac{u'(q_H)}{c'(q_H)} - 1\right)\frac{1-\alpha}{\underline{\gamma}} + \left(\frac{u'(q_L)}{c'(q_L)} - 1\right)\frac{\alpha}{\bar{\gamma}}\right\}, \tag{7.6}$$

where $\hat{\imath} \equiv \beta^{-1} - [(1-\alpha)/\underline{\gamma} + \alpha/\bar{\gamma}]$.(Notice that $i[(1-\alpha)/\underline{\gamma} + \alpha/\bar{\gamma}] = \hat{\imath}$.) Equation (7.6) determines a unique value for $\phi_{t-1} m_t = \phi_{t-1} M_t$ (from the clearing of the money market). If $(1-\alpha)/\underline{\gamma} + \alpha/\bar{\gamma} = \beta^{-1}$, then $i = \hat{\imath} = 0$ and $q_L = q_H = q^*$, which means that the Friedman rule achieves the efficient level of DM output in both inflation states. The fact that the money growth rate is stochastic does not matter for implementing the efficient level of DM output, provided that the expected rate of return of money is equal to the (gross) discount rate.

In summary, when agents are symmetrically informed, there is either no correlation between inflation and output, or a negative one, depending on whether agents are imperfectly or perfectly informed, respectively.

7.2 Bargaining Under Asymmetric Information

We now consider situations where buyers and sellers are asymmetrically informed in the DM regarding the money growth rate that will prevail for that period. At the beginning of the DM of period t, buyers receive a perfectly informative private signal, $\chi \in \{L, H\}$, regarding the value of money or, equivalently, the money growth rate for period t. If $\chi = L$, then buyers learn that the value of money will be low, $\phi_t = \phi_L = \phi_{t-1}/\bar{\gamma}$; if $\chi = H$, then buyers learn that the value of money will be high, $\phi_t = \phi_H = \phi_{t-1}/\underline{\gamma}$. A buyer will be called an H-type buyer if he receives the signal H and an L-type buyer if he receives the signal L. Although sellers do not receive any informative signals in the DM, they understand the stochastic process that drives the money supply and will learn the actual money growth rate at the beginning of the CM. The relevant timing of events for a typical period is illustrated in Figure 7.1.

Consider a match between a buyer holding m units of money and a seller holding no money in the DM of period t. Assume that the buyer's money holdings are common knowledge in the match. This simplifies the presentation since agents have no incentives to misrepresent their money holdings. The bargaining game between a buyer and a seller in the DM has the structure of a signaling game. This game is illustrated in Figure 7.2, where the label N represents the player Nature who chooses the money growth rate—or, equivalently, the value of money—the label B represents the buyer, and the label S represents the seller. A strategy

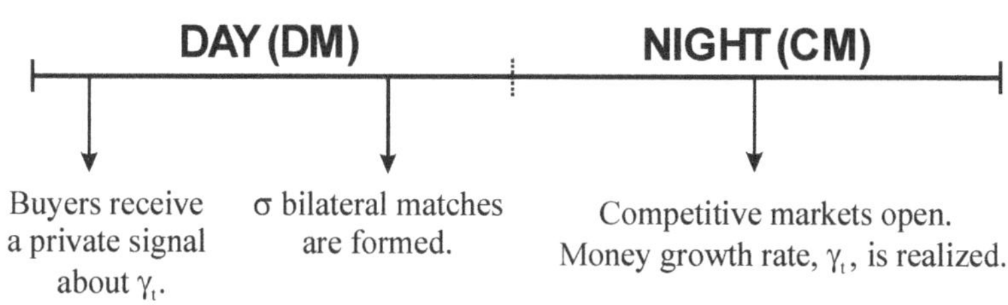

Figure 7.1
Timing of a representative period, t, under asymmetric information

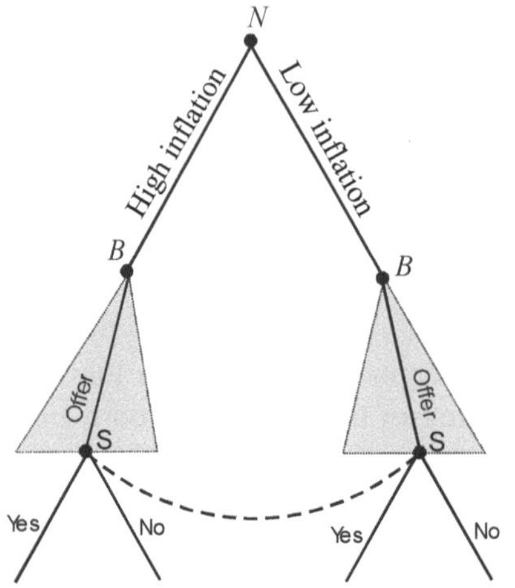

Figure 7.2
Game tree of the bargaining game in the DM

for the buyer specifies an offer $(q,d) \in \mathbb{R}_+ \times [0,m]$, where q is the output produced by the seller in the DM, d is the transfer of money from the buyer to the seller. A strategy for the seller is an acceptance rule that specifies the set $\mathcal{A} \subseteq \mathbb{R}_+ \times [0,m]$ of acceptable offers.

The buyer's payoff is $[u(q) - \phi d]\,\mathbb{I}_{\mathcal{A}}(q,d)$, where $\mathbb{I}_{\mathcal{A}}(q,d)$ is an indicator function that is equal to one if $(q,d) \in \mathcal{A}$ and zero otherwise. If an offer is accepted, then the buyer enjoys the utility of consumption, $u(q)$, net of the utility he forgoes by transferring d units of money to the seller, $-\phi d$. The seller's payoff is $-c(q) + \phi d$. The seller uses the information conveyed by the buyer's offer (q,d) to update his prior belief regarding the value of money in the subsequent CM. Let $\lambda(q,d) \in [0,1]$ represent the updated belief of a seller that the value of money is high, $\phi = \phi_H$. If (q,d) corresponds to an equilibrium offer, then the updated belief $\lambda(q,d)$ is derived from the seller's prior belief according to Bayes' rule. If (q,d) is an out-of-equilibrium offer, then $\lambda(q,d)$ is, to some extent, arbitrary, as will be discussed below.

Given his updated—or posterior—belief, the seller optimally chooses to accept or reject offers. For a given belief system, λ, the set of acceptable offers for a seller, $\mathcal{A}(\lambda)$, is given by

$$\mathcal{A}(\lambda) = \{(q,d) \in \mathbb{R}_+ \times [0,m] : -c(q) + \{\lambda(q,d)\phi_H + [1-\lambda(q,d)]\phi_L\}d \geq 0\}. \tag{7.7}$$

If offer (q,d) is acceptable, then the seller's cost of production, $c(q)$, must be no greater than the expected value of the transfer of money that he receives. The buyer will choose an offer that maximizes his surplus, taking as given the acceptance rule of the seller. The buyer's bargaining problem is given by

$$\max_{q,d\leq m} \left[u(q) - \phi d\right] \mathbb{I}_{\mathcal{A}}(q,d), \tag{7.8}$$

where the value of money is $\phi \in \{\phi_L, \phi_H\}$.

A seller's belief following an out-of-equilibrium offer is somewhat arbitrary. In order to get sharper predictions, we require that the equilibrium satisfies the *intuitive criterion*. Denote U^b_χ as the surplus that a χ-type buyer, $\chi \in \{L,H\}$, receives in the proposed equilibrium of the bargaining game. A proposed equilibrium fails to satisfy the intuitive criterion—and, hence, cannot be an equilibrium—if there exists an out-of-equilibrium offer $(\tilde{q},\tilde{d})$, such that the following conditions are satisfied,

$$u(\tilde{q}) - \phi_H\tilde{d} > U^b_H \tag{7.9}$$

$$u(\tilde{q}) - \phi_L\tilde{d} < U^b_L \tag{7.10}$$

$$-c(\tilde{q}) + \phi_H\tilde{d} \geq 0. \tag{7.11}$$

According to (7.9), the offer $(\tilde{q},\tilde{d})$ would make an H-type buyer strictly better off if it were accepted, but, according to (7.10), would make an L-type buyer strictly worse off. Since the L-type buyer has no incentive to make this offer, the seller should believe that it came from an H-type buyer, and will accept it if condition (7.11) holds.

We provide a characterization of an equilibrium offer by first demonstrating what *cannot* be an equilibrium. In particular, a pooling offer—where the H- and L-type buyers make the same offer—cannot be an equilibrium. Figure 7.3 illustrates the argument. Consider a proposed pooling equilibrium, where both types of buyers make the offer $(\bar{q},\bar{d}) \neq (0,0)$ to the seller in the bargaining game, and the offer is accepted. The offer $(\bar{q},\bar{d})$ generates a surplus $U^b_L \equiv u(\bar{q}) - \phi_L\bar{d}$ for the L-type buyer and $U^b_H \equiv u(\bar{q}) - \phi_H\bar{d}$ for the H-type buyer. The indifference curves, U^b_L and U^b_H, depicted in Figure 7.3 represent a set of offers (q,d) for each type of buyer that generates a surplus equal to the equilibrium surplus associated with that buyer's type. Note that U^b_L is steeper than U^b_H since $\phi_H > \phi_L$. The participation constraint of a seller who believes he is facing an H-type buyer is represented by the

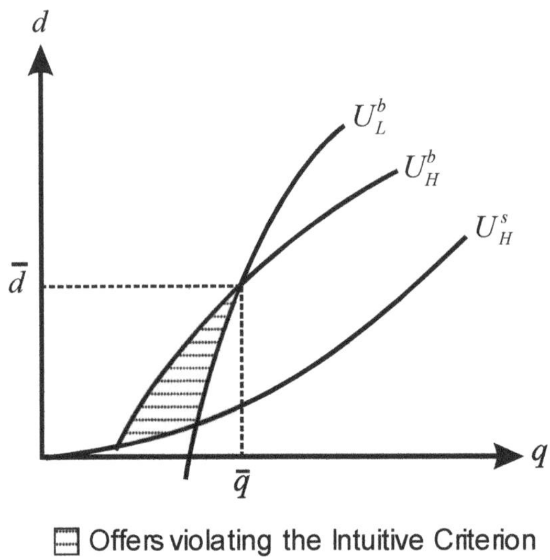

Figure 7.3
Ruling out pooling equilibria

locus $U_H^s \equiv \{(q,d) : -c(q) + \phi_H d = 0\}$. The proposed equilibrium offer $(\bar{q},\bar{d})$ lies above U_H^s since it is accepted when $\lambda(\bar{q},\bar{d}) < 1$.

The shaded area in Figure 7.3 identifies the set of offers, when compared to the proposed equilibrium, that (i) increase the surplus of an H-type buyer—offers to the right of U_H^b; (ii) reduce the surplus of an L-type buyer—offers to the left of U_L^b; and (iii) are acceptable to the seller assuming that $\lambda = 1$—offers above U_H^s. The offers in the shaded area satisfy conditions (7.9)-(7.11), which implies that the proposed equilibrium where both types of buyers offer $(\bar{q},\bar{d})$ violates the intuitive criterion. Indeed, the H-type buyer is able to make an offer different from $(\bar{q},\bar{d})$ that, if accepted, would make him better off, while making an L-type buyer strictly worse off. Moreover, provided that the seller believes that this offer is coming from an H-type buyer, then it is acceptable.

Since pooling offers are not compatible with equilibrium, if an equilibrium exists, it must be characterized by separating offers, i.e., the L- and H-type buyers make different offers. But if the offers are separating, then, in equilibrium, the seller can attribute each offer to a buyer's type. This means that, in the equilibrium, the seller knows exactly what type of money he is receiving, either low or high value.

If offers are separating, then the L-type buyer can do no worse than to make the offer that he would make under complete information, since this complete information offer is always acceptable to the seller, independent of his beliefs. The L-type buyer cannot do any better than this; otherwise, the offer would have to be pooled with an H-type buyer offer. But such offers have been ruled out as possible equilibrium outcomes. Hence, the payoff of an L-type buyer is given by

$$U_L^b = \max_{q,d \leq m} [u(q) - \phi_L d] \quad \text{s.t.} \quad -c(q) + \phi_L d \geq 0. \tag{7.12}$$

The solution to problem (7.12) is

$$q_L = \min\left[q^*, c^{-1}(\phi_L m)\right] \tag{7.13}$$

$$d_L = \min\left[\frac{c(q^*)}{\phi_L}, m\right]. \tag{7.14}$$

If the L-type buyer's money holdings are sufficiently large, then the trade in L-type matches is efficient, $q_L = q^*$. On the other hand, if the value of the money holdings is less than the cost of producing q^*—where a unit of money is valued at ϕ_L—then the L-type buyer is unable to purchase the efficient quantity of output and $q_L < q^*$. In both cases, the buyer appropriates the entire surplus of the match.

Consider now the offer made by an H-type buyer, (q_H, d_H), given the offer of the L-type buyer, (q_L, d_L). An H-type buyer's offer, (q_H, d_H), will be part of an equilibrium if the L-type buyer does not have a strict preference to offer it instead of (q_L, d_L). Hence, (q_H, d_H) solves the following problem,

$$U_H^b = \max_{q,d \leq m} [u(q) - \phi_H d] \quad \text{s.t.} \quad -c(q) + \phi_H d \geq 0 \tag{7.15}$$

$$\text{and} \quad u(q) - \phi_L d \leq U_L^b = u(q_L) - c(q_L). \tag{7.16}$$

From (7.15), the buyer maximizes his expected surplus subject to the participation constraint of the seller—where the seller has the correct belief that he faces an H-type buyer—and the incentive-compatibility condition, (7.16), that an L-type buyer cannot be made better-off by offering (q_H, d_H) instead of (q_L, d_L). Note that the solution satisfies the intuitive criterion, since there is no other acceptable offer that the H-type buyer could make that would raise his payoff and would not increase the payoff to the L-type buyer. A belief system consistent with the equilibrium offers has the seller attributing all offers that violate (7.16) to L-type buyers, and all other out-of-equilibrium

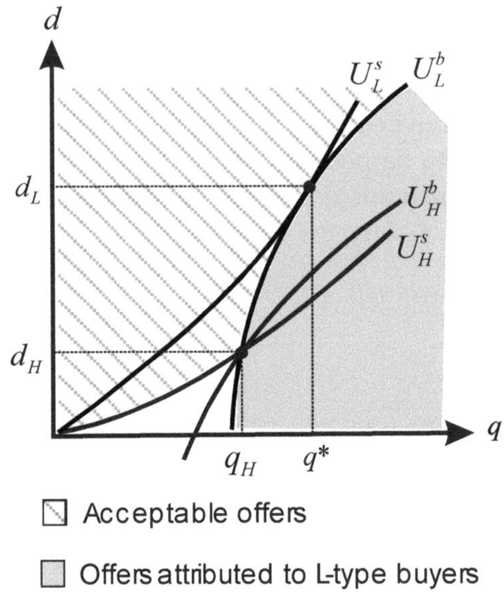

Figure 7.4
Separating offer

offers to H-type buyers, see Figure 7.4. Notice that the intuitive criterion selects the Pareto-efficient equilibrium among all separating equilibria.

The solution to (7.15)-(7.16) has both constraints binding. To see this, consider first the incentive-compatibility condition (7.16). Suppose that this condition does not bind; then, the solution, (q_H, d_H), to problem (7.15)-(7.16) is the complete information offer—given by problem (7.15)—and

$$u(q_H) - \phi_L d_H = u(q_H) - c(q_H) + (\phi_H - \phi_L) d_H > U_L^b,$$

where we have used that $c(q_H) = \phi_H d_H$. The inequality follows from the observation that, for a given m, the complete-information output in state H is $\min\{q^*, c^{-1}(\phi_H m)\}$, and, hence, the complete information payoff of an H-type buyer exceeds that of an L-type buyer. In words, the above condition states that the L-type buyer can be made better off, compared to offer (q_L, d_L), by mimicking the H-type buyers' offer, (q_H, d_H). This is not compatible with equilibrium and, hence, constraint (7.16) must bind.

Consider now the participation constraint, $-c(q)+\phi_H d \geq 0$, given in (7.15). Suppose that this constraint does not bind. Then, problem (7.15)-(7.16) becomes,

$$U_H^b = \max_{d \leq m} (\phi_L - \phi_H) d + U_L^b = U_L^b.$$

The solution to this problem is $d_H = 0$ and $U_H^b = U_L^b > 0$, which implies $q_H > 0$. But this solution violates the seller's participation constraint, which implies that the seller's participation constraint must bind.

In summary, the solution to problem (7.15)-(7.16) satisfies

$$u(q_H) - \frac{\phi_L}{\phi_H} c(q_H) = u(q_L) - c(q_L) \tag{7.17}$$

$$d_H = \frac{u(q_H) - U_L^b}{\phi_L}. \tag{7.18}$$

Using (7.15) and (7.16) with a strict equality, the payoff to an H-type buyer is

$$U_H^b = u(q_H) - \phi_H d = U_L^b - (\phi_H - \phi_L) d. \tag{7.19}$$

Substituting (7.18) for d, (7.19) can be written as

$$U_H^b = \frac{\phi_H}{\phi_L} U_L^b - \left(\frac{\phi_H - \phi_L}{\phi_L}\right) u(q_H),$$

which is decreasing in q_H. Consequently, the solution (q_H, d_H) to problem (7.15)-(7.16) corresponds to the lowest q_H that solves equation (7.17). But, note that (7.17) determines a unique q_H in the interval $(0, q_L)$. To see this, notice that if $q_H = 0$, then the left side is less than the right side; if $q_H = q_L$, then the opposite is true. Moreover, for all $q_H \leq q^*$ the left side is increasing in q_H. Hence, (7.17) has a unique solution $q_H \in (0, q_L)$. Given q_H, d_H is determined by (7.18). The most notable feature of this solution is that $q_H < q_L$, which implies $c(q_H) = \phi_H d_H < c(q_L) = \phi_L d_L$, and hence $d_H < d_L \leq m$. The lower velocity of money in the H-state is a consequence of H-type buyers separating themselves from L-type buyers.

If we adopt the functional forms $c(q) = q$ and $u(q) = 2\sqrt{q}$ we can obtain closed-form solutions for the expression of the quantities traded in the DM. From (7.13) $q_L = \min[1, \phi_L m]$ and (7.17) becomes

$$\frac{\phi_L}{\phi_H} q_H - 2\sqrt{q_H} + 2\sqrt{q_L} - q_L = 0.$$

The smallest value of q_H that solves this equation is

$$q_H = \left(\frac{\phi_H}{\phi_L}\left(1 - \sqrt{1 - \frac{\phi_L}{\phi_H}\left(2\sqrt{q_L} - q_L\right)}\right)\right)^2. \tag{7.20}$$

It is clear from this expression that the quantities traded in the H-state depend on the discrepancy of the value of money in the different states, ϕ_H/ϕ_L, and on the quantity traded in the L-state, q_L. Note that if $\phi_H = \phi_L$, then $q_H = q_L$.

The buyers' offers are illustrated in Figure 7.4, for the case where the constraint $d_L \leq m$ does not bind. The offer of the L-type buyer is given by the point where the iso-surplus curve of the seller who knows that he is facing an L-type buyer, $U_L^s \equiv \{(q,d) : -c(q) + \phi_L d = 0\}$, is tangent to the iso-surplus curve of the L-type buyer, U_L^b. In order for the H-type buyer to satisfy the seller's participation constraint, $c(q_H) - \phi_H d_H = 0$, and condition (7.16) with an equality, he must make an offer that is in the region to the left of (and including) curve U_L^b and above (and including) curve U_H^s. This region is identified as "Acceptable offers" in Figure 7.4. The utility-maximizing offer in this region is given by the intersection of the U_L^b and U_H^s curves.

7.3 Equilibrium Under Asymmetric Information

The terms of trade in the DM of period t are a function of the buyer's private signal and the money balances he accumulated in the CM of period $t-1$. Using (7.2), the buyer's choice of money holdings in the CM of period $t-1$ is given by

$$\max_{m\geq 0}\left\{-\phi_{t-1}m + \beta\sigma\left\{\alpha\left[u(q_L) + \frac{\phi_{t-1}}{\bar{\gamma}}(m - d_L)\right] + (1-\alpha)\left[u(q_H) + \frac{\phi_{t-1}}{\underline{\gamma}}(m - d_H)\right]\right\}\right\}.$$

Since $(\phi_{t-1}/\bar{\gamma})d_L = c(q_L)$, $(\phi_{t-1}/\underline{\gamma})d_H = c(q_H)$ and $\phi_t^e = \alpha(\phi_{t-1}/\bar{\gamma}) + (1-\alpha)(\phi_{t-1}/\underline{\gamma})$, this problem becomes

$$\max_{m\geq 0}\{-\phi_{t-1}m + \beta\sigma\{\alpha[u(q_L) - c(q_L)] + (1-\alpha)[u(q_H) - c(q_H)]\} + \beta\phi_t^e m\}, \tag{7.21}$$

where q_L and q_H solve,

$$q_L = \min\left[q^*, c^{-1}\left(\frac{\phi_{t-1}m}{\bar{\gamma}}\right)\right],$$

and

$$u(q_H) - \frac{\underline{\gamma}}{\bar{\gamma}}c(q_H) = u(q_L) - c(q_L), \tag{7.22}$$

where (7.22) is identical to (7.17) since

$$\frac{\phi_L}{\phi_H} = \frac{\phi_{t-1}/\bar{\gamma}}{\phi_{t-1}/\underline{\gamma}} = \frac{\underline{\gamma}}{\bar{\gamma}}.$$

According to (7.21), the buyer accumulates $\phi_{t-1}m$ real balances in the CM of period $t-1$. With probability α, the value of money in t is low and the buyer consumes q_L, and with probability $1-\alpha$ it is high and the buyer consumes q_H. In both cases, the buyer enjoys the whole surplus of the match in the DM of period t. Finally, the buyer can resell any money he has left when entering the CM of t at the expected price $\phi_t^e = [\alpha/\bar{\gamma} + (1-\alpha)/\underline{\gamma}]\phi_{t-1}$.

By grouping the m terms and then dividing by β, (7.21) can be rearranged as

$$\max_{m\geq 0}\left\{-\hat{\imath}\phi_{t-1}m + \sigma\left\{\alpha\left[u(q_L) - c(q_L)\right] + (1-\alpha)\left[u(q_H) - c(q_H)\right]\right\}\right\}, \tag{7.23}$$

where $\hat{\imath} \equiv \beta^{-1} - [\alpha/\bar{\gamma} + (1-\alpha)/\underline{\gamma}]$. The buyer chooses his money holdings in order to maximize his expected surplus in the DM, net of the cost of holding real balances. The cost of holding real balances, $\hat{\imath}$, is the difference between the gross rate of time preference and the expected gross rate of return of money, the surplus in the L-state is $S_L = u(q_L) - c(q_L)$ and the surplus in the H-state is $S_H = u(q_H) - c(q_H)$.

Observe that both S_L and S_H are increasing functions of DM output in the L-state, q_L, and are strictly increasing if $q_L < q^*$. This can be seen by differentiating the buyer's surpluses in the low and high states with respect to q_L:

$$\frac{dS_L}{dq_L} = u'(q_L) - c'(q_L) \geq 0, \tag{7.24}$$

$$\frac{dS_H}{dq_H} = [u'(q_H) - c'(q_H)]\frac{dq_H}{dq_L} \tag{7.25}$$

$$= \left[\frac{u'(q_H) - c'(q_H)}{u'(q_H) - \frac{\underline{\gamma}}{\bar{\gamma}}c'(q_H)}\right][u'(q_L) - c'(q_L)] \geq 0,$$

where, from (7.22), we used

$$\frac{dq_H}{dq_L} = \left[u'(q_H) - \frac{\gamma}{\bar{\gamma}}c'(q_H)\right]^{-1} [u'(q_L) - c'(q_L)] \geq 0. \tag{7.26}$$

The value of an additional unit of output in the low state, $S_L^{'}$, is simply the marginal match surplus, $u'(q_L) - c'(q_L)$, which gives us (7.24). An additional unit of output in state L relaxes incentive-compatibility constraint (7.16), which allows the buyer to raise his consumption by the amount given in (7.26) in state H. Since the buyer obtains the whole surplus of the match, each additional unit of consumption in the DM raises his surplus by $u'(q_H) - c'(q_H)$, which gives us (7.25).

Since the surpluses in both the H- and L-states are increasing functions of q_L, and since the buyer will never bring more money than what is required to buy q_L in the L-state because it is costly to hold money and $q_H < q_L$, we can re-express the buyer's problem (7.23) as a choice of q_L. Given that the buyer chooses $\phi_{t-1}m = \bar{\gamma}c(q_L)$, the buyer's problem can be expressed as

$$\max_{q_L \in [0,q^*]} \{-\hat{\imath}\bar{\gamma}c(q_L) + \sigma \{\alpha [u(q_L) - c(q_L)] + (1-\alpha) [u(q_H) - c(q_H)]\}\}. \tag{7.27}$$

From (7.24) and (7.25), the marginal surplus functions dS_L/dq_L and dS_H/dq_H are decreasing in q_L and q_H for all $q_H, q_L \in [0, q^*]$. Since q_H is increasing with q_L, we can deduce that the buyer's objective function in problem (7.27) is concave in q_L. The first-order (necessary and sufficient) condition for the buyer's choice of output in the L-state is given by

$$\hat{\imath} = \sigma \left\{ (1-\alpha) \left[\frac{u'(q_H) - c'(q_H)}{\bar{\gamma}u'(q_H) - \gamma c'(q_H)} \right] + \frac{\alpha}{\bar{\gamma}} \right\} \left(\frac{u'(q_L)}{c'(q_L)} - 1 \right). \tag{7.28}$$

The cost of holding money, the left side of (7.28), must be equal to the marginal benefit from holding money in the DM, which is the right side of (7.28). The right side of (7.28) varies from $+\infty$ to 0 as q_L varies from 0 to q^*. Hence, there is a unique q_L that solves (7.28). Market-clearing requires that $m = M_t$, so that the value of money in period $t-1$ is uniquely determined by $c(q_L) = (\phi_{t-1}/\bar{\gamma})M_t$, i.e., $\phi_{t-1} = \bar{\gamma}c(q_L)/M_t$.

Finally, notice that (7.24) and (7.25) imply that

$$\frac{dS_H}{dq_H} = \left[\frac{u'(q_H) - c'(q_H)}{u'(q_H) - \frac{\gamma}{\bar{\gamma}}c'(q_H)} \right] \frac{dS_L}{dq_L}. \tag{7.29}$$

Since there is a one-to-one relationship between q_L and $\phi_{t-1}m$, i.e., $q_L = c^{-1}[(\phi_{t-1}/\bar{\gamma})m]$, one can interpret S_H' and S_L' as the liquidity value of real balances in the H- and L-states, respectively. Hence, since the squared bracketed term on the right side of (7.29) is less than one, the liquidity value of an additional unit of real balances is lower in the H-state than it is in the L-state, i.e., $S_H' \leq S_L'$ (and with a strict inequality when $q_L < q^*$). So, paradoxically, the liquidity value of money is lower when its market price is high or, equivalently, when inflation is low.

7.4 The Inflation and Output Trade-Off

We now discuss some basic properties of the equilibrium when there is asymmetric information. The model makes some predictions regarding correlations between inflation, output, and the velocity of money. First, the model predicts a positive correlation between output and inflation. If $\gamma_t = \bar{\gamma}$, then $q_t = q_L \leq q^*$; if $\gamma_t = \underline{\gamma}$, then $q_t = q_H < q_L$. Consequently, the model generates an upward-sloping Phillips curve, and an apparent trade-off between inflation and output.

Second, the model predicts a positive correlation between the velocity of money and inflation. If $\gamma_t = \underline{\gamma}$, then $d_t = d_H < M_t$; if $\gamma_t = \bar{\gamma}$, then $d_t = d_L = M_t$. Buyers spend all their money holdings in the high-inflation state, but only a fraction of it in the low-inflation state. These correlations are illustrated in Figure 7.5, where we plot the quantities traded and the money transfers in the DM as a function of the inflation rate.

A short-run Phillips curve emerges because of the informational asymmetry that prevails between buyers and sellers regarding the future value of money. When buyers learn the inflation rate is low and the value of fiat money is high, they signal this information to sellers by retaining a fraction of their (valuable) money holdings, and reducing their DM consumption. It is because buyers are willing to hold onto their money balances that sellers can be convinced that fiat money has a high value. If the inflation rate is high, and the value of fiat money is low, buyers do not have to signal its value and, hence, they spend it all in the DM.

The structure of the asymmetric information mechanism in our model suggests a new explanation for the non-neutrality of money and the inflation-output trade-off. A related explanation, based on agents' imperfect information about monetary policy, suggests that output rises when inflation is high because agents are unable to disentangle nominal and real shocks. Agents who face this "signal extraction problem" attribute a high nominal price for the good they produce to both an increase in the real price of this good and an increase in the stock of money. The precise division between the real and nominal components will depend on how often the monetary authority generates high inflation. So, the reason why output is high when inflation is high is because agents incorrectly attribute an increase in the price of the good they produce to real factors as opposed to monetary ones. In contrast, the positive correlation between output and inflation in our model is not due to agents being mistaken, since, in equilibrium, both buyers and sellers know the true value of fiat money.

Another popular explanation for changes in the money supply having real effects is the presence of price rigidities. If, for some reason, producers set nominal prices and can only adjust these prices infrequently, then an unanticipated increase in the money supply can lead to a higher demand for those goods whose prices have not been adjusted. In our model the real effects of monetary policy are not based on any notions of nominal rigidities that might arise from the existence of informational asymmetries. To see this, suppose that the seller's cost function

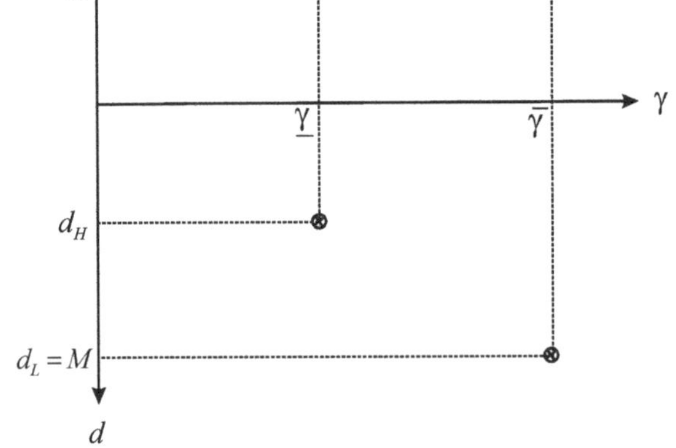

Figure 7.5
Output, velocity, and inflation.

in the DM is linear, $c(q) = q$. Then, according to (7.12) and (7.15), the price of output in the DM of period t is defined as the monetary payment divided by the output traded, and is given by

$$\frac{d_H}{q_H} = \frac{1}{\phi_H} = \frac{\underline{\gamma}}{\phi_{t-1}},$$
$$\frac{d_L}{q_L} = \frac{1}{\phi_L} = \frac{\bar{\gamma}}{\phi_{t-1}}.$$

In both the high and low inflation states, the nominal price is proportional to the money growth rate.

We now ask whether the monetary authority can take advantage of the apparent trade-off between inflation and output by implementing the high money growth rate more often. Suppose that the monetary authority increases the frequency for the high money state; i.e., it increases α. The equilibrium condition (7.28) can be compactly reexpressed as $\Gamma(\alpha, q_L) = 0$, where

$$\Gamma(\alpha, q_L) = \beta^{-1} - \left(\frac{1-\alpha}{\underline{\gamma}} + \frac{\alpha}{\bar{\gamma}}\right)$$
$$-\sigma\left\{(1-\alpha)\left[\frac{u'(q_H) - c'(q_H)}{\bar{\gamma}u'(q_H) - \underline{\gamma}c'(q_H)}\right] + \frac{\alpha}{\bar{\gamma}}\right\}\left(\frac{u'(q_L)}{c'(q_L)} - 1\right),$$

and, from (7.17), q_H is an increasing function of q_L. By totally differentiating the equilibrium condition, we obtain that $dq_L/d\alpha = -\Gamma_\alpha/\Gamma_{q_L}$, where Γ_α and Γ_{q_L} are the partial derivatives of Γ with respect to α and q_L, respectively. Using the fact that Γ is increasing in q_H and q_L, it can easily be seen that $\Gamma_{q_L} > 0$. Differentiating $\Gamma(\alpha, q_L)$ with respect to α, we obtain

$$\Gamma_\alpha = \frac{1}{\underline{\gamma}} - \frac{1}{\bar{\gamma}} + \sigma\left[\frac{u'(q_H) - c'(q_H)}{\bar{\gamma}u'(q_H) - \underline{\gamma}c'(q_H)} - \frac{1}{\bar{\gamma}}\right]\left(\frac{u'(q_L)}{c'(q_L)} - 1\right).$$

Consider the case where $\hat{\imath}$ is close to zero so that q_L is close to q^*, see equation (7.28). This implies that the liquidity premium in the low state, $u'(q_L)/c'(q_L) - 1$, is close to zero and, hence, $\Gamma_\alpha \approx 1/\underline{\gamma} - 1/\bar{\gamma} > 0$. Consequently, for $\hat{\imath}$ close to zero, an increase in α reduces the value of money and the output in all states. If the policy maker attempts to exploit the trade-off between inflation and output in a more systematic way, then agents will change their expectations about the occurrence of the different states, which, in turn, will adversely affect the value of money and output in the different states.

The overall effect of increasing the frequency of the high inflation state on expected aggregate output, however, is ambiguous because the high-inflation state, which is associated with a higher level of output, occurs more often. To see this, suppose that $\underline{\gamma} = \beta < \bar{\gamma}$ and $\alpha \approx 0$. Then, $\hat{\imath} = \beta^{-1} - ((1-\alpha)/\underline{\gamma} + \alpha/\bar{\gamma}) \approx 0$ and $q_H < q_L = q^*$. From (7.17),

$$\left.\frac{dq_H}{d\alpha}\right|_{\alpha\approx 0+} = \frac{[u'(q_L) - c'(q_L)]\, dq_L/d\alpha}{u'(q_H) - \underline{\gamma}c'(q_H)/\bar{\gamma}} = 0.$$

A change in α affects q_H indirectly through the buyer's surplus in the L-state. Since $q_L = q^*$, a change in α only has a second-order effect on the buyer's surplus in the L-state and, hence, on the quantities traded in the H-state. Let $Y = \sigma\,[\alpha q_L + (1-\alpha)q_H]$. Then,

$$\left.\frac{dY}{d\alpha}\right|_{\alpha\approx 0+} = \sigma\,(q_L - q_H) > 0.$$

If the rate of return on money is close to the rate of time preference, and if the high money growth rate occurs infrequently, then an increase in the frequency of the high money growth rate can lead to higher aggregate output.

The existence of this trade-off has also implications for social welfare measured here by the expected surplus in the DM, $\mathcal{W} = \sigma\,\{\alpha\,[u(q_L) - c(q_L)] + (1-\alpha)\,[u(q_H) - c(q_H)]\}$. By the same reasoning as above,

$$\left.\frac{d\mathcal{W}}{d\alpha}\right|_{\alpha\approx 0+} = \sigma\,\{[u(q_L) - c(q_L)] - [u(q_H) - c(q_H)]\} > 0.$$

By increasing the frequency of the high-money-growth-rate state, the policy maker can raise welfare. When $\gamma = \underline{\gamma} = \beta$ and $\alpha \approx 0$, prices (on average) fall over time. In this situation, buyers do not want to spend all of their cash (in state H) and prefer to wait until the subsequent CM, where the value of money is realized. This description is loosely related to a common-held view that deflation hurts society because agents hoard their money balances when they anticipate the value of money will increase over time, and a small expected inflation will increase output and welfare since agents will spend their money holdings faster. While this view is difficult to capture in our environment with symmetric information, it is quite natural when information is asymmetric.

It is worth emphasizing that the allocations and output levels are not continuous at $\alpha = 0$. If α is exactly equal to zero, then the money growth rate is deterministic, and there is no uncertainty about the value of money. There is no informational asymmetry in the DM and buyers do not need to signal the value of money to sellers. In that case, if $\underline{\gamma} = \beta$, then $q_H = q^*$. In contrast, if there is a chance that the policy maker chooses a high money growth rate, this possibility affects the quantities traded in the low-money-growth-rate state no matter how small α is. The mere possibility that the policy maker might implement a high money growth rate, even it is a very rare event, has a non-vanishing negative externality on the quantities traded in the low inflation state. This feature of the model is a consequence of a separating equilibrium—selected by the intuitive criterion—where the terms of trade in the low inflation state are determined by the incentive-compatibility condition, (7.16). If the intuitive criterion for equilibrium selection is dropped, then the discontinuity may no longer exist in a pooling (perfect Bayesian) equilibrium. But in that case, there would be no correlation between inflation and output.

The analytical results obtained so far, regarding the effect that monetary policy has on aggregate output and welfare, are valid for small values of α. We now use a simple numerical example to investigate the case where α is not close to 0. We take the functional forms $c(q) = q$ and $u(q) = 2\sqrt{q}$, and set $\sigma = 1$ and $\beta = 0.9$. We assume that $\underline{\gamma} = \beta$, and take three possible values for the high inflation state, $\bar{\gamma} \in \{1.1, 1.5, 2\}$. In Figure 7.6 we plot aggregate output and welfare—as measured by the expected match surplus in the DM—as a function of α, the frequency with which the high-money-growth-rate state occurs. Provided that the difference between the money growth rates in the two states is not too large, the model predicts that there is an exploitable trade-off between inflation and output. Moreover, increasing the frequency at which the monetary authority implements the high money growth rate can raise society's welfare.

The reasoning behind this exploitable trade-off is as follows. In the low-money-growth-rate state, buyers hoard money balances in order to signal the high value of money to sellers. As a result, output in the DM is quite low, and this is costly for society. In contrast, in the high-money-growth-rate state, since buyers do not hoard any cash, output is higher than it is in the low-money-growth-rate state. If we assume that the value of money is fixed, then by implementing the high-money-growth-rate state more often, the monetary authority can reduce the welfare cost associated with signaling. We will refer to this as the (positive) output-composition effect associated with increasing α. But, of course, the value of money does not remain fixed if the monetary

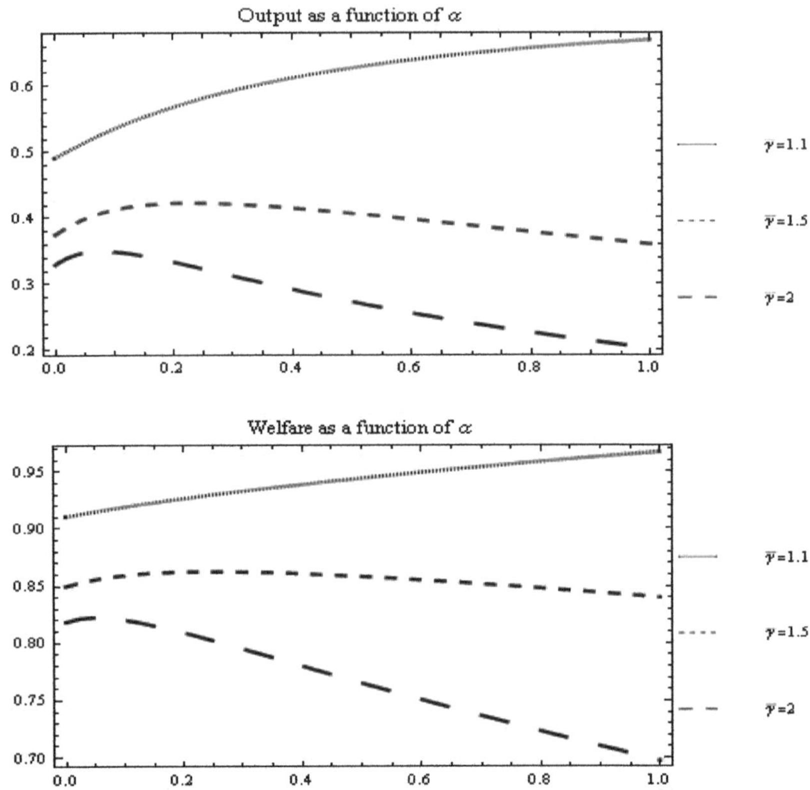

Figure 7.6
The inflation-output trade-off

authority implements the high-money-growth-rate state more often; it falls. As a result, the amount of output that is purchased in both the high- and low-money-growth states falls. We will refer to this as the inflation tax effect associated with increasing α. If the output-composition effect dominates the inflation tax effect, then increasing the frequency of the high inflation state actually increases output and welfare.

Our numerical examples indicate that if the difference between money growth rates is not too big, then the output-composition effect can dominate the inflation tax effect for all values of $\alpha \neq 0$. When the difference between money growth rates is not too big, e.g., $\bar{\gamma} = 1.1$ in our numerical example, if the monetary authority cannot implement $\gamma = \underline{\gamma}$ with certainty, then, in fact, it is optimal to choose the high money growth rate with probability one. If, however, the difference between monetary growth rates is not small, e.g., $\bar{\gamma} = 1.5$ or $\bar{\gamma} = 2$ in our numerical example, then output and welfare are non-monotonic in α. This means that as the monetary authority increases the frequency of the high-money-growth-rate state, at some point the inflation tax effect dominates the output-composition effect, which implies that output and welfare will fall. For these cases, there is an optimal frequency to implement the high-money-growth-rate state, and it is less than one.

Up to this point, the policy takes the form of a choice of α, taking $\underline{\gamma}$ and $\bar{\gamma}$ as given. Now, let's examine the optimal monetary policy when the policy maker can also choose $\underline{\gamma}$ and $\bar{\gamma}$. One may wonder if the inflation-output trade-off justifies a deviation from the Friedman rule. We saw in Chapter 6 that the optimal monetary policy in an environment where the money supply is growing at a constant rate sets the cost of holding real balances to zero. In our model, this version of the Friedman rule would require that $\beta^{-1} = \frac{1-\alpha}{\underline{\gamma}} + \frac{\alpha}{\bar{\gamma}}$. Since, at the Friedman rule, the expected rate of return of fiat money must equal the gross rate of time preference, we have

$$\underline{\gamma} < \beta < \bar{\gamma},$$

if $\alpha \in (0,1)$ and $\underline{\gamma} \neq \bar{\gamma}$. Hence, the ex-post rate of return of fiat money is larger than the rate of time preference in the low-inflation state, but it is smaller in the high-inflation state. From (7.28), the quantity traded in the high-inflation state approaches the first-best level, q^*, as the expected cost of holding real balances, i, approaches zero. And, from (7.17), the quantity traded in the low-inflation state, q_H, solves

$$u(q_H) - \frac{\underline{\gamma}}{\bar{\gamma}} c(q_H) = u(q^*) - c(q^*). \tag{7.30}$$

Since $\frac{\underline{\gamma}}{\bar{\gamma}} < 1$, the smallest solution to (7.30) has $q_H < q^*$. So equalizing the expected rate of return of currency to the rate of time preference is not enough to implement the efficient allocation. The informational asymmetry between buyers and sellers causes the quantity traded in the low-inflation state to be inefficiently low at the Friedman rule. This inefficiency can only be removed if the monetary authority eliminates the fluctuations of the money supply, i.e., if

$$\underline{\gamma} = \beta = \bar{\gamma}. \tag{7.31}$$

Clearly, if (7.31) holds, then, from (7.30), $q_H = q^*$. Hence, targeting the nominal interest rate is not sufficient to ensure that the efficient allocation is implementable; the optimal policy consists in targeting the rate of growth of money supply. This is one instance where the distinction between the two policies—targeting nominal interest rates versus money growth rates—really matters.

7.5 An Alternative Information Structure

Thus far we have assumed that buyers receive an informative signal about the rate of growth of money supply and, hence, the future value of money, while sellers do not. This assumption is consistent with the view that agents have greater incentives or opportunities to learn about the future value of the assets they hold. It is equally plausible that sellers receive prior information regarding monetary policy.

To see how the information structure affects the relationship between inflation and output, we will now suppose that sellers are informed about monetary policy, while buyers are not. The bargaining game that occurs in the DM, which is illustrated in Figure 7.7, has the structure of a screening game. The assumption that buyers are uninformed about monetary policy is captured by the dotted line in Figure 7.7 that represents an information set.

An offer by the buyer consists of a menu of various terms of trades. Since there are two possible signals that the seller can receive, we need only consider menus with two items, $\{(q_H,d_H),(q_L,d_L)\}$, where (q_H,d_H)

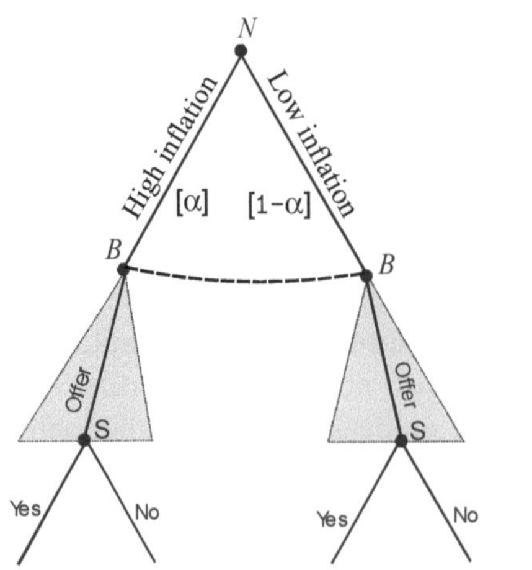

Figure 7.7
Bargaining game when buyers are uninformed

is the terms of trade intended for sellers in the low-inflation state—when the value of fiat money is high—and (q_L, d_L) is the terms of trade for sellers in the high-inflation state. A buyer holding m units of money offers a menu $\{(q_H, d_H), (q_L, d_L)\}$ that solves

$$\max_{q_H, q_L, d_H, d_L} \{(1-\alpha)\left[u(q_H) - \phi_H d_H\right] + \alpha\left[u(q_L) - \phi_L d_L\right]\}, \tag{7.32}$$

subject to $d_L \leq m$, $d_H \leq m$ and

$$-c(q_H) + \phi_H d_H \geq 0, \tag{7.33}$$

$$-c(q_L) + \phi_L d_L \geq 0, \tag{7.34}$$

$$-c(q_H) + \phi_H d_H \geq -c(q_L) + \phi_H d_L, \tag{7.35}$$

$$-c(q_L) + \phi_L d_L \geq -c(q_H) + \phi_L d_H. \tag{7.36}$$

According to (7.32)-(7.36), the buyer maximizes his expected surplus, subject to individual rationality and incentive compatibility constraints. The conditions (7.33) and (7.34) are the individual rationality constraints for sellers in the low-inflation and high-inflation states, respectively, while conditions (7.35) and (7.36) are the incentive-compatibility constraints. According to (7.35), a seller who knows that the money growth rate will be low in the current period prefers allocation (q_H, d_H) to the terms of trade intended for the high-inflation-type seller. Inequality (7.36) has a similar interpretation.

In the Appendix we show that the solution to (7.32)-(7.36) has individual-rationality constraint (7.34) and incentive-compatibility constraint (7.35) binding, i.e.,

$$-c(q_L) + \phi_L d_L = 0, \tag{7.37}$$

$$-c(q_H) + \phi_H d_H = -c(q_L) + \phi_H d_L > 0. \tag{7.38}$$

From (7.37), buyers leave no surplus to sellers in the high-inflation state. In contrast, from (7.38), the seller is able to extract a positive surplus, or informational rent, in the low-inflation state which is equal to

$$-c(q_H) + \phi_H d_H = -c(q_L) + \phi_L d_L + (\phi_H - \phi_L)\, d_L = (\phi_H - \phi_L)\, d_L. \tag{7.39}$$

Intuitively, a seller in the low-inflation state, state H, is the one who has an incentive to misrepresent his private information since when the value of money is low, he does not have to produce much for the same transfer of money. This incentive to lie by the seller in state H explains why his incentive-compatiblity constraint is binding. And, since a seller has no incentive to claim that inflation is low, state H, when it is actually high, state L, the buyer is able to extract all of the match surplus in the high-inflation state. This is why the individual-rationality constraint for the seller binds in state L.

One can check (see the Appendix) that $d_L \leq d_H$ and $q_L \leq q_H$, and that either $d_L = d_H$ and $q_H = q_L$ or $d_L < d_H$ and $q_H > q_L$. So, when the allocation is a separating one, both output and velocity are negatively correlated with inflation. Hence, the nature of the informational asymmetry between buyers and sellers is crucial for the sign of the correlation between inflation and output. If buyers are informed, then there is a positive correlation between inflation and output. This trade-off emerges because buyers signal the high value of money by retaining a fraction of their money holdings. If, on the other hand, sellers are informed, then the correlation between inflation and output is negative. In this situation, buyers reduce their cost of extracting sellers' information by spending less money in the high-inflation state, which reduces sellers' rent.

Consider a policy where the cost of holding real balances is zero, $i = 0$. For this policy, the buyer's problem (7.32)-(7.36) can be greatly simplified. First, buyers will accumulate sufficient real balances so that they are unconstrained in all states, which implies that the constraints $d_L \leq m$ and $d_H \leq m$ can be ignored. Second, since the seller receives an informational rent equal to $(\phi_H - \phi_L) d_L$ in the low inflation state, the buyer's objective function, (7.32), thanks to (7.39), can be written as

$$(1-\alpha)\left[u(q_H) - c(q_H) - (\phi_H - \phi_L) d_L\right] + \alpha\left[u(q_L) - \phi_L d_L\right].$$

And finally, since the seller does not receive any surplus in the high-inflation state, (7.37), the buyer's objective function can be further rewritten as

$$(1-\alpha)\left[u(q_H) - c(q_H) - \frac{(\phi_H - \phi_L)}{\phi_L} c(q_L)\right] + \alpha\left[u(q_L) - c(q_L)\right]. \tag{7.40}$$

The buyer's problem, therefore, is simply to choose q_H and q_L so as to maximize (7.40). The first-order conditions for this problem with respect to q_H and q_L are $u'(q_H) = c'(q_H)$ or $q_H = q^*$ and

$$\frac{u'(q_L)}{c'(q_L)} = 1 + \left(\frac{1-\alpha}{\alpha}\right)\left(\frac{\bar{\gamma}}{\underline{\gamma}} - 1\right), \tag{7.41}$$

respectively. When the Friedman rule is implemented, the quantity traded in the low-inflation state is socially efficient, while the quantity traded in the high-inflation state is inefficiently low, provided that

$\underline{\gamma} < \bar{\gamma}$. As in the previous section, a policy that consists in setting the expected cost of holding real balances equal to zero is not sufficient to obtain the efficient allocation when buyers and sellers are asymmetrically informed. In order to implement the efficient allocation, the money growth rate must also be constant, $\bar{\gamma} = \underline{\gamma}$.

7.6 Further Readings

Lucas (1972, 1973) introduces models with imperfect information to explain how unanticipated monetary shocks affect output. Lucas (1972) adopts an overlapping generations model, in which young producers are divided unevenly across markets and the supply of money is stochastic. The producers observe the price on their market, but they do not know the average price level. Therefore, conditional on the price they observe, producers will have to disentangle real from nominal disturbances. A tractable version of the model with aggregate shocks is provided by Wallace (1992). Benassy (1999) provides analytical solutions to the model. Wallace (1997) considers an unanticipated change of the money supply in a random matching model, and shows that the short-run effects are predominantly real while the long-run effects are predominantly nominal. Faig and Li (2009) introduce the Lucas signal extraction problem into the Lagos-Wright model and estimate the welfare costs of expected and erratic inflations.

Araujo and Camargo (2006) consider a search-theoretic model in which information about the value of indivisible fiat money is imperfect and learning is decentralized. Araujo and Shevshenko (2006) consider an economy where agents have incomplete information with respect to the value of money, and they learn from private experiences.

Models with sticky prices include Taylor (1980), Rotemberg (1982), and Calvo (1983). Benabou (1988) and Diamond (1993) introduce menu costs in search-theoretic models without money and show that inflation can be welfare improving. Craig and Rocheteau (2008) develop a continuous-time version of Lagos-Wright with menu costs. The optimal monetary policy corresponds to a deflation. Aruoba and Schorfheide (2011) also introduce nominal rigidities into a search model with divisible money. Head, Liu, Menzio, and Wright (2012) generate price dispersion and infrequent price adjustments in a New Monetarist model with perfectly flexible prices where consumers are heterogenously informed, as in the Burdett and Judd (1983) model of price dispersion. Rocheteau, Weill, and Wong (2015b) consider the same environment as the one in this book where buyers are subject to the constraint $y \leq \bar{y}$. When this constraint binds, equilibria feature a non-degenerate distribution of money holdings. Following a one-time money injection prices do not increase as much as the increase in the money supply and output can go up even though prices are fully flexible and there is no market segmentation.

In the context of a search model with divisible money, Williamson (2006) assumes that agents participate only infrequently in the competitive market where monetary injections take place. Finally, Sanches, and Williamson (2011) introduce an asymmetry of information regarding the seller's value of money in the context of the Lagos-Wright model.

Appendix

A. Informed sellers and uninformed buyers

Consider a match between a buyer holding a portfolio of m units of money and a seller. The buyer is uninformed about the future value of money, but he knows that with probability α the value of money is ϕ_L while with probability $1-\alpha$ the value of money is ϕ_H. The seller is informed about the value of money.

The buyer offers a menu $\{(q_H, d_H), (q_L, d_L)\}$ where (q_H, d_H) are the terms of trade for the seller in the high state and (q_L, d_L) are the terms of trade for the seller in the low state. The buyer commits to these terms of trade. The buyer's problem is:

$$\max_{(q_H,d_H),(q_L,d_L)} \{\alpha [u(q_L) - \phi_L d_L] + (1-\alpha) [u(q_H) - \phi_H d_H]\}, \tag{7.42}$$

subject to the feasibility constraints $d_H \in [0, m]$, $d_L \in [0, m]$, and the following incentive constraints:

$$-c(q_L) + \phi_L d_L \geq 0 \tag{7.43}$$

$$-c(q_H) + \phi_H d_H \geq 0 \tag{7.44}$$

$$-c(q_L) + \phi_L d_L \geq -c(q_H) + \phi_L d_H \tag{7.45}$$

$$-c(q_H) + \phi_H d_H \geq -c(q_L) + \phi_H d_L. \tag{7.46}$$

The conditions (7.43) and (7.44) are individual rationality constraints for sellers in the low and high states, respectively. Conditions (7.45) and (7.46) are incentive-compatibility constraints.

We now establish that for any optimal menu, (7.43) and (7.46) are binding, i.e.,

$$-c(q_L) + \phi_L d_L = 0 \tag{7.47}$$

$$-c(q_H) + \phi_H d_H = -c(q_L) + \phi_H d_L = (\phi_H - \phi_L) d_L. \tag{7.48}$$

First, (7.44) and (7.46) cannot both hold with a strict inequality since if this were the case the buyer could raise his expected surplus by increasing q_H and keeping (q_L, d_H, d_L) unchanged without upsetting (7.43)-(7.46). By identical reasoning, (7.43) and (7.45) cannot both hold with strict inequality. Second, (7.46) must bind. To see this assume the contrary, i.e., that (7.46) holds with a strict inequality. Then (7.46) and (7.43) imply that

$$-c(q_H) + \phi_H d_H > -c(q_L) + \phi_H d_L \geq 0.$$

This set of inequalities implies that whenever (7.46) holds with a strict inequality, then so does (7.44). A contradiction with our first point. Hence, (7.46) must bind. Third, to show that (7.43) binds assume to the contrary that (7.43) holds with a strict inequality. Then, from the reasoning above, (7.45) must bind. From (7.46) and (7.45) at equality,

$$\phi_L\left(d_H - d_L\right) = c(q_H) - c(q_L) = \phi_H\left(d_H - d_L\right).$$

This implies that the menu offered by the buyer is pooling, $d_H = d_L$ and $q_L = q_H$. But then (7.43) cannot be slack since otherwise the seller would be able to increase his expected payoff by lowering q_L and q_H without upsetting any constraint (7.43)-(7.46). A contradiction.

The reasoning above shows that buyers leave no surplus to sellers in the low state whereas sellers in the high state can extract an informational rent equal to $(\phi_H - \phi_L)d_L$. Moreover, sellers in the low state transfer less money than sellers in the high state, $d_L \leq d_H$. To see this, rearrange (7.45) and (7.46) to read

$$\phi_L(d_H - d_L) \leq c(q_H) - c(q_L) \leq \phi_H\left(d_H - d_L\right). \tag{7.49}$$

It also implies that $q_L \leq q_H$.

We will make use of the previous insights to reduce the buyer's problem to the maximization of (7.42) subject to the constraints (7.47) and (7.48). From (7.48), it is immediate that (7.44) holds. Moreover, from (7.47)-(7.48), (7.45) holds whenever $d_L \leq d_H$, which, as we demonstrated above, is the case.

The buyer's maximization problem can be divided into two steps. First, taking d_L as given, the buyer chooses the terms of trade in the H-state subject to the constraint that sellers must receive a surplus equal to $(\phi_H - \phi_L)d_L$. The buyer's surplus in the H-state solves:

$$\mathcal{S}_H^b(d_L) = \max_{(q_H, d_H)} \left[u(q_H) - \phi_H d_H\right] \tag{7.50}$$

$$\text{s.t.} \ -c(q_H) + \phi_H d_H = (\phi_H - \phi_L)d_L \tag{7.51}$$

$$d_H \in [0, m]. \tag{7.52}$$

Substituting $\phi_H d_H$ from (7.51) into (7.50) the buyer's surplus in the high state becomes

$$\mathcal{S}_H^b(d_L) = \max_{q_H} \left[u(q_H) - c(q_H)\right] - (\phi_H - \phi_L)d_L$$

$$\text{s.t.} \ c(q_H) + (\phi_H - \phi_L)d_L \in [0, \phi_H m].$$

If $c(q^*) + (\phi_H - \phi_L)d_L \leq \phi_H m$, then $q_H = q^*$ and $\phi_H d_H = c(q^*) + (\phi_H - \phi_L)d_L$. If the buyer holds enough money balances, he will compensate the seller for producing q^* and he will offer him an informational rent to guarantee that he chooses the terms of trade intended for the H-state. If $c(q^*) + (\phi_H - \phi_L)d_L > \phi_H m$, then the feasibility constraint $d_H \leq m$ is binding and $q_H = c^{-1}(\phi_H m - (\phi_H - \phi_L)d_L)$. Consequently,

$$\mathcal{S}_H^b(d_L) = u(q^*) - c(q^*) - (\phi_H - \phi_L)d_L \text{ if } c(q^*) + (\phi_H - \phi_L) d_L \leq \phi_H m. \tag{7.53}$$

$$= u \circ c^{-1}(\phi_H m - (\phi_H - \phi_L)d_L) - \phi_H m \text{ otherwise.} \tag{7.54}$$

It is immediate from (7.53)-(7.54) that $\mathcal{S}_H^b(d_L)$ is a decreasing function of d_L and it is differentiable:

$$\mathcal{S}_H^{b\prime}(d_L) = -(\phi_H - \phi_L) \text{ if } c(q^*) + (\phi_H - \phi_L)d_L \leq \phi_H m.$$
$$= -\frac{u'(q_H)}{c'(q_H)}(\phi_H - \phi_L) \text{ otherwise.}$$

Moreover, since q_H is a decreasing function of d_L, it is easy to check that $\mathcal{S}_H^b(d_L)$ is a concave function of d_L.

In the second step, the buyer chooses the terms of trade in the L-state in order to maximize his expected surplus. The buyer's expected surplus is

$$\mathcal{S}^b = \max_{q_L, d_L} \left\{ (1-\alpha)\mathcal{S}_H^b(d_L) + \alpha \left[u(q_L) - \phi_L d_L\right] \right\} \tag{7.55}$$

$$\text{s.t.} \quad -c(q_L) + \phi_L d_L = 0 \tag{7.56}$$

$$d_L \in [0, m]. \tag{7.57}$$

According to (7.55) the buyer takes into account that the surplus in the H-state depends on the transfer of money in the L-state through the incentive-compatibility conditions. Substitute $\phi_L d_L$ from (7.56) into (7.55) to rewrite this problem as:

$$\mathcal{S}^b = \max_{q_L} \left\{ (1-\alpha)\mathcal{S}_H^b\left(\frac{c(q_L)}{\phi_L}\right) + \alpha \left[u(q_L) - c(q_L)\right] \right\}$$
$$\text{s.t. } c(q_L) \in [0, \phi_L m].$$

If the constraint $c(q_L) \leq \phi_L m$ does not bind, then the choice of q_L is given by the following first-order condition:

$$-(1-\alpha)\frac{u'(q_H)}{c'(q_H)}\left(\frac{\phi_H - \phi_L}{\phi_L}\right)c'(q_L) + \alpha\left[u'(q_L) - c'(q_L)\right] = 0. \tag{7.58}$$

We distinguish three cases.

1. $d_H \leq m$ and $d_L \leq m$ are not binding.
From (7.53), $q_H = q^*$ and from (7.58) q_L solves

$$\frac{u'(q_L)}{c'(q_L)} = 1 + \left(\frac{1-\alpha}{\alpha}\right)\left(\frac{\phi_H - \phi_L}{\phi_L}\right). \tag{7.59}$$

Let $\tilde{q}_L < q^*$ denote the solution to (7.59). From (7.56), $d_L = \frac{c(\tilde{q}_L)}{\phi_L}$ and from (7.51) $d_H = d_L + [c(q^*) - c(\tilde{q}_L)]/\phi_H$. This condition $d_H \leq m$ is equivalent to $m \geq c(\tilde{q}_L)/\phi_L) + [c(q^*) - c(\tilde{q}_L)]/\phi_H$.

2. $d_H \leq m$ is binding and $d_L \leq m$ is not binding.
From (7.54), $q_H = c^{-1}[\phi_H m - (\phi_H - \phi_L)c(q_L)/\phi_L]$. From (7.58) q_L solves

$$\frac{u'(q_L)}{c'(q_L)} = 1 + \left(\frac{1-\alpha}{\alpha}\right)\frac{u'(q_H)}{c'(q_H)}\left(\frac{\phi_H - \phi_L}{\phi_L}\right). \tag{7.60}$$

The left side of (7.60) is decreasing from ∞ to 1 as q_L increases from 0 to q^* and the right side of (7.60) is increasing in q_L (since q_H is decreasing in q_L) and is greater than 1 when $q_L = 0$. Consequently, there is a unique $q_L = \hat{q}_L \in [0, q^*]$ that solves (7.60). The condition $d_L \leq m$ is equivalent to $c(q_L) \leq \phi_L m$, which can be rearranged as $q_L \leq q_H$. It can be checked that q_L and q_H are increasing in m. Moreover, from (7.60), $[u'(q_L)/c'(q_L)]/[u'(q_H)/c'(q_H)]$ is increasing in m. Hence, there is a threshold for m below which $d_L \leq m$ binds. This threshold is defined from (7.60) where $q_L = q_H = q = c^{-1}(\phi_L m)$,

$$\frac{u'(q)}{c'(q)}\left[\frac{\phi_L - (1-\alpha)\,\phi_H}{\alpha\phi_L}\right] = 1.$$

This threshold exists if $\phi_L > (1-\alpha)\,\phi_H$.

3. $d_H \leq m$ and $d_L \leq m$ are binding.
From (7.54), $q_H = c^{-1}[\phi_H m - (\phi_H - \phi_L)c(q_L)/\phi_L]$ and from (7.56), $q_L = c^{-1}(\phi_L m)$. This gives $q_H = q_L = c^{-1}(\phi_L m)$.

Now that we have determined the terms of trade in a bilateral match, we can solve for the buyer's choice of money holdings in the CM of period t. In this case, $\phi_H = \phi_t/\underline{\gamma}$ and $\phi_L = \phi_t/\bar{\gamma}$. The buyer's problem is

$$\max_{m \geq 0}\left\{-\hat{\imath}\phi_t m + \sigma(1-\alpha)\left[u(q_H) - c(q_H) - \left(\frac{\bar{\gamma}-\underline{\gamma}}{\underline{\gamma}}\right)c(q_L)\right]\right.$$
$$\left. + \sigma\alpha\left[u(q_L) - c(q_L)\right]\right\}, \tag{7.61}$$

where $\hat{\imath} = \beta^{-1} - [\alpha/\bar{\gamma} + (1-\alpha)/\underline{\gamma}]$, where we used that the buyer's surplus in the H-state is the whole match surplus net of the informational rent received by the seller, $(\phi_H - \phi_L)d_L$, and where q_H solves

$$q_H = q^* \text{ if } \phi_t m \geq \underline{\gamma} c(q^*) + (\bar{\gamma} - \underline{\gamma})\, c(q_L)$$
$$q_H = c^{-1}\left(\frac{\phi_t m}{\underline{\gamma}} - \left(\frac{\bar{\gamma} - \underline{\gamma}}{\underline{\gamma}}\right) c(q_L)\right) \text{ otherwise,}$$

and q_L solves

$$q_L = \min\left[c^{-1}\left(\frac{\phi_t m}{\bar{\gamma}}\right), \hat{q}_L\right].$$

Since it is costly to hold money, it is immediate that the constraint $d_H \leq m$ must be binding, in which case $q_H = c^{-1}[\phi_t m/\underline{\gamma} - (\bar{\gamma} - \underline{\gamma})c(q_L)/\underline{\gamma}]$. The first-order condition with respect to $\phi_t m$ gives

$$\frac{\hat{\imath}}{\sigma} = \left(\frac{1-\alpha}{\underline{\gamma}}\right)\left[\frac{u'(q_H)}{c'(q_H)} - 1\right] + \left\{\frac{\alpha}{\bar{\gamma}}\left[\frac{u'(q_L)}{c'(q_L)} - 1\right] - \left(\frac{1-\alpha}{\bar{\gamma}}\right) \frac{u'(q_H)}{c'(q_H)}\left(\frac{\bar{\gamma} - \underline{\gamma}}{\underline{\gamma}}\right)\right\}. \quad (7.62)$$

If the constraint $d_L \leq m$ does not bind, then the second term on the right side is 0 and $q_L = \hat{q}_L$. As i tends to 0, then q_H approaches q^* and q_L approaches $\tilde{q}_L < q^*$.

8 Money and Credit

The key distinction between monetary and credit trades is that monetary trades are quid pro quo, i.e., goods and services are exchanged simultaneously for currency, and do not involve future obligations, while credit trades are intertemporal and involve a delayed settlement. In reality, some trades are conducted through credit arrangements; other trades are based on monetary exchange. The coexistence of these different forms of payment raises some interesting questions such as: are the frictions that make monetary exchange essential, e.g., lack of commitment and record-keeping, compatible with the existence of credit? How does the presence of monetary exchange affect the use and the availability of credit? And, how does the availability of credit affect the value of money? We address these questions in this chapter.

A straightforward way to model the coexistence of monetary exchange and credit arrangements is to introduce some heterogeneity between trading matches. For example, suppose that in some markets there is no record-keeping technology, while in others there is a record-keeping technology and agents' identities can be costlessly verified. In the former markets, agents can only trade with money, while in the latter they can resort to credit arrangements. We consider such an environment, where there is a costless technology that enforces debt contracts in some markets but not in others. In this kind of economy we do obtain coexistence of money and credit, but there is a dichotomy between the monetary and credit sectors. The amount of output that is traded with credit is determined independently from the amount of output that is traded with money. Moreover, monetary policy has no effect on credit use.

Since this dichotomy is an artifact of costless enforcement, we break it by introducing limited commitment under imperfect monitoring. Only a fraction of buyers are monitored while the remaining ones are either not monitored or are untrustworthy to repay their debt. This economy with limited commitment displays three types of equilibria. For low inflation rates credit is not incentive feasible and all transactions are conducted with money only. For intermediate inflation rates there is coexistence of money and credit: monitored buyers pay with credit while unmonitored buyers use fiat money. Moreover, endogenous debt limits depend on monetary policy: debt limits increase with inflation. Finally, for large inflation rates agents stop using money so that all transactions occur with credit.

Alternatively, we capture a notion of commitment by using the idea of reputation. We do so by assuming that some decentralized market matches are short-lived, lasting only for that period, while others are longer-lived and can be productive for many periods. The use of credit is not incentive-feasible in short-lived matches, since, owing to the lack of commitment and record-keeping, the buyer will always default on repaying his obligation. In contrast, the buyer's behavior in a longer-lived match is disciplined by reputational considerations that will trigger the dissolution of a valuable relationship following a default. In this environment, we show that the availability of credit depends on the value of money and monetary policy, as well as the extent of the trading frictions.

In order to explain the composition between credit and monetary trades we make the use of record-keeping both costly and a choice variable of the individual. Assuming that the gains from trade vary across matches in the decentralized market, the mix between monetary and credit transactions is endogenous, and depends on monetary policy. Credit is used for large transactions and money is used for smaller ones, and, as inflation increases, the fraction of credit transactions increases. As well, if verification requires that sellers undertake an ex ante investment, then multiple equilibria can emerge, where different equilibria are characterized by different payment arrangements. In this situation, a transitory change in monetary policy can lead to a permanent change in payment arrangements. Because of this, we conclude that the emergence of a payment system depends not only on fundamentals and policies, but also on histories and social customs.

The sort of lending and borrowing that we have considered so far have agents borrowing goods and repaying with goods. That is, a credit transaction does not involve money. We consider an environment with a market for loanable funds, where agents borrow and lend money. This market is useful in the presence of idiosyncratic shocks since it allows liquid assets to be reallocated from agents with low liquidity needs to agents with high liquidity needs.

8.1 Dichotomy Between Money and Credit

In this section, we modify the model with divisible money described in Chapter 3.1 by dividing the day market into two subperiods: a morning (DM1) and an afternoon (DM2). The morning and afternoon subperiods are similar in terms of agents' preferences and specialization—buyers can consume in both subperiods but cannot produce, while sellers can produce but cannot consume—and in terms of the trading process—buyers and sellers trade in bilateral matches. The buyer's instantaneous utility function is

$$U^b(q_1, q_2, x, h) = v(q_1) + u(q_2) + x - h,$$

where q_1 is the consumption in the first subperiod, q_2 is the consumption in the second subperiod, x is the consumption of the general good in the third subperiod, and h is the utility cost of producing h units of the general good. The utility functions $v(q)$ and $u(q)$ are strictly increasing and concave, with $v(0) = u(0) = 0$, $v'(0) = u'(0) = +\infty$, and $v'(+\infty) = u'(+\infty) = 0$. Without loss of generality, we assume that there is no discounting between subperiods. The discount factor across periods is β.

The utility function of a seller is

$$U^s(q_1, q_2, x, h) = -\psi(q_1) - c(q_2) + x - h,$$

where $\psi(q)$ and $c(q)$ are strictly increasing and convex, with $\psi(0) = c(0) = 0$, $\psi'(0) = c'(0) = 0$, and $\psi'(+\infty) = c'(+\infty) = +\infty$. We denote q_1^* the solution to $v'(q) = \psi'(q)$ and q_2^* the solution to $u'(q) = c'(q)$. These are the quantities that maximize the match surpluses in the first two subperiods. The timing and preferences in a representative period are described in Figure 8.1.

Both the morning market, DM1, and the afternoon market, DM2, are characterized by search frictions. A buyer meets a seller in the DM1 with probability $\sigma_1 \in [0, 1]$, and in the DM2 with probability $\sigma_2 \in [0, 1]$, where buyer-seller matches in the morning and the afternoon are independent events. The DM1 and DM2 differ in the following important dimension: in the former, there is a record-keeping technology and all agents' identities are known to all other agents, while in the latter there

	MORNING (DM 1)	AFTERNOON (DM 2)	NIGHT (CM)
Utility of consumption:	$\upsilon(q_1)$	$u(q_2)$	x
Disutility of production:	$-\psi(q_1)$	$-c(q_2)$	$-h$
	Record-keeping Enforcement	Anonymity	Record-keeping Enforcement

Figure 8.1
Timing of a representative period

is no record-keeping and all agents are anonymous. Moreover, any contract written in the DM1 will be enforced at night since agents who renege on their obligations can be subject to arbitrarily large fines in the CM. As a result, buyers can get output in the DM1 by using credit—or, equivalently, by issuing an IOU—to be repaid at night.

We will assume that all the IOUs are one period in nature in that they are repaid in the subsequent competitive night market, CM. Moreover, the authenticity of the IOUs issued in DM1 cannot be verified in DM2, and hence they cannot be used as a medium of exchange in the afternoon (e.g., because fake IOUs can be produced at zero cost). Since buyers are anonymous in the DM2, sellers will not accept IOUs for output produced in the subperiod because buyers would renege on these at night. The anonymity of agents in the DM2 implies that money has an essential role in this environment.

We assume that the stock of money grows at a constant rate $\gamma \equiv M_{t+1}/M_t$, and that this is accomplished by a lump-sum transfers to buyers in the CM. We focus on stationary equilibria where real balances and the quantities traded in the different subperiods are constant over time. The former implies that $\phi_{t+1}/\phi_t = M_t/M_{t+1} = \gamma^{-1}$.

Consider a buyer at the beginning of the CM who holds $z = \phi_t m$ units of real balances and has issued b units of IOUs in the previous DM1, where each unit is normalized to be worth one unit of general good. The value function for this buyer, $W^b(z, -b)$, is given by

$$W^b(z, -b) = \max_{x,h,z'} \left\{ x - h + \beta V^b(z') \right\} \tag{8.1}$$

$$x + b + \gamma z' = z + h + T, \tag{8.2}$$

where V^b is the value of a buyer at the beginning of the day market. According to (8.2), the buyer finances his night time consumption, x, the repayment of his IOU, b, and his next-period real balances, $\gamma z'$, with his current real balances, z, his labor income, h, and the lump-sum transfer from the government (expressed in terms of the general good), $T = \phi_t (M_{t+1} - M_t)$. Recall that the rate of return of real balances is $\phi_{t+1}/\phi_t = \gamma^{-1}$. Hence, in order to hold z' units of real balances in the next period, the buyer must acquire $\gamma z'$ units of real balances in the current period. Substituting $x - h$ from (8.2) into (8.1), we get

$$W^b(z, -b) = z - b + T + \max_{z' \geq 0} \left\{ -\gamma z' + \beta V^b(z') \right\}. \tag{8.3}$$

As before, the value function is linear in the buyer's current portfolio, and the buyer's choice of real balances is independent of his current portfolio.

The value function of a seller who holds z units of real balances and b IOUs at the beginning of the CM period is denoted by $W^s(z, b)$. Since sellers have no incentive to accumulate real balances at night, this value function is given by

$$W^s(z, b) = z + b + \beta V^s, \tag{8.4}$$

where V^s is the value function of a seller at the beginning of the next period. Recall that sellers do not receive transfers in the CM.

Consider now a bilateral match in the DM2 between a buyer holding z units of real balances and a seller. The buyer is anonymous and cannot use credit. Hence, he can transfer at most z units of real balances to the seller in exchange for afternoon output. We assume that the buyer makes a take-it-or-leave-it offer. Because real balances enter the beginning-of-the-night value functions of the buyer and seller in a linear fashion, the buyer's offer to the seller is given by the solution to the following simple problem,

$$\max_{q_2, d_2} [u(q_2) - d_2] \text{ s.t. } -c(q_2) + d_2 \geq 0 \text{ and } d_2 \leq z,$$

where the first inequality represents the seller's participation constraint and the second is a feasibility constraint. The solution to this maximization problem is

$$q_2 = \min\left[q_2^*, c^{-1}(z)\right], \tag{8.5}$$

$$d_2 = c(q_2), \tag{8.6}$$

that is, the buyer purchases the efficient level of output if he has sufficient real balances; otherwise he spends all of his balances on output.

The value function of a buyer with z units of real balances and b units of debt at the beginning of DM2 is

$$V_2^b(z,-b) = \sigma_2 \{u[q_2(z)] - c[q_2(z)]\} + W^b(z,-b). \tag{8.7}$$

Similarly, the value function of a seller is $V_2^s(z,b) = W^s(z,b)$.

We can now turn to the buyer's bargaining problem in DM1. The buyer who holds z units of real balances makes a take-it-or-leave-it offer that solves:

$$\max_{q_1,d_1,b_1} \left[\upsilon(q_1) + V_2^b(z-d_1,-b_1) \right]$$

$$\text{s.t.} \quad -\psi(q_1) + W^s(d_1,b_1) \geq W^s(0,0)$$

$$d_1 \leq z.$$

Using the linearity of $W^s$and the seller's participation at equality, $d_1 + b_1 = \psi(q_1)$, the buyer's problem can be simplified to

$$\max_{d_1,b_1} \left[\upsilon \circ \psi^{-1}(d_1+b_1) + V_2^b(z-d_1,-b_1) \right], \tag{8.8}$$

The first-order conditions, ignoring the constraint $d_1 \leq z$, are

$$\frac{\upsilon'(q_1)}{\psi'(q_1)} - 1 \leq 0, \text{ `` $=$ '' if } b_1 > 0 \tag{8.9}$$

$$\frac{\upsilon'(q_1)}{\psi'(q_1)} - \sigma_2 \left[\frac{u'(q_2)}{c'(q_2)} - 1 \right] - 1 \leq 0, \text{ `` $=$ '' if } d_1 > 0. \tag{8.10}$$

If $q_2 < q_2^*$, then it is immediate that $d_1 = 0$. If the buyer is constrained by his real balances in the DM2, he should not spend them in the DM1 and he should trade with credit only. If $q_2 = q_2^*$, then the buyer is indifferent between using credit or cash as long as he keeps enough real balances to purchase q_2^* in DM2. So, with no loss in generality, we can assume that in the DM1 the buyer trades with credit only. From (8.9), it is immediate that $q_1 = q_1^*$.

We can now write the value function of a buyer at the beginning of a period:

$$V^b(z) = \sigma_1 \left\{ \upsilon(q_1^*) + V_2^b[z, -\psi(q_1^*)] \right\} + (1-\sigma_1) V_2^b(z,0). \tag{8.11}$$

Using the linearity of V_2^b with respect to its second argument, and substituting $V_2^b(z,0)$ from its expression given by (8.7) into (8.11), we obtain

$$\begin{aligned} V^b(z) &= \sigma_1 [\upsilon(q_1^*) - \psi(q_1^*)] + V_2^b(z,0) \\ &= \sigma_1 \{\upsilon(q_1^*) - \psi(q_1^*)\} + \sigma_2 \{u[q_2(z)] - c[q_2(z)]\} + z + W^b(0,0). \end{aligned} \tag{8.12}$$

If we substitute $V^b(z)$ from (8.12) into (8.3), then the buyer's portfolio problem in the CM can be represented by

$$\max_{z \geq 0} \{-iz + \sigma_2 \{u[q_2(z)] - c[q_2(z)]\}\}, \tag{8.13}$$

where $i \equiv (\gamma - \beta)/\beta$. Note that the buyer's real balances only affects his surplus in the DM2. The first-order (necessary and sufficient) condition for problem (8.13) is

$$\frac{u'(q_2)}{c'(q_2)} = 1 + \frac{i}{\sigma_2}. \tag{8.14}$$

This expression for the output traded in the DM2 is identical to the one we derived in Chapter 6.1, i.e., (6.8).

An equilibrium is a list $(q_1, q_2, b_1, d_2, \{\phi_t\})$ that solves $q_1 = q_1^*$, $b_1 = \psi(q_1^*)$, (8.6), (8.14), and $\phi_t = c(q_2)/M_t$. The allocation is dichotomic in the sense that the output traded in the DM1, q_1, is independent of both the quantity traded in the DM2, q_2, and the value of money, ϕ_t. As well, when inflation increases, q_1 is unaffected and remains at the efficient level, while q_2 decreases; see equation (8.14). So there are no interactions between the DM1 and the DM2.

Another noteworthy feature of the model is that in the DM1, a fraction σ_1 of the buyers issue debt, while at the same time they hold a positive amount of money. Credit is a preferred means of payment because it involves no opportunity cost. However, credit can only be used in transactions when agents' identities are known and debt contracts can be enforced. Buyers will hold money, even though it is more costly than credit, because it allows them to consume in the DM2 when they are anonymous.

Finally, as the cost of holding money, i, approaches zero, the quantity traded in the DM2 approaches its efficient level, q_2^*. When the cost of holding money is exactly equal to zero, there is no cost associated with holding real balances, and buyers will be indifferent between trading with money and credit in the DM1.

8.2 Money and Credit Under Limited Commitment

We now assume, as in Chapter 2.4, that buyers cannot commit in the DM. In this situation, sellers are only willing to extend credit to buyers if debt repayment is self-enforcing. Clearly, some sort of public recording keeping device is needed if debt repayment is to be self-enforcing.

We assume that there exists an imperfect public record-keeping device and only a fraction ω of buyers can be monitored by the device. The record-keeping device is imperfect in the following sense: if a monitored buyer defaults on his debt repayment, then a default is entered into the public record with probability $\rho \in [0,1]$. The parameter ρ can be thought of as measuring the sophistication and reliability of the financial system. If $\rho = 0$, then defaults are never recorded and sellers have no incentive to extend loans to buyers; if $\rho = 1$, then all defaults are publicly recorded. Independent of the value of ρ, the $1-\omega$ buyers that are not monitored are never able to borrow. We assume that the buyer's type—monitored or unmonitored—is public information.

An alternative interpretation of this economy is that all buyers are monitored and we focus on (asymmetric) equilibria where a fraction ω of buyers are viewed as being trustworthy and $1-\omega$ as untrustworthy. Only trustworthy buyers are extended credit, subject to a debt limit. Untrustworthy buyers cannot borrow because sellers rationally anticipate that they will default on their loans. Recall that in pure credit economies there are a continuum of such equilibria, where ω varies over $[0,1]$.

Let $W^b(z,-b)$ be the value function of a monitored buyer that enters the CM holding z real balances and debt obligation b from the previous DM. The debt obligation is measured in terms of the CM good. The CM value function is given by the solution to

$$W^b(z,-b) = z - b + T + \max_{z' \geq 0} \left\{ -\gamma z' + \beta V^b(z') \right\}, \tag{8.15}$$

where V^b is the value function of a monitored buyer at the beginning of the DM. The interpretation of (8.15) is similar to that of (8.3). Notice that the value function W^b is linear in total wealth, $z-b$, i.e.,

$$W^b(z,-b) = z - b + W(0,0).$$

We focus on equilibria where a monitored buyer is permanently excluded from credit transactions if a default appears on his public record. This outcome is consistent with equilibrium behavior. For example, suppose that sellers have no incentive to lend to a buyer that has defaulted in the past because they believe he will default on the loan. Since the buyer does not expect to receive a loan in the future, he will, in fact, default on the loan if, out of equilibrium, he is given one. This behavior validates sellers' beliefs. A buyer that has a recorded default is not (necessarily) in autarky: he can purchase DM goods with money.

Consider now the value function of a buyer who does not have access to credit because he is either not monitored or not trustworthy. The CM value function of a buyer who does not have access to DM credit, $\tilde{W}^b$, is given by the solution to

$$\tilde{W}^b(z) = z + T + \max_{z' \geq 0} \left[-\gamma z' + \beta \tilde{V}^b(z') \right], \tag{8.16}$$

where $\tilde{V}^b$ is the value function of a buyer who does not have access to credit in the DM. Notice that all buyers receive a lump-sum transfer, T, independent of being monitored (trustworthy) or not. In the event where $T < 0$, we assume, as in earlier chapters, that the government has an enforcement technology to ensure that taxes are paid.

Consider a match in the DM between a seller and a buyer who holds z real balances. The buyer and seller bargain over a contract (q, b, d), where q is the output produced by the seller, b is the unsecured loan that the seller extends to the buyer to be repaid in the subsequent CM, and d is the transfer of real balances from the buyer to seller. The terms of the contract are determined by proportional bargaining, where $\theta \in [0, 1]$ represents the buyer's share of the total surplus. The contract is given by the solution to

$$\max_q \theta \left[u(q) - c(q) \right] \tag{8.17}$$

$$\text{s.t. } b + d = (1 - \theta)u(q) + \theta c(q) \leq \bar{b} + z, \;\; b \leq \bar{b}, \tag{8.18}$$

where $\bar{b}$ is the buyer's endogenous debt limit. According to (8.18), the transfer of wealth from the buyer to the seller is a nonlinear function, $(1 - \theta)u(q) + \theta c(q)$, of the output produced by the seller. Given this transfer rule, DM output, q, is chosen to maximize the buyer's surplus, which is equal to a fraction θ of total match surplus. The solution to the bargaining problem is $q = q^*$ if $(1 - \theta)u(q^*) + \theta c(q^*) \leq \bar{b} + z$; otherwise $(1 - \theta)u(q) + \theta c(q) = \bar{b} + z$. If the buyer has sufficient payment capacity, $\bar{b} + z$, then agents trade the first-best level of DM output. If the buyer's payment capacity is "insufficient," then the buyer borrows up to his credit limit and spends all of his real balances. If the buyer is either not monitored or untrustworthy, then he does not have access to credit, which implies that $b = \bar{b} = 0$.

The expected discounted utility of a buyer with access to credit in the DM, $V^b(z)$, is given by,

$$\begin{aligned} V^b(z) &= \sigma \left[u(q) + W^b(z - d, -b) \right] + (1 - \sigma) W^b(z, 0) \\ &= \sigma\theta \left[u(q) - c(q) \right] + W^b(z, 0), \end{aligned} \tag{8.19}$$

where the terms of trade, (q, b, d), depend on the buyer's debt limit and real balances through the solution of the bargaining problem, (8.17)-(8.18). According to (8.19), the buyer is matched with a seller with probability σ, in which case the buyer purchases q units of output using b units of debt and d real balances. With probability $1-\sigma$, the buyer does not have a DM trading opportunity and, as a result, he enters the CM without any debt liabilities. The second line of (8.19) uses the linearity of W^b and says that if the buyer is matched, an event that occurs with probability σ, then he enjoys a fraction θ of total match surplus. Similarly, the expected lifetime utility of a buyer that does not have access to credit is given by

$$\tilde{V}^b(z) = \sigma\theta\left[u\left(\tilde{q}\right) - c(\tilde{q})\right] + \tilde{W}^b(z), \tag{8.20}$$

where the DM output, $\tilde{q}$, is determined by the solution to the bargaining problem, (8.17)-(8.18), with $\bar{b} = 0$.

The buyer's choice of real balances z is determined by substituting $V^b(z)$ by its expression given by (8.19) into (8.15) and is given by the solution to

$$\max_{z \geq 0} \left\{-iz + \sigma\theta\left[u\left(q\right) - c(q)\right]\right\}, \tag{8.21}$$

where q solves the DM bargaining problem, (8.17)-(8.18). In particular, $q = q^*$ if $\bar{b} + z \geq (1-\theta)u(q^*) + \theta c(q^*)$; otherwise, q solves $(1-\theta)u(q) + \theta c(q) = \bar{b} + z$. According to (8.21), buyers choose their real balances in order to maximize their expected surplus in the DM net of the cost of holding money. The first-order condition associated with problem (8.21) is

$$-i + \sigma\theta\left[\frac{u'\left(q\right) - c'(q)}{(1-\theta)u'(q) + \theta c'(q)}\right] \leq 0, \text{ with "} = \text{" if } z > 0. \tag{8.22}$$

The first term on the left side of (8.22) is the opportunity cost of holding an additional unit of real balances and the second term is the expected marginal benefit from holding real balances in the DM.

A buyer who does not have access to credit solves a problem that is identical to (8.21)—except z and q are replaced by $\tilde{z}$ and $\tilde{q}$, respectively—where $\tilde{q}$ is given by the solution to the bargaining problem (8.17)-(8.18) for $\bar{b} = 0$. In particular, $\tilde{q} = q^*$ if $\tilde{z} \geq (1-\theta)u(q^*) + \theta c(q^*)$; otherwise, $\tilde{q}$ solves $(1-\theta)u(\tilde{q}) + \theta c(\tilde{q}) = \tilde{z}$. The problem of an untrustworthy buyer can be rearranged to read,

$$\max_{\tilde{q} \geq 0} \left\{\left[\sigma\theta - i(1-\theta)\right] u\left(\tilde{q}\right) - \left(i + \sigma\right)\theta c(\tilde{q})\right\}. \tag{8.23}$$

Under the assumption $u'(0) = \infty$, a necessary and sufficient condition for $\tilde{q} > 0$ is $\sigma\theta > i(1-\theta)$.

We now turn to the determination of the debt limit. Consider a buyer that enters the CM with debt level, b. If the buyer does not repay his debt, then his default is recorded with probability, ρ. In the event that his default is recorded, the buyer can no longer access credit in future DM trades (although he can always trade with money). In the event that the default is not recorded, the buyer is able to access credit in the future DM. Hence, the buyer will repay his debt obligation b in the CM if

$$-b + W^b(z,0) \geq \rho \tilde{W}^b(z) + (1-\rho)W^b(z,0). \tag{8.24}$$

The left side of (8.24) is the expected lifetime utility of the buyer if he does not default: he repays his debt and enters the CM with z real balances and future access to credit. The right side is the expected lifetime utility of the buyer if he defaults: he is caught with probability ρ in which case he becomes untrustworthy. In the absence of an enforcement technology, if the buyer defaults, then his real balances cannot be confiscated. Using the linearity of W^b and $\tilde{W}^b$, the buyer's credit constraint, (8.24), can be simplified to

$$b \leq \rho \left[W^b(0,0) - \tilde{W}^b(0) \right] \equiv \bar{b}. \tag{8.25}$$

The buyer's debt, b, cannot exceed the expected cost from defaulting. The expected cost of defaulting equals the probability that the default is recorded times the difference between the lifetime utility of a buyer with access to credit and the lifetime utility of a buyer without access to credit. Notice that the endogenous debt limit $\bar{b}$ is independent of the assets the buyer holds when entering the CM: this is an implication of the quasi-linear preferences. Using (8.15) and (8.16) evaluated at $z = b = 0$, the debt limit (8.25) can be rewritten as

$$\bar{b} = \rho \left\{ \left[-\gamma z + \beta V^b(z) \right] - \left[-\gamma \tilde{z} + \beta \tilde{V}^b(\tilde{z}) \right] \right\}, \tag{8.26}$$

where z represents the optimal real balances of a buyer who has access to credit and $\tilde{z}$ is the optimal real balances of a buyer who does not have access to credit. Using (8.15) and (8.19) for V^b and (8.16) and (8.20) for $\tilde{V}^b$, we get

$$\beta V^b(z) = \frac{\sigma\theta \left[u(q) - c(q) \right] - (\gamma - 1)z + T}{r}$$

$$\beta \tilde{V}^b(\tilde{z}) = \frac{\sigma\theta \left[u(\tilde{q}) - c(\tilde{q}) \right] - (\gamma - 1)\tilde{z} + T}{r}.$$

Substituting these expressions into (8.26) we obtain,

$$r\bar{b} = \Gamma(\bar{b}), \tag{8.27}$$

where

$$\Gamma(\bar{b}) \equiv \rho\{-iz + \sigma\theta[u(q) - c(q)]\} - \rho\{-i\tilde{z} + \sigma\theta[u(\tilde{q}) - c(\tilde{q})]\}.$$

Notice that Γ is a function of the debt limit, $\bar{b}$, because when the buyer has access to credit, output in the DM, q, is a function of $z + \bar{b}$. (When the buyer does not have access to credit, output in the DM, $\tilde{q}$, is a function of only $\tilde{z}$.) The determination of the debt limit, $\bar{b}$, is illustrated in Figure 8.2. The line, $r\bar{b}$, is the flow return to the buyer from having access to credit with a limit of $\bar{b}$. The curve, $\Gamma(\bar{b})$, represents the flow cost associated with a buyer's default if the debt limit for future DM trades is equal to $\bar{b}$. It is equal to the probability of having the default recorded, ρ, times the loss associated with not having access to credit. This flow cost increases with the size of the credit line since q is increasing in $\bar{b}$; this implies that Γ is upward sloping. Notice that $\Gamma(0) = 0$, which implies there always exists an equilibrium with no unsecured credit. If a buyer anticipates that he will not have access to credit in the future, i.e., $\bar{b} = 0$, then, since there is no cost from defaulting, the buyer will default if he is extended credit. The seller understands this behavior and, as result, will not extend credit.

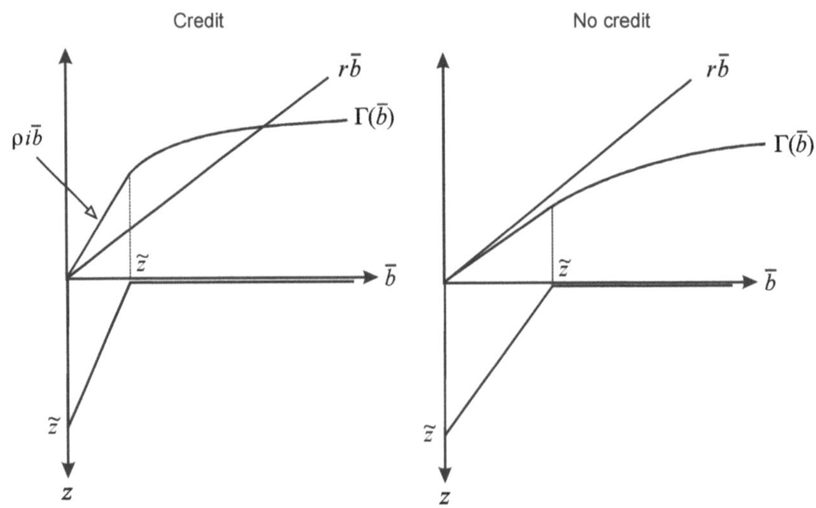

Figure 8.2
Endogenous credit limits

For a more detailed characterization of Γ, we distinguish between two cases. In the first case, the credit limit $\bar{b}$ is less than the payment capacity of a buyer who does not have access to credit, $\tilde{z}$. When $\bar{b} < \tilde{z}$, buyers with access to credit choose the same payment capacity as the one of buyers with no access to credit, i.e., $\bar{b} + z = \tilde{z}$ and $q = \tilde{q}$. Intuitively, both types of buyers face the same trade-off at the margin when $q = \tilde{q}$. Consequently, since $z = \tilde{z} - \bar{b}$, the right side of (8.27) is $\Gamma(\bar{b}) \equiv \rho i \bar{b}$. The cost from defaulting is equal to the probability ρ that the default is recorded times the quantity of real balances that the buyer has to accumulate to replace the credit line, $\tilde{z} - z = \bar{b}$, where the cost of holding a unit of real balances is equal to i. In both the left and right panels of Figure 8.2, $\Gamma(\bar{b})$ is linear for all $\bar{b} < \tilde{z}$.

In the second case, the debt limit $\bar{b}$ is greater than the payment capacity of buyers with no access to credit, $\tilde{z}$. When $\bar{b} > \tilde{z}$, $q > \tilde{q}$ and (8.22) tells us that buyers with access to credit choose not to accumulate any real balances, i.e., $z = 0$. In this case, the derivative of Γ is

$$\Gamma'(\bar{b}) \equiv \rho\sigma\theta \left[\frac{u'(q) - c'(q)}{(1-\theta)u'(q) + \theta c'(q)} \right] > 0. \tag{8.28}$$

Hence, $\Gamma(\bar{b})$ is a strictly concave function of $\bar{b}$ for all $\bar{b}$ such that $\bar{b} > \tilde{z}$ and $\bar{b} < (1-\theta)c(q^*) + \theta c(q^*)$; $\Gamma(\bar{b})$ is a constant function for all $\bar{b} \geq (1-\theta)c(q^*) + \theta c(q^*)$.

For unsecured debt to emerge as an equilibrium, the slope of $\Gamma(\bar{b})$ at $\bar{b} = 0$ must be greater than r, see the left panel of Figure 8.2. Intuitively, the cost of defaulting on an arbitrarily small credit limit must be greater than the rate of time preference. The most favorable case for which this condition holds is when buyers with no access to credit do not find it worthwhile to accumulate real balances, i.e., $\tilde{z} = 0$, which happens when $i \geq \sigma\theta/(1-\theta)$. From (8.28), we get that $\Gamma'(0) = \rho\sigma\theta/(1-\theta)$ and, as a result, credit is sustainable if $r < \rho\sigma\theta/(1-\theta)$. Buyers must be sufficiently patient and care enough about the future punishment in case of default for the repayment of debt to be self-enforcing. The threshold for the rate of time preference below which unsecured credit is incentive-feasible increases with the probability of being recorded in case of default, ρ, with the frequency of trading opportunities, σ, and with the buyer's market power in the DM, θ.

If $i < \sigma\theta/(1-\theta)$, then buyers with no access to credit have an incentive to accumulate real balances, i.e., $\tilde{z} > 0$. This makes the cost associated with defaulting lower than in the case where buyers optimally did not accumulate real balances; hence, the condition for credit to emerge as an equilibrium outcome is more stringent. Since $\Gamma(\bar{b}) = \rho i\bar{b}$ for $\bar{b} < \tilde{z}$, the condition $r < \Gamma'(0)$ can be reexpressed as $r < \rho i$. Graphically, this condition is represented in the left panel of Figure 8.2. Hence, unsecured credit can be sustained in equilibrium if the cost of holding real balances is sufficiently high. If $r > \rho i$, then there does not exist an incentive compatible credit limit $\bar{b} > 0$, see the right panel of Figure 8.2.

Finally, there is a knife-edge case where $i < \sigma\theta/(1-\theta)$ and $r = \rho i$. In this case, $r\bar{b}$ and $\Gamma(\bar{b})$ coincide, which means that there is a continuum of equilibrium debt limits $\bar{b} \in [0, \tilde{z}]$.

The model provides a channel through which inflation and monetary policy affect the equilibrium debt limit. Figure 8.3 characterizes the payment capacity of a buyer who has access to credit. If $i < r/\rho$, then unsecured credit is not incentive feasible—as in the right panel of Figure 8.2—and all buyer types choose the same real balances, $z = \tilde{z}$. Moreover, buyers' payment capacity, $z = \tilde{z}$, decreases with i;

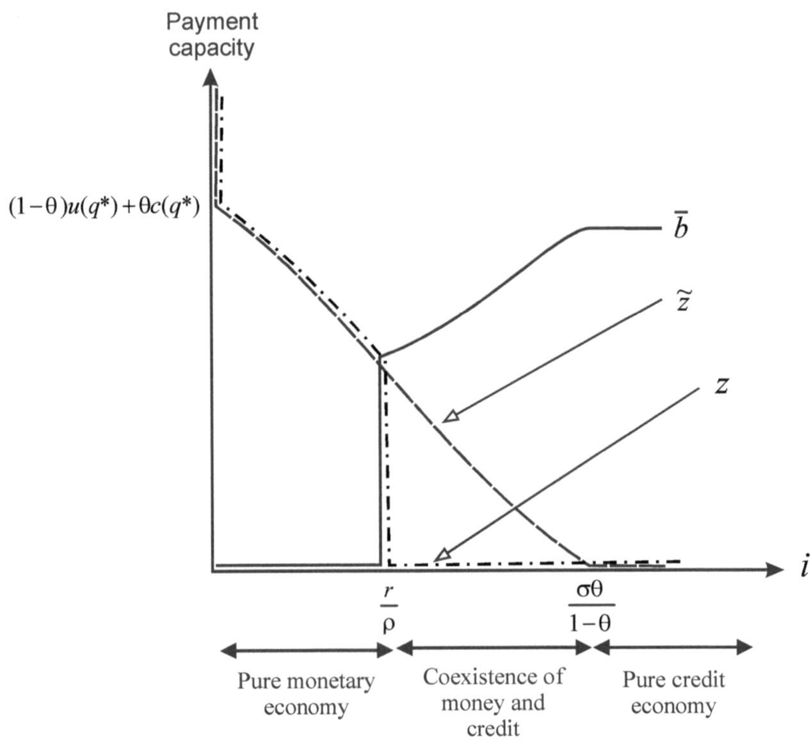

Figure 8.3
Coexistence of money and credit under limited commitment

see Figure 8.3. When $0 \leq i < r/\rho$, the economy corresponds to a pure monetary economy. If $i > r/\rho$, then unsecured credit becomes incentive feasible. As i increases, buyers who are excluded from credit become worse off as the cost of holding real money balances increases. As a result, as the nominal interest rate, i, increases, the punishment from being excluded from using credit also increases, as does the debt limit, $\bar{b}$. This outcome is illustrated in Figure 8.3 by the solid upward sloping line labelled $\bar{b}$. For all $i \in (r/\rho, \sigma\theta/(1-\theta))$ money and credit coexist as payments instruments: some buyers pay only with money, while other buyers pay only with credit. When $i > \sigma\theta/(1-\theta)$, the cost of holding money is so high that buyers who have no access to credit choose not to hold any money and live in autarky. In Figure 8.3 the dashed line, which represents money holdings for buyers that do not have access to credit, lies on the horizontal axis for nominal interest rates that exceed $\sigma\theta/(1-\theta)$. In this region, the economy is a pure credit economy.

It is also worth noting that if $i = r$—the money supply is constant—and $\rho = 1$—there is perfect monitoring—then there are a continuum of equilibria with debt limits $\bar{b} \in [0, \tilde{z}]$. Those equilibria have the same allocations and are payoff equivalent. Indeed, any change in $\bar{b}$ is offset by a change of same magnitude in real balances, z, so that the buyer's payment capacity is unchanged. This corresponds to our previous result that under perfect monitoring money plays no essential role.

8.3 Costly Record-Keeping

We now consider an environment where money and credit coexist, and monetary policy affects the composition of monetary and credit transactions. The model is similar to the one in Chapter 5.1.3, where a typical period has a decentralized market, DM; a competitive night market, CM; and the gains from trade in the DM vary across bilateral matches. To this environment we add a costly record-keeping technology. Hence, credit transactions are feasible, but costly.

The instantaneous utility function of a buyer is given by

$$U^b = \varepsilon u(q) + x - h,$$

where $\varepsilon \in \mathbb{R}_+$ is a match-specific preference shock. The preference shock, ε, is drawn from a cumulative distribution, $F(\varepsilon)$, with support $[0, \varepsilon_{\max}]$. Matched agents in the DM have the option to record a credit transaction at a utility cost of $\zeta > 0$. We assume that the buyer incurs this cost. This cost could capture the resources needed to authenticate both the buyer's identity and his IOU. If a credit transaction is recorded in the DM, we assume that its repayment is enforced at night. The value functions for buyers and sellers at the beginning of the CM, $W^b(z,-b)$ and $W^s(z,b)$, are given by equations (8.3) and (8.4), respectively.

Consider a match in the DM between a buyer with match specific preference shock ε holding z real balances, and a seller. We assume that the buyer makes a take-it-or-leave-it offer to the seller. Owing to the linearity of the buyer's and seller's CM value functions, the terms of trade, (q,b,d), are given by the solution to

$$\max_{q,d,b} \left[\varepsilon u(q) - d - b - \zeta \mathbb{I}_{\{b>0\}}\right] \text{ s.t. } -c(q) + d + b \geq 0 \text{ and } d \leq z,$$

where $\mathbb{I}_{\{b>0\}} = 1$ if $b > 0$ and $\mathbb{I}_{\{b>0\}} = 0$, otherwise. The buyer chooses his consumption, q, the amount of real balances to transfer to the seller, d, and the size of the loan, b. If the buyer chooses to use credit as a means of payment, he must incur the fixed cost ζ due to record-keeping. If the buyer incurs the fixed cost, then the solution is $q = q_\varepsilon^*$ with $d + b = c(q_\varepsilon^*)$, where q_ε^* solves $\varepsilon u'(q_\varepsilon^*) = c'(q_\varepsilon^*)$. Without loss of generality, we assume that in this case the buyer only uses credit in the transaction. If the buyer does not incur the fixed cost to use credit, then $q = q_\varepsilon(z) = \min\left\{q_\varepsilon^*, c^{-1}(z)\right\}$ and $d = c(q)$, i.e., if he has enough real balances, the buyer purchases the efficient level of output given his preference shock; otherwise he spends all of his real balances. Consequently, the buyer's surplus from a trade match in the DM is

$$S^b(z,\varepsilon) = \max\left\{\varepsilon u(q_\varepsilon^*) - c(q_\varepsilon^*) - \zeta, \varepsilon u\left[q_\varepsilon(z)\right] - c\left[q_\varepsilon(z)\right]\right\}. \tag{8.29}$$

In Figure 8.4 we illustrate the utility gain to the buyer from using a credit arrangement. The grey area represents the set of utility levels ($u^s = -c(q) + d$ for the seller and $u^b = \varepsilon u(q) - d$ for the buyer) that are incentive feasible when the buyer uses money only. The dashed line is the Pareto frontier of the bargaining set if the buyer uses credit, which excludes the fixed cost, ζ, associated with record-keeping and enforcement. This Pareto frontier is linear because the match surplus is maximum and equal to $\varepsilon u(q_\varepsilon^*) - c(q_\varepsilon^*)$. The gain for a buyer using credit can been seen on the horizontal axis: it is the distance between the intercepts of the two Pareto frontiers, the one with money only and the one with credit.

Note that $S^b(z,\varepsilon)$ is increasing in ε, i.e., both terms in the maximization problem (8.29) increase with ε. We represent each of these terms as a function of ε in Figure 8.5. From an envelope argument, the slope of the first term is $u(q_\varepsilon^*)$. The slope of the second is $u\left[q_\varepsilon(z)\right]$.

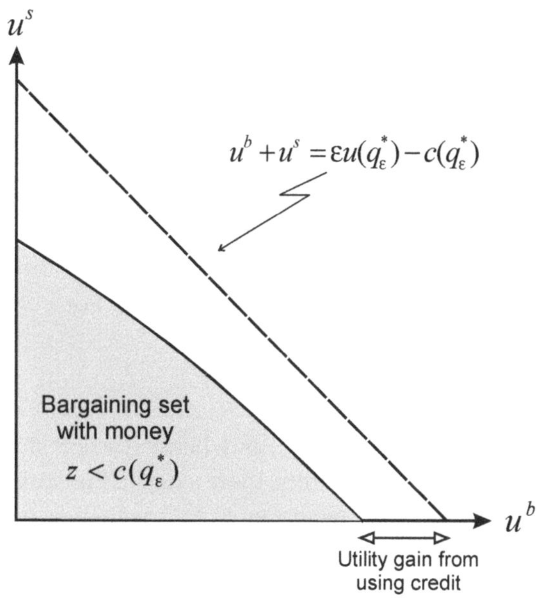

Figure 8.4
Utility gain from using credit

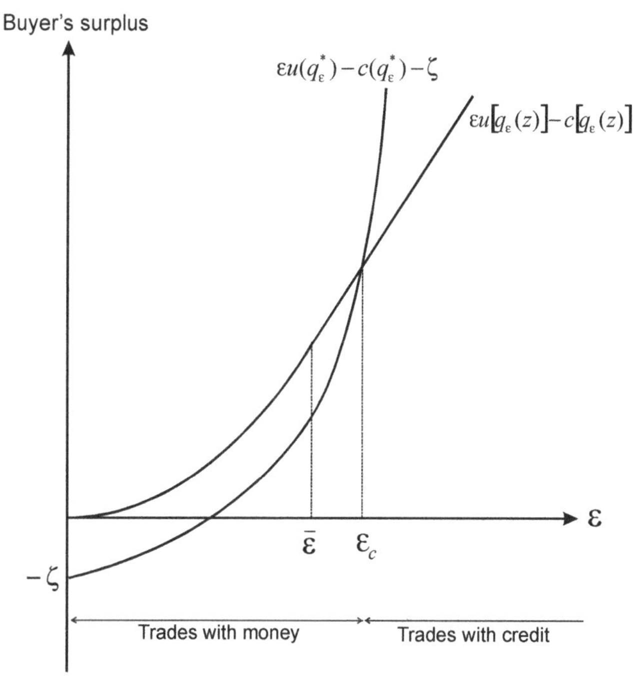

Figure 8.5
Credit vs. monetary trades

Let $\bar{\varepsilon}$ denote the value of ε such that $c(q^*_{\bar{\varepsilon}}) = z$ or, equivalently, $\bar{\varepsilon}u'\left[c^{-1}(z)\right] = c'\left[c^{-1}(z)\right]$, i.e., $\bar{\varepsilon}$ is a threshold for the idiosyncratic preference shock for a given z, below which the buyer has enough real balances to purchase the efficient level of DM output. For all $\varepsilon < \bar{\varepsilon}$, $u\left[q_\varepsilon(z)\right] = u(q^*_\varepsilon)$, which implies that the slopes of the two terms in the maximization problem (8.29) are equal. For all $\varepsilon > \bar{\varepsilon}$, $u\left[q_\varepsilon(z)\right] < u(q^*_\varepsilon)$, and the slope of the second term in the maximization problem (8.29) is independent of ε and lower than the slope of the first term. When $\varepsilon = 0$, the first term is equal to $-\zeta$, while the second is equal to zero. For $\varepsilon > \bar{\varepsilon}$ sufficiently large,

$$\{\varepsilon u(q^*_\varepsilon) - c(q^*_\varepsilon) - \zeta\} - \{\varepsilon u\left[q_\varepsilon(z)\right] - c\left[q_\varepsilon(z)\right]\} > 0,$$

since for large ε, q_ε is negligible compared to q^*_ε, and, hence, the left side of the inequality goes to infinity. Consequently, there exists a threshold $\varepsilon_c > \bar{\varepsilon}$ above which the buyer uses credit as means of payment—i.e., the first term in the maximization problem (8.29) exceeds the second—and below which he uses money. This threshold is given by,

$$\varepsilon_c u(q^*_{\varepsilon_c}) - c(q^*_{\varepsilon_c}) - \zeta = \varepsilon_c u\left[c^{-1}(z)\right] - z. \tag{8.30}$$

Graphically, the first term in the maximization problem (8.29) intersects the second term from below at $\varepsilon = \varepsilon_c$, see Figure 8.5.

It should be (re)emphasized that the value of the threshold, ε_c, is for a given level of real balances, z. From (8.30), ε_c increases with z, i.e.,

$$\frac{\partial \varepsilon_c}{\partial z} = \frac{\varepsilon_c u'\left[c^{-1}(z)\right]/c'\left[c^{-1}(z)\right] - 1}{u\left(q^*_{\varepsilon_c}\right) - u\left[c^{-1}(z)\right]} > 0,$$

since $q^*_{\varepsilon_c} > c^{-1}(z)$. Graphically, as z increases $\bar{\varepsilon}$ increases and, for all $\varepsilon > \bar{\varepsilon}$, the second term of the maximization problem (8.29) moves upward. Buyers increase their surplus by holding more real balances in all trades where they don't trade the efficient quantity. Consequently, the two terms intersect at a larger value of ε. As buyers hold more real balances, the fraction of trades conducted with credit decreases: money and credit are substitutes.

Using the linearity of W^b, the value of being a buyer at the beginning of the period, $V^b(z)$, is

$$V^b(z) = \sigma \int_0^{\varepsilon_{\max}} S^b(z,\varepsilon)dF(\varepsilon) + W^b(z,0). \tag{8.31}$$

With probability σ the buyer meets a seller, and he draws a realization for the preference shock from the distribution $F(\varepsilon)$. The buyer enjoys a surplus $S^b(z,\varepsilon)$, given by (8.29), which depends on both the buyer's real balances and the match specific component.

Substituting $V^b(z)$ from (8.31) into (8.3), and simplifying, we get

$$\max_{z\geq 0}\left[-iz+\sigma\int_0^{\varepsilon_{\max}} S^b(z,\varepsilon)dF(\varepsilon)\right]. \tag{8.32}$$

The buyer chooses his real balances in order to maximize his expected surplus in the DM, where the expectation is with respect to the random preference shock, minus the cost of holding real balances. The objective function in (8.32) is continuous and, for all $i>0$, the solution to (8.32) must lie in the interval $[0, c(q^*_{\varepsilon_{\max}})]$. If $z > c(q^*_{\varepsilon_{\max}})$, then the surplus is maximum in all matches and independent of z. But by reducing z, the buyer can reduce his cost of holding real balances without affecting his expected surplus in the DM. Since a continuous function is being maximized over a compact set, there exists a solution to (8.32).

An equilibrium corresponds to a pair (ε_c, z) that solves (8.30) and (8.32) and can be determined recursively: a value for z is determined independently by (8.32), and given this value for z, (8.30) determines a unique ε_c.

We now investigate the effects that monetary policy has on the use of fiat money and credit as means of payment. The first-order (necessary but not sufficient) condition associated with (8.32) is

$$i=\sigma\int_{\bar{\varepsilon}(z)}^{\varepsilon_c(z)}\left\{\frac{\varepsilon u'\left[c^{-1}(z)\right]}{c'\left[c^{-1}(z)\right]}-1\right\}dF(\varepsilon). \tag{8.33}$$

From (8.33), real balances have a liquidity return when the realization of the preference shock is not too low—so that the buyer's budget constraint in the match is binding—and when the preference shock is not too high—so that it is not profitable for buyers to use credit—i.e., when $\bar{\varepsilon}(z) < \varepsilon < \varepsilon_c(z)$.

Suppose that inflation and, hence, the cost of holding money, i, increases. This implies that the right side of (8.33) must also increase. One would conjecture that an increase in inflation decreases real money balances z. In order to check this conjecture consider two monetary policies with resulting nominal interest rates i and i', such that $i<i'$. (Recall that i is referred to as a nominal interest rate because it is the interest rate paid by an illiquid nominal bond that can only be traded

in the CM.) Let z and z' denote the solutions of (8.32) for i and i', respectively. From (8.32), we have

$$-iz + \sigma \int_0^{\varepsilon_{\max}} S^b(z,\varepsilon)dF(\varepsilon) \geq -iz' + \sigma \int_0^{\varepsilon_{\max}} S^b(z',\varepsilon)dF(\varepsilon), \qquad (8.34)$$

$$-i'z' + \sigma \int_0^{\varepsilon_{\max}} S^b(z',\varepsilon)dF(\varepsilon) \geq -i'z + \sigma \int_0^{\varepsilon_{\max}} S^b(z,\varepsilon)dF(\varepsilon). \qquad (8.35)$$

These inequalities imply that

$$i\,(z - z') \leq \sigma \int_0^{\varepsilon_{\max}} \left[S^b(z,\varepsilon) - S^b(z',\varepsilon)\right] dF(\varepsilon) \leq i'\,(z - z'),$$

which in turn imply $z \geq z'$ since, by assumption, $i < i'$ and $i\,(z - z') \leq i'\,(z - z')$, from the above inequality. Moreover, it can be checked that $z = z'$ when $i < i'$ is inconsistent with (8.33). Hence, $z > z'$. An increase in inflation reduces buyers' real balances and increases the use of costly credit. As the cost of holding real balances approaches zero, it is immediate from (8.32) that real balances approach $c(q^*_{\varepsilon_{\max}})$ and buyers find it profitable to trade with money only.

8.4 Strategic Complementarities and Payments

So far, we have described environments where buyers make offers to sellers and choose the means of payment that will be used in bilateral meetings. Typically, however, in order to be able to accept credit, sellers must invest ex ante—i.e., before trades take place—in a technology that authenticate buyers' IOUs. Buyers will form rational expectations about sellers' investment decisions and choose the amount of means of payment(s) to carry into meetings. As we shall see, these decisions made by buyers and sellers create strategic complementarities for payment choices and network-like externalities.

The model with network externalities is similar to that of the previous section, but modified in the following ways. First, for simplicity, assume all matches are identical, i.e., $\varepsilon = 1$. Second, and more substantially, assume that it is the seller who invests in the record-keeping technology and that this investment is undertaken at the beginning of the DM before matches are formed. The utility cost to invest in this technology is $\zeta > 0$. The pricing mechanism must be changed from the previous section to one that permits sellers to extract a fraction of the match surplus; otherwise sellers could not recover their ex ante investment costs and would have no incentive to invest in the record-keeping technology. We will adopt the proportional bargaining solution described in Chapter 3.2.3, where the buyer receives a constant share $\theta \in [0,1)$ of the match surplus, while the seller gets the remaining share, $1-\theta > 0$.

We start by describing the determination of the terms of trade in a bilateral match in the DM, depending on whether sellers have invested or not in the record-keeping technology. Consider first a match between a buyer holding z real balances and a seller who has invested in the technology. The terms of trade are given by the solution to the following problem:

$$\max_{q,d,b} \left[u(q) - d - b\right] \tag{8.36}$$

$$\text{s.t.} \quad -c(q) + d + b = \frac{1-\theta}{\theta}\left[u(q) - d - b\right], \tag{8.37}$$

$$d \leq z, \tag{8.38}$$

where we have used the linearity of the buyer's and seller's value functions with respect to their wealth. According to problem (8.36)-(8.38), the buyer maximizes his utility of consuming the DM good net of the transfer of real balances, d, and IOUs, b, subject to the constraints that (i) the seller's payoff is equal to $(1-\theta)/\theta$ times the buyer's payoff and (ii) the buyer cannot transfer more money than he has. Since b is unconstrained—buyers can borrow as much as they want in the DM—it should be obvious that $d \leq z$ never constrains the purchase of q. When sellers have invested in the record-keeping technology, buyers can finance all of their day time purchases with credit alone. Because of this, the output produced in the DM will be at the efficient level, $q = q^*$, and $d + b = (1-\theta)\,u(q^*) + \theta c(q^*)$, i.e., the seller gets the fraction $1-\theta$ of match surplus. Without loss of generality, assume that $d = 0$, so that the trade is conducted with credit only.

Consider next the case where the seller has not invested in the record-keeping technology. The terms of trade are still determined by the problem (8.36)-(8.38), but with the added constraint that $b = 0$. If $z \geq (1-\theta)\,u(q^*) + \theta c(q^*)$, then the buyer holds sufficient money balances to purchase the efficient level of output and $q = q^*$; otherwise, the level of DM output, $q(z)$, satisfies

$$z = z(q) \equiv (1-\theta)\,u(q) + \theta c(q), \tag{8.39}$$

where $q\,(z) < q^*$.

We now turn to the seller's decision to invest in the record-keeping technology. We consider situations where all buyers hold the same real balances, z. It is optimal for a seller to invest in the technology if

$$\sigma(1-\theta)\left[u(q(z))-c(q(z))\right] \leq \sigma(1-\theta)\left[u(q^*)-c(q^*)\right]-\zeta, \tag{8.40}$$

where we have used the linearity of the value function of the seller in the CM. The left side is the seller's expected payoff if he does not invest in the record-keeping technology. In this case the seller can only accept the buyer's real balances and does not provide credit. The right side is the seller's expected payoff if he invests in the technology to accept IOUs. From (8.40), the flow cost to invest in the record-keeping technology must be less than the increase in the seller's expected surplus associated with accepting credit instead of money. The left side of (8.40) is increasing in z: it equals 0 if $z=0$ and $\sigma(1-\theta)\left[u(q^*)-c(q^*)\right]$ if $z \geq (1-\theta)u(q^*)+\theta c(q^*)$. Consequently, if $\zeta < \sigma(1-\theta)\left[u(q^*)-c(q^*)\right]$, then there exists a threshold $z_c > 0$ for the buyer's real balances, below which sellers invest in the record-keeping technology. This threshold is given by the solution to

$$u\left[q(z_c)\right]-c\left[q(z_c)\right]=u(q^*)-c(q^*)-\frac{\zeta}{\sigma(1-\theta)}. \tag{8.41}$$

Let Λ be the measure of sellers who invest in the record-keeping technology. Then,

$$\Lambda\begin{cases} =1 \\ \in[0,1] \\ =0 \end{cases} \text{if } z\begin{cases} < \\ = \\ > \end{cases} z_c. \tag{8.42}$$

The seller's reaction function is depicted in Figure 8.6. It is a step function that is decreasing with the buyer's real balances. As buyers hold more money, sellers have less incentives to invest in the costly record-keeping technology.

In Figure 8.7 we illustrate the gains from using credit for the buyer and the seller. The grey area represents the set of surpluses that are incentive feasible when the buyer uses money only, while the dashed line is the Pareto frontier of the bargaining set if the buyer uses credit. The outcome to the proportional bargaining problem is given by the intersection of the line $u^s/u^b=(1-\theta)/\theta$ with the relevant Pareto frontier. The seller's gain is the vertical distance between the intersections of the Pareto frontiers with the line $(1-\theta)/\theta$, and the gain for the buyer is given by the horizontal distance. It follows that the buyer's gain

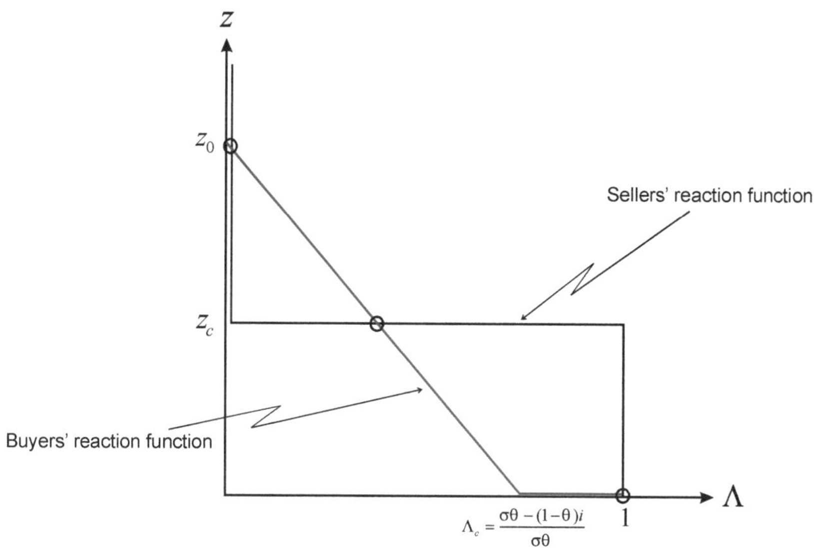

Figure 8.6
Buyers' and sellers' reaction functions

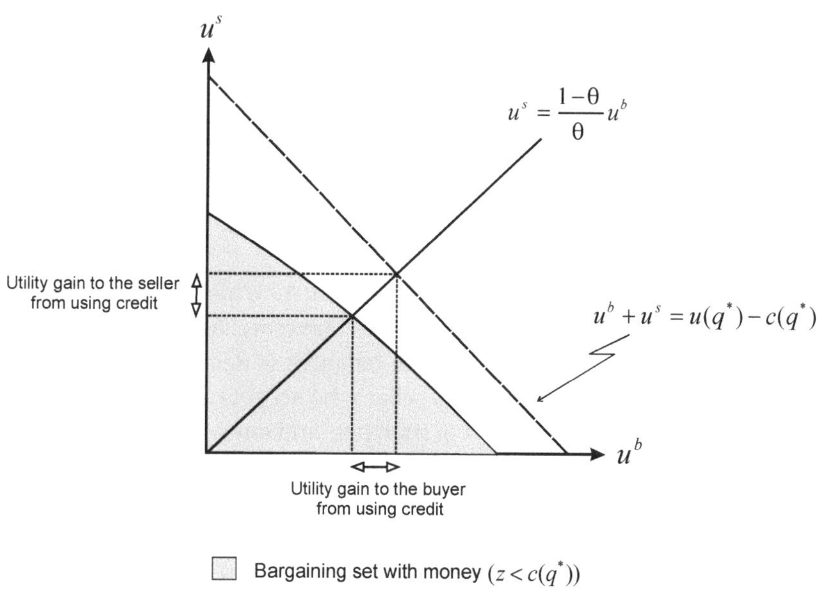

Figure 8.7
Gains from using costly credit

from using credit is $\theta/(1-\theta)$ times the seller's gain. The fact that the seller cannot appropriate the entire gain from using the credit technology, which requires an ex ante investment, creates a standard holdup problem.

Given the seller's decision to invest in the record-keeping technology, (8.42), we now consider the buyer's decision to hold real balances. Following a similar line of reasoning as in Chapter 6.3, the buyer's decision problem is given by

$$\max_{z\geq 0}\left\{-iz+\sigma(1-\Lambda)\theta\left\{u[q(z)]-c\left[q(z)\right]\right\}+\sigma\Lambda\theta\left\{u(q^*)-c(q^*)\right\}\right\}. \quad (8.43)$$

The buyer chooses his real balances in order to maximize his expected surplus in the DM, net of the cost of holding real balances. The buyer obtains a fraction θ of the entire match surplus in all meetings. From (8.43) the buyer's surplus depends on his real balances only if the seller does not have the recording-keeping technology, an event that occurs with probability $1-\Lambda$. If the seller has the technology to accept credit, an event that occurs with probability Λ, the match surplus is at its maximum and the quantity traded is q^*. The first-order condition for problem (8.43) is

$$\frac{\left[\sigma(1-\Lambda)\theta-i\left(1-\theta\right)\right]u'(q)-\left[i+\sigma(1-\Lambda)\right]\theta c'(q)}{\left(1-\theta\right)u'(q)+\theta c'(q)}\leq 0, \quad (8.44)$$

and holds with an equality if $z>0$. If $z>0$, then the numerator of (8.44) is equal to zero, and

$$\frac{u'\left(q\right)}{c'\left(q\right)}=\frac{\left[i+\sigma\left(1-\Lambda\right)\right]\theta}{\left[i+\sigma(1-\Lambda)\right]\theta-i}. \quad (8.45)$$

The right side of (8.45) is increasing with Λ, which implies that an increase in Λ decreases q, and, hence, z. Therefore, as illustrated in the Figure 8.6, the buyer's choice of real balances is decreasing in Λ. Intuitively, if it is more likely to find a seller who accepts credit, then money is needed in a smaller fraction of matches, and since it is costly to hold money, buyers find it optimal to hold fewer real balances. Moreover, there is a critical value for Λ above which buyers hold no real balances, and this happens when the denominator of equation (8.45) is equal to zero, or when $\Lambda_c=[\sigma\theta-(1-\theta)i]/\sigma\theta$, where $\Lambda_c>0$ if $i<\sigma\theta/(1-\theta)$.

A stationary symmetric equilibrium is a pair (z,Λ) that solves (8.42) and (8.43). If $\varsigma>\sigma(1-\theta)\left[u(q^*)-c(q^*)\right]$, then it is a strictly dominant strategy for sellers not to invest in the record keeping technology. In this case, there is a unique equilibrium where $\Lambda=0$. Let's now consider the case where $\zeta < \sigma(1-\theta)\left[u(q^*) - c(q^*)\right]$. From (8.41), $z_c \in (0, (1-\theta)\,u(q^*) + \theta c(q^*))$. Let z_0 be the solution to (8.43) when $\Lambda = 0$, i.e., z_0 is the buyer's money holdings if no seller invests in the record-keeping technology. If $z_0 > z_c$, which happens if i is sufficiently low, then there are multiple equilibria. This can be seen in Figure 8.6, where the buyers' and sellers' reaction functions intersect three times. There exists a pure monetary equilibrium with $\Lambda = 0$ and $z > 0$; a pure credit equilibrium, with $\Lambda = 1$ and $z = 0$; and a "mixed" monetary equilibrium, where buyers use both credit and money, accumulating $z_c > 0$ real balances, and a fraction $1 - \Lambda \in (0, 1)$ of sellers accept only money, while other sellers, $\Lambda \in (0, 1)$ of them, are willing to accept both money and credit.

The multiplicity of equilibria arises from the strategic complementarities between the buyers' decisions to hold real balances and the sellers' decisions to invest in the record-keeping technology. To understand this, suppose, for example, that buyers believe that all sellers have invested in the record-keeping technology. Then, they have no need to hold real balances. But, if sellers think that buyers are not holding any money, then they have an incentive to invest in the record keeping technology, assuming, of course, that the cost of the technology is not too high. And, for exactly the same fundamentals, buyers may anticipate that sellers choose not to invest in the record-keeping technology. In this situation, buyers will hold a large quantity of real balances. But if sellers believe that buyers hold enough real balances, then they do not have an incentive to invest in the record-keeping technology.

Given the existence of multiple equilibria, history is able to explain why seemingly identical economies can end up with different payment systems. Consider, for example, an economy with a low inflation where agents play the pure monetary equilibrium. Suppose that this economy subsequently experiences a period of high inflation. In terms of Figure 8.6, the buyer's reaction function shifts downward and, provided that the increase in the inflation rate is sufficiently large, $z_0 < z_c$. With this higher level of inflation, the equilibrium is unique and all sellers invest in the record-keeping technology, $\Lambda = 1$. Suppose that the high-inflation episode is temporary, and inflation reverts back to its initial low level; will agents go back to playing the pure monetary equilibrium? Since the pure credit equilibrium is still an equilibrium, one can imagine that agents will continue to coordinate on this equilibrium after the inflation rate reverts back to its initial level. Interestingly, even though the change in inflation was temporary, the change in the payment system has become permanent: the payment system exhibits *hysteresis*.

We conclude this section by turning to some normative considerations. When there are multiple equilibria, which one is preferred from the society's viewpoint? If society's welfare is measured by the surpluses of all matches in the DM minus the real resource cost incurred by sellers to accept credit, then social welfare is given by

$$\mathcal{W} = \sigma\Lambda\left\{u(q^*) - c(q^*)\right\} + \sigma(1-\Lambda)\left\{u\left[q(z)\right] - c\left[q(z)\right]\right\} - \Lambda\zeta.$$

Consider a case where z_0 is greater than but close to z_c. There is a pure monetary equilibrium with $z = z_0$, $\Lambda = 0$, and social welfare is $\mathcal{W}_0 = \sigma\left\{u\left[q(z_0)\right] - c\left[q(z_0)\right]\right\}$. There is also a pure credit equilibrium with $\Lambda = 1$ and social welfare is $\mathcal{W}_1 = \sigma\left\{u(q^*) - c(q^*)\right\} - \zeta$. Then, given the definition of z_c in (8.41),

$$\begin{aligned}\zeta &\approx \sigma(1-\theta)\left\{\left[u(q^*) - c(q^*)\right] - \left[u(q(z_0)) - c(q(z_0))\right]\right\}\\ &< \sigma\left\{\left[u(q^*) - c(q^*)\right] - \left[u(q(z_0)) - c(q(z_0))\right]\right\},\end{aligned}$$

where we get the strict inequality because $\theta > 0$. In this case, the difference in the surpluses associated with credit and monetary transactions strictly exceeds the cost of investment in the record-keeping technology. Hence, $\mathcal{W}_1 > \mathcal{W}_0$, the pure monetary equilibrium is dominated, from a social welfare perspective, by the pure credit equilibrium. However, the socially inefficient monetary equilibrium can prevail because of a hold up externality. If a seller decides to adopt the technology to accept credit, he incurs the full cost of the technology adoption, but he only receives a fraction $1-\theta < 1$ of the increase in the match surplus. Hence, sellers fail to internalize the effect of the credit technology on buyers' surpluses, which can lead to excess inertia in the decision to adopt the record-keeping technology.

Consider next the case where the cost of holding money, i, is close to zero. In this situation, z_0 will be close to $\theta c(q^*) + (1-\theta)u(q^*)$ and $q(z_0) \approx q^*$. Hence, $\mathcal{W}_0 \approx \sigma\left\{u(q^*) - c(q^*)\right\}$. Provided that $\zeta > 0$ the pure monetary equilibrium dominates the pure credit equilibrium from a social welfare perspective. The resources allocated to the record-keeping technology are "wasted" in the sense that a monetary equilibrium avoids costs associated with record-keeping and provides an allocation that is almost as good as the credit allocation. Still, if $\zeta < \sigma(1-\theta)\left[u(q^*) - c(q^*)\right]$, agents can end up coordinating on the inferior (credit) equilibrium because of the strategic complementarities between the buyers' and sellers' choices.

8.5 Credit and Reallocation of Liquidity

In this section, we describe an economy where credit is used to reallocate liquidity from agents with an excess supply of money to agents with an excess demand for money. To do this, we introduce some heterogeneity in terms of agents' liquidity needs: some buyers need more money than others to trade in the DM. We reinterpret the matching shocks in the DM as preference shocks. With probability σ, a buyer has a positive marginal utility of consumption in the DM, while with the complement probability, $1-\sigma$, his marginal utility of consumption is zero. These shocks are realized at the beginning of a period before agents are matched and are independent across buyers and time. In the DM, after the preference shocks are realized, each buyer gets matched with a seller with probability one.

It should be clear that this model is isomorphic to the one we have been studying so far. If buyers are unable to borrow or lend before being matched, then when the money supply is constant, the quantity traded in the DM in a stationary monetary equilibrium solves the familiar equation,

$$\frac{u'(q)}{c'(q)} = 1 + \frac{r}{\sigma}. \tag{8.46}$$

An important feature of (8.46) is that the quantities traded decrease if buyers face a higher risk of a negative preference shock—i.e., if σ is lower—because a buyer's money holdings are unproductive more often.

We now modify the environment by allowing a loan market to operate at the beginning of each period, after preference shocks are realized but before bilateral matches are formed. The sequence of events is represented in Figure 8.8. In the loan market, agents cannot produce, but

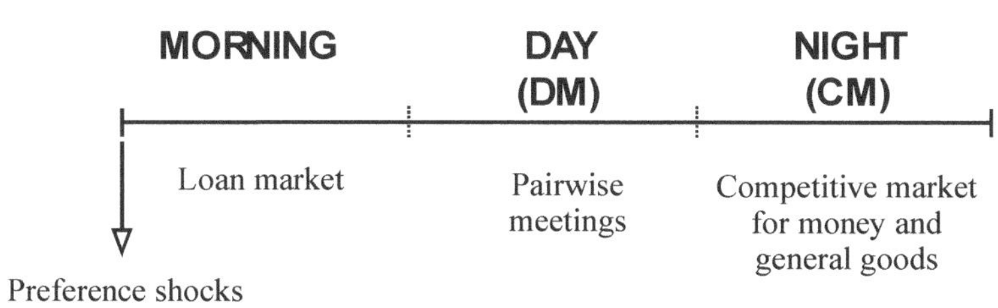

Figure 8.8
Timing

they can buy and sell loans, i.e., they can borrow or lend money for a promise to repay or receive money in the subsequent CM. The nominal interest rate on a loan is i_ℓ: a loan of one dollar is repaid in the subsequent CM for $1+i_\ell$ dollars. Finally, there is a technology to enforce the repayment of loans contracted at the beginning of a period. However, the IOU that represents a loan does not circulate in the DM because it cannot be authenticated in that market. We denote ℓ as the size of a loan. If $\ell > 0$, then the buyer is a creditor and if $\ell < 0$ then the buyer is a debtor.

Define m_ℓ as the amount of money held after the loan market closes. The expected lifetime utility of a buyer who has positive marginal utility of consumption in the DM who holds m_ℓ units of money and ℓ dollars in loans is

$$\hat{V}^b(m_\ell,\ell) = u(q) - c(q) + W^b(m_\ell,\ell), \tag{8.47}$$

where $c(q) = \min\left[c(q^*), \phi m_\ell\right]$ since we assume that buyers make take-it-or-leave-it offers to sellers. The value function of the buyer in the CM, $W^b(m_\ell,\ell)$, is given by

$$W^b(m_\ell,\ell) = \phi m_\ell + (1+i_\ell)\phi\ell + \max_{m'\geq 0}\left\{-\phi m' + \beta V^b(m')\right\}, \tag{8.48}$$

where $V^b(m)$ is the expected utility of the buyer at the beginning of a period before his preference shock is realized. According to (8.48), a buyer in the CM can sell each unit of money at the competitive price ϕ, and he receives $1+i_\ell$ dollars for each unit of loan he owns. The choice of money holdings for the next period, m', is independent of both the size of the loan, ℓ, and the amount of money held by the buyer, m_ℓ. Hence, $W^b(m_\ell,\ell) = \phi m_\ell + (1+i_\ell)\phi\ell + W^b(0,0)$.

The expected utility of the buyer at the beginning of a period who holds m units of money before his preference shock is realized, $V^b(m)$, satisfies

$$V^b(m) = \sigma \max_{\ell^d\geq 0} \hat{V}^b(m+\ell^d, -\ell^d) + (1-\sigma)\max_{\ell^s\leq m} W^b(m-\ell^s,\ell^s), \tag{8.49}$$

where we interpret $\ell^d \geq 0$ as the demand of loans and $\ell^s \geq 0$ as the supply of loans. With probability σ the buyer receives a positive preference shock and wants to consume in the DM. In this case, he demands a loan of size ℓ^d. With probability $1-\sigma$ the buyer does not want to consume but he is willing to lend part or all of his money holdings. Hence, if a buyer is a borrower, $m_\ell = m + \ell^d$ and if he is a lender, $m_\ell = m - \ell^s \geq 0$.

From (8.49) the optimal demand for loans satisfies $\hat{V}^b_{m_\ell} - \hat{V}^b_\ell \leq 0$, with a strict equality if $\ell^d > 0$. ($\hat{V}^b_{m_\ell}$ and $\hat{V}^b_\ell$ represents the derivative of $\hat{V}^b$ with respect to its first and second argument, respectively.) From (8.47), the benefit from borrowing one unit of money is $\hat{V}^b_{m_\ell} = \phi u'(q)/c'(q)$, while the cost is $\hat{V}^b_\ell = (1 + i_\ell)\,\phi$. Hence,

$$\frac{u'(q)}{c'(q)} - 1 - i_\ell \leq 0, \quad \text{“}=\text{”} \text{ if } \ell^d > 0, \tag{8.50}$$

where $c(q) = \min\left[c(q^*), \phi(m + \ell^d)\right]$. Notice that if the solution to (8.50) is interior, the quantity of money held by the buyer before entering the DM is independent from his money holdings at the beginning of the period. If the solution to (8.50) is interior, then,

$$\max_{\ell^d \geq 0} \hat{V}^b(m + \ell^d, -\ell^d) = \max_{m_\ell} \left\{u \circ c^{-1}(\phi m_\ell) - (1 + i_\ell)\phi m_\ell\right\} \\ + (1 + i_\ell)\phi m + W^b(0,0).$$

From (8.49) the individual supply of loans satisfies $\ell^s = m$ whenever $i_\ell > 0$ and $\ell^s \geq 0$ if $i_\ell = 0$. Consequently,

$$\max_{\ell^s \leq m} W^b(m - \ell^s, \ell^s) = (1 + i_\ell)\phi m + W^b(0,0).$$

We will check later that sellers have no strict incentives to borrow or lend.

The equilibrium of the loan market is represented graphically in Figure 8.9. The aggregate demand for loans, $L^d = \sigma \ell^d$, is downward-sloping because as the interest rate on loans increases, the individual demand for loans decreases. If $[u' \circ c^{-1}(\phi M)]/[c' \circ c^{-1}(\phi M)] \leq 1 + i_\ell$, then the benefit of borrowing is less than its cost, and buyers do not find it profitable to borrow funds, i.e., $L^d = \ell^d = 0$. If $i_\ell = 0$, then buyers will borrow enough money to trade q^* in the DM. The size of an individual loan is greater than or equal to $[c(q^*) - \phi M]/\phi$. The aggregate supply of loans, $L^s = (1 - \sigma)\ell^s$, is vertical at $L^s = (1 - \sigma)M$.

Let us turn to the demand for money in the CM. From (8.48) and (8.49), the optimal choice of money holdings satisfies

$$\phi = \beta\left\{\sigma \frac{u'(q)}{c'(q)}\phi + (1 - \sigma)(1 + i_\ell)\phi\right\}. \tag{8.51}$$

As usual, the left side of (8.51) represents the cost of accumulating an additional unit of money, while the right side of (8.51) is the benefit from holding an additional unit of money. The benefit has two components. With probability σ the buyer has positive marginal utility of

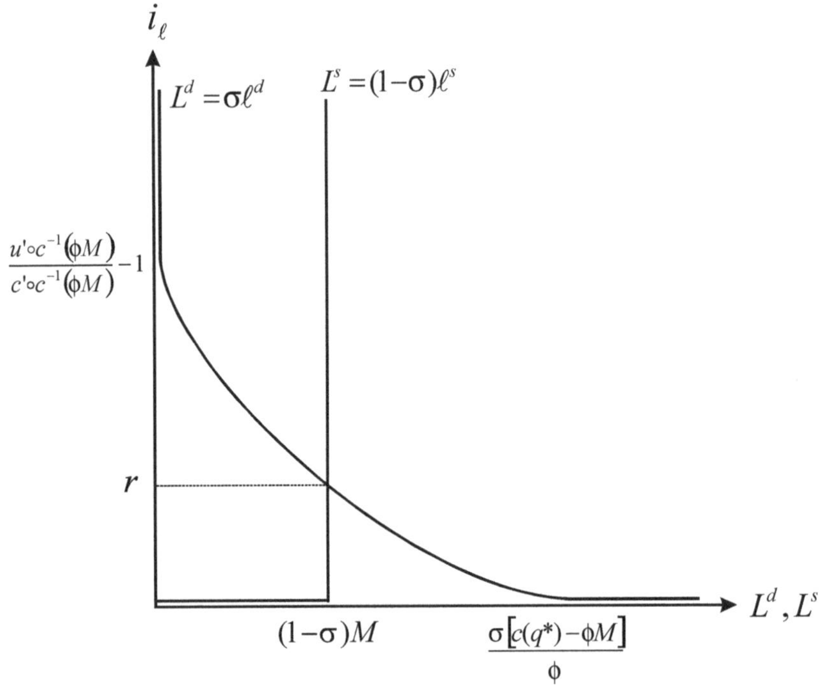

Figure 8.9
Equilibrium of the loan market

consumption, in which case he can use his marginal unit of money to buy $\phi/c'(q)$ units of output in the DM. With probability $1-\sigma$, the buyer does not want to consume, in which case he can lend his unit of money for $1+i_\ell$ units of money in the CM. So, compared to the environment where there is no borrowing or lending, the buyer can obtain an additional return on his money holdings if he does not have an opportunity to consume. This additional return tends to make money more valuable.

We now show that the loan market is active. To see this, suppose that, instead, $\ell^s = \ell^d = 0$. Since $\ell^d = 0$, (8.51) represents the demand for money, as does (8.46); and buyers with a low marginal utility of consumption do not lend their money balances, i.e., $\ell^s = 0$, only if $i_\ell = 0$. This implies that

$$\frac{u'(q)}{c'(q)} - 1 - i_\ell = \frac{u'(q)}{c'(q)} - 1 = \frac{r}{\sigma} > 0.$$

But this inequality violates (8.50). Clearly, at $i_\ell = 0$, buyers who have a positive marginal utility of consumption have an incentive to borrow some money in order to relax their budget constraint in a bilateral match. As a result, the loan market is active: $i_\ell > 0$ and $\ell^s = m$.

From (8.50) and (8.51), we can solve for the quantities traded in the DM and the interest rate on loans,

$$\frac{u'(q)}{c'(q)} = 1 + r \tag{8.52}$$

$$i_\ell = r. \tag{8.53}$$

A comparison between (8.46) and (8.52) reveals that the quantities traded when the loan market is active are greater than the quantities traded when there is no loan market to reallocate the liquid assets. This implies that the existence of a loan market after preference shocks are realized but before agents are matched in the DM is welfare improving. So the use of credit plays an essential role to reallocate the liquidity that is needed to trade in the DM. Notice also that the allocation that is obtained with an active loan market is the one that would prevail if buyers knew the realization of their preference shocks in the CM, at the time when they choose their money holdings. In this situation, there would be no precautionary demand for money holdings.

The market clearing for loans requires that $\sigma\ell^d = (1-\sigma)\ell^s$. Since, in equilibrium, $\ell^s = M$, the size of the buyer's loan is

$$\ell^d = \left(\frac{1-\sigma}{\sigma}\right) M.$$

Since we assume that buyers make a take-it-or-leave-it offer to sellers, the quantity traded in the DM solves $c(q) = \phi(M + \ell^d)$. Consequently, the value of money in equilibrium is

$$\phi = \frac{\sigma c(q)}{M}. \tag{8.54}$$

The stock of money per active buyer is M/σ. As σ increases, the quantity of money per active buyer decreases and, hence, the value of money increases.

According to (8.53) the interest rate on a loan is exactly equal to the rate of time preference, r. Buyers with a high marginal utility of consumption are willing to pay up to the rate of time preference to borrow an additional unit of money, which is the marginal benefit of money holdings in the DM.

We can now check that sellers have no strict incentives to participate in the loan market. It is clear that sellers do not want to borrow money at a positive interest rate since they don't need it in the DM. And they are indifferent in terms of accumulating money or not in the CM and lending it in the next DM at the interest r.

In the presence of a growing money supply, it can be checked that the nominal interest on the loans is $i_\ell = i \equiv (\gamma - \beta)/\beta \approx (\gamma - 1) + r$. According to the Fisher effect, an increase in the inflation rate, $\gamma - 1$, has a one-to-one effect on the nominal interest rate.

8.6 Short-Term and Long-Term Partnerships

As in Section 8.2, we assume that there is no enforcement technology and buyers cannot commit to repay their debt. Therefore, debt contracts must be self-enforcing. In contrast to Section 8.2 there is no public record-keeping technology. However, we allow for repeated interactions with a seller so that a buyer can generate a reputation for paying his debts, and the buyer's desire for this reputation results in contracts being self enforced.

We allow for the possibility of both short-term and long-term partnerships, and model this by combining the pure monetary environment with short-term partnerships in Chapter 3.1 with the long-term partnership environment described in Chapter 2.7. At the beginning of a period, unmatched agents can enter into a long-term trade match with probability σ_L or a short-term trade match with probability σ_S. A short-term match corresponds to a situation where the buyer and the seller know they will not meet again in the future. In contrast, in a long-term match the buyer and the seller have a chance to stay together for more than one period. We assume that $0 < \sigma_L + \sigma_S < 1$. A short-term match is destroyed with probability one at the beginning of the CM, while a long-term match will be exogenously destroyed with probability $\lambda < 1$ at the beginning of the CM. In addition, either party to a long-term match that is not exogenously destroyed can always choose to terminate the relationship at the beginning of the DM.

The timing of the relevant events are described in Figure 8.10. Buyers enter the day market, DM, either attached, i.e., in a long-term trade match, or unattached. At this time matched buyers and sellers in a long-term partnership simultaneously decide whether to continue or split apart. Unattached buyers and sellers participate in a random matching process. Since the measures of buyers and sellers are equal, there are

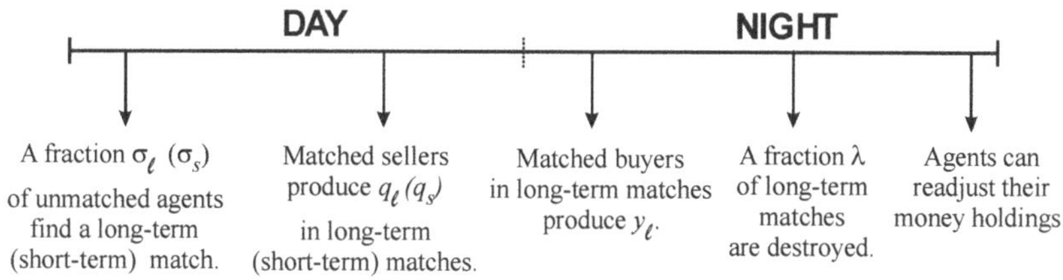

Figure 8.10
Timing of a representative period

also equal measures of unattached buyers and unattached sellers. After the matching process is completed, all matched sellers—those in either a long-term or short-term relationship—produce the DM good for buyers. The night period begins with buyers *who are in a long-term partnership* producing the general good for sellers if trade was mediated by credit in the previous DM. A fraction λ of buyers in the long-term partnership then realize a shock which dissolves the relationship they have with their currently matched seller, and all of the short-term partnerships are destroyed. This is followed by the opening of the CM, where the general good and money are traded. In terms of pricing mechanisms, we assume that buyers make take-it-or-leave-it offers to sellers in the DM, and that the night market is competitive, where one unit of money trades for ϕ_t units of the general good.

We restrict our attention to a particular class of equilibria that exhibit two features. First, money is valued, but is only used in short-term trade matches. Second, the buyer's incentive-compatibility constraint in long-term matches—that the buyer is willing to produce the general good for the seller to extinguish his debt obligation—is not binding. This latter assumption implies that a buyer in a long-term partnership is able to purchase the efficient quantity of the DM good, q^*, with credit alone. So these equilibria are such that money and credit coexist but are used in different types of meetings, as in the previous sections, but we do not need to impose enforcement or commitment.

The value of being an unmatched buyer in the CM, $W_u^b(z)$, is given by

$$W_u^b(z) = z + T + \max_{z' \geq 0}\{-\gamma z' + \beta V_u^b(z')\}, \tag{8.55}$$

where $V_u^b(z')$ is the value of being an unmatched buyer holding z' units of real balances at the beginning of a period. The buyer can consume z units of general good from his z units of real balances; he receives a lump-sum transfer (tax) of real balances if $\gamma > 1$ ($\gamma < 1$), and he accumulates $\gamma z'$ units of real balances in the current period in order to start the next period with z' real balances, where $\gamma^{-1} = \phi_{t+1}/\phi_t$ is the rate of return on money in a steady-state equilibrium.

The value function of an unmatched buyer in the DM who holds z units of real balances, $V_u^b(z)$, is given by

$$V_u^b(z) = \sigma_L V_L^b(z) + \sigma_S V_S^b(z) + (1 - \sigma_L - \sigma_S) W_u^b(z). \tag{8.56}$$

With probability σ_L, the buyer finds a long-term partnership with value $V_L^b(z)$ and, with probability σ_S, he finds a short-term match whose value is $V_S^b(z)$. With probability $1 - \sigma_L - \sigma_S$, the buyer remains unattached and enters the night market with his z units of real balances that provide value $W_u^b(z)$.

Following a similar reasoning, the expected lifetime utility of an unmatched seller at night is

$$W_u^s(z) = z + \beta V_u^s, \tag{8.57}$$

where we take into account that sellers have no incentives to hold real balances in the DM. So an unmatched seller with z units of real balances at night consumes z units of general goods and starts the next period unmatched and with no money. In the DM, the value of an unmatched seller is

$$V_u^s = \sigma_L V_L^s + \sigma_S V_S^s + (1 - \sigma_L - \sigma_S) W_u^s(0), \tag{8.58}$$

where V_L^s (V_S^s) is the value of a seller in a long-term (short-term) match in the DM. The interpretation of (8.58) is similar to (8.56), except that sellers at the beginning of the DM do not hold real balances.

The buyer in a short-term trade match makes a take-it-or-leave-it offer, (q_S, d_S), to the seller, where q_S is the amount of the DM good that the seller produces and d_S is the amount of real balances transferred from the buyer to the seller. The value function of a buyer holding z units of real balances in a short-term trade match, $V_S^b(z)$, is given by

$$V_S^b(z) = u\left[q_S(z)\right] + W_u^b\left[z - d_S(z)\right] = u\left[q_S(z)\right] - d_S(z) + z + W_u^b(0), \tag{8.59}$$

where the second equality is obtained from the linearity of W_u^b. The buyer consumes q_S units of the search good in the day and enters the competitive general goods market with $z - d_S$ units of real balances. Similarly, the value function of a seller (with no real balances) in a short-term trade match is

$$V_S^s = -c\left[q_S(z)\right] + d_S(z) + W_u^s(0), \tag{8.60}$$

where z represents the buyer's real balances. The take-it-or-leave-it offer by the buyer maximizes the buyer's surplus, $u(q_S) - d_S$, subject to the seller's participation constraint, $-c(q_S) + d_S \geq 0$, and the feasibility constraint, $d_S \leq z$. It is characterized by either $q_S(z) = q^*$ and $d_S(z) = c(q^*)$ if $z \geq c(q^*)$, or $q_S = c^{-1}(z)$ if $z < c(q^*)$. Hence, (8.59) becomes

$$V_S^b(z) = u[q_S(z)] - c[q_S(z)] + z + W_u^b(0), \tag{8.61}$$

and, from (8.60), $V_S^s = W_u^s(0)$.

The value function for a buyer in a long-term relationship holding z units of real balances at the beginning of the period is

$$V_L^b(z) = u[q_L(z)] + W_L^b[z - d_L(z), -y_L(z)], \tag{8.62}$$

where $W_L^b(z - d_L, -y_L)$ is the value of the matched buyer at night holding $z - d_L$ units of real balances, with a promise to produce y_L units of the general good for his trade-match partner. So a buyer in a long-term partnership consumes q_L units of search goods in exchange for d_L units of real balances and a promise to repay y_L units of general goods. Even though we allow the terms of trade (q_L, d_L, y_L) to depend on the buyer's real balances, z, we consider equilibria where buyers don't use money in long-term partnerships, $d_L = 0$ and (q_L, y_L) is independent of z. The value function of a buyer in a long-term partnership at the beginning of the night, $W_L^b(z, -y_L)$, satisfies

$$\begin{aligned} W_L^b(z, -y_L) = z - y_L + T + \lambda \max_{z' \geq 0}\{-\gamma z' + \beta V_u^b(z')\} + \\ (1-\lambda) \max_{z'' \geq 0}\left\{-\gamma z'' + \beta V_L^b(z'')\right\}. \end{aligned} \tag{8.63}$$

At the beginning of the night, the buyer fulfills his promise and produces y_L units of the general good for the seller. If the trade match is not exogenously destroyed, then the buyer produces in order to hold z'' real balances in the CM. If the partnership breaks up at night—an event that occurs with probability λ—then the buyer produces to hold z' real balances in the CM before he proceeds to the next period in search of a new trading partner.

By a similar reasoning, the value function for a seller in a long-term relationship at the beginning of the period is

$$V_L^s = -c[q_L(z)] + W_L^s[d_L(z), y_L(z)]. \tag{8.64}$$

The seller produces q_L for the buyer in the DM in exchange for a promise to receive y_L units of general good at night and d_L units of real balances (where z represents the buyer's real balances). The value function of the seller at night is

$$W_L^s(z, y_L) = z + y_L + (1-\lambda)\beta V_L^s + \lambda\beta V_u^s. \tag{8.65}$$

The seller receives y_L units of general goods from the buyer he is matched with and he spends his z real balances in the CM. With probability λ the long-term partnership is destroyed, in which case the seller starts the next period unmatched.

We now turn to the formation of the terms of trade in long-term partnerships. We will assume that the buyer makes a take-it-or-leave-if offer, (q_L, y_L, d_L). If the offer is rejected, no trade takes place in that period, but the buyer and the seller remain matched in the subsequent period unless an exogenous destruction shock occurs with probability λ. (In equilibrium, sellers are indifferent between being matched and unmatched.) Moreover, the offer must satisfy the incentive-compatibility constraint according to which the buyer is willing to repay his debt at night. So the buyer chooses (q_L, y_L, d_L) in order to maximize $V_L^b(z)$ subject to the seller's participation constraint, $-c(q_L) + W_L^s(d_L, y_L) \geq W_L^s(0,0)$, and the incentive-compatibility constraint, $W_L^b(z - d_L, -y_L) \geq W_u^b(z - d_L)$. The incentive-compatibility constraint states that the buyer is better-off paying his debt than walking away from his partnership. From (8.62) and using the linearity of W_L^s, W_L^b, and W_u^b, the buyer's problem can be expressed as

$$\max_{q,y,d} [u(q) - y - d] \text{ s.t. } -c(q) + y + d \geq 0, \quad d \leq z, \tag{8.66}$$

$$y \leq W_L^b(0,0) - W_u^b(0). \tag{8.67}$$

We focus on equilibria where the incentive-compatibility constraint (8.67) does not bind for all values of z. As a result, $q_L = q^*$ and $y_L + d_L = c(q^*)$. So the terms of trade in long-term partnerships are independent of the buyer's real balances. Without loss of generality, we can assume that buyers pay with credit only, $d_L = 0$. It is also immediate from (8.62) and (8.63) that a buyer in a long-term partnership at night will not accumulate real balances (in (8.63) $z'' = 0$).

Let us consider the choice of real balances by unmatched buyers. From (8.55)-(8.63), the optimal choice of real balances at night, z, for a buyer who is not in a long-term relationship satisfies

$$\max_{z \geq 0} \{-iz + \sigma_S \{u[q_S(z)] - c[q_S(z)]\}\}. \tag{8.68}$$

Since real balances are not needed in long-term partnerships, the buyer only takes into account his expected surplus in a short-term match when choosing his money holdings. This leads to the familiar first-order condition,

$$\frac{u'(q_S)}{c'(q_S)} = 1 + \frac{i}{\sigma_S}. \tag{8.69}$$

The last thing we need to check is that the incentive-compatibility condition, (8.67), is not binding. Using that $y_L = c(q^*)$, (8.67) becomes

$$c(q^*) \leq W_L^b(0,0) - W_u^b(0). \tag{8.70}$$

With the help of equations (8.56)-(8.63), and after some rearranging (see the Appendix), inequality (8.70) can be rewritten as

$$c(q^*) \leq (1-\lambda)\beta\left\{(1-\sigma_L)u(q^*) + ic(q_S) - \sigma_S\left[u(q_S) - c(q_S)\right]\right\}, \tag{8.71}$$

where q_S satisfies (8.69). If inequality (8.71) holds, then there exists an equilibrium where buyers and sellers in long-term relationships consume and produce $q_L = q^*$ units of the search good during the day and $y_L = c(q^*)$ units of the general good at night, using credit arrangements to implement these trades. Buyers and sellers in short-term partnerships trade q_S units of the search good for $y_S = c(q_S)$ units of real balances during the day.

Perhaps not surprisingly, if $\sigma_S = 0$, then from (8.69), $q_S = 0$ and the incentive condition (8.71) is identical to the one obtained in a model where money was absent and trade in long-term relationships was supported by reputation, see the definition of $\mathcal{A}^R$ given by (2.61) in Chapter 2.7. If the frequency of short-term matches, σ_S, increases, then, from (8.69), agents will increase their real balance holdings; as a result the incentive-constraint (8.71) becomes more difficult to satisfy. Hence, the availability of monetary exchange in the presence of a long-term partnership increases the attractiveness of defaulting on promised performance. However, if inflation increases, then, from the envelope theorem, the term $-ic(q_S) + \sigma_S\left[u(q_S) - c(q_S)\right]$ decreases, which relaxes the incentive-constraint (8.71). Hence, a higher inflation rate reduces the buyer's incentive to default on this long-term partnership obligations.

8.7 Further Readings

Shi (1996) considers a search-theoretic environment where fiat money and credit can coexist, even though money is dominated by credit in the rate of return. A credit trade occurs when two agents are matched and the buyer in the match does not have money. Collateral is used to make the repayment incentive-compatible, and debt is repaid with money. In this approach, monetary exchange is superior to credit in the sense that monetary exchange allows agents to trade faster. Li (2001) extends Shi's model to allow private debt to circulate and she investigates various government policies, including open-market operations.

Telyukova and Wright (2008) develop a model similar to that in Section 8.1 where IOUs are issued in a competitive market. They show that such a model can explain the credit card debt puzzle, the observation that a large fraction of U.S. households owe a sizeable amount of credit card debt and hold liquid assets at the same time. In Camera and Li (2008), agents are anonymous, and choose between using money and credit to facilitate trade. There exists a costly technology that allows limited record-keeping and enforcement. Money and credit can coexist if the cost of using the technology is sufficiently small.

The model in Section 8.2 with money and credit under limited commitment is based on Bethune, Rocheteau, and Rupert (2015). An earlier treatment with different punishments for default and theft of money is provided by Sanchez and Williamson (2010). Rojas Breu (2013) shows that an increased access to credit has an ambiguous effect on welfare by decreasing the value of outside money. Lotz and Zhang (2016) extend the model to have costly investment in a record-keeping technology as in Section 8.4. Hu and Araujo (2016) apply a mechanism design approach to study the coexistence of money and credit under limited commitment and some policy implications. See Cavalcanti and Wallace (1999) and Deviatov and Wallace (2014) for earlier versions in the context of the Shi-Trejos-Wright model. Berentsen and Waller (2011) compare allocations in economies with outside liquidity and economies with pure credit (inside bonds) and show that any allocation in the economy with credit can be replicated in the economy with outside liquidity but that the converse is not true. Gu, Mattesini, and Wright (2016) provide an overview of this literature and some of its challenges.

Lucas and Stokey (1987) propose a model where the distinction between goods purchased with cash and goods purchased with credit is exogenous. Schreft (1992) and Dotsey and Ireland (1996) endogenize the composition of trades involving cash or credit. They assume that agents trade in different markets where they can hire the services of a financial intermediary who can verify the buyer's identity. The cost paid to the intermediary is higher the greater the distance between the borrower's and the lender's home locations. This formalization is also related to the model by Prescott (1987) and Freeman and Kydland (2000), where some goods are bought with cash and others with demand deposits. The second means of payment involves a fixed cost of record-keeping associated with bank drafts. Li (2011) proposes a related search model with currency and checking deposits. Gomis-Porqueras and Sanches (2013) consider a scheme where the government pays interest on money holdings in order to induce agents to pay the cost of the record-keeping technology. Gomis-Porqueras, Peralta-Alva, and Waller (2014) explain the cost of credit by the fact that agents who trade with money are anonymous and can avoid paying taxes. When buyers receive a large liquidity shock they are willing to ask for trade credit even though they will be taxed.

Townsend (1989) investigates the optimal trading mechanism in an economy with different locations, where some agents stay in the same location and other agents move from one location to another. The optimal arrangement implies the coexistence of currency and credit: currency is used between strangers, i.e., agents whose histories are not known to one another, and credit is used among agents who know their histories. Kocherlakota and Wallace (1998) consider a random-matching economy with a public record of all past transactions that is updated only infrequently. They show that in this economy there are roles for both monetary transactions and some form of credit. Jin and Temzelides (2004) consider a search-theoretic model with local and faraway trades. There is record-keeping at the local level so that agents in local meetings can trade with credit. In contrast, agents from different neighborhoods need to trade with money. Li (2007) considers an environment with a random-matching sector and organized markets in which bills of exchange circulate as a general medium of exchange. Araujo and Minetti (2011) consider an economy where some agents (institutions) are relatively trustworthy, because they can be better monitored. When trade is limited, these institutions sustain cooperation even without banking. However, when trade expands, banking and inside money become essential.

The model on credit and the reallocation of liquidity has been inspired from the work by Berentsen, Camera, and Waller (2007) on banking. Instead of considering a loan market, they introduce banks that make loans and accept deposits. Another interpretation is the one from Kocherlakota (2003) on the societal benefits of illiquid bonds. In Kocherlakota's model, agents trade their excess liquidity for interest-bearing illiquid government bonds. Kahn (2009) uses a similar model to study round-the-clock private payments arrangements. Ferraris and Watanabe (2008, 2011) extend the model to have loans collateralized with capital.

Williamson (1999) constructs a model where banks intermediate a mismatch between the timing of investment payoffs and when agents wish to consume; claims on banks may serve as media of exchange, i.e., private money. Cavalcanti, Erosa, and Temzelides (1999) develop a model of money and reserve-holding banks where private liabilities can circulate as media of exchange. Li (2006) studies competition between inside and outside money in economies with trading frictions and financial intermediation.

Corbae and Ritter (2004) consider a model of long-term and short-term partnerships similar to the one presented in Section 8.6. Williamson (1998) constructs a dynamic risk-sharing model where there is private information about agents' endowments. Risk-sharing is accomplished though dynamic contracts involving credit transactions and monetary exchange. Aiyagari and Williamson (2000) construct a dynamic risk-sharing model where agents can enter into a long-term relationship with a financial intermediary. They introduce a transaction role for money, by assuming random limited participation in the financial market. In each period, agents can defect from their long-term contracts and trade in a competitive money market thereafter. Aiyagari and Williamson show that the value of this outside option depends on monetary policy.

Appendix

Derivation of (8.71)
From (8.62) and (8.63),

$$W_L^b(0,0) = T + (1-\lambda)\beta\left[u(q^*) - c(q^*) + W_L^b(0,0)\right] + \lambda\left[-\gamma z + \beta V_u^b(z)\right], \tag{8.72}$$

where z is the optimal choice of real balances of an unmatched buyer, and buyers in long-term partnerships do not accumulate real balances. From (8.55),

$$W_u^b(0) = T - \gamma z + \beta V_u^b(z). \tag{8.73}$$

From (8.72) and (8.73),

$$W_L^b(0,0) - W_u^b(0) = (1-\lambda)\beta\left\{u(q^*) - c(q^*) + W_L^b(0,0) - \left[-\frac{\gamma}{\beta}z + V_u^b(z)\right]\right\} \tag{8.74}$$

From (8.56), (8.61), and (8.62),

$$V_u^b(z) = \sigma_L\left[u\left(q^*\right) - c(q^*) + W_L^b\left(0,0\right) - W_u^b(0)\right]$$
$$+ \sigma_S\left[u\left(q_S\right) - c\left(q_S\right)\right] + z + W_u^b(0).$$

Substituting $V_u^b(z)$ by its expression into (8.74),

$$\left[1-(1-\lambda)\left(1-\sigma_L\right)\beta\right]\left[W_L^b(0,0) - W_u^b(0)\right] =$$
$$(1-\lambda)\beta\left\{\left(1-\sigma_L\right)\left[u(q^*) - c(q^*)\right] - \left[-iz + \sigma_S\left[u\left(q_S\right) - c\left(q_S\right)\right]\right]\right\},$$

where we have used that $i \equiv (\gamma - \beta)/\beta$. The condition (8.70), $c(q^*) \leq W_L^b(0,0) - W_u^b(0)$, can then be expressed as

$$\left[1-(1-\lambda)\left(1-\sigma_L\right)\beta\right]c(q^*) \leq$$
$$(1-\lambda)\beta\left\{\left(1-\sigma_L\right)\left[u(q^*) - c(q^*)\right] - \left[-iz + \sigma_S\left[u\left(q_S\right) - c\left(q_S\right)\right]\right]\right\},$$

and simplified to

$$c(q^*) \leq (1-\lambda)\beta\left\{(1-\sigma_L)u(q^*) + ic(q_S) - \sigma_S\left[u\left(q_S\right) - c\left(q_S\right)\right]\right\},$$

where we used that $z = c(q_S)$.

9 Firm Entry, Unemployment, and Payments

"The 'natural rate of unemployment'... is the level that would be ground out by the Walrasian system of general equilibrium equations, provided there is imbedded in them the actual structural characteristics of the labor and commodity markets, including market imperfections, stochastic variability in demands and supplies, the cost of gathering information about job vacancies and labor availabilities, the cost of mobility, and so on."

Milton Friedman (1969)

According to Milton Friedman (1969), the natural or steady-state rate of unemployment depends on frictions—such as imperfect competition, costs of gathering information, and mobility costs—that plague goods and labor markets. The labor market model of Mortensen and Pissarides (1994) formalizes Friedman's concept in a parsimonious and elegant way by incorporating bargaining power and search and matching frictions. Their model, however, abstracts from liquidity considerations, such as money and credit, that provide powerful linkages between goods and labor markets. In this chapter we incorporate money and credit into a model of frictional labor and goods markets.

We will accomplish the integration of our model of money and credit and the Mortensen-Pissarides model of unemployment in two steps. In our first step, we introduce firms into our benchmark model. We assume that there is a large number of firms that can participate in the goods market but at a cost. A firm can try to sell its divisible output in a decentralized goods market characterized by search and bargaining. If the firm is unlucky and does not meet a buyer, or if it meets a buyer but does not sell all its output, then it can sell its inventory of goods in the centralized market. This simple generalization of our benchmark model generates several new insights. First, due to strategic complementarities between buyers' choice of real balances and firms' decision to participate in the goods market, there may exist multiple steady-state equilibria. This multiplicity disappears in "cashless" economies, where all trades are conducted with perfect credit. Second, equilibria are generically inefficient even at the Friedman rule because a firm's decision to participate in the goods markets generates "search" externalities. These externalities can only be internalized for a particular value of the buyers' bargaining power. Third, entry is higher in an economy with perfect credit relative to a pure currency economy because buyers have a larger payment capacity in the former than the latter. However, the relationship between firm entry and credit might not be monotone.

Our second step consists in formalizing explicitly the labor market based on the canonical model of Mortensen and Pissarides (1994). In order to produce output, a firm must hire a worker in a labor market that is subject to search and matching frictions. The total surplus generated by the worker and firm is split according to a bargaining protocol, which makes the description of the labor market symmetric to that of the goods market. The model can generate multiple steady-state equilibria, where employment and the value of money are positively correlated across the equilibria. At the "high" equilibrium—the equilibrium with the highest value of money and highest employment—an increase in inflation increases unemployment. Hence, the model predicts a long-run, upward-sloping Phillips curve, a possibility discussed in Friedman's (1977) Nobel lecture. We also show that an economy with perfect credit has a lower unemployment rate than a pure currency economy.

We conclude the chapter by considering the case of credit under limited commitment. We show that the availability of credit, as captured by endogenous debt limits, depends on the state of the labor market. If unemployment is low, then the measure of firms in the goods market is high, trading opportunities are frequent, and hence access to credit is very valuable. As a result, credit limits are high. This linkage between credit limits and unemployment also generates multiple steady-state equilibria.

9.1 A Model with Firms

We now interpret a seller as a firm. A firm is a technology that produces $\bar{q} \geq q^*$ units of output. The firm's output can be sold in either the DM or CM. If the firm sells $q < \bar{q}$ in a DM bilateral match, the remaining output, $\bar{q} - q$, can be sold in the CM. Hence, the opportunity cost of selling q units of output in the DM, measured in terms of the CM good, is equal to q, i.e., $c(q) = q$ and $u'(q^*) = 1$. The production and sales of goods are described in Figure 9.1.

We assume that there is a large measure of firms that can choose to participate in the market. The measure of participating firms is denoted by n. (Notice that n has a different meaning than the one in previous chapters.) A firm can participate in the goods markets of period $t+1$ only if it incurs a cost $k > 0$ at the end of period t, where k is measured in terms of the CM good in period t. For now, we can think of k as an entry or participation cost for the firm. We provide an alternative interpretation of this cost in the subsequent section, when we introduce workers. In this section we assume that $k > \beta\bar{q}$; this implies that firms have no incentive to pay the entry cost if, with probability one, they are unable to sell any output in the DM.

In previous chapters, the measures of buyers and sellers are assumed to be equal. Here, the measure of sellers (or firms), n, is endogenous and, in general, will not be equal to the unit measure of buyers. We, therefore, need to be more explicit about the process that matches buyers and sellers. (We will sometimes refer to firms as sellers as they sell their output in the DM.) The number of matches is given by the matching function $\mathcal{M}(B,S)$, where B is the measure of buyers and S is the measure of sellers. The matching function is strictly increasing and concave in both of its arguments, and exhibits constant returns to scale. The probability that a buyer is matched with a seller is $\sigma \equiv \mathcal{M}(B,S)/B = \mathcal{M}(1,S/B)$ and the probability that a seller is matched with a buyer is $\mathcal{M}(B,S)/S = \mathcal{M}(B/S,1)$. Since $\mathcal{M}$ exhibits constant returns to scale, the matching probabilities are a function of the ratio S/B. We will refer to

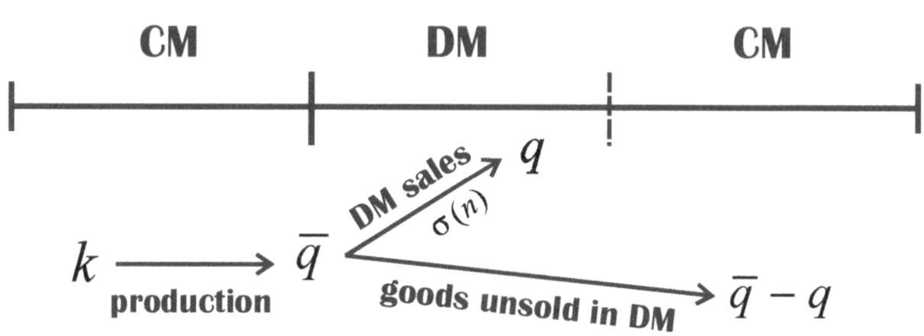

Figure 9.1
Production and sales

the ratio S/B as "market tightness." Since we normalize the measure of buyers to one and the measure of sellers is n, market tightness in the goods market is simply n. The properties of the matching function imply that $\sigma'(n) > 0$ and $\sigma''(n) < 0$. In addition, we assume that $\sigma(n) \leq \min\{1,n\}, \sigma(0) = 0, \sigma'(0) = 1$ and $\sigma(\infty) = 1$. The matching probability of a buyer in the DM increases with the measure of firms in the market due to a "thick-market" externality. The matching probability of a firm, which is $\sigma(n)/n$, is decreasing in the measure of firms due to a "congestion" externality.

Buyers can use two forms of means of payment: money and credit. In a fraction μ of the matches, buyers' debt obligations are recorded and there exists a perfect enforcement mechanism for the repayment of debt. Hence, unsecured credit can be used in those matches. (We will relax the perfect enforcement mechanism assumption at the end of the chapter.) In a fraction $1-\mu$ of matches, there does not exist an enforcement technology and buyers are not monitored. In these matches credit is not incentive feasible and only money can serve as means of payment. Whether credit is accepted or not in a match is not firm specific: all firms have equal access to the enforcement technology. As a result, the acceptability of credit is a random event that occurs whenever a match is formed and firms are ex ante identical. (For alternative ways to approach the coexistence of money and credit, see Chapter 8.) The supply of money, M_t, grows at the gross growth rate γ, i.e., $M_{t+1}/M_t = \gamma$. We focus on steady-state equilibria, where the rate of return of money is $\phi_{t+1}/\phi_t = 1/\gamma$.

9.2 Firm Entry and Liquidity

We assume that buyers own the firms. We denote firms' profits per buyer as Δ, where profits are the proceeds from the firms' sales net of their entry costs. Claims on firms' expected revenue are assumed to be illiquid and cannot be used as means of payment in the DM. (We will allow claims on productive assets to be liquid in the following chapters.)

Let's start with the buyer. The expected discounted lifetime utility for a buyer holding z real balances at the beginning of the CM *after* all his debts have been repaid, $W(z)$, is given by

$$W(z) = \max_{x,y,z' \geq 0} \{x - y + \beta V(z')\} \tag{9.1}$$

$$\text{s.t. } x + \gamma z' = y + z + \Delta + T, \tag{9.2}$$

where T is a lump-sum transfer. The buyer chooses net CM consumption, $x - y$, and next-period real balances, z', subject to the budget constraint, (9.2). The buyer's DM Bellman equation, $V(z)$, is given by

$$\begin{aligned} V(z) &= \sigma(n)\left\{\mu\left[u\left(q^c\right) - b^c + W(z)\right] + (1-\mu)\left[u\left(q\right) + W(z-d)\right]\right\} \\ &\quad + \left[1 - \sigma(n)\right] W(z) \\ &= \sigma(n)\left\{\mu\left[u\left(q^c\right) - b^c\right] + (1-\mu)\left[u\left(q\right) - d\right]\right\} + W(z), \end{aligned} \tag{9.3}$$

where (q^c, b^c) is the terms of trade in credit matches—where the buyer consumes q^c in exchange for a promise to repay b^c CM goods—and (q, d) is the terms of trade in money matches—where the buyer consumes q in exchange for d real balances. The buyer gets to consume in the DM with probability $\sigma(n)$. With probability μ the buyer can pay for his DM consumption with credit and with probability $1 - \mu$ he must use money. (In credit matches, the buyer could use a mix of money and credit but this arrangement is payoff-equivalent to using only credit. Without loss of generality, we assume buyers use only credit in credit matches.)

The terms of trade in bilateral matches in the DM are determined by the proportional bargaining solution, where the buyer's share in the match surplus is θ. As we shall see below, it is important to give some bargaining power to firms in order to link liquidity in the goods market and firms' entry decisions. In credit matches, the proportional bargaining solution implies that (q^c, b^c) solves,

$$\max_{q^c \leq \bar{q}, b^c} \left[u\left(q^c\right) - b^c\right] \text{ s.t. } u\left(q^c\right) - b^c = \frac{\theta}{1-\theta}\left(b^c - q^c\right). \tag{9.4}$$

According to (9.4), (q^c, b^c) maximizes the buyer's surplus subject to the constraint that the buyer's surplus is $\theta/(1-\theta)$ times the firm's surplus. The buyer's surplus is the utility of consumption, $u\left(q^c\right)$, net of the disutility of repaying the debt in CM goods, b^c. The firm's surplus is equal to the revenue of the firm, b^c, minus the revenue it would obtain by selling the same output, q^c, in the CM. Because repayment can be enforced, b^c is not subject to a debt limit. The solution to (9.4) is $q^c = q^*$ and $b^c = (1-\theta)u(q^*) + \theta q^*$.

In monetary matches (q, d) is given by the solution to

$$\max_{q \leq \bar{q}, d} \left[u\left(q\right) - d\right] \text{ s.t. } u\left(q\right) - d = \frac{\theta}{1-\theta}\left(d - q\right) \text{ and } d \leq z. \tag{9.5}$$

Notice that problem (9.5) is similar to problem (9.4) with the additional constraint that a buyer cannot spend more real balances than he holds, i.e., $d \leq z$. The solution to (9.5) is $q = q^*$ and $d = (1-\theta)u(q^*) + \theta q^*$ if $z \geq (1-\theta)u(q^*) + \theta q^*$ and $d = z = (1-\theta)u(q) + \theta q$ otherwise, where $q \leq q^*$.

Using the above terms of trade in (9.4), $V(z)$ can be written as

$$V(z) = \sigma(n)\theta\left\{\mu\left[u\left(q^*\right) - q^*\right] + (1-\mu)\left[u\left(q\right) - q\right]\right\} + W(z). \tag{9.6}$$

A buyer is matched with probability $\sigma(n)$ and receives the fraction θ of match surplus, which is $u\left(q^*\right) - q^*$ in credit matches and $u\left(q\right) - q \leq u\left(q^*\right) - q^*$ in monetary matches.

If we substitute (9.2) into (9.1), the buyer's problem is to choose real balances in the CM so as to maximize $-\gamma z + \beta V(z)$. Using (9.6), recognizing that $W(z) = z + W(0)$, the solution to the buyer's problem—assuming it is interior—is given by

$$i = \sigma(n)(1-\mu)\theta\left[\frac{u'\left(q\right) - 1}{\theta + (1-\theta)u'(q)}\right]. \tag{9.7}$$

Notice that (9.7) implies there is a positive relationship between q and n. As the measure of firms, n, increases, buyers face more consumption opportunities in the DM, and as a result they increase their real balances, z, and their DM consumption, q.

Let's now turn to the firm's problem. The expected revenue of a firm within a period is

$$\rho = \frac{\sigma(n)}{n}\left[\mu\left(b^c + \bar{q} - q^c\right) + (1-\mu)\left(d + \bar{q} - q\right)\right] + \left[1 - \frac{\sigma(n)}{n}\right]\bar{q}. \tag{9.8}$$

A firm has an opportunity to sell its output in the DM if it meets a buyer, an event that occurs with probability $\sigma(n)/n$. If credit is acceptable, an event that occurs with probability μ, the firm sells q^c in the DM in exchange for b^c CM goods and the remaining $\bar{q} - q^c$ goods are sold in the CM at a unit price. Similarly, if the firm meets a buyer, then with probability $1-\mu$ it is in a monetary match and its revenue is $d + \bar{q} - q$. If a firm is not matched with a consumer in the DM, then it sells all of its output, $\bar{q}$ units, in the CM. Using the solutions to the bargaining problems—(9.4) and (9.5)—the expected revenue of the firm can be reexpressed as

$$\begin{aligned}\rho &= \frac{\sigma(n)}{n}\left[\mu\left(b^c - q^c\right) + (1-\mu)\left(d - q\right)\right] + \bar{q} \\ &= \frac{\sigma(n)}{n}(1-\theta)\left\{\mu\left[u\left(q^*\right) - q^*\right] + (1-\mu)\left[u\left(q\right) - q\right]\right\} + \bar{q}.\end{aligned} \tag{9.9}$$

The first term on the right side of (9.9) is the expected surplus of the firm in the DM. The firm receives a fraction $1-\theta$ of the match surpluses. The last term, $\bar{q}$, is the firm's output measured in CM goods.

It is optimal for a firm to enter the market as long as the cost to participate, k, is no greater than the expected discounted revenue in the following period, $\beta\rho$. This "free-entry" condition can be written as,

$$-k+\beta\rho\leq 0,\ \text{“}=\text{” if } n>0. \tag{9.10}$$

The firm's expected revenue is discounted at rate $r=\beta^{-1}-1$, which is the real interest rate associated with an illiquid asset. Indeed, recall that claims on firms' revenue cannot serve as means of payment in the DM—they are illiquid. Notice that our assumption that $-k+\beta\bar{q}<0$ implies that firm entry is bounded. Substituting ρ by its expression (9.9) and assuming an interior solution, the free-entry condition becomes

$$\frac{\sigma(n)}{n}(1-\theta)\left\{\mu\left[u\left(q^{*}\right)-q^{*}\right]+(1-\mu)\left[u\left(q\right)-q\right]\right\}+\bar{q}=(1+r)k. \tag{9.11}$$

The left side of (9.11) is the firm's expected revenue and the right side is the "capitalized" cost of entry. Since $u(q)-q$ is increasing with z, it follows that the measure of firms entering the market is increasing in the real balances of buyers. Indeed, if buyers hold larger balances, then firms anticipate they will be able to sell more output in the DM at a price higher than the unit price that prevails in the CM. This increases their incentive to participate in the goods market. If the buyer has all of the bargaining power, $\theta=1$, the goods market shuts down because the firm's expected revenue, $\bar{q}$, is less than the capitalized entry cost, $(1+r)k$.

A steady-state equilibrium can be described by a pair (q,n) that solves (9.7) and (9.11). Consider first the situation where there is perfect enforcement in all matches, i.e., $\mu=1$, and, hence, credit is used in all matches. Money plays no essential role, $z=q=0$. The measure of firms, n, is uniquely determined by (9.11). There is a strictly positive measure of firms, $n>0$, if and only if

$$(1-\theta)\left[u\left(q^{*}\right)-q^{*}\right]+\bar{q}>(1+r)k.$$

The firm's expected revenue must be greater than the cost of entry. Notice that (9.11) implies that entry, n, decreases with the consumer's bargaining share, θ, and increases with both the gains from DM trade, $u\left(q^{*}\right)-q^{*}$, and the firm's productivity, $\bar{q}$.

Consider now the situation where an enforcement technology does not exist in any match, i.e., $\mu=0$. In this situation money must be used as means of payment in all matches. A steady-state equilibrium is a pair (q,n) that satisfies (9.7) and (9.11). Both conditions give a positive relationship between q and n. If money is not valued, $z=0$, then there is no entry of firms—since $(1+r)k>\bar{q}$—and the market shuts down. For firm entry to occur, buyers' real balances must be sufficiently large so that $q \geq q_0$, where q_0 solves

$$(1-\theta)\left[u\left(q_0\right)-q_0\right]+\bar{q}=(1+r)k.$$

If $q=q^*$ then the measure of firms equals the measure that would exist in an economy with perfect credit, which we denote as n_1.

Assuming that $u'(0)=+\infty$, buyers have an incentive to accumulate real balances in the CM if $n>n_0$, where n_0 is implicitly given by

$$i=\sigma(n_0)\frac{(1-\mu)\theta}{(1-\theta)}. \tag{9.12}$$

If $i<(1-\mu)\theta/(1-\theta)$, then such a n_0 exists. As the measure of firms go to infinity, the quantity traded in the DM approaches q_1, where q_1 solves

$$i=(1-\mu)\theta\left[\frac{u'\left(q_1\right)-1}{\theta+(1-\theta)u'(q_1)}\right]. \tag{9.13}$$

From (9.13), provided that $i>0$, $q_1<q^*$. Even if buyers are able to find a firm with certainty in the DM, they will consume less than q^* when money is costly to hold. Moreover, $q_1>0$ if $i<(1-\mu)\theta/(1-\theta)$.

In Figure 9.2 we represent the choice of DM consumption as a function of n, (9.7), and the entry of firms as a function of q, (9.11). From the above discussion, the curve representing the free-entry condition—labeled the n-curve—is located above the curve representing the DM consumption—labeled the q-curve—at $n=n_0$ and $n=n_1$. Hence, there are generically an even number of equilibria. The intuition that underlies the multiplicity of steady-state equilibria is as follows. Suppose firms anticipate that buyers hold large real balances. Then, they believe that q will be high in DM matches and, as a result, their expected revenue, ρ, will also be high. Therefore, a large number of firms have an incentive to participate in the market; n is high. But if n is high, then the frequency of consumption opportunities in the DM, $\sigma(n)$, is also high and buyers will find it optimal to hold large real balances, which supports firms' beliefs. Alternatively, if firms anticipate that buyers will hold small real balances, then firm entry will be small. As a result, $\sigma(n)$ is low and buyers hold low real balances.

We now focus on the "high" equilibrium—the equilibrium that has the highest q and the highest n—and perform some comparative statics.

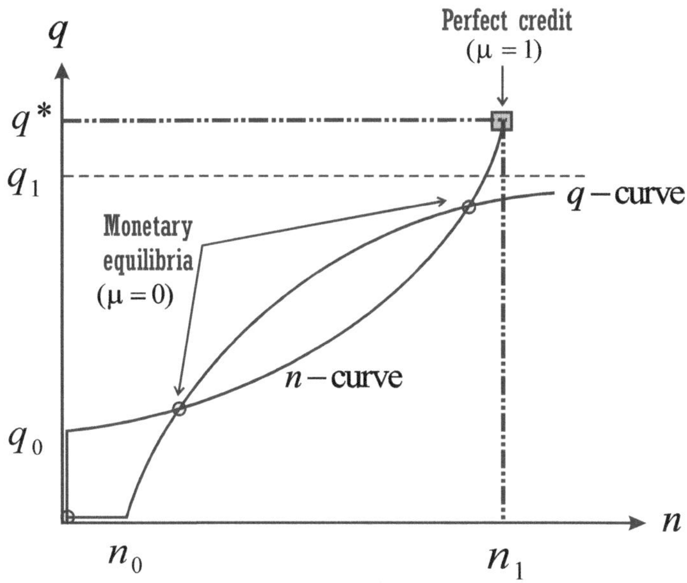

Figure 9.2
Pure monetary equilibria under free-entry of firms

From (9.11), if the cost of entry, k, decreases, or the firm's productivity, $\bar{q}$, increases, then the n-curve moves to the right. As a result, both q and n increase. In terms of monetary policy, described by the choice of i, from (9.7) we see than an increase in i shifts the q-curve down, which implies that both q and n decrease. (The n-curve is not a function of the nominal interest and hence is unaffected by a change in i.) A higher inflation rate increases the cost of holding money, which induces households to reduce their real balances. As a result, firms sell less output in DM matches, their expected revenue falls, and firm entry decreases.

When the perfect enforcement technology is available in $\mu \in (0, 1)$ of the matches, the resulting equilibrium outcomes can be represented in a diagram that is similar to Figure 9.2. An increase in the ability to use credit, μ, shifts the q-curve down and the n-curve to the right. The effect on the equilibrium is ambiguous because, even though an increase in credit tends to raise firms' expected revenue, and hence their incentive to enter, it also tends to reduce buyers' incentives to accumulate real balances, and hence firms' revenue in monetary matches. It is, however, unambiguous that a transition from a pure monetary economy, $\mu = 0$, to a pure credit economy, $\mu = 1$, raises firms' expected revenue and leads to more firm entry.

In Figure 9.3 we consider a numerical example with the following functional forms and parameter values: $u(q) = 2\sqrt{q}$, $\sigma(n) = n/(1+n)$, $\theta = 0.5$, $(1+r)k - \bar{q} = 0.4$, $i = 0.01$. The solid lines correspond to equilibrium conditions with $\mu = 0.5$ while the dashed lines correspond to $\mu = 0.8$. First, one can notice that there are multiple steady-state equilibria. Second, the highest equilibrium is such that both q and n decrease as μ increases. So even though firms enjoy larger profits in credit matches, a higher frequency of such matches reduces overall profits because buyers accumulate fewer real balances.

We conclude by examining welfare. We measure society's welfare by the discounted sum of all buyers' utilities starting in the CM of $t = 0$:

$$\mathcal{W} = x_0 - y_0 + \sum_{t=1}^{+\infty} \beta^t \left\{\sigma(n_t)\left[\mu u(q_t^c) + (1-\mu)u(q_t)\right] + x_t - y_t\right\}. \tag{9.14}$$

A planner maximizes $\mathcal{W}$ with respect to $\{(q_t, q_t^c, n_t)\}_{t=1}^{+\infty}$, subject to the feasibility condition

$$\sigma(n_t)\left[\mu q_t^c + (1-\mu)q_t\right] + x_t + kn_{t+1} = y_t + n_t\bar{q} \text{ for all } t \geq 0, \tag{9.15}$$

together with the feasibility constraints in bilateral matches, $q_t^c \leq \bar{q}$, $q_t \leq \bar{q}$. Because the economy starts in the CM of $t = 0$ we set $n_0 = q_0^c =$

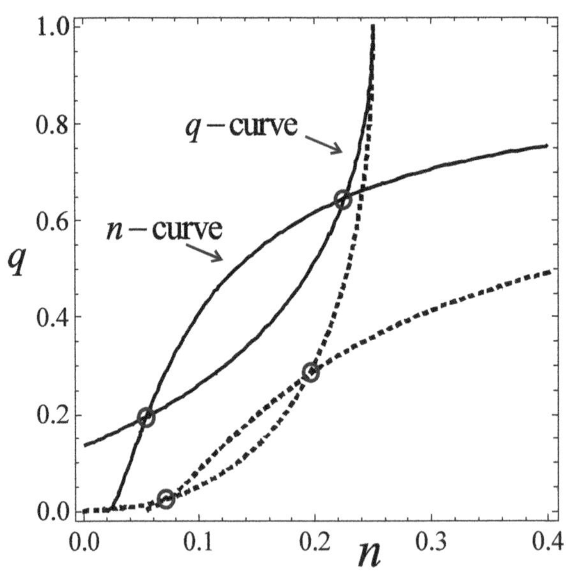

Figure 9.3
Equilibrium conditions. Plain curves: $\mu = 0.5$. Dashed curves: $\mu = 0.8$.

$q_0 = 0$. The right side of (9.15) is the amount of goods produced by buyers, y_t, and firms, $n_t\bar{q}$. Some of these goods are consumed in the DM, $\sigma(n_t)\left[\mu q_t^c + (1-\mu)q_t\right]$, in the CM, x_t, or are invested into firms, kn_{t+1}. The solution to the planning problem is,

$$q_t = q_t^c = q^* \tag{9.16}$$

$$(1+r)k = \sigma'(n_t)\left[u(q^*) - q^*\right] + \bar{q}. \tag{9.17}$$

The level of DM output maximizes match surpluses, $u(q) - q$, and is independent of the availability of credit in those matches. The socially-optimal measure of firms equates the *net* entry cost, $(1+r)k - \bar{q}$, with the marginal contribution of an entering seller to the creation of matches, $\sigma'(n)$, times the DM match surplus.

Can an equilibrium achieve the outcomes associated with the above planner's solution? From (9.7), $q_t = q^*$ if and only if $i = 0$. That is, quantities traded in DM matches are socially optimal if and only if the Friedman rule is implemented, a situation where holding real balances is not costly. The entry conditions (9.11) and (9.17) coincide if and only if

$$\frac{\sigma'(n)n}{\sigma(n)} = 1 - \theta. \tag{9.18}$$

Notice that

$$\frac{d\mathcal{M}(B,S)/\mathcal{M}(B,S)}{dS/S} = \frac{\sigma'(n)n}{\sigma(n)},$$

which means that the firm entry decision is socially optimal if the elasticity of the matching function with respect to the measure of sellers equals the seller's share in the match surplus. This condition for efficiency in search models is known as the Hosios condition. Therefore, the socially optimal allocation can be an equilibrium outcome if and only if monetary policy implements the Friedman rule and the Hosios condition holds. For a related result, see Section 6.5.

9.3 Frictional Labor Market

We now introduce a new category of agents called workers. A worker has one indivisible unit of labor and he values CM consumption according to linear preferences, x. There is a unit measure of such agents. We also change the firm's technology so that the production of $\bar{q}$ units of output requires one unit of worker's labor. Moreover, worker's labor cannot be used outside of the firm. Hence, it can be mutually beneficial for workers and firms to form bilateral matches in order to produce output. The labor status of the worker is $e \in \{0,1\}$, where $e=0$ if the worker is unemployed and $e=1$ if he is employed. The preferences and behavior of the buyer are the same as in Section 9.2.

There are two equivalent interpretations of the model. First, as described above, one can think of the buyer and worker as separate agents, each with their own budget constraints. Alternatively, the economy can be populated with a unit measure of households composed of one buyer and one worker. Each household maximizes the sum of the utilities of its members subject to the combined budget constraint of the buyer and worker given by

$$x + \gamma z' = y + ew_1 + (1-e)w_0 + \Delta + T, \tag{9.19}$$

where w_1 is the wage payment from the firm to an employed worker—measured in terms of CM goods—and $w_0 < w_1$ is the income payment of an unemployed worker. Notice that the choice of z' by the household is unaffected by the worker's income payments because there is no wealth effect.

The firm can hire a worker in a labor market that is subject to search-matching frictions. The labor market, called LM, opens at the beginning of the period, before the DM, see Figure 9.4. Each firm that paid k in the previous CM can post a vacancy and search for an unemployed worker. We can interpret k as being the cost of advertising a vacant position. There is a matching technology $\mathcal{H}(U,V)$ that matches vacant jobs, V, with job seekers, U. ($\mathcal{H}$ stands for "Hires.") The matching technology is increasing and concave in both of its arguments and is characterized by constant returns to scale. We define market tightness in the labor market as the measure of vacancies per job seekers,

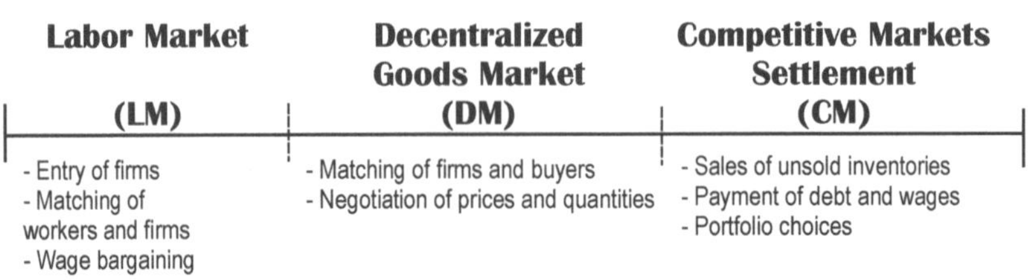

Figure 9.4
Timing of events with three subperiods

and we denote it $\tau \equiv V/U$. The probability that an unemployed worker finds a job is $f(\tau) \equiv \mathcal{H}(U,V)/U = \mathcal{H}(1,\tau)$ and the probability that a job vacancy finds an unemployed worker is $f(\tau)/\tau$. Our assumptions on $\mathcal{H}$ imply that $f'(\tau) > 0, f''(\tau) < 0$ and we assume that $f(\tau) \leq \min\{1,\tau\}$, $f(0) = 0$, $f'(0) = 1$, and $f(\infty) = 1$. Hence, the job finding probability, $f(\tau)$, is increasing in market tightness and the vacancy filling probability, $f(\tau)/\tau$, is decreasing in market tightness. In the LM stage each existing filled job is destroyed with probability $\delta \in [0,1]$. An employed worker who loses his job becomes unemployed and can only start searching again in the following period.

It is important to highlight some differences between the costs incurred by firms in this section and in Section 9.2. In Section 9.2, a firm must incur a participation cost of k in period $t-1$ for every period t in which it produces. In this section, a firm incurs the cost k to post a vacancy. Once a worker is hired, the firm does not incur the k cost but it must make a wage payment w_1 in every period it has a worker.

We measure the lifetime expected utility of a worker at the end of the LM, after the labor matching phase is completed, and before the DM goods market opens. Denote the lifetime expected utility of a worker by U_e, where $e \in \{0,1\}$ is the labor market status of the worker. Consider first a worker who is employed at the beginning of DM, i.e., $e = 1$. The worker's lifetime expected utility, U_1, is given by the Bellman equation

$$U_1 = w_1 + (1-\delta)\beta U_1 + \delta\beta U_0. \tag{9.20}$$

The employed worker receives a wage, w_1, in the CM in exchange for the labor services he offered to the firm in the previous LM. With probability $1-\delta$ the worker remains employed and his continuation lifetime expected utility is βU_1. With probability δ the worker loses his job and his continuation lifetime expected utility is βU_0. The expected lifetime utility of an unemployed worker at the beginning of the DM is

$$U_0 = w_0 + (1-f)\beta U_0 + f\beta U_1. \tag{9.21}$$

The unemployed worker receives an income, w_0, which can be interpreted as unemployed benefits (and is financed with lump-sum taxation). In the following LM, the worker finds a job with probability f and becomes employed; with probability $1-f$ he remains unemployed.

The Bellman equation describing the expected discounted sum of profits of a filled job, denoted J, is

$$J = \rho - w_1 + \beta(1-\delta)J, \tag{9.22}$$

where ρ is the firm's expected revenue generated in both the DM and CM, expressed in terms of the CM good. The value of a filled job, J, is equal to the expected revenue of the firm net of the wage it pays the worker plus the expected discounted profits of the job if it is not destroyed, an event that occurs with probability $1-\delta$. As in Section 9.2, the rate at which future profits are discounted is equal to the agents' rate of time preference, $r=\beta^{-1}-1$, since claims on firms' profits are illiquid. Solving for J from (9.22), we get

$$J=\frac{\rho-w_1}{1-\beta(1-\delta)}. \tag{9.23}$$

The value of a job is equal to the discounted sum of per-period profits, where the discount rate is adjusted by the probability of a job destruction.

The free entry of firms implies that, in equilibrium, the cost of posting a vacancy equals the probability of filling the vacancy in the next LM times the discounted value of a filled job,

$$k=\beta\frac{f(\tau)}{\tau}J. \tag{9.24}$$

The wage is determined by bargaining between the worker and the firm. We use the proportional bargaining solution (or, equivalently in this context, the generalized Nash solution), where $\lambda\in[0,1]$ represents the worker's bargaining power. The wage is set so that the worker receives λ of the total match surplus and the firm receives $1-\lambda$, i.e.,

$$U_1-U_0=\frac{\lambda}{1-\lambda}J. \tag{9.25}$$

The surplus from being employed, U_1-U_0, can be expressed in terms of wages from the Bellman equation (9.20),

$$U_1-U_0=\frac{w_1-(1-\beta)U_0}{1-(1-\delta)\beta}. \tag{9.26}$$

The term $(1-\beta)U_0$ is the worker's reservation wage: it is the value of the wage such that the worker is indifferent between being employed or unemployed. Hence, the surplus from being employed, U_1-U_0, is the discounted sum of the difference between the wage and the reservation wage, where the discount rate, as in (9.23), is adjusted by the probability of job destruction. Now, using (9.23), the worker surplus (9.25) can also be expressed as

$$U_1-U_0=\frac{\lambda}{1-\lambda}\left[\frac{\rho-w_1}{1-\beta(1-\delta)}\right]. \tag{9.27}$$

Hence, equating the left sides of (9.26) and (9.27), we get

$$w_1 - (1-\beta)U_0 = \frac{\lambda}{1-\lambda}(\rho - w_1). \tag{9.28}$$

According to (9.28), the bargaining solution applies to per-period surpluses: the per-period surplus of a worker, $w_1 - (1-\beta)U_0$, equals $\lambda/(1-\lambda)$ times per-period profits of a firm, $\rho - w_1$. We can obtain an expression for wages from (9.28), i.e.,

$$w_1 = \lambda\rho + (1-\lambda)(1-\beta)U_0. \tag{9.29}$$

The wage is a weighted average of the firm's expected revenue, ρ, and the worker's reservation wage, $(1-\beta)U_0$. From (9.21), the reservation wage of a worker can be expressed as

$$(1-\beta)U_0 = w_0 + f\beta(U_1 - U_0). \tag{9.30}$$

A worker's reservation wage is equal to the income when unemployed plus the discounted surplus from the expectation of being employed. To obtain an expression for $U_1 - U_0$ on the right side of (9.30) in terms of model parameters and market tightness, note that the bargaining rule (9.25) is a simple function of J, which implies from (9.24) that

$$U_1 - U_0 = \frac{\lambda}{1-\lambda}\left[\frac{k\tau}{\beta f(\tau)}\right].$$

Substituting this expression into the right side of (9.30), we get

$$(1-\beta)U_0 = w_0 + \frac{\lambda}{1-\lambda}k\tau. \tag{9.31}$$

We can obtain an expression for wages in terms of model parameters and market tightness, τ, by substituting the reservation wage given by (9.31) into the wage equation (9.29), i.e.,

$$w_1 = \lambda\rho + (1-\lambda)w_0 + \lambda k\tau. \tag{9.32}$$

The first two terms of (9.32) are a weighted average of the firm's expected revenue and the worker's income when unemployed. (For now we treat the expected firm revenue ρ as an exogenous parameter. Later, it will be explained by the goods market activity.) The third term is a fraction λ of the total recruiting cost per worker. Interestingly, if the worker has some bargaining power he can take advantage of the existence of recruiting costs to ask for a higher wage by threatening to leave the firm. This last term is rather important because it creates a link between the wage and the state of the labor market, τ.

We now determine the equilibrium labor market tightness. We first obtain an expression for market tightness as a function of model parameters and the wage, w_1, by substituting J, given by its expression (9.23), into the free-entry condition (9.24),

$$(r+\delta)k = \frac{f(\tau)}{\tau}(\rho - w_1). \tag{9.33}$$

Substitute the wage given by (9.32) into (the free-entry) condition (9.33) and simplify to get

$$\frac{\tau}{f(\tau)}(r+\delta)k + \lambda k\tau = (1-\lambda)(\rho - w_0). \tag{9.34}$$

Notice that the left side of (9.34) is increasing in τ. Provided that $(r+\delta)k > (1-\lambda)(\rho - w_0)$, labor market tightness is positive, increases with ρ, and decreases with w_0, λ, and k.

An alternative measure (to τ) of the state of the labor market is the measure of unemployed workers at the start of the DM, which we denote as u. The law of motion for u are:

$$u_{t+1} = u_t(1 - f_{t+1}) + \delta(1 - u_t) \tag{9.35}$$

The measure of unemployed workers in $t+1$ is equal to the measure of unemployed workers in t minus those who found a job in the LM of $t+1$, $f_{t+1}u_t$, plus the measure of employed workers who lost their job, $\delta(1-u_t)$. (Recall that there is a unit measure of workers.) The steady-state level of unemployment is such that $u_{t+1} = u_t = u$, which from (9.35) gives

$$u = \frac{\delta}{f(\tau)+\delta}. \tag{9.36}$$

Hence, the steady-state unemployment rate is a decreasing function of labor market tightness, τ, and an increasing function of the job destruction probability, δ.

In Figure 9.5 we represent (9.36) by the downward-sloping curve BC (for Beveridge curve). The free-entry condition, (9.34), is represented by the horizontal line VS (for vacancy supply). Equilibrium in the labor market is uniquely determined by the intersection of these two curves. Note that an increase in firms' expected revenue, ρ, shifts the VS curve upward, which leads to a higher labor market tightness, τ, and a lower unemployment rate, u.

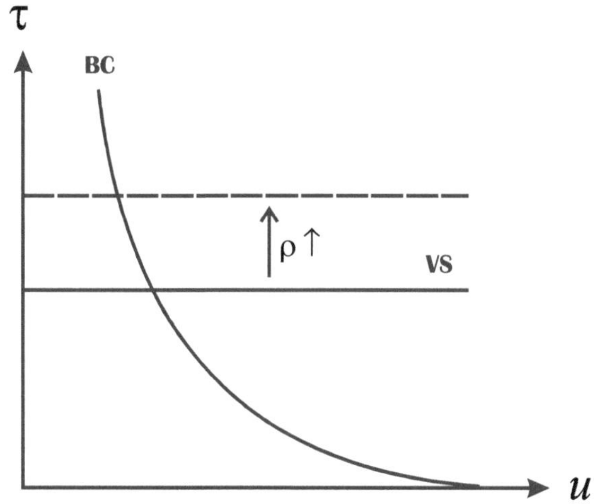

Figure 9.5
Equilibrium of the labor market

9.4 Unemployment, Money, and Credit

The previous section treats the firm's revenue, ρ, as exogenous. To characterize a general equilibrium we relax this assumption by combining the analysis of the goods and money markets of Section 9.2 with the analysis of the labor market of Section 9.3. An equilibrium can be characterized by four endogenous variables: labor market tightness, τ, unemployment, u, firm's expected revenue, ρ, and buyers' DM consumption, q.

For a given revenue, ρ, market tightness is given by the solution to (9.34),

$$\frac{\tau}{f(\tau)}(r+\delta)k + \lambda k\tau = (1-\lambda)(\rho - w_0). \tag{9.37}$$

For given DM consumption—q^* in credit matches and q in monetary matches—a firm's expected revenue is given by (9.9),

$$\rho = \frac{\sigma\left[n(\tau)\right]}{n(\tau)}(1-\theta)\left\{\mu\left[u\left(q^*\right)-q^*\right]+(1-\mu)\left[u\left(q\right)-q\right]\right\}+\bar{q}, \tag{9.38}$$

where, from (9.36), the measure of firms in the DM goods market is

$$n(\tau) = 1-u = \frac{f(\tau)}{f(\tau)+\delta}. \tag{9.39}$$

Combining (9.37) and (9.38), we obtain a positive relationship between labor market tightness, τ, and DM consumption in monetary matches, q, or, equivalently, buyers' real balances, z:

$$\frac{\tau}{f(\tau)}(r+\delta)k+\lambda k\tau$$
$$=(1-\lambda)\left\{\frac{\sigma\left[n(\tau)\right]}{n(\tau)}(1-\theta)\left\{\mu\left[u\left(q^{*}\right)-q^{*}\right]+(1-\mu)\left[u\left(q\right)-q\right]\right\}+\bar{q}-w_{0}\right\}. \tag{9.40}$$

The left side of (9.40) is increasing in τ while the right side of (9.40) is decreasing in τ. Hence, for given q, there is a unique solution to (9.40). The novelty relative to the canonical labor market model is that an increase in labor market tightness, τ, generates a competition effect in the goods market, $n'(\tau)>0$, which reduces firms' expected sales since $\sigma\left[n(\tau)\right]/n(\tau)$ is decreasing in τ. An increase in q raises the right side of (9.40). Consequently, (9.40) implies τ must increase when buyers' real balances increase. Intuitively, if buyers hold larger real balances, they can consume more output in the DM, which increases firms' revenues; increased revenues give firms incentives to open more vacancies.

The DM consumption in monetary matches is given by (9.7), rewritten here as

$$i=\sigma\left[n(\tau)\right](1-\mu)\theta\left[\frac{u'\left(q\right)-1}{\theta+(1-\theta)u'(q)}\right]. \tag{9.41}$$

The equilibrium condition, (9.41), gives a positive relationship between labor market tightness and DM output. Intuitively, if labor market tightness, τ, increases, the steady-state measure of firms in the DM goods market, n, increases and, as a result, the frequency of trading opportunities in the DM is higher for buyers. Buyers respond by accumulating more real balances, which raises DM output. Thus, an equilibrium can be reduced to a pair, (τ,q), that solves (9.40) and (9.41).

We describe some special cases. Consider first a pure credit economy, $\mu=1$. From (9.40), market tightness is determined uniquely by:

$$\frac{\tau}{f(\tau)}(r+\delta)k+\lambda k\tau=(1-\lambda)\left\{\frac{\sigma\left[n(\tau)\right]}{n(\tau)}(1-\theta)\left[u\left(q^{*}\right)-q^{*}\right]+\bar{q}-w_{0}\right\}. \tag{9.42}$$

The model provides linkages between the goods and labor markets. For example, a decrease in buyer's bargaining power in the DM goods market, θ, shifts the VS curve upward, which leads to higher labor market tightness and lower unemployment.

Consider next a pure monetary economy, $\mu = 0$. We represent the two equilibrium conditions, (9.40) and (9.41), in Figure 9.6. The quantity τ_0 is the labor market tightness below which the demand for real balances is zero—because the measure of sellers in the goods market is too low (see the q-curve in Figure 9.6). The quantity τ_1 is the market tightness given by the free-entry condition when DM output is at its efficient level, $q = q^*$ (see the τ-curve in Figure 9.6). If $(1 - \lambda)(\bar{q} - w_0) < (r + \delta)k$, then there is a threshold for DM output, q_0, below which firms cease to open vacancies, $\tau = 0$, because their expected revenue is too low relative to their entry cost. As market tightness goes to infinity, employment is maximum and the demand for real balances generates a level for DM consumption equal to q_1. It is possible, as in Section 9.2, to have multiple steady states across which labor market tightness, employment, and the value of money are positively correlated.

For comparative statics, we focus on the highest equilibrium with high real balances, high market tightness, and low unemployment. An increase in the inflation rate only affects the q-curve, which shifts downward. As a result, real balances are lower, labor market tightness is lower, and unemployment is higher. Hence, our model predicts a positive relationship between inflation and unemployment in the long run. Intuitively, inflation is a tax on trades in the DM and the tax reduces the amount of liquidity that buyers hold and the quantities that they purchase from firms. As a result, firms' expected revenues decline, which makes jobs less profitable. Firms open fewer vacancies and unemployment increases.

Conversely, the model predicts that labor market policies can spillover into the goods market and affect the value of money. For example, an increase in unemployment benefits, w_0, shifts the τ-curve to the left; this reduces both market tightness and the value of money (since q decreases), and increases unemployment. Indeed, an increase in w_0 raises wages and reduces firms' profits, see (9.34). As a result, the measure of active firms in the goods markets declines, which reduces the frequency of trading opportunities in the DM. Buyers reduce their real balances and the value of money falls. Similarly, if worker's bargaining power, λ, increases, then market tightness and the value of money fall, while unemployment increases.

Finally, consider an economy with both money and credit, $\mu \in (0,1)$. Suppose first that buyers have all the bargaining power in the DM goods market, $\theta = 1$. From (9.38) the firm's expected revenue is simply $\rho = \bar{q}$. This means that labor market tightness is determined by

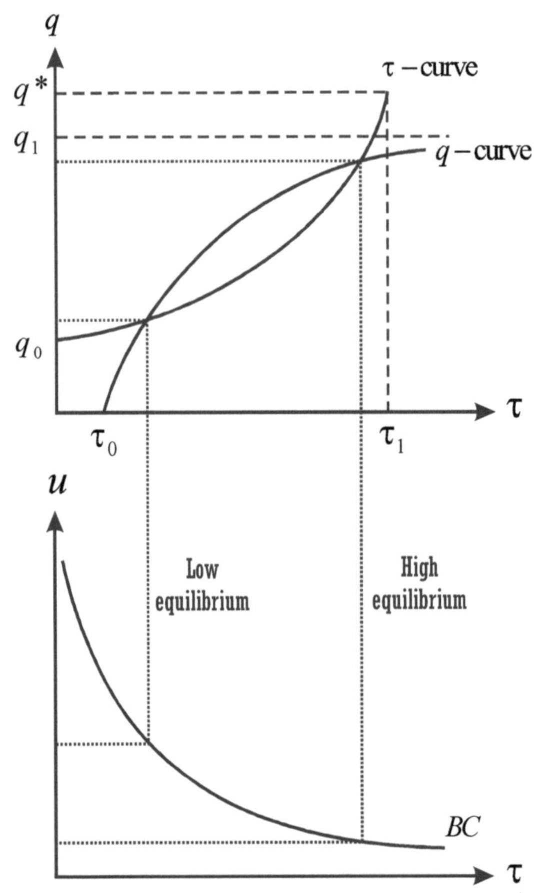

Figure 9.6
Pure monetary equilibrium with frictional labor market

(9.37) and is independent of liquidity considerations. In Figure 9.6 the τ-curve is vertical. In the more general case where $\theta \in (0,1)$, the τ-curve is upward sloping and the determination of the equilibrium is similar to the one in Figure 9.6.

9.5 Unemployment and Credit under Limited Commitment

Thus far we have assumed that credit is perfect, i.e., there is an enforcement technology that ensures debt repayment. As a result, in credit matches agents trade q^*. Suppose that such an enforcement technology does not exist, but there does exist a record-keeping technology that keeps track of buyers' individual trading histories. Now buyers cannot be forced to repay their debt. If debt is used in the DM, the repayment of the debt has to be self-enforcing. The existence of a public monitoring technology allows firms to punish buyers who default on their debt obligations by excluding those buyers from all future credit trades. For simplicity, and because money is not essential when there is perfect monitoring, in the following we abstract from monetary trades and hence assume $\mu = 1$.

We denote $\bar{b}$ the buyer's debt limit, which is defined as the maximum amount that a buyer is willing to repay. The highest debt limit that is consistent with buyer's incentives to repay solves $\bar{b} = \beta V$. The gain from defaulting, $\bar{b}$, is equal to the continuation value if the buyer has access to credit. Following the same reasoning as in Chapter 2.4, $\bar{b}$ solves:

$$r\bar{b} = \sigma(n)\theta\left[u\left(q^c\right) - q^c\right], \tag{9.43}$$

where q^c is obtained from the proportional bargaining solution,

$$\begin{aligned} q^c &= q^* \text{ if } \theta q^* + (1-\theta)u(q^*) \leq \bar{b} \\ \bar{b} &= \theta q^c + (1-\theta)u(q^c) \text{ otherwise.} \end{aligned}$$

The left side of (9.43) is linear in $\bar{b}$ while the right side is increasing and concave. Provided that $r < \sigma(n)\theta/(1-\theta)$ (using that $u'(0) = +\infty$), there is a unique $\bar{b} > 0$ solution to (9.43). Moreover, the right side of (9.43) increases with n. Therefore, the debt limit increases with the measures of firms in the goods market. Indeed, if there are more sellers in the market, then buyers have more frequent trading opportunities and hence having access to credit is more valuable, i.e., the punishment from being sent to autarky is harsher. It follows that the debt limit is higher.

From (9.38), the expected revenue of a firm in this pure credit economy is given by

$$\rho(\bar{b}) = \frac{\sigma\left[n(\tau)\right]}{n(\tau)}(1-\theta)\left\{u\left[q^c(\bar{b})\right] - q^c(\bar{b})\right\} + \bar{q}. \tag{9.44}$$

Since the match surplus increases with the buyer's debt limit, it follows that ρ increases with $\bar{b}$. Intuitively, if buyers have a higher borrowing capacity, then they can buy larger quantities in the DM, which raises firms' expected revenue. From (9.37) it follows that labor market tightness is an increasing function of $\bar{b}$.

A steady-state equilibrium can be reduced to a pair, (q^c, τ), that solves (9.37) and (9.43). These two conditions can be represented by two upward-sloping curves as in Figure 9.6. Just like in pure monetary economies, it is possible to have multiple steady-state equilibria. If firms believe that buyers have a large borrowing capacity, then they expect high sales in the DM and they find it optimal to open a large number of vacancies. As a result the number of productive jobs is large and buyers receive frequent trading opportunities in the DM. Because buyers trade often, the cost from being excluded from future transactions is large. Hence, the threat of autarky allows buyers to borrow large amounts in accordance with firms' initial beliefs.

9.6 Further Readings

The model with free-entry of producers is due to Rocheteau and Wright (2005). Relative to that model we add credit and we adopt the proportional bargaining solution. The model with frictional goods and labor market is based on Shi (1998) and Berentsen, Menzio, and Wright (2011). Shi constructs a model where large households insure their members against idiosyncratic risks in both labor and goods markets. Berentsen, Menzio, and Wright (2011) assume that individuals are endowed with quasi-linear preferences and readjust their money holdings in a competitive market that opens periodically as in Lagos and Wright (2005). In Rocheteau, Rupert, and Wright (2007) only the goods market is subject to search frictions but unemployment emerges due to indivisible labor. Mei (2011) adopts the notion of competitive search equilibrium to study the relationship between inflation and unemployment. Gomis-Porqueras, Julien, and Wang (2013) study optimal monetary and fiscal policies. In all of these models credit is not incentive feasible because of the lack of record-keeping and, therefore, fiat money plays a role in overcoming a double-coincidence of wants problem in the goods market. Other models of unemployment and inflation based on the Mortensen-Pissarides framework include Cooley and Quadrini (2004) and Lehmann (2012). Models with both frictional goods and labor markets also include Lehmann and Van der Linden (2010) and Petrosky-Nadeau and Wasmer (2015). Williamson (2015b) develops a model of monetary/labor search where economic agents have trouble splitting the surplus from exchange appropriately, and considers monetary and fiscal policies that correct this Keynesian inefficiency.

Models of unemployment and credit include Bethune, Rocheteau, and Rupert (2015) and Branch, Petrosky-Nadeau, and Rocheteau (2014). In the former, credit is unsecured and the debt limit is endogenous. Moreover, only a fraction of households have access to credit while the remaining ones can accumulate a liquid asset. In the latter, credit is collateralized with housing assets and the labor market has two sectors: a general good sector and a construction sector where homes are produced. Silva (2016) studies the link between endogenous debt limits and product variety: greater debt limits spur demand for goods and encourage entry of firms selling new goods; more varieties increase the opportunity cost of default and thus raise the equilibrium debt level. Similar to our model, Guerrieri and Lorenzoni (2009) identify a coordination element in spending and production in a decentralized model of trade, where agents may use money or credit to buy goods. This leads to greater aggregate volatility and greater comovement across producers. Beaudry, Galizia, and Portier (2015) develop a model with unemployment and costly credit that delivers endogenous limit cycles.

Wasmer and Weil (2004) and Petrosky-Nadeau (2013) extend the Mortensen-Pissarides model to incorporate a credit market where firms search for investors in order to finance the cost of opening a job vacancy. Dromel, Kolakez, and Lehmann (2010) show how credit frictions can affect the persistence of unemployment.

10 Money, Negotiable Debt, and Settlement

In large value payment systems, such as the Federal Reserve's Fedwire, participants make and receive payments throughout the day. In an ideal world, the payments process would be seamless in the sense that agents receive payments at, or just before, the time they have to make them. In such a world, agents will always have sufficient liquidity on hand to make their required payments. In practice, however, the payments process is not so perfectly synchronized; agents may have insufficient liquidity on hand when they wish to, or have to, make a payment. In such circumstances, the agent can always wait for an incoming payment. But waiting may be costly. Alternatively, the payments network may provide the agent with liquidity, say, via a daytime loan, so that the agent can make time critical payments without delay, and loans can be paid back when the agent receives (the delayed) payments. The importance of the timing of payments is not confined to large value payment systems. This issue also arises in short-term money markets, such the tri-party repos, in the clearing and settlement of financial securities and so on.

In this chapter we examine the implications associated with settlement frictions and possible policy responses if the frictions have adverse implications for the economy. To do so, we modify the economic environment so that fiat money plays a dual role: it serves both as a medium of exchange to facilitate trade and as an instrument to settle debt, i.e., to make a payment on a prior obligation. We introduce frictions in the settlement of private debt that give rise to negotiable debt. Negotiable debt is debt that can be sold to a third party, and is honored by the issuing debtor when presented for redemption. The settlement friction is that an agent may have an immediate need for liquidity or money, but presently has no liquidity and is awaiting a payment. The agent can always sell the obligation that represents this incoming payment for the liquidity that he currently desires. Depending on the extent of the frictions, the market for negotiable debt may be sufficiently liquid so that the seller of negotiable debt receives the full value of his claim. In this situation, the market for negotiable debt overcomes the settlement frictions. But this need not always be the case, and liquidity problems associated with settlement frictions can arise.

When the market for negotiable debt fails to overcome the settlement frictions, the liquidity problems that arise in settlement will spill over into credit and product markets, and will have negative implications for the real economy. In this case, there is a welfare enhancing role for central bank intervention. A central bank can pursue either open-market or discount window operations to provide additional liquidity in the settlement phase of the economy. A properly designed policy provides liquidity during the settlement phase, but has no long-run effects on the supply of money: any injection of money for liquidity purposes is immediately undone when the private debt, held by the central bank, is redeemed. If the central bank follows a policy along these lines, then an efficient allocation will be restored. This line of reasoning provides support to the notion of an elastic supply of currency, which is one of the founding principles of the establishment of the Federal Reserve System. We find that our basic insights are not altered when there is an exogenous risk of default on behalf of the debtors.

10.1 The Environment

We consider an environment where credit and money coexist, and money is used to settle debt obligations. In order to present the ideas in the most economical way, we modify the benchmark model. A period is now divided into *four* subperiods: morning, day, night, and late night.

As in the benchmark model, the day subperiod is a decentralized market, DM, characterized by bilateral matching and exchange of the search good, and the night subperiod is a competitive market, CM_2, where the general good is produced and traded. In terms of the two new subperiods, the morning subperiod, like the night subperiod, is a competitive market, CM_1, where the general good is produced and traded. In the late-night subperiod, production and consumption are not feasible. In this subperiod, agents have the opportunity to settle any debts that were incurred in previous subperiods. If agents choose to settle their debts in the late-night subperiod, the debts must be settled with money since production is not possible.

In order to capture the coexistence of money and credit, and settlement of debt obligations with money, we make the following assumptions:

1. Agents live for only four subperiods. Buyers are born at the beginning of a period, in the morning, and die after the settlement phase in the late night of the same period. Sellers are born at the beginning of the day subperiod and die at the end of the morning subperiod, CM_1, in the subsequent period.
2. Buyers are heterogenous in terms of *when* they can produce. Half of the buyers can only produce in the CM_1, and the other half can only produce in the CM_2. We call the former *early producers* and the latter *late producers*.
3. In the DM bilateral match, the seller has a technology to verify the identity of the issuer. In the late-night subperiod, there is a technology that authenticates IOUs issued in the DM and enforces the repayment of the IOUs.
4. In the CMs, IOUs cannot be authenticated and can be costlessly counterfeited.

Assumption 1 implies that in any particular CM_1, the economy is populated with young buyers and old sellers; in all other subperiods, the economy is populated with buyers and sellers who are born in the same period. The assumption of finitely-lived buyers is convenient since all buyers start the period with no money balances. Otherwise, buyers who anticipate they cannot produce in the CM_1 may want to accumulate money balances in previous periods. Assumptions 1 and 2 imply that if late producers trade in the DM they can only do so by issuing IOUs, since it is not possible for them to accumulate money balances. Assumption 3 implies that in a DM match, an IOU can be issued. Assumption 4 implies that IOUs issued and authenticated in the DM will not circulate as a means of payment in the CMs, and new IOUs will not be issued, because of the recognizability problem that exists in those subperiods. Collectively, the above assumptions imply that early producers can use money or debt in the DM; late producers only use debt in the DM; and all debts will be settled with money in the late-night settlement period. (Note that this structure is similar in spirit to that of Chapter 6.6, where the important link between that structure and the structure in this chapter is that buyers are heterogeneous in terms of their ability to produce.)

Buyers are able to produce the general good in either the CM_1 or CM_2, depending upon their type, but have no desire to consume the general good. They are unable to produce the search good, but want to consume it. The preferences for the buyer are described by the instantaneous utility function

$$U^b(q,y) = u(q) - y,$$

where y is the buyer's production of the general good—either in the CM_1 or in the CM_2, depending on the buyer's type—and q is the consumption of the search good.

Sellers are able to produce the search good in the DM, but have no desire to consume it. They are unable to produce the general good, but want to consume it. The preferences for the seller are given by

$$U^s(q,x) = -c(q) + x,$$

where x is the seller's consumption of the general good—in the CM_1 and the CM_2—and q is the amount of the search good that is produced. Note that agents do not discount utility across subperiods over their lifetime.

During the DM, buyers and sellers are matched, where buyers consume the search good and sellers produce it. For simplicity, we eliminate any search-matching frictions by setting the matching probability σ to one.

The timing of events and the pattern of trade in a representative period are summarized in Figure 10.1. At the beginning of a period, a measure one of buyers are born. Half of them, the early producers, can produce in the CM_1. In the CM_1, these young buyers produce general goods in exchange for money, and old sellers exchange money for the general good. Old sellers die at the end of the morning, and are replaced by a measure one of newborn sellers at the beginning of the DM. In the DM, each buyer is matched with a seller. Half of the buyers, the early producers, trade with money and the other half, the late producers, trade with credit. (Although it is not indicated in Figure 10.1, in order to simplify the exposition, early producers also have the option to trade with credit in the DM). In order to settle their debts in the late-night subperiod, buyers who traded with credit produce general goods in exchange for money in the CM_2; sellers exchange money for the general good. In the late night settlement period, buyers and sellers arrive in a meeting place for the purpose of settling debts. Sellers who receive

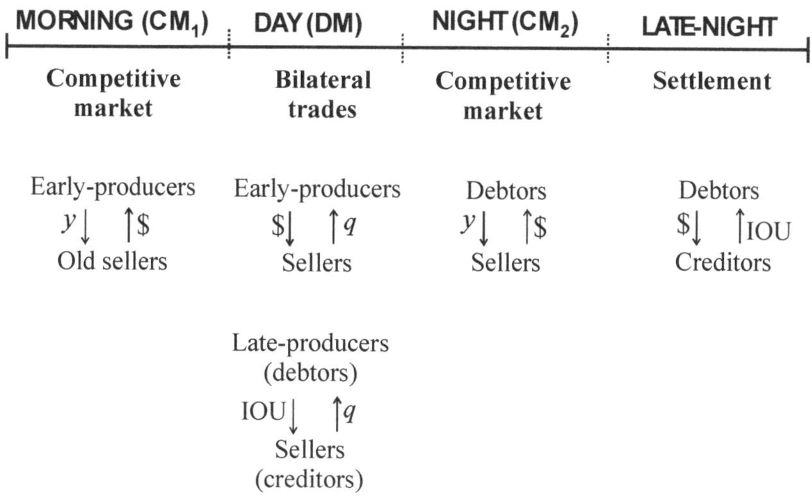

Figure 10.1
Timing and pattern of trade

money in the late-night settlement subperiod will spend it in CM_1 of the next period, before they die.

We focus on stationary equilibria. Since money is traded for general goods in competitive markets in the two different subperiods, we distinguish two prices for money. Let ϕ_1 be the price of money in terms of general goods in the CM_1, and ϕ_2 the price of money in the CM_2.

10.2 Frictionless Settlement

We first examine an economy where there are no frictions in the settlement phase. In particular, all debtors and creditors arrive simultaneously at a central meeting place in the late-night subperiod, and all debts are settled instantaneously.

Consider first a match in the DM, between a buyer who is an early producer and a seller. This buyer produced general goods in the morning to get m units of money. Suppose that the buyer spends his money m units of money in a bilateral match in the day for q^m units of the search good. The quantity q^m is determined by a take-it-or-leave-it offer by the buyer. The seller's participation constraint is

$$-c(q^m) + \max(\phi_1, \phi_2)m \geq 0. \tag{10.1}$$

A seller values a unit of money at $\max(\phi_1, \phi_2)$ because he has the option to spend his money either in the CM_2, at the price ϕ_2, or in the following

CM_1, at the price ϕ_1. We can use a simple equilibrium argument to show that $\max(\phi_1, \phi_2) = \phi_2$. If $\phi_2 < \phi_1$, then sellers will spend their money in the following CM_1. But this outcome is inconsistent with the clearing of the CM_2, since late producers need to acquire money at night to settle their debts. Therefore, the seller's participation constraint (10.1) simplifies to $-c(q^m) + \phi_2 m \geq 0$. Note also that an early-producing buyer has no incentive to accumulate money in the CM_1 *and* issue debt in the DM because sellers prefer (weakly) to receive money that they can spend in CM_2.

Since buyers do not value consumption of the general good, an early buyer's offer to the seller in the DM is given by the solution to,

$$\max_{q^m} u(q^m) \tag{10.2}$$

$$\text{s.t. } c(q^m) = \phi_2 m \tag{10.3}$$

The solution to this problem is $q^m(m) = c^{-1}(\phi_2 m)$; i.e., the buyer spends all of his money, subject to satisfying seller participation.

In the CM_1, the early-producing buyer's problem of choosing his money holdings, m, is given by the solution to

$$\max_{m} \left[-\phi_1 m + u(q^m(m))\right]. \tag{10.4}$$

The solution to (10.4) is

$$\frac{u'(q^m)}{c'(q^m)} = \frac{\phi_1}{\phi_2}, \tag{10.5}$$

since, from (10.2)-(10.3), $dq^m/dm = \phi_2/c'(q^m)$. From (10.5), $q^m = q^*$ if and only if $\phi_1 = \phi_2$; if $\phi_2 > \phi_1$, then $q^m > q^*$. The demand for money from early-producers in the CM_1 is then

$$m = \frac{c(q^m)}{\phi_2}. \tag{10.6}$$

The supply of money in the CM_1 comes from old sellers who hold the entire stock of money, M. Since there is a measure $1/2$ of early-producing buyers, equilibrium in the CM_1 money market implies that $M = m/2$ and, from (10.6), q^m satisfies

$$c(q^m) = 2M\phi_2. \tag{10.7}$$

Now let's turn to the problem of a late-producing buyer in a bilateral match in the DM. In his bilateral match, a late-producing buyer must issue an IOU to pay for the search good, which will be repaid in the late-night settlement subperiod. Recall that a buyer is able to issue an IOU in a bilateral match because the IOU and his identity can be authenticated, and the only other place where the authenticity of the IOU can be established is in the settlement subperiod. The buyer repays the debt by producing output for money in the CM_2. The terms of trade in the match are determined by a take-it-or-leave-it offer (q^b, b) by the buyer, where q^b is the amount of search good produced by the seller and b is the amount of dollars that the buyer commits to repay in the late-night settlement subperiod. (It might be convenient to think of the "m" in q^m as referring to a buyer who uses money to purchase search goods and the "b" in q^b as referring to a buyer who issues a bond or IOU.) The buyer's offer is given by the solution to

$$\max_{q^b, b} \left[u(q^b) - \phi_2 b\right] \tag{10.8}$$

$$\text{s.t.} \ -c(q^b) + \phi_1 b = 0. \tag{10.9}$$

The seller values the buyer's debt at the price ϕ_1 since the money he receives in the late-night settlement subperiod can only be spent in the next morning. The solution to the buyer's problem (10.8)–(10.9) is

$$\frac{u'(q^b)}{c'(q^b)} = \frac{\phi_2}{\phi_1}. \tag{10.10}$$

From (10.10), $q^b = q^*$ if and only if $\phi_1 = \phi_2$. If $\phi_1 < \phi_2$, then $q^b < q^*$. From (10.9), the amount of nominal debt issued by the buyer in the match is

$$b = \frac{c(q^b)}{\phi_1}. \tag{10.11}$$

Consider the equilibrium in the CM_2. If $\phi_2 > \phi_1$, then sellers holding money at the beginning of the CM_2 will spend all of it so that at the end of the night all of the money is held by the late-producing buyers, i.e., $b/2 = M$. If $\phi_2 = \phi_1$, then sellers holding money are indifferent between spending it in the CM_2 or in the following CM_1. In this case, $b/2 \leq M$. In summary,

$$b \begin{Bmatrix} = \\ \leq \end{Bmatrix} 2M \quad \text{if} \quad \phi_2 \begin{Bmatrix} > \\ = \end{Bmatrix} \phi_1. \tag{10.12}$$

A steady-state equilibrium is a list $(q^m, q^b, \phi_1, \phi_2, b)$ that satisfies (10.5), (10.7), (10.10), (10.11), and (10.12). It can be easily demonstrated that $q^m = q^b = q^*$, $b = 2M$ and $\phi_1 = \phi_2 = c(q^*)/2M$ is an equilibrium. If $\phi_1 = \phi_2$, then from (10.5) and (10.10) $q^m = q^b = q^*$. And from (10.7), $\phi_1 = \phi_2 = c(q^*)/2M$. From (10.11), $b = 2M$, which is consistent with (10.12). We show in the Appendix that this is the unique equilibrium for some specifications u and c, e.g., $u(q) = 2\sqrt{q}$ and $c(q) = q$. In what follows, we will focus on specifications for which the equilibrium under frictionless settlement is unique. In this equilibrium, the price of money is the same in the CM_1 and CM_2, and the efficient quantity of the search good q^* is traded in all matches.

10.3 Settlement and Liquidity

We now introduce settlement frictions. Settlement frictions are captured by having debtors and creditors arrive and leave the late-night settlement period at different times. To be more specific, the timing during the late-night settlement period is as follows: all of the creditors—who are sellers—and a fraction α of debtors—who are late-producing buyers—arrive at a central meeting place at the beginning of the settlement period. Then a fraction δ of the creditors depart, after which the remaining $1-\alpha$ debtors arrive. Finally, the remaining $1-\delta$ creditors and all of the debtors leave the settlement period. At this point all of the buyers die, and all of the sellers move into the morning of the next period. The timing of arrivals and departures is illustrated in Figure 10.2. We will sometimes refer to creditors (debtors) as being early-leaving (-arriving) and late-leaving (-arriving), where the meaning is obvious. These arrival and departure frictions will create a need

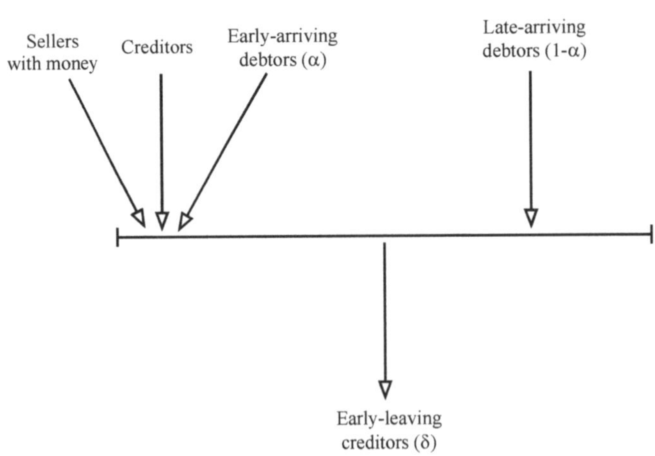

Figure 10.2
Frictions in the settlement phase

for a resale market for debt during the late-night settlement period. We assume that this resale market for debt is competitive, where ρ is the price of one-dollar of debt in terms of money.

Sellers who produce the DM good for money are neither creditors nor debtors. These sellers may have an incentive to forgo (some) consumption in the CM_2, and instead provide liquidity in the settlement period. They can do so by buying the IOUs of early-leaving creditors that will be repaid by late-arriving debtors. For simplicity, we assume that sellers with money who do not spend all of it in the CM_2 always arrive at the beginning of the settlement period, and always stay until the end; see Figure 10.2. The logic of our arguments would go through if a fraction δ of the sellers holding money had to leave the settlement stage early: in that case a seller with money would be able to buy a second-hand debt with probability $1-\delta$.

The DM bargaining problem of the buyer must now take into account the possibility that a seller who receives money for producing the DM goods may want to use some of it to purchase debt in the settlement period. In particular, a seller who receives one unit of money in a bilateral match during the DM can spend it in the CM_2 for ϕ_2 units of the general good, or he can buy $1/\rho$ IOUs in the settlement period and then purchase ϕ_1/ρ units of the general good in the following CM_1. In equilibrium, sellers must be willing to spend some of their money in the CM_2 in order to allow late-producing buyers to acquire money to settle their debt in the late-night subperiod. Since $\phi_2 \geq \phi_1/\rho$ is required for equilibrium in the CM_2, the seller's participation constraint is still given by $c(q^m) = \phi_2 m$. Hence, the early-producing buyer's bargaining problem is the same as in the frictionless settlement environment, where solution to this problem is characterized by (10.5), and the quantity produced in this match, q^m, satisfies (10.7).

Consider now the late-producing buyer's bargaining problem. The participation constraint of a seller who trades output for debt will be affected by the frictions in the settlement phase. More specifically, creditor sellers may have to sell their IOUs at a discount if they need to leave the settlement phase before their debtors arrive. Let ϖ denote the expected value to the seller of a one-dollar IOU expressed in dollars. The buyer's bargaining problem can be represented by

$$\max_{q^b,b}\left[u(q^b)-\phi_2 b\right] \tag{10.13}$$

$$\text{s.t.}\ -c(q^b)+\varpi\phi_1 b = 0, \tag{10.14}$$

where ϖ satisfies

$$\varpi = \delta\left[\alpha + (1-\alpha)\rho\right] + (1-\delta)\left[\frac{\alpha}{\rho} + (1-\alpha)\right]. \tag{10.15}$$

From (10.13), the buyer maximizes his utility of consumption net of the cost of producing $\phi_2 b$ units of general good in the CM_2 in order to repay his debt in the settlement period. The seller's participation constraint, (10.14), specifies that the expected value of the IOUs in terms of the general good traded in the next CM_1 must cover the disutility of production of the seller in the DM.

Equation (10.15) has the following interpretation. With probability δ, a seller holding a one-dollar IOU must leave the settlement place early. If his debtor has already arrived, an event which occurs with probability α, the IOU is redeemed for one dollar. Otherwise, the IOU is sold at the price ρ. With probability $1-\delta$, the seller with a one-dollar IOU does not need to leave early. Therefore, the IOU that he holds is redeemed for one dollar, independent of the arrival time of his debtor. However, if the debtor of a seller arrives early, an event which occurs with probability α, the creditor can use the dollar he receives to buy $1/\rho$ IOUs that will be redeemed for $1/\rho$ dollars at the end of the settlement phase. The expected values for an IOU, conditional on arrival and departure outcomes, and the probabilities associated with the outcomes, are presented in the following table.

The solution to the late-producing buyer's bargaining problem (10.13)–(10.14) is given by

$$\frac{u'(q^b)}{c'(q^b)} = \frac{\phi_2}{\varpi\phi_1}. \tag{10.16}$$

The quantities traded in the DM in exchange for IOUs are efficient if $\phi_2 = \varpi\phi_1$. From (10.14), the quantity of debt issued by buyers in

Table 10.1
Value of \$1 IOU in the settlement period (no default)

Debtor arrives... / **Creditor leaves...**	**early (α)**	**late ($1-\alpha$)**
early (δ)	1	ρ
late ($1-\delta$)	$1/\rho$	1

the DM is

$$b = \frac{c(q^b)}{\varpi \phi_1}. \tag{10.17}$$

Consider the equilibrium of the CM_2. Denote Δ as the funds that each seller with money—and there is a measure $1/2$ of such sellers—retains at night so that he can purchase second-hand IOUs in the late-night settlement period. The total amount of money supplied in the CM_2 is equal to the total stock, M, minus money held by sellers to purchase existing IOUs in the settlement period, $\Delta/2$. The demand for money comes from buyers who need to settle their debt, equal to $b/2$. Hence, equilibrium in the CM_2 requires that

$$\frac{b}{2} + \frac{\Delta}{2} = M. \tag{10.18}$$

If $\phi_2 > \phi_1/\rho$, then sellers who hold money at the beginning of the night prefer to spend it in the CM_2 rather than the following CM_1. If, however, $\phi_2 = \phi_1/\rho$, then sellers are indifferent between spending money in the CM_2 or in the next CM_1. To summarize,

$$\Delta \begin{cases} = 0 \text{ if } \phi_2 > \frac{\phi_1}{\rho} \\ \geq 0 \text{ if } \phi_2 = \frac{\phi_1}{\rho} \end{cases}. \tag{10.19}$$

Let's now turn to the equilibrium for the existing-debt market in the settlement period. Note that ρ, the price of IOUs in the settlement period cannot be greater than one; $\rho > 1$ implies that anyone who purchases the IOU will get a strictly negative net payoff. Therefore, $\rho \leq 1$. There are two possible sources for the supply of funds to purchase existing IOUs in the settlement period. First, there are the creditors who are repaid early and leave late, who hold in total $(1-\delta)\alpha b/2$ units of money. (Recall that half of the sellers in the DM are paid with IOUs.) Second, there are sellers who received money during the DM and supply $\Delta/2$ units of money in the settlement period. The demand for funds from early-leaving creditors is $\rho\delta(1-\alpha)b/2$. If the supply of funds, $(1-\delta)\alpha b/2 + \Delta/2$, is greater than the volume of second-hand IOUs to be purchased, $\delta(1-\alpha)b/2$, then buyers of those IOUs will bid up the price until it reaches $\rho = 1$. Otherwise, the price of second-hand IOUs will adjust so that the supply of funds, $(1-\delta)\alpha b/2 + \Delta/2$, is equal to the demand, $\delta(1-\alpha)b\rho/2$. To summarize, the market-clearing price of second-hand debt, ρ, satisfies

$$\rho = \begin{cases} 1 & \text{if } (1-\delta)\alpha\frac{b}{2} + \frac{\Delta}{2} \geq \delta(1-\alpha)\frac{b}{2} \\ \frac{(1-\delta)\alpha b+\Delta}{\delta(1-\alpha)b} & \text{otherwise} \end{cases}. \tag{10.20}$$

If the supply of funds is large enough to redeem the IOUs of early-leaving creditors at face value, then the price of existing debt is one. If there is a shortage of funds, then existing debt will be sold at a discount.

A steady-state equilibrium is a list $(\phi_1, \phi_2, \rho, q^m, q^b, b, \Delta)$ that satisfies (10.5)–(10.7) and (10.16)–(10.20). We distinguish between two types of equilibria: one where $\rho = 1$ and one where $\rho < 1$. If $\rho = 1$, then there is no liquidity shortage in the settlement period: existing IOUs are sold at par, $\rho = 1$ and, from (10.15), the expected value of a one dollar IOU in the DM is one, i.e., $\varpi = 1$. As a result, the equilibrium conditions are identical to those of the economy without any frictions in the settlement period, i.e., $q^m = q^b = q^*$, $\phi_1 = \phi_2 = c(q^*)/2M$, $b = 2M$ and $\Delta = 0$. Note that from (10.20), $\rho = 1$ requires that $(1-\delta)\alpha/\delta(1-\alpha) \geq 1$ or, equivalently, $\alpha \geq \delta$. Intuitively, there is no liquidity shortage if the measure of debtors who arrive early in the settlement place, α, is larger than the measure of creditors who leave early, δ. Creditors who are repaid by early-arriving debtors can use this money to purchase the IOUs of creditors who need to sell them, the earlier-leaving creditors.

Consider now equilibria where existing debt is sold at a discount in the settlement period, i.e., where $\rho < 1$. From (10.20), we have

$$\rho = \frac{(1-\delta)\alpha b + \Delta}{\delta(1-\alpha)b}.$$

The equilibrium is liquidity-constrained in the sense that the amount of money available at the settlement period just prior to the departure of the early-leaving creditors is insufficient to clear debts at their par value. An important result here is that if $\rho < 1$, then $\Delta > 0$, which implies that sellers with money provide additional liquidity in the settlement period by only spending a fraction of their money balances in the CM_2. To see this, suppose to the contrary that $\Delta = 0$. Then, from (10.20), $\rho = (1-\delta)\alpha/\delta(1-\alpha) < 1$ and, from (10.15), $\varpi = 1$. But this implies that the equations that determine $(q^m, q^b, \phi_1, \phi_2)$ are identical to those derived for the model that had no settlement frictions, and, as a result, that $\phi_2 = \phi_1$. (Recall that we are focusing on specifications for which the equilibrium under frictionless settlement is unique). But $\phi_2 = \phi_1$ contradicts the no-arbitrage condition, $\phi_2 \geq \phi_1/\rho$, since $\rho < 1$. Therefore, it must be that $\Delta > 0$ whenever $\rho < 1$.

When $\rho < 1$ and $\Delta > 0$, condition (10.19) implies that $\phi_2 = \phi_1/\rho$, which means that sellers with money are indifferent between spending money in the CM_2 or the following CM_1.

Let's turn to the effect that the liquidity shortage has on the equilibrium allocation. From (10.15), $\varpi < 1/\rho$ and, hence, $\phi_2/\varpi\phi_1 > \rho\phi_2/\phi_1 = 1$. Together with the fact that $\phi_2 > \phi_1$, (10.5) and (10.16) imply that

$$\frac{u'(q^m)}{c'(q^m)} = \frac{\phi_1}{\phi_2} < 1 < \frac{u'(q^b)}{c'(q^b)} = \frac{\phi_2}{\varpi\phi_1}.$$

The quantities traded in the DM must satisfy $q^b < q^* < q^m$: buyers who trade with money in the DM receive more output than those who trade with credit. Intuitively, a seller who is paid with money can use it to buy interest-bearing debt in the settlement period; in contrast, a seller paid with debt is facing the risk of having to sell his IOUs at a discount in the settlement period.

The liquidity shortage during the settlement period affects the allocation of resources by making money more valuable in the CM_2 than in the CM_1. Indeed, since unsettled debts are sold at a discount during the settlement period, there is an additional demand for liquidity at night. The fact that money is more valuable in the CM_2 allows early-producing buyers to consume more, whereas the consumption of late-producing buyers falls.

10.4 Settlement and Default Risk

We now introduce an idiosyncratic risk of late-producing buyers defaulting on their debt. We formalize the default risk by assuming that a debtor is able to produce at night with probability ϱ and, with probability $1 - \varrho$, is unable to produce and, hence, defaults on his debt obligation. Assume that a debtor does not know if he will default before the night period. This assumption implies that during the DM, buyers and sellers have symmetric information in their bilateral matches. We assume that debtors who are unable to produce and, therefore, default on their debt do not show up at the settlement period. This implies that early-leaving creditors who sell their IOUs do not know whether or not these IOUs will be repaid.

The bargaining and choice of money holdings problems for an early-producing buyer are still given by (10.2)–(10.3) and (10.4), respectively, since the risk of default is irrelevant for transactions conducted with money. The bargaining problem for a late-producing buyer, however, is now given by

$$\max_{q^b,b} \left[u(q^b) - \varrho\phi_2 b\right] \tag{10.21}$$

$$\text{s.t.} \; -c(q^b) + \varpi\phi_1 b = 0. \tag{10.22}$$

According to (10.21), the buyer receives q^b from the seller, and is able to produce at night with probability ϱ, in which case he can repay his debt. According to (10.22), the seller who receives a promise of b dollars can expect to get ϖb dollars at the end of the period, which can be spent the following morning, where ϖ, the expected value of a one-dollar IOU, now reflects not only any settlement frictions but also the possibility of default. The solution to problem (10.21)–(10.22) implies that

$$\frac{u'(q^b)}{c'(q^b)} = \frac{\varrho\phi_2}{\varpi\phi_1}. \tag{10.23}$$

In the absence of any settlement frictions, it will be the case that $\varpi = \varrho$. Then, (10.23) is identical to (10.10), and the outcome is similar to the one of the economy without default risk. The default risk is simply reflected in the (higher) amount of money that the buyer commits to repay, and the quantity of output traded in bilateral matches remains efficient. This result is reminiscent of the exogenous default result in Chapter 2.2.

Consider now a seller who has money at the beginning of the settlement period, and who contemplates buying existing IOUs from early-leaving creditors when there is a possibility of settlement frictions. The seller must assess the probability that an existing IOU will be repaid, conditional on the fact that the debtor did not arrive early. This probability is,

$$\begin{aligned}\Pr[\text{no default}\,|\text{no early arrival}] &= \frac{\Pr[\text{no default} \cap \text{no early arrival}]}{\Pr[\text{no early arrival}]} \\ &= \frac{\varrho(1-\alpha)}{1-\varrho+\varrho(1-\alpha)} \\ &= \frac{\varrho(1-\alpha)}{1-\varrho\alpha}.\end{aligned}$$

We have used the fact that there are three possible events for an IOU in deriving the above conditional probability: an IOU is not repaid, which occurs with probability $1-\varrho$; it is repaid early, which occurs with probability $\varrho\alpha$; or it is repaid late, which occurs with probability $\varrho(1-\alpha)$. The maximum price an agent is willing to pay for a unit face value of existing IOU in the settlement period is the actuarial price, ρ^*, that is equal to the conditional probability of repayment, i.e.,

$$\rho^* = \frac{\varrho(1-\alpha)}{1-\varrho\alpha}. \tag{10.24}$$

The expected value of a one-dollar IOU in the DM, when the possibility of settlement frictions exists, is

$$\varpi = \varrho\alpha\left(\delta + (1-\delta)\frac{\rho^*}{\rho}\right) + \varrho(1-\alpha)(1-\delta) + \delta(1-\varrho\alpha)\rho, \tag{10.25}$$

or, equivalently from (10.24),

$$\varpi = \varrho\left(\delta\alpha + (1-\delta)\alpha\frac{\rho^*}{\rho} + (1-\delta)(1-\alpha) + \delta(1-\alpha)\frac{\rho}{\rho^*}\right). \tag{10.26}$$

Equation (10.25) has the following interpretation: the debtor arrives early with probability $\varrho\alpha$. With probability δ, the creditor leaves early, in which case he gets the par value of the IOU. With probability $1-\delta$, he can stay late and use his dollar to buy a second-hand IOU at the price ρ, i.e., he buys $1/\rho$ IOUs. The probability that the second-hand IOU is repaid is ρ^*. The debtor arrives late with probability $\varrho(1-\alpha)$. If the creditor can wait, with probability $1-\delta$, he receives one dollar at the end of the settlement phase. Finally, if the debtor does not arrive early, because he either defaults or because he arrives late, an event that occurs with probability $1-\varrho\alpha$, and if the creditor leaves early, an event that occurs with probability δ, then the creditor can sell his IOU at the price ρ. The expected value for an IOU for different events are presented in the following table.

Following the same reasoning as in Section 10.3, the clearing of the CM_2 requires

$$\frac{\Delta}{2} + \frac{\varrho b}{2} = M, \tag{10.27}$$

Table 10.2
Expected value of \$1 IOU in the settlement period (Default)

Debtor arrives... / Creditor leaves...	early ($\varrho\alpha$)	late ($\varrho(1-\alpha)$)	never ($1-\varrho$)
early (δ)	1	ρ	ρ
late ($1-\delta$)	ρ^*/ρ	1	0

where, as above, Δ represents the funds that a seller with money (there is a measure 1/2 of such sellers) retains at night so that he can purchase existing IOUs in the settlement period. The demand of money in the CM_2 comes from the late-producing buyers who need to acquire b units of money in order to redeem their IOUs in the settlement period. The only difference with respect to the market clearing condition (10.18) is that only a fraction ϱ of the late-producing buyers are able to produce in the CM_2 in order to repay their debt. If $\phi_2 > (\rho^*/\rho)\phi_1$, the sellers with money at the end of the DM strictly prefer buying in the upcoming CM_2. As a result, the supply of funds from a seller who holds money at the beginning of the CM_2, Δ, satisfies

$$\Delta \begin{cases} = 0 & \text{if } \phi_2 > \frac{\rho^*}{\rho}\phi_1 \\ \in [0, 2M] & \text{if } \phi_2 = \frac{\rho^*}{\rho}\phi_1 \end{cases}. \tag{10.28}$$

The only difference associated with this expression, (10.28), compared to that given by (10.19), is that in the former an existing IOU is redeemed with probability ρ^*, while in the latter it is with probability one.

Finally, we consider the clearing of the market for existing debt. The market-clearing price, ρ, satisfies

$$\rho = \begin{cases} \rho^* & \text{if } \frac{(1-\delta)\alpha\varrho b}{2} + \frac{\Delta}{2} \geq \frac{\delta(1-\varrho\alpha)b\rho^*}{2} \\ \frac{(1-\delta)\alpha\varrho b + \Delta}{\delta(1-\varrho\alpha)b} & \text{otherwise} \end{cases}. \tag{10.29}$$

If the supply of funds is large enough—the left side of the inequality on the top line—to redeem the IOUs of early-leaving creditors at their actuarial price—the right side of the inequality—then the price of second-hand debt is ρ^*. If there is a shortage of funds, then existing debt will have to be sold at a discount for the market to clear. Substituting $1 - \varrho\alpha$ by its expression given by (10.24) into (10.29) and rearranging, we get

$$\frac{\rho}{\rho^*} = \begin{cases} 1 & \text{if } \frac{(1-\delta)\alpha\varrho b}{2} + \frac{\Delta}{2} \geq \frac{\delta(1-\alpha)\varrho b}{2} \\ \frac{(1-\delta)\alpha\varrho b + \Delta}{\delta(1-\alpha)\varrho b} & \text{otherwise} \end{cases}. \tag{10.30}$$

An equilibrium of the model with default risk is a list $(\phi_1, \phi_2, \rho, q^m, q^b, b, \Delta)$ that satisfies (10.2)–(10.3), (10.4), (10.22), (10.23), (10.27), (10.28), and (10.30). It can be checked that the probability of no-default, ϱ, affects the equilibrium conditions only through the variables ϱb, ρ/ρ^*, and ϖ/ϱ. For example, ρ/ρ^* given by (10.30) coincides with ρ given by (10.20) when ϱb is replaced by b. Hence, $(\phi_1, \phi_2, q^m, q^b, \Delta)$ coincide with their values in the no-default economy. The value of money and the quantities traded in the DM are not affected by the probability of default, which is taken into account in the price of bonds and the transfer of bonds in the DM. See the Appendix for further details.

The equilibrium is not liquidity-constrained whenever the supply of liquidity from the late-leaving creditors who had their IOUs redeemed by early-arriving debtors, $\varrho\alpha(1-\delta)b/2$, is greater than the demand of liquidity from early-leaving creditors, $\delta(1-\alpha\varrho)\rho^* b/2$. From (10.24), the condition $\varrho\alpha(1-\delta) \geq \delta(1-\alpha\varrho)\rho^*$ is equivalent to $\alpha \geq \delta$. This is precisely the condition we had in the absence of default risk. The fact that the rate of repayment ϱ does not influence the condition for a liquidity shortage can be explained as follows: consider an increase in the repayment rate. On the one hand, the number of creditors who are repaid early, $\varrho\alpha(1-\delta)/2$, increases, so there is more liquidity in the late-night settlement period. On the other hand, the demand for liquidity, $\delta\rho^*(1-\alpha\varrho)b/2 = \delta\varrho(1-\alpha)b/2$, increases with ϱ as well. When $\alpha = \delta$ these two effects just cancel each other.

In summary, the presence of an idiosyncratic default risk does not make it more likely that the settlement frictions will generate a shortage of liquidity and, hence, a misallocation of resources.

10.5 Settlement and Monetary Policy

When liquidity is "plentiful" in the settlement subperiod, the efficient allocation; i.e., the allocation that maximizes the surpluses in the DM, can be implemented as an equilibrium, and this is independent of default probabilities. If, however, there is a liquidity shortage, then the allocation is no longer efficient, i.e., $q^b < q^* < q^m$. Is it possible for monetary policy to improve matters in this situation?

In addressing this question, we assume that there is no default risk, i.e., $\varrho = 1$, because, as we have seen, the default risk is simply internalized in the pricing mechanism. When there is a liquidity shortage—which occurs when the fraction of creditors who depart early, δ, is greater than the fraction of debtors who arrive early, α—the market clearing price for debt in the settlement period, ρ, will be less than one, and this ultimately leads to inefficient levels of production in the DM.

Suppose now that there exists a monetary authority, or central bank, that can provide "liquidity" to the settlement period. More specifically, the central bank purchases $\Delta^{\mathrm{cb}} \leq \delta(1-\alpha)b/2$ amount of IOUs from early-leaving creditors in exchange for fiat money. When the late-arriving debtors come to the settlement period, the central bank will exchange the IOUs for fiat money. Provided that the IOUs are sold at the price $\rho = 1$, this operation is neutral for the stock of fiat money. Recall that the supply of funds by creditors who are paid early and stay late is $(1-\delta)\alpha b/2$ and that the face value of bonds of the creditors who leave early and whose issuers arrive late is $\delta(1-\alpha)b/2$. If

$$(1-\delta)\alpha\frac{b}{2} + \Delta^{\mathrm{cb}} \geq \delta(1-\alpha)\frac{b}{2},$$

then the liquidity problem is solved: the supply of funds by late-leaving creditors and the central bank is enough to satisfy the demand of funds by early-leaving creditors. In this case IOUs are traded at their face value, $\rho = 1$, and sellers spend all their money in the CM_2 so that $b/2 = M$. Consequently, in order to implement an efficient outcome as an equilibrium when there is a liquidity shortage in the absence of a central bank, the supply of liquidity by the central bank must satisfy

$$(\delta-\alpha)M \leq \Delta^{\mathrm{cb}} \leq \delta(1-\alpha)M.$$

The supply of funds by the central bank is large enough to cover the difference between the IOUs supplied by early-leaving creditors and the demand of IOUs that comes from late-leaving creditors, $(\delta-\alpha)M$, but it is not larger than the liquidity needs of early-leaving creditors, $\delta(1-\alpha)M$.

This temporary supply of liquidity by the monetary authority resembles either a discount window policy or an open-market operation. As an open-market operation, the central bank purchases $(\delta-\alpha)M$ units of bonds before the early-leaving creditors depart and sells the bonds back after the late-arriving debtors arrive. As a discount window policy, the central bank stands ready to purchase existing IOUs at their par value, with the understanding that the IOUs have to be repurchased at their par value by the late-arriving debtors before the settlement period ends. The increase in the money supply that results from the open-market operation or discount window policy is not inflationary, since the IOUs purchased by the monetary authority are all redeemed within the period so that the stock of money remains constant across periods. This policy is consistent with the real bills doctrine, which says that the stock of money should be allowed to fluctuate to meet the needs of trade by means of self-liquidating loans.

A central bank is not necessarily needed to overcome the liquidity problem. Suppose that a late-leaving creditor, say a *clearinghouse*, purchases the debt of early-leaving creditors with his own IOUs, with the understanding that the IOUs of the clearinghouse can be exchanged for money in the next morning. (This assumes that in the next period repayment by the clearing house can be enforced.) When the late-arriving debtors arrive, the clearinghouse will exchange the debt that it holds for money. In the next morning, the clearinghouse can repurchase its debt with money. Hence, as long as the clearinghouse is able to repurchase the debt it has issued, the liquidity problem that arises due to the settlement frictions can be overcome by private agents.

10.6 Further Readings

The model of settlement presented in this section is closely related to Freeman (1996a,b). Freeman considers an overlapping-generations economy with heterogenous agents. Some agents trade with debt, while others trade with money. Freeman (1999) extends the model to allow for aggregate default risk. Green (1999) shows that the role of the Central Bank as a clearinghouse can be undertaken by ordinary private agents. Zhou (2000) discusses this literature.

Temzelides and Williamson (2001) consider two related models: a model with spatial separation and a random matching model. They investigate different types of payment arrangements, such as, monetary exchange, banking with settlement, and banking with interbank lending. They show that payment systems with net settlement generate efficiency gains, and interbank lending can support the Pareto-optimal allocation in the absence of idiosyncratic shocks.

Koeppl, Monnet, and Temzelides (2008) develop a dynamic general equilibrium model of payments that incorporates private information frictions and that uses mechanism design. As in Lagos and Wright (2005), there is a periodic round of centralized trading, the settlement stage, where agents have linear preferences and can trade a general good. There is no currency, but there is a payments system that can record individual transactions and assign balances to its participants. Because some bilateral meetings are not monitored, the payments system relies on individuals reporting their trades truthfully. This type of model can be used to determine the optimal settlement frequency, and the trade-off between trade sizes and settlement frequency. Chiu and

Wong (2015) also adopt a mechanism design approach to study payment systems.

Kahn and Roberds (2009) provide a survey on the payments literature. They identify the payments problems as being associated with temporal mismatches in trading demands and limited enforcement of promises. They focus on mixtures of two kinds of payment systems: store of value systems, which includes money, and account based systems, which includes credit. In terms of the latter, they point out that collateral can be useful in facilitating payments. They also discuss issues associated with net and gross settlement, and provide a brief overview to the industrial organization of retail payments.

Appendix

Equilibrium of the Economy with Frictionless Settlement when $c(q) = q$ and $u(q) = 2\sqrt{q}$.
From (10.5) and (10.10),

$$q^m = \left(\frac{\phi_2}{\phi_1}\right)^2, \tag{10.31}$$

$$q^b = \left(\frac{\phi_1}{\phi_2}\right)^2. \tag{10.32}$$

From (10.7) and (10.11),

$$q^m = 2M\phi_2, \tag{10.33}$$

$$q^b = b\phi_1. \tag{10.34}$$

Substitute q^m by its expression given by (10.33) into (10.31) to get

$$\phi_2 = 2M(\phi_1)^2. \tag{10.35}$$

Similarly, substitute q^b by its expression given by (10.34) into (10.32) to obtain

$$\phi_1 = b(\phi_2)^2. \tag{10.36}$$

There is a unique positive solution to (10.35)-(10.36) and it is

$$\phi_2 = \frac{1}{(2M)^{\frac{1}{3}} b^{\frac{2}{3}}},$$

$$\phi_1 = \frac{1}{(2M)^{\frac{2}{3}} b^{\frac{1}{3}}}.$$

Hence,

$$\frac{\phi_2}{\phi_1} = \left(\frac{2M}{b}\right)^{\frac{1}{3}}. \tag{10.37}$$

From (10.12),

$$b \begin{Bmatrix} = \\ \leq \end{Bmatrix} 2M \quad \text{if} \quad \frac{\phi_2}{\phi_1} \begin{Bmatrix} > \\ = \end{Bmatrix} 1. \tag{10.38}$$

From (10.37) and (10.38), the unique solution is such that $b = 2M$ and $\frac{\phi_2}{\phi_1} = 1$. Consequently, $\phi_2 = \phi_1 = \frac{1}{2M}$ and $q^b = q^m = 1$.

Equivalence Between the Equilibrium Conditions of the Models with and without Default

Redefine the endogenous variables as $\tilde{b} = \varrho b$, $\tilde{\rho} = \frac{\rho}{\rho^*}$, and $\tilde{\varpi} = \frac{\varpi}{\varrho}$. The equilibrium conditions (10.22), (10.23), (10.26), (10.27), (10.28), and (10.30) can be reexpressed as

$$-c(q^b) + \tilde{\varpi}\phi_1\tilde{b} = 0$$

$$\frac{u'(q^b)}{c'(q^b)} = \frac{\phi_2}{\tilde{\varpi}\phi_1}$$

$$\tilde{\varpi} = \delta\alpha + \frac{(1-\delta)\alpha}{\tilde{\rho}} + (1-\delta)(1-\alpha) + \delta(1-\alpha)\tilde{\rho}.$$

$$\frac{\Delta}{2} + \frac{\tilde{b}}{2} = M$$

$$\Delta \begin{cases} = 0 & \text{if } \phi_2 > \tilde{\rho}\phi_1 \\ \in [0, 2M] & \text{if } \phi_2 = \tilde{\rho}\phi_1 \end{cases}$$

$$\tilde{\rho} = \begin{cases} 1 & \text{if } \frac{(1-\delta)\alpha\tilde{b}}{2} + \frac{\Delta}{2} \geq \frac{\delta(1-\alpha)\tilde{b}}{2} \\ \frac{(1-\delta)\alpha\tilde{b} + \Delta}{\delta(1-\alpha)\tilde{b}} & \text{otherwise} \end{cases}$$

It can be checked that these equilibrium conditions are identical to (10.14), (10.16), (10.15), (10.18), (10.19), and (10.20), respectively, where $\left(\tilde{b}, \tilde{\rho}, \tilde{\varpi}\right)$ is replaced by (b, ρ, ϖ).

11 Money and Capital

Even though fiat money plays a major role in facilitating exchange in practice, there exists a large variety of assets and commodities that can be, and are, used as means of payment. For example, commodities, such as gold and silver, and financial assets, such as demand deposits, checkable mutual funds, and, to some extent, government securities are used for transaction purposes. There is also a plethora of assets (e.g., capital, claims on capital, and stocks) that could be used as means of payment but are not, or only to a limited extent.

The presence of competing media of exchange raises the "central issue in the pure theory of money," which is to explain why fiat money is valued in the presence of interest-bearing assets. In John Hicks's (1935, p.5) own words,

> "The critical question arises when we look for an explanation of the preference for holding money rather than capital goods. For capital goods will ordinarily yield a positive rate of return, which money does not. What has to be explained is the decision to hold assets in the form of barren money, rather than of interest- or profit-yielding securities."

This famous quote is a statement of the so-called rate-of-return dominance puzzle. Most macroeconomic models that incorporate multiple assets—such as money, bonds, and capital—*evade* this question. Typically, money is introduced in these models either via a cash-in-advance constraint—the requirement that a subset of consumption goods must be purchased with money—or as an argument of the utility function. The role of assets as means of payment is then assumed rather than explained. According to Hicks,

> "[T]he great evaders would not have denied that there must be some explanation of the fact. But they would have put it down to "frictions," and since there was no adequate place for frictions in the rest of their economic theory, a

theory of money based on frictions did not seem to them a promising field for economic analysis."

Following Hicks's advice, our approach is to look "the frictions in the face." In this chapter and the next we explain why fiat money can be useful even when other assets can be used as media of exchange. This chapter focuses on real, capital goods (as in Hicks's quote above) while the following one is devoted to nominal assets (multiple currencies and nominal bonds). We will first show that in the absence of fiat money, agents will, from a social perspective, over-accumulate capital if the stock of capital is insufficiently large to satisfy their liquidity needs; i.e., liquidity is scarce. When fiat money is introduced into the economy and valued, the capital stock decreases since less capital is now required for transactions purposes. Moreover, there is a positive relationship between capital and inflation: this is the so-called Tobin (1965) effect.

Under standard trading mechanisms (e.g., Nash and proportional bargaining) money and capital must share the same rate of return in order to coexist. Hence, the benchmark model fails to generate the rate of return dominance described by Hicks. However, if the trading mechanism in pairwise meetings is chosen optimally so as to maximize social welfare, as in Chapter 4, then capital dominates money in its rate of return in the constrained efficient allocation. The optimal mechanism departs from standard bargaining solutions in that it is not restricted to treat money and capital symmetrically in pairwise meetings, thereby allowing for rate-of-return differences across assets. A higher-return capital is optimal because it relaxes the participation constraint of buyers in the centralized market, which gives them higher incentives to accumulate liquidity. Hence, rate-of-return dominance is not a puzzle: it is a feature of good allocations in monetary economies.

11.1 Linear Storage Technology

The most direct way for a buyer to purchase the DM good from a seller in a bilateral match in the decentralized market is to give the seller what he values: the CM good which is produced in the centralized market. In the benchmark model, a barter trade is technologically infeasible since it is assumed that goods are perishable, i.e., they fully depreciate at the end of the subperiod in which they are produced. The good that is produced in the CM cannot be carried into the next day DM to pay for the DM good. We now modify the economic environment of the benchmark model by assuming that agents have access to a storage technology that enables them to carry the CM good from one period into the next. The storage technology is represented by a function f. An agent who stores k units of the CM good obtains $f(k)$ units in the subsequent period. The DM good is still assumed to be perishable, and fully depreciates at the end of the DM.

We first consider the case where the storage technology f is linear, meaning that one unit of the stored CM good at night generates $R \geq 0$ units of general good in the following period. We will refer to a CM good that is stored as *capital*. The gross rate of return from storage is R: k units of capital at night will turn into $f(k) = Rk$ units of CM goods the following period. The Rk units of the CM good can be used as a medium of exchange in the DM, and can be either consumed and/or used as capital at night. The technology f corresponds to pure storage if $R = 1$, a productive technology if $R > 1$, and one that is characterized by depreciation if $R < 1$.

In addition to capital, an agent can also use fiat money as a store of value. One unit of money balances at date t has real value ϕ_t in the CM and has a real gross rate of return from period t to period $t+1$ equal to ϕ_{t+1}/ϕ_t. The evolution of the real value of a portfolio (m,k), consisting of m units of fiat money and k units of capital, between the night of period t, and the day of period $t+1$, is described in Figure 11.1.

Assume, for the time being, that the money supply is constant, and focus on steady-state equilibria where the value of fiat money is also constant. Consider a buyer with portfolio (m,k) at the beginning of the DM. Denote (q, d_m, d_k) as the terms of trade in a bilateral match in the DM, where q is the amount of the DM good that the buyer receives from the seller, d_m is the transfer of (nominal) money balances from the

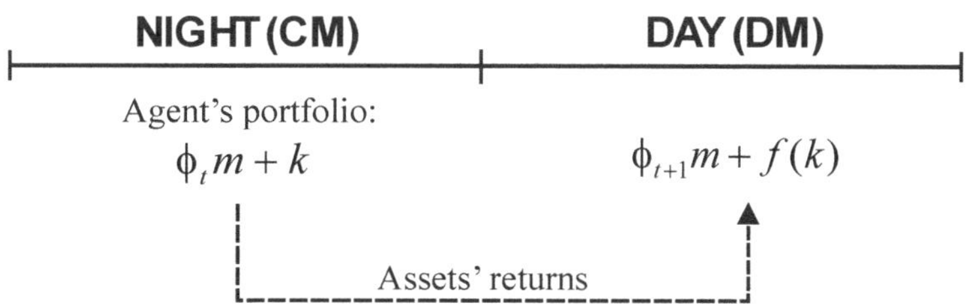

Figure 11.1
Timing and assets' returns

buyer to the seller, and d_k is the transfer of capital. We consider a pricing mechanism where the terms of trade, (q, d_m, d_k), depend only on the the buyer's portfolio. A buyer with portfolio (m,k) at the beginning of the period has a lifetime expected utility, $V^b(m,k)$, given by

$$V^b(m,k) = \sigma \left\{ u\left[q(m,k)\right] + W^b\left[m - d_m(m,k), k - d_k(m,k)\right] \right\} \\ +(1-\sigma)W^b(m,k). \tag{11.1}$$

According to (11.1), a buyer who meets a seller consumes q units of the DM good, and transfers d_m units of money balances and d_k units of capital to the seller. The value function for a buyer holding a portfolio (m,k) at the beginning of the CM, $W^b(m,k)$, obeys

$$W^b(m,k) = \phi m + k + \max_{m',k'} \left\{ -\phi m' - k' + \beta V^b(m', Rk') \right\}. \tag{11.2}$$

The cost of adjusting the buyer's portfolio in the CM is $\phi(m'-m) + k' - k$, where the k' units of general good that are stored at the end of the CM will generate Rk' units of general goods in the next DM. As it is by now standard, the value function $W^b(m,k)$ is linear in the buyer's wealth.

The terms of trades in a bilateral match are determined by a take-it-or-leave-it offer by the buyer. (We will characterize the optimal mechanism in Section 11.4.) If the buyer holds a portfolio (m,k) in the DM, his optimal offer to the seller is given by the solution to

$$\max_{q,d_m,d_k} \left[u(q) - d_k - \phi d_m\right] \quad \text{s.t.} \quad -c(q) + d_k + \phi d_m \geq 0, \tag{11.3}$$
$$d_m \leq m, \qquad d_k \leq k;$$

i.e., the buyer will maximize his surplus, subject to covering the seller's cost. The solution to problem (11.3) is

$$q(m,k) = \begin{cases} q^* \\ c^{-1}(\phi m + k) \end{cases} \text{if } \phi m + k \begin{Bmatrix} \geq \\ < \end{Bmatrix} c(q^*),$$

which implies that $\phi d_m + d_k = c(q^*)$ if $\phi m + k \geq c(q^*)$, and $(d_m, d_k) = (m,k)$, otherwise. Note that if the buyer has insufficient resources to purchase the efficient level of output, then $\partial q/\partial m = \phi/c'(q)$ and $\partial q/\partial k = 1/c'(q)$.

If we substitute V^b, given by (11.1), into W^b, given by (11.2), recognizing that the buyer extracts all of the surplus from a trade match, the buyer's optimal portfolio is given by the solution to

$$\max_{m\geq 0,k\geq 0}\left\{-\left(\frac{1-\beta}{\beta}\right)\phi m-\left(\frac{1-\beta R}{\beta R}\right)Rk+\sigma\left\{u\left[q(m,Rk)\right]-c\left[q(m,Rk)\right]\right\}\right\}. \tag{11.4}$$

The expression in the brackets should look familiar: the first two terms represent the cost of taking money and capital, respectively, into the subsequent DM. More specifically, the cost of having an additional unit of real balances into the DM is $\beta^{-1}-1$, and the cost of having an additional unit of unit of capital in the DM is $(\beta R)^{-1}-1$, (since one needs to invest only R^{-1} units of capital at night to get one unit in the DM.) The third term in (11.4) represents the expected surplus in the DM. The first-order (necessary and sufficient) conditions associated with problem (11.4) are

$$-r+\sigma\left[\frac{u'(q)}{c'(q)}-1\right]\leq 0,\quad \text{“}=\text{”}\ \text{if}\ m>0, \tag{11.5}$$

$$-\frac{1-\beta R}{\beta R}+\sigma\left[\frac{u'(q)}{c'(q)}-1\right]\leq 0,\quad \text{“}=\text{”}\ \text{if}\ k>0. \tag{11.6}$$

According to (11.5) and (11.6), a buyer equalizes the cost of having an additional unit of the asset in the DM with its expected liquidity return in the DM. The liquidity return of an asset corresponds to the increase in the buyer's surplus if he had an additional unit of the asset in the DM. This liquidity return is $u'(q)/c'(q)-1$ for both capital and real balances. To see this, note that the increase in the buyer's surplus if he accumulates an additional unit of real asset in the DM is $[u'(q)-c'(q)]\,\partial q/\partial k=[u'(q)-c'(q)]\,\partial q/\partial(\phi m)$. When $q<q^*$, $\partial q/\partial k=\partial q/\partial(\phi m)=1/c'(q)$ since $\phi m+k=c(q)$; when $q=q^*$, the liquidity return for both assets is zero.

Up to this point we have only considered the buyer's portfolio problem. The seller's choice of asset holdings is given by the solution to

$$\max_{m\geq 0,k\geq 0}\left\{-\left(\frac{1-\beta}{\beta}\right)\phi m-\left(\frac{1-\beta R}{\beta R}\right)Rk\right\},$$

since, by our choice of trading mechanism, the seller's asset holdings do not affect the terms of trade in bilateral matches. A seller will never accumulate money in the CM since $\beta<1$. If $\beta R=1$, then sellers are indifferent between accumulating capital or not.

It should be obvious from conditions (11.5) and (11.6) that buyers are willing to hold *both* money and capital if and only if $R=1$, since this implies that both assets offer the same real return. If $R > 1$, then capital dominates money in its rate of return, and buyers will hold only capital goods to make transactions. In this case, fiat money will not be valued, and the quantity traded in the DM satisfies

$$\frac{u'(q)}{c'(q)} = 1 + \frac{1-\beta R}{\sigma \beta R}. \tag{11.7}$$

The quantity of DM goods traded in bilateral matches increases with the rate of return on capital. And, as the rate of return of the storage technology, $R-1$, approaches the discount rate, r, (equivalently, $R\beta$ approaches one) the quantity traded, q, approaches its efficient value, q^*. (Note that $R\beta$ cannot be greater than 1, otherwise the buyer's problem does not have a solution.) Since $R\beta < 1$, the socially efficient level of capital in a frictionless economy is zero. Hence, one can view the buyer as "over-accumulating" capital in our economy: he does so because capital is needed for transaction purposes in the DM. This result is reminiscent to the over-production result in Section 4.3.

If $R < 1$, then the rate of return on capital is lower than that of fiat money, and, in a steady-state equilibrium, buyers will only use money for transaction purposes, i.e., buyers will not store any of the general good. It should be pointed out that there exist nonstationary equilibria where output is constant and where money and capital coexist. In such nonstationary equilibria, the rate of return on fiat money is constant and equal to $R < 1$. This implies that aggregate real balances shrink over time. But the quantity traded in the DM, q, is determined by (11.7) and, hence, is constant. Since $c(q) = Rk_t + \phi_{t+1}M$ is also constant, capital k_t must be growing over time.

In a monetary equilibrium, where money and capital coexist as means of payments, the quantities traded in the DM correspond to those traded in the monetary economy examined in the previous section, i.e., q solves $u'(q)/c'(q) = 1 + r/\sigma$. Since money and capital are perfect substitutes, which implies $R = 1$, the composition of a buyer's portfolio, in terms of money and capital holdings, will be indeterminate. The total value of the portfolio, however, is pinned down by $\phi M + k = c(q)$. Consequently, the value of money can be anywhere in the interval $(0, c(q)/M)$. This indeterminacy, however, is not neutral in the following sense. If fiat money completely replaces capital as a means of payment, then society's welfare improves because there will be a one-time gain from consuming all of the capital that was accumulated to be used as a medium of exchange. This is the kind of argument that has been put forth to favor a fiat money regime over a commodity standard.

11.2 Concave Storage Technology

When the storage technology is linear and the money supply is constant over time, money and capital coexist only in the knife-edge case where $R=1$ in a steady-state equilibrium where the value of money is constant. Coexistence can be made more robust if the storage technology is strictly concave. Consider now a storage technology that converts k units of general good in the CM into $f(k)$ units of general good at the start of the subsequent period, where $f(0)=0$, $f'>0$, and $f''<0$. For simplicity, we impose the Inada conditions $f'(0)=+\infty$ and $f'(+\infty)=0$.

The buyer's portfolio choice problem, (11.4), is now given by the solution to

$$\max_{m\geq 0,k\geq 0}\left\{-\left(\frac{1-\beta}{\beta}\right)\phi m-\frac{k-\beta f(k)}{\beta}+\sigma\left[u\left(q\right)-c\left(q\right)\right]\right\}, \tag{11.8}$$

where, from the buyers-take-all bargaining assumption, $c(q)=\min\{c(q^*),f(k)+\phi m\}$. The middle term of (11.8) represents the cost of having $f(k)$ units of capital in the DM; to get $f(k)$ units in the DM, k units must be stored in the CM, the (net) cost being $k\beta^{-1}-f(k)$. The first-order conditions associated with (11.8) are

$$-r+\sigma\left[\frac{u'(q)}{c'(q)}-1\right]\leq 0, \quad \text{“}=\text{” if } m>0 \tag{11.9}$$

$$-\frac{1-\beta f'(k)}{\beta f'(k)}+\sigma\left[\frac{u'(q)}{c'(q)}-1\right]\leq 0, \quad \text{“}=\text{” if } k>0. \tag{11.10}$$

If $q=q^*$, then, from (11.10) with an equality, $k=k^*$ where k^* solves $\beta f'(k)=1$. The quantity k^* also corresponds to the quantity that would be chosen by a social planner who can dictate the allocations in both the CM and the DM. But from (11.9) it is immediate that this is inconsistent with a monetary equilibrium.

11.2.1 Nonmonetary Equilibria

Consider first a nonmonetary equilibrium. From the Inada conditions on f, the solution to (11.10) is interior and the buyer's capital stock satisfies

$$\frac{1}{\beta f'(k)}-1=\sigma\left[\frac{u'\circ c^{-1}[f(k)]}{c'\circ c^{-1}[f(k)]}-1\right]^{+}, \tag{11.11}$$

where $[x]^+ \equiv \max(x,0)$. The left side of (11.11) is increasing in k from -1, when $k=0$, to infinity, when $k=\infty$ and is equal to zero when $k=k^*$; the right side is decreasing in k from infinity, when $k=0$, to 0, when $f(k) \geq c(q^*)$. Consequently, as illustrated in Figure 11.2, there is a unique $k^n \geq k^*$ that solves (11.11).

It can easily be seen that if $f(k^*) \geq c(q^*)$, then the right side of (11.11) intersects the horizontal axis in Figure 11.2 at a lower value than the left side, and hence $k^n = k^*$. A buyer who holds $f(k^*)$ units of general goods in the DM has sufficient resources to purchase the efficient level of the DM good, q^*, if he is matched. This implies that the right side of (11.11) is zero. And, the left side of (11.11) also equals zero, since $\beta f'(k^*) = 1$.

If, instead, $f(k^*) < c(q^*)$, then the socially-efficient stock of capital, k^*, is not large enough to allow buyers to purchase q^* in the DM. In this situation, buyers will over-accumulate capital, i.e., $k^n > k^*$ as depicted in Figure 11.2. Here, buyers are willing to accept a lower rate of return because the capital they hold generates a positive liquidity return by serving as means of payment in bilateral matches in the DM.

Now we turn to the seller's choice of capital. Sellers do not need to accumulate a means of payment. They will, therefore, choose a level of

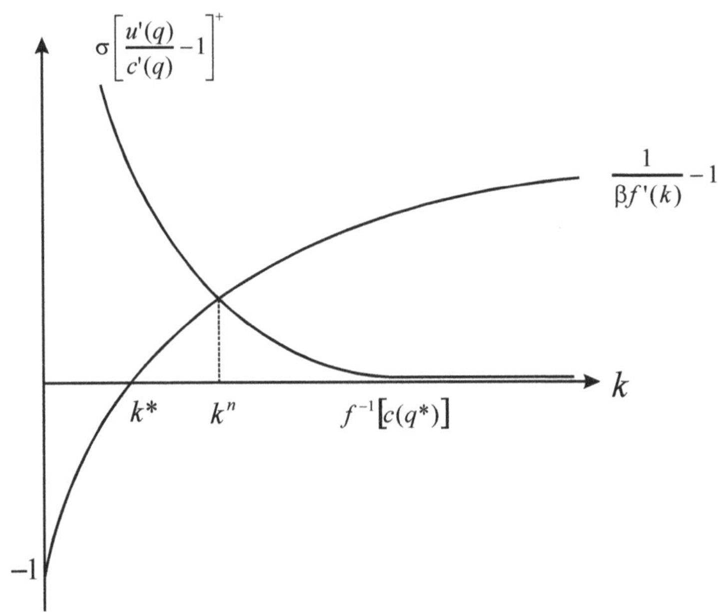

Figure 11.2
Nonmonetary equilibrium

capital that is independent of any liquidity considerations, which is the same choice that an agent would make in a frictionless economy. The seller maximizes $-k+\beta f(k)$, and his capital choice is k^*.

11.2.2 Monetary Equilibria

Consider next equilibria where fiat money is valued. Condition (11.9) holds with an equality, which, from (11.10), implies that

$$\frac{1-\beta}{\beta}=\frac{1-\beta f'(k)}{\beta f'(k)}$$

and hence $f'(k)=1$. Define $k^m>k^*$ as the solution to $f'(k)=1$, i.e., $k^m=f'^{-1}(1)$. In a monetary equilibrium, buyers are willing to hold both capital and real balances since both assets have the same expected liquidity return at the margin in the DM, $\sigma u'(q)/c'(q)-1$, and they have the same rate of return across CMs, $f'(k)-1$. Consequently, our model is able to explain the coexistence of fiat money and capital as means of payment, but does not explain the rate-of-return dominance puzzle.

The output in the DM, q, is given by the solution to (11.9) at equality, i.e.,

$$\frac{u'(q)}{c'(q)}=1+\frac{r}{\sigma},$$

and the value of money is given by $f(k^m)+\phi M=c(q)$, i.e., $\phi=[c(q)-f(k^m)]/M$. Since a necessary condition for a monetary equilibrium is $\phi>0$, which in turn implies that $c(q)>f(k^m)$, a monetary equilibrium can exist if

$$\frac{u'\circ c^{-1}[f(k^m)]}{c'\circ c^{-1}[f(k^m)]}>1+\frac{r}{\sigma} \tag{11.12}$$

or, equivalently,

$$\sigma\left[\frac{u'\circ c^{-1}[f(k^m)]}{c'\circ c^{-1}[f(k^m)]}-1\right]>\frac{1}{\beta f'(k^m)}-1, \tag{11.13}$$

since $f'(k^m)=1$. A comparison of (11.13) with (11.11) reveals that the capital stock in a monetary equilibrium, k^m, is less than that in a nonmonetary equilibrium, k^n. Hence, if condition (11.12) (or (11.13)) holds, then the (gross) rate of return of capital in the nonmonetary equilibrium is less than one, since $f'(k^m)=1$. In this situation, the introduction of a valued fiat money allows buyers to reduce their inefficiently high capital stock and to raise their consumption of the DM good.

11.3 Capital and Inflation

In order to study the effect that inflation has on capital accumulation and output, we let the money supply grow or shrink at a constant rate. As in Chapter 6, money is injected (withdrawn) through lump-sum transfers (taxes) to buyers in the CM. The money growth rate is $\gamma \equiv M_{t+1}/M_t > \beta$. We will focus on stationary equilibria, where the rate of return of money, ϕ_{t+1}/ϕ_t, is constant and equal to γ^{-1}.

Taking the same approach as in previous sections, the buyer's portfolio problem in the CM of period t, assuming the buyer makes a take-it-or-leave-it offer in the DM, is given by

$$\max_{m\geq 0,k\geq 0} \{-\phi_t m - k + \beta \{\sigma [u(q) - c(q)] + \phi_{t+1} m + f(k)\}\},$$

where $c(q) = \min\{c(q^*), f(k) + \phi_{t+1} m\}$. This problem can be rearranged to

$$\max_{m\geq 0,k\geq 0} \left\{-i\phi_{t+1} m - \frac{k - \beta f(k)}{\beta} + \sigma [u(q) - c(q)]\right\}. \tag{11.14}$$

The buyer's portfolio problem here is identical to problem (11.8), but now prices must be indexed by time, and the opportunity cost of holding money is $i = (\gamma - \beta)/\beta$. (As shown in Chapter 6.1, the opportunity cost of money, i, can be interpreted as a nominal interest rate since this is the interest that would be paid on an illiquid nominal bond that cannot be used as means of payment in the DM.) The first-order conditions to problem (11.14) are

$$-i + \sigma \left[\frac{u'(q)}{c'(q)} - 1\right] \leq 0, \quad \text{“}=\text{” if } m > 0, \tag{11.15}$$

$$-\frac{1 - \beta f'(k)}{\beta f'(k)} + \sigma \left[\frac{u'(q)}{c'(q)} - 1\right] \leq 0, \quad \text{“}=\text{” if } k > 0. \tag{11.16}$$

Note that conditions (11.15) and (11.16) generalize (11.9) and (11.10), since $i = r$ when the money stock is constant, $\gamma = 1$.

If a monetary equilibrium exists, then both (11.15) and (11.16) hold at equality, which implies

$$\frac{1 - \beta f'(k)}{\beta f'(k)} = i$$

or

$$f'(k) = \gamma^{-1}, \tag{11.17}$$

i.e., the rate of return of capital is equal to the rate of return of fiat money. Once again, the rate-of-return-equality principle holds. In a monetary equilibrium, the capital stock is $k^m = f'^{-1}(\gamma^{-1})$. Note from (11.17) that as the inflation rate, $\gamma - 1$, increases, the rate of return on fiat money falls, and buyers accumulate more capital to serve as means of payment. Hence, monetary policy can affect capital accumulation when capital is used as a means of payment. Monetary policy can also affect the level of output in the DM, which is given by the solution to

$$\frac{u'(q)}{c'(q)} = 1 + \frac{i}{\sigma}.$$

The determination of a monetary equilibrium is illustrated in Figure 11.3. The top left panel depicts the relationship between the capital stock, k, and the return to capital, $f'(k)$. The top right panel represents the relationship between the rate of return on fiat money, γ^{-1}, and the cost of holding real balances, $i = (\gamma - \beta)/\beta$. Finally, the bottom panel plots the expected liquidity return of assets in the DM, $\sigma[u'(q)/c'(q) - 1]$, as a function of the output traded in that market, q.

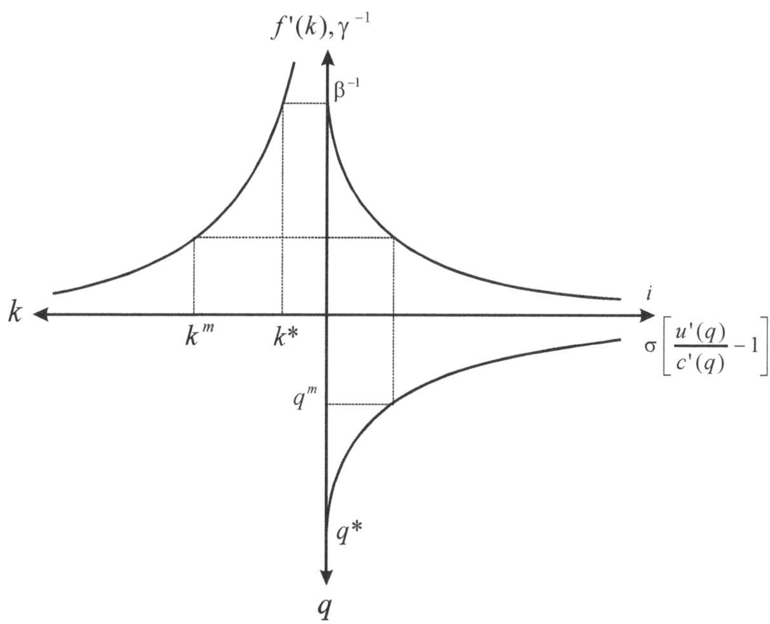

Figure 11.3
Determination of the monetary equilibrium

For a given return on money, γ^{-1}, the equilibrium capital stock, k^m, is determined in the top left panel. The associated cost of holding real balances can be read on the horizontal axis in the top right panel. Given the cost of holding real balances, the equilibrium output in the DM, q^m, is determined in the bottom right panel.

A monetary equilibrium exists if $\phi_t M_t = c(q) - f(k^m) > 0$ or, equivalently, if inequality (11.12) holds where r is replaced by i. As in the previous section, this requires that k^n be greater than k^m. As γ approaches β, k^m tends to k^*, and the condition for a monetary equilibrium becomes $k^n > k^*$. Fiat money has a welfare improving role whenever buyers in the nonmonetary equilibrium accumulate more capital than the socially-efficient level. In that case, society's welfare is at a maximum if fiat money is valued and the Friedman rule, $\gamma = \beta$, is implemented: at the Friedman rule, $q^m = q^*$ and $k^m = k^*$.

11.4 A Mechanism Design Approach

In contrast to previous sections, but as in Chapter 4, the trading mechanism in DM pairwise meetings is now chosen optimally by a planner, or "mechanism designer," taking into account agents' incentives to participate in the mechanism. A general trading mechanism for pairwise meetings specifies an offer (q, d_z, d_k), where d_z is a payment in real balances ($z = \phi m$ represents real balances), d_k is a payment in capital, k, and both d_z and d_k are functions of the buyer's portfolio, (z, k). The offer (q, d_z, d_k) must be individually rational—meaning that both the buyer and the seller are willing to accept it—and pairwise Pareto-efficient—meaning that the buyer and the seller cannot find another outcome that would make both of them better off. Notice that all of the mechanisms that we have studied so far, e.g., buyers-take-all bargaining, Nash and proportional solutions, satisfy these two properties.

For simplicity we focus on a linear technology, $f(k) = Rk$, where k units of capital accumulated in the CM of period t generates Rk units of the general good in the CM of period $t+1$. (Notice that without loss of generality we now assume that capital goods pay off in the CM instead of the beginning of the DM.) The objective of the mechanism designer is to maximize social welfare. Our measure of social welfare is given by

$$\sigma[u(q) - c(q)] + Rk - (1 + r)k. \tag{11.18}$$

In words, social welfare is given by the sum of the surpluses in the DM, $\sigma[u(q) - c(q)]$, and the CM output produced by the capital stock,

Rk, net of the capitalized investment cost incurred in the previous CM, $(1+r)k$. The incentive-feasibility constraints require that any DM offer is acceptable to both buyers and sellers, which implies that

$$u(q) - d_z - Rd_k \geq 0 \tag{11.19}$$

$$-c(q) + d_z + Rd_k \geq 0. \tag{11.20}$$

According to (11.19), the buyer's utility of DM consumption, $u(q)$, must exceed the value of the assets transferred to the seller, $d_z + Rd_k$, (each unit of capital held in the DM generates R units of output in the subsequent CM). Similarly, the value of assets that the seller receives must exceed the cost of DM production, (11.20). The mechanism designer must also ensure that buyers are willing to accumulate the portfolio (z,k) in the CM. A necessary condition for the buyer to hold portfolio (z,k) is

$$-iz - (1+r-R)k + \sigma[u(q) - d_z - Rd_k] \geq 0. \tag{11.21}$$

Condition (11.21) says that the cost of holding the portfolio (z,k), as measured by $iz + (1+r-R)k$, must be smaller than the buyer's expected surplus in the DM, $\sigma[u(q) - d_z - Rd_k]$. Provided that $R < 1+r$, if (11.21) holds, then (11.19) also holds. (In fact, it must be the case that $R \leq 1+r$; otherwise, buyers will accumulate an infinite amount of capital and will receive an infinite net payoff.) So the mechanism designer will choose a mechanism for the DM to implement as *an equilibrium outcome* a DM offer, (q^p, d_z^p, d_k^p), and a portfolio that buyers accumulate in the CM, (z^p, k^p).

Along the equilibrium path we can assume without loss of generality the offer (q^p, d_z^p, d_k^p) is chosen so that the seller is indifferent between accepting and rejecting it, i.e., $c(q) = d_z + Rd_k$. Indeed, such an offer relaxes the buyer's CM participation constraint, (11.21). Off-the-equilibrium-path offers will be chosen so as to punish buyers who do not accumulate the portfolio chosen by the mechanism designer. In particular, the mechanism assigns zero surplus to a buyer if he does not hold a portfolio of assets composed of $z \geq z^p$ and $k \geq k^p$, i.e.,

$$u(q) - d_z - Rd_k = 0 \text{ if } z < z^p \text{ or } k < k^p.$$

If the buyer accumulates more assets than z^p or k^p, then the mechanism does not increase the buyer's surplus, i.e.,

$$u(q) - d_z - Rd_k = u(q^p) - d_z^p - Rd_k^p \text{ if } z \geq z^p \text{ and } k \geq k^p.$$

If the buyer accumulates less than (z^p, k^p) assets, then he receives no surplus in the DM and, as a result, his net utility is negative. If the buyers accumulates more than (z^p, k^p) assets, then his DM surplus does not increase and the cost of holding the portfolio (weakly) increases. Therefore, if the mechanism satisfies (11.21), then it is optimal for the buyer to accumulate (z^p, k^p) assets.

The equilibrium outcome chosen by the mechanism designer can be reduced to a triple, (q^p, z^p, k^p). Given this triple, one can always back out an offer that satisfies $c(q^p) = d_z^p + Rd_k^p$. The triple is chosen to solve the following maximization problem:

$$\max_{q,z,k} \{\sigma[u(q) - c(q)] + Rk - (1+r)k\} \tag{11.22}$$

$$\text{s.t. } \sigma[u(q) - c(q)] - iz - (1+r-R)k \geq 0 \tag{11.23}$$

$$-c(q) + z + Rk \geq 0. \tag{11.24}$$

The outcome, (q^p, z^p, k^p), is incentive feasible if it satisfies the participation constraints for buyers, (11.23), and sellers, (11.24). According to (11.23), the sum of the costs of holding real balances and capital cannot exceed the buyer's expected surplus of a DM match; otherwise the DM offer would not induce buyers to hold the portfolio (z^p, k^p). According to (11.24), the value of real balances and capital in the DM, $z + Rk$, must be greater than the seller's disutility cost; otherwise the seller would not be compensated for his disutility of work.

The first-best allocation is the one where the planner is not subject to incentive-feasibility constraints—the planner has the power to enforce trades. From (11.22), the first-best allocation has $q = q^* = \arg\max\{u(q) - c(q)\}$ and $k = k^* = \arg\max\{Rk - (1+r)k\}$. Given our assumption that $R < 1 + r$, we have $k^* = 0$.

Let's now turn to incentive-feasible allocations. We first determine the conditions under which the first-best outcome, $(q^p, z^p, k^p) = (q^*, c(q^*), 0)$, is implementable. By construction, the seller's participation constraint, (11.24), is satisfied. From the buyer's participation constraint, (11.23), we have

$$\sigma[u(q^p) - c(q^p)] - iz^p \geq 0 \Leftrightarrow i \leq i^* \equiv \frac{\sigma[u(q^*) - c(q^*)]}{c(q^*)},$$

or, equivalently, $\gamma \leq \gamma^*$ where

$$\gamma^* = \beta\left\{1 + \frac{\sigma\left[u\left(q^*\right) - c(q^*)\right]}{c(q^*)}\right\}. \tag{11.25}$$

(Recall that $i = \gamma/\beta$.) Provided that the inflation rate, γ, is not too large, the first-best allocation can be implemented with fiat money as the only medium of exchange. The threshold for the money growth rate, γ^*, below which the first-best allocation is implementable is the same as the one in a pure currency economy in Chapter 4. It can be interpreted as follows. The term $\gamma^*/\beta - 1$ is the cost of holding real balances due to inflation and discounting. The term on the right side of (11.25), $\sigma\left[u\left(q^*\right) - c(q^*)\right]/c(q^*)$, is the expected nonpecuniary rate of return of money, i.e., the probability that a buyer has an opportunity to trade in the DM times the first-best surplus expressed as a fraction of the cost of producing q^*. The first-best allocation is implementable if the cost of holding real balances is no greater than the expected nonpecuniary return of money. Since $\gamma^* > \beta$, notice that the Friedman rule is not necessary to implement the first-best allocation: there is a range of low inflation rates that can achieve the highest possible welfare.

Let's consider next the case where $\gamma > \gamma^*$. Clearly, the first-best allocation, that has $q^p = q^*$ and $k^p = 0$, is not implementable. In this case the optimum has both (11.23) and (11.24) holding with equality. Indeed, if either (11.23) or (11.24) holds as a strict inequality, then the mechanism designer can either reduce k^p or increase q^p and raise welfare. Suppose first that $\gamma^{-1} \geq R$, which means that the rate of return of money is larger than the rate of return of capital. Given that capital is a socially inefficient means of payment with a low rate of return (relative to fiat money), it follows that a constrained-efficient allocation in that case must have $k^p = 0$. From (11.23) and (11.24) at equality, $z^p = c(q^p)$, where $q^p \in (0, q^*)$ is the unique positive solution to

$$-ic(q^p) + \sigma\left[u\left(q^p\right) - c(q^p)\right] = 0. \tag{11.26}$$

The output level is the highest one that is consistent with the buyer's participation constraint.

Consider next the case where $\gamma > \gamma^*$ and $\gamma^{-1} < R$; the latter inequality implies that fiat money has a lower rate of return than capital. There is now a nontrivial trade-off for the mechanism designer when choosing the buyer's portfolio. The use of real balances has no social cost but it tightens the buyer's participation constraint when money is substituted for capital since money has a lower rate of return than capital. In contrast, capital has a social cost because its rate of return is lower than agents' rate of time preference. Because (11.23) holds at equality, the mechanism designer's objective function reduces to

$$\sigma[u(q) - c(q)] + Rk(q) - (1+r)k(q) = iz(q).$$

Social welfare is equal to the cost of holding real balances. The planner would like the buyer to hold as much real balances as is (incentive) feasible because that would economize on holding capital. The mechanism designer's problem can be further simplified—essentially reducing it to a choice of q—since we can restrict our attention to outcomes that satisfy both (11.23) and (11.24) at equality. For any given q, the constraints (11.23) and (11.24) at equality have a unique solution given by

$$k(q) = \beta \left\{ \frac{\sigma[u(q) - c(q)] - ic(q)}{R\gamma - 1} \right\} \tag{11.27}$$

$$z(q) = \beta \left\{ \frac{\sigma R[u(q) - c(q)] - (1 + r - R)\, c(q)}{R\gamma - 1} \right\}. \tag{11.28}$$

Thus, the mechanism designer's maximization problem, (11.22)-(11.24), can be rewritten as

$$\max_{q \geq 0} \{iz(q)\} \quad \text{s.t. } k(q) \geq 0. \tag{11.29}$$

Suppose first that the nonnegativity constraint, $k(q) \geq 0$, is not binding, i.e., $k(q) > 0$. Maximizing $z(q)$ given by (11.28) yields $q = \tilde{q}$ where $\tilde{q} \leq q^*$ solves

$$u'(\tilde{q}) = \left[1 + \left(\frac{1 + r - R}{\sigma R}\right)\right] c'(\tilde{q}). \tag{11.30}$$

Note that $\tilde{q}$ is the output level that a buyer would obtain in an economy with capital as the only medium of exchange, see (11.7). So one can think of the mechanism designer as choosing the allocation in two steps. First, it determines the amount of output that would be optimal to finance with capital only. This quantity corresponds to $\tilde{q}$ and the wedge between $u'(\tilde{q})$ and $c'(\tilde{q})$ arises from the cost of holding capital. Second, the mechanism designer reduces the inefficiently high capital stock by requiring that the buyer accumulates real balances up to the point where he is just indifferent between participating and not participating, which corresponds to $z(\tilde{q})$. The condition $k(\tilde{q}) \geq 0$ can be rewritten as $\gamma \geq \tilde{\gamma}$ where

$$\tilde{\gamma} = \beta \left\{ 1 + \frac{\sigma \left[u(\tilde{q}) - c(\tilde{q})\right]}{c(\tilde{q})} \right\}. \tag{11.31}$$

It can be shown that $\tilde{\gamma} > \gamma^*$ and $\lim_{R \to 1+r} \tilde{\gamma} = \gamma^*$. Since $1/\tilde{\gamma} < R$ and money and capital coexist as a means of payment when $\gamma > \tilde{\gamma}$, capital has a higher rate of return than money, i.e., $1/\gamma < 1/\tilde{\gamma} < R$. In this sense, rate-of-return dominance is a property of "good" allocations in monetary economies.

Finally, when $\gamma \in (\gamma^*, \tilde{\gamma}]$, inflation is not low enough for the first-best allocation to be implementable but it is not high enough to require the accumulation of capital as means of payment. Indeed, in that case $\tilde{q}$ can be implemented with money only since, by construction,

$$-\frac{\gamma - \beta}{\beta} c(\tilde{q}) + \sigma \left[u(\tilde{q}) - c(\tilde{q}) \right] \geq 0.$$

As a result, when $\gamma \in (\gamma^*, \tilde{\gamma}]$, the capital stock is zero, $k^p = 0$, DM output, q^p, solves (11.26) and real balances z^p, are given by $c(q^p)$.

The allocations chosen by the mechanism designer are diagrammatically characterized in Figure 11.4. For low inflation rates, $\gamma \in (\beta, \gamma^*)$, the first-best allocation can be implemented with money alone: $q^p = q^*$, $k^p = k^* = 0$ and $z^p = c(q^*)$. As the inflation rate increases above γ^*, the first-best allocation is no longer implementable. The mechanism designer reduces q^p below q^* but maintains the capital stock at its

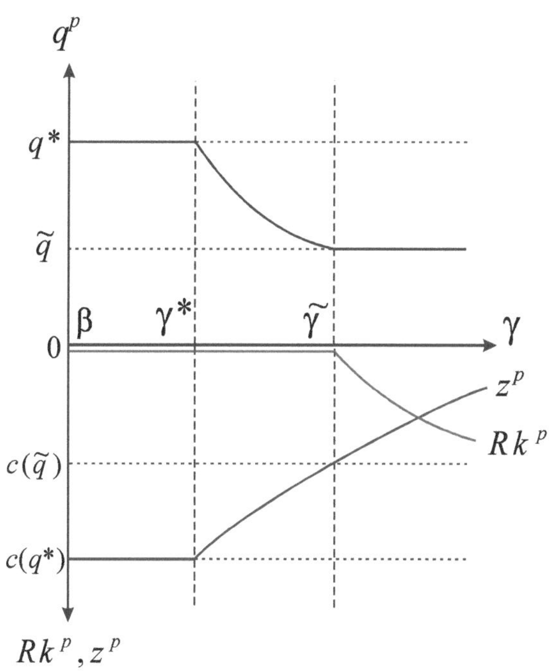

Figure 11.4
Constrained-efficient allocations

first-best level, $k^p = 0$. If the money growth rate is above $\tilde{\gamma}$, then it is optimal to accumulate capital in order to save on real balances and maintain output at its level in an economy with capital only, $q^p = \tilde{q}$. All this implies that, under the optimal mechanism, inflation leads to overaccumulation of capital only when inflation rates are sufficiently high. In this case, the mechanism designer has agents substituting away from money—that is too costly to hold—into accumulating capital.

A key finding of our analysis is that under an optimal mechanism, whenever money and capital coexist, money has a lower rate of return than capital, which implies that rate of return dominance is part of an optimal arrangement. We illustrate this result in Figure 11.5. The rate of return on capital is measured on the horizontal axis, while the rate of return of fiat money is measured on the vertical axis. There is rate-of-return equality on the 45° line; rate-of-return dominance is characterized below the 45° line. In Section 11.1, under buyers-take-all bargaining, an equilibrium in which fiat money and capital coexist can only occur in the knife-edge case where the two assets have the same rate of return, $R = \gamma^{-1}$. In contrast, under an optimal mechanism, agents never hold capital if there is rate-of-return equality, even if DM

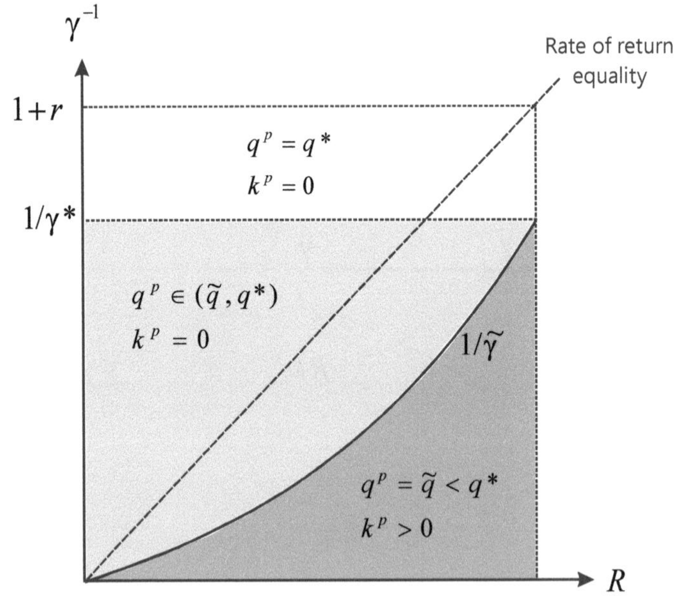

Figure 11.5
Rate-of-return dominance under an optimal mechanism

output is inefficiently low. Equilibria in which both fiat money and capital are held (the dark grey area) only exist below the 45° line, where capital has a strictly higher rate of return than fiat money.

11.5 Further Readings

Kiyotaki and Wright (1989) construct an environment where commodities are storable and can serve as means of payment but they differ in terms of their storage costs. They show that the goods that emerge as media of exchange depend on the storage costs, as well as preferences and technologies through the pattern of specialization.

Models of commodity monies include Sargent and Wallace (1983), Li (1995), Burdett, Trejos, and Wright (2001), and Velde, Weber, and Wright (1999). The existence of a monetary equilibrium when agents have access to a linear storage technology is studied by Wallace (1980) in the context of an overlapping-generations model.

The model in this chapter is from Lagos and Rocheteau (2008) who study how money and capital can compete as means of payment in a search environment. Shi (1999a, 1999b), Aruoba, and Wright (2003), Molico and Zhang (2006), Aruoba, Waller, and Wright (2011), and Waller (2011) describe search economies where agents can accumulate capital, but capital is illiquid in the sense that it cannot be used as a means of payment in bilateral matches. Ferraris and Watanabe (2012) consider the case where part of the returns of capital can be pledged. Andolfatto, Berentsen, and Waller (2016) study the use of asset-backed money in a model with illiquid capital. The effect of inflation on capital accumulation was studied in reduced-form monetary models by Tobin (1965) and Stockman (1981). Aruoba (2011) study business cycles for different versions of the model. Aruoba, Davis, and Wright (2015) interpret capital as homes and study the effect of anticipated inflation on the production of houses (construction).

The section on mechanism design is taken from Hu and Rocheteau (2013) who adopt a mechanism design approach to study the coexistence of money and capital in economies with pairwise meetings and the optimality of outcomes that feature rate-of-return dominance. Hu and Rocheteau (2015) consider the case where capital goods (Lucas trees) are in fixed supply.

12 Exchange Rates, Nominal Bonds, and Open Market Operations

In Chapter 11 we studied the coexistence of money and productive capital. In this chapter we study the coexistence of fiat money and nominal assets, either another currency or a nominal bond, and its implications for exchange rates and monetary policy. We first consider an economy with two currencies. We show that for standard pricing mechanisms, the nominal exchange rate is indeterminate: there are a continuum of equilibria with identical allocations but different relative prices between the two currencies. This result should not be surprising since the exchange rate between two intrinsically useless objects can be whatever agents believe it to be. This indeterminacy breaks down if the trading mechanism does not treat the two currencies symmetrically. We propose a Pareto-efficient trading mechanism that is biased in favor of the domestic currency: an agent can obtain better terms of trade by offering the domestic currency as means of payment, and this mechanism leaves no room for renegotiation. In this case, agents will, in equilibrium, hold only the domestic currency—thereby rationalizing cash-in-advance constraints—and the exchange rate is determined by fundamentals and monetary factors.

In an economy with fiat money and nominal government bonds, if the two assets are perfect substitutes as means of payment then they have the same rate of return. It means that liquid bonds do not pay interest; the purchase price of a bond is its face value. It is a manifestation of the rate-of-return dominance puzzle. If, however, bonds are less liquid than money—for example, they are only partially-acceptable for transactional purposes—then bonds dominate money in terms of their rates of return.

Arguably, assuming that bonds are not as liquid as money is not a satisfactory answer to the rate-of-return dominance puzzle. We rationalize the illiquidity of bonds in two ways. First, we assume that bonds suffer from a recognizability problem. As a result, sellers will only accept bonds for payment up to some endogenous limit. As agents must be compensated for holding bonds they cannot use for transactions purposes, the rate of return on bonds will exceed that of money. Open-market operations in this environment have no effect on output levels. Our second explanation is analogous to the one we used to address the indeterminacy of the exchange rate: agents trade according to a Pareto-efficient mechanism that provides the buyer with a greater surplus for transacting in money instead of bonds.

Finally, in order to investigate open market operations we study an economy with segmented markets, where in one market both money and bonds can serve as means of payment and in the other fiat money is the only medium of exchange. For instance, fiat money is the only payment instrument in the retail sector, let's say because retailers cannot authenticate bonds, while money and government bonds can serve as media of exchange in trades among firms or financial institutions. We show that open-market operations are ineffective when the relative supply of bonds is either too low or too high. For intermediate levels, an open-market sale of bonds raises real and nominal interest rates and it increases output levels. Our model can generate "liquidity traps," where the nominal interest rate on government bonds is zero and money and bonds are perfect substitutes.

12.1 Dual Currency Payment Systems

In this section we examine the coexistence of two intrinsically worthless objects as means of payment. This is a relevant exercise because actual economies have many different currencies, including "virtual currencies" (unregulated digital money.) This raises the questions of whether multiple currencies can be valued and used in payments, whether there is a role for multiple currencies, and how the exchange rate is determined. Models in international macroeconomics typically explain the determination of the value of a currency by using exogenous restrictions on payments, such as cash-in-advance constraints. Although we remove these exogenous restrictions, we show how they may endogenously arise.

12.1.1 Indeterminacy of the Exchange Rate

Consider an economy where two fiat monies—called money 1 and money 2—can be used as media of exchange. For convenience, one can think of money 1 as dollars and money 2 as euros. The stocks of both monies, M_1 and M_2, are fixed, and agents are free to use either currency. One unit of money 1 buys ϕ_1 units of the CM good, and one unit of money 2 buys ϕ_2 units of the CM good. We will focus on stationary equilibria where ϕ_1 and ϕ_2 are constant over time.

Consider a buyer holding m_1 units of money 1 and m_2 units of money 2 in the DM. His beginning-of-period value function, $V^b(m_1,m_2)$, satisfies

$$V^b(m_1,m_2) = \sigma \left\{ u\left[q(m_1,m_2)\right] + W^b\left[m_1 - d_1(m_1,m_2), m_2 - d_2(m_1,m_2)\right] \right\} \\ +(1-\sigma)W^b(m_1,m_2). \tag{12.1}$$

The interpretation of the value function (12.1) is similar to that of value function $V^b(m,k)$ given in (11.1). The value function of the buyer at the beginning of the CM is given by

$$W^b(m_1,m_2) = \phi_1 m_1 + \phi_2 m_2 + \max_{\hat{m}_1 \geq 0, \hat{m}_2 \geq 0} \left\{ -\phi_1 \hat{m}_1 - \phi_2 \hat{m}_2 + \beta V^b(\hat{m}_1,\hat{m}_2) \right\}, \tag{12.2}$$

where the interpretation is similar to that of $W^b(m,k)$ given in (11.2). The terms of trade in the DM are determined by a take-it-or-leave-it offer by the buyer, i.e.,

$$q(m_1,m_2) = \begin{cases} q^* \\ c^{-1}(\phi_1 m_1 + \phi_2 m_2) \end{cases} \text{if } \phi_1 m_1 + \phi_2 m_2 \begin{Bmatrix} \geq \\ < \end{Bmatrix} c(q^*),$$

where $\phi_1 d_1 + \phi_2 d_2 = c(q^*)$ if $\phi_1 m_1 + \phi_2 m_2 \geq c(q^*)$, and $(d_1,d_2) = (m_1,m_2)$ otherwise. Substituting $V^b(m_1,m_2)$ from (12.1) into (12.2), and using the solution to the buyer's bargaining problem, the buyer's portfolio problem is given by

$$\max_{m_1 \geq 0, m_2 \geq 0} \left\{ -r(\phi_1 m_1 + \phi_2 m_2) + \sigma \left\{ u\left[q(m_1,m_2)\right] - c\left[q(m_1,m_2)\right] \right\} \right\}. \tag{12.3}$$

The buyer chooses his portfolio (m_1,m_2) so as to maximize his expected surplus in the DM, net of the cost of holding real balances as measured by the rate of time preference, r. Because the terms of trade depend only on the real value of the buyer's portfolio, $\phi_1 m_1 + \phi_2 m_2$, the solution to (12.3) does not pin down a unique composition of the portfolio. From the first-order conditions of (12.3), q satisfies

$$\frac{u'(q)}{c'(q)} = 1 + \frac{r}{\sigma}, \tag{12.4}$$

where, $c(q) = \phi_1 m_1(j) + \phi_2 m_2(j)$ and $j \in [0,1]$ indicates the name of a buyer. Integrating over j, we get

$$c(q) = \phi_1 \int_{[0,1]} m_1(j)dj + \phi_2 \int_{[0,1]} m_2(j)dj,$$

and market clearing, $M_1 = \int_{[0,1]} m_1(j)dj$ and $M_2 = \int_{[0,1]} m_2(j)dj$. Therefore, in equilibrium,

$$c(q) = \phi_1 M_1 + \phi_2 M_2. \tag{12.5}$$

Equation (12.4) uniquely determines the value of q, and equation (12.5) is left to determine both ϕ_1 and ϕ_2. Obviously, there does not exist unique values for ϕ_1 and ϕ_2. There are stationary equilibria where only one currency is valued, i.e., either $\phi_1 = 0$ or $\phi_2 = 0$, and there are equilibria where both currencies are valued. Across these equilibria, both the quantities traded in the DM and social welfare are the same. For any exchange rate, $\varepsilon = \phi_1/\phi_2$, that expresses the value of currency 1 in terms of currency 2, e.g., the number of euros per dollar, there exists a price for money 2 that solves (12.5), i.e., $\phi_2 = c(q)/[\varepsilon M_1 + M_2]$. Consequently, the nominal exchange rate ε is indeterminate. This indeterminacy result should not come as a surprise. The two fiat currencies are, after all, intrinsically useless objects whose relative price depends on beliefs.

12.1.2 Cash-in-Advance with a Twist in a Two-Country Model

International macroeconomic models usually adopt the restriction that, in the home country, agents trade with their domestic currency. This cash-in-advance constraint allows the exchange rate to be determined and, hence, the exchange rate can be related to fundamentals, such as preferences and technologies, and policies. This approach, however, is not entirely satisfactory because it assumes, rather than explains, why some agents only use a subset of currencies available to them as means of payment. The cash-in-advance restriction seems particularly unappealing when currencies have different inflation rates, and hence, different rates of return. In this section we will suggest a simple approach that generates similar insights as traditional international macroeconomic models but without imposing constraints on the use of currencies as means of payment. The basic idea is to choose a trading mechanism in the DM that has good efficiency properties, but treats domestic and foreign currencies asymmetrically.

We now consider a two-country version of our model. The economy is composed of country 1 and country 2, where each country has the same structure as our benchmark environment. All relevant variables are indexed by the name of the country. While fundamentals can vary across countries, we assume that all agents have the same rate of time preference, r. In the CM, agents can trade the CM good and the two currencies in an integrated competitive market. Hence the law of one price holds, i.e., $\phi_1 = \varepsilon\phi_2$. (The dollar price of the CM good is $1/\phi_1$ while the euro price is $1/\phi_2$. Given that a dollar is worth ε euros, $\varepsilon/\phi_1 = 1/\phi_2$.) In the DM, agents can only trade in their home market.

In order to eliminate the indeterminacy of the nominal exchange rate, we depart from determining the terms of trade in the DM by take-it-or-leave-it offers by buyers. Instead, we adopt a trading mechanism that captures the intuitive notion that one obtains better terms of trade in a country by using the domestic money rather than the foreign money. For example, if a buyer offers to spend euros in the US, then the euro will be accepted by the seller, because he knows he can sell them in the CM, but for less output than what the buyer could obtain with dollars. The key insight is that despite this asymmetric treatment of the two currencies, there will not be any unexploited gains from trade in the DM. In contrast to cash-in-advance models, we do not impose any constraint on the use of a currency as means of payment, and the induced DM allocations is pairwise Pareto-optimal.

A key component of the model is the pricing mechanism in the DM, which we now describe in detail. Consider a match between a buyer of country 1 and a seller of the same country. The buyer's portfolio is denoted by (m_1, m_2). Conceptually, one can think of the pricing mechanism in two stages. In the first stage, the buyer's payoff is set to be equal to the payoff he would obtain if he were to make a take-it-or-leave-it offer to the seller but were restricted to use only the domestic money as means of payment, as in a cash-in-advance economy. In the second stage, all the restrictions on the use of currencies as means of payment are removed, and the actual allocation is determined so that it is pairwise Pareto-efficient and the buyer's payoff is equal to his first stage payoff. This captures the notion that the buyer gets no extra surplus from using the foreign money, but agents do not leave gains from trade unexploited, as in a cash-in-advance world.

The buyer's payoff, or surplus, from the first stage of the pricing mechanism, $U_1^b(m_1, m_2)$, is given by

$$U_1^b(m_1, m_2) = \max_{q,d_1} [u_1(q) - \phi_1 d_1] \text{ s.t. } c(q) \leq \phi_1 d_1 \text{ and } d_1 \leq m_1. \tag{12.6}$$

As in a cash-in-advance economy, the buyer's payoff is obtained by choosing his consumption and the transfer of domestic currency so as to maximize his surplus, subject to the cost of consumption not exceeding the value of the transfer and transfer not exceeding what the buyer holds. It is important to note that the terms of trade chosen in the above problem are not (necessarily) the actual terms of trade that will be implemented. The purpose of the first stage is only to pin down a surplus or payoff level for the buyer. An important property of the buyer's surplus, defined in (12.6), is that it is independent of the buyer's holdings of foreign money, m_2.

We can now move to the second stage, which determines the actual terms of trade, as well as the seller's surplus. The final allocation is chosen so as to maximize the seller's surplus, subject to the constraint that the buyer's surplus is at least equal to $U_1^b(m_1, m_2)$, i.e.,

$$U_1^s(m_1, m_2) = \max_{q,d_1,d_2} [-c_1(q) + \phi_1 d_1 + \phi_2 d_2] \tag{12.7}$$

$$\text{s.t. } u_1(q) - \phi_1 d_1 - \phi_2 d_2 \geq U_1^b(m_1, m_2) \tag{12.8}$$

$$d_1 \leq m_1, d_2 \leq m_2. \tag{12.9}$$

This two-stage pricing procedure guarantees that the allocation is pairwise Pareto-efficient, meaning that there is no other allocation that can raise the payoffs to both the buyer and the seller in a bilateral match. Importantly, from (12.9), agents are not restricted to use the domestic money as the only means of payment in the DM.

The determination of the buyer's and seller's surpluses is represented in Figure 12.1. The upper straight-line, which consists of dotted parts, specifies combinations of buyer and seller surpluses when $q = q^*$. The intermediate solid-line frontier, which consists of a curved and straight line segments, represents the Pareto-frontier when the buyer can use both domestic and foreign currencies as means of payment in the DM. On the curved portion of this frontier, the buyer transfers his entire portfolio to the seller in exchange for the DM good, and as one moves in a northwest direction along the frontier, the amount of DM good traded falls. The position of this frontier depends upon the value of the buyer's portfolio (m_1, m_2). The intermediate frontier

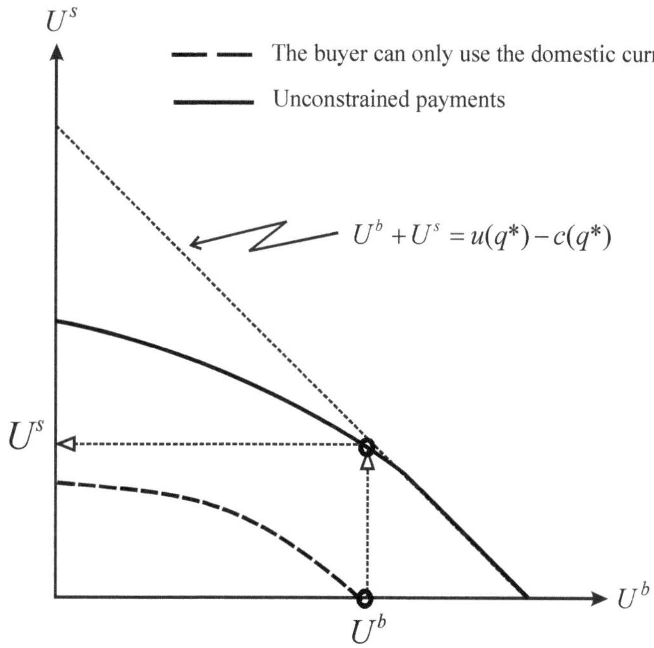

Figure 12.1
Determination of terms of trade

depicted in Figure 12.1 assumes that $\phi_1 m_1 + \phi_2 m_2 > c(q^*)$. If, alternatively, it is assumed that $\phi_1 m_1 + \phi_2 m_2 < c(q^*)$, then the entire intermediate frontier would be curved and would lie below the upper frontier. The lower dashed line frontier represents the pairs of utility levels that can be achieved when the buyer is restricted to use only the domestic currency as means of payment. For this frontier it is assumed that $\phi_1 m_1 < c(q^*)$. In terms of Figure 12.1, our pricing mechanism specifies that the buyer's surplus is given by the intersection of the dashed lower frontier and the horizontal axis: it is the maximum surplus that the buyer can extract if he can only use the domestic currency in trade. Given the buyer's surplus, U^b, the seller's surplus, U^s, lies on the Pareto frontier directly above the point $(U^b, 0)$. Note that (U^b, U^s) is pairwise Pareto-efficient, given the buyer's portfolio (m_1, m_2).

We now turn to the buyer's portfolio choice problem in the CM. Using the same kind of reasoning that led to (12.3), the portfolio choice problem of a buyer who resides in country 1 is given by,

$$\max_{m_1 \geq 0, m_2 \geq 0} \left\{ -r(\phi_1 m_1 + \phi_2 m_2) + \sigma_1 U_1^b(m_1, m_2) \right\}.$$

Since, from (12.6), m_2 has no affect on the buyer's surplus, it is immediate that the buyer will choose $m_2 = 0$. As a result, our model rationalizes a cash-in-advance constraint, one where buyers hold only the domestic currency. From (12.6), $U_1^b(m_1, m_2) = u(q_1) - c(q_1)$ where $c(q_1) = \min\left[c(q_1^*), \phi_1 m_1\right]$. The first-order condition with respect to m_1 for the buyer's portfolio problem is

$$\frac{u_1'(q_1)}{c_1'(q_1)} = 1 + \frac{r}{\sigma_1}, \tag{12.10}$$

with $c_1(q_1) = \phi_1 M_1$. By analogy, a buyer's choice of money holdings in country 2 is

$$\frac{u_2'(q_2)}{c_2'(q_2)} = 1 + \frac{r}{\sigma_2}, \tag{12.11}$$

with $c_2(q_2) = \phi_2 M_2$.

The intuition for the result that buyers hold only their domestic currency is straightforward. If a buyer purchases goods with foreign currency, he will obtain terms of trade that are worst than those associated with holding the domestic currency. More specifically, from (12.6), with an additional unit of real domestic currency, i.e., $1/\phi_1$ units of money 1, the buyer in country 1 can obtain $1/c_1'(q_1)$ units of output. According to (12.8), with an additional unit of real foreign currency, i.e., $1/\phi_2$ units of money 2, the buyer obtains $1/u_1'(q_1) < 1/c_1'(q_1)$ units of output. This implies that the marginal surplus from using the foreign currency, $u_1'(q_1)[\partial q_1/\partial(\phi_2 m_2)] - 1$, is zero, while it is strictly positive from using the domestic currency. As a result, agents in each country will only hold the domestic currency, even though there are no restriction on which currencies can be used as means of payment, and there is no cost associated with trading in the foreign exchange market.

The nominal exchange rate, $\varepsilon \equiv \phi_1/\phi_2$, is equal to

$$\varepsilon = \frac{c_1(q_1)}{c_2(q_2)} \frac{M_2}{M_1}. \tag{12.12}$$

This exchange rate depends on technologies and preferences through the first term, and on monetary factors in the two countries through the second term. In order to obtain an expression for the exchange rate which is easier to interpret, we adopt the following functional forms. Agents in both economies have the same utility function for DM goods, $u_1(q) = u_2(q) = q^{1-a}/(1-a)$ with $a \in (0, 1)$. The disutility of production is $c_j(q) = A_j q$, which implies that a productive country has a low A. From (12.10) and (12.11), $q_j = A_j^{-1/a}(1 + \frac{r}{\sigma_j})^{-1/a}$. From (12.12), the expression for the exchange rate is then

$$\varepsilon = \left(\frac{A_2}{A_1}\right)^{\frac{1-a}{a}} \left(\frac{1 + r/\sigma_2}{1 + r/\sigma_1}\right)^{\frac{1}{a}} \frac{M_2}{M_1}. \tag{12.13}$$

If country 1 becomes more productive, or if its supply of money shrinks, then its currency appreciates vis-a-vis the currency of country 2. The exchange rate depends also on trading frictions. If it becomes easier to find trading partners in country 1, then the exchange rate increases.

The model can be readily extended to account for the effects that monetary policies in each country have on the exchange rate. Let $\gamma_j \equiv M_{j,t+1}/M_{j,t} > \beta$ denote the gross growth rate of the money supply for country $j = 1, 2$. (If agents from the two countries have different discount factors, then the money growth rate in each country must be greater than the discount factor of the most patient agents.) The cost of holding real balances in country j is i_j, where $1 + i_j = (1 + r)\gamma_j$. Since a buyer gets zero surplus in the DM from holding the foreign money, he will only accumulate the domestic money, even if its inflation rate is higher than that of the foreign money. Hence, the model can explain a version of the rate-of-return dominance puzzle, where agents trade with their domestic money even if it is dominated in its rate of return by foreign money. The DM output in each country is given by an equation analogous to (12.10) and (12.11), i.e.,

$$\frac{u_j'(q_j)}{c_j'(q_j)} = 1 + \frac{i_j}{\sigma_j}, \quad j = 1, 2.$$

Using the same functional forms as described above, the expression for the exchange rate in period t becomes

$$\varepsilon_t = \left(\frac{A_2}{A_1}\right)^{\frac{1-a}{a}} \left(\frac{1 + i_2/\sigma_2}{1 + i_1/\sigma_1}\right)^{\frac{1}{a}} \frac{M_{2,t}}{M_{1,t}}.$$

The (gross) growth rate of the exchange rate, $\varepsilon_{t+1}/\varepsilon_t$, is equal to γ_2/γ_1.

12.2 Money and Nominal Bonds

In the previous section we looked at economies with multiple intrinsically useless objects—fiat currencies—that serve as means of payment. We now consider economies with fiat money and nominal bonds, which are claims on fiat money. The presence of nominal bonds allows us to determine a key policy variable, the nominal interest rate. We first show that under the standard assumptions used so far, the model predicts that the nominal interest rate is zero. This result constitutes a puzzle—the so-called rate-of-return dominance puzzle—since, in reality, bonds dominate money in terms of rate of return. We then provide conditions under which the rate-of-return dominance puzzle can be resolved, and discuss the implications of the resolution of the puzzle for the determinants of the nominal interest rate.

12.2.1 The Rate-of-Return Dominance Puzzle

Consider an economy where agents can use both money and government bonds as media of exchange. A one-period government bond is issued in the CM and is redeemed for one unit of money in the subsequent CM. The flow of bonds sold by the government each period is constant and equal to B. We will also assume that the aggregate money supply is constant, i.e., $M_{t+1} = M_t$, or equivalently, $\gamma = 1$. Government bonds are of the pure discount variety, perfectly divisible, payable to the bearer, and default-free. These assumptions make money and bonds close substitutes. Since matured bonds are exchanged for money one-for-one, the price of matured bonds, in terms of CM goods, is ϕ. Let ω be the price of newly-issued bonds in terms of CM goods. If $\omega < \phi$, then newly-issued bonds are sold at a discount for money. The one-period real rate of return on newly issued bonds is

$$r_b = \frac{\phi}{\omega} - 1. \tag{12.14}$$

Indeed, one unit of CM good purchases $1/\omega$ units of bond where each unit of bond pays off one unit of money worth ϕ units of good in the following period. In the absence of inflation the real interest on government bonds is also the nominal interest rate (denoted i_b later in the chapter). If $r_b > 0$, then the government finances the interest payments on bonds by lump-sum taxation in the CM. The tax per buyer is $(\phi - \omega) B = r_b \omega B$.

We assume that the terms of trade in bilateral matches in the DM are determined by a take-it-or-leave-it offer by the buyer. Using the same reasoning as in the previous sections the expected lifetime utility of a buyer holding a portfolio (m, b), composed of m units of money and b units of bonds at the beginning of the period, is

$$V^b(m,b) = \sigma \{u[q(m,b)] - c[q(m,b)]\} + W^b(m,b), \tag{12.15}$$

where $q(m,b) = q^*$ if $\phi(m+b) \geq c(q^*)$ and $q(m,b) = c^{-1}[\phi(m+b)]$, otherwise. The expected lifetime utility of a buyer entering the CM with portfolio (m,b) is

$$W^b(m,b) = \phi(m+b) + T + \max_{m' \geq 0, b' \geq 0} \left\{ -\phi m' - \omega b' + \beta V^b(m',b') \right\}, \tag{12.16}$$

where T represents a lump-sum transfer in terms of general goods by the government in the CM. If the government needs to finance the interest payment on bonds, then $T = -r_b \omega B < 0$. Note that this equation is similar to (12.2) in the context of two currencies. If we substitute V^b from (12.15) into (12.16), then the buyer's portfolio problem becomes,

$$\max_{m \geq 0, b \geq 0} \left\{ -r\phi m - \left(\frac{r - r_b}{1 + r_b} \right) \phi b + \sigma \left\{ u\left[q(m,b)\right] - c\left[q(m,b)\right] \right\} \right\}, \tag{12.17}$$

where the cost of holding nominal bonds is

$$\frac{\omega - \beta\phi}{\beta\phi} = \frac{r - r_b}{1 + r_b},$$

which is approximately equal to the difference between the real interest rate of illiquid bonds and the real interest rate of liquid bonds. The first-order (necessary and sufficient) conditions for problem (12.17) are

$$-r + \sigma \left[\frac{u'(q)}{c'(q)} - 1 \right] \leq 0, \quad \text{“} = \text{” if } m > 0 \tag{12.18}$$

$$-\frac{r - r_b}{1 + r_b} + \sigma \left[\frac{u'(q)}{c'(q)} - 1 \right] \leq 0, \quad \text{“} = \text{” if } b > 0. \tag{12.19}$$

If bonds are sold at a discount, i.e., if $r_b > 0$, then the cost of holding bonds is less than that of money, since $(r - r_b)/(1 + r_b) < r$. But then, from (12.18) and (12.19), buyers would only hold bonds, and fiat money would not be valued. This, however, cannot be an equilibrium outcome since a nominal bond is a claim to fiat money. Consequently, in equilibrium, fiat money and newly issued bonds must be perfect substitutes, i.e., $\omega = \phi$ and $r_b = 0$. Therefore, if there are no restrictions on the use of bonds as means of payment, then *interest-bearing* government bonds cannot coexist with fiat money. This is the rate-of-return dominance puzzle.

The output in the DM is given by the solution to (12.18) or (12.19) at equality, i.e.,

$$\frac{u'(q)}{c'(q)} = 1 + \frac{r}{\sigma} \tag{12.20}$$

and, from the seller's participation constraint, the value of money satisfies

$$\phi = \frac{c(q)}{M+B}. \tag{12.21}$$

The value of money decreases with the stock of money and bonds. The allocations and prices are identical to the ones in a pure monetary economy, where the stock of money in the pure monetary economy is equal to $M+B$. This implies that the composition of money and bonds, B/M, has no effect on output, prices, and the interest rate. In other words, open-market operations that consist in substituting money for bonds, or vice versa, are irrelevant because money and bonds are perfect substitutes.

12.2.2 Money and Illiquid Bonds

In an attempt to explain the rate-of-return dominance of bonds over money, we now introduce an admittedly arbitrary restriction on the use of bonds in bilateral meetings in the DM. We assume that a buyer holding a portfolio of b units of bonds can use only a fraction $g \in [0,1]$ of these bonds as a means of payment if he finds himself in a bilateral match. If $g=0$, then bonds are completely illiquid, and if $g=1$, then they are perfectly liquid. In practice, the illiquidity of bonds can result from legal restrictions, from the indivisibility of bonds, or from the presence of costs incurred to recognize bonds. While we provide foundations for this restriction in the next sections, for the time being we simply take it as given.

The value functions for buyers, $V^b(m,b)$ and $W^b(m,b)$, are given by (12.15) and (12.16), respectively, where $q(m,b)$ is now defined as follows: $q(m,b)=q^*$ if $\phi(m+gb)\geq c(q^*)$, and $q(m,b)=c^{-1}[\phi(m+gb)]$, otherwise. The buyer's portfolio problem is given by the solution to

$$\max_{m\geq 0, b\geq 0}\left\{-r\phi m - \phi b\left(\frac{r-r_b}{1+r_b}\right) + \sigma\left[u\left(q\left(m,b\right)\right) - c\left(q\left(m,b\right)\right)\right]\right\}. \tag{12.22}$$

The illiquidity of bonds affects the terms of trade in the DM by restricting the amount of wealth that buyers can transfer to sellers. The first-order conditions for problem (12.22), assuming an interior solution, are

$$\frac{u'(q)}{c'(q)} = 1 + \frac{r-r_b}{\sigma g(1+r_b)}, \tag{12.23}$$

$$\frac{u'(q)}{c'(q)} = 1 + \frac{r}{\sigma}. \tag{12.24}$$

Equating the right sides of (12.23) and (12.24), which implies that buyers are indifferent between holding money and bonds, we obtain

$$r_b = \frac{r(1-g)}{1+gr}. \tag{12.25}$$

The rate of return on bonds depends on the degree of their liquidity: if bonds are perfectly liquid, i.e., $g = 1$, then $r_b = 0$ and $\omega = \phi$. If bonds are partially illiquid, then the model is able to generate the rate of return dominance of bonds over money, i.e., if $g < 1$, then $r_b > 0$. In particular, if bonds are illiquid, i.e., if $g = 0$, then $r_b = r$. While the composition of money and bonds does not affect the interest rate or output, see equation (12.25), it does affect the value of money, since $\phi = c(q)/(M + gB)$.

12.3 Recognizability and Rate-of-Return Dominance

Thus far, we have shown that *interest-bearing* bonds and fiat money can coexist if there are restrictions on the use of bonds as means of payment. We have not, however, explained the origin of such restrictions. In earlier literatures, physical properties have been used to motivate why bonds are not as liquid as money. A classic motivation is that bonds are available only in large denominations and, therefore, are not useful as a means of payment for typical (small) transactions. We too will appeal to a physical property, and that is the recognizability or *counterfeitability* of a bond. The notion of imperfect recognizability of assets seems plausible at times when bonds are produced on paper, just like banknotes.

We suppose that fiat money cannot be counterfeited, or only at a very high cost, while bonds can. Agents can produce any amount of counterfeit government bonds in the CM by incurring a fixed real disutility cost of $\kappa > 0$. The technology to produce counterfeits in period t becomes obsolete in period $t+1$, so paying the cost only allows buyers to produce counterfeit assets for one period. In the DM, a seller is unable to recognize the authenticity of bonds. The government has a technology to detect and confiscate counterfeits: any counterfeit bonds produced in period t are detected and confiscated before agents enter the CM of period $t+1$. Consequently, the only outlet for a counterfeit bond produced in period t is in the DM of period $t+1$. To simplify the exposition, we assume that there are no search frictions in the DM, i.e., $\sigma = 1$, and the terms of trade, (q, d_m, d_b), are determined by a take-it-or-leave-it offer by the buyer, where q represents the output produced by the seller, d_m is the transfer of money, and d_b is the transfer of bonds—genuine or counterfeit—from the buyer to the seller.

The counterfeiting game is similar to the one analyzed for the recognizability of money in Chapter 5.3, except that it is bonds, and not money, that can be counterfeited. Following the same reasoning as in Chapter 5.3, the buyer's offer in the DM, (q, d_m, d_b), must satisfy a no-counterfeiting constraint,

$$-\omega d_b - \phi d_m + \beta u(q) \geq -\kappa - \phi d_m + \beta u(q). \tag{12.26}$$

The left side of (12.26) is the buyer's payoff if he does not produce counterfeits. The buyer accumulates d_b units of genuine bonds at the price ω, and d_m units of money at the price ϕ, and enjoys the utility of consuming q units of DM output. The right side of (12.26) is the payoff to a buyer who chooses to produce counterfeit bonds. By producing counterfeits, the buyer saves the cost of investing into bonds, ωd_b, but he incurs the fixed cost, κ, of producing counterfeits. From (12.26), a buyer in the CM at date $t-1$ who anticipates he will be making the offer (q, d_m, d_b) in the DM at date t will accumulate genuine bonds instead of counterfeits if

$$\omega d_b \leq \kappa. \tag{12.27}$$

Inequality (12.27) is an endogenous liquidity constraint that specifies an upper bound on the quantity of bonds that buyers can transfer in the DM. The real value of the newly-issued bonds cannot be greater than the fixed cost of producing counterfeits. If it is more costly to produce counterfeits, then the liquidity constraint (12.27) is relaxed.

Buyers in the CM choose a portfolio of money and genuine bonds in order to maximize their expected surplus in the subsequent DM, net of the cost of holding the assets. They anticipate that the offer they make in the DM must satisfy both the seller's participation constraint and the no-counterfeiting constraint, (12.27). Because of the opportunity cost of holding money, buyers do not hold more money than they intend to spend in the DM; hence, $d_m = m$. Moreover, if $\omega > \beta\phi$, then holding genuine bonds is costly, and buyers choose to hold the exact amount they spend in the DM; hence, $d_b = b$. If $\omega = \beta\phi$, then buyers can hold more bonds than they spend in the DM, i.e., $b \geq d_b$. Using these observations, the buyer's portfolio problem is

$$\max_{q, d_m, d_b, b} \left\{ -r\phi d_m - \left(\frac{\omega/\phi - \beta}{\beta} \right) \phi b + u(q) - \phi \left(d_m + d_b \right) \right\} \tag{12.28}$$

$$\text{s.t.} \quad -c(q) + \phi(d_m + d_b) \geq 0 \tag{12.29}$$

$$\omega d_b \leq \kappa, \tag{12.30}$$

$$d_b \leq b,$$

where b is the buyer's bond holdings. According to (12.28), the cost of holding money is $(1-\beta)/\beta = r$, the rate of time preference, while the cost of holding bonds is $(\omega/\phi - \beta)/\beta$. According to inequality (12.29), the offer must be acceptable to sellers, given that sellers interpret all offers satisfying (12.30) as coming from non-counterfeiting buyers.

The Lagrangian associated with this problem is

$$\max_{d_m, d_b, b} \left\{ -r\phi d_m - \left(\frac{\omega/\phi - \beta}{\beta} \right) \phi b + u \circ c^{-1} \left[\phi(d_m + d_b) \right] - \phi \left(d_m + d_b \right) \right.$$
$$\left. + \lambda \left(\frac{\phi \kappa}{\omega} - \phi d_b \right) + \mu \phi (b - d_b) \right\},$$

where λ is the Lagrange multiplier associated with the liquidity constraint and μ is the Lagrange multiplier associated with the feasibility constraint on the transfer of bonds. The first-order (necessary and sufficient) condition with respect to d_m determines the output traded in the DM:

$$\frac{u'(q)}{c'(q)} = 1 + r. \tag{12.31}$$

The first-order condition with respect to d_b is

$$\frac{u'(q)}{c'(q)} - 1 - \lambda - \mu \leq 0. \tag{12.32}$$

From (12.31) and (12.32), $r - \lambda - \mu \leq 0$. So $\lambda = \mu = 0$ cannot occur in equilibrium. If the solution is interior, then (12.31)-(12.32) imply that

$$r = \lambda + \mu. \tag{12.33}$$

It can easily be checked that $d_b = 0$ only if $\omega = \phi$, i.e., bonds don't pay interest, in which case buyers are indifferent between holding money and bonds so that (12.33) still holds at equality. Finally, the first-order condition with respect to b, assuming an interior solution (since in equilibrium the bonds market must clear) is

$$\mu = \frac{\omega/\phi - \beta}{\beta}. \tag{12.34}$$

Together with (12.33) this gives

$$\lambda = \frac{1-\omega/\phi}{\beta}. \tag{12.35}$$

The prices of money and bonds, ϕ and ω, are determined so as to clear the markets in the CM. Since the portfolio choice of the buyer need not necessarily be unique, we focus on symmetric equilibria. The demand for money is equal to d_m and, hence, the market-clearing condition for the money market is

$$d_m = M. \tag{12.36}$$

The market-clearing for the bond market requires that

$$b = B. \tag{12.37}$$

We consider the following three cases:

1. The no-counterfeiting constraint is not binding, $\lambda = 0$.
   The buyer's problem is, then, identical to problem (12.17), where there is no restriction on the use of bonds as means of payment. From (12.35), bonds and money are perfect substitutes, i.e., $\lambda = 0$ implies that $\omega = \phi$. From (12.34), $\mu = r > 0$ and hence $d_b = b = B$. From (12.29) at equality, $\phi(M+B) = c(q)$, meaning that the value of money decreases if the total stock of liquid assets, $M+B$, increases. The no-counterfeiting constraint (12.27) is not binding if

$$\frac{B}{M+B}c(q) \leq \kappa. \tag{12.38}$$

   If the cost of counterfeiting bonds is sufficiently high, then bonds are perfect substitutes for fiat money, and they do not pay interest. The condition (12.38) also depends on the relative supplies of money and bonds; the no-counterfeiting constraint will not bind, if bonds are not too abundant in supply, relative to fiat money. Figure 12.2 illustrates the relationship between the relative supply of bonds, $B/(M+B)$, and the relative price of bonds, ω/ϕ. When the relative supply of bonds is less than $\kappa/c(q)$, then bonds and money trade at the same price, i.e., $\omega/\phi = 1$.
2. The no-counterfeiting constraint binds, $\lambda > 0$, but buyers are not constrained by their bonds holdings, $\mu = 0$.
   Then, $\omega d_b = \kappa$. The output produced in the DM solves (12.31) and it is independent of the quantity of bonds that buyers can use as means of payment. From (12.34), $\omega = \beta\phi$. Buyers must be compensated for

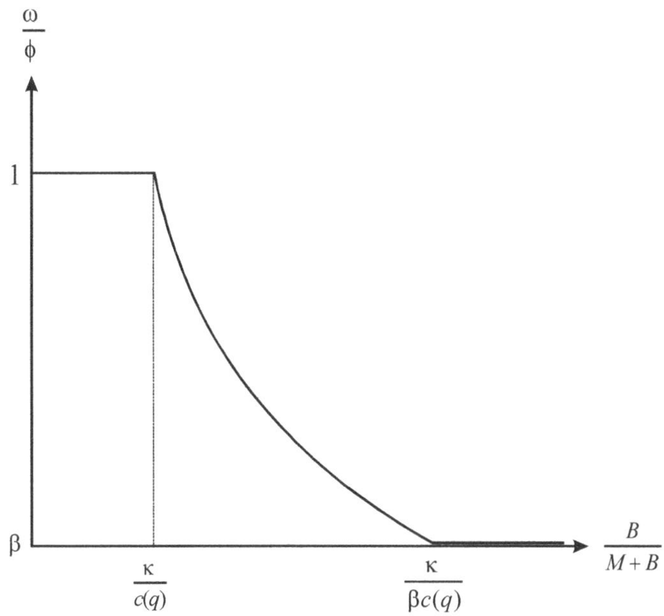

Figure 12.2
Price of bonds

their rate of time preference, and the interest rate paid by bonds is $r_b = \phi/\omega - 1 = \beta^{-1} - 1 = r$. In this case, bonds have a higher rate of return than fiat money. The no-counterfeiting constraint (12.27), along with (12.29), both at equality, implies that

$$\phi = \frac{c(q) - \kappa/\beta}{M}. \tag{12.39}$$

The value of money decreases with the cost of producing counterfeits. This implies that the value of fiat money depends not only on its own characteristics, but also on the physical properties of the competing asset. As the cost of producing counterfeit bonds increases, buyers can use a larger fraction of their bond holdings as means of payment, which reduces the value of fiat money. If counterfeited bonds can be produced at no cost, $\kappa = 0$, then, from (12.27), bonds cannot be used as means of payment and the value of money is the one that prevails in a pure monetary economy. When the no-counterfeiting constraint binds, the condition $d_b \leq B$ requires

$$\frac{\kappa}{\beta} \leq \frac{B}{M+B} c(q). \tag{12.40}$$

If the cost to produce counterfeits is sufficiently low, and if bonds are abundant relative to fiat money, then bonds are fully illiquid at the margin and they offer an interest rate equal to the rate of time preference. This result can be seen in Figure 12.2, where $\omega/\phi = \beta$ if the relative supply of bonds, $B/(B+M)$, exceeds $\kappa/[\beta c(q)]$.

3. The no-counterfeit constraint binds, $\lambda > 0$, and buyers are constrained by their bonds holdings, $\mu > 0$.
Conditions (12.27) and (12.29) at equality give

$$\frac{\omega}{\phi} = \frac{\kappa}{c(q)} \frac{M+B}{B}, \tag{12.41}$$

$$\phi = \frac{c(q)}{M+B}. \tag{12.42}$$

From (12.41), the relative price of bonds is a function of the relative supply of bonds, $B/(M+B)$. As the relative supply of bonds increases, the relative price of newly-issued bonds decreases, implying that the interest rate on bonds increases—see Figure 12.2. To understand this result notice that if the buyer receives an additional bond, under the previously prevailing market price of bonds, he cannot spend it in the DM. The price of bonds thus must decrease to reflect the fact that this illiquidity makes the no-counterfeiting constraint more strict. The price of bonds will decrease to the point where the no-counterfeiting constraint binds again. Intuitively, the stock of bonds is sufficiently large so that the no-counterfeiting constraint binds at $\omega = \phi$. In order to get buyers to hold all of the bonds, the price of bonds must fall so that $\omega < \phi$. Although it is less costly to use bonds for transactions in the DM than money, buyers do not demand any additional bonds since they cannot use them in the DM, as that would violate the no-counterfeiting constraint and they do not get compensated for their rate of time preference. From (12.34), the condition $d_b \leq B$ binds if $\mu = (\omega/\phi - \beta)/\beta > 0$, i.e., $\omega > \beta\phi$. From (12.35), $\lambda = (1 - \omega/\phi)\beta > 0$, i.e., $\phi > \omega$. From (12.41) these conditions can be reexpressed as

$$\frac{\kappa}{c(q)} < \frac{B}{M+B} < \frac{\kappa}{\beta c(q)}. \tag{12.43}$$

We can summarize our results using Figure 12.2. We can see that bonds will pay interest provided that the supply of bonds is sufficiently large, relative to the cost of producing counterfeits, i.e., when

$B/(M+B) > \kappa/c(q)$. Moreover, bonds are more likely to be sold at a discount if the cost to produce counterfeits is low (κ is low).

Although the conduct of monetary policy affects the interest rate, it has no effect on the real allocation and welfare. When bonds are relatively scarce, money and bonds are perfect substitutes and $\omega/\phi = 1$. Obviously, in that case a change in the composition of money and bonds is irrelevant for the allocation. When bonds are more abundant, the constraint on the transfer of bonds is binding. An open-market operation affects the price of bonds, but the output is still determined so that the marginal benefit of an additional unit of real balances is equal to its cost.

12.4 Pairwise Trade and Rate-of-Return Dominance

In the previous section, we used the recognizability property of money and bonds to provide an explanation for the rate-of-return dominance puzzle. In this section, we argue that even if fiat money and bonds have the same physical properties—both are divisible and recognizable—the model is still able to generate equilibria with outcomes that are consistent with the rate-of-return dominance puzzle. This explanation is based on the idea that social conventions can play a role in explaining the superior liquidity properties of some assets. For example, buyers may prefer to trade with money instead of bonds because the social convention dictates that they receive better terms of trade in the DM when using money as a means of payment. As in Section 12.1.2, we exploit the fact that the set of pairwise Pareto-efficient allocations in bilateral matches is large, and we construct a trading mechanism that generates asset prices that are consistent with those in Section 12.2.2, where there we simply *restricted* the use of bonds as means of payment.

We construct a mechanism where buyers get the same payoff they would in the economy with exogenous liquidity constraints described in Section 12.2.2. As in Section 12.1.2, the mechanism can be thought of as a two-step procedure. The first step determines the buyer's surplus in the DM, $U^b(m,b)$. It corresponds to what the buyer would obtain if he was making a take-or-leave-it offer, but was able to transfer at most a fraction g of his bond holdings to the seller, i.e.,

$$U^b(m,b) = \max_{q,d_m,d_b} \left[u(q) - \phi(d_m + d_b)\right] \tag{12.44}$$

$$\text{s.t.} \quad -c(q) + \phi\,(d_m + d_b) \geq 0 \tag{12.45}$$

$$d_m \in [0,m], \quad d_b \in [0,gb]. \tag{12.46}$$

The buyer's payoff is uniquely determined, and satisfies,

$$U^b(m,b) = \begin{cases} u(q^*) - c(q^*) \text{ if } \phi(m+gb) \geq c(q^*) \\ u \circ c^{-1}[\phi(m+gb)] - \phi(m+gb) \text{ otherwise.} \end{cases} \quad (12.47)$$

Once again, it is important to emphasize that this first step determines the surplus that the buyer will receive, and not the terms of trade that will be implemented. The latter is determined in the second step.

The second step of the pricing procedure determines the seller's surplus, $U^s(m,b)$, and the actual terms of trade, (q, d_m, d_b), as functions of the buyer's portfolio in the match, (m,b), and the first stage surplus, $U^b(m,b)$. By construction, the terms of trade are chosen so that the allocation is pairwise Pareto-efficient. The allocation solves the following problem,

$$U^s(m,b) = \max_{q,d_m,d_b} [-c(q) + \phi(d_m + d_b)] \quad (12.48)$$

$$\text{s.t. } u(q) - \phi(d_m + d_b) \geq U^b(m,b) \quad (12.49)$$

$$0 \leq d_m \leq m, \quad 0 \leq d_b \leq b. \quad (12.50)$$

It is important to emphasize that the use of bonds as means of payment is unrestricted; see condition (12.50). Moreover, $U^s(m,b) \geq 0$ since the allocation determined in the first step of the pricing procedure is still feasible in the second step. If $\phi(m+b) \geq u(q^*) - U^b(m,b)$, then the terms of trade in a bilateral meeting in the DM satisfy

$$q = q^* \quad (12.51)$$

$$\phi(d_m + d_b) = u(q^*) - U^b(m,b); \quad (12.52)$$

otherwise, the terms of trade are given by

$$q = u^{-1}\left[\phi(m+b) + U^b(m,b)\right] \quad (12.53)$$

$$(d_m, d_b) = (m,b). \quad (12.54)$$

The seller's payoff and output in the DM are uniquely determined. The composition of the payment between money and bonds is unique if the output produced in the DM is strictly less than the efficient level, q^*. If, however, $\phi(m+b) > u(q^*) - U^b(m,b)$, then there are a continuum of transfers (d_m, d_b) that can achieve (12.52). As before, the determination of the terms of trade is illustrated in Figure 12.1. The lower (dashed) frontier corresponds to the pair of surplus utility levels in the first step of the pricing protocol, where the buyer cannot spend more than a fraction g of his bond holdings. The upper frontier corresponds to the pair of utility levels in the second step of the procedure, where payments are unconstrained.

Given this pricing mechanism, the expected lifetime utility of the buyer holding portfolio (m, b) in the DM is given by

$$V^b(m,b) = \sigma U^b(m,b) + W^b(m,b). \tag{12.55}$$

With probability σ the buyer is matched, in which case he enjoys the surplus $U^b(m,b)$. If we substitute $V^b(m,b)$ from (12.55) into the buyer's portfolio problem, (12.16), and rearrange, the buyer's choice of portfolio is given by the solution to

$$\max_{m\geq 0, b\geq 0}\left\{-r\phi m - \left(\frac{r-r_b}{1+r_b}\right)\phi b + \sigma U^b(m,b)\right\},$$

where, as above, $(r-r_b)/(1+r_b)$ represents the cost of holding bonds. Note that this portfolio problem is identical to (12.22). Consequently, the buyer's demands for money and bonds are identical to the ones in the liquidity-constrained economy described in Section 12.2.2, and the rate of return of bonds is given by (12.25).

Our model with bilateral trades is able to generate a rate-of-return differential between money and risk-free bonds, even though there are no restriction on the use of bonds as means of payment. Fiat money and bonds share the same physical properties in terms of divisibility and recognizability, and the allocations in bilateral matches are pairwise Pareto-efficient. The explanation for the rate-of-return dominance is that different assets command different liquidity premia. Indeed, from (12.47), if the buyer holds an additional unit of money his surplus increases by $\phi\,[u'(q)/c'(q) - 1]$ whereas if he holds an additional unit of bonds, his surplus increases by $\phi g\,[u'(q)/c'(q) - 1]$. Hence, the marginal unit of bond commands a surplus which is g times the surplus that the marginal unit of money generates.

12.5 Segmented Markets, Open Market Operations, and Liquidity Traps

We now investigate the coexistence of money and bonds in the context of an economy with segmented markets. We assume that there are two types of sellers: type-1 sellers can only recognize and only accept money, while type-2 sellers accept both money and bonds. Similarly, there are two types of buyers, where type-1 buyers only meet type-1 sellers and type-2 buyers only meet type-2 sellers. One can interpret type-1 agents as being households and retail firms who adopt money as the only means of payments and type-2 agents as being (financial) firms that can use bonds as collateral to secure various obligations and money as a means of payments. There is a unit measure of each type of buyers and sellers. (So, the total measure of buyers is 2 and the total measure of sellers is 2.) The utility functions, $u_j(q_j)$ and $c_j(q_j)$, and the frequency of trade, σ_j, are indexed by agent type $j \in \{1,2\}$.

The money supply, M_t, and the supply of one-period nominal bonds, B_t, grow at the same constant rate γ, i.e., $M_{t+1}/M_t = B_{t+1}/B_t = \gamma$. As a result, B_t/M_t is constant over time. In the following we interpret an open-market operation as a one-time change in the ratio B/M. We denote T_t as the real transfer to type-1 or type-2 buyers in the CM. (In the absence of wealth effects, who receives the transfer of money is irrelevant.) The budget constraint of the government is

$$T_t + \phi_t B_t = \phi_t (M_{t+1} - M_t) + \omega_t B_{t+1},$$

where ω_t is the price (in terms of date-t CM good) of a government bond issued at date t and redeemed for one dollar in date $t+1$. The government finances the transfer to type-1 buyers, T_t, and the repayment of matured bonds, B_t, by printing money, $M_{t+1} - M_t$, and by issuing new bonds, B_{t+1}.

We distinguish between two nominal interest rates. The nominal interest rate on an *illiquid* bond, i, is given by the Fisher equation,

$$i = \frac{\gamma}{\beta} - 1,$$

where the real interest rate has to equal the rate of time preference, $\beta^{-1} - 1 = r$, for such a bond to be held. Consider next *liquid* bonds. One dollar in period t buys ϕ_t units of goods, and it takes ω_t units of goods to buy a bond that pays off a dollar in $t+1$. Hence, the dollar price of a one-period *liquid* bond is ω_t/ϕ_t and the nominal interest rate is

$$i_b = \frac{1 - \omega_t/\phi_t}{\omega_t/\phi_t} = \frac{\phi_t}{\omega_t} - 1. \tag{12.56}$$

We obtain the real interest rate of a one-period liquid bond from (12.56) and the Fisher equation, $1 + i_b = (\phi_t/\phi_{t+1})(1 + r_b)$, i.e., $r_b = \phi_{t+1}/\omega_t - 1$. Since the nominal interest rate on money is zero, any equilibrium must have $i_b \geq 0$ as otherwise bonds would not be held.

Let's first consider the CM problem of a type-1 buyer. His choice of real balances, z_1, is given by the solution to

$$\max_{z_1 \geq 0} \{-iz_1 + \sigma_1 [u_1(q_1) - c_1(q_1)]\},$$

where $c_1(q_1) = z_1$, since buyers makes take-it-or-leave-it offers. The first-order condition for z_1 is

$$i = \sigma_1 \left[\frac{u_1'(q_1)}{c_1'(q_1)} - 1\right]. \tag{12.57}$$

There is a unique q_1 that solves (12.57), where q_1 is a decreasing function of i.

Consider now the problem of a type-2 buyer in the CM of period t. The buyer chooses his real balances for period $t+1$, $z_2 = \phi_{t+1} m_2$, and real bond holdings, $z_b = \phi_{t+1} b$, by solving

$$\max_{z_2 \geq 0, z_b \geq 0} \{-iz_2 - \varrho z_b + \sigma_2 [u_2(q_2) - c_2(q_2)]\},$$

where

$$c_2(q_2) = \min\{z_2 + z_b, c_2(q^*)\}, \tag{12.58}$$

and the cost of holding bonds is

$$\varrho = \frac{\omega_t - \beta\phi_{t+1}}{\beta\phi_{t+1}}. \tag{12.59}$$

The cost of holding bonds is measured by the difference between the purchase price of a newly-issued bond and the discounted resale price of a matured bond, $\omega_t - \beta\phi_{t+1}$, expressed as a fraction of the discounted price of a matured bond. If we divide the numerator and denominator of (12.59) by ϕ_t and rearrange, the cost of holding bonds can be expressed as

$$\varrho = \frac{i - i_b}{1 + i_b}. \tag{12.60}$$

The cost of holding bonds is approximately equal to the difference between the nominal interest rate on illiquid bonds and the nominal interest rate on liquid bonds. Since $i_b \geq 0$, it is necessarily the case that $i \geq \varrho$. The first-order condition for z_b (assuming an interior solution, which will be guaranteed by market clearing) is

$$\varrho = \sigma_2 \left[\frac{u_2'(q_2)}{c_2'(q_2)} - 1\right]. \tag{12.61}$$

From (12.61) q_2 increases with i_b. The demand for real balances from type-2 agents, z_2, solves

$$i \geq \sigma_2 \left[\frac{u_2'(q_2)}{c_2'(q_2)} - 1 \right], \quad \text{"="} \text{ if } z_2 > 0. \tag{12.62}$$

It follows immediately from (12.61) and (12.62) that type-2 buyers hold both money and bonds only if they have the same holding costs, $\varrho = i$, which implies that $i_b = 0$. If bonds pay interest, $i_b > 0$, then bonds have a higher rate of return than money, and type-2 buyers find it optimal to hold only bonds.

The money supply is held by type-1 and type-2 buyers, which implies that

$$\phi_t M_t = z_1 + z_2. \tag{12.63}$$

Given the individual demands for real balances, z_1 and z_2, and the aggregate money supply, M_t, (12.63) pins down the value of money, $\phi_t = (z_1 + z_2)/M_t$. Similarly, the supply of liquid bonds is held by type-2 buyers, which gives

$$\phi_t B_t = z_b. \tag{12.64}$$

Given ϕ_t, (12.64) determines z_b, which from (12.61) gives the nominal interest on liquid bonds:

$$i_b = \frac{i - \sigma_2 \left[u_2'(q_2)/c_2'(q_2) - 1 \right]}{1 + \sigma_2 \left[u_2'(q_2)/c_2'(q_2) - 1 \right]}. \tag{12.65}$$

Finally, from (12.59), we can determine the (real) price of a bond, i.e.,

$$\begin{aligned} \omega_t &= \beta \phi_t (1 + \varrho)/\gamma \\ &= \frac{\beta}{\gamma} \phi_t \left\{ 1 + \sigma_2 \left[\frac{u_2'(q_2)}{c_2'(q_2)} - 1 \right] \right\}, \end{aligned} \tag{12.66}$$

where we used the expression for ϱ given by (12.61). We can now characterize the various equilibrium outcomes by distinguishing three regimes.

Equilibrium when bonds are plentiful: Rate-of-return dominance Suppose that bonds are abundant so that $q_2 = q_2^*$. This implies, from (12.61) that $i_b = i$. Hence, we have rate-of-return dominance for bonds (over money). A marginal unit of a bond has no liquidity value in DM matches since type-2 buyers are already consuming the efficient amount. Therefore, the price of liquid bonds is the same as the price of illiquid bonds. Hence, $\varrho = 0 < i$, which implies, from (12.62), that type-2 buyers do not hold money, $z_2 = 0$. From (12.58) and (12.64), $\phi B \geq c_2(q_2^*)$: the real supply of bonds must be sufficiently abundant to compensate type-2 sellers for their disutility of production. From (12.63) we have that $\phi M = z_1$; this condition along with $\phi B \geq c_2(q_2^*)$ can be rewritten as

$$\frac{B}{M} \geq \frac{c_2(q_2^*)}{c_1(q_1)}, \tag{12.67}$$

where q_1 is a decreasing function of i. Therefore, for a given i, bonds can be said to be abundant if the ratio of bonds to money exceeds some threshold that increases with i.

An open-market sale (purchase) of government bonds increases (decreases) the B/M ratio. If the supply of bonds is sufficiently large so as to satiate the liquidity needs of type-2 agents, then a small change in the ratio B/M has no effect on the equilibrium. As long as bonds are still abundant, type-2 DM output remains at q_2^* and $i_b = i$. Moreover, q_1, which is independent of B/M, is unaffected. Therefore, when bonds are abundant, a (small) open-market operation is ineffective, i.e., the open market operation does not affect interest rates or output levels.

Suppose now that the rate of growth of the money supply, γ, is increased (by a small amount), while keeping the B/M ratio constant. From the Fisher equation, $i = \gamma/\beta - 1$, increases which implies, from (12.57), that q_1 decreases. If the increase in γ is small, then condition (12.67) will continue to be satisfied and $q_2 = q_2^*$. Finally, (12.61) implies that $i_b = i$, which means that i_b increases but the real rate is unaffected, i.e., $r_b = \phi_{t+1}/\omega_t - 1 = 1/\beta - 1$ since $\omega_{t+1} = (1+\varrho)\beta\phi_{t+1}$.

Equilibrium when bonds are scarce: Rate-of-return dominance Consider now a regime where bonds are scarce in the sense that type-2 agents cannot trade the socially-efficient quantities, $q_2 < q_2^*$. From (12.61), this implies that $\varrho > 0$ and $i_b < i$. Liquid bonds are now costly to hold. Let's assume that $i_b > 0$. Since $\varrho < i$, (12.61) and (12.62) imply that type-2 buyers do not hold real balances, $z_2 = 0$. It follows from (12.58) and (12.63) that q_2 solves

$$c_2(q_2) = \phi B = c_1(q_1)\frac{B}{M}. \tag{12.68}$$

Since q_1 is a decreasing function of i, q_2 is a decreasing function of i and an increasing function of B/M. Figure 12.3 graphically characterizes the determination of the output levels. The equilibrium condition (12.57) is represented by the horizontal curve $Q1$, while the condition (12.68) is

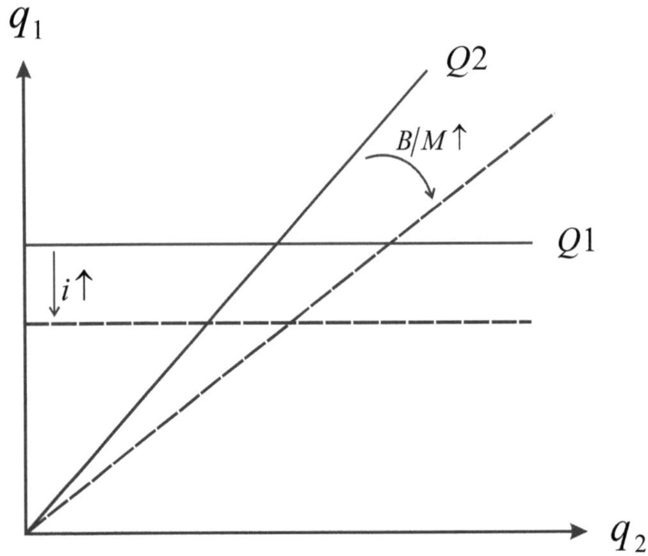

Figure 12.3
Output levels under segmented markets

represented by the upward-sloping curve Q2. An open-market sale of bonds increases q_2 and, from (12.61), raises the nominal interest rate on liquid bonds, i_b. Graphically, Q2 pivots clockwise from the origin. An increase in the money growth rate reduces output levels for all types of matches. Graphically, Q1 shifts downward.

The condition $i_b > 0$ holds provided that $q_2 > q_2^0$, where q_2^0 is the solution to (12.61) with $\varrho = i$ and $i_b = 0$. Hence, we obtain an equilibrium with $0 < i_b < i$ whenever

$$\frac{c_2(q_2^0)}{c_1(q_1)} < \frac{B}{M} < \frac{c_2(q_2^*)}{c_1(q_1)}. \tag{12.69}$$

A "liquidity trap" equilibrium: Rate-of-return equality Finally, we consider an equilibrium where type-2 agents are indifferent between holding money and bonds. From (12.61) and (12.62), this indifference requires that $i_b = 0$: bonds do not pay interest and have the same rate of return as fiat money. Hence, in this equilibrium q_2 and q_1 solve

$$i = \sigma_2\left[\frac{u_2'(q_2)}{c_2'(q_2)} - 1\right] = \sigma_1\left[\frac{u_1'(q_1)}{c_1'(q_1)} - 1\right]. \tag{12.70}$$

Given i, both q_1 and q_2 are uniquely determined. It should be noted that for all $i > 0$, $q_2 = q_2^0 < q^*$. Even though the nominal interest rate on *liquid* bonds is zero, the outcome is quite different from what is obtained under the Friedman rule, which generates a zero interest rate on *illiquid* bonds. Indeed, when $i_b = 0 < i$, holding liquidity is costly because the rate-of-return difference between liquid and illiquid assets is equal to $i > 0$. The Friedman rule, on the other hand, implies that holding any form of liquidity—money or bonds—is costless since the interest rate on illiquid bonds is zero. From (12.63), we have that

$$c(q_1) + c(q_2^0) = \phi(M + B). \tag{12.71}$$

A liquidity trap occurs when $\phi B \leq c(q_2)$, which from (12.71) can be reexpressed as

$$\frac{B}{M} \leq \frac{c_2(q_2^0)}{c_1(q_1)}. \tag{12.72}$$

From (12.70) a change in B/M does not affect q_1 and q_2 and hence, from (12.71), it does not affect aggregate real liquidity as measured by $\phi(M + B)$. An increase in the inflation rate reduces both q_1 and q_2, it reduces ϕ, and it increases i_b.

In Figure 12.4 we represent the typology of equilibria in $(i, B/M)$ space. We assume that type-1 and type-2 agents are identical in terms of fundamentals, i.e., they have the same preferences, $u_1(q) = u_2(q)$ and $c_1(q) = c_2(q)$, and the same meeting frequency, $\sigma_1 = \sigma_2$. It follows that $q_2^0 = q_1$ and, hence, liquidity trap equilibria occur when $B/M < 1$. We indicate the regimes with abundant bonds and liquidity traps by grey areas. In both of these regimes open-market operations are ineffective. When the ratio B/M is neither too high or too low, i.e., when $c_2(q_2^0)/c_1(q_1) = 1 < B/M < c_2(q_2^*)/c_1(q_1)$, the interest rate on a liquid bond is positive but less than the rate on an illiquid bond. In such equilibria a change in B/M affects the rate-of-return difference between liquid and illiquid bonds and, hence, the output traded in type-2 matches.

In Figure 12.5 we represent the output levels and the interest rate on liquid bonds when the supply of bonds varies, assuming that $i > 0$. For low values of B/M, the nominal interest rate, i_b, is zero and, assuming that the fundamentals for type-1 and type-2 agents are identical, output levels across matches are identical, $q_1 = q_2$, and less than q^*. As B/M increases above 1, i_b rises above zero. There is more liquidity in type-2 matches and, as result, q_2 increases while q_1 remains unchanged. If B/M increases above the threshold $c(q^*)/c(q_1)$, then $q_2 = q^*$ and $i_b = i$.

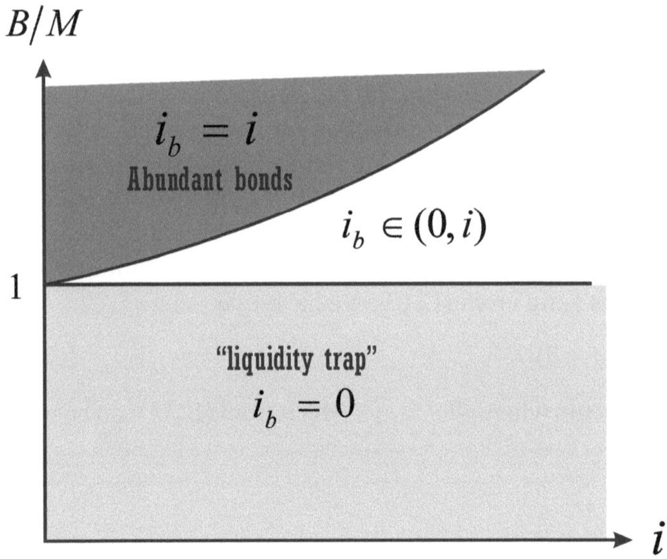

Figure 12.4
Typology of equilibria with segmented markets

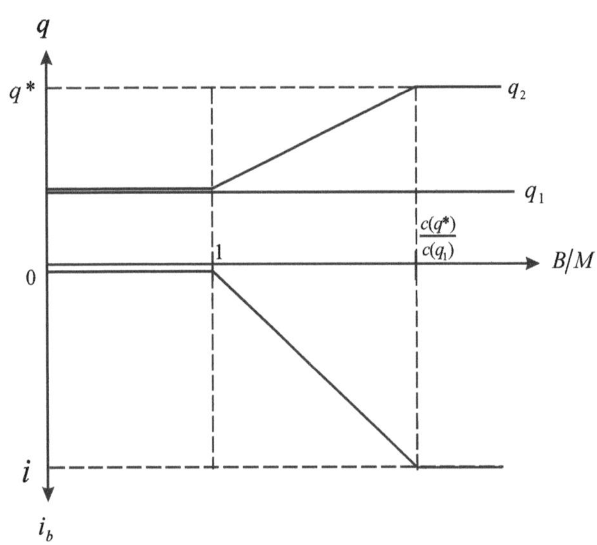

Figure 12.5
Output levels and interest rate

12.6 Further Readings

Two-country cash-in-advance models are described in Obstfeld and Rogoff (1996, Appendix 8A). The first search-theoretic environment with two currencies was proposed by Kiyotaki, Matsui, and Matsuyama (1993) and extended by Zhou (1997) to allow for currency exchange. These authors consider two-country economies and establish conditions on parameters for which one currency is used as an international currency. They also show that a uniform currency dominates in terms of welfare. Other models with multiple currencies include Head and Shi (2003), Camera and Winkler (2003), Craig and Waller (2004), Camera, Craig, and Waller (2004), Liu, Qing, and Shi (2006), Ales, Carapella, Maziero, and Weber (2008), and Fernández-Villaverde and Sanches (2016). The proposition about the indeterminacy of the exchange rate is established by Kareken and Wallace (1981) in the context of an overlapping-generations economy. Our method to determine the exchange rate adopts the trading mechanism proposed in Zhu and Wallace (2007). Another method uses legal restrictions as in Li and Wright (1998), Curtis and Waller (2000, 2003), Li (2002), Lotz and Rocheteau (2002), and Lotz (2004). Zhang (2014) and Gomis-Porqueras, Kam, and Waller (2014) break the curse of Kareken and Wallace by assuming that currencies can be counterfeited. Kocherlakota and Kruger (1999), Kocherlakota (2002), and Dong and Jiang (2010) discuss the usefulness of two currencies. Fernández-Villaverde and Sanches (2016) build a model of competition among privately issued fiat currencies. They show that there exists an equilibrium in which price stability is consistent with competing private monies, but also that there exists a continuum of equilibrium trajectories with the property that the value of private currencies monotonically converges to zero. Trejos and Wright (1996) and Craig and Waller (2000) survey the search literature on dual-currency payment systems.

The coexistence of money and bonds is discussed in Bryant and Wallace (1979), Wallace (1980), Aiyagari, Wallace, and Wright (1996), Kocherlakota (2003), Shi (2005, 2014), Zhu and Wallace (2007), Andolfatto (2011), and Lagos (2013). See also Rojas Breu (2016). Aiyagari, Wallace, and Wright (1996) introduce government agents to explain why government bonds are sold at a discount. Kocherlakota (2003), Boel and Camera (2006), and Shi (2008) show that illiquid bonds can raise society's welfare when agents are subject to idiosyncratic shocks. The approach in this chapter to explain the coexistence of money and interest-bearing bonds due to the counterfeitability of bonds is taken from Li and Rocheteau (2009) and Hu (2013).

The description of open-market operations in an economy with segmented markets is similar to Rocheteau, Wright, and Xiao (2015). Williamson (2012) developed a related model where the participation in the two types of markets (the one where only fiat money is accepted and the one where both money and bonds are accepted) is random but intermediaries offer some insurance contract. Rocheteau and Rodriguez (2014) study open-market operations in the context of a continuous-time economy with a frictional labor market where claims on Pissarides's firms are part of the effective liquidity of the economy, which provides an interest-rate channel through which monetary policy affects firm entry. Similarly, Herrenbrueck (2014) develop a model with money and (partially liquid) government bonds and physical capital to study quantitative easing and the liquidity channel of monetary policy.

13 Liquidity, Monetary Policy, and Asset Prices

In this chapter, we study the determination of asset prices in monetary economies. We first examine an environment with a fixed supply of real assets and no money. The real asset is like a Lucas (1978) tree that bears fruits (dividends) in the centralized market. It, or claims to it, can also serve as a medium of exchange in decentralized trades, just like fiat money did in earlier chapters. When the amount of real assets is relatively low, then there is a shortage of liquidity and the asset price is higher than its fundamental value defined as the discounted sum of its dividends. The difference between the asset price and the fundamental value represents the liquidity value (or premium) of the asset. This liquidity premium also depends on agents' liquidity needs, the sizes of the gains from trade that are exploitable with a medium of exchange, and the extent of trading frictions in asset markets. A prediction of the model is that asset prices tend to be higher in markets where it is easier to find a counterparty for a trade and where asset holders have a high bargaining power.

In order to study the effects of inflation on asset prices, we introduce fiat money in this environment. Fiat money can be valued if the supply of real assets is low relative to agents' liquidity needs and if the inflation rate is not too large. In a monetary equilibrium, the rate of return of the real asset is equal to the rate of return of fiat money. This rate-of-return equality implies a positive relationship between asset prices and inflation.

The rate-of-return equality breaks down if the real asset pays a risky dividend despite agents being risk neutral in terms of their CM consumption. The rate of return of the real asset rises above the rate of return of fiat money—it pays a risk premium—because its riskiness reduces its usefulness as a medium of exchange. More precisely, the risky asset pays a high dividend when liquidity needs are low (because liquid wealth is high), and a low dividend when liquidity needs are high (because liquid wealth is low). This feature makes the risky asset less attractive as a medium of exchange, compared to risk-free assets such as fiat money or government bonds. In contrast, in a perfect credit economy where agents can commit to repay their debt, the risk premium on the Lucas tree is zero. This suggests that liquidity considerations can provide an explanation for abnormally high-risk premia.

Finally, we explain rate-of-return differences across multiple assets (money and Lucas trees) as stemming from liquidity differences. Just as in Chapter 12, these liquidity differences can arise from bargaining conventions or social norms, which affect the terms at which these assets are traded. Similar to Section 8.4, where there is a cost to authenticate and accept private IOUs, the liquidity differences can also reflect that accepting an asset requires a costly ex ante investment. Finally, assets can have different liquidity premia because of informational asymmetries regarding the intrinsic value of those assets. We will show how this approach can generate a liquidity structure of asset yields and an endogenous three-tier categorization of assets: illiquid, partially liquid, and liquid assets. Assets across the categories differ in regard to their resalability, price, and sensitivity to shocks and policy interventions.

13.1 A Monetary Approach to Asset Prices

In this section, we provide a simple model, where monetary considerations matter for asset prices. Consider an economy that is identical to the one studied in previous chapters, where agents trade alternatively in centralized, CM, and decentralized markets, DM. See Figure 13.1. The economy is endowed with a single real asset, e.g., a tree, that is in fixed supply, $A > 0$, and can be traded in both markets. One can think of the bilateral matches in the DM as an over-the-counter asset market. We will elaborate on the description of an over-the-counter asset market in Chapters 15 and 16. At the beginning of each night period, before the CM opens, each unit of the real asset generates a dividend payoff equal to $\kappa > 0$ units of the general, or CM, good, e.g., the fruits of the tree. Consequently, the asset in the CM is traded ex-dividend: the dividend belongs to the agent who holds the asset at the beginning of the CM. Note that if κ approaches 0, then the asset becomes intrinsically useless, and is similar to fiat money. The price of the asset, measured in terms of the CM good in period t, is denoted by p_t. We consider stationary equilibria, where p_t is constant over time.

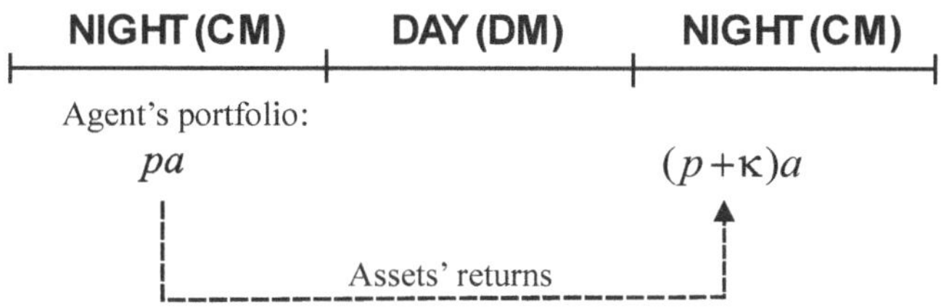

Figure 13.1
Timing and assets' returns

The value function of a buyer entering the CM holding a portfolio of a units of the real asset is,

$$W^b(a) = \max_{x,y,a'} \left\{ x - y + \beta V^b(a') \right\} \tag{13.1}$$

$$\text{s.t. } pa' + x = y + a(p+\kappa). \tag{13.2}$$

According to (13.1), in the CM the buyer chooses his net consumption of the CM good, $x - y$, and the quantity of assets, a', he will bring into the subsequent DM. Equation (13.2) is the buyer's budget constraint expressed in terms of the CM good. In the CM, one unit of the real asset generates κ units of the CM good and can be sold at the competitive price, p; see Figure 13.1. Substituting $x - y$ from the budget constraint into (13.1) and rearranging, we get

$$W^b(a) = a(p+\kappa) + \max_{a' \geq 0} \left\{ -pa' + \beta V^b(a') \right\}. \tag{13.3}$$

The CM value function is linear in the buyer's wealth, $a(p+\kappa)$, and his choice of asset holdings, a', is independent of the assets, a, he brought into the CM.

If a buyer is matched with a seller in the DM, he makes a take-it-or-leave-it offer (q, d_a), where d_a represents the assets that the buyer transfers to the seller in exchange for q units of the DM good. An alternative interpretation is that the asset is used as collateral for a secured loan, and it is only transferred to the seller if the buyer defaults in the CM. Suppose that the buyer brings a units of the asset to the DM. The value of these assets in the subsequent CM is $a(p+\kappa)$. If $a(p+\kappa) \geq c(q^*)$, then the buyer's offer is characterized by $q = q^*$ and $d_a = c(q^*)/(p+\kappa)$, where d_a is sufficient to compensate the seller for producing q^*. If, however, $a(p+\kappa) < c(q^*)$, then the buyer's offer is given by $q = c^{-1}[a(p+\kappa)]$ and $d_a = a$, i.e., the buyer spends all his asset holdings to get q.

Consequently, the value function of a buyer holding a units of asset at the beginning of the DM is,

$$V^b(a) = \sigma\left[u(q) + W^b(a - d_a)\right] + (1-\sigma)W^b(a)$$
$$= \sigma\left[u(q) - c(q)\right] + a(p+\kappa) + W^b(0), \tag{13.4}$$

where $(p+\kappa)d_a = c(q) = \min\left[c(q^*), a(p+\kappa)\right]$. In going from the first to the second equality, above, we used the fact that W^b is linear and that the buyer receives all of the surplus from exchange. According to (13.4), the buyer is in a DM match with probability σ, in which case he extracts the entire match surplus, $u(q) - c(q)$. Substituting $V^b(a)$ from (13.4) into (13.3), the buyer's choice of asset holdings solves

$$\max_{a\geq 0}\left\{-ar(p-p^*) + \sigma\left[u(q) - c(q)\right]\right\}, \tag{13.5}$$

where $p^* \equiv \kappa/r$ is the discounted sum of dividends, i.e., the price of the asset in a frictionless economy. The price p^* will be referred to as the fundamental value of the asset. The buyer maximizes his expected surplus in the DM, net of the cost of holding the real asset. The cost of holding the asset is the difference between the price of the asset and its fundamental value, times the discount rate, r.

The first-order condition from the buyer's problem (13.5), assuming an interior solution, is

$$-r(p-p^*) + \sigma\left[\frac{u'(q)}{c'(q)} - 1\right](p+\kappa) = 0. \tag{13.6}$$

If $p < p^*$, then (13.5) has no solution; in this situation there would be an infinite demand for the asset. If $p = p^*$, then, $u'(q) = c'(q)$, i.e., $q = q^*$. In this situation any $a \geq \frac{c(q^*)}{p^*+\kappa}$ is a solution to the buyer's problem; the buyer has sufficient wealth to purchase the efficient level of the DM good. Finally, if $p > p^*$, then there is a unique a that solves (13.6), and it is decreasing with p. To see this note that $r(p-p^*)/(p+\kappa)$ is increasing in p, and that $u'(q)/c'(q)$ is decreasing in p and a. Moreover, $p > p^*$ implies $\sigma\left[u'(q)/c'(q) - 1\right] > 0$, where $q = c^{-1}\left[a(p+\kappa)\right]$, and hence $q < q^*$. When the price of the asset is above its fundamental value, it is costly to accumulate the asset, and buyers will not hold enough of the asset to purchase the efficient level of output in the DM, q^*.

Since sellers do not obtain any surplus in the DM, their choice of asset holdings in the CM is simply given by $\max_{a\geq 0}\left\{-ar(p-p^*)\right\}$. Since, in any equilibrium, $p \geq p^*$, sellers will be willing to hold the asset only if its price is equal to its fundamental value and, at that price, they are indifferent between holding and not holding the asset. Because of this, and without loss in generality, we assume that, in equilibrium, sellers do not hold assets.

Let the set of all buyers be the interval $[0,1]$ and let $a(j)$ be buyer j's, $j \in [0,1]$, demand for the asset. The aggregate demand correspondence for the asset is

$$A^d(p) = \left\{ \int_{[0,1]} a(j)dj : a(j) \text{ is a solution to (13.5)} \right\}.$$

The clearing of the asset market requires

$$A \in A^d(p), \tag{13.7}$$

where A is the fixed supply of the real asset. The market-clearing price, denoted p^e, is illustrated in Figure 13.2. The aggregate demand correspondence, $A^d(p)$, is single-valued for all $p > p^*$—see equation (13.6)—and is equal to $[c(q^*)/(p^* + \kappa), +\infty)$ for $p = p^*$. Consequently, there is a unique $p \geq p^*$ that solves (13.7). Graphically, the solution is given by the intersection of the aggregate demand correspondence, $A^d(p)$, and the fixed supply of the real asset, A.

If $A \geq c(q^*)/(\kappa + p^*)$, then there is enough wealth in the economy, $(p^* + \kappa)A$, to purchase the efficient level of the DM good, q^*. In this case, the asset is priced at its fundamental value, $p = p^*$, because the expected increase in the buyer's surplus associated with an additional unit of the real asset at the beginning of the DM, $\sigma [u'(q)/c'(q) - 1](p + \kappa)$, is equal to zero. In other words, the asset has no liquidity value at the margin.

In contrast, if $A < c(q^*)/(\kappa + p^*)$, then there is insufficient wealth in the economy to purchase the efficient quantity of the DM good. Here, the expected increase in the buyer's surplus associated with an additional unit of the real asset is strictly positive, which implies that the price of the real asset, p, is above its fundamental value, p^*; see equation (13.6). Buyers are now willing to pay more than the fundamental value for the asset because an additional unit of the asset provides liquidity in the DM. This difference between p and p^* would be viewed as an anomaly in a frictionless economy since in that economy an additional unit of the asset would not provide any additional surplus in the DM.

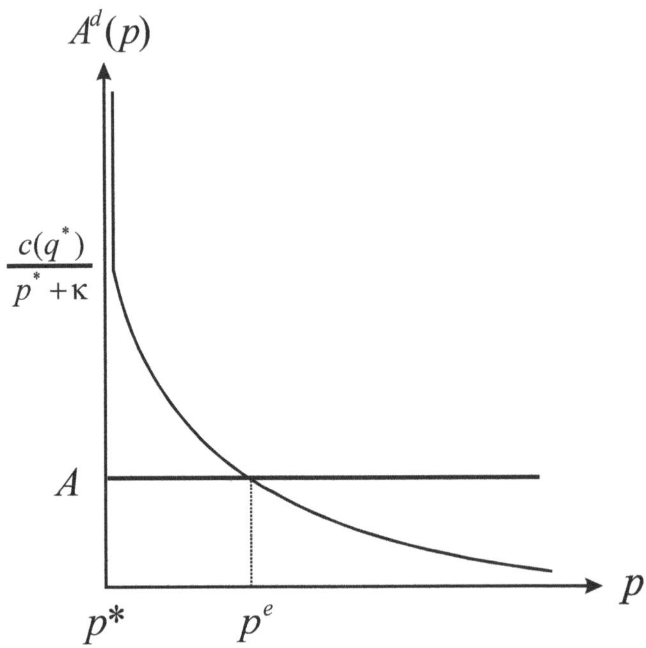

Figure 13.2
Equilibrium of the asset market

This simple model has predictions regarding the effect that trading frictions and the supply of the asset has on the asset price. The expression for the asset price, (13.6), can be rewritten as

$$p = p^* + \sigma \left[\frac{u'(q)}{c'(q)} - 1 \right] \left(\frac{p+\kappa}{r} \right), \tag{13.8}$$

where $c(q) = \min [c(q^*), A(p+\kappa)]$. The first term on the right side of (13.8) represents the fundamental value of the asset and the second term is the liquidity value of the asset, i.e., the increase in the expected surplus of the buyer in the DM from holding an additional unit of asset. Assuming that $q < q^*$, as the trading friction σ is reduced, the asset price increases, i.e., $\partial p/\partial \sigma > 0$, since the asset can be used more often as means of payment and, as a consequence, its liquidity value goes up. As well, as agents become more impatient, the asset price falls, i.e., $\partial p/\partial r < 0$. In this case, agents discount both the dividend of the asset and its future liquidity returns more heavily, which results in lower asset values. Finally, as κ tends to zero, the asset becomes like fiat money since $p^* \to 0$, and, from (13.6), its price is given by the solution to

$$-r+\sigma\left[\frac{u'(q)}{c'(q)}-1\right]=0.$$

Perhaps, not surprisingly, as the value of the dividend approaches zero, the price of the asset approaches the value of fiat money that was derived in Chapter 3.1, i.e., see equation (3.14) when $\phi_{t+1}=\phi_t$.

13.2 Monetary Policy and Asset Prices

What is the relationship between monetary policy and asset prices? Does monetary policy affect asset prices, and what is the optimal monetary policy when asset prices respond to a change in the money growth rate? We use the model developed in the previous section to answer these questions. In order to talk about monetary policy, we must reintroduce fiat money into our economy. We assume that the stock of money grows at the constant rate, $\gamma=M_{t+1}/M_t$, and is injected or withdrawn via lump-sum transfers to buyers in the CM. We focus on stationary monetary equilibria, where real balances are constant over time, i.e., $\phi_{t+1}M_{t+1}=\phi_t M_t$, and ϕ_t is the amount of the CM good that one unit of fiat money can buy in period t.

The value function of a buyer holding portfolio (a,z) at the beginning of the CM, where a represents the buyer's holdings of the real asset and $z=\phi_t m$ represents his holding of *real* money balances, generalizes (13.3) in the obvious way. This value function, $W^b(a,z)$, is given by

$$W^b(a,z)=a(p+\kappa)+z+T+\max_{a'\geq 0,z'\geq 0}\left\{-pa'-\gamma z'+\beta V^b\left(a',z'\right)\right\},\quad(13.9)$$

where the lump-sum transfer or tax received by buyers, $T\equiv\phi_t(M_{t+1}-M_t)$, is expressed in terms of the CM good. As above, the buyer's CM value function is linear in his wealth, which now includes his real balance holdings. Note that if the buyer wishes to hold $z'=\phi_{t+1}m'$ units of real balances in period $t+1$, he must produce $\phi_t m'=\phi_t/\phi_{t+1}z'=\gamma z'$ in period t; see Figure 13.3.

Since the terms of trade in the DM are determined by the buyer making a take-it-or-leave-it offer to the seller, the value function for a buyer holding portfolio (a,z) at the beginning of the period, which generalizes (13.4), is given by

$$V^b\left(a,z\right)=\sigma\left[u(q)-c(q)\right]+a(p+\kappa)+z+W^b(0,0),\quad(13.10)$$

where $c(q)=\min\left[c(q^*),a(p+\kappa)+z\right]$.

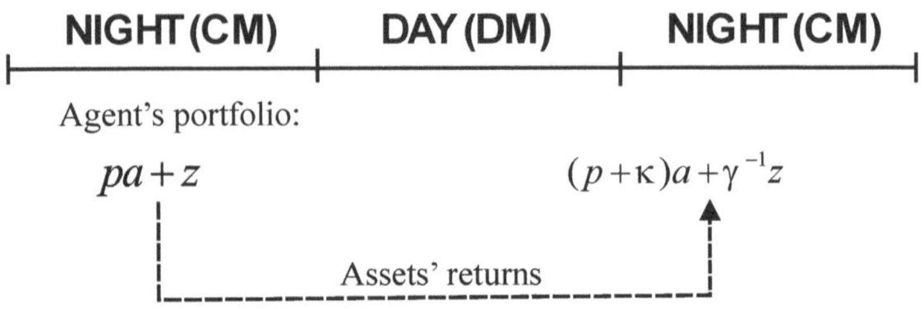

Figure 13.3
Timing and assets' returns

The buyer's portfolio problem—which is described by the last term in (13.9)—can be reexpressed by substituting the expression for $V^b(a,z)$ given by (13.10) into (13.9), and simplifying, i.e.,

$$\max_{a\geq 0, z\geq 0} \{-iz - ar(p-p^*) + \sigma[u(q) - c(q)]\}, \tag{13.11}$$

where $i = (\gamma - \beta)/\beta$ is the cost of holding real balances. Note that this problem generalizes (13.5) in the previous section. The buyer chooses his portfolio, composed of money and the real asset, in order to maximize his expected surplus in a bilateral match, net of the cost of holding the real asset and money.

In order to characterize the buyer's asset demand correspondence, it will be convenient to define $\ell \equiv z + a(p+\kappa)$ as the buyer's *liquid* wealth that is available to purchase the DM good in a bilateral match. The buyer's portfolio problem, (13.11), can be, equivalently, written as

$$\max_{a,\ell} \{-i\ell - [(r-i)p - (1+i)\kappa]a + \sigma[u(q) - c(q)]\}, \tag{13.12}$$

$$\text{s.t. } a(p+\kappa) \leq \ell \tag{13.13}$$

where $c(q) = \min[c(q^*), \ell]$. The squared bracketed term that premultiplies a in problem (13.12) has an interesting and intuitive interpretation. This term can be rearranged to read as $-[r(p-p^*) - i(\kappa+p)]$. The first term in this difference, $r(p-p^*)$, is the cost of holding a unit of the real asset between one CM and the next, and the second term is the cost of holding the equivalent amount of real balances. Hence, $r(p-p^*) - i(\kappa+p)$ represents the relative cost of holding wealth in the real asset compared to holding it in fiat money.

There are three cases to consider.

1. $r(p-p^*) < i(\kappa+p)$: Money is more costly to hold than the real asset. The constraint $a(p+\kappa) \leq \ell$ will bind, which implies that $z = 0$. If we substitute $z = 0$ into (13.11), then the buyer's problem is exactly the

same as problem (13.5), and, therefore, his choice of asset holdings, a, is given by (13.6).

2. $r(p - p^*) > i(\kappa + p)$: The real asset is more costly to hold than money. Buyers will demand only real balances and $a = 0$.

3. $r(p - p^*) = i(\kappa + p)$: Money and the real asset are equally costly to hold, which implies that the buyer is indifferent between holding the real asset and fiat money. In this case, the value of the portfolio, ℓ, solves the first-order condition,

$$i = \sigma \left[\frac{u' \circ c^{-1}(\ell)}{c' \circ c^{-1}(\ell)} - 1 \right], \tag{13.14}$$

and the asset price is

$$p = \frac{(1+i)\kappa}{r - i}. \tag{13.15}$$

We denote $\ell(i)$ as the solution to (13.14); $\ell(i)$ is the demand for liquid assets, as a function of the nominal interest rate.

The aggregate asset demand correspondence, $A^d(p)$, is illustrated in Figure 13.4. The correspondence is constructed assuming that $i > 0$. If $p = p^*$, then, necessarily, $z = 0$—since the real asset is costless to hold but money is not—and problem (13.11) or, equivalently, (13.12) simplifies to $\max_a \sigma\left[u(q) - c(q)\right]$, which implies that any $a \geq c(q^*)/(p^* + \kappa)$ is a solution and that $q = q^*$. If $p \in (p^*, (1+i)\kappa/(r-i))$, then $z = 0$, and a is the unique solution to (13.6), and is decreasing in p. In this situation, although the real asset is costly to hold, money is even more costly. This part of the asset demand correspondence is identical to the one in Figure 13.2. If $p = (1+i)\kappa/(r-i)$, then any $a \in [0, \ell(i)/(p+\kappa)]$ is a solution to (13.12) since the buyer is indifferent between holding the real asset and money, i.e., the real asset and money are equally costly to hold. In this case, the real value of the buyer's portfolio, $\ell(i)$, is given by solution to (13.14). Finally, if $p > (1+i)\kappa/(r-i)$, then it is cheaper to hold money than the real asset and, as a result, $a = 0$.

Market clearing in the asset market requires that $A \in A^d(p)$. The asset price is uniquely determined by the intersection of the aggregate demand correspondence, $A^d(p)$, and the horizontal supply, A; see Figure 13.4. A monetary equilibrium exists if $A < r - i/[\kappa(1+r)]\ell(i)$. A necessary, but not sufficient, condition for money to be valued is that the stock of real assets is less than $c(q^*)/(p^* + \kappa))$ or, in other words, the supply of the real asset must not be large enough to allow agents to trade the efficient quantity in the DM. In a monetary equilibrium, $r - i > 0$, which implies that the inflation rate must be negative or that,

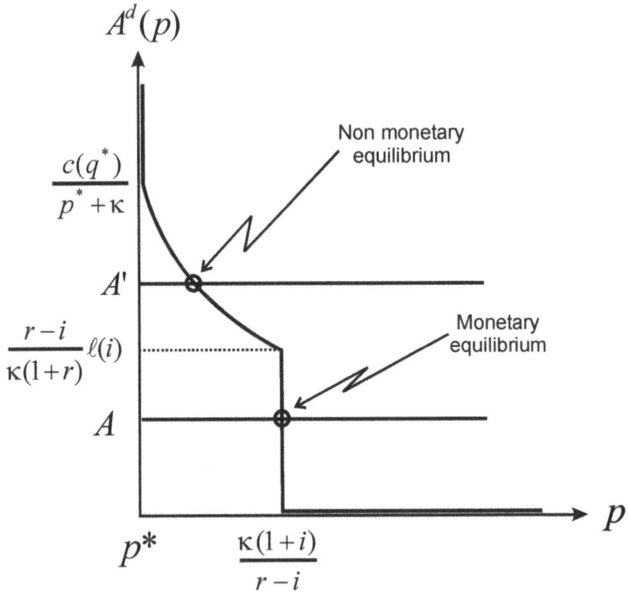

Figure 13.4
Fiat money and the demand for assets

equivalently, the money supply must contract, i.e., $\gamma < 1$. Note that in Figure 13.4, if the supply of assets is A', then the inflation rate is too large for fiat money to be valued.

In a monetary equilibrium, the price of the real asset is increasing with the rate of inflation, see (13.15), where $\partial p/\partial i > 0$. Graphically, as i increases the vertical portion of the aggregate demand curve $A^d(p)$ moves to the right. As inflation increases, it becomes more costly to hold real balances, and buyers demand a higher quantity of real assets to be used as means of payment, which, in turn, drives asset prices up. Notice the difference here—where the asset supply is fixed—compared to the analysis in Chapter 11.1—where capital goods could be produced one-for-one from the CM good. In that case, an increase in inflation did not affect the price of capital—which was always equal to one—but, instead, resulted in buyers over accumulating capital.

The gross rate of return of the real asset is $R_a = (p+\kappa)/p = 1 + \kappa/p$. In a monetary equilibrium, the rate of return of the real asset can, from (13.15), be expressed as

$$R_a = \frac{1+r}{1+i} = \gamma^{-1}, \tag{13.16}$$

i.e., the rate of return of the real asset equals the rate of return of fiat money. We have seen this principle of the equality of rates of return on assets earlier in Chapter 11.1. Since $R_a = (p+\kappa)/p > 1$, then the gross growth rate of money must be less than one, $\gamma < 1$. This is an alternative way to see that in order for money to be valued, the money supply must contract, i.e., there must be a deflation.

In a monetary equilibrium, the optimal monetary policy will drive the cost of holding real balances, i, to zero. From (13.14), as i tends to zero, the buyer's liquid wealth, ℓ, tends to $c(q^*)$, and the output traded in bilateral matches approaches its efficient level, q^*. In this situation, the asset price converges to its fundamental value, see (13.15), since real balances are costless to hold and, as a result, at the margin, the real asset does not provide any additional liquidity. When the asset price converges to its fundamental value, the gross rate of return on all assets will converge to one plus the rate of time preference, $1+r$.

13.3 Risk and Liquidity

So far, we have assumed that the real asset is risk-free in the sense that it provides a constant flow of dividend in every period. Given agents' quasi-linear preferences, the riskiness of the asset is irrelevant for asset pricing provided that one of the following two conditions is valid: (i) the real asset plays no role as a means of payment, or (ii) the value of the dividend is not realized until after the DM closes. In this section we assume that neither condition (i) nor (ii) hold, i.e., the real asset is useful for facilitating exchange and the dividend realization is known at the time of bilateral exchange. These assumptions allow us to uncover a new channel through which the riskiness of an asset affects its liquidity and price.

We assume that the dividend of the real asset follows a simple stochastic process: with probability π_H, the dividend payment is high, κ_H , and with complementary probability $\pi_L \equiv 1-\pi_H$, it is low, κ_L, where $\kappa_L < \kappa_H$. The dividend shocks are independent across time. We denote the expected dividend by $\bar{\kappa} = \pi_H\kappa_H + \pi_L\kappa_L$ and assume that buyers and sellers learn the dividend realization at the beginning of the period, before they are matched in the DM. The timing and information structure are illustrated in Figure 13.5.

At the beginning of the CM, the value function of a buyer is similar to (13.9), i.e., $W^b(a,z,\kappa) = a(p+\kappa) + z + W^b(0,0,\kappa)$. We introduce κ as an explicit argument since it is no longer constant over time.

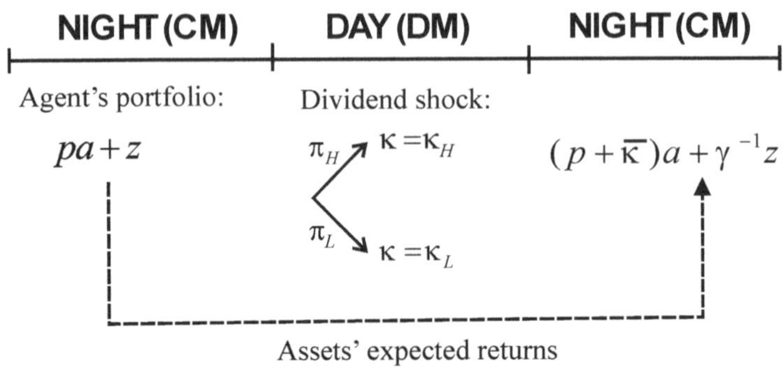

Figure 13.5
Timing and assets' returns

The terms of trade in a bilateral match in the DM are determined by a take-it-or-leave-it offer by the buyer to the seller. The output traded solves $c(q_H) = \min[c(q^*), a(p+\kappa_H)+z]$ in the high-dividend state and $c(q_L) = \min[c(q^*), a(p+\kappa_L)+z]$ in the low-dividend state. The value function for a buyer holding portfolio (a,z) at the beginning of the DM, *before the dividend realization is known*, $V^b(a,z)$, is given by

$$\begin{aligned} V^b(a,z) &= \sigma\pi_H\left[u(q_H) + W^b(a-d_{a,H}, z-d_{z,H}, \kappa_H)\right] + \\ &\quad \sigma\pi_L\left[u(q_L) + W^b(a-d_{a,L}, z-d_{z,L}, \kappa_L)\right] + \\ &\quad (1-\sigma)\left[\pi_H W^b(a,z,\kappa_H) + \pi_L W^b(a,z,\kappa_L)\right] \\ &= \sigma\left\{\pi_H[u(q_H)-c(q_H)] + \pi_L[u(q_L)-c(q_L)]\right\} + \\ &\quad a(p+\bar{\kappa}) + z + \pi_H W^b(0,0,\kappa_H) + \pi_L W^b(0,0,\kappa_L), \end{aligned} \tag{13.17}$$

where $(d_{a,H}, d_{a,L}, d_{z,H}, d_{z,L})$ is a vector of asset transfers in the two dividend states. Going from the first equality to the second equality in (13.17) we have used the linearity of W^b. According to (13.17), independent of the realization of the dividend, the buyer always extracts the entire surplus of the match. With probability π_H, the realization of the dividend is high and agents trade q_H in the DM, and with probability π_L, the dividend is low and agents trade q_L. If $a(p+\kappa_L)+z < c(q^*)$, then the quantity traded in the low dividend state is less than that traded in the high-dividend state, i.e., $q_L < q_H$.

If we substitute $V^b(a,z)$ from (13.17) into (13.9), then the buyer's portfolio problem in the CM can be expressed as,

$$\max_{a\geq 0, z\geq 0}\left\{-iz - ar(p-p^*) + \sigma\left\{\pi_H[u(q_H)-c(q_H)] + \pi_L[u(q_L)-c(q_L)]\right\}\right\},$$

where now $p^* = \bar{\kappa}/r$. The first-order (necessary and sufficient) conditions for this problem are

$$-i+\sigma\left\{\pi_H\left[\frac{u'(q_H)}{c'(q_H)}-1\right]+\pi_L\left[\frac{u'(q_L)}{c'(q_L)}-1\right]\right\}\leq 0, \tag{13.18}$$

$$-r(p-p^*)+\sigma\left\{\pi_H(p+\kappa_H)\left[\frac{u'(q_H)}{c'(q_H)}-1\right]+\pi_L(p+\kappa_L)\left[\frac{u'(q_L)}{c'(q_L)}-1\right]\right\}\leq 0, \tag{13.19}$$

where (13.18) holds at equality if $z>0$, and (13.19) holds at equality if $a>0$. The terms $(p+\kappa_H)[u'(q_H)/c'(q_H)-1]$ and $(p+\kappa_L)[u'(q_L)/c'(q_L)-1]$ represent the liquidity values of having an additional unit of the real asset in the high and low dividend states, respectively, for a buyer in a trade match. According to (13.18) and (13.19), the buyer chooses his portfolio so as to equalize the cost of holding an asset with its expected liquidity return in the DM.

In any equilibrium, the fixed stock of real assets must be held and, therefore, (13.19) must hold at equality. The asset price, p, satisfies

$$p=p^*+\frac{\sigma}{r}\left\{\pi_H(p+\kappa_H)\left[\frac{u'(q_H)}{c'(q_H)}-1\right]+\pi_L(p+\kappa_L)\left[\frac{u'(q_L)}{c'(q_L)}-1\right]\right\}. \tag{13.20}$$

The first component on the right side of (13.20) is the fundamental value of the asset, while the second component is the expected discounted liquidity value of the asset in the DM.

We first consider the case where the efficient allocation, $q_H=q_L=q^*$, can be achieved. From the pricing equation (13.20), this implies that $p=p^*$ and, from (13.18), fiat money will not be valued for any $i>0$. A sufficient condition for q^* to be implementable in all states is that the real value of the stock of assets in the low-dividend state is large enough to compensate sellers for their costs of producing q^*, i.e.,

$$A(p^*+\kappa_L)\geq c(q^*). \tag{13.21}$$

If (13.21) holds, then the efficient allocation can be implemented as an equilibrium without fiat money.

If condition (13.21) fails to hold and $i>0$, then $q_L<q^*$, and the price of the asset rises above its fundamental value. Provided that i is sufficiently small, fiat money can have a strictly positive value. In any monetary equilibrium (13.18) and (13.19) imply that $i\leq(p-p^*)/(p+\kappa_L)r<r$.

To see this, divide (13.19) by $(p+\kappa_L)$ to obtain

$$-r\left(\frac{p-p^*}{p+\kappa_L}\right)+\sigma\left\{\pi_H\left(\frac{p+\kappa_H}{p+\kappa_L}\right)\left[\frac{u'(q_H)}{c'(q_H)}-1\right]+\pi_L\left[\frac{u'(q_L)}{c'(q_L)}-1\right]\right\}\le 0.$$

Since $(p+\kappa_H)/(p+\kappa_L)>1$ and $u'(q_H)/c'(q_H)-1\ge 0$, (13.18) and (13.19) will hold at equality only if $r(p-p^*)/(p+\kappa_L)\ge i$. Hence, as in the previous section, any monetary equilibrium will be characterized by a negative inflation rate.

In order to understand the pricing relationship between fiat money and the real asset, it is useful to introduce the covariance of the value of the real asset at the beginning of the period, $p+\kappa$, and the marginal return of wealth in the DM, $u'(q)/c'(q)-1$. Denote this covariance as ρ, where, by definition,

$$\rho=\pi_H(\kappa_H-\bar{\kappa})\left[\frac{u'(q_H)}{c'(q_H)}-\frac{\overline{u'}}{c'}\right]+\pi_L(\kappa_L-\bar{\kappa})\left[\frac{u'(q_L)}{c'(q_L)}-\frac{\overline{u'}}{c'}\right], \tag{13.22}$$

and $\overline{u'}/c'=\pi_H u'(q_H)/c'(q_H)+\pi_L u'(q_L)/c'(q_L)$. Using (13.18) and (13.22), the price for the real asset, p, given by (13.20), can be expressed simply as

$$p=\frac{(1+i)\bar{\kappa}+\sigma\rho}{r-i}, \tag{13.23}$$

where the derivation of this asset price can be found in the Appendix.

For the derivation of this asset price, see the Appendix. Comparing this expression for the price of the real asset with the expression (13.15)—where there was no information revealed regarding the dividend payoff before the opening of the CM—we see that the former has an additional component, $\sigma\rho/(r-i)$, which is proportional to the covariance between the risky dividend and the marginal utility of wealth in the DM. To determine the sign of the covariance term, note that $\pi_H(\kappa_H-\bar{\kappa})+\pi_L(\kappa_L-\bar{\kappa})=0$ and, since $q_H>q_L$, $u'(q_H)/c'(q_H)<u'(q_L)/c'(q_L)$. These two observations imply that

$$\begin{aligned}\rho&=\pi_H(\kappa_H-\bar{\kappa})\left[\frac{u'(q_H)}{c'(q_H)}-\frac{\overline{u'}}{c'}\right]+\pi_L(\kappa_L-\bar{\kappa})\left[\frac{u'(q_L)}{c'(q_L)}-\frac{\overline{u'}}{c'}\right]\\&=\pi_H(\kappa_H-\bar{\kappa})\left(\frac{u'(q_H)}{c'(q_H)}-\frac{u'(q_L)}{c'(q_L)}\right)<0.\end{aligned}$$

We now discuss the effect that this new component has on the asset pricing. Let's first compare the (gross) rates of return on money, γ^{-1}, with the return of the real asset, $R_a=(p+\bar{\kappa})/p$. The rate of return on the real asset, using equation (13.23), can be expressed as

$$R_a = \frac{(1+r)\bar{\kappa}+\sigma\rho}{(1+i)\bar{\kappa}+\sigma\rho} = \gamma^{-1}\left(1+\frac{(\gamma-1)}{\bar{\kappa}(1+i)+\sigma\rho}\sigma\rho\right), \tag{13.24}$$

since $(1+r)=(1+i)\gamma^{-1}$. From (13.23), in any monetary equilibrium $r>i$, which implies $\gamma<1$. Since $(\gamma-1)\sigma/[\bar{\kappa}(1+i)+\sigma\rho]<0$, the rate of return differential $R_a-\gamma^{-1}$ has the opposite sign of ρ. Since the covariance, ρ, is negative, from (13.24),

$$R_a > \gamma^{-1}. \tag{13.25}$$

Therefore, the risk-free real asset with a dividend payment equal to $\bar{\kappa}$, will be more expensive than a risky real asset that delivers an expected dividend of $\bar{\kappa}$, see equation (13.23).

When real assets can be used for transactions purposes and agents know the dividend realization in the DM matches, the rate-of-return-equality principle no longer holds. A rate-of-return differential arises because the real asset is used as a means of payment in the DM and individuals are risk-averse. The real asset yields a high dividend in matches where the marginal value of wealth is low, and a low dividend in matches where the marginal value of wealth is high. In contrast, the rate of return of money is constant and uncorrelated with the marginal utility of wealth in the DM. Consequently, money has a higher liquidity return than the real asset, and hence a lower rate of return than that of the real asset.

Finally, as $i\to 0$, $q_H\to q^*$ and $q_L\to q^*$, which implies that $\rho\to 0$ and $R_a=\gamma^{-1}=\beta^{-1}$. In words, at the Friedman rule, fiat money and the real asset will have the same rate of return equal to the (gross) rate of time preference, and the first-best allocation is obtained.

13.4 The Liquidity Structure of Assets' Yields

In this section, we examine the structure of assets' yields and how it is affected by monetary policy. We extend the model in Section 13.2 to allow for a finite number $K\geq 1$ of infinitely-lived real assets indexed by $k\in\{1,...,K\}$. Denote $A_k>0$ as the fixed stock of asset $k\in\{1,...,K\}$, κ_k as its expected dividend in terms of the CM good, and p_k as its price in terms of the CM good. In contrast to Section 13.3, we assume that agents do not learn the dividend realization (if the dividend is risky) until the beginning of the CM. Consequently, the terms at which the asset is traded in the DM will only depend on its expected dividend, κ_k.

In order to generate rate-of-return differentials, we now assume that a buyer in a bilateral match can only transfer a fraction $\nu_k \in [0,1]$ of his holdings of asset k to the seller: Asset k is said to be partially illiquid if $0 < \nu_k < 1$, and is more liquid than asset k' if $\nu_k > \nu_{k'}$. The parameters ν_k can be interpreted as capturing either institutional constraints or informational frictions that make some assets harder to liquidate than others. In the subsequent section, we will deal with these liquidity constraints more formally (see also Chapters 12.3 and 12.4).

Consider a buyer in a bilateral match in the DM with a portfolio $(\{a_k\}_{k=1}^K, z)$, where a_k is the quantity of the kth real asset and z is real balances. We assume that the terms of trade are determined by the buyer making a take-it-or-leave-it offer, $(q, d_z, \{d_k\}_{k=1}^K)$, to the seller, where q is the buyer's consumption of the DM good, d_z is the transfer of real balances, and d_k is the transfer of the asset k. The buyer's surplus from a match in the DM is given by

$$U^b = \max_{q, d_z, \{d_k\}} \left[u(q) - d_z - \sum_{k=1}^{K} d_k(p_k + \kappa_k) \right] \tag{13.26}$$

$$\text{s.t.} \quad -c(q) + d_z + \sum_{k=1}^{K} d_k(p_k + \kappa_k) \geq 0 \tag{13.27}$$

$$d_z \leq z, \quad d_k \leq \nu_k a_k. \tag{13.28}$$

According to (13.26), the buyer maximizes his utility of consumption net of the transfer of assets. The transfer of one unit of real balances is worth one unit of the CM good, while the transfer of one unit of asset k is worth $p_k + \kappa_k$ units of the CM good. Condition (13.27) is the seller's participation constraint. The final constraint, (13.28), is a feasibility condition that says the buyer cannot transfer more than his real balances and a fraction ν_k of asset k. The solution to (13.26)-(13.28) is

$$U^b(\ell) = \begin{cases} u(q^*) - c(q^*) & \text{if } \ell \geq c(q^*) \\ u \circ c^{-1}(\ell) - \ell & \text{otherwise} \end{cases}, \tag{13.29}$$

where $\ell = z + \sum_{k=1}^{K} \nu_k a_k (p_k + \kappa_k)$ is the value of the assets that the buyer can transfer to the seller in exchange for the DM good. We will refer to ℓ as the buyer's liquid portfolio. If the value of this liquid wealth is greater than $c(q^*)$, then the buyer can ask for the efficient quantity

q^*; otherwise, he will transfer all his liquid wealth in exchange for a quantity q of output less than q^*.

Suppose that the buyer's liquidity constraint $d_z + \sum_{k=1}^{K} d_k(p_k + \kappa_k) \leq \ell$ is binding, so that $c(q) = \ell$. Then,

$$\frac{\partial U^b}{\partial a_k} = \nu_k(p_k + \kappa_k)\left[\frac{u'(q)}{c'(q)} - 1\right],$$

$$\frac{\partial U^b}{\partial z} = \frac{u'(q)}{c'(q)} - 1,$$

which implies that

$$(p_k + \kappa_k)^{-1}\frac{\partial U^b}{\partial a_k} = \nu_k\frac{\partial U^b}{\partial z}.$$

In words, $1/(p_k + \kappa_k)$ units of the kth asset, which is a claim to one unit of CM good, allows the buyer to raise his surplus in a bilateral match in the DM by a fraction ν_k of what he would obtain if he would accumulate one additional unit of real balances. In this way, the parameter ν_k is a measure of the liquidity of the asset k, and the extent to which it allows buyers to capture a fraction of the gains from trade in the DM market. If we assume that the liquidity coefficients are ranked as $\nu_1 \geq \nu_2 \geq ... \geq \nu_K$, then fiat money is the most liquid asset and the asset K is the least liquid.

The buyer's portfolio problem in the CM is a straightforward generalization of the problem with two assets, (13.11), and is given by the solution to

$$\max_{\{a_k\},z}\left\{-iz - r\sum_{k=1}^{K} a_k\left(p_k - p_k^*\right) + \sigma U^b(\ell)\right\}, \tag{13.30}$$

where $p_k^* = \kappa_k/r$ represents the fundamental price of asset k. According to (13.30), the buyer maximizes the expected surplus in the DM, net of the cost of holding the different assets in his portfolio. The cost of holding asset k is the difference between the price of the asset and its fundamental value times the discount rate, r, while the cost of holding real balances is $i = (\gamma - \beta)/\beta$. Since $z = \ell - \sum_{k=1}^{K} \nu_k a_k(p_k + \kappa_k)$, the buyer's portfolio choice problem, (13.30), can be rewritten as

$$\max_{\{a_k\},\ell}\left\{-i\ell + \sum_{k=1}^{K} a_k\left[i\nu_k(p_k + \kappa_k) - r\left(p_k - p_k^*\right)\right] + \sigma U^b(\ell)\right\} \tag{13.31}$$

$$\text{s.t.} \sum_{k=1}^{K} \nu_k a_k (p_k + \kappa_k) \leq \ell. \tag{13.32}$$

In a monetary equilibrium, constraint (13.32) does not bind since $z > 0$, and the first-order condition with respective to ℓ is

$$i = \sigma \left[\frac{u' \circ c^{-1}(\ell)}{c' \circ c^{-1}(\ell)} - 1 \right].$$

Let $\ell(i)$ denote the solution to this equation. The demand for liquid assets decreases with i, i.e., $\ell'(i) < 0$. In a monetary equilibrium, buyers must be indifferent between holding asset k and fiat money; hence, $i\nu_k(p_k + \kappa_k) - r\left(p_k - p_k^*\right) = 0$, or

$$p_k = \frac{1 + i\nu_k}{r - i\nu_k}\kappa_k, \tag{13.33}$$

for all $k \in \{1, ..., K\}$. Notice the similarities between (13.31), (13.32), and (13.33)—where the real asset is not "fully liquid"—and (13.12), (13.13), and (13.15), respectively, where it is. From (13.33), it is obvious that $r > i\nu_k$ for the asset price to be non-negative. In contrast to the previous section, where the real asset is assumed to be fully liquid, it is now possible to have a monetary equilibrium with a strictly positive inflation rate.

From (13.32) and (13.33), fiat money is valued if

$$\sum_{k=1}^{K} \nu_k A_k \left(\frac{1 + r}{r - i\nu_k} \right) \kappa_k < \ell(i). \tag{13.34}$$

For money to be valued, the total *liquid* stock of real assets, the left side of (13.34), must be less than the quantity of real balances that a buyer would accumulate in a pure monetary economy, $\ell(i)$. Otherwise, the buyer would have no incentive to complement his portfolio of real assets with real balances given the cost of holding money.

Now, let's examine the effect that monetary policy has on asset prices. From (13.33),

$$\frac{\partial \ln p_k}{\partial i} = \frac{\nu_k (1 + r)}{(1 + i\nu_k)(r - i\nu_k)}.$$

The price of real asset k increases with inflation, provided that $\nu_k > 0$, as buyers try to substitute the real asset for real balances when inflation is higher, and money is more costly to hold. If $\nu_k = 0$, then the asset is completely illiquid—in the sense that it cannot be used as means of payment in the DM—and monetary policy has no affect on its price. In this situation it should be obvious that the asset will be priced at its fundamental value, κ_k/r. Note that $\partial \ln p_k/\partial i$ is increasing with ν_k, which means that inflation has a bigger effect on the price of assets that are more liquid.

The gross rate of return of asset $k \in \{1,...,K\}$ is

$$R_k = \frac{\kappa_k + p_k}{p_k} = \frac{1+r}{1+i\nu_k}. \tag{13.35}$$

If the nominal interest rate, i, is strictly positive, then the model predicts a nondegenerate distribution of rates of return, where the ordering depends on the liquidity coefficients $\{\nu_k\}$. In any monetary equilibrium, $R_K \geq R_{K-1} \geq ... \geq R_1 \geq \gamma^{-1}$, where

$$\frac{R_{k'}}{R_k} = \frac{1+i\nu_k}{1+i\nu_{k'}} > 0 \text{ for } \nu_k > \nu_{k'}. \tag{13.36}$$

It is both interesting and important to point out that these rate-of-return differentials emerge in an environment where agents are essentially risk-neutral, i.e., they have linear preferences over the CM good. The nondegenerate structure of asset yields arise because the different assets are used in different degrees as means of payments.

We now examine the effect that monetary policy has on the structure of asset yields. From (13.35), we have

$$\frac{\partial \ln R_k}{\partial i} = -\frac{\nu_k}{1+i\nu_k}.$$

Provided that $\nu_k > 0$, as inflation increases, the rates of return of the real assets decrease, and real asset prices are bid up. As a consequence, in any monetary equilibrium, the structure of asset yields $\{R_k^i\}_{k=1}^K$ associated with a cost of money i dominates $\{R_k^{i'}\}_{k=1}^K$ associated with $i' > i$ in a first-order stochastic sense. Moreover, $|\partial \ln R_k/\partial i|$ increases with ν_k, so that the effect of inflation on an asset's rate of return is larger if the asset is more liquid. Note that

$$\ln R_{k'} - \ln R_k \approx i\left(\nu_k - \nu_{k'}\right),$$

which means that the rate of return differences across assets reflect the liquidity differences in the assets, and inflation acts as a scaling factor that amplifies these liquidity differences.

Finally, consider two assets k and k' such that $\nu_k > \nu_{k'}$. If $i > 0$, then $R_{k'} - R_k > 0$. Using (13.36),

$$\frac{\partial \ln (R_{k'} - R_k)}{\partial i} = \frac{1 - i^2 \nu_k \nu_{k'}}{i (1 + i\nu_k)(1 + i\nu_{k'})}.$$

Hence, $\partial \ln (R_{k'} - R_k) / \partial i > 0$ if and only if $1 - i^2 \nu_k \nu_{k'} > 0$. That is, the premia paid to the less liquid asset, $R_{k'} - R_k$, increases with inflation, provided that i is not too large. In the case where $\nu_{k'} = 0$, i.e., the least liquid asset is illiquid, then $\partial \ln (R_{k'} - R_k) / \partial i > 0$ always holds.

So far, we have taken the liquidity coefficients $\{\nu_k\}$ as exogenous. Although it has been useful to describe how liquidity differences across assets can generate differences in asset returns and different responses to changes in monetary policy, taking $\{\nu_k\}$ as exogenous is not satisfactory. One would like to understand what frictions in the economy would generate such restrictions on the use of assets as means of payment, and how these frictions might interact with monetary policy.

The differences in assets' liquidity may be the result of the pricing mechanism in the DM. Indeed, as shown in Chapter 12.4, one can construct a pricing mechanism that generates the same payoff for the buyer as the one in problem (13.26)-(13.28), but the constructed pricing mechanism is pairwise Pareto-efficient, and does not restrict the transfer of assets in a bilateral match, as does problem (13.26)-(13.28). For this kind of pricing mechanism, one could interpret the differences in liquidity among assets as coming from a convention that allows some assets to be traded at better terms of trades than others. The following sections provide alternative explanations that may underlie the liquidity coefficients $\{\nu_k\}$ based on informational frictions.

13.5 Costly Acceptability

In this section, we endogenize the recognizability and, hence, the liquidity of an asset. We adopt the economic environment of Chapter 13.2, where fiat money and a single risk-free real asset coexist. We assume that the real asset is not portable, but agents can trade claims on it. In the DM, agents have the technology to counterfeit those claims instantly and at zero cost. In contrast, fiat money cannot be counterfeited. If the seller is unable to distinguish genuine claims from counterfeits, then claims on the real asset will not be traded since sellers understand that it is a dominant strategy for buyers to try to pass counterfeits once an offer has been accepted. (See Chapter 12.3 for a more formal argument.) In contrast to Chapters 5.3 and 12.3, sellers can choose to be informed or not.

At the beginning of each period, a seller can invest in a costly technology that allows him to recognize genuine claims from counterfeited ones. The cost of this technology is $\psi > 0$, measured in terms of utility. We denote $\nu \in [0,1]$ as the fraction of informed sellers. It is common knowledge in the match whether the seller invested in the technology. The parameter ν, which is related to the parameter ν_k of the previous section, will also indicate the probability that a claim on the real asset is accepted in payment by a random seller in the DM.

Equilibrium If buyers make take-it-or-leave-it offers to sellers in the DM, then sellers have no incentive to invest in the costly technology that allows them to recognize counterfeits since they do not receive any surplus from their DM trades. We will, therefore, adopt the proportional bargaining solution; see Chapter 3.2.3, where sellers receive the share $1-\theta > 0$ of the total match surplus.

Consider a buyer in the DM holding z units of real balances and a units of the real asset. Denote ℓ the maximum wealth that the buyer can transfer to the seller in a match. If the seller is informed, then $\ell = z + (p+\kappa)a$; if he is not, then $\ell = z$ since uninformed sellers will not accept claims on the real asset. Under the proportional bargaining scheme, the quantity traded in informed matches, q, solves

$$\omega(q) = \min\left\{\omega(q^*), z + (p+\kappa)a\right\}, \tag{13.37}$$

where $\omega(q) \equiv \theta c(q) + (1-\theta)u(q)$ is the transfer of wealth from the buyer to the seller. In uninformed matches, the quantity traded, q^u, solves

$$\omega(q^u) = \min\left\{\omega(q^*), z\right\}. \tag{13.38}$$

The right sides of (13.37) and (13.38) differ because the liquid wealth of a buyer in an informed match is composed of money and the real asset, while it is only money in an uniformed match.

The value of being a buyer in the DM with portfolio (a,z) is given by

$$\begin{aligned} V^b(a,z) = \sigma\nu\theta\left[u(q) - c(q)\right] + \sigma(1-\nu)\theta\left[u(q^u) - c(q^u)\right] \\ + z + a(p+\kappa) + W^b(0,0), \end{aligned} \tag{13.39}$$

where, to simplify matters, we use the linearity of the value function W^b and the fact that $u(q) - \omega(q) = \theta\left[u(q) - c(q)\right]$. According to (13.39), the buyer meets a seller with probability σ. The seller is informed with probability ν. In an informed match, the seller produces q, and in an uninformed match he produces q^u. The buyer receives a fraction θ of the total surplus in all trade matches.

If we substitute V^b from (13.39) into (13.9), the buyer's value function at the beginning of the CM, then the buyer's portfolio problem is given by

$$\max_{a\geq 0, z\geq 0}\left\{-iz-ar\left(p-p^*\right)+\sigma\nu\theta\left[u(q)-c(q)\right]+\sigma(1-\nu)\theta\left[u(q^u)-c(q^u)\right]\right\}, \tag{13.40}$$

which is a straightforward generalization of (13.11). In the Appendix we show that problem (13.40) is concave. The first-order (necessary and sufficient) conditions are:

$$-\frac{i}{\sigma\theta}+\nu\left[\frac{u'(q)-c'(q)}{\theta c'(q)+(1-\theta)u'(q)}\right]+(1-\nu)\left[\frac{u'(q^u)-c'(q^u)}{\theta c'(q^u)+(1-\theta)u'(q^u)}\right]\leq 0, \tag{13.41}$$

$$-\frac{r\left(p-p^*\right)}{\sigma\theta(p+\kappa)}+\nu\left[\frac{u'(q)-c'(q)}{\theta c'(q)+(1-\theta)u'(q)}\right]\leq 0, \tag{13.42}$$

where we have used that

$$\frac{\partial q}{\partial z}=\frac{1}{p+\kappa}\frac{\partial q}{\partial a}=\frac{1}{\omega'\left(q\right)}=\frac{1}{\theta c'\left(q\right)+\left(1-\theta\right)u'\left(q\right)},$$
$$\frac{\partial q^u}{\partial z}=\frac{1}{\omega'\left(q^u\right)}=\frac{1}{\theta c'\left(q^u\right)+\left(1-\theta\right)u'\left(q^u\right)},$$

and $\partial q^u/\partial a=0$. Condition (13.41) is satisfied with an equality if $z>0$, as is condition (13.42) if $a>0$. An important difference between (13.41) and (13.42) is that a buyer can spend his marginal unit of real balances in both informed and uninformed matches, but a claim on the marginal unit of the real asset can only be transferred in informed matches. We focus on symmetric equilibria where all buyers make the same portfolio choice.

We now turn to the seller's problem. Without loss of generality, we assume that sellers do not hold assets, since they have no strict incentive to do so. At the beginning of each period, a seller must choose whether or not to invest in the technology to recognize claims on the real asset. The seller makes this choice by comparing his lifetime expected utility if he does invest in the technology with that if he does not invest. So, the seller's problem is

$$\max\left\{-\psi+\sigma(1-\theta)\left[u(q)-c(q)\right],\sigma(1-\theta)\left[u(q^u)-c(q^u)\right]\right\}. \tag{13.43}$$

Note that we omit the continuation value of the seller in the CM , $W^s(0,0)$, from both expressions in the above maximization problem. According to (13.43), if the seller chooses to be informed, then he incurs the disutility cost ψ, which allows him to accept claims on the real asset. In this case, the quantity traded is q, and the seller extracts a fraction $1-\theta$ of the match surplus. If the seller chooses to be uninformed, then he only accepts money, and the quantity traded is q^u. From (13.43), the measure of informed sellers will satisfy

$$\nu \begin{cases} = 1 \\ \in [0,1] \\ = 0 \end{cases} \text{if } -\psi + \sigma(1-\theta)\left[u(q)-c(q)\right] \begin{Bmatrix} > \\ = \\ < \end{Bmatrix} \sigma(1-\theta)\left[u(q^u)-c(q^u)\right]. \tag{13.44}$$

A stationary symmetric equilibrium is a list (q,q^u,z,p,ν) that satisfies conditions (13.37) with $a=A$, (13.38), (13.41), (13.42), and (13.44).

Equilibria with recognizable assets Consider, first, equilibria where all sellers get informed, i.e., $\nu=1$. Except for the pricing mechanism in the DM, these equilibria are essentially the same as those in Chapter 13.2, where fiat money and claims on the real asset are equally liquid. From (13.41), the output traded in the DM in a monetary equilibrium, q_1, is solution to

$$\frac{i}{\sigma\theta} = \frac{u'(q_1)-c'(q_1)}{\theta c'(q_1)+(1-\theta)u'(q_1)}, \tag{13.45}$$

which is identical to equation (3.43) in Chapter 3.2.3. The subscript "1" refers to an equilibrium with $\nu=1$. When $\nu=1$, the price of the real asset is

$$p_1 = \frac{(1+i)\kappa}{r-i},$$

since the cost of investing in one unit of the asset, $r(p_1-p^*)$, must equal the cost of obtaining an equivalent payoff by holding money, $i(p_1+\kappa)$. In a monetary equilibrium, the buyer's real balances are

$$z_1 = \omega(q_1) - (p_1+\kappa)A > 0. \tag{13.46}$$

The right side of (13.46) is decreasing in i. Note that if $i=0$, then $z_1 = \omega(q^*) - (p^*+\kappa)A$, and as i approaches r, z_1 approaches minus infinity. Consequently, if $(p^*+\kappa)A < \theta c(q^*) + (1-\theta)u(q^*)$, then there is a $\bar{\imath} \in (0,r)$, such that for all $i < \bar{\imath}$ there is an equilibrium with informed sellers and valued fiat money. If $i > \bar{\imath}$, then the equilibrium will be a nonmonetary one, and the asset price will be given by the solution to (13.42) at equality, with $\omega(q) = (p+\kappa)A$.

If $(p^* + \kappa)A \geq \theta c(q^*) + (1-\theta)u(q^*)$, then fiat money is not valued and $q_1 = q^*$ in all matches. In this equilibrium, the stock of real asset is sufficiently large to satiate the economy's need for a medium of exchange. It should be emphasized that even if $q_1 = q^*$, the equilibrium is not socially efficient since sellers incur a real cost associated with being informed.

We now need to verify that it is optimal for sellers to get informed. From (13.44), $\nu = 1$ requires

$$\psi \leq \psi_1 \equiv \sigma(1-\theta)\left\{[u(q_1) - c(q_1)] - [u(q_1^u) - c(q_1^u)]\right\}, \tag{13.47}$$

where q_1^u represents output in the DM if a seller chooses not to get informed when all other sellers are informed, and is given by the solution to $\omega(q_1^u) = z_1$ if the equilibrium when all sellers are informed is monetary, and $q_1^u = 0$ if it is not. Hence, there exists an equilibrium where all sellers are informed, provided that the cost to be informed is sufficiently low, i.e., lower than $\psi_1 > 0$.

Equilibria with unrecognizable assets Now, let's consider equilibria where all sellers are uninformed, i.e., $\nu = 0$. In this case, genuine and counterfeit claims on the real asset cannot be distinguished by sellers in the DM and, hence, they will not be accepted as means of payment. The only medium of exchange is fiat money, i.e., the model generates an endogenous cash-in-advance constraint.

The equilibrium outcome is similar to the pure monetary economy described in Chapter 3.2.3. From (13.41), the output traded in the DM is q_0^u solution to

$$\frac{i}{\sigma\theta} = \frac{u'(q_0^u) - c'(q_0^u)}{\theta c'(q_0^u) + (1-\theta)u'(q_0^u)} \tag{13.48}$$

and, from (13.42) with $\nu = 0$, the price of the real asset is

$$p_0 = p^*.$$

The subscript "0" refers to an equilibrium with $\nu = 0$. The asset is priced at its fundamental value since it cannot be used as medium of exchange owing to its lack of recognizability. The buyer's real balances are $z_0 = \omega(q_0^u)$. Condition (13.44) implies that it is optimal for sellers to remain uninformed with regard to claims on the real asset if

$$\psi \geq \psi_0 \equiv \sigma(1-\theta)\left\{[u(q_0) - c(q_0)] - [u(q_0^u) - c(q_0^u)]\right\}, \tag{13.49}$$

where q_0 represents output in the DM if a seller chooses to get informed when all other sellers are not informed and is given implicitly by (13.37), with $p = p_0 = p^*$, $a = A$ and $z = z_0$. From (13.48), if i tends to 0, then q_0^u approaches q^*, and z_0 approaches $\theta c(q^*) + (1-\theta)u(q^*)$. Consequently, $q_0 = q^*$ and $\psi_0 = 0$. Hence, if the monetary authority implements the Friedman rule, then there exists an equilibrium where agents trade the first-best level of output in all matches, and fiat money is the only means of payment. Note that this equilibrium is socially efficient because sellers do not need to invest in a costly recognition technology; fiat money, in conjunction with the Friedman rule, allows society to save on information costs.

Multiple monetary equilibria If $\psi_0 < \psi_1$, then there will exist multiple equilibria—an equilibrium where sellers get informed and one where they do not—for any $\psi \in [\psi_0, \psi_1]$ since conditions (13.47) and (13.49) can be simultaneously satisfied. We now demonstrate that $\psi_0 < \psi_1$.

First, notice that the asset price is higher in an equilibrium where sellers are informed compared to one where they are uninformed, i.e., $p_1 \geq p_0 = p^*$. This is because the price of the real asset can rise above its fundamental value only if it is recognizable and is used as medium of exchange. Hence, $(p_0 + \kappa)A \leq (p_1 + \kappa)A$. Moreover, if we assume that the conditions for a monetary equilibrium are satisfied when $\nu = 1$, then from (13.45) and (13.48), the quantities traded in the DM in a monetary equilibrium with informed sellers and in a monetary equilibrium with uninformed sellers are the same, $q_0^u = q_1$. This implies that $z_1 + (p_1 + \kappa)A = z_0$ from (13.37) and (13.38). In addition, the surplus $\mathcal{S}(\ell) \equiv u[q(\ell)] - c[q(\ell)]$ as a function of the buyer's liquid wealth, ℓ, is concave, and strictly concave if $\ell < \theta c(q^*) + (1-\theta)u(q^*)$. Therefore,

$$\sigma(1-\theta)\mathcal{S}'(z_0)(p_1+\kappa)A < \sigma(1-\theta)\{[u(q_1) - c(q_1)] - [u(q_1^u) - c(q_1^u)]\} \equiv \psi_1, \tag{13.50}$$

and

$$\psi_0 \equiv \sigma(1-\theta)\{[u(q_0) - c(q_0)] - [u(q_0^u) - c(q_0^u)]\} < \sigma(1-\theta)\mathcal{S}'(z_0)(p^* + \kappa)A. \tag{13.51}$$

See Figure 13.6. Since $(p_1+\kappa)A \geq (p^*+\kappa)A$, conditions (13.50) and (13.51) imply that $\psi_0 < \psi_1$. Consequently, if a monetary equilibrium exists with $\nu = 1$, and $\psi \in [\psi_0, \psi_1]$, then there is also a monetary equilibrium with $\nu = 0$ and $p = p^*$.

There are two other interesting cases to consider. The first case assumes that i is close to 0 and $(p^*+\kappa)A < \omega(q^*)$. In an equilibrium with uninformed sellers, z_0 approaches $\theta c(q^*) + (1-\theta)u(q^*)$, and the asset price is its fundamental value, $p_0 = p^*$. Consequently, $q_0^u = \omega^{-1}(z_0) = q^*$, $q_0 = \min\left[q^*, \omega^{-1}(z_0 + (p^*+\kappa)A)\right] = q^*$, and $\psi_0 = 0$. In a monetary equilibrium with informed sellers, $z_1 = \omega(q^*) - (p^* + \kappa)A$ and $q_1 = q^*$ while $q_1^u = \omega^{-1}\left[(p^*+\kappa)A\right] < q^*$. Hence, $\psi_1 = \sigma(1-\theta)\left\{\left[u(q^*) - c(q^*)\right] - \left[u(q_1^u) - c(q_1^u)\right]\right\} > 0 = \psi_0$. If the cost of acquiring information is sufficiently small, then there are multiple equilibria. In this case, an equilibrium where sellers are uninformed and, therefore, money is the only means of payment dominates from a social welfare viewpoint an equilibrium where sellers are informed, since information acquisition is costly.

The second case illustrates the existence of multiple equilibria when $(p^*+\kappa)A \geq \omega(q^*)$. The equilibrium with informed sellers is such that

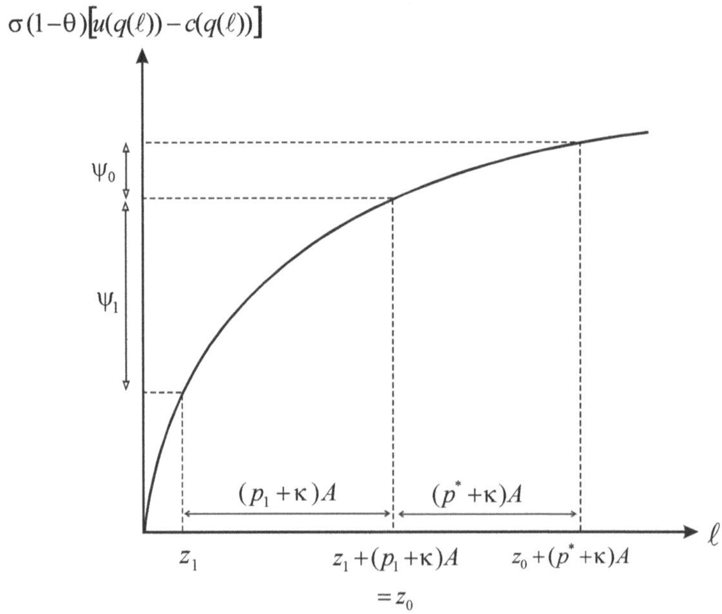

Figure 13.6
Information acquisition and multiple equilibria

$q_1 = q^*$ and money is not valued , so that $q_1^u = 0$. If i is sufficiently small to allow for the existence of a monetary equilibrium in the case where sellers are uninformed, then it is immediate that

$$\psi_1 = \sigma(1-\theta)\,[u(q^*) - c(q^*)] > \psi_0 = \sigma(1-\theta)\,\{[u(q_0) - c(q_0)] - [u(q_0^u) - c(q_0^u)]\},$$

since $q_0 = \min\left[q^*, \omega^{-1}\left(z_0 + (p^* + \kappa)A\right)\right] = q^*$ and $q_0^u > 0$.

The intuition that underlies the multiplicity of equilibria is as follows. Suppose that sellers believe that buyers hold few real balances. Then, sellers have incentives to be informed because otherwise they will only be able to accept the reduced real balances of the buyers. But if buyers believe that all sellers are informed, it is optimal for them to reduce their real balances and bid up for the real asset until the rates of return of money and the real asset are equalized. On the other hand, if sellers believe that buyers hold a large amount of real balances, then they do not need to acquire costly information to recognize claims on the real asset because the use of those assets would not increase the match surplus by more than the cost of information. And if all sellers are uninformed, it becomes optimal for buyers to accumulate large amount of real balances provided that inflation is not too high. This multiplicity of equilibria captures the strategic complementarities that make the liquidity of an asset a self-fulfilling phenomenon and is similar to the viability of credit being a self-fulfilling phenomenon in Chapter 8.4.

13.6 Pledgeability and the Threat of Fraud

We now propose a theory to endogenize resalability constraints based on the imperfect recognizability of assets and the threat of fraud. Just as in Section 13.4, this theory allows us to explain liquidity and rate-of-return differences across assets. In contrast to Section 13.4, we will show that liquidity (or resalability) constraints depend on monetary policy and market fundamentals. This will generate new insights for the relationship between liquidity and asset prices.

We now assume there are $K \geq 1$ one-period Lucas trees (or one-period real bonds) indexed by k, and we denote $\boldsymbol{K} = \{1, \ldots, K\}$ the set of all Lucas trees. Each buyer receives a lump-sum endowment A_k of asset k at the beginning of each CM. (Given that preferences are quasi-linear, the assumption of symmetric endowments is without loss of generality.) Each asset k pays a dividend equal to one unit of good at the beginning of the subsequent CM, after which it fully depreciates. The price of the asset k, measured in terms of the CM good, is denoted by p_k.

As in Chapters 5.3 and 12.3, we introduce the possibility of counterfeiting or asset fraud. Specifically, at the end of each CM subperiod, buyers can produce any quantity of fraudulent asset of type k for a fixed cost ψ_k. The cost is common knowledge. Fraudulent assets produced in period t do not pay a dividend in the CM of $t+1$ precisely because they are fraudulent. Like their genuine conterparts, any fraudulent asset produced in t fully depreciates at the end of $t+1$. In the DM, sellers are unable to distinguish genuine from fraudulent assets. We assume, in contrast to Chapter 5.3, that the cost of counterfeiting money is infinite, i.e., money is the only asset that is perfectly recognizable. Sellers are unable to recognize or authenticate assets that they may acquire in the DM. For example, if we interpret the asset as being an asset-backed security, then asset fraud may represent deficiencies in lending, securitization, and ratings practices, as well as outright mortgage fraud. The cost associated with originating the fraudulent securities, ψ_k, can represent the cost of producing false documentation about the underlying asset and the cost of gaming the procedures used by rating agencies. A seller is unable to detect any of these fraudent practices by "looking" at the asset.

The terms of trade in the DM are determined by the following bargaining game: in the CM of period $t-1$, the buyer chooses an offer, $(q, d_z, \{d_k\}_{k=1}^K)$, that he makes in the DM of period t if he is matched, where the offer specifies the amount of DM good q that the seller produces in exchange for d_z units of real balances and d_k units of asset $k \in \mathbf{K}$. Then, given this offer, the buyer decides whether to produce counterfeits for each asset k or to purchase genuine units of these assets. Finally, if the buyer is matched in the DM, the offer $(q, d_z, \{d_k\}_{k=1}^K)$ is extended to the seller, which he either accepts or rejects.

The bargaining game can be solved by backward induction since there is a proper subgame that follows the offer, $(q, d_z, \{d_k\}_{k=1}^K)$. Notice that the buyer does not observe the seller's acceptance decision when he chooses the composition of his portfolio in terms of genuine and fraudulent assets and the seller cannot observe the quality of the buyer's portfolio when he makes his acceptance decision. It can be shown that in any equilibrium the buyer does *not* produce counterfeits and the offer $(q, d_z, \{d_k\}_{k=1}^K)$ is accepted with probability one.

Consider the offer $(q, d_z, \{d_k\}_{k=1}^K)$ that a buyer chooses before he makes his counterfeiting decision. If the following incentive-compatibility condition holds, then the buyer does not have an incentive to produce counterfeits of a particular asset $\tilde{k} \in \boldsymbol{K}$,

$$-\sum_{k\in\boldsymbol{K}} p_k d_k - \gamma d_z + \beta\left\{\sigma u(q) + (1-\sigma)\left[\sum_{k\in\boldsymbol{K}} d_k + d_z\right]\right\} \geq$$
$$-\psi_{\tilde{k}} - \sum_{k\in\boldsymbol{K}\setminus\{\tilde{k}\}} p_k d_k - \gamma d_z + \beta\left\{\sigma u(q) + (1-\sigma)\left[\sum_{k\in\boldsymbol{K}\setminus\{\tilde{k}\}} d_k + d_z\right]\right\}. \tag{13.52}$$

The left side of (13.52) is the buyer's payoff if he does not produce a fraudent $\tilde{k}$ asset. In the CM, the buyer purchases d_k units of asset k at a unit price of p_k and accumulates γd_z real balances. In the subsequent period, the buyer is matched in the DM with probability σ, in which case he transfers $\sum_{k\in\boldsymbol{K}} d_k + d_z$, measured in terms of the subsequent CM good, to the seller in exchange for q units of DM output. With complementary probability, $1-\sigma$, the buyer is not matched and keeps all his assets. The right side of (13.52) is the expected payoff to the buyer who produces a fraudulent asset of type $\tilde{k}$ and purchases genuine assets of type $k \neq \tilde{k}$. In this situation, the buyer incurs a fixed cost $\psi_{\tilde{k}}$ and does not accumulate any genuine units of asset $\tilde{k}$ for DM trading. Since the asset of type $\tilde{k}$ is fraudulent, it does not provide a dividend.

The incentive compatibility constraint, (13.52), can be simplified to read

$$\left[p_{\tilde{k}} - \beta(1-\sigma)\right] d_{\tilde{k}} \leq \psi_{\tilde{k}}. \tag{13.53}$$

The left side of (13.53) is the cost of paying with genuine assets of type $\tilde{k}$, where the cost has two components. There is the holding cost of the asset, $(p_{\tilde{k}} - \beta)d_{\tilde{k}}$, and there is the cost of giving up the asset in the event of a trade, $\beta\sigma d_{\tilde{k}}$. The right side of (13.53) is the fixed cost associated with producing counterfeits assets of type $\tilde{k}$. Hence, a buyer has no incentive to commit fraud if the cost of producing counterfeits is greater than the cost of paying for DM consumption with genuine assets.

The incentive-compatibility constraint, (13.53), takes the form of a "resalability" constraint that specifies an upper bound that the asset of type $k \in \boldsymbol{K}$ can be resold in the DM by a buyer to a seller,

$$d_k \leq \frac{\psi_k}{p_k - \beta(1-\sigma)} \quad \text{for all } k \in \boldsymbol{K}. \tag{13.54}$$

The resalability constraint, (13.54), depends on the cost of producing fraudulent assets, ψ_k; the holding cost of an asset, $p_k - \beta$; and the frequency of trades in the DM, σ. An asset that is more susceptible to fraud is subject to a more stringent resalability constraint and this depends on, among other things, how costly it is to produce a counterfeit asset, ψ_k. The upper bound of the resalability constraint also depends on the frequency of trade in the DM, σ. Increasing the frequency of trade exacerbates the threat of fraud because the trade surplus of a counterfeiting buyer, $u(q)$, is greater than the match surplus of an honest buyer, $u(q) - c(q)$, and can be obtained with a higher probability. Hence, the upper bound must be lowered if σ increases to keep the buyer's incentives in line. For example, if the process of securitization implies that an asset can be retraded more frequently, then an increase in securitization raises the threat of fraud and makes resalability constraints more likely to bind. Notice also that the holding cost of the asset, $p_k - \beta$, enters the resalability constraint since, due to the lack of commitment (to repay debts), buyers must accumulate assets before their liquidity needs occur. An increase in the asset price raises the holding cost, which increases the buyer's incentives to produce a counterfeit version of the asset. Therefore, holding all else constant, higher asset prices imply lower upper bounds on the resalability constraint.

Up to this point, we have focused the offer that a buyer makes in the DM, $(q, d_z, \{d_k\}_{k=1}^K)$. Now let's turn to the buyer's CM portfolio decision, $(\{a_k\}_{k=1}^K, z)$, where a_k represents the buyer's CM demand for asset k and z is his real balance holdings. If money is costly to hold, i.e., $i > 0$, then the buyer chooses $z = d_z$. Similarly, if $p_k > \beta$, then asset k is costly to hold and, as a consequence, $a_k = d_k$, i.e., the buyer does not hold more than what he intends to use as a means of payment. If, however, $p_k = \beta$, then there is no holding cost for asset k and, therefore, $a_k \geq d_k$. The solution to the following problem determines both the buyer's offer, $(q, d_z, \{d_k\}_{k=1}^K)$, and his CM portfolio, $(\{a_k\}_{k=1}^K, z)$,

$$\max_{q,z,d_z,\{d_k,a_k\}} \left\{ -iz - \sum_{k \in \mathbf{K}} \left[\frac{p_k - \beta}{\beta}\right] a_k + \sigma\left[u(q) - c(q)\right] \right\} \tag{13.55}$$

subject to

$$c(q) = \sum_{k \in \mathbf{K}} d_k + d_z \tag{13.56}$$

$$d_k \leq \frac{\psi_k}{p_k - \beta(1-\sigma)}, \quad \text{for all } k \in \mathbf{K} \tag{13.57}$$

$$d_k \in [0, a_k], \quad \text{for all } k \in \mathbf{K}, \tag{13.58}$$

and $d_z \leq z$. Since an asset pays a single dividend equal to 1, the fundamental value of asset k, denoted by p_k^*, equals β. Therefore, the expression in the braces of (13.55) can be rewritten as

$$-iz - (1+r)\sum_{k \in K}(p_k - p_k^*)a_k + \sigma\left[u(q) - c(q)\right].$$

Notice that this expression is almost identical to (13.30), except that the second term is multiplied by $1+r$, instead of r, which reflects the one period life of the assets. Hence, the buyer's optimal offer and portfolio choice maximizes a standard looking objective function subject to three constraints. The first constraint, (13.56), is an individual rationality constraint that says the seller's payoff is zero when the buyer's assets are genuine. The second constraint, (13.57), is an incentive compatibility or resalability constraint that specifies the maximum quantity of an asset that a seller will accept with probability one that does not give an incentive to the buyer to produce a fraudulent asset. The final constraint, (13.58), is a feasibility constraint that says that the buyer cannot transfer more assets than he holds.

Assuming an interior solution for z, the first-order conditions for the buyer's problem are

$$\xi = \sigma\left[\frac{u'(q)}{c'(q)} - 1\right] = \lambda_k + \mu_k \tag{13.59}$$

$$p_k = \beta(1+\mu_k) \tag{13.60}$$

$$i = \xi \tag{13.61}$$

for all $k \in \mathbf{K}$, where $\xi \geq 0$ is the Lagrange multiplier of the seller's participation constraint, (13.56), $\lambda_k \geq 0$ is the multiplier of the resalability constraint, (13.57), and $\mu_k \geq 0$ is the multiplier of the feasibility constraint, (13.58). The multiplier ξ measures the expected surplus of the buyer from spending one unit of asset in order to raise his DM consumption by $1/c'(q)$ units. An additional unit of consumption increases the buyer's surplus by $u'(q) - c'(q)$ if he is matched in the DM, an event that occurs with probably σ. The multiplier ξ must also be equal to the cost of transferring any asset k, which is the sum of the multipliers λ_k and μ_k. Indeed, by offering an additional unit of asset k the buyer tightens both the resalability and the feasibility constraints. From (13.61), the multiplier ξ is pinned down by the cost of holding real balances, i. Finally, the first-order condition, (13.60), is the asset pricing equation for asset k, which says that the price of the asset must be equal to its discounted dividend, β, plus its discounted liquidity value as a medium of exchange in a match as measured by $\beta\mu_k$. Taken together, (13.59) and (13.60) imply that the asset price is bounded from both above and below, i.e.,

$$\beta \leq p_k \leq \beta(1+\xi). \tag{13.62}$$

The lower bound is the fundamental value of the asset, β, since a buyer can always hold onto a unit of the asset and consume its dividend in the next CM. The upper bound is the fundamental value of the asset, β, augmented by the net utility of spending an additional unit of the asset in the DM, $\beta\xi$.

We now propose a three-tier categorization of assets based on whether the resalability and feasibility constraints for an asset are slack or binding.

Liquid assets An asset is perfectly liquid if the feasibility constraint (13.58) is binding, $\mu_k > 0$, and the resalability constraint (13.57) is slack, $\lambda_k = 0$. In this case, the asset price is equal to the upper bound, $\beta(1+\xi)$. Intuitively, an asset is perfectly liquid if the buyer can spend an additional unit of the asset in the DM without violating the resalability constraint. Substituting the market clearing condition, $a_k = A_k$, and the price equation, $p_k = \beta(1+\xi) = \beta(1+i)$, into the binding feasibility constraint and the slack resalability constraint, we get $d_k = A_k \leq \psi_k/\beta(i+\sigma)$. This inequality can be rewritten as

$$\hat{\psi}_k \geq \beta(i+\sigma),$$

where $\hat{\psi}_k \equiv \psi_k/A_k$ is the cost of fraud per unit of the asset. Notice that the rate of return on a liquid asset is $1/p_k = \gamma^{-1}$, which is also the rate of return of fiat money. Hence, there is a rate-of-return equality among all liquid assets.

Partially liquid assets An asset is partially liquid if both the resalability (13.57) and feasibility (13.58) constraints bind, which implies that $\lambda_k > 0$ and $\mu_k > 0$, respectively. In equilibrium, a buyer spends all his asset holdings in the DM. However, if he acquires an additional unit of asset k and attempts to spend it in the DM, there is a positive probability that the trade is rejected. These binding constraints immediately imply that

$$\beta < p_k < \beta(1+\xi).$$

The asset price exceeds its fundamental value but is strictly less than the price of a completely liquid asset, $\beta(1+\xi)$. From (13.57), $d_k = A_k =$

$\psi_k/[p_k - \beta(1-\sigma)]$, which implies that $p_k = \hat{\psi}_k + \beta(1-\sigma)$. The conditions for an asset to be partially liquid, $\mu_k = p_k/\beta - 1 > 0$, from (13.60), and $\lambda_k = \xi + 1 - p_k/\beta > 0$, from (13.59), can be written as

$$\beta\sigma < \hat{\psi}_k < \beta(i+\sigma).$$

An asset is partially liquid if the cost of fraud is neither too low nor too high.

Illiquid assets An asset is illiquid if the resalability constraint (13.57) binds, $\lambda_k > 0$ and the feasibility constraint (13.58) is slack, $\mu_k = 0$. In equilibrium, the buyer does not spend all of his asset holdings in the DM even though he is liquidity constrained, i.e., $q < q^*$. In this case the asset price equals the lower bound, $p_k = \beta$, which is its fundamental value. The binding resalability constraint, (13.57), implies that $d_k \leq \psi_k/\beta\sigma$. Substituting this expression into the slack feasibility constraint, (13.58), we obtain that

$$\hat{\psi}_k \leq \beta\sigma.$$

We can summarize the liquidity structure of assets by their prices and the fraction of the asset used in DM purchases, $\nu_k \equiv d_k/a_k$. For convenience let $\underline{\psi} \equiv \beta\sigma$, and $\overline{\psi} \equiv \beta(\sigma + i)$. We have,

1. *Liquid assets*: for any $k \in \boldsymbol{K}$ such that $\hat{\psi}_k \geq \overline{\psi}$,

$$p_k = \beta(1+i) \tag{13.63}$$

$$\nu_k = 1. \tag{13.64}$$

2. *Partially liquid assets*: for any $k \in \boldsymbol{K}$ such that $\hat{\psi}_k \in (\underline{\psi}, \overline{\psi})$,

$$p_k = \hat{\psi}_k + \beta(1-\sigma) \tag{13.65}$$

$$\nu_k = 1. \tag{13.66}$$

3. *Illiquid assets*: for any $k \in \boldsymbol{K}$ such that $\hat{\psi}_k \leq \underline{\psi}$,

$$p_k = \beta \tag{13.67}$$

$$\nu_k = \frac{\hat{\psi}_k}{\beta\sigma} < 1. \tag{13.68}$$

We now provide a condition for money to be valued, $z > 0$. From the above, we have

$$d_k = \nu_k A_k, \quad \text{where} \quad \nu_k = \min\left\{1, \frac{\hat{\psi}_k}{\beta\sigma}\right\}.$$

That is, the buyer either transfers all his holdings of asset k to the seller in the DM if he is matched, or the maximum amount consistent with the resalability constraint and the no-arbitrage restriction that $p_k \geq \beta$. Substituting the above expression for d_k into the seller's binding participation constraint, (13.56), we get

$$c(q) = \sum_{k \in K} \nu_k A_k + z \equiv L, \tag{13.69}$$

where L can be interpreted as aggregate liquidity. Aggregate liquidity is a weighted average of asset supplies, where the weights are endogenous and depend on trading frictions and assets' characteristics. A monetary equilibrium exists if

$$\frac{u' \circ c^{-1}\left[\sum_{k \in K} \nu_k A_k\right]}{c' \circ c^{-1}\left[\sum_{k \in K} \nu_k A_k\right]} > 1 + \frac{i}{\sigma}. \tag{13.70}$$

That is, for money to be valued, the weighted sum of all asset supplies must be sufficiently small relative to the liquidity needs of the economy, and the inflation rate cannot be too high.

Whenever money is valued and $i > 0$, liquidity is scarce and assets with identical cash flows can have different prices because different assets have different counterfeiting costs, ψ_k. Figure 13.7 describes the price of asset as a function of counterfeiting cost per unit of genuine asset supply. Assets with high unit counterfeiting costs are liquid, with low unit counterfeiting costs are illiquid, and with intermediate unit counterfeiting costs are partially liquid. This departure from the Law of One Price is an alternative formulation of the rate-of-return dominance puzzle which says monetary assets coexist with other assets that have similar risk characteristics but generate a higher yield. In our model, price differentials across assets are attributed to differences in the cost of fraud. An asset that is less sensitive to fraudulent activities is used more intensively to finance spending opportunities. Relative to assets that have a lower cost of fraud, the asset with a low cost of fraud generates some nonpecuniary liquidity services, μ_k, also referred to as a convenience yield, and is sold at a higher price, see (13.60).

Our model offers insights regarding cross-sectional differences in transactions velocity, a standard measure of liquidity in monetary economies. In our model, transactions velocity in the DM is $\mathcal{V}_k \equiv \sigma d_k / A_k = \sigma \nu_k$. Our model predicts a positive relationship between the price of an asset and its velocity. The most liquid assets—any asset k such that $\hat{\psi}_k \geq \bar{\psi}$—trade at the highest price and their velocities are

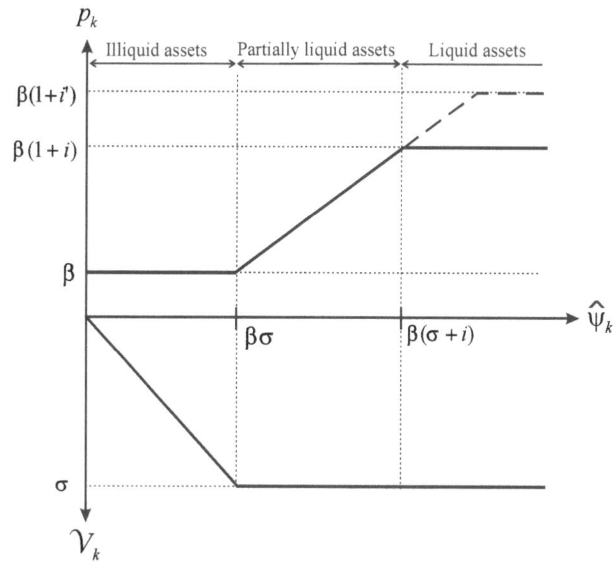

Figure 13.7
Liquidity and asset prices under the threat of fraud

maximum and equal to the frequency of spending opportunities in the DM, σ. Illiquid assets—any asset k such that $\hat{\psi}_k < \underline{\psi}$—trade at the lowest price, which is equal to their fundamental value, and have lower velocities. Figure 13.7 describes transactions velocity as a function of $\hat{\psi}_k$. Note that liquidity differences as measured by differences in velocity are not enough to explain differences in rates of return. For instance, partially liquid assets have a higher rate of return than liquid assets but have the same velocity.

The effect of monetary policy on the price of an asset depends on the degree of liquidity of that asset. Suppose the cost of holding money increases from i to $i' > i$. As is standard, a reduction in the rate of return of currency also reduces real balance holdings, z, and DM output, q. As illustrated in Figure 13.7, a reduction in the rate of return on currency also affects the sets of liquid and partially-liquid assets. Indeed, since $\overline{\psi} = \beta(\sigma + i)$ increases, the set of liquid assets shrinks and the set of partially-liquid assets expands. Although the prices of illiquid and partially-liquid assets are unaffected by a change in the inflation rate, the price of the liquid assets increases so that their rate of return can equal the (lower) rate of return on currency.

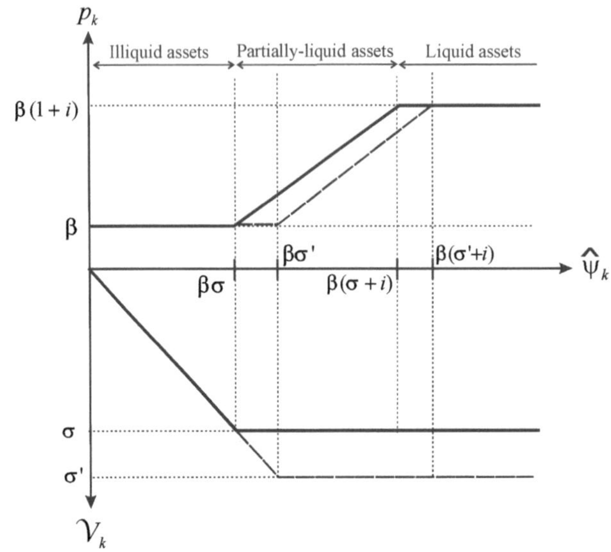

Figure 13.8
Effects of an increase in σ on prices and liquidity

Suppose next there is an increase in the frequency of trading opportunities in the DM from σ to $\sigma' > \sigma$. Because fraud becomes more profitable, the set of illiquid assets expands while the set of liquid assets shrinks; see Figure 13.8. As well, the velocity of partially liquid and liquid assets increases. Perhaps surprisingly, the prices of partially liquid assets fall even though those assets are used more frequently as media of exchange. The reason is that the higher frequency of trade exacerbates the threat of fraud and tightens the resalability constraint. The prices of liquid assets are unaffected since their prices are determined so that their rate of returns are equal to the rate of return of money.

Up to this point we have assumed that there is a fixed cost associated with producing fraudulent assets. Suppose, instead, that the cost is proportional: in order to produce a_k units of fraudulent asset k, a cost equal to $\psi_k^v a_k$ is incurred. The incentive-compatibility constraint, (13.53), is now given by,

$$(p_k - \beta) a_k + \beta \sigma d_k \leq \psi_k^v a_k. \tag{13.71}$$

In the presence of a variable cost, a buyer might want to hold more assets than what he actually spends, $a_k > d_k$, in order to signal its quality to the seller. The incentive-compatibility or resalability constraint can be rewritten as,

$$\frac{d_k}{a_k} \leq \frac{\psi_k^v - (p_k - \beta)}{\beta\sigma}.$$

The resalability constraint specifies that the quantity of an asset that a buyer uses as means of payment, d_k, is proportional to the quantity of assets that he holds, a_k, where the coefficient of proportionality is akin to a "haircut" that depends on the cost of fraud, ψ_k^v, the holding cost of the genuine asset, $p_k - \beta$, and trading frictions, σ.

13.7 Further Readings

The canonical macroeconomic model of asset pricing is due to Lucas (1978) in the context of a frictionless, exchange economy. Risk-free assets in fixed supply have been introduced into the Lagos-Wright model of monetary exchange by Geromichalos, Licari, and Suarez-Lledo (2007). The case where the asset is risky and agents are symmetrically informed about the dividend of the asset in a bilateral match has been studied by Lagos (2010b, 2011). In his model, fiat money is replaced by risk-free bonds. He adds an exogenous constraint on the use of the risky asset as means of payment, and he calibrates the model to explain the risk-free rate and equity premium puzzles following the methodology of Mehra and Prescott (1985). He shows that a slight restriction on the use of the risky asset is necessary to allow the model to match the risk-free rate and the size of the equity premium in the data for plausible degrees of risk aversion. Li and Li (2013) study liquidity and asset prices when are assets are used as collateral to secure loans.

Our model with multiple assets is related to the ones of Wallace (1996, 2000) and Cone (2005) who, in contrast to us, emphasize asset divisibility, or lack of divisibility, to explain the coexistence of money and interest-bearing assets, and the liquidity structure of asset yields. The analysis is similar to the one in Nosal and Rocheteau (2009). A related model is used by Geromichalos, Herrenbrueck, and Salyer (2016) to explain the term premium and by Venkateswarany and Wright (2013) to provide a model of financial and macroeconomic activity. Williamson (2014b) develop a model with credit, and banking in which the differential pledgeability of collateral and the scarcity of collateralizable wealth lead to a term premium. He shows that purchases of long-maturity government debt by the central bank are welfare improving.

Several explanations for the liquidity differences across assets can be found in the literature. Kiyotaki and Moore (2005) assume that the transfer of ownership of capital is not instantaneous so that an agent can steal a fraction of his capital before the transfer is effective. Similarly, Holmstrom and Tirole (1998, 2001) develop a corporate finance approach to liquidity, where a moral hazard problem prevents claims on corporate assets from being written. Freeman (1985), Lester, Postlewaite, and Wright (2012) and Kim and Lee (2008) explain the illiquidity of capital goods by the assumption that claims on capital can be costlessly counterfeited and can only be authenticated in a fraction of meetings. Following Kim (1996) and Berentsen and Rocheteau (2004), Lester, Postlewaite, and Wright (2012) endogenize this fraction of meetings by assuming that agents can invest in a costly technology to recognize claims on capital. The idea that fiat money is a substitute for information acquisition can be found in Brunner and Meltzer (1971) and King and Plosser (1986). Andolfatto, Berentsen, and Waller (2014) and Andolfatto and Martin (2013) study information disclosure regarding the value of a risky asset.

Section 13.6 on endogenous pledgeability follows Rocheteau (2009b) and Li, Rocheteau, and Weill (2012) where fraudulent assets are produced at a positive cost, and the lack of recognizability manifests itself by an endogenous upper bound on the transfer of assets in uninformed matches. Williamson (2014a) develop a model where banks have incentives to fake the quality of collateral and shows that conventional monetary easing can exacerbate these problems, in that the mispresentation of collateral becomes more profitable, thus increasing haircuts and interest rate differentials.

Asymmetries of information are used to endogenize transaction costs in financial markets (e.g., Kyle, 1985; Glosten and Milgrom, 1985), security design (e.g., DeMarzo and Duffie, 1999), and capital structure choices (e.g., Myers and Majluf, 1984). Hopenhayn and Werner (1996) develop a model with multiple indivisible assets traded in bilateral meetings under private information. Rocheteau (2009a) proposes a search-theoretic monetary model in which buyers have some private information about the future value of their risky assets. He shows that buyers in the high-dividend states retain a fraction of their asset holdings in order to signal its quality to the seller in the match. Bajaj (2015, 2016) studies a similar model under the notion of undefeated equilibrium. Guerrieri, Shimer, and Wright (2010), Chang (2014), and Davoodalhosseini (2014) study adverse selection in an asset market under competitive search and show that trading times can be used to screen assets of different qualities.

Nosal and Rocheteau (2008) extend the trading mechanism in Wallace and Zhu (2007) and show that a search-theoretic monetary model can generate rate-of-return differences among seemingly identical assets without imposing trading restrictions and without violating Pareto-efficiency in bilateral trades.

Geromichalos and Simonovska (2014) explain long-standing puzzles in international finance by studying optimal portfolio choice in a two-country model. They assume that foreign assets trade at a cost and show that agents hold relatively more domestic assets. Foreign assets turn over faster than domestic assets because the former have desirable liquidity properties, but represent inferior saving tools.

Appendix

Derivation of (13.23)

From (13.18),

$$i = \sigma \left\{ \pi_H \left[\frac{u'(q_H)}{c'(q_H)} - 1 \right] + \pi_L \left[\frac{u'(q_L)}{c'(q_L)} - 1 \right] \right\}. \tag{13.72}$$

From (13.19) at equality,

$$r(p - p^*) = (p + \bar{\kappa})\sigma \left\{ \pi_H \left[\frac{u'(q_H)}{c'(q_H)} - 1 \right] + \pi_L \left[\frac{u'(q_L)}{c'(q_L)} - 1 \right] \right\} + \sigma \left\{ \pi_H(\kappa_H - \bar{\kappa}) \left[\frac{u'(q_H)}{c'(q_H)} - 1 \right] + \pi_L(\kappa_L - \bar{\kappa}) \left[\frac{u'(q_L)}{c'(q_L)} - 1 \right] \right\}. \tag{13.73}$$

From (13.72) the first term on the right side of (13.73) is equal to $i(p + \bar{\kappa})$, and hence the expression for p can be rearranged as

$$r(p - p^*) = i(p + \bar{\kappa}) + \sigma \left\{ \pi_H(\kappa_H - \bar{\kappa}) \left[\frac{u'(q_H)}{c'(q_H)} - 1 \right] + \pi_L(\kappa_L - \bar{\kappa}) \left[\frac{u'(q_L)}{c'(q_L)} - 1 \right] \right\}. \tag{13.74}$$

It is straightforward to demonstrate that the ρ given by (13.22) is identical to the above bracketed term that is premultiplied by σ. Replacing this bracketed term with ρ, and rearranging, we get equation (13.23).

Concavity of the Problem (13.40)

The buyer's objective function is

$$\Psi(a, z) = -iz - ar(p - p^*) + \sigma\nu\theta \left[u(q) - c(q) \right] + \sigma(1 - \nu)\theta \left[u(q^u) - c(q^u) \right]$$

where q and q^u are given by (13.37) and (13.38). The partial derivatives of the buyer's objective function are

$$\Psi_z(a, z) = -i + \sigma\nu\theta \left[\frac{u'(q) - c'(q)}{\theta c'(q) + (1 - \theta)u'(q)} \right]^+ + \sigma(1 - \nu)\theta \left[\frac{u'(q^u) - c'(q^u)}{\theta c'(q^u) + (1 - \theta)u'(q^u)} \right]^+$$

$$\Psi_a(a, z) = -r(p - p^*) + \sigma\nu\theta \left[\frac{u'(q) - c'(q)}{\theta c'(q) + (1 - \theta)u'(q)} \right]^+ (p + \kappa),$$

where $[x]^+ = \max(x, 0)$. For all (a, z) such that $z + (p + \kappa)a \geq \theta c(q^*) + (1 - \theta)u(q^*)$, $q = q^*$ and $\Psi_a(a, z) = -r(p - p^*)$. The objective function

$\Psi(a,z)$ is concave, but not strictly jointly concave. If $i > 0$, then $q = q^*$ if and only if $p = p^*$. In this case the choice of real balances is uniquely determined by $\frac{u'(q^u)-c'(q^u)}{\theta c'(q^u)+(1-\theta)u'(q^u)} = \frac{i}{\sigma(1-\nu)\theta}$ and the choice of asset holdings is $z \in [\theta c(q^*) + (1-\theta)u(q^*) - z, +\infty)$.

Let us turn to the case where $p > p^*$. Then, we can restrict our attention to portfolios such that $z + (p+\kappa)a < \theta c(q^*) + (1-\theta)u(q^*)$, which implies $q < q^*$. The second and cross partial derivatives are then:

$$\Psi_{zz}(a,z) = \sigma\nu\theta\Delta + \sigma(1-\nu)\theta\Delta^u < 0$$
$$\Psi_{za}(a,z) = \sigma\nu\theta\Delta(p+\kappa) < 0$$
$$\Psi_{aa}(a,z) = \sigma\nu\theta\Delta(p+\kappa)^2 < 0$$

where

$$\Delta = \frac{u''(q)c'(q) - u'(q)c''(q)}{[\theta c'(q) + (1-\theta)u'(q)]^3}$$
$$\Delta^u = \frac{u''(q^u)c'(q^u) - u'(q^u)c''(q^u)}{[\theta c'(q^u) + (1-\theta)u'(q^u)]^3}.$$

The determinant of the Hessian matrix is then

$$\det H = (\sigma\theta)^2 \nu(1-\nu)(p+\kappa)^2\Delta\Delta^u > 0.$$

Hence, for all (a,z) such that $z + (p+\kappa)a < \theta c(q^*) + (1-\theta)u(q^*)$ the objective function $\Psi(a,z)$ is strictly jointly concave. Consequently, if $p > p^*$ then the buyer's problem has a unique solution.

14 Asset Price Dynamics

The 2001 and 2007 recessions in the U.S. were preceded by rapid increases followed by abrupt collapses in the prices of many assets. These events suggest to many observers that asset prices can rise above levels justified by fundamentals, and that price corrections can trigger or amplify fluctuations with important consequences for the macroeconomy. In this chapter we use the model from Chapter 13 to generate this type of equilibrium asset price behavior—increases above fundamental values followed by collapses, or more generally, various types of complicated dynamics. This approach seems reasonable because some assets are valued not only for their rates of return, or dividends, but also for their liquidity services. As a result, price trajectories that seem anomalous from the perspective of standard asset pricing theory might emerge naturally in models with trading frictions.

We describe an economy with an asset in fixed supply, just like the claims to trees that give off fruit as dividends in the Lucas (1978) asset-pricing model. We are agnostic about the exact nature of assets, however, and they can alternatively be interpreted as representing land and/or housing. We will assume that is has certain properties, including the fact that it is easily recognizable, that make it acceptable as means of payment or collateral. This allows us to talk about a premium on liquid assets.

Relative to Chapter 13 we investigate not only steady-state equilibria but also nonstationary equilibria, deterministic cycles, and sunspot equilibria. A key new ingredient is the decision of potential sellers to participate in decentralized trade, like in Chapter 9. This allows us to endogenize the frequency of trading opportunities, and hence the need for liquidity, which can generate multiple stationary equilibria, and dynamic equilibria where asset prices follow bubble-like paths.

As an example, our model will generate a price trajectory with the following features. First, asset prices fluctuate even though fundamentals (preferences, technologies, and government policies) are deterministic and time invariant, and agents are fully rational. Second, the price ultimately crashes, which would typically be interpreted as a bubble bursting. This asset price behavior is usually hard to obtain with real assets as the floor given by the positive fundamental value of the asset typically prevents the asset price from crashing. The fact that there are multiple steady states is key for such dynamics.

The mechanism works in part through complementarities between buyers' asset holdings and sellers' participation decisions. When there are many sellers, it is a buyers' market, and hence buyers want to hold more liquid assets. This drives up asset prices, which gives sellers greater incentives to participate. These complementarities can deliver multiple stationary equilibria, across which asset prices, output, stock market capitalization and welfare are positively related. An additional mechanism works through the intertemporal relationship between asset prices and liquidity. In equilibria where asset prices fluctuate, the liquidity premium depends negatively on the total value of liquid wealth, because a marginal asset is more useful in transactions when liquidity is scarce. Thus, in a boom, asset prices are high because agents anticipate prices will be low, and liquidity more valuable, in the future when wealth falls.

We will conclude the chapter by introducing public liquidity in the form of one-period, real government bonds. We will characterize the optimal supply of public liquidity and its implications for asset prices.

14.1 Asset Prices with Perfect Credit

We start with a special case of an economy where credit works perfectly because; e.g., there is perfect commitment and enforcement of contracts. Liquidity plays no role in this economy: buyers do not need to transfer assets to sellers or use them as collateral since, by assumption, loan repayment is guaranteed. In such an environment, assets are priced at their fundamental value.

The model in this section is identical to that of the previous chapter except that here we allow for the entry of sellers. Participation for sellers is costly: sellers incur a disutility cost $k > 0$ at the beginning of period t if they want to participate in the DM of period t. (It would be easy to interpret the sellers as firms, see Chapter 9.)

The measure of sellers that participate in the DM is n. The matching probabilities for buyers and sellers are $\alpha(n)$ and $\alpha(n)/n$, respectively. We assume that $\alpha'(n) > 0$, $\alpha''(n) < 0$, $\alpha(n) \leq \min\{1, n\}$, $\alpha(0) = 0$, $\alpha'(0) = 1$ and $\alpha(\infty) = 1$.

There is a single asset $A > 0$ that is in fixed supply. Each unit of the asset provides a payoff $\kappa > 0$ at the beginning of each CM, where the payoff is measured in terms of the CM good. One can interpret the asset as a financial security such as a fixed-income security that pays κ each period or an equity share that pays a dividend κ. One can also interpret the asset as a real asset, such as a house or a piece of land. With this interpretation, our model would be one about house price dynamics. For the housing interpretation, we can assume that buyers enjoy utility $\vartheta(h)$ for housing services, where h denotes the services provided by h units of homes. Housing services can be traded competitively at the price κ, which is measured in terms of the CM good. Hence, the demand for housing services is simply $\vartheta'(h) = \kappa$ and by market clearing we have that $\kappa = \vartheta'(A)$. While these different interpretations are strictly equivalent in terms of the analysis, we will interpret the asset as a Lucas tree.

Let $W_t^b(a)$ be the period t value function in the CM of a buyer with a units of the liquid asset *after* the repayment of any debt that was incurred in the previous DM. Similarly, let $V_t^b(a)$ be the period t value function in DM of a buyer that has a units of the asset. Hence, we have

$$W_t^b(a) = (p_t + \kappa)a + \max_{a' \geq 0} \left\{ -p_t a' + \beta V_{t+1}^b(a') \right\}, \tag{14.1}$$

where p_t is the price of the asset measured in terms of the period t CM good.

In any DM match, the seller gives the buyer output q in exchange for a promise (or debt) of b payable in the subsequent CM. To determine the terms of trade, we use the proportional bargaining solution, where $\theta \in [0, 1]$ denotes the buyer's share of the match surplus. Since buyers are able to borrow enough to purchase the efficient level of DM output, the bargaining solution is given by $q_t = q^*$ and $b_t = (1 - \theta) u(q^*) + \theta c(q^*)$.

Consider now pricing the asset. Given the linearity of W_t^b and the bargaining solution, we have

$$V_t^b(a) = \alpha(n_t)\theta \left[u(q^*) - c(q^*) \right] + (p_t + \kappa)a + W_t^b(0). \tag{14.2}$$

The buyer's expected surplus in the DM, the first term on the right side of (14.2), is independent of the buyer's asset holdings. Substituting

(14.2) into (14.1), the buyer's choice of asset holdings in period $t-1$ solves

$$\max_{a\geq 0}\left\{-\left[p_{t-1}-\beta(p_t+\kappa)\right]a\right\}.$$

Clearly, if $(p_t+\kappa)/p_{t-1}>\beta^{-1}$, then there is no solution to the problem (since agents will demand an infinite amount of the asset). If $(p_t+\kappa)/p_{t-1}\leq\beta^{-1}$, then the solution satisfies $[p_{t-1}-\beta(p_t+\kappa)]a=0$. Market clearing implies

$$\frac{p_t+\kappa}{p_{t-1}}=\beta^{-1}. \tag{14.3}$$

The solution to (14.3) is a nonnegative sequence $\{p_t\}_{t=0}^{\infty}$. We impose the transversality condition, $\lim_{t\to\infty}\beta^t p_t=0$, which states that the discounted value of the asset must be 0 as time goes to infinity, i.e., the price of the asset cannot grow faster than the rate of time preference. The price of the liquid asset, described by (14.3), satisfies the first-order difference equation:

$$p_{t-1}=\Gamma^*(p_t)=\frac{p_t+\kappa}{1+r}. \tag{14.4}$$

We plot (14.4) in the left panel of Figure 14.2. Notice that the origin is (p^*,p^*), where $p^*\equiv\kappa/r$ is interpreted as the fundamental value of the asset. The slope of $p_{t-1}=\Gamma^*(p_t)$ in (p_{t-1},p_t) space is $1+r$. Clearly, one solution to (14.4) is $p_t=p_{t-1}=p^*$. However, any other solution that has the initial asset price $p_0>p^*$ violates the transversality condition. Therefore, the only admissible solution to (14.4) consistent with $\lim_{t\to\infty}\beta^t p_t=0$ is $p_t=p^*$.

The expected value of an active seller in the DM of period t is

$$V_t^s=\frac{\alpha(n_t)}{n_t}(1-\theta)\left[u(q^*)-c(q^*)\right]+\beta\max\left\{-k+V_{t+1}^s,0\right\}. \tag{14.5}$$

In words, with probability $\alpha(n_t)/n_t$, the seller meets a buyer in the DM and sells q^* units of output for a promise of $b_t=(1-\theta)u(q^*)+\theta c(q^*)$ units of the general good in the subsequent CM. The seller will participate in the DM of period t as long as $-k+V_t^s\geq 0$. Hence, along the equilibrium path $\max\left\{-k+V_{t+1}^s,0\right\}=0$ and the measure of entrants n_t solves

$$\frac{\alpha(n_t)}{n_t}(1-\theta)\left[u(q^*)-c(q^*)\right]\leq k,\text{ and “ = ” if } n_t>0. \tag{14.6}$$

Define k^* as the critical value of the seller's entry cost such that if $k < k^*$, then $n_t > 0$ and if $k > k^*$, then $n_t = 0$, i.e., k^* solves

$$k^* = (1-\theta)\left[u(q^*) - c(q^*)\right], \tag{14.7}$$

where we have used that $\lim_{n\to 0} \alpha(n)/n = \alpha'(0) = 1$. Therefore, the solution to (14.6) has $n_t > 0$ if $k < k^*$ and $n_t = 0$ if $k > k^*$.

An equilibrium with perfect credit is a nonnegative sequence $\{(p_t, n_t)\}_{t=0}^{\infty}$ solving (14.3) and (14.6), with $\lim_{t\to\infty} \beta^t p_t = 0$. An equilibrium with perfect credit exists, is unique, and is stationary since there is a unique $n_t = n$ that solves (14.6). Hence, with perfect credit, asset prices are constant at their fundamental values, and output in pairwise meetings maximizes gains from trade. Overall efficiency holds if and only if $n = n^*$, where $\alpha'(n^*)\left[u(q^*) - c(q^*)\right] \le k$, with an equality if $n^* > 0$. That is, assuming an interior solution, the entry cost is equal to number of matches created by the marginal seller, $\alpha'(n)$, times the total surplus of the match. This condition coincides with (14.6) if and only if

$$1 - \theta = \frac{n^*\alpha'(n^*)}{\alpha(n^*)},$$

which is the Hosios condition for efficiency in search models already encountered in Chapters 6.5 and 9. For an arbitrary θ, the equilibrium is not generally efficient even with perfect credit and assets priced at their fundamental value: entry can be too high or too low due to sellers not internalizing their impact on the matching probabilities of other sellers and buyers.

14.2 Asset Prices when Liquidity is Essential

We now assume that buyers cannot commit to repay their debt and there does not exist monitoring and enforcement technologies for DM trades. As a result, buyers must use assets as a medium of exchange in the DM in order to facilitate trade. The DM bargaining problem is

$$q_t = \arg\max_q \theta\left[u(q) - c(q)\right] \tag{14.8}$$

$$\text{s.t. } d_{a,t} = \frac{(1-\theta)u(q) + \theta c(q)}{p_t + \kappa} \le a, \tag{14.9}$$

where $d_{a,t}$ represents the transfer of assets from the buyer to the seller in the DM. If $d_{a,t} \le a$ does not bind, then $q_t = q^*$ and

$d_{a,t} = [(1-\theta)u(q^*) + \theta c(q^*)] / (p_t + \kappa)$. If it does bind, then q_t is the solution to $z(q_t) = (p_t + \kappa)a$, where

$$z(q_t) \equiv \theta c(q_t) + (1-\theta)u(q_t). \tag{14.10}$$

The important point here is that q_t is now a function of the buyer's liquid wealth, $(p_t + \kappa)a$. The buyer's DM value function in period t is similar to (14.2) except that q^* is replaced by q_t,

$$V_t^b(a) = \alpha(n_t)\theta\left[u(q_t) - c(q_t)\right] + (p_t + \kappa)a + W_t^b(0). \tag{14.11}$$

The buyer's choice of asset holdings in period t, a_t, can be expressed—after substituting $V_t^b(a)$ from (14.11) into (14.1)—by

$$\max_{a_t \geq 0}\left\{-\left[r(p_{t-1} - p^*) - (p_t - p_{t-1})\right]a_t + \alpha(n_t)\theta\left[u(q_t) - c(q_t)\right]\right\}, \tag{14.12}$$

subject to $z(q_t) = \min\{(p_t + \kappa)a_t, z(q^*)\}$, where, as above, $p^* = \kappa/r$ is the fundamental value of the asset. The buyer chooses liquid assets a_t so as to maximize the expected DM surplus minus the cost of holding the assets.

Clearly, the above problem has a solution only if $r(p_{t-1} - p^*) \geq p_t - p_{t-1}$; otherwise, agents demand an infinite amount of assets. If $r(p_{t-1} - p^*) > p_t - p_{t-1}$, then $a_t = z(q_t)/(p_t + \kappa)$, where q_t is the unique solution (assumed to be interior) to

$$-\left[r(p_{t-1} - p^*) - (p_t - p_{t-1})\right] + \alpha(n_t)\theta\left\{\frac{u'(q_t) - c'(q_t)}{\theta c'(q_t) + (1-\theta)u'(q_t)}\right\}(p_t + \kappa) = 0. \tag{14.13}$$

Hence, if $(p_t + \kappa)/p_{t-1} < 1 + r$, then the solution to the buyer's problem is unique and the distribution of liquid assets across buyers in the DM is degenerate. Note that (14.13) gives a first-order difference equation for the asset price where p_{t-1} is a function of p_t. If $r(p_{t-1} - p^*) = p_t - p_{t-1}$, then the cost of holding assets is zero and any

$$a_t \in \left[\frac{(1-\theta)u(q^*) + \theta c(q^*)}{p_t + \kappa}, +\infty\right)$$

is optimal. In this case, buyers are satiated in liquidity in the sense that they each have enough liquid wealth to buy q^* in the DM. However, the exact distribution of asset holdings is not pinned down.

The expected value of a seller in period t satisfies

$$V_t^s = \frac{\alpha(n_t)}{n_t}\left[-c(q_t) + (p_t + \kappa)d_{a,t}\right] + \beta\max\left\{-k + V_{t+1}^s, 0\right\}. \tag{14.14}$$

Along the equilibrium path $\max\left\{-k+V_{t+1}^{s},0\right\}=0$ and the measure of entrants, n_t, solves

$$\frac{\alpha(n_t)}{n_t}(1-\theta)\left[u(q_t)-c(q_t)\right]\leq k, \text{ and } ``=" \text{ if } n_t>0. \tag{14.15}$$

This condition is similar to (14.6), except that q^* is replaced with q_t.

An equilibrium is a nonnegative sequence $\{(p_t,n_t)\}_{t=0}^{\infty}$ that solves (14.13) and (14.15) with $a_t=A$ and $\lim_{t\to\infty}\beta^t p_t=0$. In this section, we characterize steady-state equilibria, where (p_t,n_t) is constant for all t. Consider the stationary version of the free entry condition (14.15), and let $n(p)$ denote the solution for n given p. From (14.15), any interior solution for n solves

$$\frac{\alpha(n)}{n}=\frac{k}{(1-\theta)\left[u(q)-c(q)\right]}. \tag{14.16}$$

Since $\alpha(n)/n$ is decreasing in n, $\lim_{n\to 0}\alpha(n)/n=1$ and $\lim_{n\to\infty}\alpha(n)/n=0$, a solution $n>0$ to (14.16) exists and is unique if and only if

$$(1-\theta)\left[u\left(q\right)-c\left(q\right)\right]>k, \tag{14.17}$$

where q is a function of $(p+\kappa)A$ that solves $z(q)=\min\{z(q^*),(p+\kappa)A\}$. According to (14.17), sellers participate in the DM if and only if their surplus—which is a fraction $1-\theta$ of the total match surplus—is greater than the cost k. Moreover, if the value of the liquid assets $(p+\kappa)A$ is too small to allow agents to trade q^*, an increase in the price p increases q which, in turn, increases the total match surplus and, by (14.16), induces more sellers to participate. This is the channel by which asset prices affect sellers' utility and participation: higher asset prices increase the DM gains from trade because buyers have more liquid wealth that can be used to purchase more DM goods and higher levels of trade attract more sellers into the DM.

Consider now the stationary version of the asset-pricing condition (14.13), and let $p(n)$ denote the solution for p given n. If $(p^*+\kappa)A\geq z(q^*)$, then $p(n)=p^*$. If aggregate liquidity is sufficiently large so that buyers can purchase q^*, then the asset is priced at its fundamental value. Otherwise, the asset exhibits a liquidity premium $p(n)>p^*$, which in our terminology is a bubble. Intuitively, if n increases, it is easier for buyers to trade, so their demand for liquid assets rises; since assets are in fixed supply the liquidity premium (or bubble) for assets also increases. This is the channel through which sellers' participation decisions, n, affect asset prices.

To describe the set of stationary equilibria, we use the threshold participation cost k^* defined in (14.7) (k^* corresponds to the maximum cost consistent with $n > 0$ when $q = q^*$) and

$$\tilde{k} = (1-\theta)\left[u(\tilde{q}) - c(\tilde{q})\right],$$

where $\tilde{q}$ solves $z(\tilde{q}) = \min\{z(q^*), (p^* + \kappa)A\}$. The quantity $\tilde{k}$ is the threshold for the entry cost below which $n > 0$ when $p = p^*$. Notice that $\tilde{k} \leq k^*$, with strict inequality if $(p^* + \kappa)A < z(q^*)$.

Consider first the case where liquidity is abundant, i.e., when $(p^* + \kappa)A \geq z(q^*)$. Then, there is a unique stationary equilibrium characterized by $p = p^*$, $q = q^*$, and

$$\frac{\alpha(n)}{n} = \frac{k}{(1-\theta)\left[u(q^*) - c(q^*)\right]} \text{ if } k < k^* \text{ and } n = 0 \text{ otherwise.}$$

If there is sufficient liquidity for buyers to purchase q^* in the DM, then assets are priced at their fundamental level, just as in the perfect credit environment.

Consider now the case where liquidity is "scarce," i.e., $(p^* + \kappa)A < z(q^*)$. The free-entry condition (14.16), along with

$$\theta c(q) + (1-\theta)u(q) = (p + \kappa)A \tag{14.18}$$

is diagrammatically depicted in Figure 14.1 for three values of k. Notice that the origin in this figure is $(0, p^*)$ since the fundamental price, p^*, is the relevant lower bound on p. When $k = \tilde{k}$, the free-entry curve, by construction, intersects $(0, p^*)$; when $k < \tilde{k}$, a positive measure of entry occurs at the fundamental price; and when $k > \tilde{k}$, the price of the asset must exceed its fundamental price, p^*, before sellers have an incentive to enter. The buyer's demand for assets is given by:

$$-r(p - p^*) + \alpha(n)\theta\left\{\frac{u'(q) - c'(q)}{\theta c'(q) + (1-\theta)u'(q)}\right\}(p + \kappa) = 0. \tag{14.19}$$

It is also depicted in Figure 14.1. The intersections of the asset price and free-entry curves characterize equilibrium asset prices, p, and equilibrium entry of sellers, n.

If $k < \tilde{k}$, then the stationary equilibrium is unique and is characterized by $n > 0$ and $p > p^*$; see Figure 14.1. If $k > \tilde{k}$ and k is not too big, then there are three possible steady-state equilibria. The multiplicity of equilibria arises from the complementarities between buyers' asset choices and sellers' entry decisions discussed above, i.e., higher entry induces higher asset prices and vice versa. When $k > \tilde{k}$, there is always

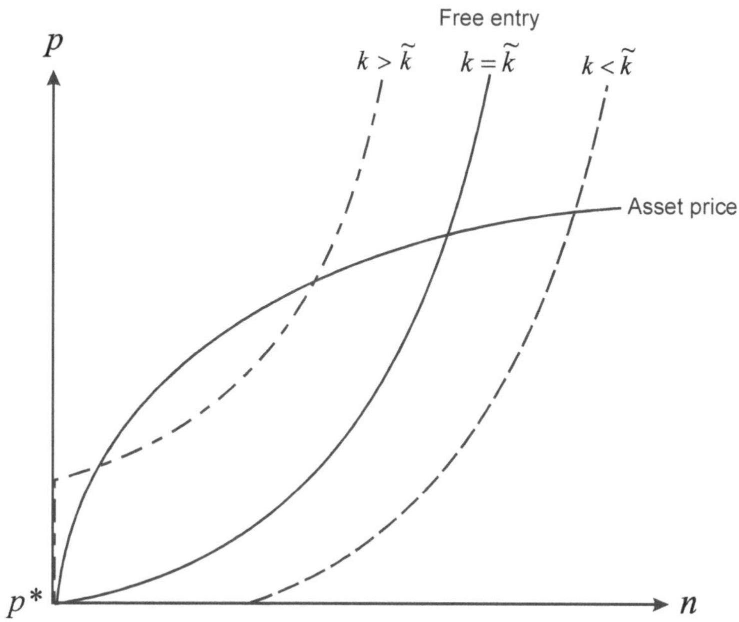

Figure 14.1
Steady-state equilibria

an inactive stationary equilibrium with $(n, p) = (0, p^*)$. In this equilibrium, the DM market shuts down and, since there is no transactions role for assets, assets are priced at their fundamental level, $p = p^*$. There are also two active stationary equilibria. In both of these equilibria, asset prices exceed their fundamental value, $p > p^*$. One equilibrium is characterized by high entry and high asset prices, while the other equilibrium has lower asset prices and lower entry. Hence, if liquid assets are in short supply, then in any equilibrium with $n > 0$, the asset bears a premium, $p > p^*$, and agents trade less than the efficient quantity, $q < q^*$, assuming, of course, that k is not too big. There is a value $\hat{k} > \tilde{k}$ for the entry cost such that the asset pricing and free-entry curves in Figure 14.1 are tangent. If $k > \hat{k}$, then there is a unique stationary equilibrium where the DM shuts down and assets are priced at their fundamental level, $p = p^*$.

The model generates predictions concerning asset prices and trade volume, where trade volume in the DM is measured by the fraction of A used for transactions each period, $\mathcal{V} = \alpha(n)d_a/A$. If there is no shortage of liquidity, then $\mathcal{V} = \alpha(n)z(q^*)/(p^* + \kappa)A$. If liquidity is scarce,

$\mathcal{V} = \alpha(n)$. When there are multiple equilibria, $\mathcal{V}$ and p are positively related across equilibria.

To investigate the efficiency of equilibria, we define welfare, $\mathcal{W}$, to be

$$\mathcal{W} = \frac{\alpha(n)\left[u(q) - c(q)\right] - nk + A\kappa}{1-\beta}, \tag{14.20}$$

which is the discounted sum of the surpluses in all matches net of the entry cost of sellers plus total dividends. It is easy to see that $\mathcal{W}$ is increasing with p across equilibria. Equilibria where p is low have low entry and low output while those with higher p have higher entry and higher output. Assuming an interior solution, efficiency requires $u'(q_t) = c'(q_t)$, i.e., $q_t = q^*$, and $\alpha'(n_t)\left[u(q^*) - c(q^*)\right] = k$, or $n_t = n^*$. Equilibrium is characterized by $q_t = q^*$ if and only if $A \geq z(q^*)/(p^* + \kappa)$ and, from (14.15), $n_t = n^*$ if and only if $[\alpha(n^*)/n^*](1-\theta) = \alpha'(n^*)$. Therefore, an equilibrium is efficient if and only if

$$A \geq \frac{\theta c(q^*) + (1-\theta)u(q^*)}{p^* + \kappa} \text{ and } \theta = 1 - \frac{n^*\alpha'(n^*)}{\alpha(n^*)}.$$

So efficiency requires that liquidity is abundant and the Hosios (1990) condition holds.

14.3 Dynamic Equilibria

We now examine nonstationary equilibria. From (14.13), the price of the liquid asset satisfies the first-order difference equation

$$p_{t-1} = \Gamma(p_t) \equiv \frac{p_t + \kappa}{1+r}\left\{1 + \alpha(n_t)\theta\left[\frac{u'(q_t) - c'(q_t)}{\theta c'(q_t) + (1-\theta)u'(q_t)}\right]\right\}, \tag{14.21}$$

where

$$q_t = \min\left\{q^*, z^{-1}\left[(p_t + \kappa)A\right]\right\}, \tag{14.22}$$

$$n_t = \psi^{-1}\left(\min\left\{\frac{k}{(1-\theta)\left[u\left(q_t\right) - c\left(q_t\right)\right]}, 1\right\}\right), \tag{14.23}$$

$\psi(n) \equiv \alpha(n)/n$ and $z(q) \equiv \theta c(q) + (1-\theta)u(q)$. The function $\Gamma(p)$ is continuous. The price of the liquid asset at $t-1$ equals the discounted sum of the price plus dividend at t, $(p_t + \kappa)/(1+r)$, multiplied by a liquidity factor, the term in braces in (14.21). Any equilibrium $\{p_t\}_{t=0}^{+\infty}$ must also satisfy the transversality condition and $p_t \geq p^*$, since the price cannot be less than the fundamental price.

To analyze $p_{t-1} = \Gamma(p_t)$, we define two thresholds. The first is the price above which buyers have enough liquidity to buy q^*,

$$\bar{p} = \frac{z(q^*)}{A} - \kappa.$$

The second is the price below which sellers stop participating in the DM,

$$\underline{p} = \begin{cases} \frac{z\left[\Delta^{-1}\left(\frac{k}{1-\theta}\right)\right]}{A} - \kappa \text{ if } \frac{k}{1-\theta} \leq u(q^*) - c(q^*) \\ p^* \qquad\qquad\qquad \text{otherwise} \end{cases}$$

where $\Delta(q) = u(q) - c(q)$ for $q \in [0, q^*]$.

If $k \geq k^*$, then $\Gamma(p) = (p + \kappa)/(1 + r)$ for all p. Indeed, if the cost of entry is too high, then sellers, independent of the price of the asset, have no incentive to participate and, as a result, the DM shuts down, $n_t = 0$. In this case there is no role for liquidity. Suppose next that $k < k^*$. If the asset price is low, $p_t < \underline{p}$, then buyers do not hold enough liquidity to get sellers to participate and $n_t = 0$. If the price of the asset is sufficiently high, $p_t > \bar{p}$, liquidity is abundant and $q_t = q^*$. Finally, if $p_t \in \left(\underline{p}, \bar{p}\right)$, then the asset price in period $t-1$ exceeds the discounted sum of the period t asset price and the dividend because the asset facilitates DM trade and it is in short supply. Hence, the nonlinear part of $\Gamma(p_t)$ reflects the existence of a liquidity premium or bubble.

We now examine some simple examples. Consider the case where liquidity is abundant, $A \geq z(q^*)/(p^* + \kappa)$. Then, there are two subcases, $k < k^*$ and $k > k^*$. The phase diagram for $k < k^*$ is as shown in the left panel of Figure 14.2. In this case $p_{t-1} = \Gamma(p_t) = (p_t + \kappa)/(1 + r)$ is linear with slope $1 + r$, so any nonstationary solution to $p_{t-1} = \Gamma(p_t)$ grows asymptotically at rate r, which violates the transversality condition. The unique equilibrium is $p_t = p^*$, which is the same as the equilibrium with perfect credit. When $k > k^*$ sellers do not enter and the unique equilibrium is $p_t = p^*$ and $n_t = 0$. The phase diagram in this case still looks like the left panel of Figure 14.2.

Now consider the case where liquidity is scarce, $A < z(q^*)/(p^* + \kappa)$. If $k \in (\hat{k}, k^*)$, then the unique stationary equilibrium has $n = 0$ but there are values of p in a dynamic equilibrium where sellers enter. Entry would occur at prices $p_t > \underline{p}$, as shown by the nonlinear part of $p_{t-1} = \Gamma(p_t)$ in the right panel of Figure 14.2. However, the unique equilibrium is still $p_t = p^*$ since any proposed dynamic equilibrium with entry violates the transversality condition. In contrast, if the entry cost is sufficiently low, $k < \tilde{k}$, then in any equilibrium the DM is active and the

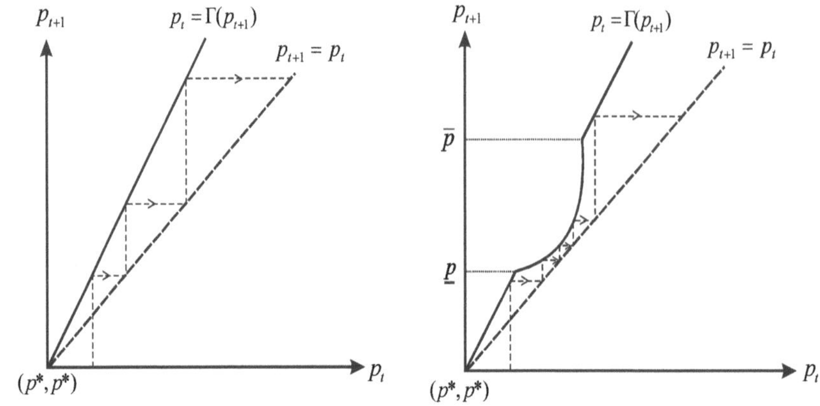

Figure 14.2
Phase diagrams. Left: high entry cost or abundant liquidity. Right: intermediate entry cost.

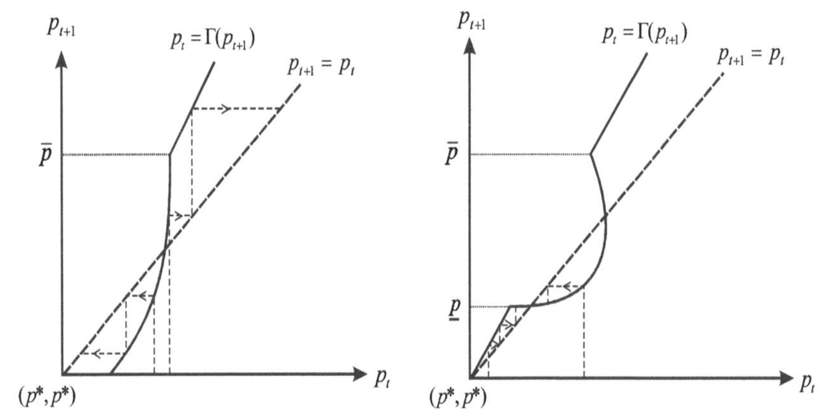

Figure 14.3
Phase diagrams. Left: low cost of entry; Right: intermediate cost of entry and multiple steady states.

price of the liquid asset is above its fundamental value. Moreover, if Γ looks like the left panel of Figure 14.3—i.e. its slope at the stationary equilibrium is greater than one—the equilibrium is unique and stationary. When there are multiple stationary equilibria, this occurs when $k \in (\tilde{k}, \hat{k})$, there can also be multiple nonstationary equilibria, as depicted in the right panel of Figure 14.3. In this case, there are a continuum of trajectories, starting from different initial prices, p_0, between the fundamental price and the higher stationary price, that all converge to an intermediate stationary equilibrium.

In the equilibria described so far, p_t varies monotonically over time. There can also be equilibria with cycles, where p_t, n_t, and q_t fluctuate over time. We proceed by way of an explicit example, using $c(q) = q$, $\alpha(n) = 1 - e^{-n}$ and

$$u(q) = \frac{(q+0.1)^{1-\eta} - 0.1^{1-\eta}}{1-\eta}.$$

For this example, we fix $r = 0.1$, $\kappa = 0.1$ and $\theta = 0.4$, and vary the other parameters. In particular, if the utility parameter η is large, Γ bends backwards, as illustrated in Figure 14.4. In this case, an increase in p_{t+1} has two effects: first, it drives p_t up, as in any standard model; second, it reduces the period t liquidity premium. If η is sufficiently large, the second effect dominates, and the slope of Γ is negative when it crosses the 45° line. In this case, if the slope of Γ is less than 1 in absolute value, there exists a continuum of initial prices, p_0, in the neighborhood of steady state such that p_t and n_t converge nonmonotonically to steady state. Consequently, even when the stationary equilibrium is unique, as in the right panel of Figure 14.4, we can have indeterminacy of dynamic equilibria, and fluctuations in prices and quantities.

Moreover, when the slope of Γ on the 45° line passes -1, the system experiences a flip bifurcation, giving rise to two-period cycles. In the left panel of Figure 14.4, two-period cycles are fixed points of the second iterate of the system, $p_t = \Gamma^2(p_{t+2})$. Alternatively, as in the right panel, the cycles can be found at the intersection of $p_t = \Gamma(p_{t+1})$ and its inverse. The simple intuition for a two-period cycle is as follows.

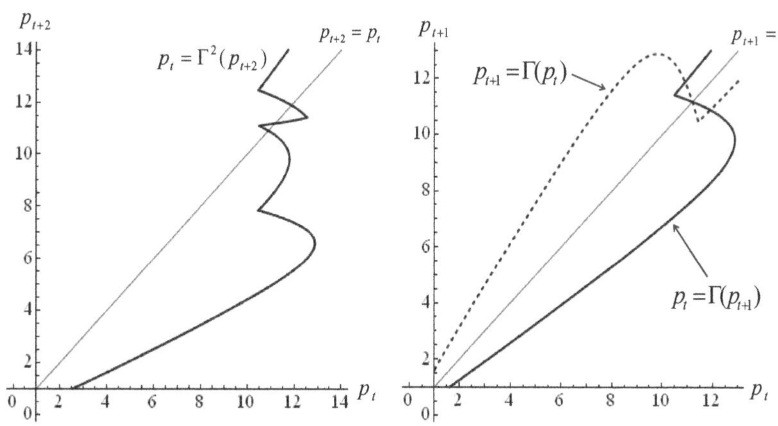

Figure 14.4
Two-period cycles

When p is low, agents anticipate it will increase and liquid wealth will rise—hence, a marginal unit of the asset will have a small liquidity premium. Conversely, if p is high, agents anticipate it will fall and liquidity will become scarce—hence, a big liquidity premium. While Figure 14.4 has a unique stationary equilibrium with a two-period cycle around it, Figure 14.5 has multiple stationary equilibria with a two-period cycle around the highest one. In both cases p alternates between a situation where buyers are liquidity constrained and one where they are not.

There are trajectories with fluctuating asset prices followed by a "crash," as illustrated in Figure 14.6. This trajectory corresponds to an example like the one in Figure 14.5 with parameter values $\eta = 3$, $A = 1.5$, and $k = 20$. During the expansion phases, the return on the liquid asset is equal to the rate of time preference and buyers are not liquidity constrained, but the price cannot keep on increasing, or it would violate transversality. We again have fluctuations around a high-price stationary equilibrium, but now the economy crashes at some point toward a lower-price equilibrium. The timing of the crash is indeterminate—we can make it happen whenever we like. All agents in the model know the bubble will burst, and they know exactly when, in this perfect foresight equilibrium, but there is nothing they can do to either avoid it or profit from it.

Moreover, as η increases further, the system can generate periodic equilibria of higher order, including three-cycles, as shown in

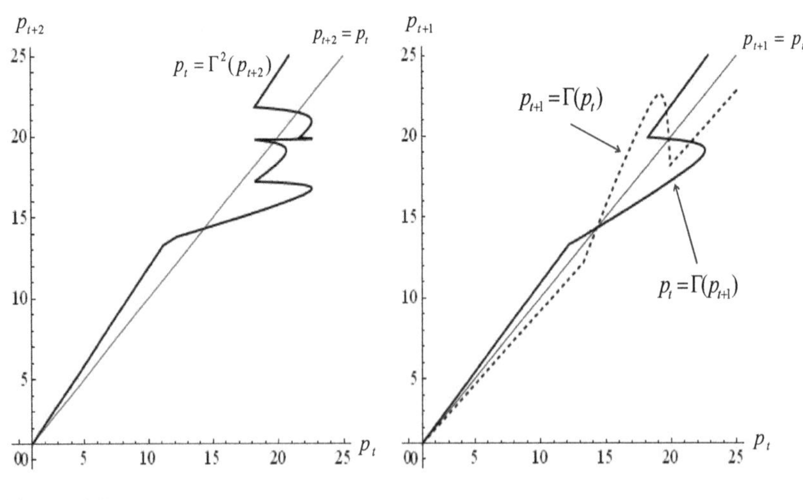

Figure 14.5
Multiple steady states and cycles

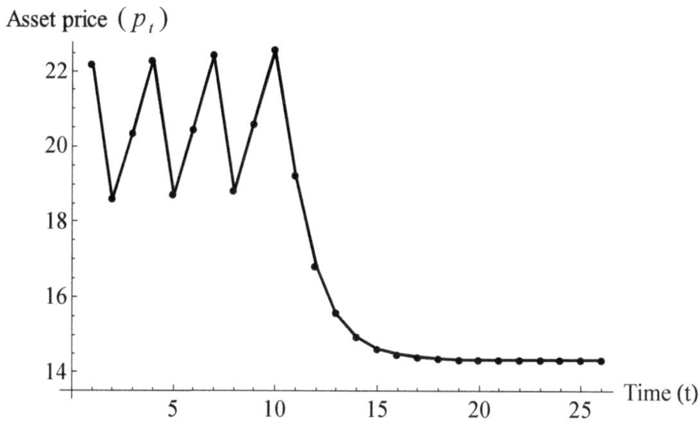

Figure 14.6
One trajectory of the asset price that resembles a bubble bursting

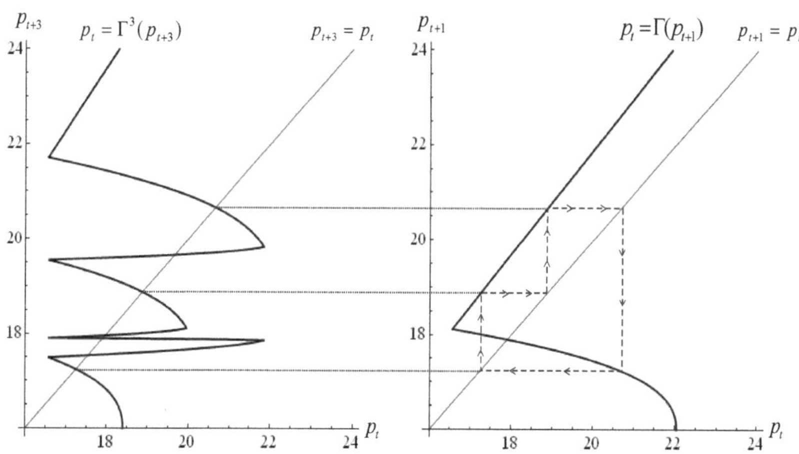

Figure 14.7
Three-period cycles

Figure 14.7. Once three-cycles exist, then all periodic orbits exist, including ∞-cycles, or chaotic dynamics.

14.4 Stochastic Equilibria

So far we have described deterministic equilibria, where agents have perfect foresight. In this section we introduce extrinsic uncertainty, by way of a sunspot, to construct equilibria where the economy fluctuates randomly between states that have different asset prices, trade volumes, and outputs. The sample space of the sunspot variable s is $S = \{\ell, h\}$ and s follows a Markov process with $\lambda_{ss'} = \Pr[s_{t+1} = s' | s_t = s]$, i.e., $\lambda_{ss'}$ is the probability that the period t sunspot s changes to sunspot s' in period $t+1$. We assume that s is observed by all agents at the start of each CM. We focus on proper stationary sunspot equilibria, i.e., equilibria where p_s and n_s are time-invariant functions of s, where prices and/or allocations are different in the two states $s = \ell$ and $s = h$. Of course, there also exist equilibria where agents ignore s.

Following our standard reasoning, we can write the buyer's CM asset accumulation problem as

$$\max_{a \geq 0} \{-p_s a + \beta\alpha(n_s)\theta [u(q_s) - c(q_s)] + \beta(\mathbb{E}_s p_{s'} + \kappa)a\}, \tag{14.24}$$

where q_s is a function of $(p_s + \kappa)a$ and $\mathbb{E}_s p_{s'} = \sum_{s' \in S} \lambda_{ss'} p_{s'}$. The seller's free entry condition is

$$\frac{\alpha(n_s)}{n_s}(1-\theta)[u(q_s) - c(q_s)] \leq k, \tag{14.25}$$

with an equality if $n_s > 0$. The expected value of one unit of a before entering the next CM is $\mathbb{E}_s p_{s'} + \kappa$, where $\mathbb{E}_s p_{s'}$ is the expected price conditional on current s. The first-order condition of the buyer together with $a = A$ yields

$$p_s = \beta(\mathbb{E}_s p_{s'} + \kappa)\left\{1 + \alpha(n_s)\theta\left\{\frac{u'(q_s) - c'(q_s)}{(1-\theta)u'(q_s) + \theta c'(q_s)}\right\}\right\}. \tag{14.26}$$

A proper, stationary, two-state sunspot equilibrium has $(p_t, n_t) = (p_s, n_s)$ in state s, satisfying (14.25) and (14.26), with $(p_\ell, n_\ell) \neq (p_h, n_h)$.

Although other outcomes are possible, for dramatic effect consider equilibria with $n_\ell = 0$ and $n_h > 0$, where the DM completely shuts down whenever $s = \ell$, and reopens whenever "animal spirits" stochastically switch back to $s = h$. Note that in any such equilibrium, $p_\ell > p^*$ because of the expectation that it will reopen at some random date. Hence, there is a positive liquidity premium or bubble component to the asset price even when the DM is inactive. For all $k \in (\tilde{k}, \hat{k})$, if $\lambda_{\ell h}$ and $\lambda_{h\ell}$ are sufficiently small, i.e., there is a very high probability that we remain in the current state, there exists a sunspot equilibrium where $0 = n_\ell < n_h$ and $p^* < p_\ell < p_h$. These sunspot equilibria are obtained by continuity from the multiple steady states, the inactive one and the one with the highest n.

14.5 Public Liquidity Provision

So far, we have seen that scarce liquidity can generate various types of endogenous instability, including periodic and stochastic equilibria. Here we investigate the effects of public liquidity provision on the equilibrium set and price dynamics. Suppose the government can issue one-period real bonds backed by its ability to tax: each bond issued in the CM at t is a claim to 1 unit of CM good at $t+1$. In contrast to private IOUs, bonds are recognizable (non-counterfeitable), which means that they can be traded, in the DM. The supply of bonds is B. The fundamental price of bonds is $p_b^* = \beta$.

The buyer's problem can now be written

$$\max_{a \geq 0, b \geq 0} \{-r\left[(p_{t-1} - p^*) - (p_t - p_{t-1})\right] a - \left[(1+r)p_{b,t-1} - 1\right] b$$
$$+ \alpha(n_t)\theta\left[u\left(q_t\right) - c\left(q_t\right)\right]\},$$

where $q_t = q^*$ if $z(q^*) \leq (p_t + \kappa)a + b$ and $z(q_t) = (p_t + \kappa)a + b$ otherwise. (Notice that we use the same notation for public debt that we previously used for private debt, b.) The first-order conditions imply

$$\frac{r\left(p_{t-1} - p^*\right) - \left(p_t - p_{t-1}\right)}{p_t + \kappa} = (1+r)p_{b,t-1} - 1$$
$$= \alpha(n_t)\theta \frac{u'(q_t) - c'(q_t)}{\theta c'(q_t) + (1-\theta)u'(q_t)}. \tag{14.27}$$

Since Lucas trees and government bonds are equally liquid, they must have the same return, $(p_t + \kappa)/p_{t-1} = 1/p_{b,t-1}$. Moreover, notice that the real interest rate on either the liquid asset or government bond, $(1 - p_{b,t-1})/p_{b,t-1}$, is less than the discount rate, r, whenever $q_t < q^*$.

When there is a shortage of private assets, $z(q^*) > (p^* + \kappa)A$, the government could supplement the stock of liquidity by supplying a sufficient amount of bonds so that buyers are satiated in liquidity. In this situation, agents can trade q^* in the DM and the liquidity premium vanishes, $p = p^*$. Although such a policy implies DM trade is efficient, the measure of active sellers in the DM will generically be inefficient.

If the government policy is not optimal, an increase of B might not reduce p. Figure 14.8 provides an example where, in the absence of intervention, there exist one inactive and two active stationary equilibria. Suppose now that the government introduces some bonds, but the total supply of liquid assets is insufficient to allow agents to trade q^* in the DM. This eliminates the inactive and the "low" equilibria, but

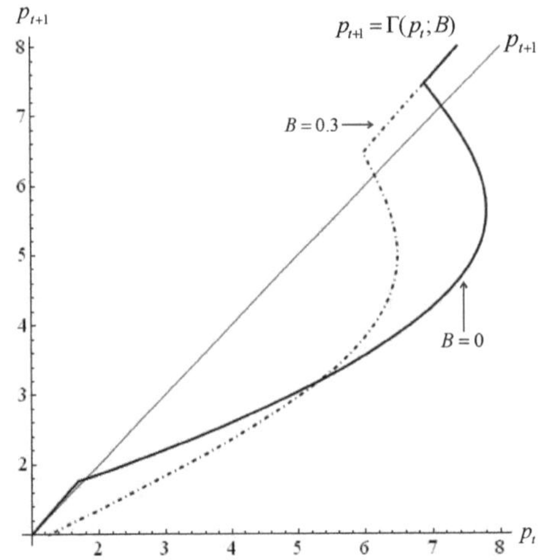

Figure 14.8
Public liquidity provision and asset prices

the high equilibrium remains. Therefore, if the economy was initially at the (active) low price equilibrium, an increase in liquidity can actually result in a higher asset price.

Finally, the result that the provision of liquidity is optimal when agents are satiated, in the sense that $q = q^*$, is not robust to the choice of the DM pricing mechanism. If we use a Walrasian pricing mechanism instead of proportional bargaining, it can be optimal for some parameters to keep liquidity scarce and have $q_t < q^*$. This can happen because sellers entering the DM do not internalize the congestion that their entry decision has on other sellers; entry can be too high. A policy can mitigate this effect by making liquid assets costly to hold, which requires the asset price p to be above its fundamental value.

14.6 Further Readings

This chapter is based on Rocheteau and Wright (2013), which extends Rocheteau and Wright (2005) to have Lucas trees instead of fiat money and studies dynamic equilibria and not simply steady states. He, Wright, and Zhu (2015) reinterpret the asset as homes by introducing it in the utility function. Ferraris and Watanabe (2011) have a related model where assets play a role as collateral. Branch, Petrosky-Nadeau, and Rocheteau (2015) incorporate this description of the goods market into a two-sector model of the labor market to study qualitatively and quantitatively the effects of home-equity extraction on housing prices, unemployment, and labor flows. Branch (2015) adopts a similar model to show the existence of bubbles under adaptive learning. Beaudry, Galizia, and Portier (2015) develop a model where agents want to concentrate their purchases of goods at times when purchases by others are high, since in such situations unemployment is low and therefore taking on debt is perceived as being less risky. They show that their model can generate endogenous limit cycles that are consistent with U.S. business cycle fluctuations in employment and output.

There is a related literature based on OLG models, such as Wallace (1980), Grandmont (1985), and Tirole (1985). See Azariadis (1993) for a textbook treatment. Kiyotaki and Moore (1997, 2005) and Kocherlakota (2008, 2009) also have assets playing dual roles, as factors of production and collateral.

LeRoy (2004) surveys papers on bubbles. Other models of bubbles include Allen and Gale (2000) and Barlevy (2008), who emphasize agency problems. Farhi and Tirole (2012) consider an OLG version of the corporate finance model in Holmstrom and Tirole (2011), where agency problems prevent firms from borrowing against future output. They show that bubbles are more likely when the supply of outside liquidity is scarce and corporate income is less pledgeable.

15 Trading Frictions in Over-the-counter Markets

"Liquidity is the ability to trade large size quickly, at low cost, when you want to trade. It is the most important characteristic of well-functioning markets. ... Liquidity—the ability to trade—is the object of a bilateral search in which buyers look for sellers and sellers look for buyers. The various liquidity dimensions are related to each other through the mechanics of this bilateral search. Traders must understand these relations in order to trade effectively."

Larry Harris, *Trading and Exchanges: Market Microstructure for Practitioners* (2003, Chapter 19)

In previous chapters, we defined the liquidity of an asset in terms of its ability to function as a medium of exchange in goods markets that are characterized by trading frictions. In this chapter, we revisit the notion of liquidity. In contrast to previous chapters, there are no trading frictions associated with the purchase and consumption of goods and, as a result, the asset does not play any role as a means of payment. Instead, trading frictions are introduced directly into an asset market best described as an over-the-counter market, with bilateral matches between investors and dealers. Our simple model will be able to capture different dimensions of liquidity that have been identified in the finance literature, such as the volume of trade, bid-ask spreads, and trading delays.

We consider an economy where investors accumulate capital goods to produce a general consumption good, as in Chapter 11.1. But idiosyncratic productivity shocks give investors a reason to want to reallocate their asset holdings. In particular, investors with low productivity want to sell their capital holdings to agents with high productivity. Investors, however, do not have direct access to a centralized market where they can readjust their asset holdings instantly. Instead, they adjust their asset holdings via a network of dealers.

An investor's asset demand depends not only on his productivity at the time he is able to access the market, but also on his expected productivity over the period of time that he does not have the opportunity to adjust his asset holdings. When asset markets are illiquid, investors put more weight on their future expected productivity and, as a result, will adjust their asset positions in a way that reduces their need to trade. Conversely, a reduction in trading frictions makes the investor less likely to remain locked into an undesirable asset position and, therefore, induces him to put more weight on his current productivity when determining his asset position. As a result, a reduction in trading frictions induces an investor to demand a larger asset position if his current productivity is relatively high, and a smaller position if it is relatively low.

This effect on the dispersion of the distribution of asset holdings is a key channel through which trading frictions determine trade volume, bid-ask spreads, and trading delays. If it is easier to trade the asset, or if dealers have less bargaining power, investors take more extreme asset positions, which leads to a higher volume of trade. As well, bid-ask spreads tend to be lower, and trading delays shorter. We also examine how asset market frictions affect asset prices.

Finally, we endogenize trading frictions by allowing free entry of dealers in the market-making sector. As the number of dealers increases, trading delays fall. We show that the presence of complementarities between investors' asset holding decisions and dealers' entry decisions can lead to multiple equilibria, so that liquidity in the market can dry up because of self-fulfilling beliefs.

15.1 The Environment

We depart from the standard environment along a number of dimensions. We now assume time is continuous. This assumption simplifies the analysis; e.g., on a small time interval, we can rule out the possibility of multiple events occurring. Even though we must drop the assumption that periods are divided into day and night subperiods, as this distinction is meaningless in continuous time, there still exist centralized and decentralized markets.

There is one type of consumption good, the general good. There are two types of infinitely-lived agents, called investors and dealers, with a unit measure of each type. Both agents consume the general good, where the utility of consuming x units of the general good is x. Agents discount future utility at rate r.

The general good can be produced with two different technologies. One technology has h units of the general good being produced from h units of labor, (and h units of labor generates h units of disutility). The general good can also be produced by a technology that uses capital as an input, and depends on the investor's productivity. This technology is described by $f_i(k)$, where $k \in \mathbb{R}_+$ represents capital invested, $i \in \{1,...,I\}$ indexes the productivity of the investor who operates the capital, and $f_i(k)$ is twice continuously differentiable, strictly increasing, and strictly concave. Capital is a durable, perfectly divisible asset that is in fixed supply, $K \in \mathbb{R}_+$. With instantaneous probability equal to δ, each investor receives a productivity shock. This means that productivity shocks occur according to a Poisson process with arrival rate δ, i.e., the inter-arrival time between two shocks is exponentially distributed with mean $1/\delta$. Conditional on receiving this shock, the investor draws productivity type $j \in \{1,...,I\}$ with probability $\pi_j > 0$, where $\sum_{i=1}^{I} \pi_i = 1$. These δ shocks capture the idea that investors' productivities vary over time, which results in investors wanting to rebalance their asset positions.

Dealers do not have access to the capital technology to produce the general good, and do not hold positions in capital. Dealers can, however, trade capital assets continuously in a competitive market. Investors do not have direct access to the competitive asset market, but they do have periodic contact with dealers who can trade in this market

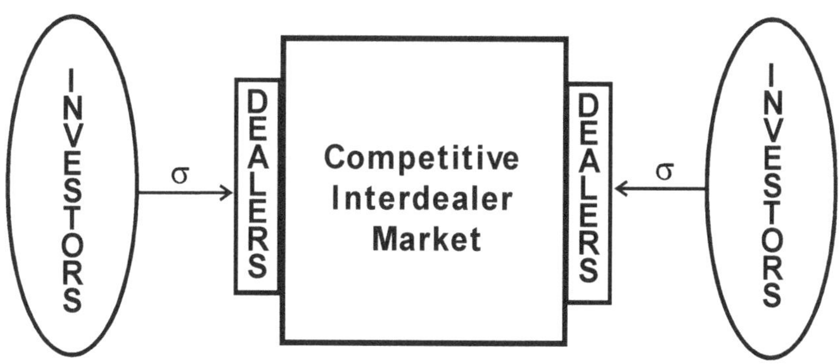

Figure 15.1
Trading arrangement

on their behalf. The arrival rate with a dealer for the investor is $\sigma > 0$. The bilateral matching process between investors and dealers plays the part of the decentralized market in earlier chapters. The trading process for the capital asset is depicted in Figure 15.1. Once a dealer and an investor have contacted one another, they negotiate over the quantity of assets that the dealer will acquire in competitive markets on behalf of the investor, and the intermediation fee that the dealer charges for his services.

15.2 Equilibrium

Let $V_i(k)$ denote the maximum expected discounted utility attainable by an investor who is of productivity type i and is holding k units of the asset. The flow Bellman equation that determines $V_i(k)$ is

$$\begin{aligned} rV_i(k) &= f_i(k) + \sigma \{V_i(k_i) - V_i(k) - p(k_i - k) - \phi_i(k)\} \\ &\quad + \delta \sum_{j=1}^{I} \pi_j [V_j(k) - V_i(k)]. \end{aligned} \tag{15.1}$$

The flow Bellman equation can be interpreted as an asset pricing equation, where the asset to be priced is an investor in state (i,k). The left side is the opportunity cost from holding this asset, while the right side is the dividends and capital gains or losses from holding the asset. According to (15.1), an investor with productivity type i and asset holdings k produces $f_i(k)$ of the general good, which can be interpreted as a flow dividend. With instantaneous probability σ, the investor contacts a dealer, and readjusts his asset holdings from k to k_i. This readjustment raises his lifetime expected utility by $V_i(k_i) - V_i(k)$, which can be interpreted as a capital gain, net of the fee, $\phi_i(k)$, he pays to the dealer and the value of the assets he purchases, $p(k_i - k)$. We will show that the intermediation fee, ϕ_i, depends on the capital stock held by the investor, but the desired capital stock, k_i, does not. With instantaneous probability δ he receives a productivity shock: conditional on receiving this shock, his productivity type becomes $j \in \{1,...,I\}$ with probability $\pi_j > 0$.

The maximum expected discounted utility attained by a dealer is denoted by V^d and solves

$$rV^d = \sigma \int \phi_i(k) dH(k,i), \tag{15.2}$$

where H represents the distribution of investors across asset holdings and preference types states. With instantaneous probability σ, the dealer meets an investor who is drawn at random from the population of investors. The dealer trades in the competitive asset market on behalf of the investor and receives an intermediation fee, $\phi_i(k)$, for his services. The size of the intermediation fee depends on the productivity type of the investor, i, and his asset holdings at the time he contacts the dealer, k.

We now examine the determination of the terms of trade in a bilateral meeting between a dealer and an investor. Suppose that the investor's productivity type is i, and he holds k units of capital. The terms of trade will specify a new asset position for the investor, k', and the intermediation fee, ϕ, paid to the dealer. If agreement (k', ϕ) is reached, then the payoff to the investor is

$$V_i(k') - p(k' - k) - \phi. \tag{15.3}$$

The investor enjoys the expected lifetime utility associated with his new stock of capital, $V_i(k')$, minus the cost of his investment in capital, $p(k' - k)$, and the intermediation fee paid to the dealer, ϕ. The payoff of the dealer is simply

$$V^d + \phi. \tag{15.4}$$

If no agreement is reached, the payoff of the investor is $V_i(k)$, and the payoff of the dealer is V^d. We assume that the agreement (k', ϕ) is given by the solution to a generalized Nash bargaining problem, where the dealer's bargaining power is $\theta \in [0, 1]$. This agreement is given by

$$[k_i, \phi_i(k)] = \arg\max_{(k', \phi)} [V_i(k') - V_i(k) - p(k' - k) - \phi]^{1-\theta} \phi^{\theta}. \tag{15.5}$$

The solution to (15.5) is

$$k_i = \arg\max_{k'} [V_i(k') - pk'], \tag{15.6}$$

$$\phi_i(k) = \theta[V_i(k_i) - V_i(k) - p(k_i - k)]. \tag{15.7}$$

According to (15.6), the choice of capital is the one that an investor would make if he could trade directly in the competitive asset market at the price p: it maximizes the value of the investor, net of the cost of acquiring the capital. According to (15.7) the intermediation fee is chosen so that the dealer gets a fraction θ of total match surplus.

If we substitute $\phi_i(k)$, given by its expression in (15.7), into (15.1), we get

$$rV_i(k) = f_i(k) + \sigma(1-\theta)\left[V_i(k_i) - V_i(k) - p(k_i - k)\right] + \delta \sum_{j=1}^{I} \pi_j \left[V_j(k) - V_i(k)\right]. \tag{15.8}$$

The investor's flow payoff, given by (15.8), is equivalent what he would receive in an economy where he is able to extract the entire surplus from his match with a dealer, but meets a dealer with an instantaneous probability equal to only $\sigma(1-\theta)$. Thus, from the investor's point of view, the stochastic trading process and the bargaining solution are payoff-equivalent to an alternative trading arrangement, in which he has all the bargaining power in bilateral negotiations with dealers, but only gets to meet dealers with instantaneous probability $\sigma(1-\theta)$.

We now proceed to provide a closed-form solution for the investor's value function. We can rearrange (15.8) to read as,

$$\left[r + \delta + \sigma(1-\theta)\right] V_i(k) = f_i(k) + \sigma(1-\theta)pk + \delta \sum_{j=1}^{I} \pi_j V_j(k) + \Omega_i, \tag{15.9}$$

where $\Omega_i \equiv \sigma(1-\theta)\max_{k'}\left[V_i(k') - pk'\right]$. If we multiply both sides of (15.9) by π_i, sum across i's, and rearrange, we get

$$\sum_{i=1}^{I} \pi_i V_i(k) = \frac{\sum_{i=1}^{I} \pi_i f_i(k) + \sigma(1-\theta)pk + \bar{\Omega}}{r + \sigma(1-\theta)}, \tag{15.10}$$

where $\bar{\Omega} \equiv \sum_{i=1}^{I} \pi_i \Omega_i$. By substituting (15.10) into (15.9), we are able to get a closed-form solution for the value function of investors,

$$V_i(k) = \frac{\bar{f}_i(k) + \sigma(1-\theta)pk}{r + \sigma(1-\theta)} + \Gamma_i, \tag{15.11}$$

where

$$\Gamma_i \equiv \frac{\Omega_i}{r + \delta + \sigma(1-\theta)} + \frac{\delta \bar{\Omega}}{\left[r + \delta + \sigma(1-\theta)\right]\left[r + \sigma(1-\theta)\right]}$$

and

$$\bar{f}_i(k) = \frac{(r + \sigma(1-\theta)) f_i(k) + \delta \sum_j \pi_j f_j(k)}{r + \sigma(1-\theta) + \delta}. \tag{15.12}$$

From (15.12), we see that $\bar{f}_i(k)$ is a weighted average of the productivities in the different states. The weights on the current productivity, $f_i(k)$, and future ones, $f_j(k)$, are functions of the transition rates σ and δ, the discount rate r, and the dealer's bargaining power, θ. As the trading frictions vanish, i.e., as σ goes to infinity, $\bar{f}_i(k)$, approaches the current productivity, $f_i(k)$. It can be shown, from (15.11), that $V_i(k)$ is continuous and strictly concave in k. From (15.6) and (15.11), the optimal choice of capital is given by

$$k_i = \arg\max_{k_i \geq 0}[\bar{f}_i(k_i) - rpk_i]. \tag{15.13}$$

From the strict concavity of $\bar{f}_i(k)$, k_i is uniquely determined. Moreover, from (15.7) and (15.11) the expression for the intermediation fee is

$$\phi_i(k) = \frac{\theta}{r + \sigma(1-\theta)} \left\{ \left[\bar{f}_i(k_i) - \bar{f}_i(k) \right] - rp\,(k_i - k) \right\}. \tag{15.14}$$

The intermediation fee depends on the dealer's bargaining power, θ, the discount factor, r, and the transition rates, σ and δ. It also varies with the change in the investor's asset position. Intuitively, the intermediation fee is proportional to the gain that the investor enjoys from readjusting his asset holdings.

We now characterize the steady-state distribution of investors' types, $H(k,j)$. The individual state of an investor is the pair $(k,j) \in \mathbb{R}_+ \times \{0,...,I\}$, where k is his current asset holdings and j his productivity type. Note that any state (k,j) such that $k \notin \{k_i\}_{i=1}^I$ is transient since whenever an investor adjusts his asset holdings in a steady-state he chooses $k \in \{k_i\}_{i=1}^I$. Thus, the set of ergodic states is $\{k_i\}_{i=1}^I \times \{1,...,I\}$. This allows us to simplify the exposition by denoting state (k_i,j) by $ij \in \{1,...,I\}^2$. Hence, for state ij, i represents the quantity of capital the investor currently has, i.e., the one corresponding to the productivity shock he had at the time he last rebalanced his asset holdings, and j represents his current productivity shock. The measure of investors in state ij is denoted n_{ij}.

In a steady state, the flow of investors entering state ij must equal the flow of investors leaving state ij:

$$\delta\pi_j \sum_{k \neq j} n_{ik} - \delta(1-\pi_j)n_{ij} - \sigma n_{ij} = 0, \quad \text{if } j \neq i, \tag{15.15}$$

$$\sigma \sum_{k \neq i} n_{ki} + \delta\pi_i \sum_{k \neq i} n_{ik} - \delta(1-\pi_i)n_{ii} = 0. \tag{15.16}$$

According to (15.15), the measure of investors in state $ij, j \neq i$, increases whenever an investor in some state ik, $k \neq j,i$, receives a productivity shock j, which occurs with instantaneous probability $\delta\pi_j$. The measure of investors decreases whenever an investor in state ij receives a new productivity shock different from j, which occurs with instantaneous probability $\delta(1-\pi_j)$, or whenever such an investor is able to readjust his asset holdings, which occurs with instantaneous probability σ. Equation (15.16) has a similar interpretation for agents in state ii.

The flows between states is depicted in Figure 15.2 for $I=3$. Each circle represents a state. The horizontal arrows represent flows due to productivity shocks, whereas the vertical arrows indicate flows due to asset holdings readjustments. The individual states shaded in grey, which lie on the diagonal, are those states for which there is no mismatch between the investor's current productivity type and his capital holdings.

It can be shown that the steady-state distribution $(n_{ij})_{i,j=1}^{I}$ satisfies

$$n_{ij} = \frac{\delta\pi_i\pi_j}{\sigma+\delta}, \quad \text{for } j \neq i, \tag{15.17}$$

$$n_{ii} = \frac{\delta\pi_i^2 + \sigma\pi_i}{\sigma+\delta}. \tag{15.18}$$

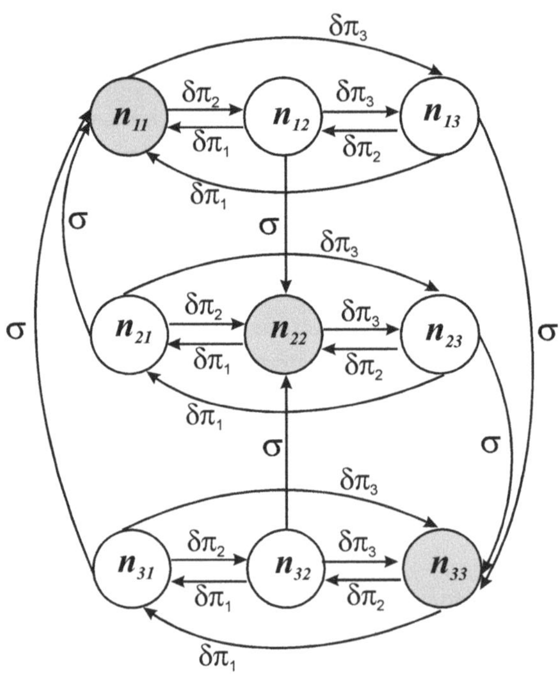

Figure 15.2
Flows across states

The marginal distributions, defined by $n_{i.} = \sum_j n_{ij}$ and $n_{.j} = \sum_i n_{ij}$, have the property that $n_{i.} = n_{.i} = \pi_i$. So the measure of investors with productivity type i is equal to π_i, the probability of drawing productivity shock i, conditional on getting a productivity shock. Note that the distribution of probabilities across states is symmetric, i.e., $n_{ij} = n_{ji}$. Note also that $\partial n_{ij}/\partial\sigma < 0$ if $i \neq j$ and $\partial n_{ii}/\partial\sigma > 0$, which means that the measure of investors who are matched to their desired capital increases as the rate at which investors get to meet dealers increases.

The only remaining equilibrium variable to be determined is the price of capital in the competitive market, p. This price equates the demand and supply of assets, i.e., $\sum_{i,j} n_{ij}k_i = K$. Using that $\sum_j n_{ij} = \pi_i$, this market-clearing condition can be expressed as

$$\sum_i \pi_i k_i = K. \tag{15.19}$$

The intuition behind equation (15.19) is the following. In a steady state, the measure of investors that have productivity type i is π_i. Each investor of type i demands k_i independent of his stock of capital at the time he meets a dealer. Hence, the aggregate demand of capital, in flow terms, is $\sigma \sum_i \pi_i k_i$. From the Law of Large Numbers, the flow supply of capital is the average capital stock held by the investors who contact dealers, σK.

There exists a unique steady-state equilibrium. The distribution of investors across asset holdings and productivity types is given by (15.17) and (15.18). The individual choices of asset holdings, the k_i's in (15.13), depend negatively on p, the equilibrium price in the interdealer market. Assuming an interior solution,

$$k_i = \bar{f}_i'^{-1}(rp).$$

Given these individual demands, the market-clearing condition (15.19) determines a unique price, the solution to

$$\sum_i \pi_i \bar{f}_i'^{-1}(rp) = K.$$

To illustrate how a reduction in trading frictions affects the equilibrium, consider the limiting case where search frictions vanish, i.e., where $\sigma \to \infty$. Investors can trade in the asset market continuously. In the limit, from (15.12) and (15.13), we get

$$\frac{f_i'(k_i)}{r} = p \tag{15.20}$$

for $i = 1,...,I$. From (15.14) we see that $\phi_i(k) \to 0$ for all k and i when $\sigma \to \infty$. Combining (15.19) and (15.20), we see that the price of the asset converges to the solution to $\sum_i \pi_i f_i'^{-1}(rp) = K$. The limiting distribution of investors across asset holdings and productivity types is $n_{ii} = \pi_i$ for each i, and $n_{ij} = 0$ for $j \neq i$. In this case, investors with productivity i choose k_i continuously by equating the marginal return from the asset, $f_i'(k_i)$, to its flow price, rp. When search frictions vanish, the equilibrium fee, asset price, and distribution of asset positions are the ones that would prevail in a Walrasian economy.

15.3 Trading Frictions and Asset Prices

In Chapter 13 we looked at asset prices in economies with trading frictions. We established that the price of an asset can depart from its "fundamental" value if the asset has a role in facilitating trade in the DM, that is, the asset can be used as a medium of exchange. In this case, the asset price will decrease if trading frictions in the DM increase. The approach we take in this chapter is different. The asset is not used to facilitate trade, but trading frictions plague the asset market itself. In this section we will revisit the effects that trading frictions have on asset prices.

We assume the following specification for the technology that investors possess:

$$f_i(k) = A_i k^{\alpha}, \quad 0 < \alpha < 1,$$

and $A_1 < A_2 < ... < A_I$. Let $\bar{A} = \sum_j \pi_j A_j$ denote the average productivity. From (15.13) the demand for capital by an investor with productivity type j is

$$k_j = \left(\frac{\alpha}{rp} \frac{(r + \sigma(1-\theta)) A_j + \delta \bar{A}}{r + \sigma(1-\theta) + \delta} \right)^{1/(1-\alpha)}. \tag{15.21}$$

It is easy to see from (15.21) that, for a given price of capital, p, k_j increases with σ as long as $A_j > \bar{A}$. That is, investors with a productivity shock above average increase their demand for capital when σ increases.

Agents with $A_j > \bar{A}$ have a current marginal productivity that is higher than what they expect it to be in the future. Because of search frictions, their choice of capital, k_j, will be lower than $k_j^{\infty} = (\alpha A_j / rp)^{1/(1-\alpha)}$, which is what they would choose in a world with no trading frictions. If investors' productivity is equal to $\bar{A}$, then the investor's choice of capital is $\bar{k} = \left(\alpha\bar{A}/rp\right)^{1/(1-\alpha)}$. Since A_j is higher than $\bar{A}$, the investor anticipates that his productivity is likely to revert toward $\bar{A}$ in the future; when this happens, he may be unable to rebalance his asset holdings for some time. As a result, the investor's optimal choice of capital holdings is a weighted average of the optimal holdings for productivities A_j and $\bar{A}$, i.e.,

$$k_j = \left(\frac{r+\sigma(1-\theta)}{r+\sigma(1-\theta)+\delta} \left(k_j^{\infty}\right)^{1-\alpha} + \frac{\delta}{r+\sigma(1-\theta)+\delta} \left(\bar{k}\right)^{1-\alpha} \right)^{1/(1-\alpha)}.$$

An increase in σ means that it will be easier for the investor to find a dealer in the future, and this makes him put more weight on his current marginal productivity from holding the asset relative to its expected value. Hence, as σ increases so does k_j. Conversely, investors with a productivity shock below the average, $A_j < \bar{A}$, reduce their demand for capital when σ increases.

From all of this, we can conclude that, for given p, as σ increases, the dispersion of asset holdings will also increase. Figure 15.3 illustrates the effect that a reduction on trading frictions has on the distribution of asset holdings. The black bars represent the distribution of asset holdings when the frequency of meetings with dealers is σ, while the grey bars represent the distribution when $\sigma' > \sigma$.

From the market-clearing condition (15.19), the asset price is given by

$$p = K^{-(1-\alpha)} \left[\sum_{j=1}^{I} \pi_j \left(\frac{\alpha}{r} \frac{(r+\sigma(1-\theta))\,A_j + \delta\bar{A}}{r+\sigma(1-\theta)+\delta} \right)^{1/(1-\alpha)} \right]^{1-\alpha}. \tag{15.22}$$

Note that the expected value of the terms in round brackets, $\sum_{j=1}^{I} \pi_j (\alpha/r)[(r+\sigma(1-\theta))\,A_j + \delta\bar{A}]/[r+\sigma(1-\theta)+\delta]$, is constant and equal to $\alpha\bar{A}/r$, and that the function $x^{1/(1-\alpha)}$ is convex in x when $0 < \alpha < 1$. If σ increases, the dispersion of the $[(r+\sigma(1-\theta))\,A_j + \delta\bar{A}]/[r+\sigma(1-\theta)+\delta]$ terms in (15.22) increases but their mean remains constant. From the convexity of the function $x^{1/(1-\alpha)}$ the asset price will increase. Therefore, when $f_i(k) = A_i k^{\alpha}$, $0 < \alpha < 1$, our model predicts a negative relationship between asset prices and trading frictions, just as in Chapter 13. The reasoning behind these negative relationships is, however, different. In Chapter 13, asset prices decrease as trading frictions become more severe because the asset is used less frequently as a means of payment. In this section, trading frictions generate a mismatch between investors' productivities and their capital holdings,

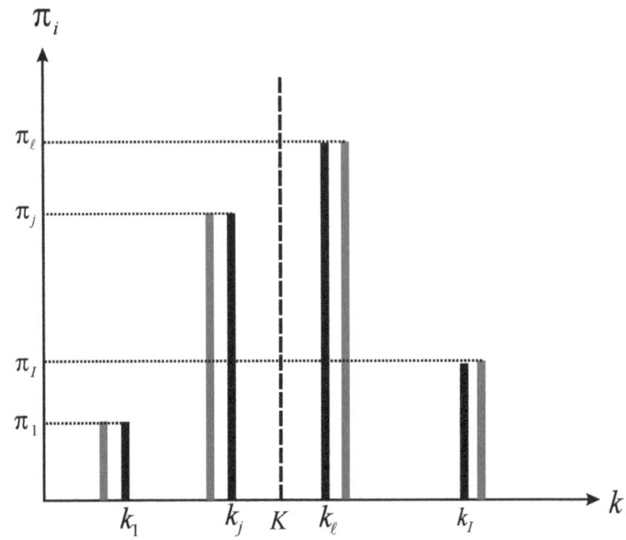

Figure 15.3
Trading frictions and distribution of asset holdings

so when frictions increase, asset prices will fall because mismatches increase.

It should be emphasized that the negative relationship between trading frictions and asset prices derived above is not a general proposition; the relationship depends on the specification of the production function, $f_i(k)$. To see this, suppose that the production function is logarithmic, $f_i(k) = A_i \ln(1+k)$. Then, the demand for capital goods, assuming an interior solution, is given by

$$k_j = \frac{(r+\sigma(1-\theta))\,A_j + \delta\bar{A}}{[r+\sigma(1-\theta)+\delta]\,rp} - 1. \tag{15.23}$$

In this case, the demand for the asset is linear in the productivity. As a consequence, the market clearing price is

$$p = \frac{\bar{A}}{r(1+K)}. \tag{15.24}$$

The asset price is now independent of the speed at which investors can access the market and dealers' bargaining power. The price given by (15.24) is, in fact, the Walrasian price that would prevail in an economy without trading frictions. This suggests that the price of an asset is a poor indicator of the trading frictions that prevail in the market for the asset. The reason why σ does not affect the asset price is quite simple. As one aggregates the individual changes in demands induced by an increase in σ, the increases in k_j for investors with values of A_j larger than $\bar{A}$ cancel out the decreases in k_j for investors with values of A_j lower than $\bar{A}$. As a result, σ has no effect on the aggregate demand for assets and, therefore, on the equilibrium price, even though the quality of the match between the stock of capital and investors is affected.

We will close this section with the special case where the investors' technologies are linear, i.e., $f_i(k) = A_i k$. From (15.13),

$$\frac{(r+\sigma(1-\theta))\,A_i+\delta\bar{A}}{r+\sigma(1-\theta)+\delta}-rp\leq 0,$$

with an equality if $k_i > 0$. Market clearing implies $k_j = 0$ for all $j < I$ so that only investors with the highest productivity demand the asset. In this case, the asset price is given by

$$p=\frac{[r+\sigma(1-\theta)]\,A_I+\delta\bar{A}}{r\,[r+\sigma(1-\theta)+\delta]}. \tag{15.25}$$

The price is a weighted average of the marginal productivity of the highest investor type and the average marginal productivity in the market. The weight on the marginal productivity of the highest productivity investor—and hence the asset price—is increasing in σ, and decreasing in θ and δ.

15.4 Intermediation Fees and Bid-Ask Spreads

An asset is said to be liquid if it can be readily bought or sold at a low transaction cost. We can measure this notion of liquidity by the intermediation fee that investors pay to dealers or, equivalently, by bid-ask spreads. In this section we study how changes in trading frictions affect intermediation fees. In the subsequent section, we will examine alternative measures of liquidity, such as trading delays.

We specialize the analysis to the production function , $f_i(k) = A_i k^\alpha$ for $\alpha \in (0,1)$. From (15.14), the equilibrium fee that a dealer charges an investor who holds a capital stock k_i and wishes to hold k_j is

$$\phi_j(k_i)=\frac{\theta}{r+\sigma(1-\theta)}\left\{\frac{[r+\sigma(1-\theta)]\,A_j+\delta\bar{A}}{r+\sigma(1-\theta)+\delta}\left(k_j^\alpha-k_i^\alpha\right)-rp\left(k_j-k_i\right)\right\}, \tag{15.26}$$

where k_j and p are given by (15.21) and (15.22), respectively. We see that an increase in σ has opposing effects on the intermediation fee. On the one hand, a higher σ implies more competition among dealers, which tends to reduce the fees they charge for any given trade size. This effect is captured by the first term on the right side of (15.26). But on the other hand, a higher σ also induces investors to conduct larger asset holding reallocations every time they trade, and this translates into larger fees for dealers, on average.

To show that the intermediation fees can vary in a nonmonotonic fashion with the trading frictions, consider the case where r is small, i.e., agents are infinitely patient. From (15.21)

$$k_j \approx \left(\frac{\alpha}{rp} \frac{\sigma(1-\theta)A_j + \delta \bar{A}}{\sigma(1-\theta)+\delta} \right)^{1/(1-\alpha)}.$$

If σ tends to infinity, i.e., the asset market is very liquid, it is clear from (15.26) that $\phi_j(k_i)$ approaches 0. If σ tends to zero, i.e., the asset market is very illiquid, then $k_j \approx \left(\frac{\alpha}{rp}\bar{A}\right)^{\frac{1}{1-\alpha}}$ which is independent of j. So when it takes a very long time to readjust one's asset position, investors choose asset holdings that reflect their average productivity and not their current one. As a consequence, they don't need to readjust their asset holdings as their idiosyncratic productivities change, and the intermediation fee, $\phi_j(k_i)$, goes to 0. Finally, when σ is neither too small nor too large, then $k_i \neq k_j$ for all $i \neq j$ so that intermediation fees are positive. This demonstrates that intermediation fees will be maximum for an intermediate level of the trading frictions.

So far we have interpreted transaction costs in terms of intermediation fees, i.e., the total amount paid by the investor to the dealer to readjust his asset holdings. Alternatively, one can interpret the results in terms of bid-ask spreads, which provides a measure of transaction costs per unit of asset traded. Consider the limiting case where $\alpha \to 1$, i.e., technologies are linear. In this case we showed above that $k_j \to 0$ for all $j \neq I$ and $rp \to [(r+\sigma(1-\theta))A_I + \delta\bar{A}]/[r+\sigma(1-\theta)+\delta]$. This implies that (15.26) yields $\phi_j(k_i) \to 0$ for all $(i,j) \notin \{I\} \times \{1,...,I-1\}$. Obviously, dealers do not obtain any fee when investors do not want to readjust their portfolios. Perhaps more surprisingly, when investors are buying the asset ($i \neq I$ and $j = I$), dealers do not charge a fee either. The reason is that when buying capital, the investor pays his marginal product for the asset, and since the technology is linear, this means that he is indifferent between holding or not holding the asset. Finally, investors in state ij, where $i = I$ and $j \neq I$, are holding k_I units of capital but wish to hold $k_j \to 0$. From (15.26), we find that

$$\phi_j(k_I) = \frac{\theta(A_I - A_j)}{r + \sigma(1-\theta) + \delta} k_I, \tag{15.27}$$

i.e., the fee is proportional to the quantity traded.

Since the intermediation fee (15.27) is linear in the quantity traded, the previous results can be readily interpreted in terms of bid-ask spreads. The fact that an investor pays no fee when buying from the dealer is equivalent to a transaction in which the dealer charges an ask-price p^a equal to the price of the asset in the competitive market, i.e., $p^a = p$. When an investor of type $j < I$ sells his capital holdings k_I through a dealer, the investor receives $pk_I - \phi_j(k_I)$. Using (15.27), this transaction is equivalent to one in which the dealer pays investors of type j a bid price $p_j^b = p - [\theta(A_I - A_j)]/[r + \sigma(1-\theta) + \delta] < p$. The difference between the effective price at which the dealer sells, p^a, and buys, p_j^b, is akin to a bid-ask spread of

$$p^a - p_j^b = \frac{\theta(A_I - A_j)}{r + \sigma(1-\theta) + \delta}.$$

This spread is decreasing in the rate at which investors can rebalance their asset holdings, σ. As σ increases, it is quicker for an investor to find a dealer, which tends to raise the investor's disagreement point in the bargaining. This competition effect reduces the per unit fees that dealers can ask for. The bid-ask spread also decreases with δ, since the value of rebalancing one's asset holdings is lower when productivity shocks are more frequent. The spread increases with the dealer's bargaining power, θ, and with the difference between the marginal productivity of the most productive investor and that of the investor involved in the trade. Dealers buy assets at a lower effective price from investors with low marginal productivity because these investors incur a larger opportunity cost from holding on to their capital.

15.5 Trading Delays

In this section, we endogenize the speed at which investors can rebalance their asset holdings by extending the model to allow for free entry of dealers. The Poisson rate at which an investor contacts a dealer is σ and, since all matches are bilateral, the Poisson rate at which a dealer serves an investor is σ/v, where v is the measure of dealers in the market. Suppose that σ is a continuously differentiable function of v, where $\sigma(v)$ a strictly increasing function and $\sigma(v)/v$ a strictly decreasing function of v. As well, assume that $\sigma(0)=0$, $\sigma(\infty)=\infty$ and $\sigma(\infty)/\infty=0$. As v increases, investors' orders are executed faster, but the flow of orders per dealer decreases due to a congestion effect.

There is a large measure of potential dealers who can choose to participate in the market. Dealers who choose to operate incur a flow cost of $\kappa>0$ that represents the ongoing costs of running the dealership, e.g., the cost of searching for investors, advertising their services, and so on. The free-entry of dealers implies that, in equilibrium,

$$\frac{\sigma(v)}{v}\int_{i,j}\phi_j(k_i)dH(k_i,j)=\kappa; \tag{15.28}$$

i.e., the expected instantaneous profit of a dealer equals his flow operation cost. Using (15.14) this condition can be rewritten as

$$\frac{\sigma(v)}{v}\frac{\theta}{r+\sigma(1-\theta)}\sum_{i,j}n_{ij}\left[\bar{f}_j(k_j)-\bar{f}_j(k_i)\right]=\kappa, \tag{15.29}$$

since $\sum_{i,j}n_{ij}\left(k_j-k_i\right)=0$.

It can be shown that there exists a steady-state equilibrium with free entry, provided that dealers have some bargaining power, $\theta>0$. If dealers have no bargaining power, then intermediation fees would equal zero in every trade, and dealers would be unable to cover their operating costs, κ. In this case, $v=0$.

Suppose instead that $\theta>0$. As the measure of dealers becomes large, the instantaneous probability that a dealer meets an investor is driven to zero, which implies that the expected profit for a dealer becomes negative, since the cost to participate in the market is strictly positive. Conversely, if the measure of dealers approaches zero, then the rate at which a dealer meets an investor grows without bound, and the expected profit of dealership becomes arbitrarily large. Expected profits are positive because investors with different productivities choose different capital stocks even when $\sigma=0$, provided that $r>0$; see, e.g., equation (15.21). Consequently, since a dealer's expected profit is continuous in the contact rate, there exists an intermediate value of v such that the expected profit of a dealer equals zero.

Before we proceed, consider the level of dealer entry for the limiting case where the dealer's operating cost, κ, tends to zero. Since the average fee is positive and bounded away from zero for any $\sigma<\infty$, the free-entry condition (15.29) implies $v \to \infty$. This in turn implies that $\sigma \to \infty$, so the equilibrium converges to the frictionless competitive equilibrium.

Although the equilibrium need not be unique when $\kappa > 0$, we now analyze two cases where the equilibrium with entry is, in fact, unique. Suppose first that $\theta = 1$, i.e., dealers receive the entire surplus from trade. From (15.29), the free-entry condition becomes

$$\frac{\sigma(v)}{v} \sum_{i \neq j} \frac{\delta \pi_i \pi_j}{\sigma(v) + \delta} \frac{\bar{f}_j(k_j) - \bar{f}_j(k_i)}{r} = \kappa. \tag{15.30}$$

Since $\theta = 1$ implies that $\bar{f}_j$ and k_j are independent of σ, from (15.12) and (15.13), the average fee depends on $\sigma(v)$ through the distribution of investors and the dealer's contact rate. As the number of dealers increases, a larger measure of investors hold their desired portfolios, which reduces dealers' opportunities to intermediate trades, i.e., an increase in v increases $\sigma(v)$, which in turn decreases n_{ij} for $i \neq j$. Clearly, the left side of (15.30) is a strictly decreasing function of v, which implies uniqueness of the steady-state equilibrium with entry. We obtain the comparative static result that higher operation costs, by reducing expected profits, reduce the measure of active dealers, i.e., $dv/d\kappa < 0$.

Suppose now that $0 < \theta < 1$ but that, in the limit, investors' technologies are linear, i.e., $f_i(k) \to A_i k$. Let $A_1 < A_2 < ... < A_I$, and recall that in this case only investors with the highest marginal productivity, A_I, want to hold assets. From (15.29),

$$\frac{\sigma(v)}{v} \frac{\theta}{r + \sigma(1-\theta)} \sum_{i=I, j<I} \frac{\delta \pi_i \pi_j}{\sigma(v) + \delta} (-\bar{f}_j(k_I)) + \sum_{i<I, j=I} \frac{\delta \pi_i \pi_j}{\sigma(v) + \delta} \bar{f}_I(k_I) = \kappa.$$

From market clearing, $k_I = K/\pi_I$. From (15.12) the previous equation becomes

$$\frac{\sigma(v)}{v} \frac{\theta}{r + \sigma(1-\theta) + \delta} \sum_j \frac{\delta \pi_j}{\sigma(v) + \delta} (A_I - A_j) K = \kappa.$$

Simplify the sum to obtain

$$\frac{\sigma(v)}{v} \frac{\delta \theta (A_I - \bar{A})}{[r + \sigma(1-\theta) + \delta]\,[\sigma(v) + \delta]} K = \kappa. \tag{15.31}$$

Since the left side of (15.31) is decreasing in v, the steady-state equilibrium with entry is unique. Using (15.31), it is straightforward to verify that $\partial \upsilon/\partial \kappa < 0$, $\partial \upsilon/\partial \theta > 0$, $\partial \upsilon/\partial K > 0$, and $d\upsilon/d\delta \gtrless 0$. Lower operation costs naturally imply more entry of dealers. Higher bargaining power for dealers means that they can extract a larger share from the gains from trade in a meeting with an investor, so the measure of dealers increases. Similarly, if the stock of assets increases, the size of each trade is larger and dealers make more profit. Finally, an increase in the frequency of productivity shocks has an ambiguous effect on the equilibrium measure of dealers. On the one hand, a higher δ generates more mismatch, which raises the return to intermediation. But, on the other hand, since with larger δ the investor's current productivity reverts back to the mean productivity, $\bar{A}$, faster, an increase in δ lowers the expected utility of the highest-productivity investor relative to the lower-productivity investors, which implies smaller gains from trade and consequently lower intermediation fees.

We have examined two special cases for which the equilibrium with entry is unique. In general, however, the steady-state equilibrium with free entry need not be unique. The basic reason behind multiple steady-state equilibria is as follows. An increase in the number of dealers leads to an increase in $\sigma(\upsilon)$. Faster trade means more competition among dealers, which tends to reduce intermediation fees. But as we have pointed out earlier, an increase in $\sigma(\upsilon)$ also induces investors to take on more extreme asset positions, i.e., more in line with their current as opposed to the mean productivity shock. This means that dealers will, on average, intermediate larger asset holding reallocations, which implies larger fees, as fees are increasing in the volume traded. If this second effect is sufficiently strong, then the model will exhibit multiple steady states. It should now be clear what drives the uniqueness result in the two examples provided above: in both cases this second effect is absent.

In Figure 15.4 we provide a typical representation of a dealer's expected profit, $[\sigma(\upsilon)/\upsilon]\sum_{i,j} n_{ji}\phi_{ji} - \kappa$, where $\phi_{ji} = \phi_i(k_j)$, as a function of the measure of dealers, υ. As υ approaches zero, the contact rate for dealers goes to infinity, while $\sum_{i,j} n_{ii}\phi_{ij}$ stays bounded away from zero. Therefore, dealers' expected profits are strictly positive for small υ. As υ goes to infinity, the dealers' expected profits approach $-\kappa$. Thus, generically, there will be an odd number of steady-state equilibria. In our numerical examples, we typically find either one or three equilibria. In case of multiple equilibria, the market can be stuck in a low-liquidity equilibrium—an equilibrium where few dealers enter and investors engage in relatively small transactions. The low-liquidity equilibrium

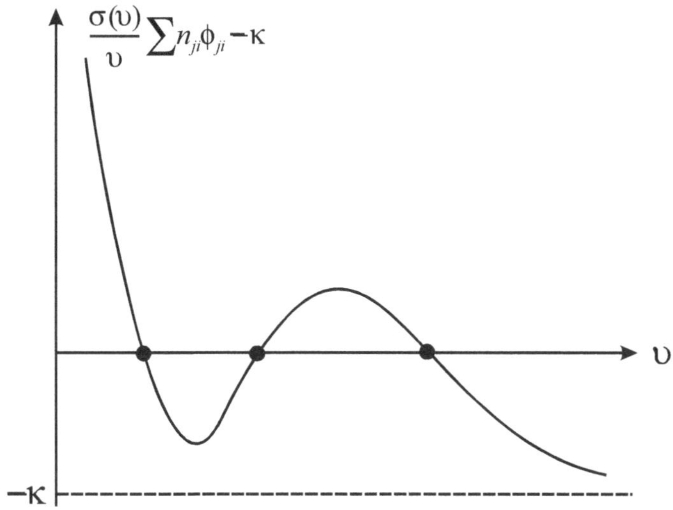

Figure 15.4
Multiple steady states

exhibits large bid-ask spreads, small trade volume, and long trade-execution delays.

The high and low equilibria share the following comparative static: a decrease in the participation cost of dealers increases the measure of dealers in the market. And, if the decrease in the participation cost is large enough, the multiplicity of equilibria can be removed. To see this, note that the expected profits curve in Figure 15.4 shifts upward when κ decreases.

We conclude this section by considering a linear matching function, $\sigma(\upsilon) = \sigma_0 \upsilon$, with $\sigma_0 > 0$. For this specification, there is no congestion effect associated with the entry of dealers: the rate at which dealers find orders to execute, $\sigma(\upsilon)/\upsilon = \sigma_0$, is independent of the measure of dealers in the market. From the free-entry condition, $\upsilon = 0$ if $\sigma_0 \bar{\phi} < \kappa$, $\upsilon = \infty$ if $\sigma_0 \bar{\phi} > \kappa$ and $\upsilon \in [0, \infty]$ if $\sigma_0 \bar{\phi} = \kappa$, where $\bar{\phi}$ represents the average fee of the dealer. If the average fee as a function of υ, $\bar{\phi}(\upsilon) = \sum_{i,j} n_{ij} \phi_{ij}$, is hump-shaped, then the number of equilibria will be either one or three.

To see that $\bar{\phi}(\upsilon)$ can be hump-shaped, recall that when r is close to 0 individual fees, ϕ_{ij}, vary in a nonmonotonic fashion with the trading frictions. If the market is either very liquid or very illiquid, then fees are close to 0; for an intermediate level of the trading frictions, fees are strictly positive. The same property holds for the average fee, $\bar{\phi}$. If the

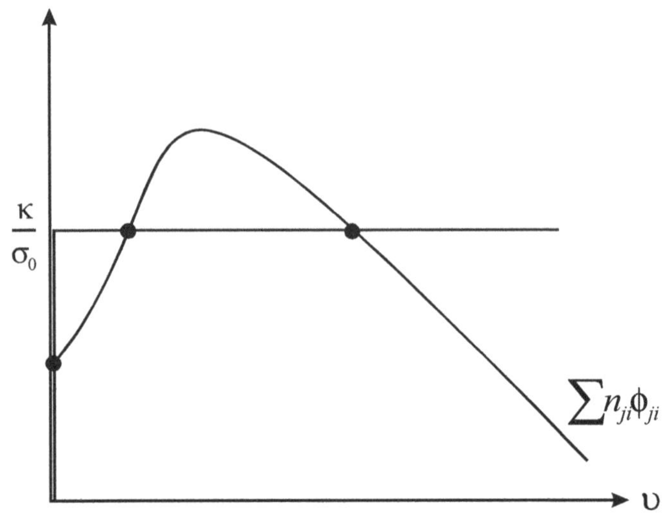

Figure 15.5
Linear matching and multiple steady states

measure of dealers is very large, the competition effect drives the average fee to zero. If the measure of dealers is very small and investors are very patient, then they choose asset positions that reflect their average productivity so that trade sizes are close to zero. In this case, the average fee is also close to zero. The average fee is highest for intermediate levels of the trading frictions. If there are multiple equilibria, then one of the equilibria is $\upsilon = 0$, as illustrated in Figure 15.5. Note that by reducing the cost of dealership κ, or by improving the efficiency of the matching technology σ_0, it is possible to eliminate the multiplicity of equilibria.

15.6 Further Readings

Duffie, Gârleanu, and Pedersen (2005, 2007) are the first to propose a description of over-the-counter markets based on a search-theoretic model, and to use this approach to explain bid-ask spreads. The model is extended by Weill (2007) to allow for dealers' inventories and by Hugonnier, Lester, and Weill (2015) to allow for any distribution of valuations for the asset in an OTC market with pairwise meetings only. The version in this chapter is based on Lagos and Rocheteau (2007, 2009). In contrast to earlier models, this version relaxes the asset holding restrictions imposed by Duffie, Gârleanu, and Pedersen, i.e., investors can hold general asset holdings, not just 0 or 1 units of the asset. Moreover, it incorporates more general forms of investor heterogeneity, and it endogenizes the measure of dealers. Gârleanu (2009) also has a version of the model with endogenous asset holdings, and he shows that trading frictions have a second-order effect on asset prices. Lagos, Rocheteau, and Weill (2011) consider a model with both endogenous asset holdings and dealers' inventories. They investigate how dealers respond to a crash and a stochastic recovery. Pagnotta and Philippon (2015) analyze trading speed and fragmentation in asset markets. Lester, Rocheteau, and Weill (2015) study a version of the model with competitive search in order to explain endogenous market segmentation. Üslü (2015) extends the model to have only pairwise meetings (no interdealer market), unrestricted holdings, and a rich heterogeneity in investor characteristics and analyzes, among other things, the determinants of price dispersion and endogenous intermediation patterns in OTC markets.

Vayanos and Weill (2008) use a search model to explain the on-the-run phenomenon according to which government securities with identical cash flows can trade at different prices. Weill (2008) develops a search-theoretic model of the cross-sectional distribution of asset returns, abstracting from risk premia and focusing exclusively on liquidity. Ashcraft and Duffie (2007), Afonso and Lagos (2015), and Bech and Monnet (2016) use a search-theoretic approach to study the market for federal funds; Gavazza (2009) studies the effects of trading frictions in the commercial aircraft markets; Geromichalos and Jung (2015) formalize the foreign exchange market; and Atkeson, Eisfeldt, and Weill (2015) focus on derivatives markets. Other papers in this search-theoretic approach to liquidity and finance include Miao (2006), Rust and Hall (2003), Vayanos and Wang (2002), Kim (2008), and Afonso (2011). Also related is the work of Spulber (1996), who considers a search environment where middlemen intermediate trade between heterogenous buyers and sellers.

Geromichalos and Herrenbreuck (2016) formalize explicitly the liquidity motive for holding assets in over-the-counter markets and study the effects of monetary policy on asset prices. Lagos and Zhang (2014) introduce monetary exchange in the model of over-the-counter trade of Lagos and Rocheteau (2009). Trejos and Wright (2016) offer an integrated approach of search-based models of money and finance.

Berentsen, Huber, and Marchesiani (2014) ask whether there can be too much trading in financial markets. They construct a dynamic general equilibrium model where a financial market allows agents to adjust their portfolio of liquid and illiquid assets in response to idiosyncratic shocks. The optimal policy response is to restrict (but not eliminate) access to the financial market. The reason for this result is that the portfolio choice exhibits a pecuniary externality: an agent does not take into account that by holding more of the liquid asset, he not only acquires additional insurance but also marginally increases the value of the liquid asset which improves insurance for other market participants.

There is also a large non-search-based, related literature that studies how exogenously specified transaction costs affect the functioning of asset markets. This literature includes Amihud and Mendelson (1986), Constantinides (1986), Aiyagari and Gertler (1991), Heaton and Lucas (1996), Vayanos (1998), Vayanos and Vila (1999), Huang (2003), and Lo, Mamaysky, and Wang (2004). See Heaton and Lucas (1995) for a survey of this body of work.

There is a collection of papers on search environments with intermediaries, following the pioneering work by Rubinstein and Wolinsky (1987). Rubinstein and Wolinsky consider a market with search frictions in which a class of agents, called middlemen, have a higher probability of getting matched than non-middlemen. See, also, Yavas (1994) and Wong and Wright (2014). Shevshenko (2004) considers a related environment with a more general inventory problem where middlemen emerge to overcome a double-coincidence of wants problems. See, also, Camera (2001). In Li (1998, 1999) middlemen do not have an advantage in terms of their matching probability, but they invest in a technology to recognize the quality of goods in the presence of private information. See, also, Biglaiser (1993).

Finally, there is a large literature in market microstructure theory that seeks to explain liquidity and trading costs. Broadly speaking, there are two approaches: one based on inventory models, and one based on information asymmetries. Inventory-theoretic models include Amihud and Mendelson (1980), Stoll (1978), and Ho and Stoll (1983). The private information approach of trading costs was pioneered by Kyle (1985) and Glosten and Milgrom (1985).

16 Crashes and Recoveries in Over-the-counter Markets

In Chapter 15 we examined an over-the-counter (OTC) market in steady state, where dealers facilitate trades between buyers and sellers but do not hold asset inventories. In many financial markets, however, dealers supply liquidity to the market by buying or selling assets from their own inventories. While dealers' liquidity provision might be inconspicuous in normal times, it becomes critical during financial disruptions. In times of crisis it can take a long time for an investor to find a counterpart for trade when the majority of market participants are on one side of the market, either because of the technological limitations of order-handling systems and communication networks or because of the decentralized nature of the trading process. In order to take into account these considerations this chapter describes an OTC market out of steady state where dealers are allowed to hold asset inventories. We characterize dealers' optimal and equilibrium inventory policies during a market crash, described as a temporary, negative shock to investors' aggregate asset demand. We derive conditions such that dealers find it optimal to provide liquidity during the crash. We analyze how dealers' incentives to provide liquidity change with the structure of the market (e.g., dealers' bargaining strength or the magnitude of trading frictions). Lastly, we study conditions under which dealers' incentives to provide liquidity are well aligned with society's interests.

We consider a dynamic market setting similar to that of Chapter 15: investors wish to rebalance their holdings of capital in response to idiosyncratic changes in productivity, but they must engage in a time-consuming process to contact dealers. In the presence of trading frictions, there emerges a natural role for dealers to provide liquidity during a crisis. The provision of liquidity by dealers varies nonmonotonically with the magnitude of trading frictions. When frictions are small, investors with higher-than-average productivity supply sufficient liquidity to other investors so that dealers do not find it profitable to step in. If, on the other hand, trading frictions are sufficiently large, dealers do not accumulate inventories for the purpose of liquidity provision because investors have little incentive to change their asset positions in illiquid markets. If one considers a spectrum of asset markets ranging from those with very small frictions to those with very large trading frictions, one would expect dealers to accumulate asset inventories following a crash in markets that are characterized in the intermediate range of the spectrum of frictions.

16.1 The Environment

The environment is similar to that in Chapter 15. Time is continuous and the horizon infinite. There are two types of infinitely-lived agents; a unit measure of investors and a unit measure of dealers. There is a fixed supply of an asset interpreted as productive capital, $K \in \mathbb{R}_+$. The utility from consuming the general consumption good is c, where $-c > 0$ means production. Investors can also produce the general good according to the technology $f_i(k)$, where $i \in \{1,...,I\}$ indexes a productivity shock. (If one wants to think of k as a financial asset, then $f_i(k)$ is the dividend flow and hedging/liquidity services provided by that asset.) An investor's technology is subject to idiosyncratic productivity shocks that occur with Poisson arrival rate δ. Conditional on receiving the productivity shock, the investor draws productivity of type i with probability π_i. Dealers also have access to a technology $\upsilon(k)$ for producing the general good. (In Chapter 15, we assumed that $\upsilon(k) = 0$.) All agents discount at the same rate $r > 0$.

Dealers can continuously trade capital in a competitive market while investors contact dealers at random with a Poisson process arrival rate σ. When an investor and dealer make contact, they negotiate the quantity of assets that the dealer will buy or sell (in the competitive market) and the intermediation fee that the investor pays to the dealer. After completing the transaction, the dealer and the investor part ways.

16.2 Dealers, Investors, and Bargaining

We begin with the determination of the terms of trade in a bilateral match between a dealer and an investor. The bargaining problem generalizes the one from Chapter 15 to a nonstationary environment.

Suppose that at time t a dealer and an investor of type i who is holding inventory k meet. Let k' denote the investor's post-trade asset (capital) holdings and ϕ be the intermediation fee. The pair (k', ϕ) is the outcome corresponding to the Nash solution to a bargaining problem, where the dealer has bargaining power $\theta \in [0,1]$. Let $V_i(k,t)$ denote the expected discounted utility of an investor with productivity type i who is holding a quantity of asset k at time t. The expected utility of the investor is $V_i(k',t) - p(t)(k'-k) - \phi$ if an agreement on (k', ϕ) is reached and is $V_i(k,t)$ if there is disagreement. The investor's surplus is, therefore, given by $V_i(k',t) - V_i(k,t) - p(t)(k'-k) - \phi$. The dealer's surplus is equal to the intermediation fee, ϕ. The outcome of the bargaining problem is given by

$$[k_i(t), \phi_i(k,t)] = \arg\max_{(k',\phi)}[V_i(k',t) - V_i(k,t) - p(t)(k'-k) - \phi]^{1-\theta}\phi^{\theta}.$$

The investor's new asset holdings, $k_i(t)$, solves

$$k_i(t) = \arg\max_{k'}[V_i(k',t) - p(t)k'], \tag{16.1}$$

and the intermediation fee is given by

$$\phi_i(k,t) = \theta\{V_i[k_i(t),t] - V_i(k,t) - p(t)[k_i(t) - k]\}. \tag{16.2}$$

From (16.1), we see that the investor's post-trade asset holdings are the one he would have chosen if he were able to trade directly with the competitive asset market instead of through a dealer. Notice that the investor's post-trade asset holdings are independent of his pre-trade holdings while the intermediation fee is not. According to (16.2), the intermediation fee is set to give the dealer a θ share of the gains associated with readjusting the investor's asset holdings.

The value function corresponding to a dealer who is holding k_t units of capital at time t satisfies

$$W(k_t,t) = \max_{q(s),k_d(s)} \mathbb{E}\left\{\int_t^T e^{-r(s-t)}\{v[k_d(s)] - p(s)q(s)\}ds + e^{-r(T-t)}[\bar{\phi}(T) + W(k_d(T),T)]\right\}, \tag{16.3}$$

subject to $\dot{k}_d(s) = q(s)$, $k_d(s) \geq 0$, and the initial condition $k_d(t) = k_t$. Here, $k_d(s)$ represents the stock of capital that the dealer is holding and $q(s)$ is the quantity that he trades for his own account at time s. The expectations operator, $\mathbb{E}$, is taken with respect to T, which denotes the next random time the dealer meets an investor. The difference

$T-t$ is exponentially distributed with mean of $1/\sigma$. Since the intermediation fee depends on the investor's productivity type and asset holdings—and given that the investor is a random draw from the population of investors at time T—the dealer expects to receive a fee equal to $\bar{\phi}(T) = \int \phi_j(k_i, T) dH_T(j, k_i)$, where H_T denotes the distribution of investors across productivity types and asset holdings at time T. The dealer enjoys a flow utility equal to $v[k_d(s)]$ from carrying inventory $k_d(s)$ and incurs disutility equal to $p(s)q(s)$ from changing his asset holdings.

Since the intermediation fee is independent of the dealer's asset holdings, the dealer's value function can be written as

$$W(k_t, t) = \max_{q(s)} \left\{ \int_t^{\infty} e^{-r(s-t)} \left\{ v[k_d(s)] - p(s)q(s) \right\} ds \right\} + \Phi(t), \tag{16.4}$$

subject to $\dot{k}_d(s) = q(s)$, $k_d(s) \geq 0$ and $k_d(t) = k_t$. The function $\Phi(t)$ is the expected present discounted value of future intermediation fees from time t onward. This formulation makes it clear that dealers trade assets in two ways; continuously in a competitive market and at random times in bilateral negotiations with investors. Since dealers have quasi-linear preferences and can trade instantaneously and continuously in the competitive asset market, their optimal choice of asset holdings is independent of their bilateral negotiations with investors.

The current-valued Hamiltonian associated with (16.4) is given by

$$\mathcal{H}(k_d, q, \nu) = v(k_d) - pq + \mu q + \nu k_d,$$

where μ is the co-state variable and ν is a Lagrange multiplier associated with the nonnegativity constraint $k_d \geq 0$. The optimal choice of asset holdings solves $p(t) = \mu(t)$ and the co-state variable solves

$$r\mu(t) = v'[k_d(t)] + \nu(t) + \dot{\mu}(t).$$

Using $\nu(t) = r\mu(t) - \dot{\mu}(t) - v'[k_d(t)] \geq 0$ and $p(t) = \mu(t)$, we get

$$v'[k_d(t)] + \dot{p}(t) \leq rp(t), \text{ “} = \text{” if } k_d(t) > 0. \tag{16.5}$$

According to (16.5), whenever a dealer finds it optimal to hold a strictly positive inventory, the flow cost of buying the asset, $rp(t)$, must equal the direct output flow from holding the asset, $v'[k_d(t)]$, plus the capital gain, $\dot{p}(t)$. Finally, the asset (capital) price $p(t)$ must satisfy the transversality condition

$$\lim_{t\to\infty} e^{-rt} p(t) k_d(t) = 0. \tag{16.6}$$

We now analyze the investor's problem. The value function of an investor of productivity type i who is holding k assets at time t, $V_i(k,t)$, satisfies

$$V_i(k,t) = \mathbb{E}_i\left[\int_t^T e^{-r(s-t)} f_{\chi(s)}(k)ds + e^{-r(T-t)}\{V_{\chi(T)}[k_{\chi(T)}(T),T] - p(T)[k_{\chi(T)}(T)-k] - \phi_{\chi(T)}(k,T)\}\right], \tag{16.7}$$

where T denotes the next time the investor meets a dealer and $\chi(s) \in \{1,...,I\}$ denotes the investor's productivity type at time s. The expectations operator, $\mathbb{E}_i$, is taken with respect to the random variables T and $\chi(s)$ and is indexed by i to indicate that the expectation is conditional on $\chi(t) = i$. Over the time interval $[t,T]$, the investor holds k assets and enjoys the discounted sum of the output flows associated with holding these assets, which is given by the first term on the right-hand side of (16.7). The time interval $T-t$ is an exponentially distributed random variable with mean $1/\sigma$. The flow output is indexed by the productivity type of the investor, $\chi(s)$, which follows a compound Poisson process. At time T, the investor (randomly) contacts a dealer and readjusts his asset holdings from k to $k_{\chi(T)}(T)$. In this event, the dealer purchases $k_{\chi(T)}(T) - k$ units of the asset in the market (or sells if the quantity is negative) at price $p(T)$ on behalf of the investor and the investor pays the dealer an intermediation fee equal to $\phi_{\chi(T)}(k,T)$. The Bellman equation (16.7) is illustrated in Figure 16.1.

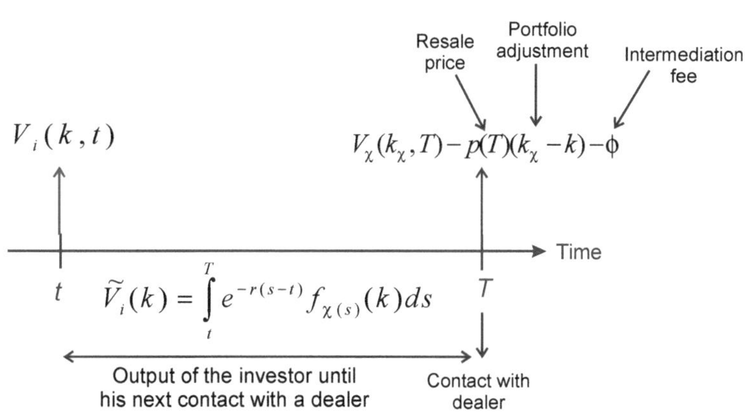

Figure 16.1
Bellman equation of the investor

The Bellman equation can be rewritten by substituting the terms of trade (16.1) and (16.2) into (16.7), i.e.,

$$V_i(k,t) = \mathbb{E}_i\left[\int_t^T e^{-r(s-t)} f_{\chi(s)}(k)ds + e^{-r(T-t)}\{(1-\theta)\max_{k'}\right. \tag{16.8}$$

$$\left.\left[V_{\chi(T)}(k',T) - p(T)(k'-k)\right] + \theta V_{\chi(T)}(k,T)\}\right].$$

The last two terms on the right-hand side of (16.9) have an interesting interpretation: they represent the payoff that the investor would receive in an economy where he meets dealers according to a Poisson process with arrival rate σ, and he extracts the whole surplus with probability $1-\theta$ while with probability θ he enjoys no gain from trade. From the investor's point of view, the stochastic trading process and the bargaining solution are payoff-equivalent to an alternative trading mechanism where the investor has all of the bargaining power in a bilateral match with a dealer but meets dealers according to a Poisson process with an arrival rate equal to $\sigma(1-\theta)$. Given this interpretation, we can rewrite (16.9) as

$$V_i(k,t) = \mathbb{E}_i\left[\int_t^{\tilde{T}} f_{\chi(s)}(k)\, e^{-r(s-t)}\, ds + e^{-r(\tilde{T}-t)}\left\{p(\tilde{T})k\right.\right.$$

$$\left.\left. + \max_{k'}[V_{\chi(\tilde{T})}(k',\tilde{T}) - p(\tilde{T})k']\right\}\right], \tag{16.9}$$

where the expectations operator, $\mathbb{E}_i$, is now taken with respect to the random variables $\tilde{T}$ and $\chi(s)$ and $\tilde{T}-t$ is exponentially distributed with mean $1/[\sigma(1-\theta)]$. From (16.9), the problem of an investor with productivity shock i who gains access to the market at time t is one of choosing $k' \in \mathbb{R}_+$ so as to maximize

$$\mathbb{E}_i\left[\int_t^{\tilde{T}} e^{-r(s-t)} f_{\chi(s)}(k')\, ds\right] - \left\{p(t) - \mathbb{E}_t\left[e^{-r(\tilde{T}-t)} p(\tilde{T})\right]\right\} k',$$

or equivalently,

$$\max_{k'} \mathbb{E}_i\left[\int_t^{\tilde{T}} e^{-r(s-t)}\left\{f_{\chi(s)}(k') - [rp(s) - \dot{p}(s)]\, k'\right\} ds\right]. \tag{16.10}$$

If an investor has continuous access to the asset market, he would choose his asset holdings so as to continuously maximize $f_i(k') - [rp(t) - \dot{p}(t)]\, k'$, which is his flow output net of the flow cost of holding the asset. Since the investor can only trade infrequently, he maximizes

(16.10) instead. Intuitively, the investor chooses his asset holdings at time t so as to maximize the present value of his output flow net of the present value of the cost of holding the asset from time t until the next time $\tilde{T}$ when he can readjust his holdings.

We can solve problem (16.10) in two steps. First, denote the first term as

$$\tilde{V}_i(k) = \mathbb{E}_i\left[\int_t^{\tilde{T}} e^{-r(s-t)} f_{X(s)}(k')ds\right], \tag{16.11}$$

which is the discounted sum of output flows until the investor has the opportunity to readjust his asset holdings at a Poisson arrival rate equal to $\sigma(1-\theta)$. Hence, (16.11) solves the following Bellman equation:

$$r\tilde{V}_i(k) = f_i(k) + \delta\sum_{j=1}^{I}\pi_j\left[\tilde{V}_j(k) - \tilde{V}_i(k)\right] - \sigma(1-\theta)\tilde{V}_i(k).$$

Using the same reasoning as in Chapter 15, it is easy to check that $\tilde{V}_i(k) = \bar{f}_i(k)/[r+\sigma(1-\theta)]$ where

$$\bar{f}_i(k) = \frac{[r+\sigma(1-\theta)]f_i(k) + \delta\sum_{j=1}^{I}\pi_j f_j(k)}{r+\delta+\sigma(1-\theta)}. \tag{16.12}$$

Second, the second term in (16.10)—after some calculations that recognize that $\tilde{T}$ is exponentially distributed, change the order of integration, and then integrate by parts—can be reexpressed as

$$\mathbb{E}_i\left[\int_0^{\tilde{T}} e^{-rs}\left[rp(t+s) - \dot{p}(t+s)\right]ds\right] = \frac{\xi(t)}{r+\sigma(1-\theta)}, \tag{16.13}$$

where

$$\xi(t) = [r+\sigma(1-\theta)]\left[p(t) - \sigma(1-\theta)\int_0^{\infty} e^{-[r+\sigma(1-\theta)]s}p(t+s)ds\right].$$

From (16.12) and (16.13), we can conclude that when an investor of type i contacts the market at time t, his choice of asset holdings solves

$$\bar{f}_i'\left[k_i(t)\right] = \xi(t). \tag{16.14}$$

Intuitively, $\bar{f}_i(k)$ is the flow expected output that the investor produces by holding k assets until his next opportunity to rebalance his holdings, and $\xi(t)$ is the cost of buying the asset minus the expected discounted resale value of the asset (expressed in flow terms).

The relationship between $\xi(t)$ and $p(t)$ is obtained by differentiating the expression for $\xi(t)$ above (with the relevant transversality condition). After some calculations, we arrive at

$$rp(t) - \dot{p}(t) = \xi(t) - \frac{\dot{\xi}(t)}{r + \sigma(1-\theta)}. \tag{16.15}$$

This expression allows us to rewrite (16.5) as

$$v'[k_d(t)] + \frac{\dot{\xi}(t)}{r + \sigma(1-\theta)} \leq \xi(t) \quad \text{“} = \text{” if } k_d(t) > 0. \tag{16.16}$$

Equations (16.14) and (16.16) illustrate an important difference between dealers and investors: dealers receive an extra return from holding the asset, captured by $\dot{\xi}(t) / [r + \sigma(1-\theta)]$, which reflects their ability to generate capital gains by exploiting their continuous access to the asset market.

16.3 Equilibrium

Irrespective of his asset holdings, each investor faces the same probability of accessing the market. Hence, we appeal to the law of large numbers to assert that the flow supply of assets by investors at time t is $\sigma[K - K_d(t)]$, where $K_d(t)$ is the aggregate stock of capital in the hands of the dealers. Notice that $K_d(t) = k_d(t)$, since there is a unit measure of identical dealers that face the same strictly concave optimization problem. The measure of investors with productivity shock i that are trading in the market at time t is $\sigma n_i(t)$, where $n_i(t)$ is the measure of investors with productivity type i at time t. Since $n_i(t)$ satisfies $\dot{n}_i(t) = \delta\pi_i - \delta n_i(t)$ for all i, we can conclude that

$$n_i(t) = e^{-\delta t} n_i(0) + (1 - e^{-\delta t})\pi_i, \qquad \text{for } i = 1, .., I. \tag{16.17}$$

The investors' aggregate demand for the asset is $\sigma \sum_i n_i(t) k_i(t)$ while the net supply of assets by investors is $\sigma[K - K_d(t) - \sum_i n_i(t) k_i(t)]$. The net demand for assets from the dealers is $\dot{K}_d(t)$, which is the change in their inventories. Market clearing, therefore, requires that

$$\dot{K}_d(t) = \sigma\left[K - K_d(t) - \sum_i n_i(t) k_i(t)\right]. \tag{16.18}$$

The market-clearing condition (16.18) determines $\xi(t)$. Using (16.9), the intermediation fees along the equilibrium path (16.2) can be expressed as

$$\phi_i(k,t) = \eta \left[\frac{\bar{f}_i[k_i(t)] - \bar{f}_i(k) - \xi(t)[k_i(t) - k]}{r + \sigma(1-\theta)} \right]. \tag{16.19}$$

Combining (16.14), (16.16) and (16.18), and assuming an interior solution for dealers' inventories, the economy can be reduced to a system of two first-order differential equations,

$$\dot{K}_d(t) = \sigma \left\{ K - K_d(t) - \sum_i n_i(t) \bar{f}_i'^{-1}[\xi(t)] \right\} \tag{16.20}$$

$$\dot{\xi}(t) = [r + \sigma(1-\theta)] \{\xi(t) - v'[K_d(t)]\}, \tag{16.21}$$

where $n_i(t)$ is given by (16.17). The steady-state equilibrium is given by $\bar{f}_i'(k_i) = v'(k_d) = \xi = rp$, where ξ is the unique solution to

$$v'^{-1}(\xi) + \sum_i \pi_i \bar{f}_i'^{-1}(\xi) = K. \tag{16.22}$$

Suppose trading frictions vanish, i.e., σ approaches ∞. From (16.15), $\xi(t) = rp(t) - \dot{p}(t)$: the investor's cost of investing in the asset is the flow cost $rp(t)$ minus the capital gain $\dot{p}(t)$. Since $\bar{f}_i(k)$ tends to $f_i(k)$ when trading frictions vanish, the investor's optimal choice of assets satisfies $f_i'(k_i) = rp(t) - \dot{p}(t)$. This is precisely the asset demand of an investor in a frictionless Walrasian market.

We now examine a very tractable special case for (16.20) and (16.21) when $n_i = \pi_i$ for all i, i.e., when the distribution of productivity types across investors is time-invariant. We represent the dynamics of the system by the phase diagram in Figure 16.2. The unique steady state, $(\bar{K}_d, \bar{\xi})$, is a saddle-point. For some initial $K_d(0)$ there is a unique trajectory, the saddle path, that sends the economy to its steady state. This trajectory also satisfies (16.6), so the saddle path is an equilibrium path.

16.4 Efficiency

We now examine the problem of a social planner who faces the trading frictions described above and aims to maximize the sum of all agents' utilities. Since at any point in time all investors access the market according to independent and identically distributed stochastic processes, the quantity of assets that a measure σ of randomly-drawn

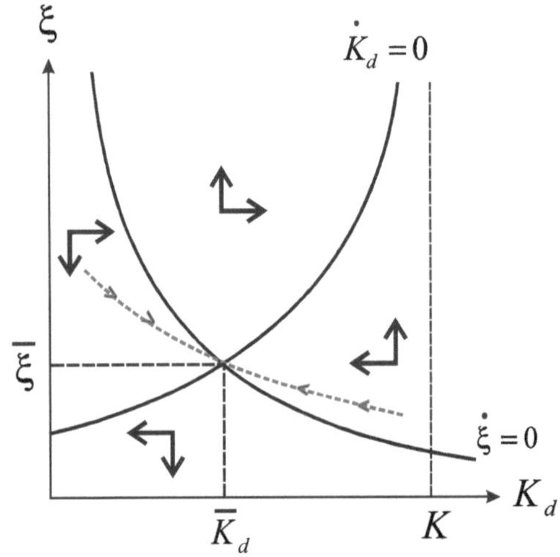

Figure 16.2
Phase diagram

investors make available to the planner is $\sigma\left[K - K_d(t)\right]$. This means that the quantity of assets available to be reallocated to agents who are in the market depends only on the mean of the distribution $H_t(i,k)$, which is $K - K_d(t)$. Although $H_t(i,k)$ is not a state variable in the planner's problem, the planner must know $n_i(t)$, the measure of investors with productivity type i at date t, in order to allocate assets across investors.

Let $\tilde{\mathcal{V}}_i(k)$ represent the expected discounted utility of an investor of type i who holds k units of the asset until the next time his portfolio can be changed, i.e.,

$$\tilde{\mathcal{V}}_i(k) = \mathbb{E}_i\left[\int_t^{t+T} f_{\chi(s)}(k)e^{-r(s-t)}ds\right]. \tag{16.23}$$

Note that $\tilde{\mathcal{V}}_i(k)$ is similar to $\tilde{V}_i(k)$ in (16.11); an important different is that the T in (16.23) has mean $1/\sigma$ while the T in (16.11) has mean $1/[\sigma(1-\theta)]$. The function $\tilde{\mathcal{V}}_i(k)$ satisfies

$$\tilde{\mathcal{V}}_i(k) = \frac{(r+\sigma)f_i(k) + \delta\sum_j \pi_{ij}f_j(k)}{(r+\sigma+\delta)(r+\sigma)}. \tag{16.24}$$

The planner's problem is given by

$$\max_{q(t),\{k_i(t)\}_{i=1}^{N}} \int \tilde{V}_i(k)dH_0(k,i) + \int_0^{\infty} e^{-rt}\left\{ v[k_d(t)] + \sigma \sum_i n_i(t)\tilde{V}_i[k_i(t)] \right\} dt \tag{16.25}$$

$$\text{s.t.} \quad q(t) = \sigma \left[K - K_d(t) - \sum_i n_i(t)k_i(t) \right], \tag{16.26}$$

$\dot{k}_d(t) = q(t)$, (16.17), and the initial conditions $n_i(0)$ and $k_i(0)$, i.e., at each date the planner chooses $q(t)$ and $k_i(t)$ in order to maximize the discounted sum of output flows that dealers and investors generate from holding assets. The first term in (16.25) captures the output that investors generate before the first time their portfolios can be reallocated. Since this term is a constant it can be ignored. Hence, the planner's current-value Hamiltonian can be written as

$$v[k_d(t)] + \sigma \sum_i n_i(t)\tilde{V}_i[k_i(t)] + \mu(t)q(t), \tag{16.27}$$

where $\mu(t)$ is the co-state variable associated with the law of motion for $k_d(t)$. From the Maximum Principle, the necessary conditions for an optimum are

$$\frac{(r+\sigma)f_i'[k_i(t)] + \delta \sum_j \pi_{ij} f_j'[k_i(t)]}{r+\sigma+\delta} = (r+\sigma)\mu(t) = \lambda(t) \tag{16.28}$$

$$v'[k_d(t)] + \frac{\dot{\lambda}(t)}{r+\sigma} = \lambda(t). \tag{16.29}$$

If we compare the equilibrium price, $\xi(t)$, with the planner's shadow price of assets, $\lambda(t)$, i.e., compare (16.5) and (16.12) with (16.28) and (16.29), notice that $\xi(t) = \lambda(t)$ if $\theta = 0$. Therefore, the equilibrium is efficient if and only if $\theta = 0$. When $\theta > 0$, an inefficiency arises from a holdup problem that is due to bargaining. Specifically, investors anticipate that they will have to pay intermediation fees for rebalancing their asset holdings in the future, where fees increase with the total trading surplus. Investors will attempt to reduce these fees by avoiding asset positions that could lead to large rebalancing in the future (even though those positions are efficient from the planner's point of view).

16.5 Crash and Recovery

We define a "market crash" as an unexpected shock that modifies the distribution of investors across productivity types $\{n_i(t)\}_{i=1}^{I}$ in a way that causes the total demand for the asset to fall unexpectedly. In analyzing a market crash, we suppose that the economy is in the steady state at the time the unexpected shock hits the economy. The recovery from the market crash is described by the evolution of the distribution of investors across productivity types as the economy reverts back to its steady state.

In order to highlight the intermediation role of dealers, we assume that initially dealers have no inventory, $k_d(0) = 0$, and that their technology is unproductive, i.e., $v(k) = 0$ for any $k > 0$. These assumptions imply that in the steady state, $K_d = 0$, i.e., dealers have no incentive to buy assets that do not generate output or capital gains. For tractability, the investors' technologies are described by $f_i(k) = A_i k^\alpha / \alpha$. This functional form implies that $\bar{f}_i(k) = \bar{A}_i k^\alpha / \alpha$, where

$$\bar{A}_i = \frac{[r + \sigma(1-\theta)]A_i + \delta \bar{A}}{r + \sigma(1-\theta) + \delta}$$

and $\bar{A} = \sum_i \pi_i A_i$. An investor with productivity type i who gains access to the market at time t has an asset demand given by

$$k_i(t) = \left[\frac{\bar{A}_i}{\xi(t)}\right]^{1/(1-\alpha)}. \tag{16.30}$$

A dealer's asset holdings satisfy

$$[rp(t) - \dot{p}(t)]\, k_d(t) = 0. \tag{16.31}$$

Since dealers do not enjoy any direct benefit from holding the asset, they will hold the asset after a market crash only if it can generate a capital gain. Clearly, dealers will not hold inventories when the price of the asset is growing at a rate that is lower than his rate of time preference. Dealers are willing to hold inventories of the asset whenever $\dot{p}(t)/p(t) \geq r$. Note, however, that $\dot{p}(t)/p(t) > r$ is inconsistent with equilibrium. Hence, dealers will hold the asset (in equilibrium) only when $\dot{p}(t)/p(t) = r$. Using (16.15), we can express the dealer's optimal asset holdings as

$$\left[\xi(t) - \frac{\dot{\xi}(t)}{r + \sigma(1-\theta)}\right] K_d(t) = 0, \tag{16.32}$$

where $\dot{\xi}(t)/\xi(t) \leq r + \sigma(1-\theta)$ and $K_d(t) \geq 0$ represents the dealers' aggregate inventories. (Notice that individual dealers do not need to hold the same inventories.)

Using (16.17) and (16.30), the market-clearing condition (16.20) can be written as

$$\dot{K}_d(t) = \sigma\left\{K - K_d(t) - \xi(t)^{-1/(1-\alpha)}\left[\bar{E} - e^{-\delta t}\left(\bar{E} - E_0\right)\right]\right\}, \tag{16.33}$$

where $\bar{E} = \sum_i \pi_i \bar{A}_i^{1/(1-\alpha)}$ and $E_0 = \sum_i n_i(0)\bar{A}_i^{1/(1-\alpha)}$. Notice there are two sources of time variation: one comes from the effective cost of purchasing the asset, $\xi(t)$, and other comes from the distribution of investors over the various productivity types, $\left[\bar{E} - e^{-\delta t}\left(\bar{E} - E_0\right)\right]$. The constant $\bar{E}$ measures investors' willingness to hold the asset in the steady state, and E_0 reflects the investors' willingness to hold the asset when the aggregate shock hits at time 0. Thus, $E_0/\bar{E}$ is a measure of the magnitude of the shock to aggregate demand for the asset.

We assume that $E_0/\bar{E} < 1$, which means that lower productivity types receive larger population weights at time 0 relative to the steady state. Thus, aggregate investor demand for the asset is lowest at $t = 0$ when the crisis hits and then gradually recovers over time as the initial distribution of productivity types $\{n_i(0)\}_{i=1}^{I}$ reverts back to the steady-state distribution $\{\pi_i\}_{i=1}^{I}$.

The dealers' optimality condition, (16.32), and the market-clearing condition, (16.33), are a pair of differential equations that can be used to solve for $\xi(t)$ and $K_d(t)$. If $K_d(t) > 0$ for all $t \in [t_1, t_2]$, then (16.32) implies that $\xi(t) = e^{[r+\sigma(1-\theta)](t-t_2)}\xi(t_2)$. Given this path for $\xi(t)$, (16.33) is a first-order differential equation that can be solved for the path of $K_d(t)$. Similarly, if $K_d(t) = 0$ over some interval, then (16.33) implies a path for $\xi(t)$.

Suppose that dealers do not hold inventories along the equilibrium path, $K_d(t) = 0$. Then (16.33) implies

$$\xi(t) = \left[\frac{\bar{E} - e^{-\delta t}\left(\bar{E} - E_0\right)}{K}\right]^{1-\alpha}. \tag{16.34}$$

Dealers have no incentive to hold inventories if $\dot{p}(t)/p(t) \leq r$, which from (16.15) can be reexpressed as $\xi(t) - \dot{\xi}(t)/[r + \sigma(1-\theta)] > 0$. From the above equation, this condition implies that

$$\bar{E} \geq e^{-\delta t}\left(\bar{E} - E_0\right)\left[\frac{\delta(1-\alpha)}{r + \sigma(1-\theta)} + 1\right].$$

It is clear that if this condition holds at $t = 0$ then it holds for all $t > 0$. Therefore, the equilibrium is characterized by $K_d(t) = 0$ for all t if

$$\frac{E_0}{\bar{E}} \geq \frac{\delta(1-\alpha)}{\delta(1-\alpha)+r+\sigma(1-\theta)}. \tag{16.35}$$

A sufficient condition for (16.35) is that $[r+\sigma(1-\theta)]/\delta$ is sufficiently large. Suppose that productivity shocks are very persistent (δ is very small). In this case the recovery is slow, the growth rate of the asset price is low, and dealers' capital gains are smaller than their opportunity cost of holding the asset. If, instead, σ becomes arbitrarily large (it goes to infinity), then the economy approaches the frictionless Walrasian benchmark. In this case, dealers no longer have a trading advantage *vis-à-vis* investors and, as a result, their ability to realize capital gains vanishes.

Now suppose that dealers hold inventories along the equilibrium path, which means that condition (16.35) does *not* hold. Dealers may be willing to hold inventories of the assets because their trading advantage over investors—they have continuous access to the market while investors do not—allows them to "time the market" continuously so as to capture capital gains that investors cannot realize. If dealers were unable to hold inventories, these capital gains would remain unexploited. In equilibrium, competition among dealers equalizes the capital gains with the opportunity cost of holding assets, i.e., $\dot{p}/p = r$.

We now provide some numerical examples to illustrate and explain how the key parameters influence the dealers' incentives to hold inventories in times of crisis. We set $r = 0.05$, $\alpha = 1/2$ and assume that the productivity shock is either $A_1 = 0$ or $A_2 = 1$ with equal probability. We assume that $\sigma = \delta = 1$ so that, on average, investors get one productivity shock and one chance to trade per unit of time. We also set $\theta = 0$ so that the equilibrium of the benchmark parametrization corresponds to the solution to the planner's problem. At time 0 the fraction of investors with low productivity rise from its steady-state value 0.5 to $n_1(0) = 0.95$.

The shaded regions in Figure 16.3 illustrate the combinations of parameter values for which dealers hold inventories in times of crisis, i.e., condition (16.35) is not satisfied. In each panel, we let the two parameters in the axes vary while holding the remaining parameters fixed at their benchmark values. Recall that the steady-state equilibrium allocations of an economy where $\theta = 0$ correspond to the efficient allocations. Figure 16.3 indicates that there are parameterizations

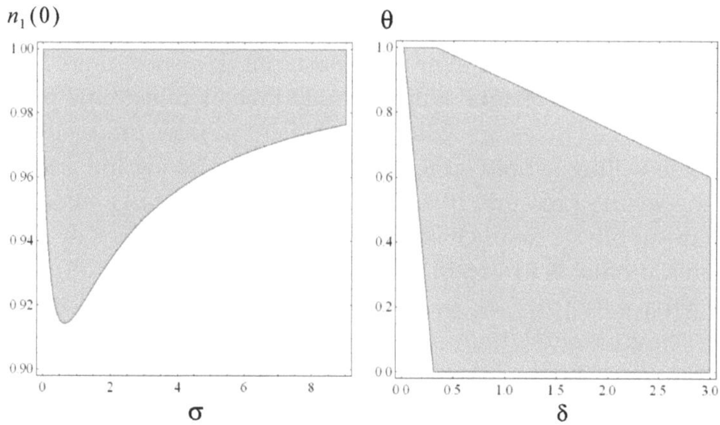

Figure 16.3
Grey area: Dealers hold inventories

involving $\theta = 0$ where dealers accumulate inventories. Dealers play a societal role by exploiting an intertemporal trade-off between the marginal productivity of investors at the current date and in the future. Since the average marginal productivity of the asset across investors is low at the outset of the crisis and higher later on, the dealers' inventories are able to smooth the marginal productivities over time.

We now examine how changes in fundamentals affect the dealers' likelihood of intervening during the crisis. The left panel in Figure 16.3 shows that for any given σ, dealers intervene if $n_1(0)$ is large enough, i.e., if the crash is sufficiently abrupt. If the shock is large, dealers expect that capital gains will compensate for their rate of time preference. The right panel shows that dealers find it optimal to intervene if the recovery is fast, i.e. δ is large. However, the figure also shows that dealers will not intervene if δ is too large when their bargaining power is high. Since δ not only measures the speed of the recovery but also the arrival intensity of idiosyncratic productivity shocks, if δ is very large, then an investor is likely to change type very quickly after trading and before reestablishing contact with dealers. Because the average type of an investor over his holding period becomes closer to the mean, $\bar{A}$, the economy is then similar to an economy without idiosyncratic productivity shocks, in which case dealers do not have an incentive to reallocate assets across time.

The left panel in Figure 16.3 shows that, for a given size of the aggregate shock, dealers provide liquidity if trading frictions are neither too severe nor too small. Consider first the case of a large σ. Investors anticipate that they can rebalance their asset positions in a short time, $1/\sigma$. This effect increases investors' willingness to take more extreme positions. In particular, investors with higher-than-average productivity become more willing to hold larger-than-average positions and absorb more of the selling pressure. In some cases, when σ is large enough, they end up supplying so much liquidity to other investors that dealers do not find it profitable to step in. If, on the other hand, σ is small, then investors behave as if $A_i \approx \bar{A}$, and they choose asset holdings closer to the mean. The economy is then similar to an economy without idiosyncratic productivity shocks, in which case dealers are not needed to help reallocate assets across time.

The right panel in Figure 16.3 reveals that for any given δ, dealers are more likely to hold inventories if their bargaining power is neither too large nor too small. Recall that if $\theta = 0$, the economy is constrained-efficient. Therefore, the right panel also shows that there are parameter values for which dealers intervene in equilibrium although the planner would not have them intervene, and there are also parameter values for which the opposite is true.

We can summarize the discussion above as follows. Dealers provide liquidity by accumulating asset inventories if: (i) the market crash is abrupt and the recovery is fast; (ii) trading frictions are neither too severe not too small; (iii) dealers' market power is not too large; and (iv) idiosyncratic productivity shocks are not too persistent.

Figure 16.3 illustrates the conditions under which dealers accumulate inventories but it is not informative about the size of dealers' intervention, e.g., how much capital they accumulate over time. Figure 16.4 addresses this issue by plotting the trajectory of dealers' inventories for the parameter values of our benchmark example.

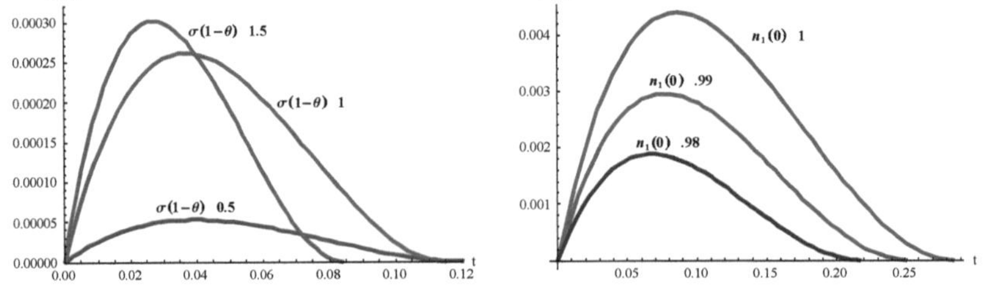

Figure 16.4
Dealers' inventories following an aggregate negative shock

The left panel illustrates the relationship between market structure, as summarized by $\sigma(1-\theta)$, and dealers' inventory policy. The length of the period of time during which dealers hold inventories is first increasing with $\sigma(1-\theta)$ because investors take more extreme positions and this increases the discrepancy between their marginal productivity at different dates. It is then decreasing for larger values of $\sigma(1-\theta)$ since liquidity is less needed when trading frictions are smaller. The maximum quantity of assets that dealers hold tends to decrease with the extent of the frictions since the measure of investors who contact the market over a small interval of time increases with σ. As σ falls, the demand for liquidity is lower.

The right panel of Figure 16.4 describes dealers' inventory behavior as a function of the severity of the aggregate shock. First, the holding period expands as $n_1(0)$ increases. Second, the quantity of assets dealers hold at any point in time tends to be larger the more severe the initial reduction in the asset demand. Hence, a more severe crash has dealers providing more liquidity for a longer period of time.

16.6 Further Readings

The model in this chapter is based on Lagos, Rocheteau, and Weill (2011). We describe a version of the model where the recovery following the aggregate shock is deterministic, as in Weill (2007), whereas Lagos, Rocheteau, and Weill (2011) describe a shock that scales down all productivities and a stochastic recovery that occurs according to a Poisson process. In contrast to Weill (2007), dealers' asset holdings are unrestricted and the model incorporates a richer heterogeneity.

Sultanum (2016) studies a version of the model where investors are organized in small coalitions called financial institutions and preference shocks for the asset are privately observed. He shows that there is a truth-telling equilibrium similar to the one in this chapter that implements an efficient risk-sharing arrangement. There are other "run equilibria," where all investors misrepresent their valuations for the asset. Such equilibria exist when search frictions are large. Inventory-theoretic models in the market microstructure literature include Amihud and Mendelson (1980), Stoll (1978), Ho and Stoll (1983).

Camargo and Lester (2014) study a dynamic, decentralized lemons market with one-time entry and show how "frozen" markets suffering from adverse selection recover endogenously over time. Camargo, Kim, and Lester (2015) study the effects of government intervention in an environment in which adverse selection causes trade to break down. They find that while some intervention is required to restore trading, too much intervention reduces the informational content of trades. Chiu and Koeppl (2016) address a similar question and find that a government can resurrect trading by buying up lemons which involves a financial loss. It can be optimal to delay the intervention to allow selling pressure to build up, thereby improving the average quality of assets for sale.

Bibliography

Afonso, Gara (2011). "Liquidity and congestion," *Journal of Financial Intermediation* 20, 324–360.

Afonso, Gara and Ricardo Lagos (2015). "Trade dynamics in the market for federal funds", *Econometrica* 83, 263–313.

Aiyagari, S. Rao and Mark Gertler (1991). "Asset returns with transactions costs and uninsured individual risk," *Journal of Monetary Economics* 27, 311–331.

Aiyagari, S. Rao and Neil Wallace (1991). "Existence of steady states with positive consumption in the Kiyotaki-Wright model," *The Review of Economic Studies* 58, 901–916.

Aiyagari, S. Rao, Neil Wallace, and Randall Wright (1996). "Coexistence of money and interest-bearing securities," *Journal of Monetary Economics* 37, 397–419.

Aiyagari, S. Rao and Stephen Williamson (1999). "Credit in a random matching model with private information," *Review of Economic Dynamics* 2, 36–64.

Aiyagari, S. Rao and Stephen Williamson (2000). "Money and dynamic credit arrangements with private information," *Journal of Economic Theory* 91, 248–279.

Alchian, Armen (1977). "Why money?" *Journal of Money, Credit, and Banking* 9, 133–140.

Ales, Laurence, Francesca Carapella, Pricila Maziero, and Warren Weber (2008). "A model of banknote discounts," *Journal of Economic Theory* 142, 5–27.

Aliprantis, Charalambos, Gabriele Camera, and Daniela Puzzello (2006). "Matching and anonymity," *Economic Theory* 29, 415–432.

Aliprantis, Charalambos, Gabriele Camera, and Daniela Puzzello (2007). "A random matching theory," *Games and Economic Behavior* 59, 1–16.

Aliprantis, Charalambos, Gabriele Camera, and Daniela Puzzello (2007). "Contagion equilibria in a monetary model," *Econometrica* 75, 277–282.

Alvarez, Fernando, and Urban Jermann (2000). "Efficiency, equilibrium, and asset pricing with risk of default," *Econometrica* 68, 775–797.

Amihud, Yakov, and Haim Mendelson (1980). "Dealership markets: Market-making with inventory," *Journal of Financial Economics* 8, 31–53.

Amihud, Yakov, and Haim Mendelson (1986). "Asset pricing and the bid-ask spread," *Journal of Financial Economics* 17, 223–249.

Andolfatto, David (2008). "The simple analytics of money and credit in a quasi-linear environment," Working Paper.

Andolfatto, David (2010). "Essential interest-bearing money," *Journal of Economic Theory* 145, 1495–1507.

Andolfatto, David (2011). "A note on the societal benefits of illiquid bonds," *Canadian Journal of Economics* 44, 133–147.

Andolfatto, David (2013). "Incentive-feasible deflation," *Journal of Monetary Economics* 60, 383–390.

Andolfatto, David, Aleksander Berentsen, and Christopher Waller (2014). "Optimal disclosure policy and undue diligence," *Journal of Economic Theory* 149, 128–152.

Andolfatto, David, Aleksander Berentsen, and Christopher Waller (2016). "Monetary policy with asset-backed money," *Journal of Economic Theory* (Forthcoming).

Andolfatto, David, and Fernando Martin (2013). "Information disclosure and exchange media," *Review of Economic Dynamics* 16, 527–539.

Araujo, Luis (2004). "Social norms and money," *Journal of Monetary Economics* 51, 241–256.

Araujo, Luis, and Braz Camargo (2006). "Information, learning, and the stability of fiat money," *Journal of Monetary Economics* 53, 1571–1591.

Araujo, Luis, and Braz Camargo (2008). "Endogenous supply of fiat money," *Journal of Economic Theory* 142, 2008, 48–72.

Araujo, Luis, and Braz Camargo (2009). "Money vs. memory," Working Paper, Michigan State University.

Araujo, Luis, Braz Camargo, Raoul Minetti, and Daniela Puzzello (2012). "The essentiality of money in environments with centralized trade," *Journal of Monetary Economics* 59, 612–621.

Araujo, Luis, and Tai-Wei Hu (2016). "Optimal monetary interventions in credit markets," Working Paper.

Araujo, Luis, and Raoul Minetti (2011) "On the essentiality of banks," *International Economic Review* 52, 679–691.

Araujo, Luis, and Andrei Shevshenko (2006) "Price dispersion, information, and learning," *Journal of Monetary Economics* 53, 1197–1223.

Arrow, Kenneth, and Gerard Debreu (1954). "Existence of an equilibrium for a competitive economy," *Econometrica* 22, 265–290.

Aruoba, S. Boragan (2011). "Money, search, and business cycles," *International Economic Review* 52, 935–959.

Aruoba, S. Boragan, and Sanjay Chugh (2008). "Optimal fiscal and monetary policy when money is essential," *Journal of Economic Theory* 145, 1618–1647.

Aruoba, S. Boragan, Morris Davis, and Randall Wright (2015). "Homework in monetary economics: Inflation, home production, and the production of homes," *Review of Economic Dynamics* (Forthcoming).

Aruoba, S. Boragan, Guillaume Rocheteau, and Christopher Waller (2007). "Bargaining and the value of money," *Journal of Monetary Economics* 54, 2636–2655.

Aruoba, S. Boragan, and Frank Schorfheide (2011). "Sticky prices versus monetary frictions: An estimation of policy trade-offs," *American Economic Journals: Macroeconomics* 3, 60–90.

Aruoba, S. Boragan, Christopher Waller, and Randall Wright (2011). "Money and capital: A quantitative analysis," *Journal of Monetary Economics* 58, 98–116.

Aruoba, S. Boragan, and Randall Wright (2003). "Search, money, and capital: A neoclassical dichotomy," *Journal of Money, Credit, and Banking* 35, 1085–1106.

Ashcraft, Adam, and Darrell Duffie (2007). "Systemic illiquidity in the federal funds market," *American Economic Review* 97, 221–225.

Atkeson, Andrew, Andrea Eisfeldt, and Pierre-Olivier Weill (2015). "Entry and exit in OTC derivatives markets," *Econometrica* 83, 2231–2292.

Azariadis, Costas (1993). *Intertemporal Macroeconomics.* Blackwell: Malden, Massachusetts.

Bailey, Martin (1956). "The welfare costs of inflationary finance," *Journal of Political Economy* 64, 93–110.

Bajaj, Ayushi (2015). "Undefeated equilibria of the Shi-Trejos-Wright model under adverse selection," mimeo.

Bajaj, Ayushi (2016). "Accounting for debasements: Indivisibility or imperfect recognizability of money," mimeo.

Banerjee, Abhijit and Eric Maskin (1996). "A Walrasian theory of money and barter," *The Quarterly Journal of Economics* 111, 955–1005.

Baranowski, Ryan (2015). "Adaptive learning and monetary exchange," *Journal of Economic Dynamics and Control* 58, 1–18.

Beaudry, Pascal, Dana Galizia, and Franck Portier (2015). "Reviving the limit cycle view of macroeconomic fluctuations," mimeo.

Bech, Morten, and Cyril Monnet (2016). "A search-based model of the interbank money market and monetary policy implementation," *Journal of Economic Theory* (Forthcoming).

Benabou, Roland (1988). "Search, price setting, and inflation," *Review of Economic Studies* 55, 353–376.

Bénassy, Jean-Pascal (1999). "Analytical solutions to a structural signal extraction model: Lucas 1972 revisited," *Journal of Monetary Economics* 44, 509–521.

Berentsen, Aleksander, Gabriele Camera, and Christopher Waller (2004). "The distribution of money and prices in an equilibrium with lotteries," *Economic Theory* 24, 887–906.

Berentsen, Aleksander, Gabriele Camera, and Christopher Waller (2005). "The distribution of money balances and the nonneutrality of money," *International Economic Review* 46, 465–487.

Berentsen, Aleksander, Gabriele Camera, and Christopher Waller (2007). "Money, credit, and banking," *Journal of Economic Theory* 135, 171–195.

Berentsen, Aleksander, Samuel Huber, and Alessandro Marchesiani (2014). "Degreasing the wheels of finance," *International Economic Review* 55, 735–763.

Berentsen, Aleksander, Samuel Huber, and Alessandro Marchesiani (2015). "Financial innovations, money demand and the welfare cost of inflation," *Journal of Money, Credit, and Banking* 47, 223–261.

Berentsen, Aleksander, Alessandro Marchesiani, and Christopher Waller (2014). "Floor systems for implementing monetary policy: Some unpleasant fiscal arithmetic," *Review of Economic Dynamics* 17, 523–542.

Berentsen, Aleksander, Guido Menzio, and Randall Wright (2011). "Inflation and unemployment in the long run," *American Economic Review* 101, 371–98.

Berentsen, Aleksander, Miguel Molico, and Randall Wright (2002). "Indivisibilities, lotteries, and monetary exchange," *Journal of Economic Theory* 107, 70–94.

Berentsen, Aleksander and Cyril Monnet (2008). "Monetary policy in a channel system," *Journal of Monetary Economics* 55, 1067–1080.

Berentsen, Aleksander and Guillaume Rocheteau (2002). "On the efficiency of monetary exchange: How divisibility of money matters," *Journal of Monetary Economics* 49, 1621–1649.

Berentsen, Aleksander and Guillaume Rocheteau (2003). "On the Friedman rule in search models with divisible money," *Contributions to Macroeconomics* 3, Article 11.

Berentsen, Aleksander and Guillaume Rocheteau (2003). "Money and the gains from trade," *International Economic Review* 44, 263–297.

Berentsen, Aleksander and Guillaume Rocheteau (2004). "Money and information," *Review of Economic Studies* 71, 915–944.

Berentsen, Aleksander, Guillaume Rocheteau, and Shouyong Shi (2007). "Friedman meets Hosios: Efficiency in search models of money," *Economic Journal* 117, 174–195.

Berentsen, Aleksander, Mariana Rojas Breu, and Shouyong Shi (2012). "Liquidity, innovation, and growth," *Journal of Monetary Economics* 59, 721–737.

Berentsen, Aleksander, and Carlo Strub (2009). "Central bank design with heterogeneous agents," *European Economic Review* 53, 139–152.

Berentsen, Aleksander, and Christopher Waller (2011). "Outside versus inside bonds: A Modigliani-Miller type result for liquidity constrained economies," *Journal of Economic Theory* 146, 1852–1887.

Berentsen, Aleksander, and Christopher Waller (2015). "Optimal stabilization policy with search externalities," *Macroeconomic Dynamics* 19, 669–700.

Bethune, Zachary, Tai-Wei Hu, and Guillaume Rocheteau (2014). "Dynamic indeterminacy and welfare in credit economies," Working Paper, University of California, Irvine.

Bethune, Zachary, Peter Rupert, and Guillaume Rocheteau (2015). "Aggregate unemployment and household unsecured debt," *Review of Economic Dynamics* 18, 77–100.

Bhattacharya, Joydeep, Joseph Haslag, and Antoine Martin (2005). "Heterogeneity, redistribution, and the Friedman Rule," *International Economic Review* 46, 437–454.

Bhattacharya, Joydeep, Joseph Haslag, and Antoine Martin (2006). "Sub-optimality of the Friedman rule in Townsend's turnpike and stochastic relocation models of money: Do finite lives and initial dates matter?" *Journal of Economic Dynamics and Control* 30, 879–897.

Biglaiser, Gary (1993). "Middlemen as experts," *The RAND Journal of Economics* 24, 212–223.

Boel, Paola and Gabriele Camera (2006). "Efficient monetary allocations and the illiquidity of bonds," *Journal of Monetary Economics* 53, 1693–1715.

Boel, Paola and Gabriele Camera (2009). "Financial sophistication and the distribution of the welfare cost of inflation," *Journal of Monetary Economics* 56, 968–978.

Boel, Paola and Gabriele Camera (2011). "The welfare cost of inflation in OECD countries," *Macroeconomic Dynamics* 15, 217–251.

Brunner, Karl and Allan Meltzer (1971). "The uses of money: Money in the theory of an exchange economy," *American Economic Review* 61, 784–805.

Bryant, John and Neil Wallace (1979). "The inefficiency of interest-bearing national debt," *Journal of Political Economy* 87, 365–381.

Burdett, Kenneth and Kenneth Judd (1983). "Equilibrium price dispersion," *Econometrica* 51, 955–969.

Burdett, Kenneth, Alberto Trejos, and Randall Wright (2001). "Cigarette money," *Journal of Economic Theory* 99, 117–142.

Branch, William (2016). "Imperfect knowledge, liquidity and bubbles," *Journal of Economic Dynamics and Control* 62, 17–42.

Branch, William, and Bruce McGough (2016). "Heterogeneous beliefs and trading inefficiencies," *Journal of Economic Theory* 163, 786–818.

Branch, William, Nicolas Petrosky-Nadeau, and Guillaume Rocheteau (2015). "Financial frictions, the housing market, and unemployment," *Journal of Economic Theory* (Forthcoming).

Calvo, Guillermo (1983). "Staggered prices in a utility-maximizing framework," *Journal of Monetary Economics* 12, 383–398.

Camargo, Braz, Teddy Kim, and Ben Lester (2015). "Information spillovers, gains from trade, and interventions in frozen markets," *Review of Financial Studies* (Forthcoming).

Camargo, Braz and Ben Lester (2014). "Trading dynamics in decentralized markets with adverse selection," *Journal of Economic Theory* 153, 534–568.

Camera, Gabriele (2001). "Search, dealers, and the terms of trade," *Review of Economic Dynamics* 4, 680–694.

Camera, Gabriele, and YiLi Chien (2016). "Two monetary models with alternating markets," *Journal of Money, Credit, and Banking* (Forthcoming).

Camera, Gabriele, and Dean Corbae (1999). "Money and price dispersion," *International Economic Review* 40, 985–1008.

Camera, Gabriele, Ben Craig, and Christopher Waller (2004). "Currency competition in a fundamental model of money," *Journal of International Economics* 64, 521–544.

Camera, Gabriele and Alessandro Gioffre (2014). "Game-theoretic foundations of monetary equilibrium," *Journal of Monetary Economics* 63, 51–63.

Camera, Gabriele and Yiting Li (2008). "Another example of a credit system that coexists with money," *Journal of Money, Credit and Banking* 40, 1295–1308.

Camera, Gabriele, Rob Reed, and Christopher Waller (2003). "Jack of all trades or master of one? Specialization, trade and money," *International Economic Review* 44, 1275–1294.

Camera, Gabriele, and Johannes Winkler (2003). "International monetary exchange and the law of one price," *Journal of Monetary Economics* 50, 1531–1553.

Carapella, Francesca, and Stephen Williamson (2015). "Credit markets, limited commitment, and government debt," *Review of Economic Studies* (Forthcoming).

Cass, David (1965). "Optimum growth in an aggregative model of capital accumulation," *The Review of Economic Studies* 37, 233–240.

Cavalcanti, Ricardo, Andres Erosa, and Ted Temzelides (1999). "Private money and reserve management in a random matching model," *Journal of Political Economy* 107, 929–945.

Cavalcanti, Ricardo and Andres Erosa (2008). "Efficient propagation of shocks and the optimal return on money," *Journal of Economic Theory* 142, 128–148.

Cavalcanti, Ricardo and Ed Nosal (2011). "Counterfeiting as private money in mechanism design," *Journal of Money, Credit and Banking* 43(S2), 625–636.

Cavalcanti, Ricardo and Neil Wallace (1999). "Inside and outside money as alternative media of exchange," Proceedings, Federal Reserve Bank of Cleveland, 443–468.

Chang, Briana (2014). "Adverse selection and liquidity distortion," Working Paper, University of Wisconsin.

Chiu, Jonathan and Thorsten Koeppl (2016). "Trading dynamics with adverse selection and search: Market freeze, intervention and recovery," *Review of Economic Studies* (Forthcoming).

Chiu, Jonathan and Cesaire Meh (2011). "Financial intermediation, liquidity, and in‡ation," *Macroeconomic Dynamics* 15, 83–118.

Chiu, Jonathan, Cesaire Meh, and Randall Wright (2015). "Innovation and growth with financial and other frictions," *International Economic Review* (Forthcoming).

Chiu, Jonathan and Miguel Molico (2010). "Liquidity, redistribution, and the welfare cost of inflation," *Journal of Monetary Economics* 57, 428–438.

Chiu, Jonathan and Miguel Molico (2011). "Uncertainty, inflation, and welfare," *Journal of Money, Credit, and Banking* 43, 487–512.

Chiu, Jonathan and Russell Wong (2015). "Payment systems: A mechanism design approach," Working Paper of the Bank of Canada.

Clower, Robert (1967). "A reconsideration of the microfoundations of monetary theory," *Western Economic Journal* 6, 1–8.

Coles, Melvyn and Randall Wright (1998). "A dynamic equilibrium model of search, bargaining, and money," *Journal of Economic Theory* 78, 32–54.

Cone, Thomas (2005). "Anticipated inflation and rates of return in a search-theoretic monetary model," *Journal of Monetary Economics* 52, 567–674.

Constantinides, George (1986). "Capital market equilibrium with transaction costs," *Journal of Political Economy* 94, 842–862.

Cooley, Thomas and Vincenzo Quadrini (2004). "Optimal time-consistent monetary policy in a Phillips-curve world", *Journal of Economic Theory* 118, 174–208.

Corbae, Dean and Joseph Ritter (2004). "Decentralized credit and monetary exchange without public record-keeping," *Economic Theory* 24, 933–951.

Craig, Ben and Guillaume Rocheteau (2008). "Inflation and welfare: A search approach," *Journal of Money, Credit and Banking* 40, 89–119.

Craig, Ben and Guillaume Rocheteau (2008). "State-dependent pricing, inflation, and welfare," *European Economic Review* 52, 441–468.

Craig, Ben and Christopher Waller (2000). "Dual-currency economies as multiple-payment systems," Federal Reserve Bank of Cleveland, *Economic Review* 36, 2–13.

Craig, Ben and Craig Waller (2004). "Dollarization and currency exchange," *Journal of Monetary Economics* 51, 671–689.

Cuadras-Morato, Xavier (1994). "Commodity money in the presence of goods of heterogeneous quality," *Economic Theory* 4, 579–591.

Curtis, Elisabeth S. and Christopher Waller (2000). "A search-theoretic model of legal and illegal currency," *Journal of Monetary Economics* 45, 155–184.

Curtis, Elisabeth S. and Christopher Waller (2003). "Currency restrictions, government transaction policies and currency exchange," *Economic Theory* 21, 19–42.

Curtis, Elisabeth, and Randall Wright (2004). "Price setting, price dispersion, and the value of money: Or, the law of two prices," *Journal of Monetary Economics* 51, 1599–1621.

Davoodalhosseini, Mohammad (2014). "Constrained efficiency with search and information frictions," Job Market Paper, PennState University.

Debreu, Gerard (1959). *Theory of Value: An Axiomatic Analysis of Economic Equilibrium.* New York: Wiley. Reprint. New Haven: Yale University Press, 1971.

DeMarzo, Peter, and Darrell Duffie (1999). *"A liquidity-based model of security design,"* *Econometrica* 67, 65–99.

Deviatov, Alexei (2006). "Money creation in a random matching model," *The B.E. Journal of Macroeconomics* 6, 1–20.

Deviatov, Alexei and Neil Wallace (2001). "Another example in which lump-sum money creation is beneficial," *Advances in Macroeconomics* 1, Article 1.

Deviatov, Alexei and Neil Wallace (2014). "Optimal inflation in a model of inside money," *Review of Economic Dynamics* 17, 287–293.

Diamond, Peter (1982). "Aggregate demand management in search equilibrium," *Journal of Political Economy* 90, 881–894.

Diamond, Peter (1984). "Money in search equilibrium," *Econometrica* 52, 1–20.

Diamond, Peter (1987a). "Credit in search equilibrium,"*Financial Constraints, Expectations, and Macroeconomics*. Eds. Meir Kohn and Sho-Chieh Tsiang. Oxford University Press.

Diamond, Peter (1987b). "Multiple equilibria in models of credit," *American Economic Review* 77, 82–86.

Diamond, Peter (1990). "Pairwise credit in search equilibrium," *Quarterly Journal of Economics* 105, 285–319.

Diamond, Peter (1993). "Search, sticky prices, and inflation," *Review of Economic Studies* 60, 53–68.

Doepke Matthias and Martin Schneider (2013). "Money as a unit of account," NBER Working Paper 19537.

Dong, Mei and Janet Jiang (2010). "One or two monies?" *Journal of Monetary Economics* 57, 439–450.

Dong, Mei and Janet Jiang (2014). "Money and price posting under private information," *Journal of Economic Theory* 150, 740–777.

Dotsey, Michael and Peter Ireland (1996). "The welfare cost of inflation in general equilibrium," *Journal of Monetary Economics* 37, 29–47.

Dromel, Nicolas, Elie Kolakez, and Etienne Lehmann (2010). "Credit constraint and the persistence of unemployment", *Labour Economics* 17, 823–834.

Duffie, Darrell, Nicolae Garleanu, and Lasse H. Pedersen (2005). "Over-the-counter markets," *Econometrica* 73, 1815–1847.

Duffie, Darrell, Nicolae Garleanu, and Lasse H. Pedersen (2007). "Valuation in over-the-counter markets," *The Review of Financial Studies* 20, 1865–1900.

Duffy, John and Daniela Puzzello (2014). "Gift exchange versus monetary exchange: Theory and evidence," *American Economic Review* 104, 1735–1776.

Duffy, John and Daniela Puzzello (2015). "Experimental evidence on the essentiality and neutrality of money in a search model," Experiments in Macroeconomics, Research in Experimental Economics, Volume 17, Bingley, UK: Emerald Group Publishing Ltd, 2015.

Dutu, Richard, Benoit Julien, and Ian King (2012), "On the welfare gains of price dispersion," *Journal of Money, Credit, and Banking*, 44, 757–786.

Engineer, Merwan and Shouyong Shi (1998). "Asymmetry, imperfectly transferable utility, and fiat money in improving the terms of trade," *Journal of Monetary Economics* 41, 153–183.

Engineer, Merwan and Shouyong Shi (2001). "Bargains, barter, and money," *Review of Economic Dynamics* 4, 188–209.

Ennis, Huberto (2001). "On random matching, monetary equilibria, and sunspots," *Macroeconomic Dynamics* 5, 132–142.

Ennis, Huberto (2004). "Macroeconomic fluctuations and bargaining," *Journal of Economic Theory* 115, 322–340.

Ennis, Huberto (2008). "Search, money, and inflation under private information" *Journal of Economic Theory* 138, 101–131.

Ennis, Huberto (2009). "Avoiding the inflation tax," *International Economic Review* 50, 607–625.

Faig, Miquel (2008). "Endogenous buyer-seller choice and divisible money in search equilibrium," *Journal of Economic Theory* 141, 184–199.

Faig, Miquel and Belen Jerez (2006). "Inflation, prices, and information in competitive search," *Advances in Macroeconomics* 6, 1313.

Faig, Miquel and Zhe Li (2009). "The welfare cost of expected and unexpected inflation," *Journal of Monetary Economics* 56, 1004–1013.

Fernández-Villaverde, Jesús and Daniel Sanches (2016). "Can currency competition work?," NBER Working Paper 22157.

Ferraris, Leo and Makoto Watanabe (2008). "Collateral secured loans in a monetary economy," *Journal of Economic Theory* 143, 405–424.

Ferraris, Leo, and Makoto Watanabe (2011). "Collateral fluctuations in a monetary economy," *Journal of Economic Theory* 146, 1915–1940

Ferraris, Leo and Makoto Watanabe (2012). "Liquidity constraints in a monetary economy," *International Economic Review* 53, 255–277.

Fisher, Stanley (1974). "Money and the production function," *Economic Inquiry* 12, 517–533.

Freeman, Scott (1985). "Transaction costs and the optimal quantity of money," *Journal of Political Economy* 93, 145–157.

Freeman, Scott (1996a). "Clearinghouse banks and banknote over-issue," *Journal of Monetary Economics* 38, 101–115.

Freeman, Scott (1996b). "The payments system, liquidity, and rediscounting," *American Economic Review* 86, 1126–1138.

Freeman, Scott (1999). "Rediscounting under aggregate risk," *Journal of Monetary Economics* 43, 197–216.

Freeman, Scott and Joseph Haslag (1996). "On the optimality of interest-bearing reserves in economies of overlapping generations," *Economic Theory* 7, 557–565.

Freeman, Scott and Finn Kydland (2000). "Monetary aggregates and output," *American Economic Review* 90, 1125–1135.

Friedman, Milton (1969). "The optimum quantity of money," in *The Optimum Quantity of Money and Other Essays*, 1–50.

Friedman, Milton (1960). *A Program for Monetary Stability*. New York: Fordham University Press.

Galenianos, Manolis and Philipp Kircher (2008). "A model of money with multilateral matching," *Journal of Monetary Economics* 55, 1054–1066.

Gavazza, Alessandro (2011). "Leasing and secondary markets: Theory and evidence from commercial aircraft," *Journal of Political Economy* 119, 325–377.

Geromichalos, Athanasios and Lucas Herrenbreuck (2016). "Monetary policy, asset prices, and liquidity in over-the-counter markets," *Journal of Money, Credit, and Banking* 48, 35–79.

Geromichalos, Athanasios, Lucas Herrenbreuck, and Kevin Salyer (2016). "A search-theoretic model of the term premium," *Theoretical Economics* (Forthcoming).

Geromichalos, Athanasios and Kuk Mo Jung (2015). "An over-the-counter approach to the FOREX market", University of California, Davis, Working Paper.

Geromichalos, Athanasios, Juan Licari, and Jose Suarez-Lledo (2007). "Monetary policy and asset prices," *Review of Economic Dynamics* 10, 761–779.

Geromichalos, Athanasios and Ina Simonovska (2014). "Asset liquidity and international portfolio choice," *Journal of Economic Theory* 151, 342–380.

Glosten, Lawrence and Paul Milgrom (1985). "Bid, ask and transaction prices in a specialist market with heterogeneously informed traders," *Journal of Financial Economics* 14, 71–100.

Gomis-Porqueras, Pedro, Benoit Julien, and Chengsi Wang (2013). "Optimal monetary and fiscal policies in a search theoretic model of money and unemployment," *Macroeconomic Dynamics* 17, 1330–1354.

Gomis-Porqueras, Pedro, Timothy Kam, and Christopher Waller (2014). "Breaking the curse of Kareken and Wallace," Working Paper of the Federal Reserve Bank of St Louis.

Gomis-Porqueras, Pedro and Adrian Peralta-Ava (2010). "Optimal monetary and fiscal policies in a search theoretic model of monetary exchange," *European Economic Review* 54, 331–344.

Gomis-Porqueras, Pedro, Adrian Peralta-Alva, and Christopher Waller (2014). "The shadow economy as an equilibrium outcome," *Journal of Economic Dynamics and Control* 41, 1–19.

Gomis-Porqueras, Pedro and Daniel Sanches (2013). "Optimal monetary policy in a model of money and credit," *Journal of Money, Credit and Banking* 45, 701–730.

Grandmont, Jean-Michel (1985). "On endogenous competitive business cycles," *Econometrica* 53, 995–1046.

Green, Edward (1999). "Money and debt in the structure of payments," Federal Reserve Bank of Minneapolis, Quarterly Review 23, 13–29.

Green, Edward and Warren Weber (1996). "Will the new $100 bill decrease counterfeiting?" Working Paper 571, Federal Reserve Bank of Minneapolis.

Green, Edward and Ruilin Zhou (1998). "A rudimentary random-matching model with divisible money and prices," *Journal of Economic Theory* 81, 252–271.

Green, Edward and Ruilin Zhou (2002). "Dynamic monetary equilibrium in a random-matching economy," *Econometrica*, 70, 929–969.

Gu, Chao, Fabrizio Mattesini, and Randall Wright (2016). "Money and credit redux," *Econometrica* 84, 1–32.

Gu, Chao, Fabrizio Mattesini, Cyril Monnet, and Randall Wright (2013a). "Banking: A New Monetarist approach," *Review of Economic Studies* 80, 636–662.

Gu, Chao, Fabrizio Mattesini, Cyril Monnet, and Randall Wright (2013b). "Endogenous credit cycles," *Journal of Political Economy* 121, 940–965.

Guerrieri, Veronica and Guido Lorenzoni (2009). "Liquidity and trading dynamics," *Econometrica* 77, 1751–1790.

Guerrieri, Veronica, Robert Shimer, and Randall Wright (2010). "Adverse selection in competitive search equilibrium," *Econometrica* 78, 1823–1862.

Harris, Larry (2003). *Trading & Exchanges, Market Microstructure for Practitioners*, Oxford University Press, New York.

Haslag, Joseph and Antoine Martin (2007). "Optimality of the Friedman Rule in an overlapping generations model with spatial separation," *Journal of Money, Credit and Banking* 39, 1741–1758.

He, Chao, Randall Wright, and Yu Zhu (2015). "Housing and liquidity," *Review of Economic Dynamics* 18, 435–455.

Head, Allen, Lucy Liu, Guido Menzio, and Randall Wright (2012). "Sticky prices: A New Monetarist approach," *Journal of the European Economic Association* 10, 939–973.

Head, Allen and Shouyong Shi (2003). "A fundamental theory of exchange rates and direct currency trades," *Journal of Monetary Economics* 50, 1555–1591.

Heaton, John and Deborah Lucas (1995). "The importance of investor heterogeneity and financial market imperfections for the behavior of asset prices," Carnegie-Rochester Conference Series on Public Policy 42, 1–32.

Heaton, John and Deborah Lucas (1996). "Evaluating the effects of incomplete markets on risk sharing and asset pricing," *Journal of Political Economy* 104, 443–87.

Herrenbrueck, Lucas (2014). "Quantitative easing and the liquidity channel of monetary policy," Working Paper, Simon Fraser University.

Hicks, John (1935). "A suggestion for simplifying the theory of money," *Economica* 2, 1–19.

Ho, Thomas and Hans Stoll (1983). "The dynamics of dealer markets under competition," *Journal of Finance* 38, 1053–74.

Holmstrom, Bengt and Jean Tirole (1998). "Private and public supply of liquidity," *Journal of Political Economy* 106, 1–40.

Holmstrom, Bengt and Jean Tirole (2001). "LAPM - a liquidity-based asset pricing model," *Journal of Finance* 56, 1837–1867.

Hopenhayn, Hugo and Ingrid Werner (1996). "Information, liquidity, and asset trading in a random matching game," *Journal of Economic Theory* 68, 349–379.

Howitt, Peter (2005). "Beyond search: Fiat money in organized exchange," *International Economic Review* 46, 405–429.

Hu, Tai-Wei (2013). "Imperfect recognizability and coexistence of money and higher-return assets," *Economic Theory* 53, 111–138.

Hu, Tai-wei, John Kennan, and Neil Wallace (2009). "Coalition-proof trade and the Friedman rule in the Lagos-Wright model," *Journal of Political Economy* 117, 116–137.

Hu, Tai-wei, and Guillaume Rocheteau (2013). "On the coexistence of money and higher return assets and its social role," *Journal of Economic Theory* 148, 2520–2560.

Hu, Tai-wei, and Guillaume Rocheteau (2015). "Monetary policy and asset prices: A mechanism design approach," *Journal of Money, Credit, and Banking* 47, 39–76.

Hu, Tai-Wei, and Cathy Zhang (2014). "Responding to the inflation tax," Working Paper.

Huang, Ming (2003). "Liquidity shocks and equilibrium liquidity premia," *Journal of Economic Theory* 109, 104–29.

Hugonnier, Julien, Benjamin Lester, and Pierre-Olivier Weill (2015). "Heterogeneity in decentralized asset markets," Working Paper of the Federal Reserve Bank of Philadelphia 15–22.

Iwai, Katsuhito (1996). "The bootstrap theory of money: A search-theoretic foundation of monetary economics," *Structural Change and Economic Dynamics* 7, 451–477.

Jacquet, Nicolas and Serene Tan (2012) "Money and asset prices with uninsurable risks," *Journal of Monetary Economics* 59, 784–797.

Jafarey, Saqib and Adrian Masters (2003). "Output, prices, and the velocity of money in search equilibrium," *Journal of Money, Credit and Banking* 35, 871–88.

Jafarey, Saqib and Peter Rupert (2001). "Limited commitment, money, and credit," *Journal of Economic Theory* 99, 22–58.

Jean, Kasie, Stanislav Rabinovich, and Randall Wright (2010). "On the multiplicity of monetary equilibria: Green-Zhou meets Lagos-Wright," *Journal of Economic Theory* 145, 392–401.

Jevons, William S. (1875). *Money and the Mechanism of Exchange.* D. Appleton and Co., New York.

Jin, Yi, and Ted Temzelides (2004). "On the local interaction of money and credit," *Review of Economic Dynamics* 7, 143–156.

Jones, Robert (1976). "The origin and development of media of exchange," *Journal of Political Economy* 84, 757–775.

Julien, Benoit, John Kennes, and Ian King (2008). "Bidding for money," *Journal of Economic Theory* 142, 196–217.

Kahn, Charles (2009). "Collateral policy in a world of round-the-clock payment," Working Paper of the University of Illinois.

Kahn, Charles and William Roberds (2009). "Why pay? An introduction to payments economics," *Journal of Financial Intermediation* 18, 1–23.

Kamiya, Kazuya and Takashi Shimizu (2006). "Real indeterminacy of stationary equilibria in matching models with divisible money", *Journal of Mathematical Economics* 42, 594–617.

Kamiya, Kazuya, Noritsugu Morishita, and Takashi Shimizu (2005). "On the existence of single-price equilibria in a matching model with divisible money and production cost," *International Journal of Economic Theory* 1, 219–231.

Kamiya, Kazuya and Takashi Sato (2004). "Equilibrium price dispersion in a matching model with divisible money," *International Economic Review* 45, 413–430.

Kamiya, Kazuya and Takashi Shimizu (2007a). "Existence of equilibria in matching models of money: A new technique," *Economic Theory* 32, 447–460.

Kamiya, Kazuya and Takashi Shimizu (2007b). "On the role of tax-subsidy scheme in money search models," *International Economic Review* 48, 575–606.

Kareken, John and Neil Wallace (1981). "On the indeterminacy of equilibrium exchange rates," *Quarterly Journal of Economics* 96, 207–222.

Kehoe, Timothy and David Levine (1993). "Debt-constrained asset markets," *Review of Economic Studies* 60, 865–888.

Kehoe, Timothy, Nobuhiro Kiyotaki, and Randall Wright (1993). "More on money as a medium of exchange," *Economic Theory* 3, 297–314.

Kim, Young (2008). "Liquidity and selection in asset markets with search frictions," mimeo.

Kim, Young Sik (1996). "Money, barter and costly information acquisition," *Journal of Monetary Economics* 37, 119–142.

Kim, Young Sik and Manjong Lee (2008). "Recognizability and liquidity," mimeo.

King, Robert and Charles Plosser (1986). "Money as the mechanism of exchange," *Journal of Monetary Economics* 17, 93–115.

Kiyotaki, Nobuhiro, Akihiko Matsui, and Kiminori Matsuyama (1993). "Toward a theory of international currency," *Review of Economic Studies* 60, 283–307.

Kiyotaki, Nobuhiro and John Moore (1997). "Credit cycles," *Journal of Political Economy* 105, 211–248.

Kiyotaki, Nobuhiro and John Moore (2002). "Evil is the root of all money," *American Economic Review, Papers and Proceedings* 92, 62–66.

Kiyotaki, Nobuhiro and John Moore (2005). "Liquidity and asset prices," *International Economic Review* 46, 317–349.

Kiyotaki, Nobuhiro and Randall Wright (1989). "On money as a medium of exchange," *Journal of Political Economy* 97, 927–954.

Kiyotaki, Nobuhiro and Randall Wright (1991). "A contribution to the pure theory of money," *Journal of Economic Theory* 53, 215–235.

Kiyotaki, Nobuhiro and Randall Wright (1993). "A search-theoretic approach to monetary economics," *American Economic Review* 83, 63–77.

Kocherlakota, Narayana (1996). "Implications of efficient risk sharing without commitment," *Review of Economic Studies* 63, 595–609.

Kocherlakota, Narayana (1998a). "Money is memory," *Journal of Economic Theory* 81, 232–251.

Kocherlakota, Narayana (1998b). "The technological role of fiat money," *Federal Reserve Bank of Minneapolis Quarterly Review* 22, 2–10.

Kocherlakota, Narayana (2002). "The two-money theorem," *International Economic Review* 43, 333–346.

Kocherlakota, Narayana (2003). "Social benefits of illiquid bonds," *Journal of Economic Theory* 108, 179–193.

Kocherlakota, Narayana (2008). "Injecting rational bubbles," *Journal of Economic Theory* 142, 218–232.

Kocherlakota, Narayana (2009). "Asset pricing implications of Pareto optimality with private information," *Journal of Political Economy* 117, 555–590.

Kocherlakota, Narayana and Thomas Krueger (1999). "A signaling model of multiple currencies," *Review of Economic Dynamics* 2, 231–244.

Kocherlakota, Narayana and Neil Wallace (1998). "Incomplete record-keeping and optimal payment arrangements," *Journal of Economic Theory* 81, 272–289.

Koeppl, Thorsten, Cyril Monnet, and Ted Temzelides (2008). "A dynamic model of settlement," *Journal of Economic Theory* 142, 233–246.

Koopmans, Tjalling (1965). "On the concept of optimal economic growth," in The Econometric Approach to Development Planning, Amsterdam, North Holland.

Kranton, Rachel (1996). "Reciprocal exchange: A self-sustaining system," *American Economic Review* 86, 830–851.

Kultti, Klaus (1996). "A monetary economy with counterfeiting," *Journal of Economics* 63, 175–186.

Kydland, Finn and Edward Prescott (1982). "Time to build and aggregate fluctuations," *Econometrica* 50, 1345–1370.

Kyle, Albert (1985). "Continuous auctions and insider trading," *Econometrica* 53, 1315–1335.

Lagos, Ricardo (2010a). "Some results on the optimality and implementation of the Friedman rule in the search theory of money," *Journal of Economic Theory* 145, 1508–1524.

Lagos, Ricardo (2010b). "Asset prices and liquidity in an exchange economy," *Journal of Monetary Economics* 57, 913–930.

Lagos, Ricardo (2011). "Asset prices, liquidity, and monetary policy in an exchange economy," *Journal of Money, Credit, and Banking* 43, 521–552.

Lagos, Ricardo (2013). "Moneyspots," *Journal of Political Economy* 121, 127–185.

Lagos, Ricardo and Guillaume Rocheteau (2005). "Inflation, output, and welfare," *International Economic Review* 46, 495–522.

Lagos, Ricardo, and Guillaume Rocheteau (2007). "Search in asset markets: Market structure, liquidity, and welfare," *American Economic Review* 97, 198–202.

Lagos, Ricardo and Guillaume Rocheteau (2008). "Money and capital as competing media of exchange," *Journal of Economic Theory* 142, 247–258.

Lagos, Ricardo and Guillaume Rocheteau (2009). "Liquidity in asset markets with search frictions," *Econometrica* 77, 403–426.

Lagos, Ricardo, Guillaume Rocheteau, and Pierre-Olivier Weill (2011). "Crises and liquidity in over-the-counter markets," *Journal of Economic Theory* 146, 2169–2205.

Lagos, Ricardo, Guillaume Rocheteau, and Randall Wright (2016). "Liquidity: A New Monetarist perspective," *Journal of Economic Literature* (Forthcoming).

Lagos, Ricardo and Randall Wright (2003). "Dynamics, cycles, and sunspot equilibria in 'genuinely dynamic, fundamentally disaggregative' models of money," *Journal of Economic Theory* 109, 156–171.

Lagos, Ricardo and Randall Wright (2005). "A unified framework for monetary theory and policy analysis," *Journal of Political Economy* 113, 463–484.

Lagos, Ricardo and Shengxing Zhang (2014). "Monetary exchange in over-the-counter markets: A theory of speculative bubbles, the Fed model, and self-fulfilling liquidity crises," Working Paper.

Laing, Derek, Victor Li, and Ping Wang (2007). "Inflation and productive activity in a multiple-matching model of money," *Journal of Monetary Economics* 54, 1949–1961.

Lehmann, Etienne (2012). "A search model of unemployment and inflation", *Scandinavian Journal of Economics* 114, 245–266.

Lehmann, Etienne and Bruno Van Der Linden (2010). "Search frictions on product and labor markets: Money in the matching function," *Macroeconomic Dynamics* 14, 56–92.

Lester, Benjamin, Andrew Postlewaite and Randall Wright (2012). "Liquidity, information, asset prices, and monetary policy," *Review of Economic Studies* 79, 1209–1238.

Lester, Benjamin, Guillaume Rocheteau, and Pierre-Olivier Weill (2015). "Competing for order flow in OTC markets," *Journal of Money, Credit, and Banking* 47, 77–126.

Levine, David (1991). "Asset trading mechanisms and expansionary policy," *Journal of Economic Theory* 54, 148–164.

Li, Victor (1994). "Inventory accumulation in a search-based monetary economy," *Journal of Monetary Economics* 34, 511–536.

Li, Victor (1995). "The optimal taxation of fiat money in search equilibrium," *International Economic Review* 36, 927–942.

Li, Victor (1997). "The efficiency of monetary exchange in search equilibrium," *Journal of Money, Credit, and Banking* 28, Article 4.

Li, Yiting (1995). "Commodity money under private information," *Journal of Monetary Economics* 36, 573–592.

Li, Yiting (1998). "Middlemen and private information," *Journal of Monetary Economics* 42, 131–159.

Li, Yiting (1999). "Money and middlemen in an economy with private information," *Economic Inquiry* 37, 1–12.

Li, Yiting (2001). "A search model of money and circulating private debt with applications to monetary policy," *International Economic Review* 42, 925–946.

Li, Yiting (2002). "Government Transaction Policy and Gresham's Law," *Journal of Monetary Economics* 49, 435–453.

Li, Yiting (2006). "Banks, private money, and government regulation," *Journal of Monetary Economics* 53, 2067–2083.

Li, Yiting (2007). "Inside money, organized markets, and specialization," *Macroeconomic Dynamics* 11, 388–404.

Li, Yiting (2011). "Currency and checking deposits as means of payment," *Review of Economic Dynamics* 14, 403–417.

Li, Ying-Syuan and Yiting Li (2013). "Liquidity and asset prices: A New Monetarist approach," *Journal of Monetary Economics* 60, 426–438.

Li, Yiting and Guillaume Rocheteau (2009). "Liquidity constraints," Working Paper.

Li, Yiting and Guillaume Rocheteau (2011). "On the threat of counterfeiting," *Macroeconomic Dynamics* 15, 10–41.

Li, Yiting, Guillaume Rocheteau, and Pierre-Olivier Weill (2012). "Liquidity and the threat of fraudulent assets," *Journal of Political Economy* 120, 815–846.

Li, Yiting, and Randall Wright (1998). "Government transaction policy, media of exchange, and prices," *Journal of Economic Theory* 81, 290–313.

Lippi, Francesco, Stefania Ragni and Nicholas Trachter (2015). " Optimal monetary policy with heterogeneous money holdings," *Journal of Economic Theory* 159, 339–368.

Liu, Lucy Qian, Liang Wang, and Randall Wright (2011). "The hot potato effect of inflation," *Macroeconomic Dynamics* 15, 191–216.

Liu, Qing and Shouyong Shi (2006). "Currency areas and monetary coordination" *International Economic Review* 51, 813–836.

Lo, Andrew, Harry Mamaysky, and Jiang Wang (2004). "Asset prices and trading volume under fixed transactions costs," *Journal of Political Economy* 112, 1054–1090.

Lomeli, Hector and Ted Temzelides (2002). "Discrete time dynamics in a random matching monetary model," *Economic Theory* 20, 259–269.

Lotz, Sebastien (2004). "Introducing a new currency: Government policy and prices," *European Economic Review* 48, 959–982.

Lotz, Sebastien and Guillaume Rocheteau (2002). "On the launching of a new currency," *Journal of Money, Credit and Banking* 34, 563–88.

Lotz, Sebastien, Andrei Shevshenko, and Christopher Waller (2007). "Heterogeneity and lotteries in monetary search models," *Journal of Money, Credit and Banking* 39, 703–712 .

Lotz, Sebastien, and Cathy Zhang (2016). "Money and credit as means of payment: A New Monetarist approach," *Journal of Economic Theory* (Forthcoming).

Lucas, Robert (1972). "Expectations and the neutrality of money," *Journal of Economic Theory* 4, 103–124.

Lucas, Robert (1973). "Some international evidence on output-inflation trade-offs," *American Economic Review* 63, 326–334.

Lucas, Robert (1978). "Asset prices in an exchange economy," *Econometrica* 46, 1429–1445.

Lucas, Robert (1980). "Two illustrations of the quantity theory of money," *American Economic Review* 70, 1005–1014.

Lucas, Robert (1990). "Liquidity and interest rates," *Journal of Economic Theory* 50, 237–264.

Lucas, Robert (1995). "Monetary Neutrality" Nobel Prize Lecture – 1995 Nobel Prize in Economics, December 7, 1995.

Lucas, Robert (2000). "Inflation and welfare," *Econometrica* 68, 247–274.

Lucas, Robert and Nancy Stokey (1987). "Money and interest in a cash-in-advance economy," *Econometrica* 55, 491–513.

Marimon, Ramon and Fabrizio Zilibotti (1997). "Unemployment vs. mismatch of talents: Reconsidering unemployment benefits," *The Economic Journal* 109, 266–291.

Mehra, Rajnish and Edward Prescott (1985). "The equity premium: A puzzle," *Journal of Monetary Economics* 15, 145–161.

Miao, Jianjun (2006): "A search model of centralized and decentralized trade," *Review of Economic Dynamics* 9, 68–92.

Moen, Espen (1997). "Competitive search equilibrium," *Journal of Political Economy* 105, 385–411.

Molico, Miguel (2006). "The distribution of money and prices in search equilibrium," *International Economic Review* 47, 701–722.

Molico, Miguel and Yahong Zhang (2006). "Monetary policy and the distribution of money and capital," *Computing in Economics and Finance* 136.

Monnet, Cyril (2005). "Counterfeiting and inflation," Working Paper Series 512, European Central Bank.

Monnet, Cyril and Daniel Sanches (2015). "Private money and banking regulation," *Journal of Money, Credit, and Banking* 47, 1031–1062.

Mortensen, Dale and Christopher Pissarides (1994). "Job creation and job destruction in the theory of unemployment," *Review of Economic Studies* 61, 397–415.

Mortensen, Dale and Randall Wright (2002). "Competitive pricing and efficiency in search equilibrium," *International Economic Review* 43, 1–20.

Myers, Stewart and Nicholal Majluf (1984). "Corporate financing and investment decisions when firms have information that investors do not have," *Journal of Financial Economics* 13, 187–221.

Nash, John (1953). "Two person cooperative games," *Econometrica* 21, 128–140.

Niehans, Jurg (1971). "Money and barter in general equilibrium with transactions costs," *American Economic Review* 61, 773–783.

Niehans, Jurg (1978). *The Theory of Money,* Baltimore: John Hopkins University Press, 1978.

Nosal, Ed (2011). "Search, welfare and the 'hot potato' effect of inflation," *Macroeconomic Dynamics* 15, 313–326.

Nosal, Ed and Guillaume Rocheteau (2008). "The economics of payments," Policy Discussion Papers, Federal Reserve Bank of Cleveland.

Nosal, Ed and Guillaume Rocheteau (2009). "Pairwise trades, asset prices, and monetary policy," *Journal of Economic Dynamics and Control* 37, 1–17.

Nosal, Ed and Neil Wallace (2007). "A model of (the threat of) counterfeiting," *Journal of Monetary Economics* 54, 994–1001.

Obstfeld, Maurice, and Kenneth Rogoff (1996). *Foundations of International Macroeconomics.* Cambridge, MA: MIT Press, Appendix 8A.

Oh, Seonghwan (1989). "A theory of a generally acceptable medium of exchange and barter," *Journal of Monetary Economics* 23, 101–119.

Osborne, Martin and Ariel Rubinstein (1990). *Bargaining and Markets.* San Diego: Academic Press.

Ostroy, Joseph (1973). "The informational efficiency of monetary exchange," *American Economic Review* 63, 597–610.

Ostroy, Joseph and Ross Starr (1974). "Money and the decentralization of exchange," *Econometrica* 42, 1093–1113.

Ostroy, Joseph and Ross Starr (1990). "The transactions role of money," *Handbook of Monetary Economics.* Eds. Benjamin Friedman and Frank Hahn. Elsevier: Amsterdam.

Pagnotta, Emiliano and Thomas Philippon (2015). "Competing on speed," NYU Working Paper.

Patinkin, Don (1965). *Money, Interest and Prices,* 2nd edition. New York: Harper & Row.

Peterson, Brian and Shouyong Shi (2004). "Money, price dispersion and welfare," *Economic Theory* 24, 907–932.

Petrosky-Nadeau, Nicolas and Etienne Wasmer (2015). "Macroeconomic dynamics in a model of goods, labor and credit market frictions," *Journal of Monetary Economics* 72, 97–113.

Phillips, William (1958). "The relationship between unemployment and the rate of change of money wages in the United Kingdom 1861–1957," *Economica* 25, 283–299.

Pissarides, Christopher (2000). *Equilibrium Unemployment.* Cambridge, USA: MIT Press (2nd edition).

Prescott, Edward (1987). "A multiple means-of-payment model," *New Approaches to Monetary* Economics. Eds. W. Barnett and K. Singleton. Cambridge, UK: Cambridge University Press.

Quercioli, Elena and Lones Smith (2015). "The economics of counterfeiting," *Econometrica* 83, 1211–1236.

Rauch, Bernhard (2000). "A divisible search model of fiat money: A comment," *Econometrica* 68, 149–156.

Redish, Angela and Warrenn Weber (2011), "Coin sizes and payments in commodity money systems," *Macroeconomic Dynamics* 15, 62–82.

Reed, Robert and Christopher Waller (2006). "Money and risk sharing," *Journal of Money, Credit, and Banking* 38, 1599–1618.

Renero, Juan M (1998). "Unstable and stable steady-states in the Kiyotaki-Wright model," *Economic Theory* 11, 275–294.

Renero, Juan M (1999). "Does and should a commodity medium of exchange have relatively low storage costs?" *International Economic Review* 40, 251–264.

Rocheteau, Guillaume (2008). "Money and competing assets under private information," Working Paper 0802, Federal Reserve Bank of Cleveland.

Rocheteau, Guillaume (2009a). "A monetary approach to asset liquidity," Working Papers 09-01, Federal Reserve Bank of Cleveland.

Rocheteau, Guillaume (2009b). "Information and liquidity: A discussion," Working Papers, Federal Reserve Bank of Cleveland 09-02.

Rocheteau, Guillaume (2012). "The cost of inflation: A mechanism design approach," *Journal of Economic Theory* 147, 1261–1279.

Rocheteau, Guillaume and Antonio Rodriguez-Lopez (2014). "Liquidity provision, interest rates, and unemployment," *Journal of Monetary Economics* 65, 80–101.

Rocheteau, Guillaume, Peter Rupert, and Randall Wright (2007). "Inflation and unemployment in general equilibrium," Scandavian *Journal of Economics* 109, 837–855.

Rocheteau, Guillaume, Peter Rupert, Karl Shell, and Randall Wright (2008)."General equilibrium with nonconvexities and money," *Journal of Economic Theory* 142, 294–317.

Rocheteau, Guillaume, Russell Wong, and Pierre-Olivier Weill (2015a). "A tractable model of monetary exchange with ex-post heterogeneity," NBER Working Paper 21179.

Rocheteau, Guillaume, Russell Wong, and Pierre-Olivier Weill (2015b). "Working through the distribution: Money in the short and long run," NBER Working Paper 21779.

Rocheteau, Guillaume and Randall Wright (2005). "Money in search equilibrium, in competitive equilibrium, and in competitive search equilibrium," *Econometrica* 73, 175–202.

Rocheteau, Guillaume and Randall Wright (2009). "Inflation and welfare in models with trading frictions," *Monetary Policy in Low Inflation Economies.* Eds. Ed Nosal and Dave Altig. Cambridge University Press.

Rocheteau, Guillaume and Randall Wright (2013). "Liquidity and asset market dynamics," *Journal of Monetary Economics* 60, 275–294.

Rocheteau, Guillaume, Randall Wright, and Sylvia Xiaolin Xiao (2015). "Open-market operations," Working Paper.

Rocheteau, Guillaume, Randall Wright, and Cathy Zhang (2016). "Corporate finance and monetary policy," Working Paper.

Rojas Breu, Mariana (2013). "The welfare effect of access to credit," *Economic Inquiry* 51, 235–247.

Rojas Breu, Mariana (2016). "Debt enforcement and the value of money," Working Paper, University Paris Dauphine.

Rotemberg, Julio (1982). "Sticky prices in the United States," *Journal of Political Economy* 90, 1187–1211.

Rubinstein, Ariel and Asher Wolinsky (1987). "Middlemen," *Quarterly Journal of Economics* 102, 581–594.

Rupert, Peter, Martin Schindler, and Randall Wright (2000). "The search-theoretic approach to monetary economics: A primer," *Federal Reserve Bank of Cleveland Economic Review* 36, 10–28.

Rust, John, and George Hall (2003). "Middlemen versus market makers: A theory of competitive exchange," *Journal of Political Economy* 111, 353–403.

Samuelson, Paul (1958). "An exact consumption-loan model of interest with or without the social contrivance of money," *Journal of Political Economy* 66, 467.

Sanches, Daniel and Stephen Williamson (2010). "Money and credit with limited commitment and theft," *Journal of Economic Theory* 145, 1525–1549.

Sanches, Daniel and Stephen Williamson (2011). "Adverse selection, segmented markets, and the role of monetary policy," *Macroeconomic Dynamics* 15, 269–292.

Sargent, Thomas and Neil Wallace (1983). "A model of commodity money," *Journal of Monetary Economics* 12, 163–187.

Sargent, Thomas and Neil Wallace (1985). "Interest on reserves," *Journal of Monetary Economics* 15, 279–290.

Schreft, Stacey (1992). "Transaction costs and the use of cash and credit," *Economic Theory* 2, 283–296.

Shevshenko, Andrei (2004). "Middlemen," *International Economic Review* 45, 1–24.

Shevshenko, Andrei and Randall Wright (2004). "A simple search model of money with heterogeneous agents and partial acceptability," *Economic Theory* 24, 877–885.

Shi, Shouyong (1995). "Money and prices: A model of search and bargaining," *Journal of Economic Theory* 67, 467–496.

Shi, Shouyong (1996). "Credit and money in a search model with divisible commodities," *Review of Economic Studies* 63, 627–652.

Shi, Shouyong (1997a). "A divisible search model of fiat money," *Econometrica* 65, 75–102.

Shi, Shouyong (1997b). "Money and specialization," *Economic Theory* 10, 99–113.

Shi, Shouyong (1998). "Search for a monetary propagation mechanism," *Journal of Economic Theory* 81, 314–352.

Shi, Shouyong (1999a). "Search, inflation, and capital accumulation," *Journal of Monetary Economics* 44, 81–103.

Shi, Shouyong (1999b). "Money, capital, and redistributive effects of monetary policies," *Journal of Economic Dynamics and Control* 23, 565–590.

Shi, Shouyong (2001). "The extent of the market and the optimal degree of specialization," mimeo.

Shi, Shouyong (2005). "Nominal bonds and interest rates: The case of one-period bonds," *International Economic Review* 46, 579–612.

Shi, Shouyong (2006). "Viewpoint: A microfoundation of monetary economics," *Canadian Journal of Economics* 39, 643–688.

Shi, Shouyong (2008). "Efficiency improvement from restricting the liquidity of nominal bonds," *Journal of Monetary Economics* 55, 1025–1037.

Shi, Shouyong (2014). "Liquidity, interest rates, and output," *Annals of Economics and Finance* 15, 1–43.

Shi, Shouyong and Weimin Wang (2006). "The variability of velocity of money in a search model," *Journal of Monetary Economics* 53, 537–571.

Silva, Mario (2015). "New Monetarism with monopolistic competition: Dixit-Stiglitz meets Lagos-Wright," Working Paper of the University of California at Irvine.

Silva, Mario (2016). "Limited commitment, variety, and unemployment," Working Paper of the University of California at Irvine.

Silveira, Rafael and Randall Wright (2010). "Search and the market for ideas," *Journal of Economic Theory* 145, 550–1573.

Silveira, Rafael and Randall Wright (2015). "Venture capital: A model of search and bargaining," *Review of Economic Dynamics* 19, 232–246.

Smith, Bruce (1989). "Limited information, money, and competitive equilibrium," *Canadian Journal of Economics* 19, 780–797.

Smith, Bruce (1991). "Interest on reserves and sunspot equilibria: Friedman's proposal reconsidered," *Review of Economic Studies* 58, 93–105.

Spulber, Daniel (1996). "Market microstructure and intermediation," *Journal of Economic Perspectives* 10, 135–152.

Starr, Ross (1972). "The structure of exchange in barter and monetary economies," *Quarterly Journal of Economics* 86, 290–302.

Stockman, Alan (1981). "Anticipated inflation and the capital stock in a cash-in-advance economy," *Journal of Monetary Economics* 8, 387–393.

Stoll, Hans (1978). "The supply of dealer services in securities markets," *Journal of Finance* 33, 1133–1151.

Sultanum, Bruno (2016). "Financial fragility and over-the-counter markets," Mimeo.

Taber, Alexander and Neil Wallace (1999). "A matching model with bounded holdings of indivisible money," *International Economic Review* 40, 961–984.

Taylor, John (1980). "Aggregate dynamics and staggered contracts," *Journal of Political Economy* 88, 1–23.

Telyukova, Irina and Randall Wright (2008). "A model of money and credit, with application to the credit card debt puzzle," *Review of Economic Studies* 75, 629–647.

Temzelides, Ted and Stephen Williamson (2001). "Payments systems design in deterministic and private information environments," *Journal of Economic Theory* 99, 297–326.

Tirole, Jean (1985). "Asset bubbles and overlapping generations," *Econometrica* 53, 499–1528.

Tobin, James (1965). "The monetary interpretation of history," *American Economic Review* 55, 464–485.

Townsend, Robert (1980). "Models of money with spatially separated agents," *Models of Monetary* Economies. Eds. John Kareken and Neil Wallace. Federal Reserve Bank of Minneapolis, 265–303.

Townsend, Robert (1987). "Economic organization with limited communication," *American Economic Review* 77, 954–971.

Townsend, Robert (1989). "Currency and credit in a private information economy," *Journal of Political Economy* 97, 1323–1344.

Trejos, Alberto (1999). "Search, bargaining, money and prices under private information," *International Economic Review* 40, 679–695.

Trejos, Alberto and Randall Wright (1993). "Search, bargaining, money and prices: Recent results and policy implications," *Journal of Money, Credit, and Banking* 25, 558–576.

Trejos, Alberto and Randall Wright (1995). "Search, bargaining, money, and prices," *Journal of Political Economy* 103, 118–141.

Trejos, Alberto and Randall Wright (1996). "Search-theoretic models of international currency," *Federal Reserve Bank of St. Louis Review* 78, 117–32.

Trejos, Alberto and Randall Wright (2016). "Search-based models of money and finance: An integrated approach," *Journal of Economic Theory* (Forthcoming).

Üslü, Semih (2015). "Pricing and liquidity in decentralized asset markets." Working paper. University of California at Los Angeles.

Vayanos, Dimitri (1998). "Transaction costs and asset prices: A dynamic equilibrium model," *Review of Financial Studies* 11, 1–58.

Vayanos, Dimitri and Jean-Lu Vila (1999). "Interest rate and liquidity premium with transaction costs," *Economic Theory* 13, 509–539.

Vayanos, Dimitri and Tan Wang (2002). "Search and endogenous concentration of liquidity in asset markets," *Journal of Economic Theory* 136, 66–104.

Vayanos, Dimitri and Pierre-Olivier Weill (2008). "A search-based theory of the on-the-run phenomenon," *Journal of Finance* 63, 1361–1398.

Velde, François, Warren Weber, and Randall Wright (1999). "A model of commodity money, with applications to Gresham's law and the debasement puzzle," *Review of Economic Dynamics* 2, 291–323.

Venkateswarany, Venky and Randall Wright (2013). "A New Monetarist model of financial and macroeconomic activity," *NBER Macro Annual*, 227–270.

Wallace, Neil (1980). "The overlapping generations model of fiat money," *Models of Monetary* Economies. Eds. John Kareken and Neil Wallace. Federal Reserve Bank of Minneapolis, 49–82.

Wallace, Neil (1992). "Lucas's signal extraction model: A finite-state exposition with aggregate real shocks," *Journal of Monetary Economics* 30, 433–447.

Wallace, Neil (1996). "Questions concerning rate-of-return dominance and indeterminacy in absence-of-double-coincidence models of money,"mimeo.

Wallace, Neil (1997). "Short-run and long-run effects of changes in money in a random-matching model," *Journal of Political Economy* 105, 1293–1307.

Wallace, Neil (1998). "Introduction to modeling money and studying monetary policy," *Journal of Economic Theory* 81, 223–231.

Wallace, Neil (2000). "Knowledge of individual histories and optimal payment arrangements," *Federal Reserve Bank of Minneapolis Quarterly Review* 24, 11–21.

Wallace, Neil (2001). "Whither monetary economics?" *International Economic Review* 42, 847–869.

Wallace, Neil (2010). "The *Mechanism-Design* approach to Monetary Theory," In Benjamin Friedman and Michael Woodford (eds.), *Handbook of Monetary Economics, Second Edition.* Amsterdam: North-Holland.

Wallace, Neil (2014). "Optimal money creation in pure currency economies: A conjecture," *Quarterly Journal of Economics* 129, 259–275.

Wallace, Neil and Ruilin Zhou (1997). "A model of a currency shortage," *Journal of Monetary Economics* 40, 555–572.

Waller, Christopher (2011). "Random matching and money in the neoclassical growth model: Some analytical results," *Macroeconomic Dynamics* 15, 293–312.

Wang, Liang (2014). "Endogenous search, price dispersion, and welfare," UH Manoa Department of Economics WP 14-29R.

Weill, Pierre-Olivier (2007). "Leaning against the wind," *Review of Economic Studies* 74, 1329–1354.

Weill, Pierre-Olivier (2008). "Liquidity premia in dynamic bargaining markets," *Journal of Economic Theory* 140, 66–96.

Williamson, Stephen (1998). "Payment systems with random matching and private information," *Journal of Money, Credit, and Banking* 30, 551–569.

Williamson, Stephen (1999). "Private money," *Journal of Money, Credit, and Banking* 31, 469–491.

Williamson, Stephen (2002). "Private money and counterfeiting," *Federal Reserve Bank of Richmond, Economic Quarterly* 88, 37–57.

Williamson, Stephen (2006). "Search, limited participation, and monetary policy," *International Economic Review* 47, 107–128.

Williamson, Stephen (2012). "Liquidity, monetary policy, and the financial crisis: A New Monetarist approach," *American Economic Review* 102, 2570–2605.

Williamson, Stephen (2014a). "Central bank purchases of private assets," Working Paper of the Federal Reserve Bank of St. Louis 2014-026.

Williamson, Stephen (2014b). "Scarce collateral, the term premium, and quantitative easing," Working Paper of the Federal Reserve Bank of St. Louis 2014-008.

Williamson, Stephen (2015a). "Interest on reserves, interbank lending, and monetary policy," Working Paper of the Federal Reserve Bank of St. Louis 2015-024.

Williamson, Stephen (2015b). "Keynesian inefficiency and optimal policy: A New Monetarist approach," *Journal of Money, Credit, and Banking* 47, 197–222.

Williamson, Stephen and Randall Wright (1994). "Barter and monetary exchange under private information," *American Economic Review* 84, 104–123.

Williamson, Stephen and Randall Wright (2010a). "New monetarist economics: Methods," *Federal Reserve Bank of St. Louis Review* 92, 265–302.

Williamson, Stephen and Randall Wright (2010b). "New monetarist economics: Models," In Benjamin Friedman and Michael Woodford (eds.), Handbook of Monetary Economics, Second Edition. Amsterdam: North-Holland.

Wong, Tsz-Nga (2015). "A tractable monetary model under general preferences," *Review of Economic Studies* 83(1), 402–420.

Wong, Tsz-Nga (2016). "Monetary exchange and the irreducible cost of inflation," *Journal of Economic Theory* (Forthcoming).

Wong, Yuet-Yee and Randall Wright (2014). "Buyers, sellers, and middlemen: Variations on search-theoretic themes," *International Economic Review* 55, 375–398.

Woodford, Michael (1990). "The optimum quantity of money," *Handbook of Monetary Economics* 2, 1067–1152.

Woodford, Micheal (2003). *Interest and Prices: Foundations of a Theory of Monetary* Policy, Princeton University Press.

Wright, Randall (2010). "A uniqueness proof for monetary steady state," *Journal of Economic Theory* 145, 382–391.

Yavas, Abdullah (1994). "Middlemen in bilateral search markets," *Journal of Labor Economics* 12, 406–429.

Zhang, Cathy (2014). "An information-based theory of international currency," *Journal of International Economics* 93, 286–301.

Zhou, Ruilin (1997). "Currency exchange in a random search model," *Review of Economic Studies* 64, 289–310.

Zhou, Ruilin (1999). "Individual and aggregate real balances in a random-matching model," *International Economic Review* 40, 1009–1038.

Zhou, Ruilin (2000). "Understanding intraday credit in large-value payment systems," *Federal Reserve Bank of Chicago, Economic Perspectives*, 29–44.

Zhu, Tao (2003). "Existence of a monetary steady state in a matching model: Indivisible money," *Journal of Economic Theory* 112, 307–324.

Zhu, Tao, (2005). "Existence of a monetary steady state in a matching model: Divisible money," *Journal of Economic Theory* 123, 130–160.

Zhu, Tao (2008). "An overlapping-generations model with search," *Journal of Economic Theory* 142, 318–331.

Zhu, Tao and Neil Wallace (2007). "Pairwise trade and coexistence of money and higher-return assets," *Journal of Economic Theory* 133, 524–535.

Index

Printed by Libri Plureos GmbH in Hamburg,
Germany